909.0971241 O98
The Oxford history of the
British Empire
45148

THE OXFORD HISTORY OF THE BRITISH EMPIRE

THE OXFORD HISTORY OF THE BRITISH EMPIRE

Volume I. *The Origins of Empire*
EDITED BY Nicholas Canny

Volume II. *The Eighteenth Century*
EDITED BY P. J. Marshall

Volume III. *The Nineteenth Century*
EDITED BY Andrew Porter

Volume IV. *The Twentieth Century*
EDITED BY Judith M. Brown and Wm. Roger Louis

Volume V. *Historiography*
EDITED BY Robin W. Winks

909.0971241
O98
v.1

THE OXFORD HISTORY OF THE BRITISH EMPIRE

Wm. Roger Louis, D.Litt., FBA
Kerr Professor of English History and Culture, University of Texas, Austin and Honorary Fellow of St Antony's College, Oxford
EDITOR-IN-CHIEF

VOLUME I

The Origins of Empire

British Overseas Enterprise to the Close of the Seventeenth Century

Nicholas Canny, Ph.D., MRIA
Professor of History, National University of Ireland, Galway
EDITOR

Alaine Low, D.Phil.
ASSISTANT EDITOR

Oxford New York
OXFORD UNIVERSITY PRESS
1998

045148

Oxford University Press, Great Clarendon Street, Oxford OX2 6DP
Oxford New York
Athens Auckland Bangkok Bogotá Bombay
Buenos Aires Calcutta Cape Town Dar es Salaam
Delhi Florence Hong Kong Istanbul Karachi
Kuala Lumpur Madras Madrid Melbourne
Mexico City Nairobi Paris Singapore
Taipei Tokyo Toronto Warsaw
and associated companies in
Berlin Ibadan

Oxford is a trade mark of Oxford University Press

Published in the United States by
Oxford University Press Inc., New York

© *Oxford University Press 1998*

All rights reserved. No part of this publication may be reproduced, stored in a retrieval system, or transmitted, in any form or by any means, without the prior permission in writing of Oxford University Press. Within the UK, exceptions are allowed in respect of any fair dealing for the purpose of research or private study, or criticism or review, as permitted under the Copyright, Designs and Patents Act, 1988, or in the case of reprographic reproduction in accordance with the terms of the licences issued by the Copyright Licensing Agency. Enquiries concerning reproduction outside these terms and in other countries should be sent to the Rights Department, Oxford University Press, at the address above

British Library Cataloguing in Publication Data
Data applied for

Library of Congress Cataloging in Publication Data
The Oxford history of the British Empire / editor-in-chief, Wm. Roger Louis; assistant editor, Alaine Low. p. cm.
Includes bibliographical references.
Contents: v. 1. The origins of empire / editor, Nicholas Canny
1. Great Britain—Colonies—History. 2. Imperialism—History.
I. Louis, William Roger, 1936– . II. Low, Alaine M. III. Canny, Nicholas P.
DA16.095 1998
909′.0971241–dc21 97–36299

ISBN 0–19–820562–7 (v. 1)

1 3 5 7 9 10 8 6 4 2

Typeset by Puretech India Ltd, Pondicherry
Printed in Great Britain on acid-free paper by
Bookcraft Ltd, Midsomer-Norton,
Nr. Bath, Somerset

The Editor-in-Chief and Editors of the *Oxford History of the British Empire* acknowledge with gratitude support from

The Rhodes Trust

The National Endowment for Humanities, Washington, DC

St Antony's College, Oxford

The University of Texas at Austin

FOREWORD

From the founding of the colonies in North America and the West Indies in the seventeenth century to the reversion of Hong Kong to China at the end of the twentieth, British imperialism was a catalyst for far-reaching change. British domination of indigenous peoples in North America, Asia, and Africa can now be seen more clearly as part of the larger and dynamic interaction of European and non-western societies. Though the subject remains ideologically charged, the passions aroused by British imperialism have so lessened that we are now better placed than ever to see the course of the Empire steadily and to see it whole. At this distance in time the Empire's legacy from earlier centuries can be assessed, in ethics and economics as well as politics, with greater discrimination. At the close of the twentieth century, the interpretation of the dissolution of the Empire can benefit from evolving perspectives on, for example, the end of the cold war. In still larger sweep, the *Oxford History of the British Empire* as a comprehensive study helps us to understand the end of the Empire in relation to its beginning, the meaning of British imperialism for the ruled as well as the rulers, and the significance of the British Empire as a theme in world history.

It is nearly half a century since the last volume of the large-scale *Cambridge History of the British Empire* was completed. In the mean time the British Empire has been dismantled and only fragments such as Gibraltar and the Falklands, Bermuda and Pitcairn, remain of an Empire that once stretched over a quarter of the earth's surface. The general understanding of the British Imperial experience has been substantially widened in recent decades by the work of historians of Asia and Africa as well as Britain. Earlier histories, though by no means all, tended to trace the Empire's evolution and to concentrate on how it was governed. To many late-Victorian historians the story of the Empire meant the rise of world-wide dominion and imperial rule, above all in India. Historians in the first half of the twentieth century tended to emphasize constitutional developments and the culmination of the Empire in the free association of the Commonwealth. The *Oxford History of the British Empire* takes a wide approach. It does not depict the history of the Empire as one of purposeful progress through four hundred years, nor does it concentrate narrowly on metropolitan authority and rule. It does attempt to explain how varying conditions in Britain interacted with those in many other parts of the world to create both a constantly changing territorial Empire and ever-shifting patterns of social and economic relations. The *Oxford History of the British Empire* thus deals with the impact of British imperialism on dependent peoples in a broader sense than was usually attempted in earlier historical writings, while it also takes into account the significance of the Empire for the Irish, the Scots, and the Welsh as well as the English.

To search for themes that might link the tentative ventures in transoceanic trade and settlement of the late sixteenth or of the seventeenth century with an Empire of rule that spanned the globe in more recent times is to venture on to dangerous ground. Even essential terms, such as 'British' or 'Empire' had completely different meanings. Yet certain features characterized British overseas expansion from its origins until the liquidation of the Empire in the later twentieth century. One distinguishing characteristic was that the enterprise involved all the peoples of the British Isles and changed their relations with one another in important respects. Another was that it brought the British into contact with alien peoples whose fate was to be determined by the British. Both these processes are clearly evident in this volume.

At no point in Britain's Imperial history has the dynamic of expansion been an exclusively English one, even though the English role may have been predominant, as it was in the period covered by this volume. The Scots were already involved in early expansion, though in a lesser way, and it was becoming an Irish process as well, as Irish labour crossed the Atlantic. This merging of peoples overseas was beginning to be reflected in the use of the term 'British' Empire. Before the eighteenth century the Irish were, however, far more a people colonized than colonizing. Waves of Anglo-Scottish settlement in Ireland attracted far larger numbers and much greater resources than any transatlantic enterprise. Whatever the differences of scale and environment, in the eyes of contemporaries, the 'planting' or settling of Ireland and America were seen as essentially similar operations.

Nor were fundamental differences seen between the Gaelic Irish and the native inhabitants of the new world. Both were regarded as backward and barbarous peoples who should be brought to Christian civility. A belief in superiority was thus balanced by some sense of obligation. In practice, especially in the early phases of contact in North America and throughout the period in Asian and West African ports, relations with non-European peoples involved co-operation or even dependence on the British side rather than domination. As settlement increased, however, the demands of new immigrants for land produced similar results in Ireland, North America or those parts of the West Indies where Caribs survived. Indigenous peoples were dispossessed; they were driven to retaliate in rebellion and war; Draconian punishments followed, including further dispossession. Those who laboured on the land from which native peoples had been expelled were usually servants shipped from Britain. In Barbados and later in other West Indian and southern mainland colonies, however, the supply of labour was increasingly met by Africans. This meant that English trade with West Africa came to be dominated by human cargoes, for whom the status of chattel slaves was devised by their owners. What was taken to be the imperative of inescapable need again broke down inhibitions; this time against trading in 'any that had our owne shape'. This was a pattern that was frequently to recur in the history of the British Empire.

The volumes in the *Oxford History of the British Empire* do not necessarily begin and end at the same point. Historical understanding benefits from an integration and overlap of complex chronology. Although oceanic voyages from Britain commenced as long ago as the Middle Ages, and crossings of the Atlantic took place from the end of the fifteenth century, this volume begins with the deliberate attempts to open up long-distance trade and to found colonies from the late sixteenth century. As is the case throughout the series, there is no uniform chronological ending for this volume, some chapters extending up to the end of the seventeenth century, some even beyond into the eighteenth century. Other chapters end with the Glorious Revolution of 1689, a notable landmark in the history of both Britain and the British overseas.

A special feature of the series is the Select Bibliography of key works at the end of each chapter. These are not intended to be a comprehensive bibliographical or historiographical guide (which will be found in Volume V) but rather they are lists of useful and informative works on the themes of each chapter.

The Editor-in-Chief and Editor acknowledge, with immense gratitude, support from the Rhodes Trust, the National Endowment for the Humanities in Washington, DC, St Antony's College, Oxford, and the University of Texas at Austin. We have received further specific support from the Warden of St Antony's, Lord Dahrendorf, the Dean of Liberal Arts at the University of Texas, Sheldon Ekland-Olson, and, for the preparation of maps, the University Cooperative Society. Mr Iain Sproat helped to inspire the project and provided financial assistance for the initial organizational conference. It is also a true pleasure to thank our patrons Mr and Mrs Alan Spencer of Hatfield Regis Grange, Mr and Mrs Sam Jamot Brown of Durango, Colorado, and Mr and Mrs Baine Kerr of Houston, Texas. We have benefited from the cartographic expertise of Jane Pugh and her colleagues at the London School of Economics. We are indebted to Jane Ashley for her help in preparing the index. Our last word of gratitude is to Dr Alaine Low, the Assistant Editor, whose dedication to the project has been characterized by indefatigable efficiency and meticulous care.

Wm. Roger Louis

PREFACE

The title to this volume appears without a commencement date because it is impossible to identify a moment before which people in Britain and Ireland had no interest in the known and unknown world beyond the confines of Europe. Romanticized reports of travel by Europeans in Asia and Africa circulated in both islands during the Middle Ages as they did on the continent of Europe, and there can have been no maritime community in either Britain or Ireland that did not harbour myths about lost islands, or even continents in the Atlantic, or about voyages by intrepid mariners such as the Irish St Brendan or the Welsh Prince Madoc.

Belief in such stories must have played some part in encouraging sailors to undertake voyages far into the Atlantic, and traders and fishermen from the west of England, especially from Bristol, maintained regular contact with Iceland during the medieval period. This renders the argument that Bristol sailors reached the coast of Newfoundland in 1481, at least eleven years before Columbus's first Atlantic voyage, plausible if not proven, but it would be far-fetched to suggest that such possible discoveries also laid the foundations of Britain's trading and territorial Empire.

Where trade was concerned, the vast bulk of English and Scottish commerce had been centred on the continent of Europe during the Middle Ages, while Irish trade was directed towards England, with a lesser concentration on southern Europe. Well-established trading routes supplied the peoples of Britain and Ireland with Mediterranean and Baltic commodities and with the luxury goods of Asia that were brought to Europe by the traditional overland routes. At the same time territorial controversies also focused on the continent of Europe rather than further afield, and the ambition of successive English monarchs to revive the medieval Angevin Empire did not end until 1562 with the evacuation of New Haven (Le Havre).

During the Middle Ages English and Scottish monarchs disputed the border that separated their realms. The resulting conflict persisted into the reigns of Henry VIII and Edward VI and was not finally resolved until 1603, when the two realms were brought together into a single, composite British monarchy. Scottish monarchs, who upheld the interests of the Scots-speaking population of the lowlands, also aspired to extend their authority over the Gaelic-speaking highlands, while sixteenth-century English monarchs were extensively and expensively engaged in the analogous effort to assert their influence over all parts of Ireland until the end of the century.

These preoccupations of the people of Britain and Ireland, and their rulers, go some way to explaining why, in spite of famous exploits, such as the Cabot voyages of 1497 and 1498, their role in long-distance voyaging was relatively modest before the close of the sixteenth century. The volume explains how this involvement quickened during the seventeenth century to the point where the English were the most consequential European presence in the North Atlantic, and where English merchants were the principal conveyors of African slaves across the Atlantic as well as being major participants in direct trade with Asia.

While seeking to explain this transformation in England's position in the world of long-distance trade and colonization, the volume concludes that it was more the product of accident than design. It also suggests that a shape was imposed on what had been accomplished by chance only after state authorities came to appreciate the commercial importance of the various colonies, fortified posts, and trading routes throughout the world that had been established by private adventurers. Successive chapters reveal a striking contrast between the low level of state involvement during the first half of the seventeenth century and a more active state participation in colonial endeavour from the 1650s onward, but the overall impression is that transoceanic ventures remained a low priority for all British governments to the end of the period and that the real achievements might well have been frittered away in any of the European peace negotiations of the late seventeenth century. People in the seventeenth century had little awareness that they were on the threshold of some great Imperial age.

The volume draws upon recent scholarship on the history of Britain and her colonies and incorporates original research. Thematic chapters deal with the concept of Empire in the early period. Some contemporaries viewed colonization as a way of extending civil society and were greatly influenced by knowledge of classical literature. A chapter is devoted to literature and Empire. Ethical issues and the struggle for legitimacy by the colonizers, and the relations between colonizers and Native Americans on the mainland and in the Caribbean are explored in two chapters. The impact of political, constitutional, and religious upheavals in Britain on events in the colonies is examined. By the end of the period some settlers were prepared to take up arms to defend their rights. Divisions between whites within the colonies and tensions between colonial populations and at home in the First British Empire in North America and the West Indies foreshadow the conflicts of the eighteenth century. Other themes which are given separate treatment are the growth and development of the state and its military and naval prowess, the importance of technological advance in ship design, and the expansion and specialization of British trade and manufacture. These themes are further developed in specific regional chapters.

The regional chapters are arranged in chronological order. They show how a network of communication linked the various parts of the emerging British Empire in the New World with London, and with each other through intercolonial trade. Chapters deal with colonization within Britain and Ireland as well as in the New World and attention is also given to the part played by the Scots and Irish in colonial endeavours of the English. The book indicates that contrasts between the transplanted society of New England, which has been depicted as a communal success, and those in the Chesapeake, the West Indies, and outposts such as Newfoundland, have been exaggerated in the past. However, there were real differences and four chapters discuss colonizing efforts in distinct regions of North America and illustrate the diversity of modes of government in church and state. The role of the great trading companies in Asia and West Africa and the importance of the West Indies trade is explored in three regional chapters. Britain's role in the European continental wars and her rivalry with other European colonial powers within the New World and Asia take the story up to 1713, so forming a link to the second volume in the series.

Nicholas Canny

CONTENTS

LIST OF MAPS

LIST OF FIGURES

LIST OF TABLES

LIST OF CONTRIBUTORS

VIRGINIA DEJOHN ANDERSON (Ph.D., Harvard) is an Associate Professor of History at the University of Colorado at Boulder. She is the author of *New England's Generation: The Great Migration and the Formation of Society and Culture in the Seventeenth Century.*

JOHN C. APPLEBY (Ph.D., Hull) is Lecturer in the Department of History at Liverpool Hope University College. He is the co-editor of *The Irish Sea* and editor of *A Calendar of Documents Relating to Ireland from the Records of the High Court of Admiralty, 1534–1641.* He has contributed to *Women in Early Modern Ireland* and *Europe and the Lesser Antilles.*

DAVID ARMITAGE (Ph.D., Cambridge) is Associate Professor of History at Columbia University. He has written essays on the intellectual history of the first British Empire, is co-editor of *Milton and Republicanism*, and editor of Bolingbroke's *Political Writings* and *Theories of Empire, 1450–1800.* He is completing a study of the ideological origins of the British Empire to *c.*1740.

G. E. AYLMER (D.Phil., Oxford) served in the Royal Navy in the Second World War. He was formerly Master and is an Honorary Fellow of St Peter's College, Oxford. His books include *The King's Servants . . . 1625–1642* and *The State's Servants . . . 1642–1660.* He is currently working on a similar study for the reign of Charles II (1660–85).

T. C. BARNARD (D.Phil., Oxford), FRHist. S, is Fellow and Tutor in Modern History, Hertford College, Oxford. He is the author of *Cromwellian Ireland* and *The English Republic.* With Jane Clark he has edited *Lord Burlington: Life, Art, and Architecture.* He is the author of articles on seventeenth- and eighteenth-century Anglo-Irish history.

HILARY MCD. BECKLES (Ph.D., Hull) is Professor of History and Dean of the Faculty of Arts and General Studies at the University of the West Indies. His books include *White Servitude and Black Slavery in Barbados, 1627–1715.*

MICHAEL J. BRADDICK (Ph.D., Cambridge) is Lecturer in History at the University of Sheffield. He has written on the development of the early modern English state in *Parliamentary Taxation in Seventeenth-Century England: Local Administration and Responses* and *The Nerves of State: Taxation and the Financing of the English State, 1558–1714.*

NICHOLAS CANNY (Ph.D., Pennsylvania), MRIA, is Professor of History at the National University of Ireland, Galway, and is a member of *Academia Europaea.* His publications include *The Elizabethan Conquest of Ireland* and *Kingdom and Colony: Ireland in the Atlantic World*, and he has edited *Europeans on the Move, 1500–1800.* He is currently completing *Ireland in the English Colonial System.*

RICHARD S. DUNN (Ph.D., Princeton) is Director of the Philadelphia Center for Early American Studies and Nichols Professor of American History Emeritus at the University of Pennsylvania. He is author of *Puritans and Yankees: The Winthrop Dynasty of New England, 1630–1770; Sugar and Slaves: The Rise of the Planter Class in the English West Indies, 1624–1713,* and editor of *The Journal of John Winthrop, 1630–1649.*

P. E. H. Hair (D.Phil., Oxford) former Ramsay Muir Professor of Modern History at the University of Liverpool, is President of the Hakluyt Society. He held posts in African universities, 1952–65. His recent books include *Barbot on Guinea: The Writings of Jean Barbot on West Africa, 1678–1712* and *The Founding of the Castello de São Jorge da Mina.*

James Horn (D.Phil., Sussex) is Head of the School of Historical and Critical Studies at the University of Brighton. He is the author of *Adapting to a New World: English Society in the Seventeenth-Century Chesapeake,* and editor, with Ida Altman, of *'To Make America': European Emigration in the Early Modern Period.*

Jonathan I. Israel (D.Phil., Oxford), FBA, is Professor of Dutch History and Institutions, University College, London. His books include *Race, Class and Politics in Colonial Mexico; The Dutch Republic and the Hispanic World,* and *Empires and Entrepots: the Dutch, the Spanish Monarchy, and the Jews.*

Ned C. Landsman (Ph.D., Pennsylvania) is Associate Professor of History at the State University of New York at Stony Brook. He is the author of *Scotland and Its First American Colony, 1680–1765* and of numerous articles on British provincial cultures in the eighteenth century.

Robin Law (Ph.D., Birmingham) is Professor of African History at the University of Stirling. He is author of *The Oyo Empire, c.1600–c.1836; The Horse in West African History* and *The Slave Coast of West Africa, 1550–1750.* He is an Editor of the *Journal of African History.*

Peter C. Mancall (Ph.D., Harvard) is Professor of History at the University of Kansas. His publications include *Valley of Opportunity: Economic Culture Along the Upper Susquehanna, 1700–1800; Envisioning America: English Plans for the Colonization of North America, 1580–1640s,* and *Deadly Medicine: Indians and Alcohol in Early America.*

P. J. Marshall (D.Phil., Oxford), FBA, is former Rhodes Professor of Imperial History at King's College, London. He has been Editor of the *Journal of Imperial and Commonwealth History* and is Associate Editor of *The Writings and Speeches of Edmund Burke.* His books include *The Impeachment of Warren Hastings* and *Bengal: The British Bridgehead.*

Jane H. Ohlmeyer (Ph.D., Trinity College, Dublin) is Lecturer in History at Aberdeen University. Her books include *Civil War and Restoration in the Three Stuart Kingdoms: The Political Career of Randal MacDonnell, First Marquis of Antrim.* She has edited *Ireland from Independence to Occupation, 1641–1660.*

William O'Reilly (M.St., Oxford) is Lecturer in History at the National University of Ireland, Galway, and is author of several forthcoming articles in English and German on aspects of early modern migration. He is completing his D.Phil. thesis: 'A Comparative Study of Eighteenth-Century German Migration to Pennsylvania and Hungary'. He is author of the chronology.

Anthony Pagden (D.Phil., Oxford) is Harry C. Black Professor of History at The Johns Hopkins University. His books include *European Encounters with the New World: From Renaissance to Romanticism* and *Lords of All the World: Ideologies of Empire in Spain, Britain, and France, 1500–1800.*

N. A. M. RODGER (D.Phil., Oxford) has been Assistant Keeper of the Public Records and is now Anderson Fellow of the National Maritime Museum. His books include *The Wooden World: An Anatomy of the Georgian Navy* and *The Safeguard of the Sea: A Naval History of Britain*, Vol. I, *660–1649*.

ROBERT M. WEIR (Ph.D., Case Western Reserve University) is Professor of History at the University of South Carolina. His publications include *Colonial South Carolina: A History* and *'The Last of American Freemen': Studies in the Political Culture of the Colonial and Revolutionary South.*

NUALA ZAHEDIEH (Ph.D., London School of Economics) is Lecturer in the Department of Economic and Social History, University of Edinburgh. She is the author of 'Trade, Plunder and Economic Development in Early English Jamaica', in the *Economic History Review*, and 'Privateering in Jamaica, 1655–1689', in the *Journal of Imperial and Commonwealth History.*

ABBREVIATIONS AND LOCATION OF MANUSCRIPT SOURCES

Public Record Office, London:

C	Chancery
CO	Colonial Office
Cust.	Customs
E	Exchequer
HCA	High Court of Admiralty
SP	State Papers

All other abbreviations and manuscript sources will be found in the first reference in each chapter.

1

The Origins of Empire: An Introduction

NICHOLAS CANNY

The study of the British Empire in the sixteenth and seventeenth centuries presents special difficulties because no empire, as the term subsequently came to be understood, then existed, while the adjective 'British' meant little to most inhabitants of Britain and Ireland during the years covered by this volume. During the sixteenth century England was sometimes described as an empire, but always with a view to emphasizing the long tradition of independence from foreign potentates, including the Pope, enjoyed by its monarchs through the centuries. The word 'empire', which was particularly favoured by Henry VIII after his breach with Rome, therefore called to mind the relative isolation of England through the centuries rather than its dominion over foreign territories.[1] That specific meaning was sustained when, with the Union of the Crowns in 1603, the English monarchy gave way to a composite dominion which incorporated the three kingdoms of England, Scotland, and Ireland, and the principality of Wales. King James VI and I was the first monarch of this conglomeration, and he himself chose for it the mythical name 'Britain' or 'Great Britain' in the hope that this usage would familiarize his diverse subjects in the several jurisdictions with the political alteration that had taken place, and would persuade them to shift their loyalties from their local communities to the new composite monarchy that had been created.[2] Therefore as King James established 'Britain' as the name of his multiple kingdom, phrases such as 'great Brittaines imperial crowne', or 'the Empire of Great Britaine', were but adaptations of the prevailing concept of independent authority, and had no necessary expansionist associations.[3] Educated English

This Introduction benefited greatly from comments by David Armitage, Tom Bartlett, Jack Greene, Karen O. Kupperman, P. J. Marshall, John Morrill, Geoffrey Parker, and the Editor-in-Chief. David Armitage also kindly allowed me to consult unpublished work.

[1] Richard Koebner, *Empire* (Cambridge, 1961), esp. pp. 53–55.

[2] B. Levack, *The Formation of the British State: 1603–1707* (Oxford, 1987); C. H. Firth, 'The British Empire', in *Scottish Historical Review*, XV (1918), pp. 185–89; David Armitage, 'The Empire of Great Britain: England, Scotland and Ireland, *c.*1540–1660', *The Ideological Origins of the British Empire* (Cambridge, forthcoming), chap. 2.

[3] This first phrase comes from Thomas Blennerhasset, *A Direction for the Plantation in Ulster* (London, 1610), sig. A 2, and the second from John Speed, *The Theatre of the Empire of Great Britain* (London, 1611).

people were, of course, familiar with such associations attaching to the word 'empire' in its classical usage, but while Milton's Satan, once he came to know of God's creation, aspired to have his 'Honour and Empire . . . enlarged by conquering this new world', his special source of pride was in being saluted as emperor in Hell because it 'asserted' that he had been 'ordained to govern, not to serve!'[4]

This latter definition would have been immediately intelligible to English people of the seventeenth century because the 'Union of Love' which King James wished to achieve between his English and his Scottish subjects implied a rejection of the ambition of those in England who visualized Britain as a unitary state, within which England would enjoy political, cultural, and religious dominance over Scotland.[5] The terms 'Britain' and 'British', as these were defined by King James VI and I, therefore had a precise insular connotation. In so far as the words then came to acquire expansionist associations it was in relation to the establishment in Ulster, through the process of plantation, of a settler society where Scottish and English Protestants became joint participants in a common enterprise which was described as 'British', and where Scots and English were referred to indistinguishably as 'British Protestants', or even 'Britaines'.[6] The exceptional character of this usage at the outset of the seventeenth century becomes apparent when we note that those few English advocates of transoceanic exploration and settlement who would allow Scots, Welsh, and Irish to participate in the effort to extend Crown authority beyond the frontiers of Europe did not describe the undertaking they favoured as 'British'. Rather, when Samuel Purchas encouraged what would be described today as 'British' colonial expansion, he conceived it as a plural rather than a singular endeavour which, he hoped, would result not only in the dispersal 'through the world' of 'England's out of England', but also in 'Royal Scotland, Ireland, and Princely Wales, multiplying new Scepters to his Majesty and his heirs in a New World'.[7]

[4] John Milton, *Paradise Lost*, Book IV, ll. 390–91; Book V, l. 802, in John Carey and Alastair Fowler, eds., *The Poems of John Milton* (London, 1980), pp. 636, 725.

[5] For the unitary view see Armitage, *Ideological Origins*, chap. 2; Roger A. Mason, 'Scotching the Brute: Politics, History and National Myth in Sixteenth-Century Britain', in Mason, ed., *Scotland and England, 1286–1815* (Edinburgh, 1987), pp. 60–84; Roger A. Mason, 'The Scottish Reformation and the Origins of Anglo-British Imperialism', in Mason, ed., *Scots and Britons: Scottish Political Thought and the Union of 1603* (Cambridge, 1994), pp. 161–86; this attitude was shared by Edmund Spenser, on which see 'Spenser Sets his Agenda', in Nicholas Canny, *Ireland in the English Colonial System, 1580–1650* (Oxford, forthcoming), chap. 1.

[6] The terms not only enjoyed official currency but were embraced by the settlers within the plantation, for which see 'The names of the freeholders . . .', S[cottish] R[ecord] O[ffice], Edinburgh, RH15/91/60.

[7] Samuel Purchas, *Hakluytus Posthumus or Purchas his Pilgrimes*, 20 vols. (Glasgow, 1905), I, pp. xxxvii–xxxviii.

Purchas's desire to have Irish and Scots involved was exceptional because most English propagandists for colonization conceived it as an exclusively English enterprise to which Welsh people were silently admitted. This conception was, perhaps, a reflection of reality, because there were few Scots or Irish who had the capacity to become promoters of overseas colonization until the eighteenth century. Therefore the English were precocious among the peoples who became subjects of the British Crown in 1603 in displaying an early interest in the phenomenon that, for want of a better term, is known as the Expansion of Europe. However, even the English, despite manifesting a navigational prowess which matched that of the Spanish and Portuguese, were slow to follow up their 'Discoveries' and to claim domination over foreign peoples and trading routes, as the Iberians did so spectacularly from the outset.[8] That the English were capable of overawing peoples less technically accomplished than themselves is not in doubt, and historians have striven to explain the relative tardiness of the English in making the switch from exploration to exploitation by alluding to the essential difference in wealth and social organization between the Native American peoples encountered by the English (and also the French) and those who came within the reach of Spanish explorers in the valley of Mexico and in Peru.[9] This goes some way towards explaining the perceived time-lag, even when it takes no account of the varied Portuguese experience at colonization. However, the more interesting consideration is that the supposed tardiness of the English as colonizers has come to be perceived as a problem to be explained, and that this problem derives from the widely held assumption that there was some necessary connection between exploration and exploitation and that the establishment of overseas empires was the inevitable consequence of 'Discovery'. Therefore, in historical terms, the most important aspect of the poor performance of the English as colonizers during most of the sixteenth century may well be that it proves that no such connection existed, at least at the outset of the period covered by this volume.[10]

The number of English traders who were interested in Atlantic, Asian, and African opportunities before the end of the sixteenth century was small, and the modest involvement of the English state with overseas ventures reflects a generally low level of communal interest. This is not to deny the sustained concern of some sectors, particularly the fishing and merchant communities, with the opportunities that had become available to them since the close of the fifteenth century through the recent expansion in geographic knowledge. Even allowing for this, it still appears

[8] On navigational matters see chap. by N. A. M. Rodger.

[9] Sir John Elliott, *Britain and Spain in America: Colonists and Colonized*, The Stenton Lecture, University of Reading, 1994, p. 13.

[10] See below, pp. 55–56.

that the interest of the monarchy in the new possibilities far outstripped that of the English commercial community, at least during the reign of Henry VIII. The subsequent waning of state interest in oceanic affairs is explained largely by the fragility of the regimes of Edward VI and Mary I, and also that of Queen Elizabeth I during her early years. For their part, merchants remained reasonably satisfied, even up to the closing decades of Elizabeth's reign, that they had sufficient access to the commodities of Asia, Africa, and America either through established European trading networks or through raids on Spanish shipping.

The relative passivity of the English state in relation to overseas matters went unchallenged until some politically engaged Protestants associated with Sir Francis Walsingham, Secretary of State to Queen Elizabeth and head of intelligence, and the propagandists employed by them, sought to alert the nation and the state to the advantage that their Spanish adversaries had gained over them through transoceanic exploits. This made little impression on the members of the great London merchant companies, who did not seriously contemplate the risk and expense of distant engagement until the early seventeenth century. By this time the end of privateering, combined with the disruption of customary European trading networks that had occurred during the course of the war with Spain, forced them to accept that they themselves would have to establish direct trading connections with Asia and to exploit whatever opportunities existed in America if they were to satisfy the demands of their customers for the exotic commodities from distant continents to which they had become accustomed.[11] Merchant investment in a series of new companies generated a spectacular expansion in trade which took Englishmen to the African coast, the Levant, Russia, the Indian Ocean, and elsewhere, and which added substantially to the wealth of England because of the opportunities it provided for re-exportation.[12] However, this activity was not considered either imperial or colonial in the seventeenth century, possibly because it was not associated with settlement, and because English consumers, who were already familiar with the commodities being supplied, did not appreciate the novelty of the means by which they were now being procured.

America, therefore, remained the principal concern of those who advocated overseas ventures. The most prominent of the early authors were the two Richard Hakluyts and their associates, and their disciple Samuel Purchas. On a political level these were essentially propagandists for militant Protestantism, and they perceived the promotion of trade and colonization as one necessary means both to enhance the position of Protestant rulers in the world and to check the Catholic monarchs of Spain. They were also of one mind in considering that their mon-

[11] See chap. by John C. Appleby; and below, pp. 149–51.

[12] See chaps. by P. E. H. Hair and Robin Law; P. J. Marshall; Nuala Zahedieh.

archs, as upholders of true religion, were more duty-bound than the Spanish rulers to bring the truths of Christianity to those who previously had had no access to that knowledge, and they were confident that the endeavours of those who followed their advice would be favoured by a benevolent Providence once they cast aside that 'preposterous desire of seeking rather gain than God's glory'.[13]

While describing the religious and associated nationalistic commitment of propagandists such as the Hakluyts and Purchas, one must always bear in mind that their opinions were aspirational and did not reflect the priorities of their countrymen or even their government. This becomes apparent on comparison of the preoccupations of the younger Hakluyt with those of his contemporary, Adam Winthrop of Groton Manor in Suffolk, who in 1586 (when Hakluyt was still writing), commenced a diary of the major events in his life which he would carry on intermittently until 1619.[14] During that time Winthrop did not make a single entry that concerned English long-distance voyaging, nor did he mention any literature that would have shed light on that subject apart from Sebastian Münster's *Cosmographia Universalis*, which he purchased in 1595 for 5 shillings. The matters that preoccupied him were religious, familial and local, and he could even bring the few events of national importance that he mentioned down to the parochial and personal level. For example, when noting that on 24 October 1603 'it was proclaimed that England and Scotland should be called great Brittaine', he also mentioned that on 26 May 1603 his cousin Munnyng had, at Groton, shown him 'a new book in Latin, *De Unione Britaniae*'.

Reference is made here to Adam Winthrop because the diary of this articulate, religious squire, whose family was soon to be associated with Puritan migration to New England, demonstrates how little overseas activity in the Atlantic or in Asia impinged upon the consciousness of even educated English people as late as the early decades of the seventeenth century. Adam Winthrop was naturally interested in the progress of the Protestant Reformation on the continent of Europe, but otherwise when he looked beyond his immediate environs it was to Ireland. Even that interest was explained by the presence in Ireland of several members of his immediate family who became settlers in the plantation of Munster. Adam maintained a regular correspondence with these relatives, sometimes acted as their agent in local matters, entertained them at Groton on their return visits, and occasionally, as on 9 May 1605, accompanied those departing for Ireland for some of their journey: 'I did ride with my brother [John] Winthrop into Ess[ex], and returned the 17th.'

[13] Richard Hakluyt, *Divers Voyages* (1582; London, 1850), p. 13.

[14] 'The Diary of Adam Winthrop, 1580–1630', in *Winthrop Papers*, ed. Allyn B. Forbes and others, 6 vols. (Massachusetts Historical Society, 1929–), I, pp. 39–145.

These frequent references to Ireland give the impression that that country was no more than a natural geographic extension of England, and it was certainly the ambition of those who were engaged in the establishment of a sizeable English settlement in the southerly province of Munster to make it, and represent it as, just such an extension (see Map 6.2).[15] Ireland's geographic position emerges in much the same light in the early surviving correspondence of Adam Winthrop's famous son John (later Governor of Massachusetts), as it does in the diary of the father.[16] There is, however, one significant difference; while retaining contact with his cousins in Munster, John Winthrop, through the 1620s, was more concerned with developments at the centre of government in Ireland, and he seems then to have believed that the entire kingdom of Ireland, and not just Munster, might be fashioned by the English into a truly godly society. Therefore he sent his eldest son, John Jr., to be educated at Trinity College, Dublin, out of the belief, shared by other zealous Protestants, that it had surpassed even Emmanuel College, Cambridge, on which it was modelled, in sustaining a godly curriculum and environment.[17] The progress of the College was perceived by Winthrop as only a step towards rescuing Ireland from its perverse attachment to popery,[18] but he seems to have been convinced by the settlement endeavours of his brother-in-law, Emmanuel Downing, a government official in Dublin, and of the godly clergyman Richard Olmstead, then enjoying the patronage of Sir Charles Coote, that plantation would become the instrument for redeeming the entire country. It is possible that John Winthrop invested in these ventures and visited Ireland himself in 1621, and he certainly considered making his home there: 'I wish oft God would open a way to settle me in Ireland, if it might be for his glory, Amen.'[19]

God, as it happens, decreed that John Winthrop's home should be in Massachusetts rather than in Ireland, but this episode shows that he, like thousands of other English, and also Scots, contemplated an involvement with the various state-

[15] Michael MacCarthy-Morrogh, 'The English Presence in Early Seventeenth Century Munster', in Ciaran Brady and Raymond Gillespie, eds., *Natives and Newcomers: The Making of Irish Colonial Society* (Dublin, 1986), pp. 171–90; Nicholas Canny, 'The 1641 Depositions as a Source for the Writing of Social History: County Cork as a Case Study', in Patrick O'Flanagan and Cornelius G. Buttimer, eds., *Cork: History and Society* (Dublin, 1993), pp. 249–308.

[16] The correspondence to which reference is made appears in *Winthrop Papers*, I, pp. 278–319.

[17] Ibid., pp. 281, 283–84, 288–89, 311; Alan Ford, 'The Church of Ireland, 1558–1634: A Puritan Church?', in A. Ford, J. McGuire, and K. Milne, eds., *'As By Law Established': The Church of Ireland Since the Reformation* (Dublin, 1995), pp. 52–68; Alan Ford, *The Protestant Reformation in Ireland, 1590–1641* (Frankfurt am Main, 1985).

[18] John Winthrop to John Winthrop Jr., 3 Oct. 1623, *Winthrop Papers*, I, pp. 288–89; same to same, 29 March 1624, *Winthrop Papers*, I, p. 311.

[19] Ibid., and same to same, 20 April 1623, *Winthrop Papers*, I, pp. 280–81; Francis J. Bremer, 'The Heritage of John Winthrop: Religion along the Stour Valley, 1548–1630', *The New England Quarterly*, xx (1997), on Olmstead in Ireland, see Ford, *The Protestant Reformation*, pp. 205–08.

sponsored plantations in Ireland in preference to gambling on more speculative ventures across the Atlantic or further afield. Much has been written about these interconnections between British 'domestic' and 'overseas' colonization, which have sometimes been likened to the connection between the *reconquista* of Moorish Spain and the conquest of New Spain.[20] In both instances, historians find it puzzling that procedures and justifications that they associate with overseas colonization were employed within Europe into the early modern period. This puzzlement stems from the notion that colonization was a procedure reserved by European powers to assert their authority over peoples who were 'foreign' to them, and which in turn links 'otherness' with places remote from Europe. Such assumptions are not justified, because they do not allow for the fact that all educated Europeans were conscious that colonization was a method that had been employed in ancient times by the Romans to advance their authority and civility throughout much of Europe, and in medieval times by the Anglo-Normans to extend their influence, including their involvement with England, Scotland, Wales, and Ireland.[21]

These precedents held a special appeal for the English, the lowland Scots, and the Old English in Ireland, since these were all keenly conscious that their own societies owed their origin to conquests. For these people, therefore, resort to colonial methods was almost an automatic response once it became clear that reform by persuasion had proven futile, because they were convinced, both by precedent and by the treatises of such recent theorists as Machiavelli, that the establishment of colonies was a procedure appropriate for their own time and place.[22] Moreover, it would also have appeared logical to those of Norman descent in Scotland, England, and Ireland that their first priority was to fulfil their historic civilizing mission close to home, before becoming involved in more speculative ventures for which their moral responsibility was less clear. Besides, it may have seemed to committed Protestants, such as Emmanuel Downing and John Winthrop, that the completion of this domestic agenda should enjoy priority because the Protestant Reformation had made but little progress in the outlying reaches of the King's dominions.

While we can speculate over what might have motivated John Winthrop and his associates, we have clear information on what principles guided Queen Elizabeth's learned Secretary, Sir Thomas Smith, when he became involved in a much-studied, but ultimately futile colonization venture in north-east Ulster during

[20] See chap. by Anthony Pagden.

[21] See chaps. by Jane H. Ohlmeyer and T. C. Barnard; and Anthony Pagden, *Lords of All the World* (New Haven, 1996).

[22] For references to Machiavelli, see Sir William Herbert, *Croftus sive de Hibernia Liber*, ed. Arthur Keaveney and John A. Madden (Dublin, 1992), pp. 74–77; 86–87; 92–93.

the 1570s. Smith, who is best remembered as the author of the political treatise *De Republica Anglorum*, made it clear when discussing his Ulster venture that the only means of extending this 'Commonwealth' of England beyond its historic frontiers was through military conquest followed by the erection of colonies along the lines favoured by the Romans. For Smith, a classicist and a former Professor of Civil Law, both the vocabulary and methods of colonization derived from Roman practice, and justified the hierarchical and authoritarian character of the colony that he sought to establish in Ulster. This colony would then be instrumental in civilizing the Gaelic population of Ulster in the same way that Roman colonial institutions had civilized the Ancient Britons.[23] Similar arguments were pursued by William Strachey when speaking of the responsibility of English settlers in Virginia towards the native inhabitants there, and when he also cited the Spanish example of his own times it was because this too conformed to his understanding of classical precedent.[24] These examples suggest that those Englishmen who contemplated the colonial option as a means of extending the scope of civil society looked to the precedents provided by the common store of knowledge that all educated Europeans had acquired through their study of classical literature.

Observations such as those by Smith, and more formal accounts such as those by Strachey, blunted the sharp edge associated with the word 'colony' by making it synonymous with 'plantation', a term with gentler, horticultural associations. Thus, the 'Undertakers' in the plantation of Ulster were required to 'plant or place upon a small proportion, the number of 24 able men of the age of 18 years being English or Inland Scottish'. The various English settlements in North America were known from the outset as 'plantations', and the official body established after the Restoration of the monarchy in 1660 to oversee all of these projects was called the Council of Trade and Plantations. Even more emphatically, John Milton removed any taint associated with plantation as colonization when he likened it to the Creation, praising God as 'the sovereign Planter' who had 'framed all things to man's delightful use'.[25]

Attention to the various plantation efforts in Ireland and Scotland is warranted because it shows that colonization had been a weapon in the armoury of European governments long before the so-called 'Discoveries' occurred, and that it continued to be employed within Europe long after colonization had become more

[23] Sir Thomas Smith, *De Republica Anglorum*, ed. Mary Dewar (Cambridge, 1982); Hiram Morgan, 'The Colonial Venture of Sir Thomas Smith in Ulster, 1571–5', *Historical Journal*, XXVII (1985), pp. 261–78.

[24] See below, pp. 154–56.

[25] *Conditions to be Observed by the Brittish Undertakers of the Escheated Lands in Ulster* (London, 1610); Patricia Seed, *Ceremonies of Possession in Europe's Conquest of the New World, 1492–1660* (Cambridge, 1995), pp. 25–31; John Milton, *Paradise Lost*, Book IV, ll. 691–92, in Carey and Fowler, eds., *Poems of John Milton*, p. 653.

commonly associated with far-flung, exotic places. It is interesting to identify such precedents and parallels, but one must be aware that, while these could encourage English people to adventure further afield, at the start of this period they also served to stunt colonial endeavour and even set it on false trails. Thus, English colonization in completely different climatic and economic environments frequently followed the same course during the early years of settlement, because the different promoters shared the same assumptions, derived from ancient or medieval precedent. Merchants, frequently the main sponsors of colonization, were conservative by disposition, relying on standard procedures for promoting and supervising any task in hand, regardless of the different circumstances that might prevail, and this also resulted in inflexibility. For example, comparison of the procedures followed by the London companies in meeting their responsibilities in the Ulster plantation with the orders governing the plantation efforts of the Berkeley family in both Bermuda and Virginia shows that the sponsoring body in each case appointed one person to represent its interest on the ground, and that this person was required to take detailed guidance from home before entering into any commitment that would involve financial outlay.[26] Such close monitoring resulted in formulaic letters concerning the measurement and division of plantation land in the respective colonies and the exploitation of natural resources, which were almost identical in content and made no allowance for the entirely different environments in which the agents operated.[27]

Such attachment to routine may have resulted in much wasted effort, but it also generated detailed reports and costings which provide valuable insights into colonization in practice. The ambition both in Ulster and in Bermuda and Virginia was the creation of model societies, but it was also expected that skilled, enterprising people would have the opportunity to make their fortunes in their new environment. Thus Mr Arundel's letter to Virginia of January 1622, which predicted that 'any young laborious honest man may in a short time become rich in this country', had its parallel in the prediction of Thomas Blennerhasset, a propagandist for the Ulster plantation, that all artisans or experienced husbandmen who went to Ulster would 'be in estimation and quickly enriched by [their] endeavours'. At the same time, the promoters of both enterprises warned that the unskilled and the indigent would have no place in their respective societies; the dire warning of Blennerhasset from Ulster, that 'loiterers and lewd persons in this

[26] Procedures followed by the London Companies in Ulster are best detailed in the papers relating to the Company of Ironmongers, London, Guildhall Library, MSS 17, 278(1); and those concerning the Haberdashers Company, Edinburgh, SRO, RH 15/91/33; the affairs of the Berkeley Plantations can be traced in the Smythe of Nibley Papers, N[ew] Y[ork] P[ublic] L[ibrary].

[27] Edinburgh, SRO, RH 15/91/33; Bryan Cave in Somer Isles to Mr Thorpe, 14 July 1616, Smythe of Nibley Papers, doc. no. 2, NYPL.

our new world will not endure', was matched repeatedly by similar sentiments from Bermuda and Virginia.[28]

Another shared assumption, deriving from Roman precedent, was that colonies had, of necessity, to be organized into towns or even cities if they were to remain civil and secure. Thomas Smith had sought to organize his private plantation in Ulster around its projected capital Elizabetha, and the supporters of the state-sponsored plantation in Ulster of the early seventeenth century also insisted that the settler community would have to be organized about a network of towns. For this they pleaded not only the example of the Romans spreading civility through the foundation of cities but also 'the noble precedent' whereby, at the time of the Norman Conquest of Ireland, the city of Bristol had agreed with King Henry II to take over Dublin from the Vikings and settle it with civil people, which 'plantation' not only brought fame and profit to Bristol but was 'not the least cause of civilizing and securing of that part of the country'.[29]

With similar intent, the promoters of the Berkeley Plantation in Virginia commissioned their representative Captain John Woodleefe on 4 September 1619: 'to erect and build a town called Barkley and to settle and plant our men and diverse other inhabitants there, to the honour of Almighty God, the enlarging of Christian religion, and to the augmentation and revenue of the general plantation in that country, and the particular good and profit of ourselves, men and servants as we hope'. The business of the plantation was to be conducted from this town, and Woodleefe, enjoying a trading monopoly as the chief merchant of the company, would conduct his trade from its security, 'either with the natives of Virginia, or with the English there residing'.[30]

Agents in both plantations were given detailed, and almost identical, instructions on the erection of houses and churches for the inhabitants, and the English promoters supplied much the same commodities to each initial group of settlers to get them started. These goods, regardless of climate or environment, inevitably included seeds that would enable the settlers to produce their first harvest, as well as crops that the sponsors believed would make the colony commercially viable; but these lists tell us more about the deficiencies of the English economy than about the potential of particular colonies. Thus, while the sponsors of Berkeley Plantation looked forward to their colony producing 'iron ore, silk grass, mulberry trees, vines, English wheat, maize and other Virginia corn, aniseeds, flax, [w]oade, oilseeds, and the like, as well as meadow and pasture for cattle, fish, fowl,

[28] Mr Arundle's Letter, Jan. 1621/2, Smythe of Nibley Papers, doc. no. 37; Thomas Blennerhasset, *A Direction for the Plantation of Ulster* (London, 1610), sig. B2^{v}.

[29] Blennerhasset, *Direction*, sig. B2^{v}; Mayor Sebright to Ironmongers, 1609, London, Guildhall Library, MSS, 17, 278(1), f. 3.

[30] Commission to Captain John Woodleefe, 4 Sept. 1619, Smythe of Nibley Papers, ff. 59–60.

and timber for shipping and other uses', the merchant sponsors of plantation in Ulster were confident that their acquisition would provide them with a 'store of all things for man's sustenance' which, when detailed, included many of the commodities expected of Virginia. Promoters were also given to expounding on the strategic advantage of their various colonies, as in the case of Ulster where its location was praised first because of its proximity to the 'great and profitable fishings... in the next isles of Scotland where many Hollanders do fish all the summer season', then because it was 'ready for traffic with England and Scotland', and finally (and implausibly) because it was 'open and convenient for Spain and the Straits, and nearest for Newfoundland'.[31]

The promoters of both colonies were to learn from experience that these fantasies would never be realized, but, like the English-based sponsors of other colonial ventures, they showed themselves to be slaves to precedent, persisting with inappropriate ventures and political forms, sometimes at considerable human and financial cost. Nor is this stubbornness surprising, when we note that these same assumptions about the formation of new societies were shared and popularized by England's leading literary figures. Milton may have been describing the behaviour of fallen angels rather than humans in Book I of *Paradise Lost*, but it is none the less significant that he identified their first undertaking, after they had been cast down from Heaven, as the construction of 'Pandaemonium, the high capital of Satan and his peers'.[32]

There were several instances in the English colonial experience of the seventeenth century where the rigid adherence of colonial promoters to their inherited beliefs was responsible for total failure. The more pragmatic promoters often heeded the advice of those directly involved with plantations only after their initial forays had resulted in such heavy human and financial losses that they had no other option but to follow the course that was most likely to produce some return on their investment. Once they were guided by such counsel, the forms that the various colonies assumed were very different from classical models, the most extreme example being that in the Chesapeake, which emerged as a string of riverain tobacco farms rather than a sequence of elegant plantations organized about an imagined capital like Barkley.[33]

Historians have been so impressed by the parallels between colonization enterprises in different places, and by the references to these parallels that were made by

[31] Ordinances, Directions and Instructions to Captain Woodleefe, 4 Sept. 1619, Smythe of Nibley Papers, ff. 61–62; London, Guildhall Library, MSS, 17, 278(1), ff. 0–1.

[32] John Milton, *Paradise Lost*, Book I, ll. 756–57, in Carey and Fowler, eds., *Poems of John Milton*, p. 505.

[33] See chap. by James Horn.

contemporaries, that some scholars have gone so far as to suggest that the experiences gained in Scotland and Ireland actually influenced colonial practice in the New World. It goes without saying that some transfer of knowledge must have occurred, especially when the same people were involved in different theatres of colonization, but insufficient account has been taken of the ways in which 'Internal Colonialism' hindered and distorted as well as stimulated English colonial ventures further west in the Atlantic.[34] This part of the Introduction will address such matters, but before doing so will identify some of the more potent lessons that have been disregarded by those who have studied British domestic and transoceanic colonization as a single subject.

The most obvious oversight is the extent to which the plantation in Ulster, which was the costliest British colonial undertaking of the seventeenth century, both popularized the concept of 'British' as opposed to 'English' colonization, and provided the first example of how a British colony and Empire might function.[35] Reference has already been made to the novel nomenclature that was coined to describe settlers and settlement at the very launch of the plantation in Ulster, but that experience also provided the first tangible example of ordinary lowland Scots and English people, who, despite their shared origin and religion, continued to have little contact with each other long after the Union of the Crowns, engaging upon a common enterprise.

The theory favoured by King James for the plantation in Ulster was that Scots and English should function as equal partners in a civilizing and reforming endeavour, and that Scots and English tenants would be intermixed on the property of each Undertaker. In practice, however, the plantation that emerged in Ulster was very much an English creation and was English dominated. The King, on whose support all planters ultimately relied, had taken up residence in London, and while Scots proprietors enjoyed equality of rights with English grantees in the Ulster plantation, it was in a jurisdiction where the administration and the state church were constitutionally subject to England. It is not surprising, under these circumstances, that English settlers treated their Scots partners as second best, and they accepted Scots tenants on their estates in an effort to meet plantation conditions only when English tenants were not available and where Irish customary tenants were being forced off the land by government regulation. The condescending attitude towards the Scots expressed in 1622 by Mr Taylor of Armagh, who favoured the extension of 'a plantation of British' to County

[34] The term was coined in Michael Hechter, *Internal Colonialism: The Celtic Fringe in British National Development, 1536–1966* (London, 1975).

[35] See Linda Colley, *Britons: Forging the Nation* (London, 1992), which associates the development of a British identity with the eighteenth and nineteenth centuries and more particularly with the years between Waterloo and 1837.

Monaghan (an Ulster county which had not been included within the original plantation scheme), anticipated what many English would have to say of Scots settlers in several British colonies throughout the world in future decades. Taylor recommended that the better lands to the south of County Monaghan should be reserved for English proprietors, but 'for the waste land on the north side... to which English will hardly be drawn; it were good to set it to Scotch men... the Scotch shall be as a wall betwixt them and the Irish through whose quarter the Irish will not pass to carry any stealths'.[36]

Within this Ulster context, land-hungry Scots planters had no option but to become frontiersmen, whenever this was the role assigned to them, and to show deference to the, usually English, bishops of the Church of Ireland while seeking to negotiate leases of land from them. They also had to work closely with their English planter neighbours who dominated the administration and defence of the province, while they had, at the outset, to rely upon Irish tenants or subtenants to pay rent for the estates which they hoped ultimately to develop as models of British settlement in the province. At the same time, they had to establish and maintain contact with the administration in Dublin, which was a totally English body. While they were thus forced to accept their role in the plantation as supplementary to that of the English, the Scots planters in Ulster sought to compensate for this inferiority by constructing a Scottish microcosm within the larger English-dominated plantation. To do this, they lured Scots tenants, usually from their own localities in Scotland, to take the place of the Irish tenants on their estates; they married Scottish wives and retained Scottish servants in their houses; they provided patronage, whenever this was feasible, to clergymen of their own nation; they maintained continuing contact with their homeland; and they strove to confine their associations in the public as well as in the private spheres to Scots of their own rank, both those who remained in Scotland and those who became fellow planters in Ireland. Yet however hard they tried to forge an exclusively Scottish world in Ireland, this proved impossible. For example, Sir Robert MacClelland, later Lord Kirkcudbright, whose Irish career can be documented with precision, worked assiduously to populate his Irish lands with Scots tenants and also to maintain contact with his property and kinsmen in Scotland, but he always employed some Irish people both as servants and under-tenants, and he retained the services of a Mr Winslawe and a Mr Wamsley for 'law business', because it was English common law rather than Scottish law that obtained in Ireland. From the outset, MacClelland had to send a servant on frequent expeditions to conduct business with the Dublin administration, and as the seventeenth century

[36] 'Mr. Taylor of Armagh, his Proposition for Planting my Lord of Essex's Land', Dublin, National Library of Ireland, MSS, 8014 (x).

progressed his heirs, like all Scots landowners in Ireland, had to establish connections also with the court of King Charles I because Irish issues were increasingly resolved there.[37]

Therefore, the colony-within-a-colony that MacClelland and his fellow Scots strove to fashion in Ulster during the course of the seventeenth century was never an exact replica of what they had left behind in Scotland; rather, it was a hybrid society of Scots, Irish, and English, with the balance decidedly in favour of the Scots, and it existed side by side with other micro-communities where the ethnic balance was more English or Irish depending on the nationality of the proprietors. By thus creating their own enclaves, however, the Scots in Ulster succeeded in maintaining a distance from the English who were both commercially and politically dominant within the wider planter community, and they sometimes took advantage of the resulting freedom to enter into business transactions with native proprietors rather than with well-connected English settlers. That is certainly the impression conveyed by Lord Balfour of Glenawley, when advising a fellow Scots peer, the Earl of Annandale, on the management of the fishery that Annandale had acquired in Killibegs in County Donegal. Annandale, he said, should never 'trust any English in that place', since they would merely deceive him by 'fair shows and protestations'.[38]

The Ulster experience of the first half of the seventeenth century showed that Scots and English did not operate as equals within this first 'British' settler community. Rather, the plantation society that emerged was dominated by the English, who tolerated a sequence of sub-communities where either Scots or Irish predominated, and which were expected to fulfil special functions for the benefit of the wider plantation effort. This ethnically diverse settlement was created in Ulster because it was insisted upon by the King, but even if this had not been the royal wish a mixed settlement might have come into being by default because the English planters experienced difficulty in attracting English tenants in sufficient numbers to meet the plantation conditions. The tensions that developed between the separate national groups who controlled distinct areas of settlement will strike a familiar chord with all who are acquainted with the British Atlantic World in the post-Restoration period. So also will the practices and procedures of the Scots in Ulster during the first half of the seventeenth century, because after 1660 it was the

[37] Nicholas Canny, 'Fashioning "British" Worlds in the Seventeenth Century', in Canny, Gary B. Nash, Joe Illick, and William Pencak, eds., *Empire, Society and Labor: Essays in Honor of Richard S. Dunn* (College Park, Pa., 1997, supplement no. 64 to *Pennsylvania History*), pp. 26–45; MacClelland's principal estate in Ireland went to his daughter Marion and her husband Robert Maxwell, who was forced to become a petitioner at court to uphold their interests; see Robert Maxwell to Bishop of Derry, 14 March 1639/40, Edinburgh, SRO, RH 15/91/20, no. 1.

[38] James, Lord Balfour of Glenawley to John, Earl of Annandale, 20 July 1626, in H[istorical] M[anuscripts] C[ommission] *Report of the Laing Manuscripts*, I, pp. 169–72.

Atlantic Ocean rather than the Irish Sea which bore thousands of indigent Scots families and their animals to a new home, this time in the Middle Atlantic colonies.[39]

The most potent lesson demonstrated by the Irish experience is that the establishment of colonies of settlement, on the model of those of the Romans, was feasible in the modern world, and the most distinctive feature of the future British Empire within the spectrum of European overseas empires is the prominent place enjoyed by colonies of white settlement within it. These, when they came into being, always included, in varying proportions, Scots and Irish as well as English and Welsh, and to this extent the seventeenth-century plantation experience in Ulster provided the first practical example of how a 'British' society might function. Many British colonial societies, both in North America and in the emerging British Empire of subsequent decades, would also, like that in seventeenth-century Ulster, be culturally diverse communities with a distinct place and function being assigned to English, Scots, Irish, and Welsh groups which were incorporated in a larger planter society controlled by a select group of English merchants or officials.

When taking account of this positive achievement we must also allow that what happened in Ulster, and more generally in Ireland, during the first half of the seventeenth century also served to distort, and even hinder, wider colonial developments. For example, Scottish involvement with Ulster meant that Scots could not, even if the opportunity had presented itself, become seriously engaged in colonization further afield because they lacked the resources to do so. Up to 30,000 Scottish people migrated to Ulster, mostly in family groups, in the decades prior to the Irish insurrection of 1641, and when these are added to the simultaneous exodus of Scots fighting men to the continent of Europe, it becomes clear that Scotland could not have provided any other colony with a supply of artisans and agricultural workers.[40] The engagement with Ulster must also have placed a considerable strain on the Scottish money supply, because those Scots who succeeded as landowners in Ulster bore the cost of transporting tenants, their families, and livestock to Ireland, and placing them in a house and on a farm that would comply with plantation conditions. As a consequence of this investment, many Scots planters in Ulster became heavily indebted to Scottish money-lenders, and it is likely that migrating tenants also drew upon Scottish sources of credit to meet their start-up costs. Thus, while we might regard the society that was evolving in Ulster in the decades previous to 1641 as a prototype of what would come into being on the mainland of North America (and especially in the Middle

[39] See chap. by Ned C. Landsman.

[40] T. C. Smout, N. C. Landsman, and T. M. Devine, 'Scottish Emigration in the Seventeenth and Eighteenth Centuries', in Nicholas Canny, ed., *Europeans on the Move: Studies in European Migration, 1500–1800* (Oxford, 1994), pp. 76–112.

Atlantic colonies) in the late seventeenth and the eighteenth centuries, we must also accept that what was happening in Ulster would have hindered Scottish involvement in the Atlantic both because of the demand it placed on human resources and the strain it placed on the credit supply in a backward economy.[41]

When looked at from this perspective we can see how developments in Ulster hindered, or at least retarded, more remote colonial endeavours and kept the Scots involvement to a minimum during the early part of the seventeenth century. The plantation in Ulster, together with several other Irish plantations, would also have consumed English human resources that might otherwise have been attracted to America, and it is clear that, in the seventeenth century, the revived plantation in Munster lured away large numbers of the very type of skilled settler that the sponsors of all colonies were seeking. Plantation in Munster must also, in its initial stages, have drawn heavily on English surplus capital, but a significant return would have accrued because, previous to 1641, some of the Munster settlements proved highly profitable.[42]

Not so in the case of Ulster, where the plantation was slow to become a going concern. Moreover, the plantation of Ulster required not only significant investment from the English Undertakers and their tenants, on a par with that made by their Scots counterparts, but the leading London merchant companies were also called upon by the King to accept responsibility to plant one of the six escheated counties (designated County Londonderry) under the same conditions as the Undertakers, and to erect two trading ports at Derry and Coleraine with appropriate fortifications. The costs associated with the development of the towns, the recruitment of settlers, and the simultaneous development of a sequence of manors throughout the county made the investment by the merchant companies in Ulster the single most expensive contribution of the City of London to Britain's colonial endeavour of that time. One may well imagine the disenchantment of the leading London companies and their members with all colonial enterprise when this investment, which had been forced on them by the Crown, not only failed to win them official gratitude but soon exposed them to substantial fines because they had not fully met their obligations.[43] This experience may go some considerable way towards explaining the subsequent low level of investment by established London merchants in transatlantic colonial enterprise, and their preference for

[41] David Armitage, 'Making the Empire British; Scotland in the Atlantic World, 1542–1707', *Past and Present*, CLV (1997), pp. 34–63; Canny, 'Fashioning "British" Worlds'.

[42] Michael MacCarthy-Morrogh, *The Munster Plantation: English Migration to Southern Ireland, 1583–1641* (Oxford, 1986).

[43] T. W. Moody, *The Londonderry Plantation, 1609–41* (Belfast, 1939); Canny, 'Fashioning "British" Worlds'; Jane H. Ohlmeyer, 'Strafford, the "Londonderry Business" and the "New British History"', in J. F. Merritt, ed., *The Political World of Thomas Wentworth, Earl of Strafford, 1621–41* (Cambridge, 1996), pp. 209–30.

continued involvement with trade, including in the newly developed East India Company which conducted long-distance trade with Asia. This Company had, by the end of the century, become the biggest trading concern in England and was already overtaking its Dutch equivalent as the biggest European handler of Asian goods.[44]

While these points show how, in several respects, British involvement with Ireland stifled potential colonial enterprise elsewhere, we can also see how it distorted it. The first distortion occurred because transoceanic activity, and the settlement associated with it, remained almost entirely English until the second half of the seventeenth century, despite the fact that the government that sanctioned such enterprise was self-consciously British. This is largely explained by the existence of a multitude of lesser English traders who took up the opportunities in the Atlantic that had been passed over by their disillusioned betters, but the exhaustion of the possible supply of both Scottish investment and migrants through Scotland's heavy involvement with Ulster meant that Scots were able to launch few American ventures of their own during the first half of the seventeenth century.[45] Irish investors were even less involved with Atlantic ventures, because the limited speculative capital that was available to them was usually invested in land or manufacturing enterprises at home rather than in transoceanic colonization; the only group of Irish businessmen who are known to have invested in Atlantic ventures during these years concentrated upon St Christopher (St Kitts) and the Amazon basin.[46]

The inability of Scots and Irish to participate as significant investors resulted in an effective monopoly for English promoters in 'British' overseas enterprise. English traders who gained commercial monopolies in this sphere then became determined to exclude interlopers, including Scots competitors. This brought a predictable response from the Scottish Covenanters, who demanded 'liberty of commerce and trade ... through the veins of all his Majesty's dominions', as well as free membership of trading companies, the abolition of internal customs, and mutual rights for English, Irish, and Scots traders where any one of them enjoyed 'any outtrade and dealing in any foreign places'.[47] Despite such protest, transoceanic enterprise in the name of the British Crown continued to rely upon English initiative and resources, and one purpose of the passage of the English Navigation Acts of the later seventeenth century was to preserve the English monopoly, which

[44] Robert Brenner, *Merchants and Revolution, 1550–1653* (Princeton, 1993).

[45] Armitage, 'Making the Empire British'.

[46] Joyce Lorimer, ed., *English and Irish Settlement on the River Amazon, 1550–1646* (London, 1989); Louis Cullen, 'The Irish Diaspora of the Seventeenth and the Eighteenth Centuries', in Canny, ed., *Europeans on the Move*, pp. 113–49.

[47] Transactions of the Committee of Estates of Scotland, 29 March 1641, Edinburgh University Library, MSS, DC 4.16, ff. 90^{v}–91^{v}.

persisted until the Act of Union with Scotland in 1707. Before that, the most significant contribution of Scots and Irish to Britain's overseas settlements was in populating rather than in promoting them.

Another distortion that resulted from the early concentration of English and Scottish colonial energies upon Ireland is that people with no previous experience of overseas endeavour came to think of it as a westward enterprise rather than as something that also presented opportunities in Africa and Asia. This was exemplified in the case of Adam and John Winthrop, whose mental map was first a local English one, until it was extended westwards to incorporate Ireland. Finally, after John Winthrop had traversed the ocean, his became an Atlantic world where the English presence was weak and an English godly presence weaker still. Moreover, this New World of John Winthrop was like his old one in that it was circumscribed by menacing French and Spanish papists lying respectively to the north and the south of his New England settlement, but sailing the same ocean that was the lifeline for all European settlements. Having identified the threats that were likely to come from known adversaries, Winthrop then familiarized himself with the parts of the Atlantic that were under English control, even when these were ungodly mercenary places such as Barbados and Newfoundland, or profane settlements such as Maryland, where Jesuits abounded and Mass was celebrated.[48] He took a particular interest in these colonies because they could complement or even be a source of settlers for his own community, but he also feared that even the godly settlements could become rivals and drain off settlers from Massachusetts.[49] Thus, in 1640 he remonstrated in theological terms with Lord Saye and Sele over the latter's attempt to lure settlers from New England to Providence Island, while in 1642 he warmly welcomed to Boston one Mr Bennet, a gentleman from Virginia with news of godly people there who were in urgent need of clergymen to minister to their spiritual needs.[50] And when he concluded that the survival of the godly could not be assured by English resources alone, he looked to the possibility of recruiting Protestants from Ireland and Scotland into his colony, as well as Irish Catholic servants who would be amenable to reform when placed in a godly environment.[51]

This does not mean that there were no English people (or Scots people for that matter) who could see all transoceanic enterprise as a single whole. For example, Patrick Copeland, an English clergyman serving in 1640 in Bermuda but pre-

[48] '*Winthrop's Journal, "History of New England", 1630–49*', ed. J. K. Hosmer, 2 vols. (New York, 1908), I, p. 126.

[49] Karen Ordahl Kupperman, *Providence Island, 1630–1641* (Cambridge, 1994).

[50] Lord Saye and Sele to Wentworth, 9 July 1640, *Winthrop Papers*, IV, pp. 263–67; *Winthrop's Journal*, I, pp. 334–35; II, p. 73.

[51] Malcolm Freiberg, ed., *Winthrop Papers* (Boston, 1992), VI, pp. 309, 313, 314.

viously a chaplain to the East India Company, praised the conversion methods that had been devised by Dutch Protestant missionaries in Amboina, which were an adaptation of the practices that had been used by Jesuit missionaries who worked in Asia under Spanish and Portuguese tutelage. While Copeland, like any right-thinking Protestant, decried the perversity of the Jesuits in spreading false doctrines, he admired the Dutch initiative in imitating methods that had proven effective, and he recommended the employment of a similar strategy for bringing the truths of Christianity to the American Indians in both the Chesapeake and New England.[52] However, Copeland was exceptional in both his global view and experience, and despite a major English commercial involvement with Africa and Asia, relatively few English, and even fewer Scots and Irish, settled in those continents during the seventeenth century.[53]

Many English commentators of the time took this balance for granted and, for the earlier part of the century, saw themselves as emulating the Spanish, rather than the Portuguese or the Dutch, in their continental preference. Some, for example Thomas Bowdler in his Commonplace Book for the years 1635–36, considered that England had made a deliberate and commendable choice. Bowdler had served in British embassies abroad and had debated with papist adversaries over the relative importance of overseas adventures in the struggle for power in Europe. His debates had led him to the conclusion that it was in his government's interest to discourage ventures to Asia because these resulted in the loss to England not only of bullion but also of sailors who were essential to Britain's security; 'not one in ten returning' from such voyages. On the other hand, Atlantic ventures, and particularly those to the West Indies, found favour with Bowdler, because they would 'raise another England to withstand our new Spain in America', while fostering trade 'without waste of treasure . . . and without such loss of mariners as in other places'. The remarks of Bowdler are particularly pertinent because they show how this one individual who gave thought to the subject of overseas involvements in the years immediately preceding the wars of the mid-century could see some logic in the emerging pattern of England's overseas enterprise, with the Atlantic beginning to arouse more interest than Asia, and with the West Indies enjoying pride of place within the Atlantic sector. Nor, unlike historians of today, did he identify the risks from disease in the West Indies and the Chesapeake as a necessary disadvantage. On the contrary, he considered that the high mortality of settlers (but not of sailors) in the West Indies and the Chesapeake added to the social utility of these settlements, making them 'really

[52] Patrick Copeland to John Winthrop, 4 Dec. 1640, *Winthrop Papers*, IV, *1638–44* (Boston, 1944), p. 157; Susan Kingsbury, ed., *The Records of the Virginia Company*, 4 vols. (Washington, 1906–35), I, pp. 532–39, 550–51, 581; Patrick Copeland, *A Declaration How the Monies were Disposed* (London, 1622).

[53] See chaps. by P. E. H. Hair and Robin Law; P. J. Marshall.

helpful ... as now they serve for drains to unload their populous state which else would overflow its own banks by continuance of peace and turn head upon itself or make a body fit for any rebellion'.[54]

These observations of Thomas Bowdler, Patrick Copeland, and John Winthrop might be considered individualistic or even whimsical, but one thing they shared was their recognition that the merits of overseas endeavour would come to enjoy a wider appreciation only when these would be made to appear essential to the commercial, military, or spiritual interests of their home societies. This was the same assumption from which the Hakluyts, Purchas, and the other early propagandists of colonial endeavour proceeded, but the fact that the case for colonization still needed to be reiterated in the middle of the seventeenth century indicates that the original message had made little impression in either England or Scotland, other than among committed Protestants. Not even all of these, as witnessed in the case of Adam Winthrop, were inspired by, or even interested in, colonial involvement. They were more easily convinced of its importance as a tool of foreign policy because they were caught in a time warp where the essential foreign-policy issue remained the animosity between England and Spain that had dominated the last years of the reign of Queen Elizabeth. For these Protestants, England's (and presumably Britain's) providential role was to defend the achievements of the Reformation and to oppose the power of Spain, which was identified as the bulwark of papist superstition, both in Europe and beyond. This Protestant concern to emulate Spain while attacking its Atlantic interests goes some way towards explaining why militant Protestants, such as John Winthrop and Lord Saye and Sele, were to the fore in English overseas ventures of the mid-seventeenth century, and their obsession with shadowing Spain also contributed to the continuing Atlantic focus of England's colonial thrust. For all their commitment, however, these individuals did little to advance the cause of colonization in the short term, and the futility of their efforts was symbolized by the fact that the energies that had been invested in the establishment of the colony of Providence Island (off the coast of Nicaragua), which was designed as a base from which to undermine the Spanish empire, were subsequently reinvested in the Cromwellian settlement of Ireland.

The example and the rhetoric of those who were advanced in both their Protestantism and their commitment to colonization were not lost on Oliver Cromwell, and his Western Design represented the first deployment of the military resources of the British state in the interests of transoceanic, as opposed to Irish, colonization; although not, it must be said, at the expense of Ireland, which then

[54] Commonplace Book of Thomas Bowdler, 1635–36, Edinburgh University Library, Laing MSS, La III, f. 532.

experienced the most ambitious plantation effort to date.[55] The scant return on Cromwell's Atlantic deployment is of less consequence than the way in which it directed public consciousness, more effectively than the Hakluyts or Purchas had ever done, to the economic no less than the moral importance of overseas empire. Then the employment of state resources for colonial purposes had the ironic consequence of alerting the Dutch to the threat to their trading interests that stemmed from Cromwellian aggression, and this Dutch fear ultimately contributed to a political realignment between the Protestant United Provinces and Catholic Spain against a common threat from the most stridently Protestant power in Europe.[56]

While the Cromwellian initiatives produced few lasting gains for Britain, besides the island of Jamaica, they did result in an alteration of foreign-policy priorities that was to have enduring significance. The maintenance of those colonies and trading positions that had been acquired in almost serendipitous fashion during the first half of the seventeenth century now came to be considered a matter of national interest as well as pride. Moreover, it was accepted by the Restoration government, as it had been during the Interregnum, that colonies established by foreign adversaries might be seized by force, or that their transfer to Britain might become a counter in treaty negotiations. This possibility seemed to negate the spiritual priority that had been invoked consistently to legitimize all colonization, but policy-makers were not forced to admit that they had abandoned the religious imperative because the colonies that were considered the most desirable targets for acquisition were West Indian islands devoted almost entirely to the production of sugar and populated principally by African slaves. Such, it was accepted, could be made immediately 'British', as opposed to being 'Dutch', 'French', or 'Spanish', by the simple expedient of introducing a new governing élite in place of that established by the 'foreign' power.

All of this points to secular interests taking the place of the spiritual motives that were previously invoked to justify colonization, and this reorientation of priorities was made easier for the scrupulous by declaring the successive wars against the Dutch to be essentially wars to punish a people who had failed to uphold true religion in its purest form.[57] Such propositions were no more than special pleading; the government of Charles II was keenly conscious of the need to expand its colonial interests if for no other reason than that the consequent increase in customs revenue was a vital new source of income. What was good for the Crown was also perceived to coincide with the interests of merchants, and the

[55] See chap. by T. C. Barnard. [56] See chap. by Jonathan I. Israel.

[57] See chap. by Michael Braddick. Stephen C. A. Pincus, 'Popery, Trade and Universal Monarchy: The Ideological Context of the Outbreak of the Second Anglo Dutch War', *English Historical Review*, CVII (1992), pp. 1–29.

trade statistics of the time demonstrate that this perception was an accurate reflection of reality as Britain's West Indian islands became the prime producers of customs revenue for the Crown, while they also constituted the principal overseas market for both food supplies and manufactured goods from Britain.[58]

Thus it came to be widely accepted in England in the decades after the Restoration that colonies were essential to the economic well-being of the community. As this reality became established, officials and merchants began to cast covetous eyes on places on the map that should be brought under the British Crown, either because they were economically desirable or because they were strategically important for the maintenance and development of existing colonies and trading routes across the globe. Therefore, by the end of the seventeenth century, a new concept of Empire had been established, which involved the assertion of dominion over foreign places and peoples, the introduction of white, and also black, settlement in these areas, and the monopolizing of trade with these newly acquired possessions. This concept was given formal expression in a pamphlet published in 1685, by 'R.B.' (the pseudonym of Nathaniel Cruch), called *The English Empire in America*.[59] This work looked to the economic prospects of eight mainland and eleven island settlements, traced the origin of each, and placed the early explorations of 'our brave English spirits' that had led to the establishment of all nineteen colonies in the context of 'the first discovery of the New World called America, by the Spaniards'. All of this was consistent with the standard of reporting set by the Hakluyts, but it differed essentially from their formula because it measured success principally in material terms and attached scant importance to religion in the emerging Empire. However, as is clear from his title, R.B. was, like the Hakluyts but unlike Purchas, a 'little-Englander' in that he was writing to celebrate England's achievements, and made reference to Irish and Scots only because they were numerically significant among European settlers on the islands of Montserrat and Barbados. His geographic sense was also narrow, or deliberately misleading, in that he described all of these 'Dominions' in America as being in 'the West Indies', and he devoted no attention whatever to English navigational or trading exploits in Africa or Asia.

Despite his shortcomings as a reporter, R.B. consolidated the view that an Empire of trade and dominion had been established, that this Empire was located in the Atlantic, and that it was in the national interest to cherish and defend it. Since R.B.'s nation was always England, so also was his Empire that of England:

[58] See chaps. by Michael Braddick and Nuala Zahedieh.

[59] *The English Empire in America: or the Prospect of His Majesties Dominions in the West Indies. By R.B.* (London, 1685). [The card catalogue of the Beinicke Library at Yale University states that 'R.B.' stands for Richard or Robert Burton, the pseudonym of Nathaniel Cruch or Crouch who was the printer of this work.]

because it had been acquired principally through English endeavours; because it was controlled from London; because it was managed by English people; and because, with the few exceptions mentioned above, the white population was overwhelmingly of English descent. However, even as he was writing the English character of the Empire was changing, and R.B. did not take sufficient account of the extent to which the English presence had already been diluted. Almost from the outset, the English in the West Indies had been joined by a small but significant group of Irish Catholic planters, who not only developed sugar plantations on particular islands but also played an important role in drawing indentured servants from Ireland to meet the labour requirements of planters on other islands as well as their own. This mobilization of white labour was greatly augmented by the forced migration of an Irish Catholic work-force to the West Indies in the aftermath of the Cromwellian conquest of Ireland, and it is the combination of these movements which justifies the assertion that 'the Irish constituted from mid-century the largest single flow of white immigrants to the seventeenth-century West Indies'. The dragooning of Irish labourers for Barbados by the Cromwellians is notorious, but what is not so well remembered is that the precedent for this was the transportation of significant numbers of Scottish soldiers to the West Indies after the Battles of Dunbar and Worcester in 1650–51. These were followed by some voluntary Scottish emigrants to the islands in subsequent years, and both Scots and Irish servants were joined by an ever-increasing number of African slaves. The consequent permanent change in the population balance may be one reason why the sugar islands came more frequently to be referred to as the British, rather than the English, West Indies.[60]

Another factor which contributed to the increasing flow of Scots emigrants to all the colonies, and not only to the West Indies, was that Ireland proved less attractive for settlers after 1660 than in the decades before 1641, and people who might previously have hoped to make their fortunes there now had to look further afield.[61] English adventurers were still to the fore among those who led the quest for colonial opportunity, but, in the decades after the Restoration, these were frequently joined by Scots, or by English and Scottish people who had first tried their luck with plantation in Ireland. Promoters of colonization in America encountered increasing difficulty in finding workers and settlers for their colonies because an expanding economy in England meant there were fewer people from that country who were available for menial work in the colonies. The consequent shortfall in labour in the West Indies was made good by Irish and some Scottish workers, as well as African slaves, and slaves were also employed in considerable

[60] See chap. by Hilary McD. Beckles. L. M. Cullen, 'The Irish Diaspora', in Canny, ed., *Europeans on the Move*, p. 113.

[61] See chap. by T. C. Barnard.

numbers by tobacco producers and by farmers in the Chesapeake and Carolina. For most colonies on the mainland of North America, however, and particularly for those in the buoyant Middle Atlantic sector, the work-force was drawn increasingly from Scotland where, in sharp contrast to England, economic conditions became increasingly difficult as the seventeenth century progressed. The immediate Scottish response to the collapse in the rural economy was to flee to Ulster, but this was a place of refuge rather than of opportunity in the 1690s, so some Scots began to make their way directly to mainland America while others, known to historical literature as Scotch-Irish, first went to Ulster and later made a second migration to America. Furthermore, as trade and human traffic increased between Irish and North American ports, these Protestant emigrants were joined by some Irish Catholics, and the population mix in the Middle Atlantic colonies became even more diverse with the addition of a German-speaking leaven towards the close of the seventeenth century. These various groups did no more in the Middle Colonies before 1689 than establish enclaves of their own within settlements where the tone was set by English, and English Quakers at that, but the diversity of population meant that the adjective 'English' was no longer adequate to describe the emerging Empire, and 'British' came gradually to be accepted as a more serviceable term.[62]

Even as the colonies came to be identified as British, the ever more diverse white settlers began to lay claim to the rights of Englishmen and expected to be governed through a locally elected Assembly, which they also took to be the manner of English governance. R.B. was most admiring of the legal forms in operation in New England and the island of Nevis, but he suggested that governing institutions in each of the colonies were moving towards a common English form, even in recently acquired Jamaica, where 'the Laws ... are as like those of England as the differences of the countries will admit'.[63] This warranted mention presumably because R.B. appreciated that would-be settlers would demand some assurances that their liberties would be guaranteed.

These demands reflected the reality that the law in force throughout the expanding Empire was English law, despite being sometimes administered by Scots, but they may also have stemmed from the growing recognition that legal rights of individuals could quickly be eroded as they moved into unfamiliar surroundings far removed from the support of acquaintances and kin. Moreover, it was accepted from the outset that 'savages' would be made 'civil' only under authoritarian rule, and since many Europeans who were recruited as settlers in the various colonies were considered by their superiors to be little better than savages, repeated attempts had been made to govern them also in military fashion.

[62] See chap. by Ned. C. Landsman. [63] *The English Empire*, pp. 91, 184, 209.

Such resort to authoritarian rule was hardly surprising in the narrow constraints aboard ship or in the many forts and trading stations that dotted the sailing routes of the burgeoning British Empire, but the fear always existed that the many Governors of colonies who had military backgrounds would attempt to rule their colonies as they were accustomed to rule their regiments, and would formulate codes of conduct such as 'The Laws Divine, Moral and Martiall' that were briefly and notoriously enforced in Virginia during the early years of settlement.[64] Furthermore, as slavery became an ever more common feature of Empire and as whites groped for a consensus on what codes were appropriate for the management of slave gangs, they were forced to give thought also to how their own claims to freedom might be preserved in a world where liberty was becoming the exception rather than the rule.[65]

Thus, as separate English, Scottish, and even Irish microcosms were being fashioned (as Samuel Purchas had hoped they would be) under the aegis of a common monarch, the diverse elements from the composite British monarchy were quickly to learn that the readiest means of procuring for themselves the customary or putative rights of Englishmen was to insist that they were British. This insistence explains the alacrity with which ordinary white settlers in almost all the Atlantic colonies took up arms to defend their rights, and this, as much as their rigid attachment to Protestantism, explains also the general conflagration that beset almost all of the British Atlantic World in the aftermath of the Glorious Revolution.[66] No other event better demonstrated the existence of a British Empire whose white inhabitants shared political assumptions as well as economic interests. At the same time, this episode also demonstrated that this First British Empire, which was still in the process of being defined, would be an Atlantic Empire, if only because it was impossible to envisage a similar disturbance in the interest of civil liberties occurring in any of Britain's factories or trading stations on the coastline of Africa or in Asia.

While it is possible to point to the moment when a British Empire had come into being in fact if not in name—the naming was to await the Act of Union between England and Scotland of 1707 and the publication in the following year of John Oldmixon's *The British Empire in America*—that moment can be identified only with the advantage of hindsight, and people who lived through the seventeenth century had little awareness that they were on the threshold of some great

[64] Stephen Saunders Webb, *The Governors General: The English Army and the Definition of Empire, 1569–1681* (Chapel Hill, NC, 1979); 'Laws Divine, Moral and Martiall', in Peter Force, ed., *Tracts and Other Papers Relating... to the Colonies in North America*, 4 vols. (Washington, 1836), III, no. 2.

[65] See below, pp. 227–33; 389–97.

[66] See chap. by Richard S. Dunn.

Imperial age.[67] Everything that has been said in this Introduction, and that will be detailed in the chapters which follow, makes it clear that before 1689 an English (and much more so a Scottish and Irish) transoceanic presence was always tentative and had usually been a matter of low priority. Thus, while three successive Dutch wars, fought between 1652 and 1674, demonstrated that the state was capable of mobilizing its resources to defend its commercial and colonial interests, these were exceptional interventions, and most colonial activity at the end of the seventeenth century existed, as it had done at the beginning of the sixteenth century, in a limbo between public and private spheres.[68] Indeed, the only development that marked a departure from the sixteenth-century practices was the Asian traffic pursued by the East India Company in large, purpose-built ships that were capable of carrying bulky cargoes and enduring long and hazardous voyages around the Cape of Good Hope; a journey which took an average of six months to traverse in one direction (see Map. 1.1). Everybody in the seventeenth century regarded this as an exceptional trade which was proving highly profitable for investors in the Company, but while this traffic was new to England it was recognized that it was displacing a European commerce in Asian goods that had existed for centuries—yet not even the most far-sighted could have imagined that the calicoes and spices that were being imported in ever-increasing quantities were laying the foundations for Britain's most spectacular Imperial achievement of future centuries.[69]

On the other hand, the mundane trade and colonial activity on the Atlantic came to be perceived in the later seventeenth century as an essentially English achievement which was contributing to the enrichment not only of England, but also of Scotland and Ireland. What happened there was also, in some respects, no more than a quantitative advance upon what had been under way in the sixteenth century, with trade and the passage of people being conducted in small and frequently old ships, ranging in size from twenty-five to 300 tons, that had been requisitioned from other commercial traffic, or from the fishing- and coal-fleets. The principal concerns of the captains of the multitude of little vessels that plied the Atlantic were to cover the cost of each individual voyage while making it safely to journey's end. Therefore, whenever they were forced off course by unforeseen circumstances they did not hesitate to dispose of their cargo, and even their passengers, at a destination different from that originally intended. Nevertheless,

[67] James Truslow Adams, 'On the Term "British Empire"', *American Historical Review*, XXVII (1922), pp. 485–89; John Oldmixon, *The British Empire in America, Containing the History of the Discovery, Settlement, Progress and Present State of all the British Colonies on the Continent and Islands of America*, 2 vols. (London, 1708).

[68] See chaps. by Michael Braddick and G. E. Aylmer.

[69] See chaps. by P. J. Marshall and Nuala Zahedieh.

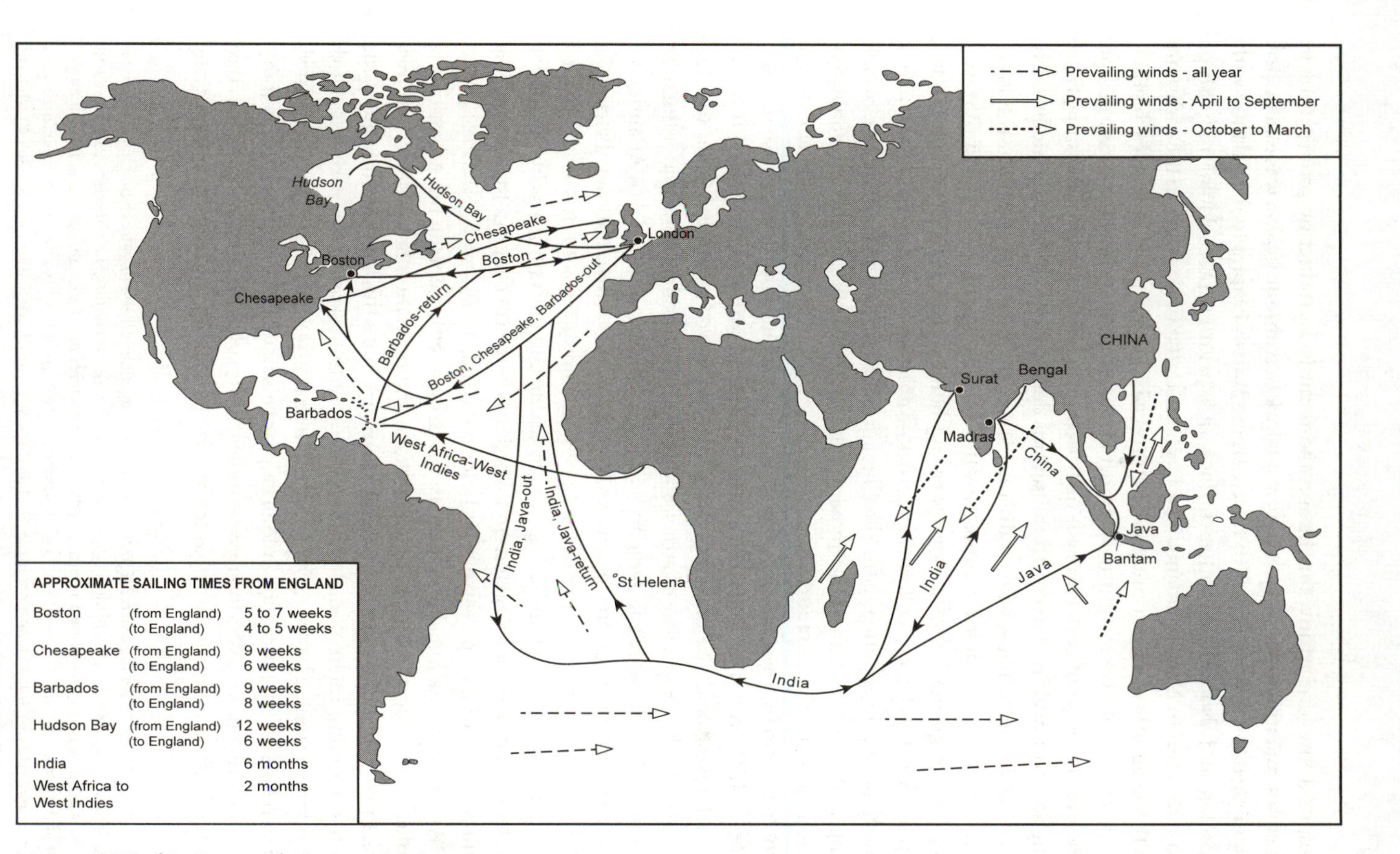
Prevailing winds - all year
Prevailing winds - April to September
Prevailing winds - October to March
Hudson Bay
Hudson Bay
Chesapeake
Boston
London
Boston
Chesapeake
Barbados-return
Boston, Chesapeake, Barbados-out
Barbados
West Africa-West Indies
India, Java-out
India, Java-return
St Helena
Surat
Bengal
CHINA
Madras
China
India
Java
Java
Bantam
India
APPROXIMATE SAILING TIMES FROM ENGLAND
Boston (from England) 5 to 7 weeks
(to England) 4 to 5 weeks
Chesapeake (from England) 9 weeks
(to England) 6 weeks
Barbados (from England) 9 weeks
(to England) 8 weeks
Hudson Bay (from England) 12 weeks
(to England) 6 weeks
India 6 months
West Africa to West Indies 2 months

MAP 1.1. Wind Systems and Communications

despite a low level of investment and the hazards presented by pirates, foreign enemies, and unpredictable weather, a network of communication was established that linked the various points of the emerging British Empire in the Atlantic with London, and also with each other through an expanding intercolonial trade. Ships bound either for Newfoundland, New England, or the Chesapeake in the early part of the seventeenth century preferred to travel within hailing distance of each other, so that they would enjoy mutual support in the event of shipwreck or assault, and towards the close of the century it had become standard practice for ships from England to travel in convoys to the several destinations in the Atlantic at fairly predictable times. Thus, while individual ships might leave England for the sugar islands in the West Indies at almost any time of year, the largest number of vessels departed in groups between November and January and reached the West Indies about sixty days later to collect the perishable muscovado sugars. Sailings of about one hundred ships annually for the Chesapeake were even more seasonal, occurring, as R.B. put it, 'from midsummer till the late end of September'. The objective was to have the ships in the Chesapeake by the beginning of November, where they would remain over winter disposing of their European exports while assembling a cargo which would be ready for return to England in the early spring. Travel to New England and the emerging ports of New York and Philadelphia was less dictated by the seasonality of crops, and the prime considerations that influenced the flow of traffic were the avoidance of winter storms in the North Atlantic and the necessity to clear the American ports for the return journey before the harbours froze over. The annual passage of as many as 175 boats to the cod-fishing grounds off Newfoundland was also as much dictated by climate as by the fishing cycle; ships usually left England on this relatively short voyage in the early spring and returned to Europe when their holds were full.[70]

As this brief account shows, the various British settlements in the Atlantic were linked by this remarkable passage of boats to and from their home ports, and they were made further conscious of being members of a common community by the ever-expanding intercolonial trade. Already by the close of our period, English traders represented by the Royal African Company had become the biggest carriers of slaves on the Atlantic, and while all ships involved with the sugar trade inevitably encountered these slavers in the West Indies, some sugar boats travelled to the coast of West Africa on the outward journey and ventured to trespass upon the slaving

[70] David Cressy, *Coming Over: Migration and Communication between England and New England in the Seventeenth Century* (Cambridge, 1987), esp. pp. 144–77; Alison Games, 'The English Atlantic World: A View from London', in Canny and others, eds., *Empire, Society and Labor*, pp. 46–72; R.B., *The English Empire*, pp. 104, 128; Ian K. Steele, *The English Atlantic, 1675–1740: An Exploration of Communication and Community* (Oxford, 1986); and on intercolonial trade see John J. McCusker and Russell R. Menard, *The Economy of British America, 1607–1789* (Chapel Hill, NC, 1985).

monopoly enjoyed by the Company. Others involved in the sugar business followed equally circuitous routes and stopped by Madeira for wine and provisions, or by the Cape Verde islands for salt. Some ships bound ultimately for the fishing grounds of Newfoundland also saw the advantage of plying a southern route in search of salt on the way out, while on their return voyage some sailed directly for the Mediterranean to sell their catch before returning to their home base.

This multi-faceted movement provided settlers and traders in all British colonies and factories with commodities and information both from home and from all parts of the ever-expanding British Atlantic World. Such regular contact made settlers and traders conscious of their interdependency and of their membership of a community from which those associated with the far-distant Asian trade were excluded by time and distance. Experience also showed that, for all its discomforts, travel on the Atlantic was reasonably safe and predictable, and that because of prevailing winds and currents, journey times were not significantly longer than those to the eastern Mediterranean.[71] Religious zealots who made their homes in America still liked to represent their first crossing as a rebirth, but it seems that this was more a literary trope than a representation of reality to judge by the frequency with which people from all settlements traversed the Atlantic on several occasions during the course of a lifetime, assured that Providence, and the technical skills of navigators, would bring them safely to their destinations.

The fact that several experiments at colonization proved to be profitable and enduring to the point where a few settlements had assumed such a 'British' appearance that settlers came to consider them as 'home', was equally important in arousing interest in colonial and imperial possibilities. This process has been dubbed 'Anglicization' in relation to the social and cultural convergence that occurred throughout the various settlements in Colonial British America during the period 1660–1760,[72] but the true significance of that development can be appreciated only when it is considered in the light of the experience of the early seventeenth century. Historians discussing the seventeenth century have frequently contrasted the transplanted society of New England, which is depicted as a communal success, with those societies created in the Chesapeake, the West Indies, the Carolinas, and such isolated outposts as Newfoundland, all of which are associated with harsh exploitation, skewed sex ratios, and high mortality. The chapters in the present volume indicate that such contrasts have been exaggerated, and that not even the most committed advocates of the New England experiment were confident at the beginning that their transplanted community would endure. Best estimates of the Great Migration to New England during the 1630s suggest it

[71] See below, pp. 85–90.

[72] Jack P. Greene, *Pursuits of Happiness: The Social Development of Early Modern British Colonies and the Formation of American Culture* (Chapel Hill, NC, 1988).

did not exceed 21,000 people,[73] and John Winthrop's misgiving that the migration was not sufficient to guarantee survival was not exaggerated, since nobody could have imagined that this base population would multiply (principally through an unprecedented rate of natural increase matched only by that of New France; Map 19.1) to reach about 90,000 people of European descent by 1689. While Winthrop and his associates had reason to fear that their society would collapse once immigration faltered, they were also seriously concerned that the colony would not be able to repay its debts, since they had difficulty in finding markets for the goods they produced. Here again the totally unexpected success of Barbados as a sugar-producing island created the demand for food that assured the survival of agrarian and fishing communities in New England, and created the need for the commercial and administrative centres that were such a vital element of New England society at the close of the seventeenth century.

This was a godsend that nobody could have anticipated in the early seventeenth century, when the islands were used either for the production of tobacco of an indifferent quality or as bases for piracy. Besides rendering New England economically solvent, the commercial success of sugar production after the 1640s also facilitated the development, first in Barbados and then in the Leeward Islands and Jamaica, of a wealthy planter plutocracy and an affluent commercial community that was the essence of Britishness in its composition and outlook. There were approximately 20,000 white people living in Barbados at the close of the period, and the road system their leaders designed, the sugar mills they erected, the mansions in which the planters dwelt, and the bustle of the port of Bridgetown all bore witness to its vibrancy as a European commercial community.[74] The profits being made from sugar were such that for most observers there would have been no English, or British, Empire in America without the West Indies, and the remarks of Thomas Bowdler show that people of the time would not have been unduly disturbed by mortality rates which were so high that it had taken a migration of approximately 150,000 white people to all the islands of the British West Indies, down to 1689, to create the white population of 20,000 who then persisted in Barbados. R.B., writing in 1685, was so indifferent to high mortality rates that he even fails to mention them, while John Oldmixon confronted the issue by suggesting that people who had not been productive at home could hardly be considered 'the wealth of a nation'. Neither were contemporaries concerned that whites in Barbados were outnumbered by 30,000 African slaves as long as there was clear evidence that the planters were ready to deal with any contingency that might arise; R.B. consoled himself with the thought that slave revolts were not

[73] See below, pp. 197, 200, where Anderson estimates the settler population in 1650 at 23,000 people.
[74] See below, pp. 226–27, 237–39.

likely so long as slaves were drawn from different regions of Africa and spoke different languages.[75]

Early settlement in the Chesapeake had also seemed unpromising, and there were several occasions on which the Virginia Company in London, and the leaders of the settlement in Virginia, contemplated abandoning the effort because of the financial and human losses that were being sustained. However, all talk of disengagement was silenced once investors recognized the economic possibilities of tobacco production, and the continued high mortality rates among European immigrants were studiously ignored. The cultivation of tobacco also produced ungainly settlement patterns that were the polar opposite to the classical ideal of a colony. Nevertheless, contemporaries found the profits that could be gained from tobacco production more impressive than the associated risks and hardships, and while it is now known that it took a total immigration of 116,000 people to produce a white settler community that numbered about 90,000 at the close of the seventeenth century, the population loss could be shrugged off by R.B. with the blithe assurance that, in the Chesapeake of the 1680s, 'the air is good and the climate so agreeable to the English, especially since the clearing it from woods, that few die of the country disease called seasoning'.[76] Therefore he, as a propagandist for Empire, believed that all shortcomings of the colonial endeavour were counterbalanced by the achievements of the emerging white creole élite, who indeed enjoyed better resistance to local epidemics and who constructed the mansions, churches, and courthouses that came to dominate the Chesapeake countryside at the close of the seventeenth century.

The symbols of prosperity that were then manifested in New England, the West Indies, and the Chesapeake, the three nodal points of settlement in Colonial British America, far outweighed the contingent and fragmented, but commercially important, outposts in Newfoundland and in Hudson Bay. Contemporaries could also look optimistically to the future because the recent urban foundations in Philadelphia, New York, and Charles Town (Charleston) were displaying early signs of economic vitality as they established commercial networks that were more broadly spread than those of the older port of Boston.[77]

When aggregated, these various colonies and settlements amounted to an empire and some authors were already referring to them collectively as such. However, it was very different from any empire or colony that had been envisaged by the Hakluyts or Samuel Purchas. The fundamental difference was that it allowed little space for the Native American population within it, so that the

[75] Oldmixon, *The British Empire*, I, pp. xxx–xxxvi; II, pp. 1–169; *The English Empire*, pp. 201–02.

[76] *The English Empire*, pp. 135–36.

[77] Gary B. Nash, *The Urban Crucible* (Cambridge, Mass., 1979); see chaps. by Ned C. Landsman and Robert M. Weir.

reforming ambition which had legitimized colonization in the first instance could be said to have been almost altogether abandoned.[78] Now it was commerce rather than religion that was invoked to justify colonial activity, and the communities being established on lands that had once belonged to American Indians were essentially colonies of white settlement populated by European emigrants from England, Scotland, Ireland, or colonies under white management which relied on African slaves for a labour force. Authors who, in the tradition of the Hakluyts and Purchas, persisted in comparing English achievements with those of Spain described the Spanish territories in the New World as 'fortunate acquisitions', whereas those of the English were due to their own daring and commercial acumen.[79] This latter attribute immediately called to mind the Dutch, who had been pathfinders in promoting a commercial empire, but the Dutch became less frequently referred to as the French supplanted them as Britain's enemy, and as propagandists of empire began to appreciate the novelty of England's, and ultimately Britain's, achievement. The pamphleteer and historian John Oldmixon acknowledged this uniqueness when, in defending Britain's proprietors in the West Indies against the charge of lacking 'pedigree', he proclaimed that 'prudence and industry' were a greater source of honour than 'a long roll of ancestry'; to give point to this assertion he averred that while there was 'no herald office, no Court of Arms in Barbados . . . there [was] no Trading County in England of that extent where there [were] so many Gentlemen of so good estates, and so good families'.

This assertion of the superiority of Barbados over England rendered superfluous any comparison with contemporary empires, and mention of the empires of Britain's political rivals was seldom made by commentators once it was claimed that British achievements had surpassed even those of the ancient Romans, who were believed to have been the only other people to have successfully advanced their imperial power through the establishment of colonies. Thus, when asking rhetorically if it 'was ever pretended that the Roman colonies dispeopled Rome', Oldmixon concluded in 1708 that 'the British Colonies are or may be much more advantageous to the Britains than the Roman Colonies . . . were to the Romans'.[80] By then Oldmixon, and many of his readers, were satisfied that a process had been completed; this volume sets out to demonstrate that the unfolding of the trial-and-error efforts of the subjects of the British Crown through the course of the seventeenth century can indeed be considered the Origins of Empire.

[78] See chap. by Peter C. Mancall.
[79] *The English Empire*, p. 27.
[80] Oldmixon, *The British Empire*, pp. xxxvi–xxxvii.

Select Bibliography

KENNETH R. ANDREWS, *Trade, Plunder and Settlement: Maritime Enterprise and the Genesis of the British Empire, 1480–1630* (Cambridge, 1984).

DAVID ARMITAGE, *The Ideological Origins of the British Empire* (Cambridge, forthcoming).

BERNARD BAILYN, *The New England Merchants in the Seventeenth Century* (Cambridge, Mass., 1955).

—— and Philip D. Morgan, *Strangers within the Realm: Cultural Margins of the First British Empire* (Chapel Hill, NC, 1991).

ROBERT BRENNER, *Merchants and Revolution: Commercial Change, Political Conflict and London's Overseas Traders, 1550–1653* (Princeton, 1993).

NICHOLAS CANNY, ed., *Europeans on the Move: Studies on European Migration, 1500–1800* (Oxford, 1994).

JACK P. GREENE, *Pursuits of Happiness: The Social Development of Early Modern British Colonies and the Formation of American Culture* (Chapel Hill, NC, 1988).

—— and J. R. POLE, eds., *Colonial British America: Essays in the New History of the Early Modern Era* (Baltimore, 1984).

DAVID HANCOCK, *Citizens of the World: London Merchants and the Integration of the British Atlantic Community, 1735–1835* (Cambridge, 1995).

MICHAEL HECHTER, *Internal Colonialism: The Celtic Fringe in British National Development* (London, 1975).

RICHARD KOEBNER, *Empire* (Cambridge, 1961).

KAREN ORDAHL KUPPERMAN, ed., *America in European Consciousness, 1493–1750* (Chapel Hill, NC, 1995).

JOHN J. MCCUSKER and RUSSELL R. MENARD, eds., *The Economy of British America, 1607–1789* (Chapel Hill, NC, 1985).

D. W. MEINIG, *The Shaping of America: A Geographical Perspective on 500 Years of History*, Vol. I, *Atlantic America, 1492–1800* (New Haven, 1986).

EDMUNDO O'GORMAN, *The Invention of America: An Inquiry into the Historical Nature of the New World and the Meaning of its History* (Bloomington, Ind., 1961).

ANTHONY PAGDEN, *Lords of All the World: Ideologies of Empire in Spain, Britain and France, c.1500–c.1800* (New Haven, 1995).

STEVEN C. A. PINCUS, *Protestantism and Patriotism: Ideologies and the Making of English Foreign Policy, 1650–1668* (Cambridge, 1996).

DAVID B. QUINN, *England and the Discovery of America, 1481–1620* (New York, 1974).

G. V. SCAMMELL, *The First Imperial Age: European Overseas Expansion, c.1400–1715* (London, 1989).

STUART B. SCHWARTZ, ed., *Implicit Understandings: Observing, Reporting, and Reflecting on the Encounters Between Europeans and Other Peoples in the Early Modern Era* (Cambridge, 1994).

PATRICIA SEED, *Ceremonies of Possession in Europe's Conquest of the New World, 1492–1640* (Cambridge, 1995).

IAN K. STEELE, *The English Atlantic, 1675–1740: An Exploration of Communication and Community* (Oxford, 1986).

2

The Struggle for Legitimacy and the Image of Empire in the Atlantic to c.1700

ANTHONY PAGDEN

The English arrived late in the Atlantic. This fact was to mark their views both of their own Imperial identity and that of their two main rivals, Spain and France, until the demise of the 'First British Empire' in the late eighteenth century. John Cabot received his instructions from Henry VII in 1496, but for all the symbolic weight which later generations were to place upon this unprofitable voyage by a migrant Italian and his son, no serious attempt was made to settle in the Americas until Sir Humphrey Gilbert's expedition of 1583. By that time not only had the Spanish empire become a reality both in the Caribbean and on the mainland, but the French had also established a settlement on the St Lawrence.

The English came late, and they began, as most newcomers do, as self-conscious imitators.[1] 'How strange a thing it is', reflected that tireless promoter of the Virginia Company, Robert Johnson, in 1609, 'that all the States of Europe have been asleep so long that for a hundred years and more the ... riches of the East and West should run ... but into one coffer.'[2] The English may have lost 'the first opportunity', but Johnson was convinced that with the Crown now anxious to join in the scramble for America, they would 'make good the common speed', for they 'are best at imitation and so do soon excel their teachers'.[3]

The English had had extensive experience in Ireland with subduing and colonizing a people they regarded with no less bewilderment and disdain than they would later display towards the Algonquian and other neighbouring Native American peoples. But for all the similarities, the English invasion of America was, in the beginning at least, conceived as a different kind of project for which the Spanish achievement provided, if not the only, then certainly the most compelling example. Like the Spanish, the English first saw themselves as conquerors, and like the Spanish they sought to legitimate their Imperial ambitions in the name of an

[1] John Elliott, *Britain and Spain in America: Colonists and Colonized*, The Stenton Lecture, University of Reading, 1994.

[2] *Nova Britannia* (London, 1609), ff. [C3^{r-v}].

[3] *The New Life of Virginea ... being the Second Part of Nova Britannia* (London, 1612), f. [E4^{v}].

obligation to convert the heathen Americans to the Christian faith.[4] 'The principal and main ends' [of this plantation], declared the author of *A True and Sincere Declaration of the Purpose and Ends of the Plantation begun in Virginia*, 'were first to preach and baptize into Christian Religion, and by propagation of that Gospel to recover out of the arms of the Devil, a number of poor and miserable souls, wrapped up unto death, in almost invincible ignorance.'[5]

Providentialism, indeed, frequently bulked as large in English discussions of Empire as it ever did in Spanish discourse, and it played a particularly heightened role in the imperialism of the Cromwellian republic. Cromwell's 'Western Design' of 1654–55, a disastrous attempt to seize Hispaniola as a base for a subsequent invasion of the Spanish-American mainland, seems to have begun as a device for exporting the Revolution of the Saints. Like the Spanish Monarchy, the English Commonwealth was to be a new Rome in the West and, as John Milton observed after its final collapse, a new Jerusalem.[6] This reference to Rome suggests that the English were as much in thrall as the Spanish had been to the image of Imperial grandeur derived from ancient models. Although Britain could never really, even in Sir Walter Ralegh, boast a true *conquistador*, and only Virginia was ever formally recognized, and that speciously, as conquered territory, the earliest promoters of the fledgling settlements in America did their best to stress the honour and glory necessarily attached to expansion overseas. 'Up then,' Richard Hakluyt urged Ralegh in Horatian fashion, 'go on as you have begun, leave to posterity an imperishable monument of your name and fame... For... no greater glory can be handed down than to conquer the barbarian, to recall the savage and the pagan to civility, to draw the ignorant within the orbit of reason.'[7] Spanish success in America, which drew a succession of European imitators, was not, however, attributed only to the supposed heroism of the *conquistadores*, much less to the dubious benefits of their religion. It was, instead, the ability of the Spanish to extract seemingly infinite quantities of precious metals from their new dominions which led other Europeans, even the staunchly Protestant Captain John Smith, to celebrate their 'unparalleled virtues'.[8] Spanish America, at least, was all that new worlds were believed to be. Spain's power and her apparent wealth all flowed from this. The greatness of Spain, wrote Ralegh, had not been gained from 'the trade of

[4] See chap. 7 by Nicholas Canny.

[5] *A True and Sincere Declaration of the... Plantation... in Virginia...* (London, 1610), pp. 2–3.

[6] David Armitage, 'The Cromwellian Protectorate and the Language of Empire', *The Historical Journal*, XXXV (1992), pp. 531–55. On Milton and America, see J. Martin Evans, *Milton's Imperial Epic* (Ithaca, NY, 1996).

[7] *A Discourse on Western Planting*, in E. G. R. Taylor, ed., *The Original Writings... of the two Richard Hakluyts*, 2 vols. (London, 1935), II, p. 368.

[8] Quoted in Karen Ordahl Kupperman, *Settling with the Indians: The Meeting of English and Indian Cultures in America, 1580–1640* (Totowa, NJ, 1980), p. 166.

sacks of Seville oranges . . . It is his Indian Gold that . . . endangereth and disturbeth all the nations of Europe.'[9]

Both the English and the French had, therefore, set off in search of Indian gold of their own. Jacques Cartier's first expedition in 1513 had gone with the aim of discovering islands and lands rich in gold.[10] Similarly, the expeditions which Martin Frobisher led to Newfoundland in 1576, 1577, and 1578 had all been in pursuit of precious metals. All had proved fruitless. Cartier's gold turned out to be iron pyrites and quartz, while Frobisher could only produce a living Eskimo as 'witness of the captain's far and tedious travel'.[11] As Adam Smith later observed, Spain's great wealth had been the consequence neither of virtue nor heroism, but merely of chance. 'Fortune', he remarked drily, 'did upon this what she has done upon very few other occasions. She realized in some measure the extravagant hope of her votaries.'[12]

The lasting recognition that there was no new Mexico or Peru still to be discovered, that Ralegh's 'Large, Rich and Beautiful Empire of Guiana' was a fiction, transformed forever the English perceptions of the kind of project their Empire in America was intended to be. Confusedly at first and then with religious, and invariably self-righteous zeal, they abandoned the vision of El Dorado and Spanish-style kingdoms overseas for that of 'colonies' and 'plantations'; places, that is, which would be sources not of human or mineral, but of agricultural and commercial wealth.

By the early eighteenth century this transition was so complete that any memory of the earlier objectives of the French and English in North America had been erased from the record. In 1748 Montesquieu could afford to view the ruin of the Spanish empire in America with quiet satisfaction. The Castilian crown, priest-ridden and murderously obsessed with religious conformity, had looked upon the Americas as 'objects of conquest'. The English and the French, 'more refined than they', had, by contrast, seen in the New World 'objects of commerce and, as such, directed their attention to them'. The goal of these new, more enlightened, settlers had been not 'the foundation of a town or of a new empire', but rather the peaceful exploitation of commerce and natural resources.[13]

[9] Robert Schomburgk, ed., *The Discoverie of the . . . Empire of Gviana, with a Relation of the . . . City of Manoa (which the Spaniards call El Dorado)* . . . (1596; London, 1848), p. xiv.

[10] Marcel Trudel, *The Beginnings of New France, 1524–1663*, trans. Patricia Claxton (Toronto, 1973), pp. 19–20.

[11] Richard Collinson, ed., *The Three Voyages of Martin Frobisher* (London, 1867), pp. 74–75; see the comments in Stephen Greenblatt, *Marvellous Possessions* (Oxford, 1991), pp. 109–18.

[12] R. H. Campbell and A. S. Skinner, eds., textual editor W. B. Todd, *An Inquiry into the Nature and Causes of the Wealth of Nations* [1776] (Vol. II of the Glasgow Edition of the Works and Correspondence of Adam Smith), 2 vols. (Oxford, 1976), II, pp. 563–64.

[13] *De l'esprit des lois*, Book XXI, chap. 21.

This new image of Empire changed the kind of enterprise the English, and subsequently the British, Empire was to become. It meant, too, that English relations with, and attitudes towards, the aboriginal peoples of the Americas was different from that of the Spanish. The Spanish sought to integrate the Indians into a miscegenated society, albeit at the lowest possible social level, and the French attempted to 'Frenchify'[14] their indigenes. The English, after decades of moralizing, sought only to exclude the Indians or, where expedient, to annihilate them. And because of their view of themselves as a commercial and agricultural, rather than a conquering people, few Europeans were so little given to moral scruples over their imperial exploits as the English. But although questions of the legitimacy of the occupation of aboriginal lands, and the frequent enslaving of the aboriginals themselves, could be, and frequently were, swept aside when more immediate interests demanded, generations of colonists found themselves unable fully to escape the painful implications of the question asked by Robert Gray in *A Good Speed to Virginia* of 1609: 'by what right or warrant we can enter into the land of these Savages, take away their rightful inheritance from them, and plant ourselves in their place, being unwronged or unprovoked by them?'[15]

One of the foundational conceptions which the modern European empires had inherited from their classical, and subsequently their Christian, ancestors was the conviction, moral as much as legal, that every expansionist state was required to legitimate its actions by appeal to some law, in most cases of either supposedly natural or divine origin. In the terms accepted by every legal system of classical and Christian origin, acts of appropriation necessarily involved the denial of those rights which all men held by virtue of their condition as men. Every such act, therefore, had to be explained so as to render those natural rights invalid. Questions of legitimation, however, only became pressing when obvious spoliation had taken place involving a sufficiently large number of persons over a sufficiently protracted period of time to draw the attention of the metropolitan power, or to become a source of contention between the colonists themselves. For this reason the British in Africa and Asia were little concerned with legitimating their actions, at least until the nineteenth century. Until that time they had no declared imperial ambitions in those places. In Africa their activities were largely confined to trade, primarily in slaves and gold, and what few settlements they did establish, although generally fortified, were in no sense 'colonies'. Legally, too, they were generally held by agreement with the indigenous rulers to whom rent or tribute was usually

[14] i.e. *franciser*—the word was coined by Mirabeau to describe Colbert's colonial policy; Anthony Pagden, *Lords of All the World: Ideologies of Empire in Spain, Britain and France, c.1500–c.1800* (New Haven, 1995), p. 151.

[15] *A Good Speed to Virginia* (London, 1609), ff. C3^{v} – [C4^{r}].

paid.[16] Similarly in Asia, where their presence was far more significant, the English, until the mid-eighteenth century, were, or believed themselves to be, wholly engaged in commerce. English factories in Asia were established with active native support, and constituted mixed communities of both English and Asian merchants. Of the three settlements which were later to grow into the major British bases in India—Madras, Calcutta, and Bombay—Madras and Calcutta were both acquired by treaty and Bombay was ceded by the Portuguese in 1661 as part of Charles II's marriage settlement. The 'aristocratic republicans' of the East India Company were firmly opposed to conquest and colonization, as expensive and ultimately ruinous. They proudly contrasted their own trading practices with the alleged violence employed by their Portuguese and Dutch rivals.[17] Had not the Dutch, asked one champion of the Company in 1685, 'killed thousands of *Indians* for one that ever died by the *English* hands'.[18] The belief of Sir Josiah Child—the Company's President in the 1680s, as well as one of the most influential political economists of the seventeenth century—that the Company should pursue a more aggressive policy towards recalcitrant native rulers, came to nothing. In the seventeenth century the British were no match for Mughal forces, and the brief skirmish with the Mughal empire between 1688 and 1689 resulted in the closure of the factory at Surat and the blockade of Bombay.[19] None of these events was sustained enough to pose lasting problems of legitimation, and none resulted in any form of colonization. Furthermore, any limited war of this kind could always be justified in terms of the claim that any attempt made to restrict trade, or to control the seaways, was contrary to natural law and had thus resulted in the loss of the natural rights of the supposed belligerents.

Legitimation only became a pressing moral and political concern when prolonged warfare became a necessary condition of expansion. Then all the British Imperial adventurers, from Ralegh to Clive, were troubled by Cicero's assertion that 'the best state never undertakes war except to keep faith or in defence of its safety'.[20] As the self-conscious heirs of the classical *imperium mundi*, all the European colonizing powers were sensitive to the need to explain their actions as directed towards peaceful ends, and thus to find reasons in natural law which would justify their all-too-frequent resort to violent means.

For this reason it was the Americas, occupied by technologically simple but powerful groups of peoples fully able, at least initially, to resist European incursions, which tested European moral and legal scruples to their limits. The Spanish were, of course, the first to confront this problem. How could the Amerindians, who, prior

[16] See below, pp. 250–51. [17] See chap. by P. J. Marshall. [18] See below, p. 280.
[19] Ibid. pp. 280–81.
[20] *De Republica*, iii. 34. See J. Barnes, 'Cicéron et la guerre juste', *Bulletin de la société française de philosophie*, LXXX (1986), pp. 41–80.

to Columbus's arrival, had had no knowledge of the Europeans' very existence, be said to have 'harmed them'? The attempts by the so-called 'School of Salamanca' in the mid-sixteenth century to find an answer to this question were prolonged, bitter, and noisy. They had far-reaching consequences and provided a background against which the other European powers tested their own claims to legitimacy well into the eighteenth century. They were even praised by Samuel Johnson, no enemy to Protestant imperial ambitions, as evidence of the possibility of enlightened humanitarianism even within papist societies. But for all their significance, they were also in one important respect unique. For the Spanish, unlike the English or the French, had from the first been engaged upon a self-styled war of conquest. Furthermore, they had pursued this conquest on the highly questionable authority of a papal grant. In 1493 Pope Alexander VI had issued five Bulls which conceded to Ferdinand and Isabella the right to occupy a region vaguely defined as 'such islands and lands . . . as you have discovered or are about to discover'. This concession was dubious, at best, since it relied upon an assumption which few, even among Catholics, were prepared to concede: that the papacy could exercise authority over secular as well as spiritual affairs, and that its jurisdiction extended to non-Christians as well as Christians. Nevertheless, the 'Bulls of Donation' remained a central component of the Spanish defence of empire until the mid-eighteenth century.

Spanish arguments over the rights of conquerors provided a point of departure for the English accounts of their activities in the Americas. Despite the fact that, even under Cromwell, the English could make no claim to have been granted their overseas possession by some higher authority, Henry VII's letters patent to John Cabot of 1496 had echoed exactly the terms of Alexander VI's Bulls of Donation by granting him rights to 'conquer and possess'[21] for the King, any territory not already in Christian hands, as, indeed, did those granted by Elizabeth I to Sir Humphrey Gilbert in 1578 and to Walter Ralegh in March 1584.[22] The argument, duly pressed by Richard Hakluyt, was that since Henry was 'Defender of the Faith', he was as entitled as any Pope to make universal concessions of sovereignty so as to 'enlarge and advance . . . the faith of Christ'.[23] This argument, however, did not win many adherents. The English, after all, were Protestants and, as many argued, even if the papal Bulls had been binding upon Catholics, nothing—including Henry's papal sobriquet—of Catholic origin could be binding upon them.

The only possible argument derived from divine dispensation which might have been available to the English was the claim often referred to as the 'Calvinist theory

[21] Quoted in Moses Finaly, 'Colonies—An Attempt at a Typology', *Transactions of the Royal Historical Society*, XXVI (1976), p. 180.

[22] Francis Jennings, *The Invasion of America: Indians, Colonialism, and the Cant of Conquest* (Chapel Hill, NC, 1975), p. 45.

[23] *Discourse on Western Planting*, p. 215.

of revolution'.[24] This argument, first attributed to the fourteenth-century theologian, John Wyclif and the Bohemian reformer Jan Huss, and subsequently associated with Luther and Calvin, maintained that since all *dominium*—that is, property-rights and sovereignty—derives from God's grace and not, as the Thomists had insisted, from God's law, no non-Christian, nor any 'ungodly' Christian, could be a bearer of rights. In terms of this assertion, the Amerindians as infidels had been denied grace and could, therefore, make no claim to *dominium*. Their properties, and even their persons, were thus forfeit to the first 'godly' person who came their way. 'Our Emigrants to *North-America*', wrote Josiah Tucker to Edmund Burke in 1775, 'were mostly Enthusiasts of a particular Stamp. They were that set of Republicans, who believed, or pretended to believe, that *Dominion was founded in Grace*. Hence they conceived, that they had the best Right in the World, both to *tax* and to *persecute* the *Ungodly*'.[25]

Although the attitudes and the behaviour of the Calvinists frequently seemed to suggest that they did indeed take such a view, few British writers ever employed this argument. For most Protestants could also see that any theory grounded upon the supposed 'godliness' of individuals—rather than on the natural law—could be used to legitimate any claimant immodest enough to think himself a 'godly ruler'. For this reason, if for no other, it was, as James Otis noted in 1764, a 'madness' which, at least by his day, had been 'pretty generally exploded and hissed off the stage'.[26]

There was another reason why the 'Calvinist theory of revolution' played so small a role in English attempts to legitimate their presence in America. Like the Spanish natural-law claims it sought to overturn, it was an argument for exercising rights over people. This meant that it could only be realized through conquest, and the English, as we have seen, had already rejected the image of their Empire as one based on conquest. It was also the case that the political culture of England, because it had itself been the creation of the Norman Conquest of 1066, was committed to the 'continuity theory' of constitutional law in which the legal and political institutions of the conquered are deemed to survive a conquest.[27] Conquest, the English believed, could therefore never confer legitimacy, and in general could only ever have deleterious consequences for conqueror and conquered alike. '*Conquest*', Locke had said, 'is as far from setting up any Government, as demol-

[24] Quentin Skinner, *The Foundations of Modern Political Thought*, 2 vols. (Cambridge, 1978), II, pp. 189–348.

[25] *A Letter to Edmund Burke, Esq . . . in Answer to his Printed Speech* (Gloucester, 1775), pp. 18–20.

[26] 'The Rights of the British Colonies Asserted and Proved' [Boston, 1764], in Bernard Bailyn, ed., *Pamphlets of the American Revolution*, Vol. I, *1750–1765* (Cambridge, Mass., 1965), p. 422.

[27] James Tully, *An Approach to Political Philosophy: Locke in Contexts* (Cambridge, 1993), pp. 257–58, and J. G. A. Pocock, *The Ancient Constitution and the Feudal Law* (Cambridge, 1987), pp. 237–38.

ishing an House is from building a new one in the place. Indeed it often makes way for a new Frame of a Common-wealth, by destroying the former; but without the Consent of the people, can never erect a new one.'[28]

Therefore, the constitution which Locke helped to draft for the Carolinas cautioned the settlers, with Spanish arguments for conquest in mind, that the Indians' 'idolatry, ignorance or mistakes gives us no right to expel or use them ill'.[29]

The English were reluctant to press their claims in this way for obvious empirical reasons. Castile had been the only European power to settle in an area both rich in natural resources and in which the aboriginal peoples had achieved the highest degree of population density and technological expertise. The complexity and the military organization of Mexican and Inka society also made them, once they had been conquered and all serious resistance crushed, relatively easy to rule. As Josiah Child noted in 1665, the Spaniards had benefited from having settled in areas where cities and plantations already existed, whereas the English had only 'wild Heathens, with whom they could not, nor ever have been known to mix'.[30] Such peoples were clearly unsuited to be the true vassals of a conquering monarch. The crowning of Powhatan may have been intended to create the image of a North American Atahualpa; it was certainly meant to emphasize the dependence of the American chieftain on the English Crown.[31] But in practice the English wars of conquest in the Americas were relatively limited affairs, generally involving various and mutually hostile aboriginal groups.

Early contacts, which had made the settlers dependent upon native agriculture, soon gave way to policies of either segregation or, when the Native Americans seemed to threaten the existence of the settlements, attempted genocide. This need to draw and enforce a frontier between the Indian lands and the lands of the Crown, in marked contrast to anything which took place in Spanish America,[32] was to have far-reaching consequences for the subsequent legal and political relationship between the two groups.

Unlike the Spanish, the English were, therefore, predominantly concerned with securing rights not over peoples but over lands. In order to make good these rights

[28] *Second Treatise*, 175, in *Locke's Two Treatises of Government* (hereafter *Two Treaties*), ed. Peter Laslett, 2nd edn. (Cambridge, 1967), p. 403.

[29] *The First Set of Fundamental Constitutions of South Carolina as compiled by Mr. John Locke* [March 1669], Act XCVII in *Historical Collection of South Carolina . . . relating to the State from its first Discovery until its Independence in the year 1776*, 2 vols. (New York, 1836), I, p. 386.

[30] *A New Discourse on Trade* (Glasgow, 1751), p. 153.

[31] Powhatan's coronation is discussed by Nicholas Canny, p. 157. *The Discourses of Conquest* On Powhatan's legal status in the eyes of the English Crown, see Robert A. Williams, *The American Indian in Western Legal Thought: The Discourses of Conquest* (New York, 1990), pp. 206–12.

[32] Elliott, *Britain and Spain*, p. 12.

they had to argue that the territories they wished to appropriate were in some sense unoccupied. The best-known, and certainly the most frequently cited, argument in favour of the expropriation of aboriginal lands in America was John Locke's claim in his *Second Treatise of Government* of 1689–90 that a man only acquired rights of ownership in a thing when he had 'mixed his *Labour* with [it]; and joyned to it something that is his own'.[33] His contribution to the debate over property rights in America was enormous.[34]

Locke's personal involvement with English colonies in America is well known. He was secretary to the Lords Proprietor of Carolina between 1668 and 1671, secretary to the Council of Trade and Plantations, 1673–74, and a member of the Board of Trade from 1696 until 1700. He had investments in the Royal African Company (whose business was slaves) and in the Company of Merchant Adventurers to trade with the Bahamas, and he was a Landgrave of the government of Carolina. His writings on America, apart from the observation in the *Two Treatises* and the *Fundamental Constitutions of Carolina* of 1669, include Carolina's agrarian laws, a reform proposal for Virginia of 1696, memoranda and policy recommendations for the boards of trade, histories of European exploration and settlement, as well as a wide range of documents, many still unpublished, covering the government and the rights of the English Crown in America.[35] His principal defence of the English colonization of America rested, however, on the main argument set out in Chapter 5 of the *Second Treatise*: 'Of Property'.

Locke's theory of property lies at the centre of his political theory, and it has been seen as a crucial development in the language of rights in early-modern Europe. However, for all its complexity, and Locke's celebration of his own originality, it is, in the first instance, a development of the argument from Roman law known as *res nullius*. This maintained that all 'empty things', which included unoccupied lands, remained the common property of all mankind until they were put to some, generally agricultural, use. 'In the Law of Nature and of Nations', John Donne told the members of the Virginia Company in 1622, 'a land

[33] *Second Treatise*, 27, p. 306.

[34] James Tully, 'Rediscovering America: The Two Treatises and Aboriginal Rights', in Tully, *An Approach*, pp. 137–76. Most of what follows is drawn from this remarkable article, and from two other works by the same author: 'Aboriginal Property and Western Theory: Recovering a Middle Ground', *Social Philosophy and Policy*, XI (1994), pp. 153–80, and *Strange Multiplicity: Constitutionalism in an Age of Diversity* (Cambridge, 1995), pp. 70–81. See also 'Property, Self-Government and Consent', *Canadian Journal of Political Science*, XXVIII (1995), pp. 105–32, and 'Placing the "*Two Treatises*"' in Nicholas Philipson and Quentin Skinner, eds., *Political Discourse in Early-Modern Britain* (Cambridge, 1993), pp. 257–58.

[35] Listed in Tully, 'Rediscovering America', pp. 140–41. See also Richard Ashcroft, 'Political Theory and Political Reform: John Locke's "Essay on Virginia"', *The Western Political Quarterly*, XXII (1969), pp. 742–58.

never inhabited by any, or utterly derelicted and immemorially abandoned by the former inhabitants, becomes theirs that will possess it.'[36]

Robert Cushman in 1621, Samuel Purchas in 1629, and Francis Higginson in New England in 1631, among others, had all used arguments which, though far cruder than those Locke was to develop, drew upon the same basic Romanized premise. In 1633 a jurisdictional dispute developed between John Winthrop, Roger Williams, and John Cotton (sometimes compared to the famous dispute in 1551 between Bartolomé de las Casas and Juan Ginés de Sepúlveda) over the competing claims of possession by occupation and possession by treaty, which was to last, in one form or another, well into the following century.

The association between the historical need to press the claim to *res nullius*, and what is sometimes called 'the agriculturalist argument' became, in effect, the basis for most English attempts to legitimate their presence in America. That so many of the examples Locke uses in his *Second Treatise* are American ones shows that his intention was to provide the settlers, for whom he had worked in so many other ways, with a powerful argument based in natural law rather than legislative decree to justify their depredations. It was, of course, not only that. Locke's objective was to solve a much-disputed problem in natural law: in his own words, how 'any one should ever come to have a Property in a thing', given that we have it on the authority of the Scriptures that 'God gave the World to *Adam* and his Posterity in common'.[37] And the answer to that question would have to be applicable to all persons everywhere. Locke's solution to this conundrum offered the colonists the most authoritative re-working of a classical legal theory which, in differing idioms, would provide the colonists with a means of characterizing their societies, and their relations with the land of America and its aboriginal inhabitants, down to, and in many cases far beyond, independence.

Locke's development of the *res nullius* argument was twofold. First, America is said to be in the same condition as all the world had been before the creation of human societies. Locke's famous remark, 'in the beginning all the world was *America*', refers immediately to the absence among the Amerindians of any form of commercial exchange.[38] But this, in turn, means that '*America* . . . is still a Pattern of the first Ages in *Asia* and *Europe*, whilst the Inhabitants were too few for the Country, and want of People and Money gave Men no Temptation to enlarge their

[36] *A Sermon Preached to the Honourable Company of the Virginia Plantation, 13 Nov. 1622* (London, 1623), p. 26. The most commonly cited source is *Digest*, XLI, 1. and the law *Ferae bestiae*, Justinian *Institutes*, II. i. 2: 'Natural reason admits the title of the first occupant to that which previously had no owner.'

[37] For the wider context of the debate, see James Tully, *A Discourse on Property: John Locke and his Adversaries* (Cambridge, 1980).

[38] *Second Treatise*, 49, p. 319.

Possessions of Land, or contest for wider extent of Ground'. Because the Amerindians are in this condition their rulers 'exercise very little Dominion, and have but a very moderate Sovereignty'.[39] They are thus still in the 'State of Nature', although in a very late stage of it. The form of political organization among the Amerindians is what was called 'individual self government'. Although this did, in Locke's view, grant their 'kings' some measure of 'dominion' and 'sovereignty', it was clearly not equal to that exercised within a fully developed political society of a European kind, where individuals had surrendered their 'natural power' to a political community and established a legal system and judiciary. Such persons lived '*in Civil Society* one with another'. Those who do not 'are still in the state of Nature, each being, where there is no other, Judge for himself, and Executioner'.[40]

This account of aboriginal American society bore no resemblance to any of the ethnographical data with which Locke certainly could have been, and probably was, familiar. But no English, and subsequently British, claim to sovereignty in the Americas paid much heed to such data. In natural law any deviation from what were assumed to be universal conditions constituted a violation of those conditions. Any alternative system of property ownership, land tenure, or rulership which the Amerindians might practise was regarded not as an alternative, but simply as an aberration.

There were, of course, areas in which Europeans and Native Americans met under less stark intellectual restraints. The experience of life in unfamiliar and threatening environments compelled many of the settlers to seek a 'middle ground', where some understanding of aboriginal customs were observed, and some kind of dialogue between native and interloper was possible.[41] But Locke and his fellow ideologues were not interested in ethnology, nor were they seeking means of accommodation. They were looking instead for ways to legitimate wholesale appropriation which would be acceptable both to other European powers and, in some measure, to their own consciences.

The major conclusion which Locke drew from his characterization of Amerindian society was that it was possible for Europeans to disregard all aboriginal forms of government, and consequently to deny them any status as 'nations'. This meant that all dealings between Europeans and Amerindians were, in effect, between legitimate political societies on the one hand and simple individuals on the other. Although Locke does not say so, this would have meant that all treaties and contracts made between the settlers, as representatives of the English Crown, and Amerindian chiefs would have been worthless.

[39] Ibid., 108, pp. 357–58. [40] Ibid., 87, p. 343.

[41] See esp. Richard White, *The Middle Ground* (Cambridge, 1991).

Locke's second claim is concerned with the Indians' right to own both 'their' lands and whatever goods they might produce. Locke's claim that it was labour which removed all commodities from the state of nature into the domain of private ownership meant that 'this... makes the Deer, that *Indian's* who hath killed it; 'tis allowed to be his goods who hath bestowed his labour upon it'.[42] The hunter and the gatherer could legally possess what they required in order to survive, although they could not, since such produce was perishable, acquire a surplus in this way.[43] With the invention of money property became mobile, and surplus-producing civil societies could, thereby, acquire rights over far more than the individual's due share without invading that of his neighbour. The Amerindians, however, who lived in a pre-commercial state could not do this. They, therefore, could legally have no right to the goods of the land beyond that needed for their own immediate survival. As John Winthrop had phrased it, 'if we leave them sufficient for their use we may lawfully take the rest, there being more than enough for them and us'.[44] Even if they did 'improve' the lands, this was never enough to establish an undisputed right over it. 'A man does not become proprietary of the sea', said John Donne, 'because he hath two or three boats fishing in it.'[45]

Furthermore, any hunter-gatherer society was condemned, no matter how rich the lands off which it lived, to perpetual poverty. The image in the early promotional literature for America, of a land of abundance where food could be had without labour, was an illusion. 'The *Americans*', wrote Locke, 'are rich in Land and poor in all the Comforts of Life', because 'for want of improving it by labour [they] have not one hundreth part of the Conveniences we enjoy.'[46] Locke seems to have shared the view of many Europeans that the comforts which the Europeans could provide, and teach the Indians how to provide for themselves, would easily compensate them for their loss of the traditional, and wasted, hunting grounds.

For Locke and the European settlers, 'the *chief matter of Property*' was not the fruits of the earth 'but the *Earth itself*'.[47] Rights in land, like rights in game or fish, were established by mingling one's labour with the goods to be acquired. In the case of land, this demanded a higher degree of technical expertise, and carried a far greater social weight. For Locke, agricultural societies were the final stage in a development which had begun with nomadic hunter-gatherer communities and then progressed through Aristotle's 'lazy pastoralists' before reaching the true *polis*, the settled political community. Civil societies were defined in terms of the modes of their political authority. Such societies could also only ever be agricultural, and

[42] *Second Treatise*, 30, p. 307. [43] *Second Treatise*, 36, p. 313.

[44] Quoted in Tully, 'Rediscovering America', p. 151.

[45] *A Sermon... to the Honourable Company of the Virginia Plantation*, p. 27.

[46] *Second Treatise*, 41, pp. 314–15; Tully, *Strange Multiplicity*, p. 75.

[47] *Second Treatise*, 32, p. 308.

subsequently commercial, ones. Agriculture constituted the final stage in the development of the social expression of human rationality, since agriculture not only transformed, in Aristotelian terms, nature's potential into actuality, it also required a high degree of co-operation, and the existence of settled communities. It carried, therefore, a quasi-sacral significance, in that by tilling and 'improving' the land men were not merely ameliorating their own condition, but were fulfilling their ends as men.[48] Because Amerindians merely roamed and foraged across the land, they did not *own* it. The Indians had only, in Robert Cushman's words, 'run over the grass as do also the foxes and wild beasts', and did nothing to add to its value by 'maturing, gathering, ordering etc.'. On the other hand, the English, by settling and by 'maturing, gathering, ordering etc.', had acquired rights of possession in the land to which the original inhabitants could make no claim.[49] The settlers had then made good those rights by 'improving', through agriculture, what were frequently described as the 'vacant places of *America*'.[50]

There was, however, a further and still more sinister point. Locke insisted that land had been given to men for the 'use of the Industrious and Rational'. Those who did not use it in this way were not only lacking in industry but might also be lacking in rationality. Locke did not press this claim, but both his argument and that of the Spanish Aristotelians, most notably Juan Ginés de Sepúlveda, who wished to argue that the Indians, because they had failed to attain the required degrees of civility, were 'slaves by nature', depend upon the same proposition that rights to land derive not from need or simple presence but from collective, and rational, human action.[51] Locke and his successors firmly denied that the Indians' failure to till the land might constitute a reason for mistreating them; indeed, the Carolina constitution explicitly denied any such assumption. But their alleged status as hunter-gatherers helped to reinforce the settlers' general contempt for the 'savage' condition of the Amerindians.[52] Also, since any man who refused to accept the Europeans' right to appropriate 'vacant' lands was in defiance of the natural law, he might 'be destroyed as a *Lyon* or a *Tyger*, one of those wild Savage Beasts, with whom Men can have no Society nor Security'.[53] The settlers might thus, Locke

[48] Ibid., 32, p. 309.

[49] *Reasons and Considerations Touching the Lawfullness of Removing out of England into Parts of America* (London, 1622), f. 2^{v}, and see William Cronon, *Changes in the Land: Indians, Colonists and the Ecology of New England* (New York, 1988), p. 56.

[50] *Second Treatise*, 36, p. 311.

[51] See Anthony Pagden, *The Fall of Natural Man*, 2nd edn. (Cambridge, 1986), pp. 27–56, 109–18.

[52] Tully also indicates similarities between Locke's argument for the enslavement of aboriginal peoples, and those used by the Spanish scholastics, although these depended upon the violations of the natural law rather than a failure to develop a natural potential. Tully, 'Rediscovering America', pp. 163–64.

[53] *Second Treatise*, 11, p. 292.

claimed in the *First Treatise of Government*, make war on the Indians 'to seek Reparation upon any injury received from them'. As in the Spanish case, such 'reparation' could, and frequently did, take the form of enslavement.[54]

The *res nullius* argument, with Locke's development of it, was, and remained until 1776, the most powerful and the most frequently cited legitimation of the British presence in America, and it was to be employed later, in a modified form, to justify British incursions into both Africa and Australia. But it was not without its critics. Some, most notably Roger Williams, rejected the entire argument on empirical grounds. Giving 'the Country to his English subjects, which belonged to the Native Indians', the King had, he claimed, committed an injustice, since in his view forest-clearing and slash-and-burn agricultural techniques did constitute a form of improvement. There was also the difficulty over the status of royal hunting grounds in England. If the King could exercise true property rights over areas of hunting land then, in natural law, so could the Indians.[55]

Williams, however, had a scarcely concealed agenda. He was defending Salem's right to purchase land from the Indians. Many years later, as the battle between the colonists and the Crown over the right to land intensified, the Amerindians found themselves some unusual allies. The 'claim by *prior discovery or pre-occupancy*', argued Jeremiah Dummer in 1721, applied only 'to derelict lands, which they [the Americas] were not, being full of inhabitants who undoubtedly had as good a title to their own country as the Europeans have to theirs'. And if the Amerindians had, indeed, been the true owners of 'their' lands, then the only legitimate way in which the colonists could have acquired them was through purchase or 'concession'. There could, Dummer insisted, be 'no other right than that in which the honest New-England planters rely on having purchased it with their money'.[56]

As late as 1781 Samuel Wharton was arguing against the government of the United States that Locke's natural rights to the means of preservation did in fact mean that the Indians had a right to their land, since it constituted their means of subsistence. Like Dummer and Williams, Wharton had an interest in defending the 'civil' status of the Indians: in his case, the survival of a number of land-speculation companies which claimed substantial areas of the state of Virginia on grounds of 'concession'.[57] For these men it was crucial that the Amerindians should enjoy natural rights of property in their lands, since only then could they

[54] See Anthony Pagden, 'Dispossessing the Barbarian: The Language of Spanish Thomism and the Debate over the Property Rights of the American Indians', in Pagden, ed., *The Languages of Political Theory in Early-Modern Europe* (Cambridge, 1987), pp. 79–98.

[55] Cronon, *Changes*, pp. 56–57.

[56] *A Defence of the New-England Charters* (London, 1721), p. 14.

[57] Tully, 'Rediscovering America', pp. 168–69.

dispose of them as they wished. No wandering hunters devoid of civil institutions would be in a position to make 'concessions' of any kind.

In general, however, the question of the status of hunting land could be resolved in terms of the widely accepted stadial theory of social development. Hunting in an agricultural and commercial stage of human development was a relic, and a mere pastime. It had nothing to do with subsistence. The King's right as the ruler of an advanced agricultural people to take possession of land for productive use also granted him the rights to retain some for leisure pursuits. The claim that 'primitive' forms of crop production constituted 'improvement', and thus provided the grounds for possession, was dismissed by John Cotton.[58]

The *res nullius* argument was widely deployed against rival European powers wielding similar arguments in the same areas. In such cases, however, it could only be made effective if it included some claim to prior discovery, since discovery constituted the necessary first step towards effective occupation. The English, in their struggle with the French, expended a great deal of effort in claims and counter-claims to property rights over territory they boasted that they had been the first to 'discover'. In general, such arguments were poorly considered and inconsistently applied. In 1609, for instance, when there was a handful of settlers in the malarial swamps of the James River, the first Royal Charter for the Virginia Company solemnly laid claim to what was, in effect, all the territory of North America not actively occupied by the Spanish.[59]

Nobody knew anything about the real extent of these regions, nor of the nature of their inhabitants. To match this, the French Crown in 1627, when there were only 107 French settlers in Canada, gathered in settlements in Acadia and the St Lawrence and completely isolated from one another, asserted its rights over a territory which reached from Florida to the Arctic Circle, nearly all of which was uncharted, and virtually none of which was, in practice, either *res nullius* or—given the Spanish presence in the south—'undiscovered'; nor could it possibly have been said to be so even in theory.[60]

The need to sustain claims to prior discovery against those made by rival powers resulted in some very far-fetched readings of the early history of the European voyages, and a prolonged debate over who had been the first to reach America. The problem for the English and the French was the primacy of Columbus's first voyage. The only way to challenge this was to find even earlier transatlantic voyages. The yoking of Welsh and English history by the accession of the Tudor dynasty and the Acts of Union of 1536 and 1543 allowed the voyages of a fictional

[58] Quoted in Cronon, *Changes*, p. 58.
[59] *The Three Charters of the Virginia Company of London* . . . , p. 1.
[60] Marcel Trudel, *New France*, p. 163.

Welshman, Prince Madoc, who had supposedly fled civil war in 1170 to what is now Alabama, to be presented as evidence that, in Hakluyt's words, 'the West Indies were discovered and inhabited 325 years before Columbus made his first journey'.[61] And if this seemed a rather weak basis for territorial occupation, he added, somewhat more plausibly, that it had been the Cabots, sailing in English ships and under English instructions, who had 'first discovered Florida [the North American mainland] for the King of England'.[62] Francis I of France referred vaguely to a land discovered by the French thirty years before Columbus's first voyage, and Henry IV's cosmographer royal, André Thevet, without reference to either the English or the Spaniards, renamed the entire American continent 'Antarctic France'. He was not above inventing 'some old papers and Pilot books', which demonstrated that Breton sailors had reached America in the reign of Charles VIII.[63]

The trouble with all these stories was not merely their obvious absurdity. In law, discovery constituted only the first step towards legitimate occupation. 'To pass by and eye', as Francis I icily informed the Spanish ambassador, 'is no title of possession.'[64] Neither were those more formal acts of occupation: setting up a stone cross (a *padrão*), as the Portuguese had on the West African coast; planting a standard, as Columbus had done in the Antilles; or removing a twig and a piece of earth 'after the custom of England', as Sir Humphrey Gilbert did in St John's Harbour in 1583.[65] To 'discover' something in the sense of acquiring rights of possession over it meant, as Hugo Grotius argued in 1633, not merely 'to seize it with the eyes [*occulis usurpare*] but to apprehend it'.[66] In order to be *rights*, claims to both property and sovereignty (*dominium*) have to be exercised. The 'agriculturalist' argument which provided the basis for all English claims to land-rights in America rested precisely upon the claim that the Europeans, unlike the Native Americans, had exercised *dominium* in the form of mingling their labour with the land. And no argument used against another European power could afford to be so radically inconsistent with one used against an aboriginal people. All those who

[61] David Armitage, 'The New World in British Historical Thought', in Karen Ordahl Kupperman, ed., *America in European Consciousness, 1492–1750* (Chapel Hill, NC, 1995), p. 59.

[62] *Discourse on Western Planting*, pp. 292–95. The English were still resorting to prior discovery in claiming Hudson Bay as late as 1670: W. J. Eccles, *Canada under Louis XIV, 1663–1701* (London, 1964), p. 111.

[63] Trudel, *New France*, p. 38, and André Thevet, *La Cosmographie universelle*, 2 vols. (Paris, 1575), II, 964^{v}–65.

[64] Quoted in Trudel, *New France*, p. 38.

[65] Patricia Seed, *Ceremonies of Possession in Europe's Conquest of the New World, 1492–1640* (Cambridge, 1995), p. 1.

[66] *Mare liberum: The Freedom of the Seas or the Right which Belongs to the Dutch to Take Part in the East India Trade*, trans. with a revision of the Latin text of 1633 by Ralph van Deman Magoffin (Oxford, 1916), p. 15.

made contact with each other in America did so, in Locke's words, 'perfectly in the State of Nature'.[67] This was also the real theoretical weakness of the arguments set out in the Bulls of Donation. For even if the Pope had been in an undisputed position to make donations of this kind, he would at best only be granting something akin to first refusal. To be masters of America the English, or the French, would have had to have exercised their mastery: something which they clearly had not done over vast tracts of it. 'Nothing but possession by a colony, a settlement or a fortress', wrote Arthur Young in 1772, 'is now allowed to give a right from discovery.'[68]

As Young recognized, few European titles for original settlement in America would stand scrutiny. It was only the continuing fact of its existence which could confer legitimacy on the European possession of the New World. Even some Spaniards, such as the jurist Juan de Solórzano y Pereira, whose *De indiarum iure* of 1629 was widely read in British America, were prepared to accept that, whether the initial claims made by the Europeans in America turned out to be just or unjust, they could only be sustained by prolonged occupation. The Roman law of prescription allowed for long-term, *de facto* occupation of a particular thing (*præscriptio longi temporis*) to be recognized *de iure* as a case of *dominium.* Thus, long-term occupation could confirm retrospective rights of property and even—although this was more dubious—of jurisdiction. It was always the objective condition which conferred legal rights and, in the end, it was legal, not natural, rights which were under discussion.[69]

Despite the generalized hostility of the common law to the notion of prescription, the English were, in general, willing to accept such arguments. For prescription was part of the same essentially existential juridical argument as *res nullius.* The legitimacy of a state or condition depended upon its continual and successful existence. The English, claimed Robert Johnson in 1609, had been there 'long since'—in fact a mere two years—without any interruption or invasion. This, in his view, was sufficient to grant James I 'rule or Dominion' over all 'those English and Indian people'. And although, like all Englishmen, he rejected the Papal Bulls of Donation, he conceded that this argument could equally be applied to the Spanish in 'their "Nova Hispania"'.[70] Accepting the Spanish presence in the South by 'right of discovery' and subsequent prescription was, as Johnson realized, an inescapable consequence of pressing the English claim in the North. Similarly, Robert Ferguson in 1699 acknowledged that the only rights which the Spaniards

[67] *Second Treatise*, 14, pp. 294–95.

[68] *Political Essays Concerning the Present State of the British Empire* (London, 1972), p. 472.

[69] The most important source for the significance of prescription to such cases was Bartolus of Sassoferato's discussion (*repetitio*) on the law *Quominus*, under the title *De fluminibus* (*Digest* 43. 12.2).

[70] *Nova Britannia*... (London, 1609), ff.B2^{r-v}.

might have had in America derived exclusively from their 'having inhabited, occupied and inherited them for 200 years without interruption, disseizure or dispossession'.[71]

Since the English were eager to insist in this way upon the peaceful origins of their settlements, and to disassociate themselves from the image of conquest, it is hardly surprising, even if we set aside for a moment the other significant differences between the political cultures of the two nations, that only the Spaniards should have engaged in prolonged and acrimonious disputes over the legitimacy of their overseas Empire. Few Englishmen believed that they had entered land belonging to anyone or had deprived anyone of their inheritance, rightful or not—unless, of course, it was some other European power. The English, declared Robert Gray, had 'no intention to take away from them [the Native Americans] by force that rightful inheritance which they have in that country, for they are willing to entertain us, and have offered to yield into our hands on reasonable conditions, more land than we shall be able this long time to plant and manure'.[72]

The only major exception to his rule was the much-discussed conquest of Virginia. This was intended to be, so far as circumstances allowed, a copy of the conquests of Mexico and Peru. The argument that justified the English Crown in authorizing the Virginia Company to invade an established ruler's territory was based, however, primarily upon Sir Edward Coke's disturbing claim that all infidels were aliens, *perpetui enemici*, 'perpetual enemies', 'for between them, as with devils, whose subjects they be, and the Christians, there is perpetual hostility, and can be no peace'.[73] This, in Coke's opinion, was a precept not of the canon law, which it so closely resembled, but of the English common law. Few Englishmen, however, were prepared to accept this, and still fewer were willing to endorse Coke's grander, and bizarre, claim that the common law of the English people was identical with the law of nature. The legitimacy of the conquest of Virginia was never seriously challenged until the eighteenth century. But the settlers there soon came to describe themselves, as 'improvers' of lands which they had either purchased or which had been 'empty', in much the same way as the inhabitants of the other colonies.

[71] Robert Ferguson, *A Just and Modest Vindication of the Scots Design, for Having Established a Colony at Darien* (N.P., 1699), pp. 72–73. He went on, however, to argue that, as the Spaniards' first incursions had been based on a conquest which, in his opinion, was nothing other than a case of 'Fraud, Violence and Usurpation', these, too, were invalid, which suggests a curious understanding of prescription.

[72] *A Good Speed to Virginia*, ff. C3^{v} – [C4^{r}].

[73] Quoted in Williams, *The American Indian in Western Legal Thought*, p. 200. See, however, *True Declaration of the Estate of the Colony in Virginia*... (London, 1610) [f. B4^{r}], which argues that the colony was only settled by force when Powhatan, after having become a subject of the English Crown, 'rebelled'.

If, as it was claimed, the English had only settled on vacant lands with the consent of the native populations—unlike the Spaniards, who had invaded territories rightly occupied by legitimate, if primitive, rulers—it followed that English colonization was mutually beneficial to migrant and native—again unlike the Spanish. Conquering and enslaving, declared the author of the *True Declaration of the Estate of the Colony of Virginia* with smug satisfaction, was simply not the way of the English, 'who by way of merchandizing and trade do buy of them pearls of the earth, and sell to them pearls of heaven'.[74]

In their own self-image the English, then, became not the conquerors of Indians but their potential saviours, not only from paganism and pre-agricultural modes of subsistence, but also from Spanish tyranny.[75] Robert Johnson invited the prospective English settler in Virginia to consider 'the great works of freeing the poor Indians from their devourers', and how the children, 'when they come to be saved, will bless the day when first their father saw your faces'.[76] By the early seventeenth century it had become common for the English colonists to represent themselves as benevolent settlers helping the benighted Indians to develop God's plenty. The Amerindians were, in Hakluyt's words, a people 'crying out to us . . . to come and help'. This sentiment was even incorporated into the seal of the Massachusetts Bay Company in 1629, on which an Indian was depicted waving a banner inscribed with the words 'Come over and Help Us'. In exchange for this much-needed help, increasingly large areas of territory for their own use was all these harbingers of European technology required. The obvious absurdity and crass instrumentality of these claims was not lost on contemporaries. But for all its transparency, the argument that the English had been welcomed by the Amerindians as liberators became a staple of the propaganda war waged against the Spaniards, and on behalf of almost every British colonization project.[77] The Spaniards, like the Turks—with whom they became increasingly identified—were depicted as having destroyed those whose ends they should have protected. Just as the English had come to the assistance of the King of Spain's unfortunate subjects in the Netherlands, so they might now rescue his subjects in the Americas from *de facto* slavery.

The quest for an apparently unassailable legitimation for the occupation of aboriginal territories was to have an enduring impact on the ways in which the British came to perceive the future of their overseas Empire. For the long discussion over legality forced upon the colonists, and the European government, the

[74] *True Declaration of the Estate of the Colony of Virginia*, f. B3.

[75] See James Axtell, *The Invasion Within: The Contest of Cultures in Colonial North America* (New York, 1985), p. 133, and more generally on the evangelical programme, pp. 131–78.

[76] *Nova Britannia*, f. C2^{v}.

[77] See Karen Ordahl Kupperman, *Providence Island, 1630–1641* (Cambridge, 1993), pp. 93–94.

recognition that any future 'British Empire' had to be based not upon conquest and tribute, but upon trade and agriculture. 'The sea', as Andrew Fletcher of Saltoun wrote at the end of the century, 'is the only empire which can naturally belong to us.'[78] Furthermore, the reliance on the 'agriculturalist argument' implied a large measure of self-determination on the part of the colonists themselves. Locke's attempted legitimation for the English colonization of America, unlike either the Spanish or even the French, depended not upon concessions made from, or on behalf of, the metropolitan power but on the actions of the settlers themselves. These had been private persons acting of their own volition and employing their own capital. They had not gone to perpetuate a European society already corrupted by the absolutist (and 'continental') ambitions of the Stuart monarchy. They had gone to build a new, more righteous one. Unlike the Spanish and French colonies, which were merely Spain and France transplanted, the English settlements had been Lockean foundations created, quite literally, out of the State of Nature. The relationship between these foundations and the 'mother country' was thus not one of dependency, as was the case in the French and Spanish empires, but of independent and voluntary allegiance. Already by 1657, English writers within a broadly republican tradition were claiming that the English Empire was a protectorate of several interests rather than a universal state.[79] The English Crown, as James Harrington expressed it, borrowing Cicero's description of the Empire of the late Roman Republic, exercised not *imperium* over its various dependencies, but *patrocinium* (protectorate).[80] The other favoured image was that of the Greek, rather than the Roman Empire. Whereas Spain, and later France, had attempted to reconstitute the Roman *imperium*, declared Fletcher, and with it the dubious claim to Universal Monarchy, the English had sought only to emulate the Achaean League, a federation of loosely independent states governed by a common assembly.[81] It is not incidental that it was this image to which James Madison and James Wilson were to appeal in their proposals for a federal structure for the United States. The English, wrote an admiring marquis de Mirabeau in 1758, had been 'the most enlightened of the peoples of Europe in their conduct in the New World'. Although he thought that their conflicting love of liberty and passion for luxury would finally destroy them, they alone, he recognized, had built

[78] 'A Discourse on Government with Relation to Militias', in *The Political Works of Andrew Fletcher Esq.* (London, 1737), p. 66.

[79] See below, pp. 119–21.

[80] J. G. A. Pocock, ed., *The Political Works of James Harrington* (Cambridge, 1977), p. 446. The distinction between *imperium* and *patrocinium* is made by Cicero, *De Officiis*, ii. 27. And see Richard Koebner, *Empire* (Cambridge, 1961), pp. 4–11.

[81] 'An Account of a Conversation Concerning the Regulation of Governments for the Common Good of Mankind', in *The Political Works of Andrew Fletcher* (London, 1737), p. 436.

their colonies upon 'the laws of Republics, Councils and Parliaments'.[82] It was this nascent republicanism—which, as Harrington and his successors had seen, was able to survive in America long after it had been crushed in Britain itself—which would also be the final undoing of the entire colonial project in America.

[82] Victor Riqueti, Marquis de Mirabeau, *L'Ami des hommes, ou traité de la population*, 3 vols. (The Hague, 1758), II, p. 213.

Select Bibliography

DAVID ARMITAGE, 'The New World in British Historical Thought', in Karen Ordahl Kupperman, ed., *America in European Consciousness, 1493–1750* (Chapel Hill, NC, 1995).

BARBARA ARNEIL, '"The Wild Indians", Venison: Locke's Theory of Property and English Colonialism in America', *Political Studies*, XLIV (1996), pp. 60–74.

JAMES AXTELL, *The European and the Indian: Essay in the Ethnohistory of Colonial North America* (Oxford, 1981).

—— *The Invasion Within: The Contest of Cultures in Colonial North America* (New York, 1985).

WILLIAM CRONON, *Changes in the Land: Indians, Colonists and the Ecology of New England* (New York, 1988).

J. MARTIN EVANS, *Milton's Imperial Epic: Paradise Lost and the Discourse of Colonialism* (Ithaca, NY, 1996).

RICHARD HAKLUYT, *A Discourse on Western Planting*, in E. G. R. Taylor, ed., *The Original Writings and Correspondence of the two Richard Hakluyts*, 2 vols. (London, 1935).

JAMES HARRINGTON, *The Political Works of James Harrington*, ed. J. G. A. Pocock (Cambridge, 1977).

FRANCIS JENNINGS, *The Invasion of America: Indians, Colonialism, and the Cant of Conquest* (Chapel Hill, NC, 1975).

RICHARD KOEBNER, *Empire* (Cambridge, 1961).

KAREN ORDAHL KUPPERMAN, *Settling with the Indians: The Meeting of English and Indian Cultures in America, 1580–1640* (Totowa, NJ, 1980).

JOHN LOCKE, *Locke's Two Treatises of Government: A Critical Edition*, with introduction and notes by Peter Laslett, 2nd edn. (Cambridge, 1967).

ANTHONY PAGDEN, *Lords of All the World: Ideologies of Empire in Spain, Britain and France, c.1500–c.1800* (New Haven, 1995).

JAMES TULLY, 'Rediscovering America: The Two Treatises and Aboriginal Rights', in *An Approach to Political Philosophy: Locke in Contexts* (Cambridge, 1993), pp. 137–76.

—— 'Placing the "*Two Treatises*"', in Nicholas Philipson and Quentin Skinner, eds., *Political Discourse in Early-Modern Britain* (Cambridge, 1993), pp. 257–58.

—— 'Aboriginal Property and Western Theory: Recovering a Middle Ground', *Social Philosophy and Policy*, XI (1994), pp. 153–80.

—— *Strange Multiplicity: Constitutionalism in an Age of Diversity* (Cambridge, 1995).

—— 'Property, Self-Government and Consent', *Canadian Journal of Political Science*, XXVIII (1995), pp. 105–32.

RICHARD WHITE, *The Middle Ground* (Cambridge, 1991).

ROBERT A. WILLIAMS, *The American Indian in Western Legal Thought: The Discourses of Conquest* (New York, 1990).

3

War, Politics, and Colonization, 1558–1625

JOHN C. APPLEBY

The foundation-stones for an English seaborne Empire were laid during the period covered by this chapter. In 1558 the bulk of English maritime activity was confined within European waters; overseas possessions were limited to tenuous toe-holds in the Channel Islands and Ireland. Interest in overseas expansion was superficial and restricted to a small group of merchants and travel-writers, such as Richard Eden, who were inspired by the example of Spain and Portugal. Within sixty years, however, English maritime enterprise had taken on a global character, paving the way for the establishment of colonial settlements in North America and the Caribbean, and a scattering of trading posts in Africa, Asia, and South America. English merchants had also developed new trades with Muscovy and the Mediterranean, and had acquired an important interest in the international fishery at Newfoundland.[1] These were considerable achievements, particularly for a small country with limited economic resources, but they should not be exaggerated. Almost any advance on the situation in 1558, when the last continental remnant of England's medieval empire was lost to France, was bound to appear impressive.

That the achievements of the period failed to match the expectations of a new generation of colonial expansionists, such as Richard Hakluyt, who envisaged the creation of an English Empire in America to rival and eventually supersede Spain's, was the result of a structural weakness in English enterprise which repeatedly influenced its character and conduct during this period. Ultimately this weakness stemmed from the lack of sustained state support for overseas expansion. As a result, the burden of colonial and commercial development was left in the hands of private adventurers whose concern for immediate gain was detrimental to the long-term planning needed to promote colonization. In any

[1] I am grateful to Emeritus Professors Kenneth R. Andrews and David B. Quinn and Professor Nicholas Canny for their comments on a draft of this chapter. For modern surveys, see Kenneth R. Andrews, *Trade, Plunder and Settlement: Maritime Enterprise and the Genesis of the British Empire, 1480–1630* (Cambridge, 1984); David B. Quinn and A. N. Ryan, *England's Sea Empire, 1550–1642* (London, 1983); and Esmond Wright, *A History of the United States of America*, Vol. I, *The Search for Liberty: From Origins to Independence* (Oxford, 1995).

case, most London merchants, particularly the powerful Merchant Adventurers, were more concerned with traditional trades in Europe than the wider world. Although a newer group of city traders began to develop a significant stake in colonial trade and settlement during the 1620s, for most of this period colonization was of marginal concern both to the city and the Crown.[2]

These difficulties were compounded by the timing of English colonizing activity. When serious interest in colonization emerged during the 1570s, Spain and Portugal had already acquired extensive empires in the west and east. The imperial monopolies claimed by the Iberian monarchies forced those who followed in their footsteps to adopt armed and aggressive methods, encouraging the growth of English and French piracy and privateering in Europe and across the Atlantic. Though unwilling to launch a direct challenge to Spain or Portugal, the English Crown was prepared to sanction much of this activity for financial and strategic considerations. The peculiar indirectness of the Crown's role during the latter part of the sixteenth century also reflected the tension between its European and oceanic concerns which influenced its conduct during the conflict with Spain after 1585. Although the war encouraged the idea of a militant Protestant imperialism that drew on widespread anti-Catholicism, it was tempered by a long-standing tradition of maritime war and plunder which favoured privateering at the expense of colonization (see Map 3.1).

This context gave English overseas expansion a contingent character, the origins of which are difficult to locate. Colonial and commercial developments were part of a broader process in the reorientation of overseas enterprise which was the product of a complex combination of economic and political circumstances. Difficulties in traditional markets, particularly in Antwerp, led to a slow but significant decline in the cloth trade during the second half of the sixteenth century. Such problems reinforced an ambition to deal directly with distant markets to acquire luxury imports. Though cloth continued to dominate overseas commerce, by the 1620s English trade was undergoing an important shift in direction.[3] The growing hostility towards Spain accompanying this change heavily influenced the oceanic development of English commerce. The links which were formed during the period between trade, privateering, and colonization established a pattern of enterprise of enduring significance for the future development of English maritime imperialism.

Little of this could have been anticipated in 1558. Although the years before the war with Spain witnessed mounting tension and unofficial conflict between England

[2] Robert Brenner, *Merchants and Revolution: Commercial Change, Political Conflict and London's Overseas Traders, 1550–1653* (Cambridge, 1993), pp. 52–140; Andrews, *Trade, Plunder and Settlement*, pp. 20–21.

[3] Andrews, *Trade, Plunder and Settlement*, pp. 7–10.

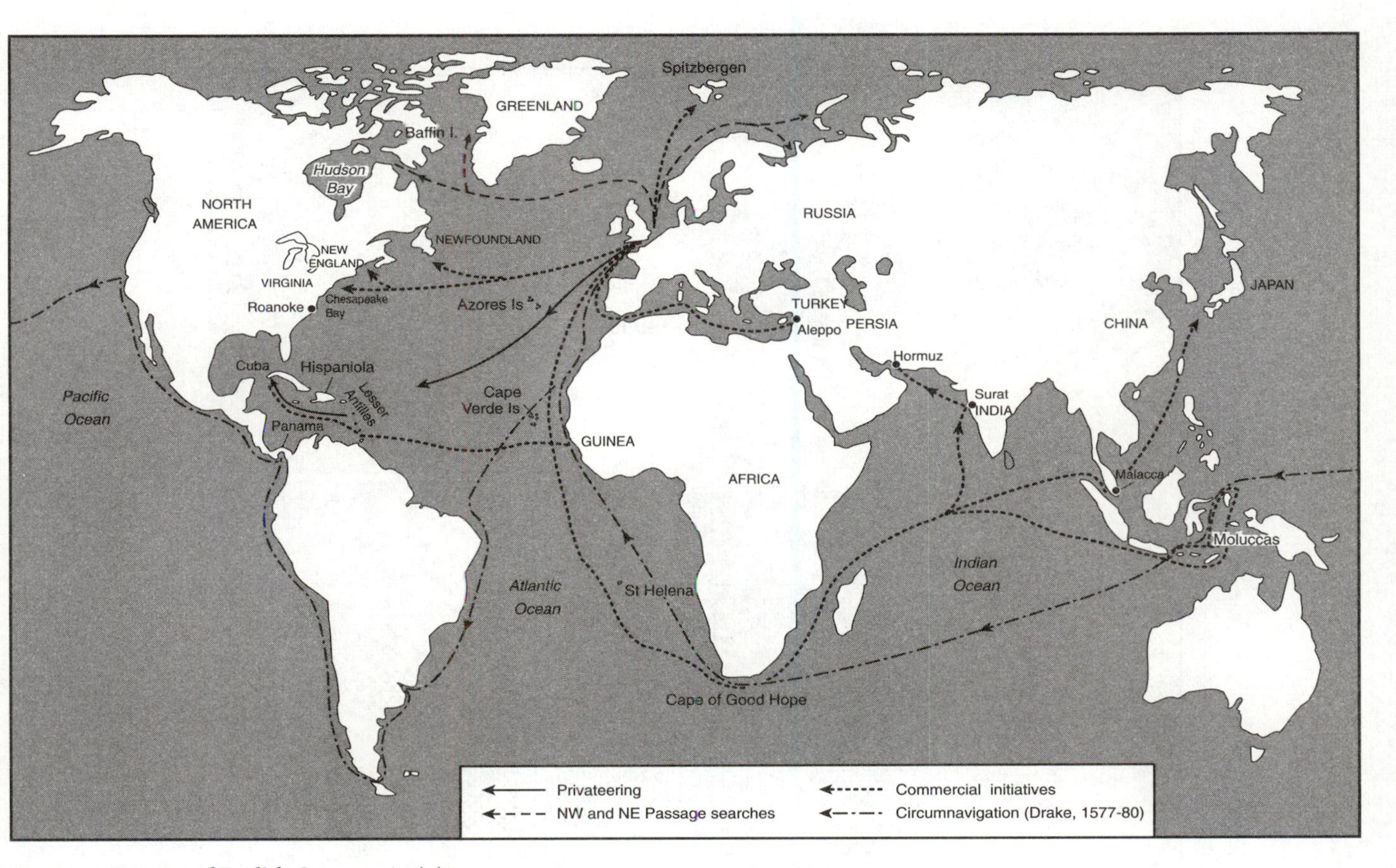

MAP 3.1. Patterns of English Overseas Activity

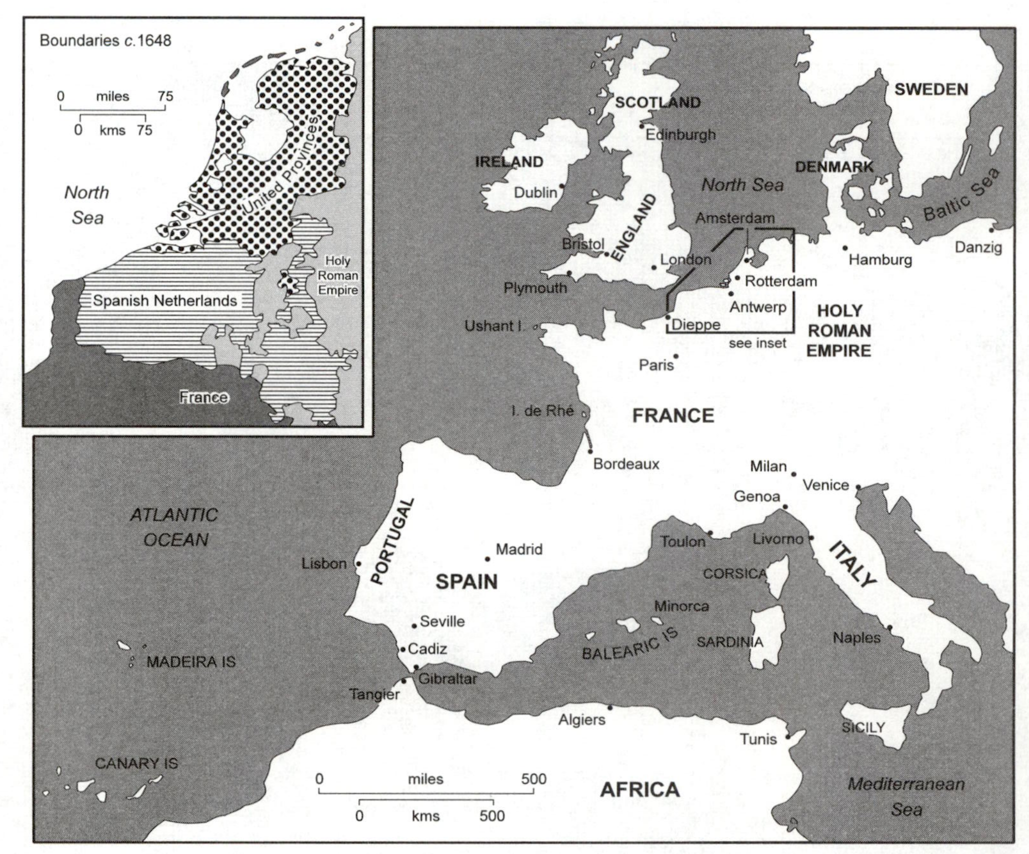

Map 3.2. Western Europe

and the Iberian world, the 'long peace' of which Drake complained in 1585 was a time of experimental initiatives in trade, exploration, and plantation ranging from Ireland to North America.[4] The major advance of this early period was the creation of an Atlantic dimension to English maritime enterprise, though it occurred against a background of widening commercial horizons. English interest in the Atlantic can be traced back to the 1480s, but it was spasmodic, small-scale, and in decline by the 1530s and 1540s.[5] Its revival grew out of various attempts to break into the lucrative trade in gold, ivory, and pepper in West Africa which were driven by the growing domestic demand for luxury goods. The Guinea trade had widespread ramifications for the development of English maritime enterprise. Portuguese hostility to the incursions of interlopers into the region led to a commercial conflict during the 1550s and 1560s, when well-armed trading fleets, occasionally of considerable size, combined trade with piracy as need or opportunity arose. The escalation in maritime violence accompanying these ventures, together with increasing international competition in West Africa, led to a contraction in the trade which lasted into the early seventeenth century. But the real significance of these enterprises does not lie in their economic success or failure, which varied from venture to venture; rather, it lies in the evidence they provide for the development of a powerful syndicate linking prominent city merchants with leading naval officials and well-placed courtiers. The Queen was also an investor in several of these ventures, providing unprecedented royal support for such an aggressive challenge to Portuguese trade in Africa.[6]

The risks inherent in this commercial activity became apparent during John Hawkins's ambitious attempts to break into the transatlantic slave trade in the 1560s. The four ventures set out by Hawkins from 1562 to 1568 received support from prominent courtiers, city magnates, and the Queen, attracted by the potential profit to be made from supplying Spanish America with African slave labour. But these were never purely peaceful commercial ventures. From the start, English slaving had an aggressive dimension which identified Africans as legitimate prey, in Hawkins's revealing description.[7] Not only was Hawkins ready to use force to acquire slaves in West Africa, but also the threat of force to dispose of them across the Atlantic. In both cases, however, such aggressive methods added to the heavy

[4] M. Oppenheim, ed., *The Naval Tracts of Sir William Monson*, 5 vols. (London, 1902–14), I, p. 123; Quinn and Ryan, *England's Sea Empire*, pp. 75–88.

[5] David Beers Quinn, *England and the Discovery of America, 1481–1620* (New York, 1974), pp. 5–23, 160.

[6] John W. Blake, *West Africa: Quest for God and Gold, 1454–1578* (London, 1977), pp. 155–56, 163–64, 173–75; Andrews, *Trade, Plunder and Settlement*, pp. 108–11.

[7] Clements R. Markham, ed., *The Hawkins' Voyages during the Reigns of Henry VIII, Queen Elizabeth, and James I* (London, 1878), p. 6; Kenneth R. Andrews, *The Spanish Caribbean: Trade and Plunder, 1530–1630* (London, 1978), pp. 108–33.

overhead costs of slaving which raised a question-mark about its profitability even before the disastrous, if overblown, clash between the English and Spanish at San Juan de Ulúa in 1568. The episode was a financial disaster for Hawkins and his backers, and did much to cool English interest in the slave trade. It also inflamed opinion in England and Spain, contributing to a breakdown in Anglo-Spanish relations that lasted from 1568 to 1572. This crisis, which was related to wider religious and political turmoil within Western Europe, had complex consequences for English maritime enterprise. Economically it strengthened the search for new overseas markets to compensate for the loss of Antwerp, a major outlet for the cloth trade. Politically, however, it encouraged an increase in the level of violence at sea, in the Channel and the Atlantic, where piracy and privateering asserted a powerful influence on English overseas enterprise.

The search for new markets had effectively begun in the early 1550s, following a catastrophic decline in cloth exports. The most significant outcome of this earlier crisis was the incorporation of a company in 1553 to search for a North-east Passage to Cathay, linking the attempt to seek out new outlets for cloth with a long-standing desire to capture the rich eastern trade in spices and silks. Although abortive, the venture initiated English contact with Russia, leading to the formation of the Muscovy Company in 1555. Thereafter the Company developed a regular trade with Russia, renewed the search for the North-east Passage, and sponsored repeated attempts to open up an overland trade with Persia, pioneered by Anthony Jenkinson in 1557 and 1561. These efforts met with mixed success. Though trade was profitable, hopes of finding a passage faded after 1580 with the failure of a voyage set out under the command of Arthur Pet and Charles Jackman, from which only one ship returned after a gruelling experience with the cold and ice. The Company's Persian interests, moreover, were overtaken by the establishment of the Turkey Company in 1581 to trade with the Levant through the Mediterranean.[8]

In contrast with these peaceful commercial initiatives in the East, English enterprise in the West rapidly assumed a more aggressive form. Piracy and privateering had grown steadily during the 1560s, as a result of the Anglo-French wars from 1557 to 1559 and 1562 to 1564. The international crisis of the later 1560s deepened the anti-Spanish character of this maritime violence. It also fostered collaboration between English pirates, French Huguenot corsairs, and Dutch 'Sea-Beggars' with the connivance of some of the Queen's ministers, who were alarmed by the threat to the Protestant cause in northern Europe from the Spanish monarchy. The seriousness of this threat encouraged transatlantic maritime enterprise aimed at cutting off Spain from its supply of treasure from the New

[8] Andrews, *Trade, Plunder and Settlement*, pp. 79–84, 88–89; C. G. A. Clay, *Economic Expansion and Social Change: England, 1500–1700*, 2 vols. (Cambridge, 1984), II, pp. 113–15, 128–29.

World. At the same time it stimulated the earliest non-Iberian attempts to establish settlements across the Atlantic, though it was a group of French Huguenots who pioneered the way with the foundation of two small, but short-lived, forts in South Carolina in 1562 and Florida in 1564.[9] Hawkins visited the French fort, shortly before its destruction by the Spanish, during his second slaving voyage of 1565. One of his backers, Sir William Winter, a prominent naval official, raided the Spanish base at San Augustin (St Augustine) in 1571.[10] At this stage, however, the English seemed content to follow in the wake of the French, though the experience of the latter suggested that in the right circumstances plunder might serve as the handmaid of western settlement.

The failure of Hawkins's last venture strengthened the piratical trend in English enterprise at a formative period in its oceanic development. Though made up of several different strands, it was Francis Drake who played a crucial role in this development, waging a private war against Spain in the Caribbean which sent shock-waves rippling throughout Spanish America. Drake's voyages during the early 1570s, and those of the French, exposed the vulnerability of the Spanish Caribbean to opportunistic raids by fairly small-scale operators. The attack on the Panama isthmus in 1573 also raised the prospect of English and French pirates acting in partnership with escaped slaves, or *cimarrones*, against Spain.[11] Drake's campaign was brought to an end by a gradual improvement in Anglo-Spanish relations, though this did little to dampen ambitions inflamed by the possibility of rich pickings in the Caribbean or the Pacific. In 1576 one of Drake's men, John Oxenham, crossed the isthmus with the help of the *cimarrones* intent on plundering treasure ships sailing along the coast from Peru. More than a year after his arrival Oxenham was captured by the Spanish and subsequently hanged as a pirate.

It was within this context that plans for American settlement emerged. In 1574 Sir Richard Grenville successfully petitioned the Queen for permission to occupy lands in the southern hemisphere not in the possession of any Christian prince. In reality the proposal seems to have been aimed at the conquest of the southernmost region of South America which, it was claimed, had been left for England 'by gods providence'.[12] Alarmed at the damage Grenville's voyage might inflict on relations with Spain, the Queen withdrew her approval for the venture. Three years later, when Anglo-Spanish relations were again deteriorating, she was prepared to support a similar plan which culminated in Drake's 'famous voyage' of 1577.[13] Although plunder was Drake's primary objective, the official purpose of the venture was to prospect the creation of colonial settlements in unoccupied parts

[9] David B. Quinn, ed., *New American World: A Documentary History of North America to 1612*, 5 vols. (London, 1979), II, chap. 33.

[10] Ibid., pp. 363–64, 575.

[11] Andrews, *Trade, Plunder and Settlement*, pp. 129–34.

[12] Ibid., p. 141.

[13] Ibid., pp. 144–58.

of South America, based on an alliance between the English and native forces hostile to Spain. The idea for the voyage apparently came from Drake and his allies in the navy, but it attracted support from officials and courtiers, such as Sir Francis Walsingham and the Earl of Leicester, as well as the Queen.

In the event, these southern settlements failed to materialize. But Drake's unplanned circumnavigation and his visit to Ternate, the first direct contact between England and the East Indies, followed by his return to London with a king's ransom in booty, was a breathtaking achievement which revealed the oceanic potential of English maritime activity. Nor was it an isolated event. On the northern margins of America the English renewed the search for the Northwest Passage to Cathay (China). The three ventures led by Martin Frobisher from 1576 to 1578 were embarrassing failures, showing how easily even well-organized expeditions were distracted by the prospect of quick profit. The apparent discovery of gold on Baffin Island aroused considerable excitement in London, but it evaporated as soon as 'it was found to be . . . dross'.[14] Even so, the Frobisher voyages are further evidence of the growing confidence and revitalized ambitions behind English maritime enterprise.

The same ambitions can be detected in the emergence of an imperial ideology during the later 1570s. It was at this time that John Dee invented the phrase 'British Impire' to describe and justify England's claim to the North Atlantic, based on the mythical conquests of King Arthur and Prince Madoc, the latter allegedly the first discoverer of North America in the twelfth century. Though Dee had wide-ranging contacts with city merchants and maritime adventurers, the impact of his ideas beyond such interested parties was limited. Imperial rhetoric and ideology failed to strike a chord either with the Queen or her people, though the notion of an imperial destiny in the West led inexorably on to the claim that colonies were warranted by 'God's direction and command', which turned the 'laborious and unpleasant taske . . . [of] subduing . . . unmanured Countreyes' into a duty.[15]

The proliferation of projects for trade, plunder, and colonization which emerged during the period from 1578 to 1584 provides convincing testimony of the growing ambitions of English overseas enterprise. The circumnavigation encouraged commercial ambitions in the East, as seen in Edward Fenton's attempted voyage to the East Indies in 1582 and Drake's abortive Moluccas project of 1584. In addition, the rapid deterioration in Anglo-Spanish relations during the

[14] William Harrison, *The Description of England*, ed. Georges Edelen (Ithaca, NY, 1968), p. 366; Andrews, *Trade, Plunder and Settlement*, pp. 168–79.

[15] [John White], *The Planters Plea* (London, 1630), pp. 1, 6; Gwyn A. Williams, *Madoc: The Legend of the Welsh Discovery of America* (London, 1979), pp. 35–38; John Parker, *Books to Build an Empire: A Bibliographical History of English Overseas Interests to 1620* (Amsterdam, 1965), pp. 65, 138–39. William H. Sherman, *John Dee* (Amherst, Mass., 1995), is the most recent study; and see below p. 114.

later 1570s created a fertile breeding-ground for new strategic ideas which anticipated aggressive action against Spain in the Atlantic. In 1577 Sir Humphrey Gilbert presented the Queen with two proposals on how to 'annoy' the King of Spain; in 1579 Hawkins drew up a plan to set out a mixed fleet of royal and private ships to seize the Spanish treasure fleet. Two years later Hawkins was involved in a scheme for an attack on the Azores, now part of the Spanish monarchy following Philip II's acquisition of Portugal in 1580. He produced another plan, in 1584, for a wide-ranging maritime assault on Spanish oceanic trade.[16] Of more practical significance were the commissions issued by Don Antonio, the Pretender to the Portuguese throne, authorizing the plunder of Spanish shipping. By 1582 at least eleven English ships were sailing under his authority.[17] Don Antonio's presence in England acted as a focal point for anti-Spanish activity, providing it with some degree of legitimacy.

These projects were accompanied by a flurry of interest in colonizing schemes involving Gilbert, Christopher Carleill, Sir George Peckham, and Walter Ralegh. Not all linked colonization with hostility to Spain, and even those schemes that did included wider social and economic matters. Carleill, for example, emphasized the commercial potential of colonization, though not to the neglect of social issues. His discourse of 1583 was dressed up in the ideology of moral reformation, promoting colonization as a way of preventing the 'good sort of people' from being troubled by the poor and disorderly.[18] The diversity of such schemes emphasizes the lack of coherence within English colonial enterprise; the one common element they all shared, a lack of state support, rendered them all ineffectual.

The Gilbert ventures clearly reveal the underlying limitations of English colonization at this time. Following his involvement in several unsuccessful colonizing schemes in Ireland during the 1560s and 1570s, Gilbert was granted a patent from the Queen for discovery and overseas plantation in 1578.[19] However, lack of additional royal support created financial difficulties, delaying and distorting plans which were always in danger of being undermined by poor leadership. Gilbert's first expedition of 1578, intended as a raid in the West Indies to be followed by the establishment of a settlement in North America, ended when the fleet split up off the coast of Ireland. Bad weather forced Gilbert back to England, while his consorts turned to piracy. Though he led another expedition to

[16] Quinn and Ryan, *England's Sea Empire*, pp. 86–88; Kenneth R. Andrews, *Drake's Voyages: A Re-Assessment of their Place in Elizabethan Maritime Expansion* (London, 1967), pp. 85–92.

[17] M. J. Rodriguez-Salgado and Simon Adams, eds., *England, Spain and the Gran Armada, 1585–1604* (Edinburgh, 1991), p. 240.

[18] Quinn, *New American World*, III, pp. 27–29, 34–55; Andrews, *Trade, Plunder and Settlement*, pp. 197–99.

[19] David B. Quinn, ed., *The Voyages and Colonising Enterprises of Sir Humphrey Gilbert*, 2 vols. (London, 1940), I, pp. 35–54, 83–88. For Ireland see chap. by Jane H. Ohlmeyer.

North America in 1583, taking formal possession of the harbour of St John's in Newfoundland, the voyage was a chronicle of disaster from start to finish, culminating in Gilbert's death on the voyage home. These colonial initiatives might well have died with Gilbert but for the intervention of his half-brother, Walter Ralegh, who received a patent from the Queen for overseas plantation in March 1584. Aware of the need for royal support, Ralegh conducted a carefully orchestrated campaign in an attempt to persuade Elizabeth to provide practical assistance for his Roanoke ventures. Arthur Barlowe's account of the first reconnaissance voyage to Roanoke in 1584, which Ralegh edited, came close to portraying the land as a garden of Eden and its people as pre-lapsarian 'naturals' who would welcome English settlers with open arms. It was followed by Hakluyt's *Discourse of Western Planting*, which was presented to the Queen in 1584.[20] Though not meant for publication, the *Discourse* elaborated a comprehensive case in favour of state support for colonization. Economic, social, religious, and strategic motives were thrown together in a mixture of sophistication and naïvety, which was reinforced by a deep hostility towards Spain. Elizabeth, however, was unwilling to play the part assigned to her either by Hakluyt or Ralegh. As a result, the first sustained efforts at colonization remained firmly in the hands of private enterprise.

It would be tempting to dismiss this early phase as a time of fruitless experimentation, when inadequate resources were squandered on ill-conceived and mismanaged projects. But the period was part of a broader reordering of maritime and colonial activity during which North America emerged as a major focus for English ambitions. As this process overlapped with a deterioration in Anglo-Spanish relations, peaceful projects for plantation were superseded by aggressive schemes based on the belief that war between England and Spain was inevitable. The establishment of Roanoke during 1585 went ahead because of its perceived potential as a naval base for raids on Spanish shipping in the Caribbean. In practice, however, the war distorted English maritime enterprise to the detriment of colonization. Hopes that the state might implement an oceanic strategy capable of nurturing transatlantic settlement were dashed by the reluctance of the Queen to risk limited resources in a distant and marginal theatre of the conflict.

This situation left Ralegh and his associates to shoulder the burden of organizing and supplying the small settlement at Roanoke. But the need to make a profit continually favoured short-term expediency over longer-term planning, as reflected in the attempt to combine colonization with privateering or in the search for gold and silver mines at the expense of more gainful pursuits. The first

[20] David B. Quinn, ed., *The Roanoke Voyages, 1584–1590*, 2 vols. (London, 1955), I, pp. 9–16, 108, 110; Richard Hakluyt, *Discourse of Western Planting*, eds. David B. Quinn and Alison M. Quinn (London, 1993), pp. 19–20, 39, and esp. 115–19.

settlement, led by Ralph Lane, managed to survive for a year until it was abandoned in June 1586. Although this was a significant achievement, it was marred by the shortcomings that became evident in the English approach to colonization. Lane's militant Protestantism, which identified Spain as the sword of Antichrist, as well as his military background, did little to prepare him for the task of colonial pioneering. His complaint that he was in charge of wild men among savages also points to deeper weaknesses concerning the type of settler employed in the venture. The inability of the English to adapt to their new surroundings also had serious consequences for their relations with the Indians.[21] During the winter these relations grew more tense as the settlers continued to demand supplies of food from Indians of the region, although the reluctance of the latter to continue feeding the English meant that by the spring Lane and his men were reduced to scouring the seashore for crustaceans. As relations between natives and newcomers collapsed, the English attacked an Indian settlement, killing Wingina, one of the chiefs of the Roanoke tribe. Lane's return to London in the summer with the survivors of the settlement was a serious setback to the colonizing movement. A shadowy, though short-lived, presence was maintained at Roanoke following Sir Richard Grenville's arrival with a relief expedition in June 1586. Delayed by privateering in the Caribbean, Grenville narrowly missed Lane; but the small party of men he left at Roanoke were subsequently killed by Indians.[22]

English colonization continued, but in a modified and more realistic manner. In 1587 John White, a survivor from the first settlement, led a mixed party of men and women, farmers and tradesmen, instead of the soldiers who had accompanied Lane, to establish a colony in Chesapeake Bay.[23] Unfortunately White and his party never reached the bay; instead, they were forced ashore at Roanoke by a crew of mariners keen to return to the Caribbean in search of plunder. Later in the year White returned to England to organize a relief expedition for the settlement. Due to a combination of misfortunes, however, his return was delayed until 1590, when he found the settlement abandoned. Unable to search for survivors, White was forced to leave the 'lost colonists' to their obscure fate.[24] Any lingering interest in Roanoke was effectively killed off by the counter-attraction of privateering.

Roanoke provided the English with an opportunity for testing their capabilities for colonization. Although the experience exposed serious limitations concerning the supply of overseas settlements, it enabled the English to acquire vital

[21] Quinn, *Roanoke Voyages*, I, pp. 203–04.

[22] David Beers Quinn, *Set Fair for Roanoke: Voyages and Colonies, 1584–1606* (Chapel Hill, NC, 1985), pp. 139–49.

[23] Andrews, *Trade, Plunder and Settlement*, pp. 214–15.

[24] Quinn, *England and the Discovery of America*, pp. 432–81.

information about the region.[25] The work of White and Thomas Hariot, based on their experience in the first settlement, provided an invaluable record of the land and its people which, in different circumstances, might have encouraged additional attempts at settlement.[26] But the timing was unpropitious for peaceful colonization. Even if Roanoke had been a suitable site for a naval base, the war at sea was overshadowed by the international conflict in the Netherlands. The prospect of Spain assuming direct control over such a sensitive strategic area forced Elizabeth into a heavy military commitment to maintain the anti-Spanish coalition in northern Europe, which grew as the conflict spread to France. From 1585 to 1597 as many as 50,000 English troops served in the garrisons and on the battlefields of France and the Netherlands.[27]

The scale of these commitments had serious consequences for maritime and colonial enterprise. Despite the hopes of Drake, Hawkins, and members of the war party at court for an oceanic campaign against Spain supported by the state, the maritime conflict degenerated into a 'little war' of privateering.[28] There was a number of important semi-official expeditions to Spain and the Caribbean, but their conduct was dependent on an uneasy alliance between public and private interests in which strategic aims were always counterbalanced by financial considerations. Drake's voyage to the West Indies in 1585 illustrates the nature of this alliance. Though sponsored by the Queen, she contributed only two ships to the expedition, out of a total of more than thirty vessels. Her investment in the venture amounted to £20,000; private adventurers provided £40,000.[29] Inevitably, these arrangements reduced royal control over the war at sea, and in such a way that it soon became a national treasure-hunt in which the state and private adventurers were competitors in a lottery for plunder and prize.

This competition deepened the confusion over maritime strategy, undermining the effectiveness of the sea war. Drake's Caribbean raid of 1585 damaged the pride and reputation of the Spanish monarchy: with Cartagena and Santo Domingo 'consumed much with fire', the West Indies seemed to be fatally exposed to English depredation.[30] But the voyage failed to fulfil its financial or strategic purpose. Indirectly the arrival of the expedition at Roanoke in June 1586, following an

[25] Quinn, *Roanoke Voyages*, I, pp. 35–60, 317–87, 390–98; see below p. 89.

[26] See below pp. 152–53.

[27] Stephen Saunders Webb, *The Governors-General: The English Army and the Definition of Empire, 1569–1681* (Chapel Hill, NC, 1979), pp. 5–6; R. B. Wernham, *After the Armada: Elizabethan England and the Struggle for Western Europe, 1588–1595* (Oxford, 1984), pp. 23–26, 77–87, 181–82, 559–68.

[28] Andrews, *Trade, Plunder and Settlement*, pp. 243–48; Rodriguez-Salgado and Adams, *England, Spain and the Gran Armada*, pp. 85–86.

[29] Mary Frear Keeler, ed., *Sir Francis Drake's West Indian Voyage, 1585–86* (London, 1981), pp. 9–10, 12–16.

[30] Ibid., p. 258.

assault on Spanish Florida, led to the abandonment of the settlement, making a mockery of any serious attempt to develop a co-ordinated strategy linking colonial and military aims. The attack on Cadiz in 1587 delayed the sailing of the Armada by one year, but any wider strategic purpose was sacrificed in the interests of financial gain (Map 3.2). The failure of the Armada, though a narrow escape for the English, did little to alter this situation. The expedition to Lisbon the following year was an impressive display of maritime strength, but the fleet failed to achieve any of its stated aims, giving Spain the opportunity to rebuild its naval and imperial defences in Europe and in the Caribbean. The difference became apparent in 1595 when Drake complained, during the course of his last voyage in the West Indies, 'that hee never thought any place could bee so changed'.[31] The failure of the venture, and the loss of Drake and Hawkins with many of their men, represented the low point of the semi-official war at sea. The Cadiz expedition of 1596, which witnessed the emergence of a new generation of courtly warriors led by the Earl of Essex, halted this disappointing trend. But subsequent attempts to seize the initiative, through the capture of a base on the coast of Spain, failed due to a combination of ill-luck, bad weather, and poor judgement. Though the war dragged on, the state gradually withdrew its support for aggressive naval action, leaving the maritime conflict in the hands of private adventurers who pursued their own interests with little effective control.

In these circumstances privateering became the main form of maritime activity during the war. Every year from 1585 onwards, between 100 and 200 vessels, ranging in size from small barques of less than 50 tons to substantial men-of-war of 300 tons, put to sea in search of prizes. Although the success and profitability of these ventures varied considerably, English privateers seized a large number of prizes, the annual value of which amounted at least to £200,000.[32] The lure of profit attracted interest from a broad range of English society. Merchants and shipowners dominated the business, but sections of the gentry and nobility were also involved in it. George Clifford, third Earl of Cumberland, set out twelve ventures to the coast of Spain, the Azores, and the Caribbean in search of honour and profit, though privateering nearly ruined him.[33] Behind such prominent promoters were hundreds of small investors such as butchers, innkeepers, shipwrights, and farmers, and propping up the whole business were the thousands of men who sailed aboard men-of-war each year, eager to profit from the conflict with Spain.

[31] Kenneth R. Andrews, ed., *The Last Voyage of Drake and Hawkins* (Cambridge, 1972), pp. 100–01; Wernham, *After the Armada*, pp. 96–105, 235–44, 445–46.

[32] Kenneth R. Andrews, *Elizabethan Privateering: English Privateering during the Spanish War, 1585–1603* (Cambridge, 1964), pp. 32–34, 128–34.

[33] G. C. Williamson, *George, Third Earl of Cumberland (1558–1605): His Life and His Voyages* (Cambridge, 1920); Andrews, *Elizabethan Privateering*, pp. 70–78.

In the short term the impact of privateering on colonization was fatal, diverting the interests of colonial promoters such as Ralegh into raiding. Over the longer term, however, it had a more positive contribution to make to colonial settlement, particularly in the West. The sea war of the 1580s and 1590s helped to forge and fashion the tools of Empire, developing the ships, men, and capital needed for seaborne expansion.[34] Privateering stimulated a shipbuilding boom which created the basis for an ocean-going merchant marine, manned and led by seamen whose knowledge of the Caribbean and eastern seaboard of North America was unrivalled. The experience of men such as Christopher Newport or William Parker, who made repeated crossings of the Atlantic, was vital to subsequent commercial and colonial advance. Equally important was the way in which the war encouraged the concentration of capital in the hands of a group of London merchants, such as John Watts and Paul Bayning, who came to dominate the business. The profit these men made out of the war was redeployed after 1604 to promote colonial and maritime enterprise in North America and the East Indies. Privateering also fostered a more favourable environment for such activity through the steady pressure placed on vulnerable points in the Spanish and Portuguese empires. Bernard Drake's raid on the Newfoundland fishery in 1585 weakened Portuguese interest in transatlantic fishing, creating an opportunity for the English to exploit. Elsewhere privateering caused local and structural damage of varying intensity, while the pressure on Spanish imperial defences in the West Indies gradually led to the neglect of peripheral areas north and south, and in the Lesser Antilles.[35] Once the war had ended it was in these areas that English trade and plantation became focused.

The war, of course, did not halt peaceful commercial development. English trade with the Levant, which had been growing steadily from the early 1570s, flourished despite the political and commercial dangers of trading in the Mediterranean and the potential for competition between the Venice and Turkey Companies, though the latter problem was effectively solved by a merger in 1592 which led to the incorporation of the Levant Company. At the same time there was a revival of interest in the search for the North-west Passage sponsored by Walsingham. Although the three voyages of John Davis between 1585 and 1587 failed, his exploration of the Arctic was one of the greatest feats of seamanship in the sixteenth century. Of more importance, economically, was the boom in English activity at the Newfoundland fishery which was under way during the 1580s and 1590s. The huge demand for fish in southern Europe led to the establishment of a profitable triangular trade, linking England and Newfoundland with

[34] Andrews, *Trade, Plunder and Settlement*, pp. 252–55; *Elizabethan Privateering*, pp. 70–78; see below, pp. 86–88.

[35] Andrews, *Elizabethan Privateering*, pp. 182–84, 224–27; Quinn, *New American World*, IV, pp. 47–55; Gillian T. Cell, *English Enterprise in Newfoundland, 1577–1660* (Toronto, 1969), pp. 24–25, 47–48.

markets in Italy, France, and Spain, despite the war. By 1604 the English were sending as many as 150 ships a year to the fishery.[36] This burgeoning trade was accompanied by growing interest in the Gulf of St Lawrence during the 1590s, when the English tried to wrest control of the rich walrus fishery from the French. Though unsuccessful, an attempt to establish a base on the Magdalen Islands in 1597 raised the novel prospect of North America being used as a haven for religious exiles. The expedition, led by Charles Leigh, planned to leave a small group of Dissenters, or 'pilgrims' as they were already being called, on one of the islands, but it was thwarted by fierce French resistance.[37]

Such initiatives were overshadowed during the closing stages of the war by growing interest in the East Indies trade. From the 1580s onwards there had been a number of attempts to establish direct contact between England and the Indies, though most were influenced by the prospect of plunder. Thomas Cavendish's circumnavigation from 1586 to 1588 was followed by a series of voyages which failed to achieve much of significance. In 1591 a group of London merchants set out a small fleet under the command of James Lancaster, in the first English attempt to reach the East by the Cape of Good Hope. The voyage turned into a disaster, however, after the ships and most of the men were lost. Serious mercantile interest revived in 1599 when England had a 'gracious-geven opportunytie of drawinge a perpetuall trade' from the East Indies, as Portuguese enterprise faltered.[38] In reality, it was Dutch activity which led to the incorporation of the East India Company in 1600. Levant traders, alarmed at the threat to their trading interests, played a prominent role in the formation of the Company, though the City 'privateering interest' was also powerfully represented in the new venture. John Watts, the leading merchant promoter of privateering in London, was the first Governor of the Company, and other members included fellow-adventurers in the maritime conflict such as Paul Bayning and the Earl of Cumberland. The Company intended its first venture of 1601 to be pursued 'in a merchantlike course', but Lancaster, the leader of the expedition, was authorized to indulge in privateering should 'any opportunity be offered without prejudice or hazard' to the voyage.[39] By these means London merchants continued to exploit the sea war in the hope of winning new markets from the enemy.

[36] A. P. Newton, 'The Beginnings of English Colonisation, 1569–1618', in J. Holland Rose and others, eds., *The Cambridge History of the British Empire*, 9 vols. (Cambridge, 1929–59), I, pp. 73–74; Quinn and Ryan, *England's Sea Empire*, pp. 138–39; Cell, *English Enterprise*, pp. 22–23.

[37] Andrews, *Trade, Plunder and Settlement*, pp. 305–07; Quinn, *New American World*, IV, pp. 66–80.

[38] Williamson, *Cumberland*, p. 222; G. V. Scammell, *The World Encompassed: The First European Maritime Empires, c.800–1650* (London, 1981), pp. 471–76; Sir William Foster, *England's Quest of Eastern Trade* (London, 1933), pp. 117–22, 127–35.

[39] G. Birdwood and W. Foster, eds., *The Register of the Letters etc. of the Governor and Company of Merchants of London Trading into the East Indies, 1600–1619* (London, 1893), pp. 195–96; Andrews, *Trade, Plunder and Settlement*, pp. 261–65.

The long Spanish war emphasized the growing divergence between maritime and colonial enterprise. During the last quarter of the sixteenth century English adventurers gained the confidence and ability to undertake oceanic seafaring, but they failed signally to establish a permanent overseas colony beyond Ireland. But if the war delayed colonization, it may have been a 'necessary pause' in a process that remained uncoordinated and poorly supported.[40] As a result of the experience gained during the 1580s and 1590s, the English were in a better position to undertake colonization than at any time in the previous fifty years. In 1599 Hakluyt anticipated a 'good & godly peace' which would stir the Queen into transporting 1,000 or 2,000 settlers to Virginia, much as Isabella of Castile had been stirred into supporting Columbus following the end of the war in Granada.[41] Though a vain hope, many of the energies which went into the privateering war were transferred into colonizing schemes after 1604. Even before the war was over the privateering interest in London was transforming itself into a small but powerful group in favour of overseas trade and colonial settlement.

With this background, however, there was a danger that colonization would be controlled by promoters more interested in 'the base and hasty drawing of profit in the first years' than in the long-term investment needed to establish self-sustaining settlements.[42] Francis Bacon's advice that colonial promoters must be prepared 'to lose almost twenty years' profit' before expecting any recompense was unwelcome to a generation of merchants accustomed to the rapid profits made from privateering. But the limited view of colonization held by private adventurers was related to the continuing lack of state support for commercial and colonial expansion. In consequence, while the peace with Spain fostered maritime enterprise, of varying shades of legality, colonizing schemes were ill-equipped to take full advantage of the opportunities which beckoned after 1604 as a result of the growing weakness of the Spanish monarchy, now struggling to maintain its imperial integrity in the face of English and Dutch pressure. The Treaty of London, which brought the war to an end, made this task more difficult by leaving the issue of commercial and colonial enterprise in America unresolved, enabling the English to claim that where land was not effectively occupied by a Christian nation, it was open for others to settle.[43] Nor was Spain in any position to prevent English transatlantic trade or settlement. Twenty years of unremitting conflict at sea left peripheral regions in North and South America,

[40] Andrews, *Elizabethan Privateering*, pp. 198–99, 232.

[41] E. G. R. Taylor, ed., *The Original Writings and Correspondence of the Two Richard Hakluyts*, 2 vols. (London, 1935), II, pp. 456–57.

[42] Alexander Brown, ed., *The Genesis of the United States*, 2 vols. (London, 1890), II, pp. 799–802.

[43] David B. Quinn, 'James I and the Beginnings of Empire in America', *Journal of Imperial and Commonwealth History*, II (1974), pp. 135–52. See above, pp. 42–44.

and in the Caribbean, exposed to commercial and colonial penetration by rival Europeans.

In these circumstances English adventurers were soon pressing forward with a variety of colonizing schemes in America. The earliest of these ventures, which focused on Guiana, grew directly out of the privateering war. During the 1590s privateers and traders visited the coast, though English interest in the region was in danger of being subverted by Ralegh's ill-fated quest for El Dorado. Nevertheless, privateering led to the emergence of more positive commercial and colonial ventures in the early seventeenth century. In 1604 Charles Leigh established a small settlement along the Wiapoco River, though it collapsed after two years of struggling in adverse conditions.[44] Similar attempts to establish settlements on the islands of St Lucia and Grenada in 1605 and 1609, which were loosely linked to English interest in the mainland, likewise failed. The hostility both settlements provoked from native Carib Indians in the Lesser Antilles effectively deterred colonization in the Caribbean until the mid-1620s, when Thomas Warner established a small tobacco colony on St Kitts (see Map 10.1).[45]

English interest in Guiana was sustained by grandiose hopes of finding gold, which sat uneasily with more practical schemes for establishing tobacco plantations and trading posts. Because of its anti-Spanish character, moreover, it was vulnerable to royal interference, particularly after 1612, when the death of Prince Henry robbed adventurers of a powerful patron at court. While several English and Irish plantations were established along the Amazon River between 1611 and 1620, the formation of the Amazon Company in 1619 aroused such fierce Spanish hostility that the Company was quickly suppressed by the King. Following so soon on the heels of Ralegh's disastrous last voyage to Guiana in 1618, it was perhaps inevitable that James I would be suspicious of the Company, despite the claim of Roger North, the leading promoter of the venture, that its purpose was to oppose the Dutch who were 'usurping' English interests in the region.[46] English and Irish activity persisted, but lack of royal support left it fatally exposed to Spanish and Portuguese hostility.

Spanish hostility was less effective further north, where Virginia soon emerged as the centre-piece of Jacobean colonization in America. Though Spain complained that the colony was little more than a 'den of thieves', the distance of Chesapeake Bay

[44] Andrews, *Elizabethan Privateering*, pp. 196–97; Joyce Lorimer, ed., *English and Irish Settlement on the River Amazon, 1550–1646* (London, 1989), pp. 10–11, 19–22.

[45] Andrews, *Spanish Caribbean*, pp. 240–42; Peter Hulme and Neil L. Whitehead, eds., *Wild Majesty: Encounters with Caribs from Columbus to the Present Day* (Oxford, 1992), pp. 62–79; Carl and Roberta Bridenbaugh, *No Peace Beyond the Line: The English in the Caribbean, 1624–1690* (New York, 1972), pp. 9–24. See below, pp. 233–34.

[46] Lorimer, *English and Irish Settlement*, pp. 36–45, 60–68, 81, 201–03.

from the Caribbean provided a protective barrier against military action, enabling the English to establish a small beachhead at Jamestown in 1607.[47] Distance from Spanish power did not guarantee success, of course, as abortive attempts to establish a colony on Newfoundland indicate. Jamestown survived, but its future was repeatedly threatened by mismanagement and misconduct among adventurers and settlers, which continued even after the discovery of a profitable cash crop in tobacco gave it a firmer economic future. Persistent problems in adjusting to new circumstances, combined with an unhealthy environment, left Virginia demographically dependent on England until the later seventeenth century.[48]

The organization of the colony was in the hands of the Virginia Company of London from its foundation in 1606 until its collapse in 1624. A similar company, based in Plymouth, with authority to settle to the north of Chesapeake Bay, was short-lived, and achieved little beyond establishing a small settlement of 120 men at Sagadahoc in Maine in 1607 which collapsed two years later. By contrast, the London Company began by vigorously promoting the colonization of Virginia, employing a wide range of sophisticated methods to achieve its purpose, including the use of sermons and lotteries.[49] The Company received widespread support from merchants, gentry, aristocrats, and others eager to share in the economic exploitation of America. Leading supporters included the Earl of Salisbury and Sir Thomas Smythe, who both played important roles behind the scenes, particularly in providing a link between the government and city. However, the failure of the Company to make a profit during its early years was deeply discouraging, and caused serious financial difficulties in the future. It was unfortunate, perhaps, that the settlement of Jamestown also coincided with the plantation in Ulster, one of several colonizing projects in Ireland which attracted close attention from the Crown at the expense of transatlantic enterprise.

Such problems were overshadowed by a confusion over aims and methods within the Virginia Company, and between it and the colony. The tension between short-term profit and long-term investment exposed uncertainty over the purpose and future of Jamestown. In spite of the peace with Spain, some shareholders saw the settlement more as a military outpost which might be of use as a base for raids on Spanish shipping, than as a self-sufficient agricultural colony.[50] The failure of

[47] Brown, *Genesis of the United States*, II, pp. 646–47; Charles M. Andrews, *The Colonial Period of American History*, 4 vols. (New Haven, 1934–38), I, pp. 98–101.

[48] Cell, *English Enterprise*, pp. 61–80; James Horn, *Adapting to a New World: English Society in the Seventeenth Century Chesapeake* (Chapel Hill, NC, 1994), pp. 11–12, 25, 139. See chap. by James Horn.

[49] Brown, *Genesis of the United States*, II, pp. 760–61; Susan Myra Kingsbury, ed., *The Records of the Virginia Company of London*, 4 vols. (Washington, 1906–35), IV, pp. 216–17, 524; Ian K. Steele, *Warpaths: Invasions of North America* (Oxford, 1994), pp. 82–84.

[50] Andrews, *Trade, Plunder and Settlement*, pp. 313–14. The military dimension to English colonization is stressed by Webb, *The Governors-General*, pp. 437–39.

the Company to develop a coherent strategy to deal with this issue had a catastrophic impact on the early development of Virginia. Lacking firm leadership, gangs of squabbling settlers preferred to search for gold and silver than to grow food for themselves. John Smith restored morale by forcing the settlers to work or go hungry, but his departure paved the way for the horrifying 'starving-time' during the winter of 1609, which was accompanied by the outbreak of hostilities between the English and Indians. Powhatan, the Indian leader, nearly succeeded in forcing the English out of Chesapeake Bay. In 1610 the surviving settlers were prevented from abandoning the settlement only by the timely arrival of a relief expedition from London. The imposition of Draconian measures, including the use of martial law, saved the colony, but it continued to struggle until the development of tobacco as a commercial crop.[51] Although the windfall profits made from the cultivation of the crop created a feverish, speculative boom which burst when prices collapsed, tobacco held out the prospect of ever-widening marketing opportunities as an item of mass consumption in European markets. From 1617 to 1621, for example, exports of tobacco from the colony increased from 20,000 to 350,000 pounds, though it was the private adventurer, not the Company, who gained most from this expansion.[52] Tobacco may have saved Virginia, providing the opportunity for a small number of planters to reap a considerable profit from its cultivation, but it did little to lay the basis for balanced economic or social development. As it encouraged the expansion of the colony, moreover, it revived Indian alarm at English intentions. The fragility of Anglo-Indian relations was destroyed in 1622 when the Indians attacked Jamestown and outlying plantations, killing about 350 settlers: the colony was 'almost shattered to pieces, and brought to a very low and calamitious condition'.[53] Though Virginia survived, the attack sounded the death-knell for the Company, which was abolished by royal decree in 1624. Thereafter it became the first royal colony in the New World, a development which had important long-term implications for English Imperial authority.[54]

By the early 1620s not only was the Company faced with mounting financial difficulties, it was also deeply embroiled in internal feuding between the supporters of Sir Edwin Sandys, the Company's treasurer, and the backers of the Earl of

[51] Andrews, *Trade, Plunder and Settlement*, pp. 315–23; Edmund S. Morgan, *American Slavery, American Freedom: The Ordeal of Colonial Virginia* (New York, 1975), pp. 71–107; Helen C. Rountree, *Pocahontas's People: The Powhatan Indians of Virginia Through Four Centuries* (Norman, Okla., 1990), pp. 53–60; 183–85.

[52] John J. McCusker and Russell R. Menard, *The Economy of British America, 1607–1789* (Chapel Hill, NC, 1985), pp. 117–19; T. O. Lloyd, *The British Empire, 1558–1983* (Oxford, 1984), pp. 16–17.

[53] Clayton Colman Hall, ed., *Narratives of Early Maryland, 1633–1684* (New York, 1925), p. 188.

[54] Gary B. Nash, *Red, White, and Black: The Peoples of Early America* (Englewood Cliffs, Fla., 1974), pp. 61–63; Robert M. Bliss, *Revolution and Empire; English Politics and the American Colonies in the Seventeenth Century* (Manchester, 1990), pp. 23–24. See above, p. 48.

Warwick, a leading member of the Company and a prominent promoter of other colonial ventures. Though heightened by personal animosity, there were deeper matters at issue between the rival groups. Warwick's Protestant imperialism was infused with a deep hostility towards Spain, which could easily be employed to justify the looting of Spanish America. But his promotion of illicit privateering across the Atlantic angered Sandys and his supporters, at a time when they were trying to encourage the agricultural and industrial development of the colony.[55] Yet the differences between the two sides should not be exaggerated. Although the ideology behind Warwick's colonizing schemes reached back to the 1580s and 1590s, his interests also placed him in the vanguard of a group of colonial entrepreneurs whose pursuit of profit had novel implications for the future development of English America. These implications were already becoming apparent on Bermuda, discovered in 1609, and settled three years later by an offshoot of the Virginia Company. Though the island colony experienced a troubled birth, when it was plagued by rats introduced by the English, within ten years it had been carved up into extensive tobacco plantations on which some planters, including Warwick's agents, were experimenting with slave labour brought to the island by Dutch privateers. Though the widespread introduction of servile labour was delayed by market forces, a similar pattern of enterprise can be detected in the subsequent activities of the Providence Island Company, in which Warwick was a leading spirit.[56]

The widening scope of English colonial activity, which the peace with Spain fostered, is demonstrated by repeated attempts to colonize Newfoundland in the early seventeenth century.[57] Growing out of well-established and wide-ranging interests, the attempted colonization of Newfoundland also reveals the potential for conflict between maritime and colonial enterprise when the exploitation of a profitable primary resource, such as fishing, was at stake. The Newfoundland Company, incorporated with the support of merchants, courtiers, and gentry, sent John Guy in 1610 to establish a small colony on the Avalon Peninsula. After a promising start, however, the settlement was attacked by English pirates and weakened by growing hostility from fishermen, who claimed that the settlers were obstructing their activities ashore. As the colony struggled to survive, the Company began to license the establishment of other settlements by private adventurers, including an attempt by Sir George Calvert to establish a Catholic

[55] Andrews, *Colonial Period*, I, pp. 153–72; Brenner, *Merchants and Revolution*, pp. 99–102.

[56] Karen Ordahl Kupperman, *Providence Island, 1630–1641: The Other Puritan Colony* (Cambridge, 1993); Brenner, *Merchants and Revolution*, pp. 154–59; Wesley Frank Craven and Walter B. Hayward, eds., *The Journal of Richard Norwood, Surveyor of Bermuda* (New York, 1945), pp. 53–56. See below, p. 204.

[57] Cell, *English Enterprise in Newfoundland*, pp. 60–79, 83–91.

colony at Ferryland from 1622 to 1628. None of these ventures was successful, though a small group of settlers struggled to survive on Newfoundland long after the demise of the Company in 1632.

The colonization of New England, towards the end of the period covered by this chapter, marked a small but potentially significant exception to the dismal pattern of English colonial enterprise in America. Following the failure of the Sagadahoc settlement, interest in the region had been limited to fishing and trading, despite John Smith's attempts to promote the colonization of the area by publicizing its rich resources.[58] This changed during 1620 with the establishment of Plymouth plantation by a small group of religious separatists. The possibility that America might be a haven for religious refugees can be traced back to Hakluyt, but its practical application was not effectively tested until William Bradford led a mixed community of men, women, and children, Puritans and non-Puritans, across the Atlantic to bring their own sense of order to what they saw as 'a vast and empty chaos'.[59] Although a group of separatists, led by Henry Jacob, attempted to establish themselves in Bermuda and Virginia during the early decades of the seventeenth century, both congregations were small and short-lived.[60] By comparison, Plymouth plantation was an unrivalled experiment in colonial development. Though it struggled to survive for many years, the idea of God's elect seeking to build a holy commonwealth in New England set a powerful precedent for the future, foreshadowing a new wave of English colonization which emerged after 1625 during the troubled reign of Charles I.

In contrast to the faltering progress of English colonial enterprise after 1604, overseas trade seemed set for a period of sustained and impressive growth. Seizing the opportunities presented by the peace with Spain, English merchant ships sailed the oceans in search of Eastern spices, Caribbean sugar and tobacco, Arctic whales, and Newfoundland fish, though trade was often accompanied by plunder, if not outright piracy.[61] But the same lack of state support for commerce, as for colonization, left many of these initiatives vulnerable to Iberian hostility and, increasingly, Dutch rivalry, and failed to halt the decline in traditional exports of cloth, though this was related to deeper changes in the nature of English overseas trade which were under way after *c.*1620. The emergence of the Dutch as a global trading power with unrivalled financial and shipping resources exacerbated

[58] David B. Quinn and Alison M. Quinn, eds., *The English New England Voyages, 1602–1608* (London, 1983); Andrews, *Colonial Period*, I, pp. 91–97.

[59] Dwight B. Heath, ed., *A Journal of the Pilgrims at Plymouth: Mourt's Relation: A Relation or Journal of the English Plantation Settled at Plymouth in New England, by Certain English Adventurers both Merchants and Others* (New York, 1963), pp. 90–92; Andrews, *Colonial Period*, I, pp. 249–84; Wright, *The Search for Liberty*, pp. 161–87.

[60] Craven and Hayward, eds., *Journal of Richard Norwood*, pp. 98, 160.

[61] Clay, *Economic Expansion*, II, pp. 130–31, 134, 139–40, for commercial developments.

the difficulties facing the older sectors of English commerce, and also threatened to disrupt the expansion of the newer oceanic trades. Within two decades Anglo-Dutch rivalry had grown so intense that commercial conflict seemed unavoidable.[62]

Dutch competition exposed serious shortcomings in English overseas trade and maritime activity. The small, but rapidly expanding whaling industry at Spitzbergen, which 'prospered strangely' from 1612 to 1617, was nearly destroyed by Dutch hostility.[63] Commercial rivalry also put at risk the development of English trading interests in the East Indies. Although the East India Company received strong support from some of the wealthiest merchants in the City of London, throughout its early years it struggled with pressing financial difficulties, made worse by the expectation of rapid returns among shareholders. Capital shortages limited the Company's operations in the East, leaving it vulnerable to Portuguese hostility and Dutch competition. In the Spice Islands, where the Company had hopes of establishing a lucrative trade, its fleets were shadowed and often threatened by those of the rival Dutch company.[64] Attempts to deal with mounting Anglo-Dutch tension at conferences in 1613 and 1615 were ineffective, and failed to prevent the outbreak of hostilities in the East during 1618. A semblance of peace was restored in 1620, but as a political solution it was unwelcome to the members of either company. The Dutch execution of ten English merchants at Amboina in 1623, a 'massacre' in the emotive language of the day, was greeted with outrage in London, and provoked demands for the issue of letters of reprisal against the Dutch.

These problems, which were compounded by the difficulties of trading in such distant regions, compelled the Company to reorganize its commercial operations in the East. Although it was establishing a commercial empire of unprecedented scope and complexity, the Company's fluctuating fortunes led to improvisation and major restructuring. Trade with Japan was abandoned in 1623, while the Spice Islands were increasingly neglected in favour of western India and Persia, where the Company conducted a valuable trade after 1614 focused, particularly on Surat. The seizure of the Portuguese fortress of Hormuz in 1622 by a Persian army, acting with the assistance of the Company, encouraged this development and provided some compensation for its disappointing record further east. Even so, it remained ill-equipped to deal with the commercial crisis of the 1620s, when a combination of falling profits and rising costs led to demands that the Indies trade should be

[62] Quinn and Ryan, *England's Sea Empire*, pp. 154–55, 161–62. On Dutch enterprise see Jonathan I. Israel, *Dutch Primacy in World Trade, 1585–1740* (Oxford, 1989), esp. pp. 101–12.

[63] *Calendar of State Papers Domestic, 1611–18*, pp. 140, 203, 252, 503, 516, 560; Gordon Jackson, *The British Whaling Trade* (London, 1978), pp. 13–14.

[64] On the spice trade see below, pp. 268–71.

abandoned altogether.[65] While the Company survived, it faced an uncertain future at the end of the reign of James I.

The difficulties facing the East India and Virginia Companies indicate that corporate enterprise was in serious disarray by the early 1620s. Lack of effective state support, one of the unifying themes of this complex period, weakened both companies and raised deeper questions concerning the role of public and private enterprise in colonial development. The failure to develop a coherent imperial policy before 1650 turned English overseas enterprise into a continuous process of trial and error, sustained by the ambitions of small groups of adventurers keen to maximize profits, but at the risk of mortgaging future progress. These cross-currents tended to heighten the long-standing importance of plunder in English maritime activity, though in the Atlantic privateering easily shaded into trade and colonization. The dynamic relationship between trade, plunder, and settlement encouraged an aggressive nationalistic approach, legitimized by hostility towards Spain, which underpinned English imperialism, at least during the first half of the seventeenth century.[66] The instability of this relationship, however, fostered subtle differences between colonial and maritime enterprise. By 1625, for example, England had become an oceanic seafaring nation capable of rivalling Spain or Portugal, but it had yet to establish an overseas colony able to reproduce itself—with the possible, but as yet insignificant, exception of Plymouth plantation. Colonial population figures are notoriously unreliable for this period, but conservative estimates of several thousand settlers in the Chesapeake, 1,500 on Bermuda, several hundred in New England and Newfoundland, and several hundred in Guiana and the Caribbean, cast some light on the limited nature of English colonization.[67] Robert Harcourt's description of the settlement of Guiana as being little more than 'a few dispersed men, being altogeather without Governement' could, without undue exaggeration, be applied to much of English America in 1625.[68] Such small, incomplete, and potentially chaotic societies were of slight concern to the state: colonies, like trade, aroused little interest unless they could be taxed or exploited for other financial purposes. In the long term, this lack of

[65] K. N. Chaudhuri, *The English East India Company: The Study of an Early Joint-Stock Company, 1600–1640* (London, 1965), pp. 21–22, 49–50, 56, 61–63, 66, 209, 217; Foster, *England's Quest*, pp. 248–53, 274–76; Clay, *Economic Expansion*, II, pp. 130–31.

[66] See the interesting comments in Daniel A. Baugh, 'Maritime Strength and Atlantic Commerce: The Uses of "a Grand Marine Empire"', in Lawrence Stone, ed., *An Imperial State at War: Britain from 1689 to 1815* (London, 1994), pp. 185–89, 195. See below, pp. 426–28.

[67] Clay, *Economic Expansion*, II, pp. 137–38; R. C. Simmons, *The American Colonies: From Settlement to Independence* (London, 1976), pp. 24, 42–43.

[68] Lorimer, *English and Irish Settlement*, p. 281; Scammell, *The World Encompassed*, pp. 480–81, 492–93; Anthony McFarlane, *The British in the Americas, 1480–1815* (London, 1994), pp. 52–53.

political interest or control was to be fatal to English interests in America. In the short term, it created a patchwork of small settlements and trading posts, populated by marginal migrants with a tenuous hold on the land, and with a future as unsettled as it was unclear.[69]

[69] The informal nature of this process was reflected in the mundane manner in which the English claimed possession of American territory: see Patricia Seed, *Ceremonies of Possession in Europe's Conquest of the New World, 1492–1640* (Cambridge, 1995), pp. 19–23, 38–40.

Select Bibliography

Charles M. Andrews, *The Colonial Period of American History*, 4 vols. (New Haven, 1934–38).

Kenneth R. Andrews, *Elizabethan Privateering: English Privateering during the Spanish War, 1585–1603* (Cambridge, 1964).

—— *The Spanish Caribbean: Trade and Plunder, 1530–1630* (London, 1978).

—— *Trade, Plunder and Settlement: Maritime Enterprise and the Genesis of the British Empire, 1480–1630* (Cambridge, 1984).

Robert Brenner, *Merchants and Revolution: Commercial Change, Political Conflict and London's Overseas Traders, 1550–1653* (Cambridge, 1993).

Gillian T. Cell, *English Enterprise in Newfoundland, 1577–1660* (Toronto, 1969).

K. N. Chaudhuri, *The East India Company: The Study of an Early Joint-Stock Company, 1600–1640* (London, 1965).

C. G. A. Clay, *Economic Expansion and Social Change: England, 1500–1700*, 2 vols. (Cambridge, 1984).

Richard Hakluyt [the younger], *The Principale Navigations, Voiages, Traffiques and Discoveries of the English Nation*, 12 vols. (1589; Glasgow, 1903–05).

Joyce Lorimer, ed., *English and Irish Settlement on the River Amazon, 1550–1646* (London, 1989).

Anthony McFarlane, *The British in the Americas, 1480–1815* (London, 1994).

Edmund S. Morgan, *American Slavery, American Freedom: The Ordeal of Colonial Virginia* (New York, 1975).

Samuel Eliot Morison, ed., *Of Plymouth Plantation, 1620–1647 by William Bradford* (New York, 1952).

David B. Quinn, ed., *The Voyages and Colonising Enterprises of Sir Humphrey Gilbert*, 2 vols. (London, 1940).

—— ed., *The Roanoke Voyages, 1584–1590*, 2 vols. (London, 1955).

—— *England and the Discovery of America, 1481–1620* (New York, 1974).

—— *Set Fair for Roanoke: Voyages and Colonies, 1584–1601* (Chapel Hill, NC, 1985).

—— and A. N. Ryan, *England's Sea Empire, 1550–1642* (London, 1983).

R. B. Wernham, *After the Armada: Elizabethan England and the Struggle for Western Europe, 1588–1595* (Oxford, 1984).

—— *The Return of the Armadas: The Last Years of the Elizabethan War Against Spain, 1595–1603* (Oxford, 1994).

4

Guns and Sails in the First Phase of English Colonization, 1500–1650

N. A. M. RODGER

Whatever triggered the remarkable expansion of European seafaring in the fifteenth and sixteenth centuries, it was not primarily or simply a matter of better ships and navigational techniques.[1] On the contrary, the Portuguese voyages down the coast of Africa, and the Spanish across the Atlantic, would not have been beyond the capacity of European ships and skills in earlier centuries, if the will to mount such expeditions had been present. When they were undertaken, the barriers to be overcome were as much political, psychological, logistical, and financial as technical. Nevertheless, ship design on the Atlantic seaboard of Western Europe was changing in the later fifteenth and sixteenth centuries, and the cumulative effect of these changes was to transform European shipping in ways which profoundly influenced the overseas expansion of every European state. Moreover, the changes operated differently in different countries, and their effect in England and Scotland was to create some distinctive and valuable advantages, as well as some disadvantages, in the competition with other countries for overseas possessions and markets. The kind of ships the English and Scots built, and the manner in which they armed them, had a real influence on the way in which their colonial Empire eventually developed. Naval architecture, naval tactics, gunnery, and navigation were fundamental technical skills upon which overseas expansion was to be built, and they have to be understood if it is to be fully accounted for.

This would be easier if the subject were distinguished by more research and fewer misconceptions. As it is, many of the critical stages in the development of sixteenth-century ship design are obscure, and at present any account of them has to rely on a good deal of conjecture. Moreover, the development of sailing-ship design is still almost invariably understood in terms laid down a century ago by the great naval historian Sir Julian Corbett. He was interested in the English Navy Royal of Queen

[1] G. V. Scammell, *The First Imperial Age: European Overseas Expansion, c.1400–1715* (London, 1989), pp. 54–55. For further discussion on the naval dimension of British colonial expansion see chap. by John C. Appleby, Jonathan I. Israel and G. E. Aylmer.

Elizabeth's reign as the origin of the navy of his own day, and in Drake as its founding father. He was especially interested in tracing the beginnings of the ship-of-the-line, and the tactics of the broadside and the line of battle associated with her. He describes Drake entering Cadiz Bay in 1587, 'ready to pit bowline and broadside against oars and chasers'.[2] This approach still dominates the narratives of almost all modern historians. The word 'broadside' (not widely used in this sense in English before the 1590s) is met with everywhere, and it still seems to be almost universally accepted that Queen Elizabeth's war with Spain marked the unequivocal triumph of the new technology of the sailing ship, armed with heavy guns mounted on the broadside, over the obsolete galley.[3] Whether this involved the immediate adoption of the line of battle, or whether that followed after an interval, remain matters of controversy, but no one doubts that there was a necessary connection between the two. Very few historians doubt that this technical revolution was also a national one, an English triumph over Spain, though it is now coming to be recognized that in some respects the Portuguese may have anticipated the English. It is now generally accepted that for particular reasons this 'broadside revolution' did not apply to the Mediterranean, where the galley preserved her predominance for another century,[4] but hardly anyone now doubts that during the sixteenth century the English led an Atlantic revolution in the design of fighting ships (which in England at this period included virtually all deep-sea merchant ships), with profound consequences for the future of English power overseas.

This simple picture needs to be substantially revised. Over a period of about two centuries, from the mid-fifteenth to the mid-seventeenth centuries, there was a series of developments in hull design, rig, the mounting and use of heavy guns, and the tactics of naval warfare, the cumulative effect of which was in the end the dominance of the ship of the line—but this was not a simple historical 'revolution' whereby a superior new type swept away an inferior old one. It was a long and complex process of interconnected changes, in the course of which the design of warships and merchantmen parted company.[5]

The first of these changes was the development in the fifteenth century of the three-masted square rig, the ancestor of the modern 'ship' rig.[6] By the end of that

[2] Julian S. Corbett, *Drake and the Tudor Navy*, 2 vols., 2nd edn. (London, 1899), II, p. 75.

[3] But see Brian Lavery, 'The Revolution in Naval Tactics (1588–1653)', in Martine Acerra, José Merino, and Jean Meyer, eds., *Les Marines de guerre européennes, XVII–XVIIIe siècles* (Paris, 1985), pp. 167–74, whose general argument I follow.

[4] J. F. Guilmartin, *Gunpowder and Galleys: Changing Technology and Mediterranean Warfare at Sea in the Sixteenth Century* (Cambridge, 1974).

[5] N. A. M. Rodger, 'The Development of Broadside Gunnery, 1450–1650', *Mariner's Mirror*, LXXXII (1996), pp. 301–24, deals with this in more detail.

[6] Ian Friel, 'The Three-Masted Ship and Atlantic Voyages', in Joyce Youings, ed., *Raleigh in Exeter 1985: Privateering and Colonisation in the Reign of Elizabeth I* (Exeter, 1985), pp. 21–37; Frank Howard,

century, the standard rig set square sails on fore and main masts, with a triangular lateen sail on the mizzen mast. The main mast continued to carry most of the canvas to drive the ship, but sail could be spread forward and aft to balance the ship on any point of sailing, and by unbalancing the rig to force her rapidly on to any desired point of sailing. In particular, it became much easier to tack, by taking in canvas forward so that the sail set on the mizzen would force the ship's head up into the wind, then backing the headsails to blow the ship's head off on to the new tack. In this and other ways very large ships could now be handled in conditions in which even small ships with a single mast and sail had hitherto been helpless, conferring an enormous advantage in both economic and military terms.[7]

At the same time a new vessel called the caravel appeared on the Atlantic coasts of Spain and Portugal. This was initially a small, two- or three-masted, lateen-rigged vessel, fast and handy, used for war, fishing, and local trade.[8] It was 'carvel-built' in the Mediterranean tradition, with a strong internal frame clad in strakes of light planking butted together and made watertight with caulking. This was quite unlike the clinker building of northern shipwrights, who formed the shell of their ships from overlapping strakes of planking riveted together, building upwards from the keel, and only added ribs to stiffen the hull after it was substantially complete.[9] As the caravel grew in size it came to be rigged with a combination of square and lateen rig on two, three, or more masts. The type seems to have been developed in this form in Brittany in the 1430s or 1440s, and from there it spread rapidly throughout northern Europe. At the same time it was carried into the Mediterranean by Catalan and Sicilian owners.[10] The new rig, applied to a fine hull, made a fast and handy ship ideal for war, trade, and piracy. It was the caravel, or carvel, which introduced carvel-building into England, but the

Sailing Ships of War, 1400–1860 (London, 1979), pp. 28–31; Gillian Hutchinson, *Medieval Ships and Shipping* (Leicester, 1994), pp. 43–44.

[7] Hutchinson, *Medieval Ships*, pp. 61–64; Howard, *Ships of War*, pp. 28–30; Fernand Braudel, *The Mediterranean and the Mediterranean World in the Age of Philip II*, trans. Siân Reynolds, 2 vols. (London, 1972), I, p. 301.

[8] Clinton R. Edwards, 'Design and Construction of Fifteenth-Century Iberian Vessels: A Review', *Mariner's Mirror*, LXXVIII (1992), pp. 419–32; C. R. Phillips, 'The Caravel and the Galleon', in Richard W. Unger, ed., *Cogs, Caravels and Galleons* (London, 1994), pp. 91–114; Martin Malcolm Elbl, 'The Portuguese Caravel and European Shipbuilding: Phases of Development and Diversity', *Revista da Universidade de Coimbra*, XXXII (1985), pp. 543–72; Roger C. Smith, *Vanguard of Empire: Ships of Exploration in the Age of Columbus* (Oxford, 1993), pp. 31–46.

[9] Hutchinson, *Medieval Ships*, pp. 5–10.

[10] Phillips, 'Caravel and Galleon'; Henri Touchard, *Le Commerce maritime breton à la fin du Moyen Âge* (Paris, 1967), pp. 316–19; Michel Mollat, *La Vie quotidienne des gens de mer en Atlantique (IXe–XVIe siècle)* (Paris, 1983), pp. 141–42; Ian Friel, *The Good Ship: Shipbuilding and Technology in England, 1200–1520* (London, 1995), pp. 171–80; Eric Rieth, 'La Question de la construction navale à franc-bord au Ponant', *Neptunia*, CLX (1985), pp. 8–21; Jacques Bernard, *Navires et gens de mer à Bordeaux (vers 1400–vers 1550)*, 3 vols. (Paris, 1968), I, pp. 359–61.

attraction of the type lay not simply in the lie of the planking, but in the combination of cheap frame construction with a highly efficient rig. As a result, the size of the average merchantman seems to have fallen, for a small, fast, and cheaply built vessel could now do more, and earn more, than bigger and clumsier vessels before. The shipping slump of the late fifteenth century hastened the economic decline of the great carracks.[11]

In military terms, however, the carrack continued to be the 'capital ship' of the early sixteenth century. Its very high freeboard, above all its towering 'forestage', conveyed an overwhelming advantage in battle in an age when all fighting was essentially hand to hand. The military threat to the carrack came not from the new carvels, but from an old type revitalized, the galley. Galleys had met sailing ships in action for centuries, and the strength and freeboard of the ship had almost always been superior, but now the case was altered, for the problem of mounting heavy guns for use at sea had been solved by the Venetians not later than the 1470s, and by 1500 all the Mediterranean galley fleets were armed with heavy artillery.[12] A generation before the quite different and considerably greater difficulties of mounting heavy guns in sailing ships had been even partially solved, the galley was securely installed in the artillery age. Neither carracks nor carvels had any defence against heavy guns, and they were swiftly displaced from Mediterranean war fleets.[13] If any of the English were disposed to play down the threat, they did so no longer after the disastrous campaign of 1513 in Brittany, where the French Mediterranean galleys sank one of Henry VIII's ships outright, badly damaged another, and killed the Lord Admiral: 'Never man saw men in greter fere then all the masters and maryners be of the galies . . .'[14] From this point the galley was, for Englishmen, the modern naval weapon-system, the one they feared and envied above all. They spent the rest of the century alternately trying to build galleys of their own, and trying to design a sailing ship which could rival the galley. Moreover, the galley was not simply the threat they had to counter, it was the only known solution to the problem of mounting and using heavy guns at sea. It represented the future; not just a challenge to be met but an example to be imitated.

[11] Phillips, 'Caravel and Galleon', p. 96; Hutchinson, *Medieval Ships*, pp. 44–46.

[12] John F. Guilmartin, Jr., 'The Early Provision of Artillery Armament on Mediterranean War Galleys', *Mariner's Mirror*, LIX (1973), pp. 257–80. The earliest heavy guns in galleys may have been those carried by the Burgundian galleys built at Antwerp in the late 1440s, for which see Kelly R. De Vries, 'A 1445 Preference to Shipboard Artillery', *Technology and Culture*, XXXI (1990), pp. 818–29; and Jacques Paviot, *La Politique navale des ducs de Bourgogne, 1384–1482* (Lille, 1995), pp. 294–300.

[13] Jan Glete, *Navies and Nations: Warships, Navies and State Building in Europe and America, 1500–1860*, 2 vols. (Stockholm, 1993), I, p. 140.

[14] Alfred Spont, ed., *Letters and Papers Relating to the War with France, 1512–1513* (Navy Records Society, X, 1897), pp. 146, 159.

Unfortunately, the galley's solution to the gun problem did not appear to be applicable to sailing ships.[15] Galleys mounted a single heavy gun (later flanked by two or four smaller pieces) on the fighting platform in the bows. No attempt was made to train and very little to elevate the gun; it was pointed by moving the whole ship, and recoiled on a slide down the central gangway of the galley. Though the mounting of a heavy gun right forward involved penalties of weight and hull stress, which in the long run helped to make the galley obsolete, it was a simple and elegant method of carrying to sea a very heavy gun—by the 1530s usually a full cannon firing a 50–60 pound ball. The commonest employment of these guns was in shore bombardment, for the galley did not cease to be what it had always been, an instrument of inshore and amphibious warfare. Galley fleets did, however, sometimes meet in battle. Since they were very vulnerable to attack from abeam, or worse still from aft, they formed in as tight a line abreast as possible, and tried to keep the enemy right ahead. Attack continued to be a matter of a preliminary bombardment, a quick dash, and boarding. Formerly the preliminary bombardment had been delivered by crossbowmen; now it consisted in one round from the heavy gun, fired at fifty yards' range or less, followed by boarding through the smoke. If boarding were impossible or too risky, as, for example, in action with a sailing ship, the galley might lie off to bombard the enemy, but the rate of fire was extremely slow.

This was the method of naval warfare with heavy guns that the northern nations were trying to imitate. They wanted heavy guns mounted low down near the waterline, in order to engage very low targets (galleys) at very close range. They wanted guns firing forward, for that was the only way they could use them to attack. Though prolonged firing might be called for against shore targets, they expected a sea battle to be decisive; that meant that they expected to fire one round from each gun that would bear as they closed the enemy to grapple and board. Heavy guns were rare and expensive, so no ship could expect to carry very many. Rate of fire was an irrelevance and reloading a minor consideration when heavy guns were expected to fire one round per battle.

Unfortunately, clinker-built hulls were ill-adapted to fitting internal decks strong enough to carry heavy guns, and to the cutting of watertight gunports, capable of being opened and closed at sea, without weakening the structure. The big carracks of the late fifteenth and early sixteenth centuries only carried large guns on deck, in the waist firing through small ports in the bulwarks, or under the forecastle and aftercastle firing through open galleries.[16] There was a limit to the

[15] On galleys the standard authorities are: Guilmartin, *Gunpowder and Galleys*, and Francisco-Felipe Olesa Muñido, *La Galera en la navigación y el combate*, 2 vols. (Madrid, 1971).

[16] Christiane Villain-Gandossi, *Le Navire médiéval à travers les miniatures* (Paris, 1985), pl. 76; Rieth, 'La Construction navale à franc-bord', p. 17; Howard, *Ships of War*, pp. 12, 26–27.

size and number of big guns which could be carried so high up in the ship, they could not easily be laid on small, low targets, and they could not be fired ahead. In practice they were fired once, to clear the enemy's decks as the ship went alongside to board. Though useful and even formidable in their way, they served essentially the same anti-personnel purpose as the numerous smaller guns carried in the upperworks. They were no solution to the problem of matching the galleys.

According to tradition, the first watertight gunport was designed by a Breton shipwright in 1501; it was presumably adapted from loading ports, which had been used for centuries.[17] At about this time northern shipbuilders began to use the square transom stern, which among other possible advantages made it possible to cut gunports in the flat, carvel planking on either side of the stern post. Here, in the flat right aft on the lowest deck (the space which very soon came to be called the 'gunroom'), the first really heavy guns began to be mounted in sailing ships in the early years of the sixteenth century.[18] The English were not the first to arrive at this solution: the Scottish navy of James IV was certainly before them,[19] and others may have been as well, but within two years of the 1513 campaign English ships were being built or rebuilt to carry two heavy guns in the gunroom. They were, in the cases we know about, large weapons (in the *Henry Grace à Dieu* breech-loaders over twenty feet long without their chambers), firing through ports cut almost at deck level and near the waterline.[20] This was the first, imperfect solution to the problem of mounting heavy guns at sea. For shore bombardment the gunroom ports served well enough, and heavy guns aft at least protected the vulnerable stern from galley attacks,[21] but it was clearly difficult to envisage a method of attack in which they could be used. Nevertheless, the stern was the point of real military strength in the early sixteenth century, and it is probably significant that most paintings of large English warships of this period portray them from aft, showing off their principal strength.

At the same time as the transom stern was adopted, or soon after, large warships began to be built or rebuilt with carvel planking and extensive internal stiffening to support load-bearing decks. This made it easier to mount heavy guns firing through broadside ports, and soon ports began to be cut in the gunroom on

[17] L. G. Carr Laughton, 'Early Tudor Ship-Guns', ed. Michael Lewis, *Mariner's Mirror*, XLVI (1960), pp. 242–85, esp. 250.

[18] Howard, *Ships of War*, pp. 45, 75; R. A. Konstam, 'Naval Artillery to 1550: Its Design, Evolution and Employment', unpublished M.Litt. thesis, St Andrews, 1987, p. 144; Margaret Rule, *The Mary Rose: The Excavation and Raising of Henry VIII's Flagship* (London, 1982), p. 152.

[19] Norman MacDougall, '"The greatest scheip that ewer saillit in Ingland or France": James IV's *Great Michael*', in MacDougall, ed., *Scotland and War, AD 79–1918* (Edinburgh, 1991), pp. 36–60, esp. 41; Konstam, 'Naval Artillery', p. 34.

[20] Laughton, 'Early Tudor Ship-Guns', pp. 252–66, 275–78, 283.

[21] Ibid., pp. 251–52; Howard, *Ships of War*, p. 45.

either side, evidently for smaller pieces mounted on higher carriages, as the sills were at the same height as in seventeenth- or eighteenth-century men-of-war.[22] Soon afterwards one or two pairs of ports began to be cut right forward, from which guns could be 'bowed' round to fire nearly right ahead. By the time of the Spithead action of 1545 the *Henry Grace à Dieu* and the *Mary Rose* had a complete row of lower-deck gunports.[23] The dangers of this must have become obvious when the *Mary Rose* flooded through open ports and sank. Furthermore, the critical problem of ahead fire had still not been solved.

Meanwhile Henry VIII's shipwrights had been experimenting with a variety of oared vessels of varying size, many with names ('galley', 'galliot', 'galleass') which clearly indicate their inspiration. They are usually seen as attempts to integrate oar and sail, which was undoubtedly part of their purpose, but there seem to have been even more attempts to provide ahead fire by building sailing ships with the characteristic low bow and beakhead of the galley.[24] The most successful of these experiments were probably the two 'galleasses' *Bull* and *Tiger*, later rebuilt without oars, which went on to long and successful careers in the Elizabethan navy, and may well have been the prototypes of the galleons of the 1570s.[25] These galleons kept relatively high upperworks aft, but had low forecastles with long beakheads like a galley. Four heavy guns could normally be mounted firing forward: two on the gun deck firing from ports cut in the hull either side of the stem, and two under the forecastle above, firing above the beakhead and either side of the bowsprit. As far as our scanty evidence goes, this hybrid 'sailing-galley' or 'galleon' type appears to have been developed by the English navy, but it may well be that it was borrowed: the Portuguese had been carrying heavy guns to sea for longer than the English; the Spaniards and others also built galleons[26] and in the Baltic War of 1563–70 the Danish and Swedish navies fought several artillery battles.[27] It is

[22] R. C. Anderson, 'The *Mary Gonson*', *Mariner's Mirror*, XLVI (1960), pp. 199–204; Laughton, 'Early Tudor Ship-Guns', pp. 264–66.

[23] L. G. Carr Laughton, 'The Square-Tuck Stern and the Gun-Deck', *Mariner's Mirror*, XLVII (1961), pp. 100–05; Rule, *Mary Rose*, p. 20.

[24] A. H. Taylor, 'Carrack into Galleon', *Mariner's Mirror*, XXXVI (1950), pp. 144–51, esp. 145–46; Phillips, 'Caravel and Galleon', pp. 91–114; Peter Kirsch, *The Galleon: The Great Ships of the Armada Era* (London, 1990), p. 14.

[25] Tom Glasgow, 'H.M.S. *Tiger*', *North Carolina Historical Review*, XLIII (1966), pp. 115–21; Howard, *Ships of War*, pp. 82–83; Corbett, *Drake*, I, pp. 25–32.

[26] Kirsch, *Galleon*, pp. 11–12; José Luis Casada Soto, *Los Barcos españoles del siglo XVI y la Gran Armada de 1588* (Madrid, 1988), pp. 187–94; Carlo M. Cipolla, *Guns and Sails in the Early Phase of European Expansion, 1400–1700* (London, 1965), pp. 80–81.

[27] Glete, *Navies and Nations*, I, p. 120; R. C. Anderson, *Naval Wars in the Baltic during the Sailing Ship Epoch, 1522–1850* (London, 1910), pp. 4–10; Niels M. Probst, 'The Introduction of Flushed-Planked Skin in Northern Europe—and the Elsinore Wreck', in Christer Westerdahl, ed., *Crossroads in Ancient Shipbuilding: Proceedings of the Sixth International Symposium on Boat and Ship Archaeology, Roskilde*

certain, however, that by the time of Queen Elizabeth's war with Spain most English warships and armed merchantmen were built more or less in this style, which was regarded as distinctively English.[28] Their qualities were speed, handiness, and relatively heavy armament. Even the biggest warships carried no guns as heavy as a galley's, and privateers were usually quite lightly armed by comparison with the Queen's ships, but they were very heavily armed by comparison with the ships of Spain or other countries.[29]

The heavy armament was made possible by the remarkable advances in the mid-sixteenth century of the English iron-founding industry. Whereas Henry VIII had had to import almost all his military supplies,[30] Queen Elizabeth had available a plentiful supply of iron guns at a time when few founders in other countries had progressed beyond bronze.[31] As it happens, bronze guns were in every respect superior as well as being easier to cast,[32] and the English Navy Royal was armed almost exclusively in bronze until the very end of the Queen's reign,[33] but iron guns cost at most one-fifth the price of bronze.[34] Whereas in other countries heavy guns were still vastly expensive princely status symbols, in England by the 1580s they had become an everyday commodity within the pocket of any would-be pirate or explorer. This striking technical advantage, which lasted in certain respects into the nineteenth century, distinctly marked the character of English expansion. It made English ships, however small, unusually ready to fight other

1991 (Oxford, 1994), pp. 143–52; Jørgen H. Barfod, 'Den danske orlogsflåde før 1560', *Historisk Tidsskrift*, XCIV (1994), pp. 261–70, at 267.

[28] Corbett, *Drake*, II, p. 179; Julian S. Corbett, *The Successors of Drake* (London, 1900), pp. 417–21; James A. Williamson, *Hawkins of Plymouth*, 2nd edn. (London, 1969), p. 250; R. Morton Nance, 'The Ship of the Renaissance', *Mariner's Mirror*, XLI (1955), pp. 180–92 and 281–98, esp. 294. Tom Glasgow, Jr., 'The Shape of the Ships that Defeated the Spanish Armada', *Mariner's Mirror*, XLIX (1963), pp. 177–98; Tom Glasgow, Jr., 'Oared Vessels in the Elizabethan Navy', *Mariner's Mirror*, LII (1966), pp. 371–77, esp. 376, where 'ram' should read 'beakhead'.

[29] Kenneth R. Andrews, *The Spanish Caribbean: Trade and Plunder, 1530–1630* (New Haven, 1978), pp. 159–61.

[30] C. S. L. Davies, 'Supply Services of the English Armed Forces, 1509–50', unpublished D.Phil. thesis, Oxford, 1963, pp. 43–64.

[31] Roger Ashley, 'The Organisation and Administration of the Tudor Office of Ordnance', unpublished B.Litt. thesis, Oxford, 1972, esp. pp. 8–14; S. B. Bull, 'The Furie of the Ordnance: England's Guns and Gunners by Land, 1600–1650', unpublished Ph.D. thesis, Wales, 1988, pp. 35–38.

[32] John F. Guilmartin, Jr., 'The Guns of the *Santissímo Sacramento*', *Technology and Culture*, XXIV (1983), pp. 559–601.

[33] William Latham, 'A Complete List of the Royal Navy of England in 1590', *Archaeologia*, XIII, 2nd edn. (1807), pp. 27–34; Michael Oppenheim, *A History of the Administration of the Royal Navy and of Merchant Shipping in Relation to the Navy... 1509 to 1660...* (London, 1896), p. 157; Brian Lavery, *The Arming and Fitting of English Ships of War, 1600–1815* (London, 1987), pp. 84–85.

[34] The differential (essentially a function of the scarcity of copper) varies a good deal in different times and places; see David B. Quinn and A. N. Ryan, *England's Sea Empire, 1550–1642* (London, 1983), p. 60, for some prices.

ships; it gave the English advantages at sea which they did not have on land; it tended to make them more successful at taking colonial products from the ships of other European powers than in developing colonies of their own.

This last was a consequence of ship design as well as gun-power. Any ship represents a balance of different qualities; superiority in one has to be bought by sacrificing others. The speed and handiness of English ships resulted from fine underwater lines; consequently they had limited carrying capacity, particularly if much of their displacement was absorbed by carrying a heavy armament. They were, as a result, ill-adapted in some respects for long ocean passages,[35] often forced to spend a great deal of time searching for food and water, incurring delays and losses which several times ruined their plans. The Spaniards comforted themselves with the reflection that the English ate so much that their ships could not carry a useful load,[36] and they were right in effect, even if they mistook the cause.

It is not certain, however, that even slow and capacious ships would in sixteenth- and seventeenth-century conditions have been able to make very long cruises with comfort. From the fourteenth century (at latest) to the nineteenth, the range of foodstuffs which could be preserved for use at sea remained the same: salt beef and pork, beer, pease, cheese and butter (all in cask), biscuit, and salt fish. The preservation and packing of all these was a skilled and chancy business, especially brewing beer and pickling meat, which could only be done in winter. The only English seaport whose markets were developed enough to victual a large expedition or a major fleet was London, and then only if money was provided early enough to pack at the right season and despatch in good time. In the best circumstances it appears that in this period victuals could not be relied upon for more than three or four months, and the best circumstances were frequently not available. In terms of ship design, Elizabethan men-of-war, both royal and private, were hardly less capable of campaigning in the West Indies (or even the East Indies) than their successors in the eighteenth century. The real difference lay in

[35] Phillips, 'Caravel and Galleon', p. 106; Kenneth R. Andrews, 'The Elizabethan Seaman', *Mariner's Mirror*, LXVIII (1982), pp. 245–62, esp. 246. The distinctive English 'whole-moulding' design method which produced the fine hull forms is discussed by Richard Barker, 'Design in the Dockyards, about 1600', in Reinder Reinders and Paul Kees, eds., *Carvel Construction Technique, Skeleton-first, Shell-first: 5th International Symposium on Boat and Ship Archaeology, Amsterdam, 1988* (Oxford, 1991), pp. 61–69, and 'Many may peruse us: Ribbands, Moulds and Models in the Dockyards', *Revista de Universidade da Coimbra*, XXIV (1987), pp. 539–59; Niels Probst, 'Nordeuropæisk spanteopslagning i 1500–og 1600-tallet. Belyst ud fra danske kilder', *Maritim Kontakt*, XVI (1993), pp. 7–42; John E. Dotson, 'Treatises on Shipbuilding before 1650', in Richard W. Unger, ed., *Cogs, Caravels and Galleons: The Sailing Ship, 1000 to 1650* (London, 1994), pp. 160–68.

[36] Florence E. Dyer, 'The Elizabethan Sailorman', *Mariner's Mirror*, X (1924), pp. 133–46, esp. 136. Jorge Calvar Gross and others, eds., *La Batalla del Mar Océano: Corpus Documental de las hostilidades entre España e Inglaterra (1568–1604)*, 3 vols. to date (Madrid, 1988–), I, p. 393.

two centuries of effort to improve the quality of victuals and the organization of victualling. This alone explains why Queen Elizabeth's navy could not have been an instrument of colonial conquest even if she had intended it to be. It also explains many of the worst difficulties of the early English colonies. Individual ships could and did reach far across, even around the globe, but reliable movement on a large scale was still badly hampered by the difficulty of preserving food.

This in turn bore on England's geographical disadvantages. The wind systems of the North Atlantic are broadly clockwise from the coast of Portugal down to the Canaries, across the Atlantic to the West Indies, up the coast of North America, and back across the North Atlantic (see Map 1.1). From the Gulf of Florida to the coasts of Europe the wind is seconded by the powerful drift of the Gulf Stream. Within the Caribbean both wind and currents set from east to west, so that ships enter through the Lesser Antilles, and leave through the Windward or Mona Passages (from the southern part of the basin), or through the Gulf of Florida. This pattern of winds and currents gave Spanish ships an easy passage to and from the New World. Sailing from Seville in the spring, they ran before the wind south-west and westerly across the Atlantic, entered the Caribbean through the Windward Islands, and dispersed to their destinations. They gathered again in the late summer (before the hurricane season) at Havana, left by the Florida Straits, and returned across the central Atlantic, breaking their voyage midway at the Azores. Unfortunately for the English, the winds of the north-eastern Atlantic do not follow the clockwise pattern: here the prevailing winds are south-westerly for most of the year, forcing any ship bound to the southward or westward to beat down Channel and across the Bay of Biscay, losing weeks or even months before picking up the favourable Trade Winds. Western ports, especially Plymouth, were popular because one could take one's departure after having got most of the way down Channel—but 'such a narrow corner of the realm, where a man would think that neither victuals were to be had, nor cask to put it in',[37] was too small to supply any large force properly. Hence English ships, and especially fleets, often ran short of food and water trying to get across the Atlantic, and were forced to waste time and incur risks landing at the Bayona Islands, the Canaries, Madeira, or the Cape Verde Islands. In principle the crossing direct to New England or Newfoundland was much shorter, but it was also directly into the prevailing winds across the most stormy and dangerous part of the North Atlantic. Here too the Basques, with a longer but easier passage, exploited the Grand Banks long before the English could mount an effective challenge. In practice, the most successful English crossings tended to be those like the 1606 Jamestown squadron which took the longer but

[37] J. K. Laughton, ed., *State Papers Relating to the Defeat of the Spanish Armada* (Navy Records Society, I and II, 1895), I, p. 199.

safer southerly route, which offered islands at regular intervals to supply food and water.

The wind systems also do much to explain why, and where, the English concentrated their early colonial ventures. Because all Spanish trade left the Caribbean through the Florida Channel and worked up the coast as far as the Carolinas before picking up the westerlies to blow them home, a base in or near Roanoke or Chesapeake Bay was perfectly placed for privateers cruising to intercept; far enough north to escape the fate of the Huguenots massacred by the Spaniards at St Augustine, but still within a hundred miles or so of the usual Spanish track. A generation later in the 1620s and 1630s the English, like the French and Dutch, profited from the Spaniards' failure to settle the Lesser Antilles by acquiring footholds which, in the fullness of time, allowed them to control the gateway to the Caribbean basin.

It is well known that the English were late-comers in overseas voyaging. Well into the 1560s, England remained an ally of Spain and the Empire, closely linked commercially and militarily. Both before and for some time after Philip II's short reign as 'Prince Consort' of England, the English navy was essentially an auxiliary of Spanish power, and he himself had something to do with the efficient state in which that fleet was left to Elizabeth.[38] The English were involved only to a limited extent in the Spanish and Portuguese Atlantic trades, no further than the Azores and Canaries, which were counted as within European waters and not part of the colonial monopoly from which foreigners were excluded. It was King Philip who encouraged the development of English navigation by giving Stephen Borough access to the secrets of the Casa de Contratación (the government office to regulate trade) in Seville.[39] At that date, and for long afterwards, the Spaniards and Portuguese were the acknowledged masters of oceanic voyaging, and the Scots and French were in advance of the English. English seamen were skilled pilots, familiar with the waters of northern Europe, but not deep-sea navigators.[40] Like Chaucer's shipman, they knew every creek in Brittany and Spain—no doubt because, like the shipman (generally supposed to be based on the notorious Dartmouth pirate, the elder John Hawley), that was where they lay in wait for their victims.[41] This sort of knowledge, derived from a lifetime of practical

[38] Tom Glasgow, Jr., 'Maturing of Naval Administration, 1556–1564', *Mariner's Mirror*, LVI (1970), pp. 3–26, and 'The Navy in Philip and Mary's War, 1557–1558', *Mariner's Mirror*, LIII (1967), pp. 321–42; Corbett, *Drake*, I, pp. 131–36.

[39] David W. Waters, *The Art of Navigation in England in Tudor and Early Stuart Times* (London, 1958), is the standard authority. See also his appendix 'The Art of Navigation in the Age of Drake', in Kenneth R. Andrews, ed., *The Last Voyage of Drake & Hawkins* (Hakluyt Society, Second Series, CXLII, 1972).

[40] Hutchinson, *Medieval Ships*, pp. 165–74.

[41] Bernard, *Navires et gens de mer*, I, p. 413, and II, p. 774; Dorothy A. Gardiner, 'John Hawley of Dartmouth', *Devonshire Association Transactions*, XCVIII (1966), pp. 173–205.

experience, was of little use in making ocean passages. For that the mariner needed to learn the new scientific techniques of celestial navigation. He had to be literate and numerate, if not learned, familiar with the new books and instruments which appeared with precocious speed in late sixteenth-century England. This was one of the most valuable fruits of the Elizabethan naval war. From the strategic point of view, and certainly from the colonial, it was a disappointment to the ardent spirits of the time, but in barely half a century the forced growth of war had endowed England with a large population of highly skilled navigators, competent to carry a ship to anywhere in the world and bring her home with no greater probability of loss than any other nation. No commercial or colonial effort overseas would have been possible without these men and the skills they had learnt.[42]

In the early seventeenth century, with the return of peace, the English found their overseas efforts still shaped by the nature of the resources available to them. Heavily armed ships with limited stowage were best adapted for cargoes of small bulk and high value, carried in dangerous waters. So the English prospered in the Levant trade, where shippers were willing to pay well for insurance against the Barbary and Christian corsairs. They opened up the East India trade, where a good armament was essential to trade in the face of Dutch and Portuguese hostility. They secured a large part of the European carrying trade as neutrals in the Thirty Years War, able to defend themselves against the privateers of every nation. In all these cases, however, the English advantage lay largely in the disordered and dangerous condition of the seas (disorder which they and their countrymen had done a great deal to generate). They stood to lose much of this trade on the coming of general peace, to carriers like the Dutch with much lower running costs. In the long term, the English tradition of heavily armed traders, pirates, or privateers, was forced to give way to designs better adapted to the cheap carriage of bulk cargoes, notably the celebrated Dutch *fluit* or flyboat.[43]

This was part of the process by which warships became more and more distinct from merchantmen, a process which helped to shape the growth of overseas empires. Our understanding of this process has been badly distorted by an obsession with the broadside. By the mid-sixteenth century English warships had a continuous row of gunports from bow to stern, and the biggest Elizabethan

[42] Kenneth R. Andrews, *Drake's Voyages: A Re-assessment of their Place in Elizabethan Maritime Expansion* (London, 1967), pp. 155–56; Andrews, 'The Elizabethan Seaman', pp. 259–60; G. V. Scammell, 'The Sinews of War: Manning and Provisioning English Fighting Ships, *c.*1550–1650', *Mariner's Mirror*, LXXIII (1987), pp. 351–67, esp. 361–64.

[43] See chap. by John C. Appleby; Ralph Davis, *The Rise of the English Shipping Industry in the Seventeenth and Eighteenth Centuries*, 2nd edn. (Newton Abbot, 1971), pp. 6–12; Kenneth R. Andrews, *Ships, Money and Politics: Seafaring and Naval Enterprise in the Reign of Charles I* (Cambridge, 1991), pp. 16–33; Richard W. Unger, 'The Fluit: Specialist Cargo Vessels, 1500 to 1650', in Unger, *Cogs, Caravels and Galleons*, pp. 115–30.

warships had two gundecks.[44] They were the lineal ancestors of the eighteenth-century ship-of-the-line; they already mounted the majority of their guns on the broadside, and it is easy for the modern commentator to treat them as 'broadside-armed' ships. Englishmen of the day, however, did not think or speak of their ships in this way. They continued to have their eyes firmly fixed on the galley, as the type they had to match, and continued to take it for granted that a naval action would be fought in galley fashion. The bow chasers were always the heaviest guns in the ship, and their fire was augmented by canting ('bowing') the broadside guns, which had especially wide ports for this purpose.[45] Otherwise the broadside guns were thought of as essentially auxiliary, to be employed if opportunity offered.[46]

Elizabethan naval tacticians took it for granted that in a naval action against other sailing ships their ships would be faster and more weatherly, and that the enemy would always be to leeward. He would be attacked in the time-honoured fashion, derived from galley-tactics and recommended by writers of all nations:[47] one bore up, 'gave him the prow' (i.e. fired all the bow chasers), and ran alongside to board. When Elizabethan seamen fought to win, this was their invariable practice.[48] When Drake took the *Nuestra Señora de la Concepcíon* in 1579, he fired two rounds before boarding.[49] Eight years later in the same waters Cavendish three times attempted to board the *Santa Ana*, and was three times beaten off with loss, before it occurred to him that he might gain some advantage against an opponent whose main armament was two muskets, by standing off and bombarding him at a distance.[50] Attacking the Portuguese *Madre de Deus* in 1592, the Earl of Cumberland's *Assurance*, 'coming up unto her, laid her aboard, discharging even withal four or five cast pieces and a volley of small shot, and ranging up along the starboard quarter of the carrack'.[51] When Richard Grenville in the *Tiger* encountered the *Santa Maria de San Vicente* in the

[44] Corbett, *Successors of Drake*, pp. 425–29.

[45] W. G. Perrin, ed., *Boteler's Dialogues* (Navy Records Society, LXV, 1929), p. 259; G. E. Mainwaring and W. G. Perrin, eds., *The Life and Works of Sir Henry Mainwaring* (Navy Records Society, LIV and LVI, 1920–22), II, p. 200.

[46] Rodger, 'Broadside Gunnery'.

[47] e.g., Alonso de Chaves (1530s), quoted by Cesáreo Fernández Duro, *Armada Española desde la unión de los Reinos de Castilla y de Aragón*, 9 vols. (Madrid, 1895–1903), I, pp. 379–81; Julian S. Corbett, ed., *Fighting Instructions, 1530–1816* (Navy Records Society, XXIX, 1905), pp. 6–16; Philip of Ravenstein, Duke of Cleves, *Instruction de toutes manières de guerroyer, tant par terre que par mer, & des choses y servantes* (Paris, 1558), pp. 135–38.

[48] Taylor, 'Carrack into Galleon', pp. 144–51, esp. 149.

[49] Calvar Gross, *La Batalla del Mar Océano*, I, p. 147; Zelia Nuttall, ed., *New Light on Drake: A Collection of Documents relating to his Voyage of Circumnavigation, 1577–1580* (Hakluyt Society, Second Series, XXXIV, 1914), pp. 164–75.

[50] Calvar Gross, *La Batalla del Mar Océano*, III, p. 1684; Richard Hakluyt, *The Principal Navigations Voyages Traffiques & Discoveries of the English Nation*, 12 vols. (Glasgow, 1903–05), XI, pp. 324–25.

[51] C. L. Kingsford, ed., 'The Taking of the *Madre de Dios*, anno 1592', in J. K. Laughton, ed., *The Naval Miscellany II* (Navy Records Society, XL, 1912), pp. 85–121, quoted at 107–08.

Caribbean in 1585, he 'bore down on them, firing her guns with the intention of disabling them', ran alongside, and boarded.[52] In 1591 he did exactly the same thing with the entire Spanish fleet: the *Revenge*'s formidable armament of heavy guns fired briefly as they closed, then they fought hand to hand for fifteen hours. When the *Revenge* finally surrendered, most of her powder was still untouched.[53] This was naval warfare in the galley style: proper, traditional, and decisive. Standing off and engaging in a gunnery duel held few attractions for those who had tried it:

> ... our enimie, playenge upon us with theyr ordinance, made our gunnors fall to it ere we were at musket shott & no nerer could I bringe them though I had no hope to take any of them but by boordinge, heere wee popt away powder and shott away to no purpose for most of our gunnors would hardly have stricken Paules steeple had it stoode there.[54]

If artillery bombardment was called for, for instance against a shore target, an Elizabethan captain would naturally choose his heaviest guns. In the lively sketch of Sir William Winter's squadron attacking the papal landing force at Smerwick in 1581, the big ships *Revenge*, *Swiftsure*, and *Aid* are anchored well out, while the smaller *Tiger*, *Achates*, and *Merlin* are under sail closer in—but every one of the six is firing either bow or stern chasers rather than her broadside.[55] Against galleys in confined waters, however, there could be no guarantee that the English could get the weather gage (i.e. the windward position), without which it would be difficult to bring their bow guns to bear. For this reason galleys were universally regarded as being at their most formidable in their natural habitat, coastal waters. Wherever coastal defence was needed, Spanish officers always demanded, and English always feared, the presence of galleys.[56] This was a serious worry for English admirals, and the explosion of joy and relief which accompanied Drake's successful attack on Cadiz in 1587 owed much to his success in dealing with galleys in just the circumstances in which they seemed to be most dangerous. The same thing happened again in 1596, and in 1602 Sir Richard Leveson cut out a carrack from Cezimbra Road, though she was defended by eight galleys and the wind was offshore: 'a precedent which has been seldom seen or heard of, for ships to be the destroyers of galleys'.[57]

[52] Irene A. Wright, ed., *Further English Voyages to Spanish America, 1583–1594*, (Hakluyt Society, Second Series, XCI, 1951), p. 13.

[53] Peter Earle, *The Last Fight of the Revenge* (London, 1992), pp. 122–24.

[54] Andrews, *Drake's Last Voyage*, pp. 104–05.

[55] Tom Glasgow, Jr., and W. Salisbury, 'Elizabethan Ships Pictured on the Smerwick Map, 1580', *Mariner's Mirror*, LII (1966), pp. 157–65.

[56] Richard Boulind, 'Shipwreck and Mutiny in Spain's Galleys on the Santo Domingo Station, 1583', *Mariner's Mirror*, LVIII (1972), pp. 297–330; Andrews, *The Spanish Caribbean*, pp. 102–05; Paul E. Hoffman, *The Spanish Crown and the Defense of the Caribbean, 1535–1585* (Baton Rouge, La., 1981), pp. 174–93; Calvar Gross, *La Batalla del Mar Océano*, I, pp. 314 and 532.

[57] M. Oppenheim, ed., *The Naval Tracts of Sir William Monson* (Navy Records Society, XXII–XXIII, XLIII, XLV, and XLVII, 1902–14), II, p. 163; cf Corbett, *Successors of Drake*, pp. 369–77, and Sir Richard Leveson's account in Historical Manuscripts Commission, *Salisbury Manuscripts*, XII, pp. 183–84.

In 1588 the English fleet faced a different tactical problem. It was obviously unwise to run alongside the ships of the Spanish Armada, loaded with troops, and attempt to board them. The English had to adopt a tactic that exploited their heavy guns but avoided close action, and one was available which in its simplest form had been in use since the fifteenth century.[58] They started in the obvious, indeed the only possible fashion, by gaining the weather gage and 'giving the prow'. Having fired their bow guns, however, instead of running aboard the enemy they luffed up (or wore) and went about on to the other tack, firing as they did so one broadside, the stern chasers, and the other broadside in succession. They then withdrew to windward to reload at leisure. After Lord Howard reorganized his fleet into four squadrons, they seem to have made at least some effort to attack in a loose line ahead, each ship following his leader into action, so that in principle the whole squadron formed a circle or figure of eight, each ship bearing down on the enemy and firing once every half or three-quarters of an hour. Thus they fought in line ahead, but not in anything like the future line of battle. This was the standard late-Elizabethan battle tactic, invoked with minor variations by all naval writers of the day.[59]

It has been argued that the English gunnery advantage in 1588, an advantage of which every witness speaks, derived from the use of truck carriages which could be easily run in and out, while the Spaniards were still using land or field carriages with unwieldy trains.[60] It is certain that this difference in mountings existed, but it is unlikely that it had the effect claimed.[61] The evidence suggests that in 1588 both English and Spanish ships probably ran their guns out and secured them there before firing 'non-recoil'. References to the gunner steering the ship in action, yawing to bring individual guns to bear, must mean that a ship's guns, like a galley's, were regarded as fixed.[62] Whether the guns were run in after firing, or loaded outboard, is not clear, but the guns' crews were so small (one or two to a gun in 1588) that in any case the guns must have been loaded one after the other.[63] To run the guns out at the beginning of an action, men had to be taken from handling the ship, which was embarrassing if, like Sir Kenelm Digby in 1628, you had to open fire unexpectedly:

[58] Rodger, 'Broadside Gunnery'.

[59] Perrin, *Boteler's Dialogues*, pp. 296–97; Thos. Birch, ed., *The Works of Sir Walter Ralegh . . .*, 2 vols. (London, 1751), I, p. cii; Corbett, *Fighting Instructions*, pp. 42, 59–60, 62; John Smith, *A Sea Grammar*, ed. Kermit Goell (London, 1970), pp. 77–78; Tom Glasgow, Jr., 'Gorgas' *SeaFight*', *Mariner's Mirror*, LIX (1973), pp. 79–85.

[60] Colin Martin and Geoffrey Parker, *The Spanish Armada* (London, 1988), pp. 50–51, 208–09.

[61] Mainwaring, *Works*, II, p. 119; Simon Adams, 'The Gran Armada: 1988 and After', *History*, LXXVI (1991), pp. 238–49, esp. 242.

[62] Mainwaring, *Works*, II, p. 184; Monson, *Naval Tracts*, IV, p. 33.

[63] Rodger, 'Broadside Gunnery'.

In the beginning of the fight I had all my gunnes in, and all my sailes out (for otherwise I could not haue reached them), so that I suffered much for want of men before I could fitt the sails and bring the gonnes to their due bearing, otherwise they sould haue had many more shottes out of my shippe.[64]

As late as 1632 expert opinion regarded four men as sufficient to handle a two-and-a-half ton demi-cannon.[65] One Elizabethan commentator deduced from the experience of 1588 that guns' crews ought to be increased to the point where they could 'traverse, run out, and haul in the guns',[66] but it does not seem that his advice was acted upon. In all actions the English practice was to withdraw out of range after firing in order to reload before resuming the action.[67] In these circumstances even the heaviest cannonade was bound to be, by modern standards, desultory, and even the exiguous ammunition allowances of English ships would be adequate for a lengthy battle.[68] The disadvantage for the Spanish ships in 1588, or at least for the quite small number of first-line ships which bore the brunt of the fighting, is that they would be under more or less continuous fire from a succession of English ships, with no opportunity of reloading in safety. The disadvantage for the English would be most evident if they were unable to withdraw from action to reload at leisure; this was how the Indiaman *Lion* was taken off Gombroon in 1625, boarded from boats while her men were trying to reload.[69]

All the surviving paintings and drawings, both of the Armada fight and of other actions of this period, show English ships attacking from the windward with their bow guns.[70] Individual broadside guns are shown firing from time to time, but the weight of visual as well as written evidence continues to emphasize the bow, and to a lesser extent the stern chasers and gunroom ports, at the expense of the other broadside guns. The broadside guns, even on occasion 'a broadside', might be fired in suitable circumstances, but in action against another warship 'a man-of-war pretends to fight most with his prow'.[71] Mounting the heaviest guns right forward and aft had serious disadvantages. It naturally made the ships pitch heavily in a

[64] John Bruce, ed., *Journal of a Voyage into the Mediterranean by Sir Kenelm Digby, A.D. 1628* (Camden Society, XCVI, 1868), p. 12.

[65] G. G. Harris, ed., *Trinity House of Deptford Transactions, 1609–35* (London Record Society, XIX, 1983), p. 116.

[66] Corbett, *Drake*, II, pp. 288–89.

[67] L. G. Carr Laughton, 'Gunnery, Frigates and the Line of Battle', *Mariner's Mirror*, XIV (1928), pp. 339–63.

[68] N. A. M. Rodger, 'Elizabethan Naval Gunnery', *Mariner's Mirror*, LXI (1975), pp. 353–54.

[69] G. V. Scammell, *The English Chartered Trading Companies and the Sea* (National Maritime Museum, [1983]), p. 26.

[70] e.g. Vroom's painting of the Armada battle in the Tiroler Landesmuseum Ferdinandeum, Innsbrück, Ryther's 'Armada Charts', or the National Maritime Museum's 'Armada Cartoon'.

[71] Mainwaring, *Works*, II, p. 131.

seaway, and it imposed considerable hogging (i.e. arching) stresses on the hull.[72] For this reason Elizabethan ships on long sea passages often dismounted some of their guns and stowed them in the hold, sometimes with embarrassing results when they met enemies unexpectedly.[73] Though it is seldom said expressly, it was probably the chasers which were struck down, or at least shifted amidships, for it was undoubtedly they which most strained the ship. For the same reason they were dismounted from ships lying in reserve.[74]

Much of our evidence about English naval tactics in the sixteenth century comes from the writings of Monson, Mainwaring, Ralegh, Smith, Boteler, and others, reflecting in retirement on their experiences during the Spanish War. As is the way with military theorists, they were good at learning the lessons of the last war, but by no means percipient about the next. Even as they wrote, during the reigns of James I and Charles I, warship design was developing in ways which were making their experience obsolete. Armed merchantmen still often mounted their heaviest guns aft,[75] but warships were being built of a size which made it impossible to mount more than a small proportion of the armament in chase. The first English three-deckers, the *Prince Royal* and the *Sovereign of the Seas*, mounted a formidable armament of chasers, but inevitably the great weight of their firepower was on the broadside.[76] Moreover, they were large and ponderous ships, with full lines to support so great a weight of metal. As contemporary critics pointed out, they could not expect to gain the weather gage and bear down on the enemy like the nimble ships of Queen Elizabeth's time.[77] How they could be handled in battle was by no means clear.

It remained unclear until the battles of the Dutch Wars. Though the evidence is obscure and the detail uncertain, it was clearly in the 1650s and 1660s that the logic of warship design as it had developed eventually forced the abandonment of the old tactic of attacking with the bow chasers, and obliged admirals to develop a formation in which their ships could develop broadside fire all at once. Thus was born the line of battle. At this point, too, if not earlier, the old methods of loading

[72] G. V. Scammell, 'European Seamanship in the Great Age of Discovery', *Mariner's Mirror*, LXVIII (1982), pp. 357–76, esp. 362 and 373; Alexander B. Grosart, ed., *The Voyage to Cadiz in 1625, being a Journal written by John Glanville* (Camden Society, New Series, XXXII, 1883), p. xliii; Mainwaring, *Works*, II, pp. 131–32.

[73] George F. Warner, ed., *The Voyage of Robert Dudley... to the West Indies, 1594–1595* (Hakluyt Society, Second Series, III, 1909), p. 59.

[74] A. P. McGowan, ed., *The Jacobean Commissions of Enquiry, 1608 and 1618* (Navy Records Society, CXVI, 1971), p. xxiii.

[75] Michael Strachan, '*Sampson*'s Fight with Maltese Galleys, 1628', *Mariner's Mirror*, LV (1969), pp. 281–89, esp. 286.

[76] Howard, *Ships of War*, p. 145.

[77] Lavery, 'Revolution in Naval Tactics', p. 169; W. Salisbury, 'A Draught of a Jacobean Three Decker: The *Prince Royal*?', *Mariner's Mirror*, XLVII (1961), pp. 170–77.

had to be abandoned, for now there was no opportunity to break off the action to reload, and strong incentive to fire as rapidly as possible.[78]

The distinctive features of English ship design in this period are largely explained by the ways in which English maritime activity developed during the sixteenth century. In many respects the Navy Royal was the best organized, most professional, and most 'modern' navy in Europe, but it was run in ways which blurred and at times obliterated the distinctions between public and private business. The same men who administered the navy as 'Officers of the Admiralty' and commanded squadrons at sea as admirals and captains, were also merchants, shipowners, privateers, shipbuilders, and naval contractors. The fleets they put to sea were normally composed of a mixture of royal and private ships, often built by the same shipwrights to the same designs, and many ships passed from one category to the other. The royal fleet was only the core of a national fleet, a 'navy' in the old sense, a great part of which was devoted to making war for profit. The Navy Royal was so much under the control of private merchants and shipowners that it was in great measure absorbed into their private naval warfare.[79]

This interpenetration of public and private was characteristic of the age; it can be seen in another form in the contract system by which Philip II raised most of his fleets.[80] The essential difference is that in Spain royal power laid burdens on the merchant fleet which steadily weakened it as a commercial force without turning it into an effective instrument of war. In little more than half-a-century, from 1550 to the early 1600s, the Spanish merchant fleet and shipbuilding industry declined from being the largest in the world to decay and impoverishment.[81] By contrast, the English hybrid system created a national fleet excellently adapted for defensive and piratical war at sea.[82] It was not, in this period, at all suitable for founding or sustaining a colonial empire overseas. It was not fit for peaceful trade on competitive terms. It was a predatory fleet developed to profit from other people's

78 Laughton, 'Gunnery, Frigates and the Line of Battle', p. 353.

79 See chap. by John C. Appleby; David Loades, *The Tudor Navy: An Administrative, Political and Military History* (Aldershot, 1992); Andrews, *Drake's Voyages*, pp. 9–13, 146–56.

80 I. A. A. Thompson, *War and Government in Habsburg Spain, 1560–1620* (London, 1976); Andrews, *The Spanish Caribbean*, pp. 90–94; Francisco-Felipe Olesa Muñido, *La Organización naval de los estados Mediterráneos y en especial de España durante los siglos XVI y XVII*, 2 vols. (Madrid, 1968), I, pp. 463–88.

81 Carla Rahn Phillips, 'The Growth and Composition of Trade in the Iberian Empires, 1450–1750', in James D. Tracy, ed., *The Rise of Merchant Empires: Long-Distance Trade in the Early Modern World, 1350–1750* (Cambridge, 1990), pp. 34–101; Carlos Gómez-Centurión Jiménez, *Felipe II, la Empresa de Inglaterra y el comercio septentrional (1566–1609)* (Madrid, 1988), pp. 125–33; Huguette and Pierre Chaunu, *Séville et l'Atlantique (1504–1650)*, 8 vols. in 11 (Paris, 1955–59), I, p. 209, and VIII, i, pp. 256–57; Lawrence A. Clayton, 'Ships and Empire: The Case of Spain', *Mariner's Mirror*, LXII (1976), pp. 235–48; Scammell, *First Imperial Age*, p. 241; Andrews, *The Spanish Caribbean*, pp. 87–88.

82 Kenneth R. Andrews, *Elizabethan Privateering* (Cambridge, 1964), pp. 227–35, and *Ships, Money and Politics*, pp. 26–29.

colonies. If empire, as Francis Xavier said, was little more than 'to conjugate the verb to rob in all its moods and tenses',[83] the English were the purest of imperialists. In so far as they were interested in colonies of their own, it was chiefly as bases for naval operations.[84] The ships used for the early colonizing expeditions were not particularly suitable for the purpose: grossly overcrowded, even by contemporary standards, and unable to carry the victuals needed for a comfortable Atlantic crossing, let alone to sustain the colonists after their arrival. The *Susan Constant*, which led the Jamestown expedition, has been reconstructed according to the best available information. She carried seventy-one passengers and about fourteen crew on a burthen of 120 tons, and was obliged to touch in the West Indies for food and water on the outward voyage.[85]

By 1650 the situation was changing rapidly. Ship design and tactics had developed in such a way as to distinguish warships more and more clearly from merchantmen. Geopolitics were tending to separate their areas of operation. The main fleets for the most part remained in European waters, influencing colonial developments indirectly by their success or failure against European rivals, while merchantmen traded across the Atlantic to the burgeoning colonial empire. Both merchantmen and men-of-war were coming to resemble more and more their counterparts in the fleets of other European colonial powers. An era was opening in which variations in ship design were to play only a minor part in the different fortunes of European empires. Not until the nineteenth century did the British once more possess ships distinctively different from those of other imperial powers, differences which once again shaped the course of Empire.

[83] Scammell, *First Imperial Age*, p. 92.

[84] See chap. by John C. Appleby; Andrews, *Elizabethan Privateering*, pp. 190–92.

[85] Brian Lavery, *The Colonial Merchantman Susan Constant, 1605* (London, 1988), pp. 24–25.

Select Bibliography

Kenneth R. Andrews, *Elizabethan Privateering: English Privateering during the Spanish War, 1585–1603* (Cambridge, 1964).

—— *Drake's Voyages: A Re-assessment of their Place in Elizabethan Maritime Expansion* (London, 1967).

—— *Ships, Money and Politics: Seafaring and Naval Enterprise in the Reign of Charles I* (Cambridge, 1991).

Jorge Calvar Gross, José Ignacio González-Aller Hierro, Marcelino de Dueñas Fontán, and María del Campo Mérida Valverde, eds., *La Batalla del Mar Océano: Corpus Documental de las hostilidades entre España e Inglaterra (1568–1604)*, 3 vols. to date (Madrid, 1988–).

Carlo M. Cipolla, *Guns and Sails in the Early Phase of European Expansion, 1400–1700* (London, 1965).

Julian S. Corbett, *Drake and the Tudor Navy*, 2 vols., 2nd edn. (London, 1899).

—— *The Successors of Drake* (London, 1900).

RALPH DAVIS, *The Rise of the English Shipping Industry in the Seventeenth and Eighteenth Centuries*, 2nd edn. (Newton Abbot, 1971).

JAN GLETE, *Navies and Nations: Warships, Navies and State Building in Europe and America, 1500–1860*, 2 vols. (Stockholm, 1993).

FRANK HOWARD, *Sailing Ships of War, 1400–1860* (London, 1979).

GILLIAN HUTCHINSON, *Medieval Ships and Shipping* (Leicester, 1994).

J. K. LAUGHTON, ed., *State Papers Relating to the Defeat of the Spanish Armada* (Navy Records Society, I and II, 1895).

BRIAN LAVERY, 'The Revolution in Naval Tactics (1588–1653)', in Martine Acerra, José Merino and Jean Meyer, eds., *Les Marines de guerre européennes, XVII–XVIIIe siècles* (Paris, 1985), pp. 167–74.

DAVID LOADES, *The Tudor Navy: An Administrative, Political and Military History* (Aldershot, 1992).

DAVID B. QUINN and A. N. RYAN, *England's Sea Empire, 1550–1642* (London, 1983).

N. A. M. RODGER, 'The Development of Broadside Gunnery, 1450–1650', *Mariner's Mirror*, LXXXII (1996), pp. 301–24.

—— *The Safeguard of the Sea: A Naval History of Britain*, Vol. I, *660–1649* (London, 1997).

G. V. SCAMMELL, 'The Sinews of War: Manning and Provisioning English Fighting Ships, *c*.1550–1650', *Mariner's Mirror*, LXXIII (1987), pp. 351–67.

A. H. TAYLOR, 'Carrack into Galleon', *Mariner's Mirror*, XXXVI (1950), pp. 144–51.

RICHARD W. UNGER, ed., *Cogs, Caravels and Galleons* (London, 1994).

DAVID W. WATERS, *The Art of Navigation in England in Tudor and Early Stuart Times* (London, 1958).

5

Literature and Empire

DAVID ARMITAGE

> Empire Follows Art & Not Vice Versa as Englishmen suppose
> (William Blake).[1]

At the height of British Imperial power, the relationship between literature and Empire seemed self-evident: the expansion of 'England' caused an explosion of English Literature, and Art followed Empire as surely as the *translatio studii* had once dogged the *translatio imperii*. 'Action and imagination went hand in hand... Shakespeare and Marlowe were, no less than Drake and Cavendish, circumnavigators of the world', stated one of England's first Professors of English Literature, Sir Walter Raleigh, in 1906.[2] English Literature and the British Empire were the twin children of the English Renaissance, that extraordinary widening of intellectual and geographical horizons during Elizabeth I's reign. 'The most romantic poetic imaginings were exceeded in wonder by the things discovered and made known... Seamen were to make literature; upon their experience was to be built much of the literature that followed', asserted the *Cambridge History of English Literature* (1910).[3] The *Cambridge History of the British Empire* (1929) concurred: 'the land vibrated with an adventurous spirit conducive to mental daring and inquisitiveness. Only the dull clod stayed at home', while Shakespeare's 'plays unquestionably quickened the *Wanderlust* of the average healthy young Englishman'.[4] Empire spurred the growth of literature, as the planting of colonies went hand-in-hand with the building of a canon.

This association of the age of reconnaissance with the era of renaissance is one of the enduring myths of modernity. Since the sixteenth century, the coincidence of

[1] William Blake, 'Annotations to Sir Joshua Reynolds' "Discourses"' (*c.*1808), in Geoffrey Keynes, ed., *The Complete Writings of William Blake* (Oxford, 1966), p. 445.

[2] Sir Walter Raleigh, *The English Voyages of the Sixteenth Century* (Glasgow, 1906), p. 155.

[3] Charles N. Robinson and John Leyland, 'The Literature of the Sea from the Origins to Hakluyt', in A. W. Ward and A. R. Waller, eds., *The Cambridge History of English Literature*, 15 vols. (Cambridge, 1907–27), IV, p. 67.

[4] J. Holland Rose and F. R. Salter, 'The Spirit of Adventure', in J. Holland Rose and others, eds., *The Cambridge History of the British Empire*, 9 vols. (Cambridge, 1929–59), I, p. 23; cf. Virginia Woolf, 'The Elizabethan Lumber Room' (1925), in Woolf, *The Common Reader: First Series*, ed. Andrew McNeillie (London, 1984), pp. 39–47.

the discovery of the routes to the Indies and the rediscovery of ancient texts has been held to mark the break between the 'middle' ages and the modern world.[5] Like the inventions of gunpowder and the stirrup, the discovery of America and the recovery of the Greek and Roman classics were held to have confirmed the moderns in their modernity and thereby condemned the ancients, along with almost all non-European peoples, to benighted backwardness.[6] According to Francis Bacon, it was not the soil, the climate, or their bodies that distinguished civilized Europeans from wild and barbarous peoples in the 'New Indies', but rather their skills [*artes*], more precisely gunpowder, printing, and the compass, those recent inventions that, more decisively than any political power, religion, or heavenly influence [*imperium aliquod... secta... stella*], had 'changed the appearance and state of the whole world: the first in literature [*in re literaria*], the second in warfare [*in re bellica*], the third in exploration [*in navigationibus*]'.[7] The myth of the Elizabethan seadogs and Gloriana's nest of singing birds was the later, and peculiarly English, version of this story. Yet only in retrospect did the Elizabethan era come to be seen as a golden age, and only with the rise of linguistic nationalism in the nineteenth century were literature and Empire traced back to common roots in the late sixteenth century.[8]

The knowledge that the new discoveries were only haltingly received into European consciousness has taken away one plank of the Renaissance myth of modernity;[9] similarly, the more particular national story of Elizabethan expansion has been sceptically unpicked. The creation of a vernacular and secular 'English literature' was halting and long-drawn-out: at least one-tenth of all publications in England before 1640 were in Latin, which remained the medium of literate culture until the later seventeenth century, and English remained a marginal language within Europe. Almost half of all books published in England during the same period were works of philosophy and religion, while audiences for sermons always far outnumbered those for the plays of Shakespeare and his contempor-

[5] On the consequences of this coincidence, see esp. Anthony Grafton, *New Worlds, Ancient Texts: The Power of Tradition and the Shock of Discovery* (Cambridge, Mass., 1992).

[6] David Armitage, 'The New World and British Historical Thought: From Richard Hakluyt to William Robertson', in Karen Ordahl Kupperman, ed., *America in European Consciousness, 1493–1750* (Chapel Hill, NC, 1995), pp. 60–63.

[7] Francis Bacon, *Instauratio Magna* (1620), in James Spedding and others, eds., *The Works of Francis Bacon*, 7 vols. (London, 1857–59), I, pp. 221–22.

[8] Jeffrey Knapp, *An Empire Nowhere: England, America, and Literature from Utopia to The Tempest* (Berkeley, 1992), p. 18; cf. Richard Helgerson, *Forms of Nationhood: The Elizabethan Writing of England* (Chicago, 1992), chaps. 3–4, which nourishes the myth by juxtaposing the Elizabethans' discovery of the English nation with their exploration of the wider world.

[9] J. H. Elliott, *The Old World and the New, 1492–1650* (1970; Cambridge, 1992); Michael T. Ryan, 'Assimilating New Worlds in the Sixteenth and Seventeenth Centuries', *Comparative Studies in Society and History*, XXIII (1981), pp. 519–38.

aries.[10] The other side of the Elizabethan myth has also crumbled: no lasting colonies were planted before 1603 (in fact, none could be said to be permanent until the late 1620s), privateering was only a euphemism for piracy, and the horizons of most Elizabethans remained firmly fixed on the Three Kingdoms and their problems rather than the wider world. The causal link between Empire and literature so blithely taken for granted by the Victorians and Edwardians has therefore not withstood scrutiny, despite its enthusiastic rediscovery in the new Elizabethan age of the 1950s.[11]

The collapse of an orthodoxy often creates a counter-orthodoxy similar in form to the old piety. This is just what has happened in the literary study of 'imperialism' and 'colonialism', as most recent scholars have taken for granted the indebtedness of English literature to the British Empire in the early-modern period. Edward Said has summarized the new consensus:

> if one began to look for something like an imperial map of the world in English literature, it would turn up with amazing insistence and frequency well before the mid-nineteenth century...There were established English offshore interests in Ireland, America, the Caribbean, and Asia from the sixteenth century on, and even a quick inventory reveals poets, philosophers, historians, dramatists, statesmen, novelists, travel writers, chroniclers, soldiers, and fabulists who prized, cared for, and traced these interests with continuing concern.[12]

Sir Walter Ralegh and Sir Philip Sidney were indeed far from the only British authors before the Restoration who were also involved in overseas activity. Sir Edward Dyer was a major financial backer of Martin Frobisher's voyage in 1576; Thomas Lodge had been on board Cavendish's circumnavigation in 1591–93; John Donne joined the Earl of Essex on his expedition to the Azores in 1596, agitated to become secretary to the fledgling Virginia Company in 1609, and was made an honorary member in 1622, while his son became military commander of St Christopher and then Muster-Master-General of Virginia; Sir William Alexander was Scotland's most prolific poet in the early seventeenth century and its leading promoter of plantation in North America; George Sandys was the Virginia Company's treasurer in Virginia, where he completed his translation of Ovid's *Metamorphoses* (1621–26); Sir William Davenant attempted to emigrate to Virginia

[10] J. W. Binns, *Intellectual Culture in Elizabethan and Jacobean England: The Latin Writings of the Age* (Leeds, 1990); Edith L. Klotz, 'A Subject Analysis of English Imprints for Every Tenth Year from 1480 to 1640', *Huntington Library Quarterly* (hereafter *HLQ*), I (1937–38), pp. 417–19; Peter McCullough, *Sermons at Court, 1558–1625: Politics and Religion in Elizabethan and Jacobean Preaching* (Cambridge, 1998).

[11] A. L. Rowse, *The Elizabethans and America* (London, 1959), pp. 188–215.

[12] Edward Said, *Culture and Imperialism* (London, 1993), pp. 98–99; for a parallel argument to mine, criticizing Said from an eighteenth-century perspective, see Linda Colley, 'The Imperial Embrace', *Yale Review*, LXXXI, 4 (1993), pp. 92–98.

in 1646; Thomas Hobbes attended the Virginia Company's council meetings as secretary to William, Lord Cavendish, and owned land in Virginia by virtue of his shareholdership in the Company.[13] Such a 'quick inventory', even if incomplete, does reveal a wide breadth of concern among early-modern writers, though it is easy to mistake the significance of their involvement. Mostly it was not evidence of the first drawing of 'an imperial map of the world in English literature', but rather of the financial opportunities offered to the gentry and nobility by overseas ventures, of the close connection between arms and letters in Elizabethan culture, and of the role played by humanistically trained secretaries in the expanding opportunity state created by their patrons in the new overseas companies.[14]

In fact, as this chapter will show, the impress of Empire upon English literature in the early-modern period was minimal, and mostly critical where it was discernible at all, while contemporaries understood literature and empire, what Bacon called *res literaria* and *imperium*, in terms far different from those adopted by modern scholars. Post-colonial studies have generated proto-colonial studies, and recent scholarship has found the literature of the sixteenth and seventeenth centuries to be deeply, because necessarily, inflected by the 'imperial' experiences of racial difference, irreducible 'otherness', assertions of hierarchy, and national self-determination.[15] However, to apply modern models of the relationship between culture and imperialism to early-modern literature and Empire demands indifference to context and inevitably courts anachronism. It is therefore necessary to be as sceptical about post-Imperial demystifications as it once was about mid-Imperial complacencies.

[13] Ralph M. Sargent, *At the Court of Queen Elizabeth: The Life and Lyrics of Sir Edward Dyer* (London, 1935), pp. 41–46; Thomas Lodge, *A Margarite for America* (1596), ed. James Clyde Addison, Jr. (Salzburg, 1980), p. 42; R. C. Bald, *John Donne: A Life* (Oxford, 1970), pp. 162, 435, 552–53; T. H. Breen, 'George Donne's "Virginia Reviewed": A 1638 Plan to Reform Colonial Society', *William and Mary Quarterly*, Third Series, XXX (1966), pp. 449–54; John G. Reid, *Sir William Alexander and North American Colonization: A Reappraisal* (Edinburgh, 1990); R. B. Davis, 'America in George Sandy's Ovid,' in *Literature and Society in Early Virginia, 1608–1640* (Baton Rouge, La., 1973), pp. 3–13; W. R. Richardson, 'Sir William Davenant as American Colonizer', *Review of English Studies*, I (1934), pp. 61–62. Noel Malcolm, 'Hobbes, Sandys, and the Virginia Company', *Historical Journal*, XXIV (1981), pp. 297–321.

[14] Theodore K. Rabb, *Enterprise and Empire: Merchant and Gentry Investment in the Expansion of England, 1575–1630* (Cambridge, Mass., 1967); Arthur B. Ferguson, *The Chivalric Tradition in Renaissance England* (Washington, 1986); Malcolm, 'Hobbes, Sandys, and the Virginia Company'.

[15] For example (to take only books), Francis Barker and others, eds., *Europe and its Others*, 2 vols. (Colchester, 1985); Peter Hulme, *Colonial Encounters: Europe and the Native Caribbean, 1492–1797* (London, 1987); Ania Loomba, *Gender, Race, Renaissance Drama* (Manchester, 1989); Stephen Greenblatt, *Marvellous Possessions: The Wonder of the New World* (Oxford, 1991); Jonathan Goldberg, *Sodometries; Renaissance Texts, Modern Sexualities* (Stanford, Calif., 1992); Emily Bartels, *Spectacles of Strangeness: Imperialism, Alienation, and Marlowe* (Philadelphia, 1993); Stephen Greenblatt, ed., *New World Encounters* (Berkeley, 1993); Margo Hendricks and Patricia Parker, eds., *Women, 'Race', and Writing in the Early Modern Period* (London, 1994); Kim F. Hall, *Things of Darkness: Economies of Race*

Both 'literature' and 'empire' are modern categories that have been projected anachronistically on to the early-modern period. Before the mid-eighteenth century, the highest form of literacy was command of the classical languages, and a long-standing cultural prejudice separated the *literatus* from the 'lewed'; 'literature' was therefore above all that body of material in which one was *literatus*, the canon of Latin and, to a lesser extent, Greek classics.[16] Except in so far as it referred to the *literae humaniores*, '"Literature" was not a clear and distinctly identifiable category of writing', while the more familiar modern conception of 'a sharply defined and autonomous realm of written objects that possess an "aesthetic" character and value' only began to emerge towards the end of the seventeenth century and would not triumph until the late eighteenth century.[17] Contemporaries would have consigned most of what has since been called literature to the realm of the frivolous and the fictitious, as being neither persuasive nor truthful, let alone true.[18] This incompatibility of categories should not make it impossible to study the poetry, drama, and prose of the period before the late seventeenth century as 'literature' in its modern sense; rather, being at once more precise in its definition, to avoid anachronism, and more expansive in its application, makes it possible to encompass writings in Latin as well as pamphlets and tracts within the category of literature.

'Empire' is no less unfamiliar a concept in early-modern usage. It was the vernacular analogue of *imperium*, a designation of authority in Roman public law which had been invested with a spatial dimension during the late Roman republic and early principate. *Imperium* originally signified the supreme authority held by a military commander, and from thence came to mean 'rule' more generally, and ultimately the territory over which such rule was exercised.[19] The early-modern meanings of empire were distilled from these Roman precedents and their later analogues. From supreme authority, *imperium* became used to

and Gender in Early Modern England (Ithaca, NY, 1995). For a trenchant critique see Dane Kennedy, 'Imperial History and Post-Colonial Theory', *Journal of Imperial and Commonwealth History* (hereafter *JICH*), XXIV (1996), pp. 345–63.

[16] E. R. Curtius, *European Literature and the Latin Middle Ages* (Princeton, 1953), p. 42; Keith Thomas, 'The Meaning of Literacy in Early Modern England', in Gerd Baumann, ed., *The Written Word: Literacy in Transition* (Oxford, 1986), pp. 100–01.

[17] Andrew Hadfield, *Literature, Politics and National Identity: Reformation to Renaissance* (Cambridge, 1994), p. 1; Michael McKeon, 'Politics of Discourse and the Rise of the Aesthetic in Seventeenth-Century England', in Kevin Sharpe and Steven N. Zwicker, eds., *Politics of Discourse: The Literature and History of Seventeenth-Century England* (Berkeley, 1987), p. 36.

[18] William K. Nelson, *Fact or Fiction: The Dilemma of the Renaissance Storyteller* (Cambridge, Mass., 1973).

[19] J. S. Richardson, '*Imperium Romanum*: Empire and the Language of Power', *Journal of Roman Studies*, LXXXI (1991), pp. 1–9; Andrew Lintott, 'What was the "Imperium Romanum"?', *Greece & Rome*, XXVIII (1981), pp. 53–67.

denote any power that recognized no superior and, by extension, a political community that was self-governing and acknowledged no higher allegiance, on the analogy of the universalist supremacy of the Roman Empire, and its Carolingian, Ottonian, and later successors.[20] It was but a short step from this to the assertion that an empire was an absolute monarchy under a single head like the Spanish monarchy, an empire in form if not in name. Empire approached most closely to its modern meaning when applied to the community of different territories and their peoples ruled by a common superior, such as the Holy Roman Empire.[21] *Imperium* remained primarily a juridical concept with its roots in Roman law well into the eighteenth century; only in the mid-nineteenth century did 'empire' become a shorthand term for its late-coined cousin 'imperialism'.[22] The avoidance of anachronism should not disable inquiry into the early-modern origins of the later European empires; instead, it shows the wider conceptual field within which contemporaries debated conceptions of order, hierarchy, independence, and political community, within the Three Kingdoms, Europe, and the wider world. Almost without exception, educated sixteenth- and seventeenth-century Britons derived their conceptual framework for considering these problems from their training in the Greek and, above all, Roman classics. The humanist curriculum of grammar, rhetoric, history, poetry, and ethics supplied the basis of all intellectual life from the early sixteenth century until well into the eighteenth century by virtue of its place at the centre of grammar school and university education, especially in England. In particular, the classical *ars rhetorica* provided indispensable techniques for those involved in the promotion of commerce and emigration and the conduct of government, whether within the Three Kingdoms or further afield.[23] Since from the very beginning neither the English nor the Scottish Crowns had supplied the financial resources to support colonization, just as investment in privateering had been personal rather than state-sponsored, most of the early literature of overseas enterprise was promotional in intent, and hence persuasive in form. It was therefore a vernacular branch of classical rhetoric, and

[20] Cf. Robert Folz, *The Concept of Empire in Western Europe from the Fifth to the Fourteenth Century* [Paris, 1953], Eng. trans. Sheila Ann Ogilvie; see above pp. 1–2 (London, 1969).

[21] John Robertson, 'Empire and Union: Two Concepts of the Early Modern Political Order', in Robertson, ed., *A Union for Empire: Political Thought and the British Union of 1707* (Cambridge, 1995), pp. 3–36; Anthony Pagden, *Lords of All the World: Ideologies of Empire in Spain, Britain and France, c.1500–c.1800* (New Haven, 1995), pp. 12–17.

[22] Richard Koebner, *Empire* (Cambridge, 1961); Richard Koebner and Helmut Dan Schmidt, *Imperialism: The Story and Significance of a Political Word, 1840–1960* (Cambridge, 1964).

[23] On the centrality of the humanist curriculum in England, see esp. Quentin Skinner, *Reason and Rhetoric in the Philosophy of Hobbes* (Cambridge, 1996), Part I, 'Classical Eloquence in Renaissance England'.

revealed its origins in its informing tropes, genres, and visions of political community.[24]

The major means by which rhetoric could persuade its audience to action was by making the absent present, the distant near, and the exotic familiar. The aim of the orator was to provide a lively image in the minds of his hearers by the force of his eloquence, reinforced by all the battery of tropes and figures at his disposal. Since the new-found lands, especially in the Americas, were previously unknown and unfamiliar to British readers, rhetoric was indispensable for conjuring a striking impression, and hence a persuasive account, of such distant discoveries.[25] The key trope for rendering the outlandish in comfortable terms was, of course, metaphor, its very etymology (meaning 'to carry across') suggesting its utility as the central technique for travel reports from distant lands. As for the earlier Spanish *conquistadores*, so for British adventurers, '[t]he challenge . . . was to convince their readers that the experiences they described were real, not invented'.[26] This also required that the fulfilment of expectations, however remarkable, made far-flung travels credible, and this may explain why Sir Walter Ralegh spent so much of his own account of his first voyage to Guiana assuring his readership that just beyond the mountains lay El Dorado, the Amazons, 'divers nations of *Canibals*, and . . . those *Ewaiponoma* without heades'.[27] To fulfil the exotic expectations of his readership would have satisfied that requirement for Ralegh, especially since he validated it (again, in line with the recommendations of the *ars rhetorica*) with the guarantee of his own status as an eye-witness: '[f]or the rest, which my selfe have seene, I will promise these things that follow and knowe to be true'.[28]

Classical oratory was divided into three major genera, the deliberative (aimed to exhort or discourage action), the judicial (deployed for accusation or defence, especially in a legal context), and the demonstrative (offering praise or blame). Since most early tracts were aimed at encouraging financial investment or individual emigration, and hence at inspiring action, they were largely cast in the genus

[24] The following account of rhetoric and discovery is indebted to Andrew Fitzmaurice, 'Classical Rhetoric and the Literature of Discovery, 1570–1630', unpublished Ph.D. thesis, Cambridge, 1995. I am grateful to Dr Fitzmaurice for permission to refer to his work; see also Andrew Fitzmaurice, 'Classical Rhetoric and the Promotion of the New World', *Journal of the History of Ideas*, LVIII (1997), pp. 121–44.

[25] Patricia Parker, *Literary Fat Ladies: Rhetoric, Gender, Property* (London, 1987), pp. 139, 143.

[26] Rolena Adorno, 'Introduction', in Irving A. Leonard, *Books of the Brave: Being an Account of Books and of Men in the Spanish Conquest and Settlement of the Sixteenth Century New World* [1949], reprint and new introduction (Berkeley, 1992), p. xxi.

[27] Sir Walter Ralegh, *The Discoverie of the Large, Rich and Bewtiful Empyre of Guiana* (London, 1596), pp. 23, 91.

[28] Ibid., p. 93; on the problem of the authority of the 'I'-witness in the New World see Anthony Pagden, *European Encounters with the New World: From Renaissance to Romanticism* (New Haven, 1993), pp. 51–87.

of deliberative oratory. Thus, Sir George Peckham claimed that he had written his 'simple shorte treatise, hoping that it shall perswade such as have beene, and yet doo continue detractors & hinderers of this journey', and 'to proove that this voyage . . . is an action tending to the lawful enlargement of her Majesties dominions, commodious to the whole Realme in general'.[29] Likewise, Lawrence Keymis's account of Guiana aimed 'to remoove all fig-leaves from our unbeleefe . . . or, if we will not be perswaded; that our selfe-wil may rest inexcusable'.[30] If successful in their rhetoric, Peckham would have hoped to have shown the 'action [of Sir Humphrey Gilbert] to be honest and profitable' and Keymis would have won 'the approbation and purses of manie Adventurers', since 'great reason it is, where assistance is to be asked due causes be yeelded, to perswade & induce them unto it'.[31] They would therefore have used the techniques of the *ars rhetorica* to achieve the great end of Roman moral philosophy—the good of the commonwealth through the promotion of action which was at once *honestum* and *utile*. In the words of the economic theorist Gerard de Malynes, writing of Virginia and Bermuda in 1622, '[t]his inducement should have wrought in their Idea, an imaginarie common-wealth'—in his case, as in the writings of the late sixteenth century, a commonwealth imagined along recognizably classical lines.[32]

The heritage of Roman moral thought, above all derived from the writings of Cicero, supplemented by Latinized versions of Aristotle, as well as by the Roman historians Sallust, Livy, and Tacitus, provided the intellectual framework for at least the first half-century of British colonial theory. The earliest Elizabethan reports of voyages to the New World, and the first tracts in favour of emigration and colonization, repeatedly invoked the language of classical republicanism as they justified their enterprises by appealing to the potential benefits to commonwealth (*res publica*). For example, George Best began his account of Martin Frobisher's first voyage in terms set by Cicero: 'Man is borne not only to serve his owne turne (as *Tullie* sayeth), but his kinsfolke, friends, and the common wealth especially, loke for some furtherance at hys handes, and some frutes of his laboure.' Navigation and the consequent expansion of both human knowledge and national trade would both benefit the commonwealth, and therefore fulfil the duties (*officia*) of humanity recommended by the leading classical moralist.[33] The greatest of all Elizabethan colonial tracts, Richard Hakluyt's 'Particuler Discourse'

[29] Sir George Peckham, *A True Reporte of the Newfound Landes* (London, 1583), sig. C^{r}.

[30] Lawrence Keymis, *A Relation of the Second Voyage to Guiana* (London, 1596), sig. [A3]^{v}.

[31] Peckham, *True Report*, sig. Biii^{v}; Keymis, *Relation of the Second Voyage to Guiana*, sig. [A4]^{r}.

[32] Gerard de Malynes, *Consuetudo, vel Lex Mercatoria, or The Ancient Law-Merchant* (London, 1622), p. 234; for Malynes's classical assumptions see esp. ibid., pp. 1–4.

[33] [George Best], *A True Discourse of the Late Voyage of Discoverie for Finding of a Passage to Cathaya* (London, 1578) (referring to Cicero, *De Officiis*, I. 53), pp. 1, 2.

(1584), was presented to Queen Elizabeth I on 5 October 1584 to affirm the merits of 'western planting'.[34] Yet the 'Discourse of Western Planting' was accompanied by a second document, written up by the same scribe on the same paper as the 'Discourse', a Latin synopsis of Aristotle's *Politics*.[35] This supplied the political and moral context within which he expected Elizabeth and her counsellors (all trained and many, like Sir William Cecil and Elizabeth herself, very much committed humanists) to judge his proposals for English colonization.

The classical moral context of early British Atlantic exploration forces a reconsideration of an iconic moment in its history, the death of Sir Humphrey Gilbert in 1583. Gilbert's companion, Edward Hayes, reported the Christian stoicism of the captain's death in the stormy waters off Newfoundland:

> Munday the ninth of September, in the afternoone, the Frigat [the *Squirrel*] was neere cast away, oppressed by waves, yet at that time recovered: and giving foorth signes of joy, the Generall sitting abaft with a booke in his hand, cried out unto us in the Hind (so oft as we did approch within hearing) We are as neere to heaven by sea as by land. Reiterating the same speech, well beseeming a souldier, resolute in Jesus Christ, as I can testifie he was.[36]

It is usually assumed that the book in Gilbert's hand was More's *Utopia* (1516),[37] in which the narrator, Raphael Hythlodæus, related that he asked to be left with the garrison at the farthest point of Vespucci's last voyage to the New World, and was happy to be abandoned because 'he was more concerned about his travels than his tomb. He would often say, "The man who has no grave is covered by the sky" [*Caelo tegitur qui non habet urnam*] and "Wherever you start from, the road to heaven is the same length" [*Undique ad superos tantundem esse viae*]'.[38] Hythlodæus alluded to Lucan (*Pharsalia*, vii. 819) and Cicero (*Tusculan Disputations*, I. xliii. 104): Cicero's tag was proverbial,[39] though More altered his 'inferos' to the less obviously pagan 'superos'. However, Gilbert's humanism should put in

[34] Richard Hakluyt, *A Particuler Discourse*... *Known as Discourse of Western Planting* (1584), ed. David B. Quinn and Alison M. Quinn (London, 1993).

[35] Richard Hakluyt, 'Analysis seu Resolutio Perpetua Octo Libris Politicorum Aristotelis' (1584), B[ritish] L[ibrary] Royal MSS, 12 G. XIII (there is another copy, in Hakluyt's own hand, BL Sloane MSS, 1982). In common with accounts of the 'Discourse of Western Planting', the only treatment of the 'Analysis' fails to make the intellectual connection between Hakluyt's two works: Lawrence V. Ryan, 'Richard Hakluyt's Voyage into Aristotle', *Sixteenth-Century Journal*, XII (1981), pp. 73–83.

[36] Edward Hayes's narrative of Gilbert's last expedition, in David B. Quinn, ed., *The Voyages and Colonising Enterprises of Sir Humphrey Gilbert*, 2 vols. (London, 1940), II, p. 420.

[37] Ibid., I, p. 89, n. 1; Samuel Eliot Morison and others, *The Growth of the American Republic*, 2 vols. [1932], 6th edn. (New York, 1969), I, p. 36; Johnemery Konecsni, 'Sir Humfrey Gilbert, *Utopia*, and America', *Moreana*, LI (1976), pp. 124–25.

[38] Thomas More, *Utopia: Latin Text and English Translation*, ed. George M. Logan and others (Cambridge, 1995), pp. 44 (Latin), 45 (English).

[39] Morris Palmer Tilley, *A Dictionary of the Proverbs in England in the Sixteenth and Seventeenth Centuries* (Ann Arbor, 1950), W171, 'The way to heaven is as ready by water as by land (alike in every place)'.

question the easy assumption that his dying words were mediated through More rather than directly from Cicero. He was committed to the humanistic ideal of the study of the classics as a training for civil and political action, and in the early 1570s he designed an 'academy' for the Queen's wards to provide a humanistic alternative to the scholastic curricula of the universities, an institute in which the scholars 'shall study matters of accion meet for present practize both of peace and warre'.[40] At around the same time, in 1570/71, he is recorded as a member of a reading-group which met to study the lessons of Livy's *Histories* in order to apply them to the problems of the English in contemporary Ireland.[41] Moreover, in 1566 he had defended his plans to search for the North-west Passage to his brother: 'you might justly have charged mee with an unsetled head if I had at any time taken in hand, to discover Utopia, or any countrey fained by imagination: But Cathaia [Cathay] is none such ...'[42] Though *Utopia* was a classic product of European humanism, Gilbert knew on which side of the line separating fact and fiction More's ideal commonwealth lay. It was thus more likely that he was drawing comfort from Cicero's stoicism than that he was rereading More's fiction in his last hours off the Newfoundland coast.

More in the *Utopia* had been the first author in Britain to recover the term *colonia* in its Roman sense of a scion transplanted from one community into an alien soil, when he described the passage of citizens from the over-populated isle of Utopia on to vacant land on the adjacent mainland (*coloniam suis ipsorum legibus propagant*).[43] Utopia's *coloniae* were justified solely on the natural jurisprudential grounds that those who supported a population by productive use of land could rightfully dispossess any who left that land idle and uncultivated. This 'agriculturalist' argument in favour of colonization and dispossession was used well into the eighteenth century, though largely in the form in which John Locke restated it in the 1680s.[44] However, More's own arguments would have had little relevance to his son-in-law John Rastell's abortive voyage to the New World in 1517. Rastell's retrospective justifications in his interlude, the *Four Elements* (*c.*1518–20), for what had been essentially a commercial venture were the extension of the King's dominions, curiosity about the natives, and their conversion to

[40] [Sir Humphrey Gilbert], 'The Erection of an Achademy in London for Educacion of Her Majesties Wardes' (*c.*1570), BL Lansdowne MSS, 98, f. 6^{v}, printed in F. J. Furnivall, ed., *Queene Elizabethes Achademy, A Booke of Precedence, &c.* (London, 1869), p. 10.

[41] Anthony Grafton and Lisa Jardine, '"Studied for Action": How Gabriel Harvey Read His Livy', *Past and Present* (hereafter *P&P*), CXXIX (1990), pp. 40–42.

[42] Sir Humphrey Gilbert to Sir John Gilbert, 30 June 1566, in Quinn, ed., *Voyages and Colonising Enterprises*, I, p. 134.

[43] More, *Utopia*, ed. Logan and others, p. 134.

[44] James Tully, 'Rediscovering America: The *Two Treatises* and Aboriginal Rights', in Tully, *An Approach to Political Philosophy: Locke in Contexts* (Cambridge, 1993), pp. 155–71; see above, pp. 45–46.

Christianity.[45] More's work set the limits to the possibility of planting overseas colonies, and appeals to the Roman model of *colonia* itself were rare before the 1620s.[46] When used at all, the vernacular term 'colony' meant only the plantation of nucleated settlements within a foreign landscape, and carried none of the negative associations with exploitation and cultural domination that are implied by the much later term 'colonialism'.[47]

At least since More's friend Erasmus had refused to edit Dante's *Monarchia* in support of Charles V's claims to the Holy Roman Empire, there had been an anti-imperial strain within European humanism.[48] The legacy of Rome on which humanism was built was divided between a legitimation of universalist ambitions, as shown by the history of the *Imperium Romanum* and enshrined in the *Digest*'s identification of the Emperor as *dominus mundi*, and a body of reflection upon the responsibilities and dangers of imperial rule.[49] For instance, Cicero called attention to Rome's duty to extend its patronage (*patrocinium*) across the world, not its authoritarian empire (*imperium*) (*De Officiis*, ii. 26). Tacitus, in his account of the invasion of Britain, put into the mouth of the chieftain Calgacus a call to arms to defend British *libertas* against the robbery, butchery, and rape which the Romans called *imperium* (*Agricola*, xxx).[50] St Augustine, protesting in similar terms against states without God which were therefore no better than robber bands, acknowledged that it had been God's design to allow Rome's expansion but warned that 'to rejoice in the extent of empire is not the characteristic of good men' (*De Civitate Dei*, iv. 15). Echoing such strictures a thousand years later in his edition of Suetonius, Erasmus saw all empires as born in blood and robbery, and the Roman Empire as vitiated by its expansion, its use of mercenaries, and its internal weakness.[51]

[45] John Rastell, *Four Elements* (*c*.1518–20), ll. 762–80, in Richard Axton, ed., *Three Rastell Plays: Four Elements, Callisto and Melebea, Gentleness and Nobility* (Cambridge, 1979), pp. 49–50; Arthur W. Reed, 'John Rastell's Voyage in the Year 1517', *Mariner's Mirror*, IX (1923), pp. 137–47.

[46] David B. Quinn, 'Renaissance Influences in English Colonization', *Transactions of the Royal Historical Society* (hereafter *TRHS*), Fifth Series, XXVI (1976), pp. 73–93.

[47] See, for example, Matthew Sutcliffe, *The Practice, Proceedings, and Lawes of Armes* (London, 1593), pp. 204–05; 'Certeyn Notes and Observations Touching the Deducing and Planting of Colonies' (*c*.1607–09), BL Cotton MSS, Titus B. X, ff. 402ʳ–09ʳ; Moses Finley, 'Colonies—An Attempt at a Typology', *TRHS*, Fifth Series, XXVI (1976), pp. 167–88; Nicholas Canny, *Kingdom and Colony: Ireland in the Atlantic World, 1560–1800* (Baltimore, 1988), pp. 13–17; see above, pp. 7–8.

[48] John W. Headley, 'Gattinara, Erasmus and the Imperial Configurations of Humanism', *Archiv für Reformationsgeschichte*, LXXI (1980), pp. 64–98; Robert P. Adams, *The Better Part of Valor: More, Erasmus, Colet and Vives on Humanism, War, and Peace, 1496–1535* (Seattle, 1965), pp. 102–03, 163.

[49] P. A. Brunt, '*Laus Imperii*', in *Roman Imperial Themes* (Oxford, 1990), pp. 288–323.

[50] Robert Sidney, 1st Earl of Leicester, brother of Sir Philip Sidney, drew attention to this passage on 'The servitu[de] under the Ro[mans]' in his copy of Justus Lipsius, ed., *C. Cornelii Taciti Opera* (Antwerp, 1585), pp. 234–35, BL shelfmark C. 142. e. 13.

[51] Erasmus to Dukes Frederick and George of Saxony, 5 June 1517, in P. S. and H. M. Allen, eds., *Opus Epistolarum Desiderii Erasmi*, 12 vols. (Oxford, 1906–58), II, pp. 579–86.

Though there was no necessary connection between humanism and humanitarianism, humanists were among the greatest critics of European overseas activity in the sixteenth century.[52] Perhaps the most prominent British humanist of the generation after Thomas More was the Scot George Buchanan, who experienced the ambivalent effects of early-modern expansion when he taught at the University of Coimbra, before suffering at the hands of the Portuguese Inquisition. Though in his early years he had obediently celebrated the Portuguese empire, in his later poetry he became a fierce critic, not only of the Portuguese but more generally of commercial expansion, territorial conquest, and the exploitation of native peoples by European powers.[53] The Portuguese were spreading disease and pollution across the globe in the wake of their maritime enterprises by means of their sodomitical clergy and avaricious merchants. At home, the commercial wealth of the Indies weakened rather than strengthened the Portuguese monarchy by making it dependent on fragile international relations and the whims of wind and weather: 'if the fury of war or the raging sea shuts down the pepper stall [*occludat piperariam tabernam*], that great king of so many names will . . . borrow money or go hungry'.[54]

Buchanan's two most famous pupils were Michel de Montaigne and James VI of Scotland, and each developed these strains of anti-imperialism in his own peculiar way. Montaigne showed himself more clearly his teacher's student with his criticisms of the destruction of the Indies, as 'the richest, the fayrest and best parte of the worlde [was] topsieturvied, ruined and defaced, for the trafficke of Pearles and Pepper: Oh mecanicall victoryes, oh base conquest'.[55] James VI became Scotland's premier colonial theorist when he espoused the internal colonization of the Highlands and Islands in the name of civilization, yet (as James I) even he condemned those of his new English subjects who had debased themselves 'so farre, as to imitate these beastly *Indians*, slaves to the *Spaniards*, refuse to the world, and as yet aliens from the holy Covenant of God' by becoming 'smoke-buyers', consumers of tobacco.[56]

[52] Anthony Pagden, 'The Humanism of Vasco de Quiroga's "Información en Derecho"', in Wolfgang Reinhard, ed., *Humanismus und Neue Welt* (Bonn, 1987), pp. 134–35, 142; cf. G. J. R. Parry, 'Some Early Reactions to the Three Voyages of Martin Frobisher: The Conflict Between Humanists and Protestants', *Parergon*, New Series, VI (1988), pp. 149–61, which nevertheless overstates the contrast between English Protestants' 'profound caution about the limits set by God upon human exploitation of resources' and humanists' 'more sustained optimism about human inventiveness' (p. 155).

[53] John R. C. Martyn, 'New Poems by Buchanan, from Portugal', in I. D. McFarlane, ed., *Acta Conventus Neo-Latini Sanctandreani* (Binghamton, NY, 1986), pp. 79–83; Arthur H. Williamson, 'George Buchanan, Civic Virtue and Commerce: European Imperialism and its Sixteenth-Century Critics', *Scottish Historical Review* (hereafter *SHR*), LXXV (1996), pp. 20–37.

[54] Arthur H. Williamson, 'Scots, Indians, and Empire: The Scottish Politics of Civilization, 1519–1609', *P&P*, CL (1996), pp. 76–82; Buchanan, 'In Polyonymum', cited in ibid., p. 80.

[55] Michel de Montaigne, 'Of Coaches', in *The Essayes*, trans. John Florio (London, 1603), p. 546.

[56] See below, p. 135; James VI and I, *A Counterblaste to Tobacco* (1604), in James Craigie, ed., *Minor Prose Works of King James VI and I* (Edinburgh, 1981), pp. 88, 97.

The first allusion to the New World in English vernacular verse had served as a humanistic reproach to scholastic folly.[57] In 1509 the Devon clergyman Alexander Barclay englished Sebastian Brant's *The Ship of Fools* (1494), which included the first mention of America in European poetry. According to Brant, the recent discovery of a new world in the west was no cause for self-congratulation; rather, it revealed the pitiful limitations of human intellect and scholastic learning, even though it had supplied the late King Ferdinand with new territory and subjects: 'Thus is it foly to tende unto the lore | And unsure science of vayne geometry | Syns none can knowe all the worlde perfytely.'[58] Barclay did not urge his new monarch, Henry VIII, to pursue the conquest of the new lands, yet in a paean added to Brant's text, Barclay praised Henry as 'moste worthy by honour to ascende | Unto a noble Diademe Imperyall'. However, this would be won by taking up partnership with James IV of Scotland to renew the crusade against the Turk rather than by competing with the Spanish monarchy in the Americas.[59] John Rastell later lamented that the Spanish had been the first to conquer the New World: 'O what a thynge had be than | Yf that they that be englyshe men | Myght have bene the furst of all | That there shuld have take possessyon' in America, rather than the Spaniard.[60] Seventy years later, Lawrence Keymis wondered who in Henry VII's reign would have believed in 'the persuasion and hope of a new found *Utopia*'?[61] The New World remained largely in the realm of fiction and fancy for Britons until at least the early seventeenth century, when Francis Bacon compared the solid success of the Ulster plantation with the risks of the new venture in Virginia, 'an enterprise in my opinion differing as much from [Ulster], as *Amadis de Gaul* differs from Cæsar's *Commentaries*'.[62]

Britons frequently recalled that Virgil, the greatest of all imperial poets, had seen them as completely cut off from the rest of the known world (*Eclogues*, i. 36: 'et penitus toto divisos orbe Britannos').[63] Like America, 'Britannia' had been a new world waiting to be discovered; its Columbus was Julius Caesar, and 'he who first of

[57] C. S. Lewis, *Poetry and Prose in the Sixteenth Century* (Oxford, 1954), p. 130.

[58] 'Of the folysshe descripcion and inquisicion of dyvers contrees and regyons', in Sebastian Brant, *The Ship of Fools*, trans. Alexander Barclay, ed. T. H. Jamieson, 2 vols. (Edinburgh, 1874), II, p. 26.

[59] Ibid., pp. 205, 209.

[60] Rastell, *Four Elements*, ll. 762–65, in Axton, ed., *Three Rastell Plays*, p. 49.

[61] Keymis, *Relation of the Second Voyage to Guiana*, sig. [A4]^{v}.

[62] Francis Bacon, 'Certain Considerations Touching the Plantation in Ireland, Presented to His Majesty, 1606', in James Spedding, ed., *The Letters and the Life of Francis Bacon*, 7 vols. (London, 1861–74), IV, p. 123; cf. Queen Henrietta Maria's verdict on Prince Rupert's plan to colonize Madagascar in 1636: 'it sounds like one of Don Quixote's romances', cited in Martin Butler, *Theatre and Crisis, 1632–1642* (Cambridge, 1984), p. 34.

[63] Josephine Waters Bennett, 'Britain Among the Fortunate Isles', *Studies in Philology*, LIII (1956), pp. 114–17; Graham Parry, *The Golden Age Restor'd: The Culture of the Stuart Court, 1603–42* (Manchester, 1981), pp. 4, 260, n. 7; Knapp, *An Empire Nowhere*, pp. 4, 64–65, 87.

all the Romans discovered it, wrote, How he had found out another world'.[64] This observation of Britain's otherness was clearly a commonplace by the end of the fifteenth century, when Erasmus alluded to 'Britain . . . | Which antiquity called another world'.[65] The changing meaning attributed to this analogy between Britain and the New World is an index of a shift from resigned indifference to civilizing confidence in England between the mid-sixteenth and early seventeenth centuries. From the time of Sir Thomas More, the trope of Britain's isolation was used to explain the lack of overseas possessions and to congratulate the English in particular on their insular self-sufficiency, their indifference to expansion (especially after the last toehold of the Angevin empire had been lost with the cession of Calais), and their ennobling distance from the scramble for territory and trade being fought between the great Catholic powers of the Continent.[66] The identification of the 'British Isles' with the Fortunate Isles of mythology added an idealistic dimension to Britain's isolation that was still being celebrated in court masques late in the reign of James VI and I.[67] However, by the 1610s the analogy had been turned around for the purpose of promoting the Virginia Company's embryonic ventures:

> Who knowes not England once was like
> a Wildernesse and savage place,
> Till government and use of men,
> that wildnesse did deface:
> And so Virginia may in time,
> be made like England now . . .

asked a ballad of 1612.[68] No longer cut off from all the world, the Britons would be the new Romans, carrying civility to the barbarians of a New World in the West. However, until the late 1620s neither the English nor the Scots had lastingly settled anywhere except Ireland, and much fictional and poetic reflection idealized the fact that (in Ben Jonson's words) 'this empire is a world divided from the world'.[69]

[64] William Camden, *Britannia* (1594), trans. Philemon Holland (London, 1610), p. 2, alluding to 'Incerti Panegyricus Constantio Cæsari Dictus', XI. 2, in R. A. B. Mynors, ed., *XII Panegyrici Latini* (Oxford, 1964), p. 222.

[65] 'Britannia . . . | Orbem vetustas quod vocavit alterum': Erasmus, 'Prosopopeia Britanniae Maioris' (1499), ll, 25–26, in C. Reedijk, ed., *The Poems of Desiderius Erasmus* (Leiden, 1956), p. 249.

[66] Knapp, *An Empire Nowhere*, p. 12.

[67] Bennett, 'Britain Among the Fortunate Isles', pp. 118–28; Ben Jonson, *The Fortunate Isles, and Their Union* (1624), in C. H. Herford and Percy and Evelyn Simpson, eds., *Ben Jonson*, 11 vols. (Oxford, 1925–52), VII, pp. 707–29. As Bennett points out ('Britain Among the Fortunate Isles', p. 114), the trope was still being staged in a celebration for Queen Victoria in 1841.

[68] 'The Second Part of London's Lotterie' [1612], in C. H. Firth, ed., *An American Garland* (Oxford, 1915), p. 24; cf. William Strachey, 'Ecclesiae et Reipub:' in Louis B. Wright and Virginia Freund, eds., *The Historie of Travell into Virginia Britania (1612)* (London, 1953), p. 6.

[69] Ben Jonson, *The King's Entertainment* (1604), in Herford and Simpson, eds., *Ben Jonson*, VII, p. 84, referring to Virgil and to Claudian, 'Panegyricus Dictus Manlio Theodoro Consuli', l. 51: 'et nostro diducta Britannia mundo'.

Until at least the 1650s, the British Empire was identified solely as the community of territories once supposedly ruled under a single head within the Atlantic archipelago, and perhaps again to be commanded by a single British emperor.[70] Only after the Restoration—'being not now as of old, *divisi ab orbe Britanni*, *separatists* from the *Universe*'[71]—did the British Empire come to include the territorial settlements of North America and the Caribbean or the factories of Africa and Asia; even then it was couched in the form 'the British Empire *in* America' or 'the British Empire *of* America', implying the territory over which the authority of the monarchy was exercised rather than a unitary political body of which England, Ireland, Scotland, and the colonies were dependent but integrated members.[72] That sense of the British Empire seems only to have appeared in the second quarter of the eighteenth century, and is an index of the slow growth of a comprehensive imperial ideology for Britons, whether in the metropolitan nations or *outre-mer*.

The British Empire in the sixteenth century was instead the congeries of kingdoms and colonies within Britain and Ireland that were controlled by an actually or aspiringly British monarchy, imagined as centred upon London, and dominated by the English. It was therefore a conscious resurrection of the Anglocentric and anti-Celtic vision of Geoffrey of Monmouth's *Historia Regum Brittaniae* (*c.*1138). This 'neo-Galfridian' conception of the British Empire was most pointedly revived by Henry VIII and the Protector Somerset in pursuit of their claims to sovereignty over Scotland in the 1540s.[73] During the course of Henry's invasion of Scotland, his ideologists grounded England's claim to feudal superiority over the Scots not only on the long history of Scottish submission but also on the Galfridian history of Brutus, from whose name the denomination of 'Britain' or the Graecized 'Brytayn' (that is, Βρυταιν) was derived. After Brutus's death, his three sons Locrine, Albanact, and Camber ruled England, Scotland, and Wales respectively, with the two younger brothers paying homage to the eldest, Locrine.[74] This mythic

[70] S. T. Bindoff, 'The Stuarts and Their Style', *English Historical Review*, LX (1945), pp. 192–216; David Armitage, 'The Cromwellian Protectorate and the Languages of Empire', *HJ*, XXXV (1992), pp. 531–32.

[71] *The Golden Coast, or A Description of Guinney* (London, 1665), pp. 1–2, cited in Knapp, *An Empire Nowhere*, p. 248.

[72] C. H. Firth, '"The British Empire"', *SHR*, XV (1918), pp. 185–89; James Truslow Adams, 'On the Term "British Empire"', *American Historical Review*, XXVII (1922), pp. 485–89; see above pp. 25–26.

[73] On this see esp. Roger A. Mason, 'The Scottish Reformation and the Origins of Anglo-British Imperialism', in Mason, ed., *Scots and Britons: Scottish Political Thought and the Union of 1603* (Cambridge, 1994), pp. 161–86.

[74] *A Declaration, Conteyning the Just Causes and Consyderations, of this Present Warre with the Scottis* (1542), in James A. H. Murray, ed., *The Complaynt of Scotlande Wyth an Exortatione to the Thre Estaits to be Vigilante in Deffens of Their Public Veil* (London, 1872), p. 199; cf. John Elder, *To the Moost Noble, Victorius, and Redoubted Prynce, Henry the Eight* (1542), in Sir Walter Scott and David Laing, eds., *The Bannatyne Miscellany... Volume One* (Edinburgh, 1827), p. 11.

genealogy affirmed the continuity of British union without conceding English superiority over the junior, and hence dependent, territories of Wales and Scotland. When Geoffrey of Monmouth was supplemented by his contemporary, Gerald of Wales, an aggressive vision of British cultural superiority stiffened this Brutan vision of English suzerainty.[75]

The attempted dynastic marriage between the English King, Edward VI, and the Scots Queen, Mary, five years later offered a further opportunity for the English aggressively to revive this vision of a 'Brutan' Empire. Somerset's ideologists once again returned to Brutus's invasion, his sons' succession, and the early British history 'to prove that al Britayn, was under one Emperor, and beeyng under one Emperor, then was Scotlande and Englande but one Empire' from the reign of Roman emperor Constantine. In light of these ancient historic claims, the Scots should submit to their superiors, and 'laie doune their weapons, thus rashely received, to fight against the mother of their awne nacion: I mean this realme now called Englande the onely supreme seat of the empire of greate Briteigne'.[76] This Edwardian idea of an empire within Britain antedated by two decades the earliest usage of the term 'British Empire', and that (by Humphrey Llwyd, in his *Commentarioli Britannicae Descriptionis Fragmentum* (1572)) derived from the same Brutan history.[77] In this light, John Dee's more famous appeals to 'this Incomparable Brytish Empire' and its inhabitants, 'the true and naturall born subjects of this Brytish Empire', that is, of 'the Queenes Majesties Dominions, of her Brytish Empire', seem positively belated.[78] However, his vision of the British Empire was expansive enough to encompass the seas around Britain even as far as the French and German coasts, the rediscovered lands on the north-east coast of America, and a claim to 'the Lawfull Possession as well as the Proprietie of the Supremacy over *Scotland*', derived in part from Henry VIII's 'little Pamphlet' of 1542.[79]

[75] John Gillingham, 'The Beginnings of English Imperialism', *Journal of Historical Sociology*, V (1992), pp. 392–409.

[76] James Henrisoun, *An Exhortacion to the Scottes to Conforme Themselves to the Honourable, Expedient, and Godly Union Betweene the Two Realmes of Englande and Scotland* [1547], in Murray, ed., *The Complaynt of Scotlande*, pp. 218–19; Nicholas Bodrugan [sc. Adams], *An Epitome of the Title that the Kynges Majestie of Englande, Hath to the Sovereigntie of Scotlande* [1548], in ibid., p. 250.

[77] Humphrey Llwyd, *Commentarioli Britannicae Descriptionis Fragmentum* (Cologne, 1572), f. 75a, and *The Breviary of Britayne*, trans. Thomas Twyne (London, 1573), f. 92a; cf. Bruce Ward Henry, 'John Dee, Humphrey Llwyd, and the Name "British Empire"', *HLQ*, XXXV (1972), pp. 189–90, which discounts the Edwardian tracts as precursors on the nominalistic grounds that they do not employ the precise form 'British Empire'.

[78] John Dee, *General and Rare Memorials Pertayning to the Perfect Arte of Navigation* (London, 1577), pp. 8, 14, 28; on Dee see esp. William H. Sherman, *John Dee: The Politics of Reading and Writing in the English Renaissance* (Amherst, Mass., 1995), chap. 7, '"This British Discovery and Recovery Enterprise": Dee and England's Maritime Empire'.

[79] John Dee, 'Brytanici Imperii Limites' (1576), BL Add. MSS, 59681, f. 28v; cf. Dee, 'ΘΑΛΑΤΟΚΡΑΤΙΑ ΒRETTANIKH' (1597), BL Harl. MSS, 249, ff. 95r–105r.

The neo-Galfridian vision of the empire of Great Britain, when combined with the Aristotelian foundations of classical moral philosophy, provided the substance of Edmund Spenser's uncompleted epic, *The Faerie Queene* (1590–96). Spenser claimed for his work the educational purpose of an 'historical fiction', and compared it to Xenophon rather than Plato, 'for that the one in the exquisite depth of his judgement formed a Commune welth such as it should be, but the other in the person of Cyrus and the Persians fashioned a government such as might best be'.[80] He envisaged a plan for his poem that would carry his readers through a course of instruction in the private ethical virtues and the public political virtues.[81] No utopian fiction, *The Faerie Queene* would provide not only an example after which 'to fashion a gentleman' but, like More's *Utopia* itself, also offer a vision of the best state of the commonwealth (*optimum status reipublicae*), in Spenser's case the commonwealth of Britain, encompassing the islands of both Britain and Ireland. Spenser's ethical purposes were accordingly at one with the aims English humanists hoped to achieve through the study of the *litterae humaniores*, while his political vision of English domination throughout Britain and Ireland presented perhaps the most ambitious and hard-line British imperial vision of its time.[82]

Spenser, in common with Sir Humphrey Gilbert, Richard Hakluyt, and John Dee, believed on Geoffrey of Monmouth's authority that Britons had colonized Ireland in the reign of King Arthur, before Arthur went on to bring Iceland, Gotland, Orkney, Norway, Denmark, and Gaul within the ambit of his British empire. (Dee and Hakluyt went even further, and included parts of the Americas in this Arthurian empire on the basis of the Welsh prince Madoc's supposed discovery of the New World in 1170.) English policy in Ireland could therefore be justified as a restoration of English dominion rather than a novel imposition.[83] The extent of Arthur's British empire gave hope that Ireland might be but the first territory to be recovered by the English, and this aspiration may have lain behind Spenser's dedication of the 1596 edition of his work 'To the Most High, Mightie and Magnificent Empresse' (in the sense of a monarch ruling diverse dependent

[80] Edmund Spenser, 'A Letter of the Authors Expounding his Whole Intention in the Course of this Work', in Edwin Greenlaw and others, eds., *The Works of Edmund Spenser: A Variorum Edition*, 11 vols. (Baltimore, 1932–57), I, p. 168.

[81] My reading of Spenser is indebted to Nicholas Canny, *Ireland in the English Colonial System* (Oxford, forthcoming), chap. 1, 'Spenser Sets His Agenda', though I have adapted his conclusions very much to my own purposes. My thanks to Professor Canny for making his work on Spenser available in typescript.

[82] Compare the other political visions of Britain before 1603 described in Hiram Morgan, 'British Policies Before the British State', in Brendan Bradshaw and John Morrill, eds., *The British Problem, c.1534–1707: State Formation in the Atlantic Archipelago* (Basingstoke, 1996), pp. 66–88.

[83] Andrew Hadfield, 'Briton and Scythian: Tudor Representations of Irish Origins', *Irish Historical Studies*, XXVIII (1993), pp. 390–92, 405–07.

territories, according to both classical and contemporary usage) 'Elizabeth by the Grace of God Queene of England Fraunce and Ireland and of Virginia'.[84]

Spenser grounded the Tudor claim to the empire of Britain on the traditional Galfridian genealogy. In Books II and III of *The Faerie Queene* he traced the line of British kings from Brutus himself down to Queen Elizabeth. In the beginning, 'The land, which warlike Britons now possesse, | And therein have their mightie empire raysd, | In antique times was salvage wildernesse, | Unpeopled, unmanured, unprov'd, unpraysd', until settled by Brutus and his followers, after which the three parts of the mainland were ruled by his three sons, Locrine, Albanact, and Camber (*FQ*, II. x. 5, 13–14). Britain was overrun first by the Romans under Julius Caesar, who, 'envying the Britons blazed fame, | (O hideous hunger of dominion) hither came', then later by the Saxons, who displaced 'The royall seed, the antique *Trojan* blood, | Whose Empire longer here, then ever any stood', until the Tudors 'shall the Briton bloud their crowne againe reclame' (*FQ*, II. x. 47; III. iii. 42, 48). According to Merlin's prophesy, the Arthurian empire of the British Isles would be restored in the reign of 'a royall virgin': 'Thenceforth eternall union shall be made | Between the nations different afore' (*FQ*, III. iii. 49). There were Britons in England, Britons in Scotland, and Britons in Ireland. All traced their ancestry back to Brutus, and all would be reunited into a single British monarchy under Elizabeth. The hierarchy of the post-Brutan multiple monarchy would thereby be recovered, with the kingdoms formerly ruled by Albanact and Camber owing their due allegiance to the senior kingdom of England and the British colonists of Ireland reunited with their parent monarchy.

A unified British monarchy of England, Scotland, and Ireland remained unachieved during Spenser's lifetime, just as his epic of moral and political education lay abandoned and truncated long before his death. The failure of both Spenser's great designs was not coincidental. The worsening situation in Ireland in the opening years of Tyrone's rebellion may have convinced him that he should offer more pointedly practical advice to achieve the British pacification of Ireland than an Aristotelian programme of moral re-education could provide. He may also have lost faith in the effectiveness of such humanist ethical edification during the darkening years of Elizabeth's last decade, a desperate period of *Sturm und Drang* on both sides of St George's Channel.[85] The political alternatives were becoming starker and more circumscribed, and Spenser attempted to

[84] Spenser, *The Faerie Queene*, 'Dedication', in Greenlaw and others, eds., *The Works of Edmund Spenser*, I, p. 2 (all further references within the text are to this edition, with quotations tagged by book, canto, and stanza). *Pace* Hadfield, 'Briton and Scythian', p. 406, Spenser's inclusion of Virginia in the royal style was unparalleled during Elizabeth's lifetime.

[85] John Guy, ed., *The Reign of Elizabeth I: Court and Culture in the Last Decade* (Cambridge, 1995); Hiram Morgan, *Tyrone's Rebellion: The Outbreak of the Nine Years' War in Ireland* (Woodbridge, 1993).

negotiate them as directly as he could in the dialogic form of *The View of the Present State of Ireland*.[86] Yet with hindsight the generic abortion of Spenser's epic appears prophetic of the repeated failure of any British author ever to produce a complete and unequivocal epic poem in the classical tradition, and hence to provide either England or Scotland with its expected literary monument to empire.

The incompleteness of *The Faerie Queene* was symptomatic of wider European cultural changes in the sixteenth and early seventeenth centuries that linked the three great modern transformations—in literature, in warfare, and in navigation—hailed by Francis Bacon. The 'Military Revolution' of the sixteenth century, with its shifts from arrows to gunpowder, from pitched battles to sieges, and from cavalry to infantry, changed the conditions under which epic and romance had traditionally been written.[87] The gunpowder revolution in particular changed the very character of heroism,[88] and rendered the traditional modes of representing the heroes of epic and romance redundant, as warfare became long-range, impersonal, and dependent less upon personal strength and valour than on superiority of technology and manpower. Only in colonial warfare did the old co-ordinates of literary chivalry still seem to be in place, as small bands of heroic warriors (so they were celebrated by their poets) fought complex, face-to-face battles against alien peoples far from home. The Portuguese and the Spanish produced the sole successful martial epics in the late sixteenth century, Camoens's *Lusiads* (1572) and Ercilla y Zuñiga's *Araucana* (1590), respectively set in the East Indies and in Chile: 'the other European nations, which lacked colonies, did not provide poets with the circumstances necessary for them to celebrate heroism', and produced either great epic fragments, like *The Faerie Queene*, or epics either without or against war, such as Milton's *Paradise Lost* (1667).[89]

There would never be a British *Aeneid*, nor even a British *Lusiads*. The closest the English came to acquiring an imperial epic was in the works of two humanist poets of the 1580s and 1590s. The English Camoens would in fact not have been English at all; he was to have been the young Hungarian humanist Stephen Parmenius, who had accompanied Sir Humphrey Gilbert on his last voyage to Newfoundland in 1583.[90] Parmenius went in search of the North-west Passage,

[86] For these suggestions see Canny, *Ireland in the English Colonial System*, chap. 1.

[87] On the military developments see Geoffrey Parker, *The Military Revolution: Military Innovation and the Rise of the West, 1500–1800*, 2nd edn. (Cambridge, 1996); Michael Murrin, *History and Warfare in the Renaissance Epic* (Chicago, 1994), brilliantly draws out their implications for the epic.

[88] See, for example, the complaints against 'th'airy Fanfaras of *Monsieur Gun*', in W.C., *Archerie Reviv'd* (Edinburgh, 1677), p. 9.

[89] Murrin, *History and Warfare*, p. 242.

[90] On whom see David B. Quinn and Neil M. Cheshire, *The New Found Land of Stephen Parmenius* (Toronto, 1972).

'minding to record in the Latine tongue, the gests and things worthy of remembrance, happening in this discoverie, to the honour of our nation, the same being adorned with the eloquent stile of this Orator, and rare Poet of our time'.[91] The poet's death off Newfoundland just ten days before that of Sir Humphrey Gilbert cut short his impeccably humanist design of an epic to celebrate Britain's *imperium*, though he had heralded the voyage with the poem *De Navigatione . . . Carmen* επιβατικων (1582) before his departure.[92] In this he signalled his desire to compose epic praise (*Ordiri heroas laudes*, l. 10) of Britain's voyagers as they went in search of the lands unknown to the ancients, and called upon Elizabeth, the mistress of the wide seas (*dominatricemque . . . | Oceani immensi*, ll. 171–72), to bestow peace upon her people so that they might extend the boundaries of their empire (*ut iam . . . possint | Augere imperii fines*, ll. 183–84). However, he ended the poem with the closest passage in British verse of the period to Adamastor's famous curse in the *Lusiads*, as America offered herself to the British, but concluded her plea with the warning that even the best-founded empires would, like Rome itself, descend into tyranny (*Et quod Romuleis crevit sub patribus olim | Imperium, diri semper minuere Nerones*, ll. 329–30). In the end, the only sixteenth-century British poem that marked an overseas venture and that proclaimed its genre as epic would be George Chapman's 'De Guiana, Carmen Epicum' (1596).[93] Chapman's hopes of '*Riches* with honour, *Conquest* without bloud' that would 'let [Elizabeth's] soveraigne Empire be encreast' (ll. 15, 63) were as vain as Ralegh's 'Large, Rich and Bewtiful Empyre of Guiana' was chimerical. An Elizabethan Empire of conquest in South America to match the Spanish viceroyalties remained as implausible as the possibility of a British equivalent to the *Lusiads*.

There was, however, an English version of the *Araucana*. Ercilla's epic of the apparently interminable conflict between the Araucanian Indians of Chile and their Spanish overlords was perhaps the most original of all sixteenth-century epics, since the poet wrote as a participant in the events represented in his poem, and also because he managed to combine a celebration of Spanish heroism along with sympathy for the Indians' cause.[94] In one of the most remarkable English colonial documents of the sixteenth century, the Elizabethan commander in Ireland, Sir George Carew, produced a prose translation of the first sixteen cantos of the *Araucana*, probably during the period 1599–1603 when he was President of

[91] Edward Hayes's narrative of Gilbert's last expedition, in Quinn, ed., *Voyages and Colonising Enterprises*, II, p. 413.

[92] Stephen Parmenius, *De Navigatione . . . Carmen* επιβατικων (1582), reprinted, with English translation, in Quinn and Cheshire, *New Found Land of Stephen Parmenius*, pp. 82–105.

[93] George Chapman, 'De Guiana, Carmen Epicum' (1596), in Phyllis Brooks Bartlett, ed., *The Poems of George Chapman* (New York, 1941), pp. 353–57.

[94] Murrin, *History and Warfare*, p. 100; David Quint, *Epic and Empire: Politics and Generic Form from Virgil to Milton* (Princeton, 1993), pp. 157–85.

Munster and charged with quelling rebellion in the province.[95] The *Araucana* was presumably of less interest to Carew for its poetry (since he reduced to prose the stanzas he translated, and shortened them by almost half their length in the process) than for its portrayal of guerrilla warfare against an occupying European power fought in inhospitable terrain. Carew understood the *Araucana* not as a poetic fiction but as a historical record and 'purposelie omitt[ed]' anything 'nott pertinent to the Araucanan warr, wch is the subject of this Historie'. The relevance of the war to the Irish situation was clear: as Carew had the Araucanian leader, Caupolican, tell his native troops, '[the Spanish] fight best in fortified places and playne groundes, we in woodes mountaynes and bogges'.[96] Perhaps Carew hoped to learn as much about his enemy through Ercilla's sympathetic account of the Araucanians and their struggle; perhaps he wanted to learn about the Spanish, whose invasion of Kinsale he repelled in 1602, just as later that year he ordered a 'Spanish Chronicle' from a merchant in Lisbon;[97] perhaps he simply sought solace in the knowledge that he was not the only European military commander in a bellicose environment, facing an intractable conflict with a hostile native population. Like *The Faerie Queene*, Carew's truncated translation of an epic narrating a war with 'no natural closure'[98] was as apt an emblem of the increasing irrelevance of epic after the Military Revolution as it was of the limits that classical poetic forms imposed on the literary representation of British overseas activity.

The last great epic by an English humanist was Milton's *Paradise Lost*.[99] Like Camoens's *Lusiads*, it was originally planned as a ten-book epic and, again like the *Lusiads*, it was structured around a narrative of exploration and colonization.[100] Yet on these grounds, Samuel Johnson argued that *Paradise Lost* was, at the very least, an unconventional epic, if indeed it could be called an epic at all: 'The subject of an epick poem is naturally an event of great importance' such as 'the destruction of a city, the conduct of a colony, or the foundation of an empire', all of which

[95] 'The Historie of Araucana Written in Verse by Don Alonso de Ercilla Translated out of the Spanish into Englishe Prose Allmost to the Ende of the 16: Canto', trans. Sir George Carew, L[ambeth] P[alace] L[ibrary], MSS, 688, ff. 186^{r}–229^{v}, printed in Frank Pierce, ed., *The Historie of Araucana... Allmost to the Ende of the 16: Canto* (Manchester, 1964).

[96] LPL MSS, 688, ff. 221^{v}, 198^{r} (Pierce, ed., *The Historie of Araucana*, pp. 43, 14). For Carew's recommendations for a defensive war against both the Irish and the Spanish (11 Aug. 1602) see [Thomas Stafford, ed.,] *Pacata Hibernia: Ireland Appeased and Reduced* (London, 1633), pp. 348–50.

[97] Sir George Carew to Lord Brockhurst, 15 Oct. 1602, LPL MSS, 620, f. 116, printed in J. S. Brewer and William Bullen, eds., *Calendar of the Carew Manuscripts, Preserved in the Archiepiscopal Library at Lambeth*, 6 vols. (London, 1867–73), IV, p. 306.

[98] Murrin, *History and Warfare*, p. 105.

[99] On Milton's humanism see Donald Lemen Clark, *John Milton at St Paul's School* (New York, 1948), and Martin Dzelzainis, 'Milton's Classical Republicanism', in David Armitage and others, eds., *Milton and Republicanism* (Cambridge, 1995), pp. 3–24.

[100] On *Paradise Lost* and the *Lusiads* see esp. Louis Martz, *Poet of Exile* (New Haven, 1980), pp. 155–68, and Quint, *Epic and Empire*, pp. 253–57, 265.

Johnson found wanting in Milton's poem.[101] Milton had followed predecessors such as Michael Drayton and Samuel Daniel in developing the 'peaceful epic' that spurned 'Wars, hitherto the only argument | Heroic deemed, chief mastery to dissect | With long and tedious havoc fabled knights | In battles feigned'.[102] More precisely, he had abandoned an early intention to write an epic on King Arthur,[103] perhaps because the matter of Britain had during the previous century been so closely identified with an aggressively Anglocentric territorial empire in the Atlantic archipelago. However, Milton did produce an epic whose secondary narrative was of Satan's exploration and colonization of a 'new world', though his continuing commitment to the political programme of English humanism ensured that his would be a consciously anti-imperial epic.[104]

Milton had expressed his disquiet with the expansion of England under the Rump Parliament and with the increasingly monarchical cast of the Cromwellian Protectorate in classical republican language drawn from Sallust, Machiavelli, and his fellow republican Marchamont Nedham. He also conspicuously failed to herald the foreign policy achievements of either Rump or Protectorate in verse, unlike Andrew Marvell, Edmund Waller, and other contemporaries.[105] Throughout his epic, Milton expressed his distaste for the expansion of Pandemonium in classical republican terms, as Satan's minions rejected the option of 'preferring | Hard liberty before the easy yoke | Of servile pomp' (*PL*, ii. 255–57) in favour of a venture '[i]n search of this new world' (*PL*, ii. 403). The denizens of Pandaemonium became creeping serpents, while the first people of Eden (found at first like the 'American so girt | With feathered cincture, naked else and wild': *PL*, ix. 1116–17, were condemned to loss of innocence, expulsion from their native territory: 'The world . . . all before them, where to choose | Their place of rest, and providence their guide' (*PL*, xii. 646–47). The angel Michael recommended 'The paths of righteousness . . . | And full of peace' (*PL*, xi. 814–15) rather than the bloody enterprise of 'subduing nations' (*PL*, xi. 792), and this was consonant with the criticisms of Interregnum foreign policy and the republican warnings against the

[101] Samuel Johnson, *The Lives of the English Poets*, ed. George Birkbeck Hill, 3 vols. (Oxford, 1905), I, p. 171.

[102] Murrin, *History and Warfare*, pp. 17, 240–45; John Milton, *Paradise Lost* (1667), ed. Alastair Fowler (London, 1968), Book IX, ll. 28–31 (all further references are to this edition, tagged by book and line number).

[103] Milton, 'Mansus' (1639?), ll. 80–84, and 'Epitaphium Damonis' (1639), ll. 162–71, in Milton, *Complete Shorter Poems*, ed. John Carey (London, 1968), pp. 264–65, 275–76.

[104] The following account of *Paradise Lost* summarizes the argument of David Armitage, 'John Milton: Poet Against Empire', in Armitage and others, eds., *Milton and Republicanism*, pp. 206–25.

[105] On which see esp. Margarita Stocker and Timothy Raylor, 'A New Marvell Manuscript: Cromwellian Patronage and Politics', *English Literary Renaissance*, XX (1990), pp. 106–62, and the important correction in Elsie Duncan-Jones, 'Marvell, R. F. and the Authorship of "Blake's Victory"', in Peter Beal and Jeremy Griffiths, eds., *English Manuscript Studies*, V (London, 1995), pp. 107–26.

dangers of territorial expansion that Milton had expressed both overtly and covertly for some fifteen years. *Paradise Lost* marked the end of the humanist epic in Britain, and subverted the classical relationship between epic and empire, as Dr Johnson recognized. However, that *Paradise Lost* contained such an imperial narrative has only been recognized at two significant post-Imperial moments—in the Early American Republic in the late eighteenth century, and after the end of the European empires in the late twentieth.[106] Perhaps only after the end of Empire is it possible to see that literature's relationship to Empire has not always been complicit or supportive, when there has existed any connection at all.

Milton in due course became part of the accepted canon of 'English Literature', as Alexander Barclay, John Rastell, George Buchanan, and Stephen Parmenius did not, either because they were not English or were deemed insufficiently 'literary'. It has been influentially argued that the creation of that canon was an imperialist project, and 'in part that the discipline of English came into its own in an age of colonialism' when the study of English Literature was prescribed in India under the terms of the Charter Act of 1813.[107] On this reading, English Literature was forged as a tool of the civilizing process, as art was made the implement of Empire. Yet it is striking that almost all of the major colonial administrators, educationalists, and missionaries involved in deploying English Literature in early nineteenth-century India were not English at all but Scots.[108] This is only what one might expect, since it was in fact the Scots who had invented the canon of English Literature in the middle of the eighteenth century, some sixty years before literary study was ever prescribed in India.[109]

The interest of Enlightenment Scots in their own cultural improvement compelled the creation of the new university subject of Rhetoric and *Belles-Lettres* to help in rendering them acceptable linguistic partners for the English within a united Britain after the Anglo-Scottish union of 1707. The first course to make use of a canon of English Literature in this curricular context was taught by a young

[106] Keith W. F. Stavely, 'The World All Before Them: Milton and the Rising Glory of America', *Studies in Eighteenth-Century Culture*, XX (1990), pp. 47–64; J. Martin Evans, *Milton's Imperial Epic: Paradise Lost and the Discourse of Colonialism* (Ithaca, NY, 1996).

[107] Gauri Viswanathan, *Masks of Conquest: Literary Study and British Rule in India* (London, 1990), pp. 2, 23; cf. Said, *Culture and Imperialism*, pp. 48–49.

[108] For example, Charles Cameron; Alexander Duff (St Andrews); Gilbert Elliot, Earl of Minto (Edinburgh); Mountstuart Elphinstone; Charles Grant; Holt Mackenzie; John Malcolm (who attended lectures at Edinburgh University, 1794–95); James Mill (Edinburgh); and Thomas Munro (Glasgow)—in fact, almost every major figure treated in Viswanathan, *Masks of Conquest*, save for William McNaughten, an Irishman, and Thomas Babington Macaulay and Charles Trevelyan, the anomalous Englishmen in this company; John M. MacKenzie, 'Essay and Reflection: On Scotland and the Empire', *International History Review*, XV (1993), p. 733.

[109] Robert Crawford, *Devolving English Literature* (Oxford, 1992), chap. 1, 'The Scottish Invention of English Literature'; P. J. Marshall, 'Imperial Britain', *JICH*, XXIII (1995), p. 393.

lecturer at Edinburgh University in 1748–51, before he moved to take up the Chair of Logic at Glasgow University. That lecturer was Adam Smith,[110] and his initiative was soon followed in the ensuing decades at all of the major Scottish universities, and thereafter in the colleges of British America and finally, in the late nineteenth century, in England itself. In light of the continuity of the humanist curriculum and of the strain of scepticism about Empire it transmitted, it should be no surprise to learn that Rhetoric gave birth to the discipline of English Literature, nor that its progenitor would become the most sophisticated metropolitan critic of the first British Empire. English Literature only belatedly became an instrument of Empire. The anti-imperialism at the heart of the classical curriculum may have encouraged absent-mindedness about Empire, while the failure of vernacular writers to imagine an expanding overseas empire for Britain may have hampered its pursuit. At least in regard to the sixteenth and early seventeenth centuries, the greatest of all British anti-imperial poets was right: Empire followed Art and not vice versa, as some students of English Literature have supposed.

[110] Adam Smith, *Lectures on Rhetoric and Belles Lettres*, ed. J. C. Bryce (Oxford, 1983).

Select Bibliography

PERCY G. ADAMS, 'The Discovery of America and European Renaissance Literature', *Comparative Literature Studies*, XIII (1976), pp. 100–16.

DAVID ARMITAGE, *The Ideological Origins of the British Empire* (Cambridge, forthcoming).

ROBERT RAWLSTON CAWLEY, *Unpathed Waters: Studies in the Influence of the Voyagers on Elizabethan Literature* (Princeton, 1940).

WAYNE FRANKLIN, *Discoverers, Explorers, Settlers: The Diligent Writers of Early America* (Chicago, 1979).

J. E. GILLESPIE, *The Influence of Overseas Expansion on England to 1700* (New York, 1920).

ANTHONY GRAFTON, *New Worlds, Ancient Texts: The Power of Tradition and the Shock of Discovery* (Cambridge, Mass., 1992).

STEPHEN GREENBLATT, *Marvelous Possessions: The Wonder of the New World* (Oxford, 1991).

—— ed., *New World Encounters* (Berkeley, 1993).

RICHARD HELGERSON, *Forms of Nationhood: The Elizabethan Writing of England* (Chicago, 1992).

PETER HULME, *Colonial Encounters: Europe and the Native Caribbean, 1492–1797* (London, 1987).

JEFFREY KNAPP, *An Empire Nowhere: England, America, and Literature from Utopia to The Tempest* (Berkeley, 1992).

RICHARD KOEBNER, *Empire* (Cambridge, 1961).

WALTER MIGNOLO, *The Darker Side of the Renaissance: Literacy, Territoriality, and Colonization* (Ann Arbor, 1995).

MICHAEL MURRIN, *History and Warfare in the Renaissance Epic* (Chicago, 1994).
JOHN PARKER, *Books to Build an Empire: A Bibliographical History of English Overseas Interests to 1620* (Amsterdam, 1965).
DAVID B. QUINN, 'Renaissance Influences in English Colonization', *Transactions of the Royal Historical Society*, Fifth Series, XXVI (1976), pp. 73–93.
DAVID QUINT, *Epic and Empire: Politics and Generic Form from Virgil to Milton* (Princeton, 1993).
WILLIAM H. SHERMAN, *John Dee: The Politics of Reading and Writing in the English Renaissance* (Amherst, Mass., 1995).
FRANCES A. YATES, *Astraea: The Imperial Theme in the Sixteenth Century* (London, 1975).

6

'Civilizinge of those Rude Partes': Colonization within Britain and Ireland, 1580s–1640s

JANE H. OHLMEYER

Howard Lamar and Leonard Thompson, editors of a seminal collection of essays on the role the frontier played in shaping the histories of North America and South Africa, recognized the significance of many types of frontier—global, national, local, economic, cultural, religious, geographical, climatic, and linguistic; but they concerned themselves largely with political frontiers that they defined 'not as a boundary or line, but as a territory or zone of interpenetration between two previously distinct societies'.[1] According to their model, the frontier 'opens' in a given region when the first representatives of the intrusive society arrive and 'closes' when a single political authority emerges in the zone; during the intervening period relations between the natives and newcomers develop and crystallize as they vie for control over territory and political ascendancy.

The extent to which these theories can be applied to Ireland, the Scottish Highlands and Islands, and along the Anglo-Scottish Borders where, during the late sixteenth and early seventeenth centuries, central government tried to establish political hegemony, remains problematic for a number of reasons (see Map 6.1).[2]

I am grateful to the members of the Scottish History Seminar at the University of Aberdeen, especially Steve Boardman, David Ditchburn, Allan Macinnes, and Grant Simpson, for their comments on this chapter. I am also indebted to Nicholas Canny, Steven Ellis, Mícheál Ó Siouchru, and Geoffrey Parker for helpful suggestions for improvement.

[1] H. Lamar and L. Thompson, eds., *The Frontier in History: North America and South Africa Compared* (New Haven, 1981), p. 7.

[2] Wales has been excluded from this survey on the grounds that, by the Act of Union (1536) between England and Wales, the political—though not of course the religious, cultural, or linguistic—frontier had closed. As Robert Bartlett's *The Making of Europe: Conquest, Colonisation and Cultural Change, 950–1350* (London, 1993) demonstrates, medieval historians have been particularly sensitive to these 'frontier' theories. Jim Lydon, Robin Frame, and Katharine Simms have examined the role that the 'frontier' played in shaping medieval Irish society, culture, and politics, while Anthony Goodman and Geoffrey Barrow have done the same for the Anglo-Scottish borders. See their essays in Robert Bartlett and Angus MacKay, eds., *Medieval Frontier Societies* (Oxford, 1989). Also see T. Barry, R. Frame, and K. Simms, eds., *Colony and Frontier in Medieval Ireland: Essays presented to J. F. Lydon* (Dublin, 1995), and Anthony Goodman, 'The Anglo-Scottish Marches in the Fifteenth Century: A Frontier Society?', in Roger A. Mason, ed., *Scotland and England, 1286–1815* (Edinburgh, 1987), pp. 18–33. For early-modern

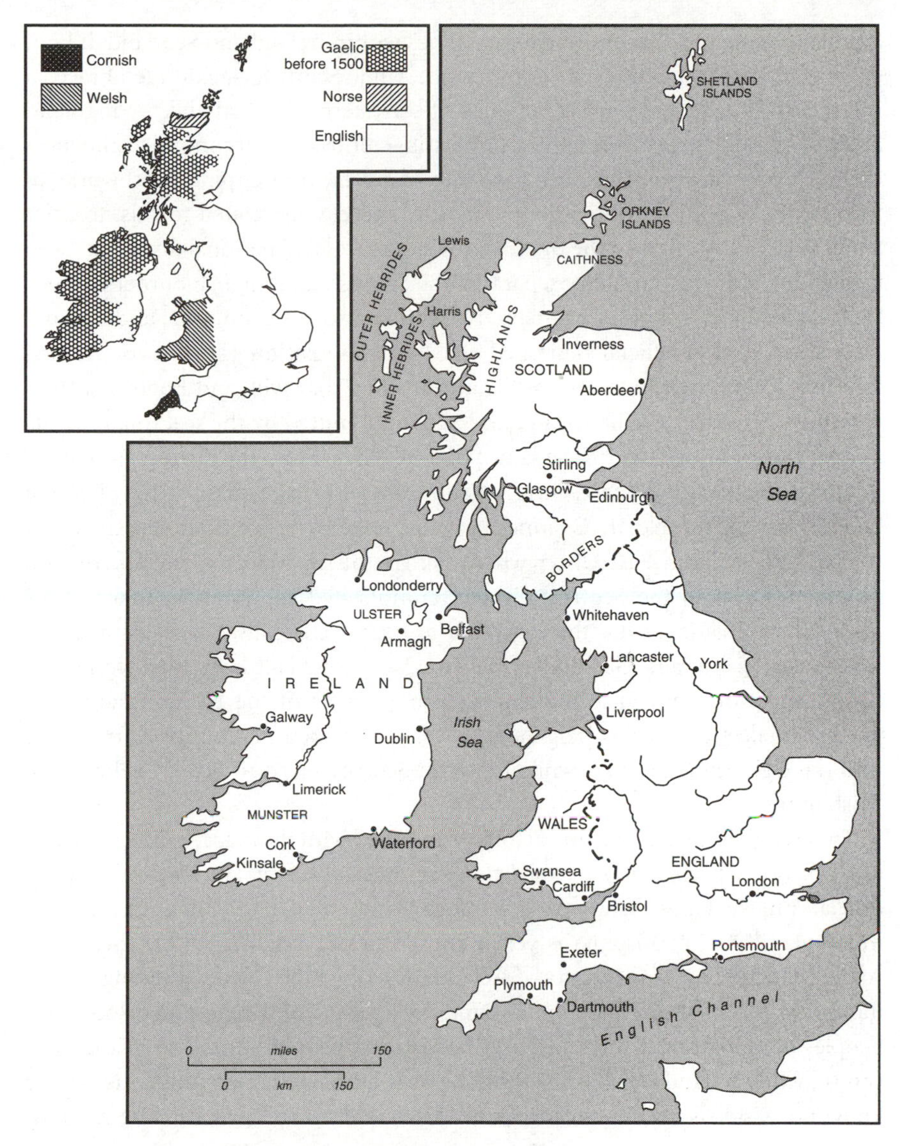

MAP 6.1. Britain and Ireland; [inset] Linguistic Divisions

First, the internal frontier constantly fluctuated as domestic and external forces interacted by pushing, especially in Ireland and Scotland, the political frontier

Ireland see David B. Quinn, 'Ireland and Sixteenth Century European Expansion', in T. D. Williams, ed., *Historical Studies*, I (London, 1958); W. J. Smyth, 'The Western Isle of Ireland and the Eastern Seaboard of America—England's First Frontiers', *Irish Geography*, XI (1978), pp. 1–23; and Steven G. Ellis, *Tudor Frontiers and Noble Power: The Making of the British State* (Oxford, 1995).

gradually westward.[3] Secondly, frontier zones within Ireland and Scotland did not constitute homogeneous units. For instance, while Scottish Gaeldom embraced a number of distinct geographic regions—the Western seaboard and the highland areas of the north-east—religious, linguistic, cultural, and economic influences criss-crossed with political ones to create complex, overlapping patchworks of frontier zones within frontier zones. Finally, and closely related to this, frontier zones within the realms of the British Crown transcended national divisions. Even though the political boundary separated the Scottish and English border regions, these communities formed a remarkably uniform social, economic, and cultural unit. One English official described the local population (known as 'reivers', 'borderers', and 'steel bonnets') as 'Scottishe when they will, and English at their pleasure'.[4] Similarly, Gaelic Ireland and Scotland, united by the sea, to all intents and purposes formed part of the same political ethos. From the thirteenth century the passage of Scottish mercenaries ('gallowglass' or 'redshanks', as they became known) across the North Channel spawned extensive informal settlement in Ireland, especially in East Ulster where the rise of the MacDonnells of Antrim, nominally loyal to the Scottish Crown, complicated the political make-up of Elizabethan Ireland, as did the eagerness of their arch-rivals, Clan Campbell, to interfere in Irish affairs. Gaeldom also formed a distinct cultural entity, with bards composing works aimed at audiences on both sides of the North Channel. A peculiar dialect, known as 'Highland Irish', was spoken in County Antrim well into the eighteenth century; while Lowland Scots referred to Scots Gaelic as the 'Irish tongue'.

These close human and cultural links, combined with the inaccessibility of these outlying areas, particularly alarmed contemporary observers. In 1609 one English official confessed that Ulster was 'heretofore as unknown to the English here as the most inland part of Virginia is yet unknown to our English colony there'.[5] Sir Arthur Chichester, Lord Deputy of Ireland, described the Gaelic-speaking inhabitants of the Scottish Highlands and Islands as 'a proud, obstinate, and disobedient people', 'a barbarous, irreligious, and headstrong people, inured to crimes and spoils'; while Ireland was, in his opinion, 'that barbarous land where the people know not God, nor care not for man'.[6] He could easily have said the same of

[3] The significance of the internal frontier is explored in Michael Hechter, *Internal Colonialism: The Celtic Fringe in British National Development, 1536–1966* (London, 1975).

[4] Quoted in G. M. Fraser, *The Steel Bonnets: The Story of the Anglo-Scottish Border Reivers* (London, 1989), p. 65. Also see Thomas I. Rae, *The Administration of the Scottish Frontier, 1513–1603* (Edinburgh, 1966), p. 225.

[5] Historical Manuscripts Commission, *Calendar of the Manuscripts of the Most Honourable the Marquess of Salisbury . . .*, Vol. XXI, *1609–1612* (London, 1970), p. 121.

[6] Cited in Maurice Lee, *Great Britain's Solomon: James VI and I in his Three Kingdoms* (Urbana, Ill., 1990), pp. 203–04.

the peoples of the Northern Isles of Shetland and Orkney, the Isle of Man, and the Anglo-Scottish Borders; for central government—whether in Dublin, Edinburgh, or London—regarded the economic, political, and cultural distinctiveness of these regions as 'uncivilized' and potentially corrosive to the English- and Scots-speaking world. Their inhabitants were classified as barbarians, rebels, and subversives intent on destabilizing the peripheries of the British monarchies.

Prior to the union of the Crowns in 1603, Elizabeth I of England and James VI of Scotland tried to manipulate the instability of these outlying regions, especially Ulster and the Borders, to their own ends. However, with James VI's accession to the English throne, the need to drive a wedge within Gaeldom, to pacify, to 'civilize', and to 'close' the internal frontiers in Ireland, the Highlands and Islands, and, above all, along the Borders, became a top priority for the Stuarts. But what was the nature of these frontier societies during the late sixteenth and early seventeenth centuries? What did they have in common and what features distinguished them from the English-speaking intruders? What relationship did they enjoy with the metropolitan administrations in Edinburgh, London, and Dublin? Did the agents of the Crown share a common expansionist agenda and mentality? What strategies did they adopt in an attempt to tame these allegedly dark corners of the three kingdoms, and with what success did they integrate them into a greater Imperial polity?

Fighting and Feasting

Though the physical environment, language, dress, political structures, and inheritance and tenurial practices varied considerably throughout the Borders and Gaeldom, these regions shared, however superficially, many features.[7] Like all frontier societies throughout pre-modern Europe, they remained sparsely populated, with widely dispersed settlements, few towns, and difficult internal communications. Pastoralism, especially cattle farming, formed the mainstay of the local economy, with the herds being moved to high pastures during the summer months (a practice known as transhumance or, in Ireland, 'booleying'). While, from the perspective of Lowland England and Scotland, this consumption-oriented, redistributive economy remained relatively unsophisticated, with trade limited to the exchange of raw material, it played a critical role in sustaining the social and political infrastructure of Gaeldom and the Borders.[8]

[7] For instance, varied patterns of landholding ensured that while partible inheritance was common in Gaelic Ireland, Orkney, Shetland, and in some Border counties, primogeniture predominated in the Western Isles. For a helpful discussion of the dangers inherent in such a comparative approach see Lamar and Thompson, eds., *The Frontier in History*, p. 5, and A. Hennessy, *The Frontier in Latin American History* (London, 1978), pp. 138–39.

[8] For an interesting discussion of transhumance and the life-styles it could support see Fernand Braudel, *The Mediterranean and the Mediterranean World of Philip II*, 2 vols. (London, 1972), I, pp. 85–94.

In the Highlands and Islands an overlapping nexus of greater and lesser clans, cemented by feudal and tenurial ties and by bonds of kinship, friendship, and manrent, determined the social order. The Anglo-Scottish Borders enjoyed a complex social structure which combined Lowland concepts of feudal land tenure with a system of kinship similar to the clans and known as 'surnames' or 'clans'. Likewise, a fragmentary patchwork of patriarchal septs (clans) ruled Ireland. A small number of powerful native Irish and Old English overlords not only controlled their own territories but also collected tribute (in the form of military service, food, lodgings, and agricultural labour) and demanded submission from neighbouring lordships. They, like their Scottish and Border counterparts, all shared a common desire to extract 'black rent' (or 'black mail') from previously independent territories and thereby extend their political control and enhance their standing within their own lordship.

Since military might determined effective lordship, maintaining and sustaining an effective army became the priority for any Irish, Highland, or Border lord. It also articulated the social order, for a lord's followers were not only obliged to feed and house soldiers but to offer military service themselves in return for a lord's protection.[9] This enabled individual lords to field substantial private forces. For instance, the rebellious Earl of Tyrone and his Ulster allies allegedly mustered 2,000 'buannachts' (or native mercenary soldiers) in 1594, and 4,000 to 6,000 ordinary swordsmen regularly enlisted for service during the later stages of the Nine Years War (1594–1603).[10] Scottish mercenaries supplemented these native soldiers, and between the 1560s and 1590s some 25,000 mercenaries found employment in militarized Ulster. This exodus of troops to Ulster dramatically impacted upon the social structure of the Western Isles, which became more 'geared to war than elsewhere in Scottish Gaeldom', with 6,000 fighting men, or 'buannachan', allegedly ready for war in the 1590s.[11] When not employed in Ireland, they formed a 'distinct parasitic class' which fed upon local clansmen (known as 'sorning') in much the same way that Irish swordsmen did. As in Gaeldom, local Border lords raised private armies and levied 'black mail' from neighbouring clans on both sides of the national frontier. At their height during the mid-sixteenth century, the Armstrongs of the West Marches could assemble raiding parties of 3,000 men well-

[9] In Ireland this elaborate system of extortion, intimidation, and protection, which sustained these private armies and underpinned society, was known to the Old English as 'coign and livery'.

[10] For further details see Ciaran Brady, 'The Captains' Games: Army and Society in Elizabethan Ireland', in Thomas Bartlett and Keith Jeffery, eds., *A Military History of Ireland* (Cambridge, 1996), pp. 144–47.

[11] Allan I. Macinnes, 'Crown, Clan and Fine: The "Civilising" of Scottish Gaeldom, 1587–1638', in *Northern Scotland*, XIII (1993), p. 33. Also see Allan I. Macinnes, *Clanship, Commerce and the House of Stuart, 1603–1788* (Edinburgh, 1996).

versed in guerrilla warfare; while in 1592 the Grahams of Cumbria allegedly rallied a force of 500.[12]

As the scattered remains of fortified stone farmhouses ('bastles') and defensive, narrow, multi-storey 'peel' towers along the Borders, or of tower houses and castles in Ireland and the Western Isles highlight, these military systems spawned violence. During the minority of James VI (1578–85) endemic lawlessness, feuds, and inter-baronial wars periodically disrupted Scottish politics, as did six aristocratic coups.[13] Feuding proved 'the great cancer of the Borders', and one English official noted with horror how reivers 'will subject themselves to no justice but in an inhumane and barbarous manner fight and kill one another'.[14] In 1597 on the West March the damage allegedly done by the Scots in England during the previous ten years was assessed at £12,000 and that by the English in Scotland at £13,000. In the winter of 1589–90 the reivers from Liddesdall alone averaged one raid a week and stole over 850 beasts and took sixty prisoners. During a ten-day rampage in the West March in 1602–03 (known as 'ill week'), these thugs killed ten men, took fourteen more for ransom, inflicted £6,750-worth of damage on local villages, and captured 5,000 cattle, sheep, and horses.

Since livestock, especially cows, served as the most important form of wealth in all of these areas (and in Ireland were used to pay mercenary troops), cattle raiding, especially in the long winter evenings, formed an integral part of the local, redistributive economy.[15] In Ireland, a successful cattle-raid also resulted in the submission of a territory which enhanced the military and political standing of a given lord and brought him increased riches in the form of tribute. As a result, 'the chief inclination of these people', as one Spanish traveller noted in 1588–89, 'is to be robbers, and to plunder each other; so that no day passes without a call to arms among them'.[16]

If 'fighting' served as one main pillar on which these societies rested, 'feasting' was another. Attention has been drawn to the importance of food and drink—

[12] R. T. Spence, 'The Pacification of the Cumberland Borders, 1593–1628', *Northern History*, XIII (1977), p. 61.

[13] However, as Keith Brown has shown, contemporary observations about feuds and criminal violence have often been overstated. For instance, bonds of manrent served as a double-edged sword: on the one hand, they fuelled lawlessness and feuds; on the other, they acted as a form of social control by seeking to harness violence and create a milieu of peace. For further details see K. M. Brown, *Bloodfeud in Scotland, 1573–1625: Violence, Justice and Politics in Early Modern Scotland* (Edinburgh, 1986).

[14] Quoted in Fraser, *Steel Bonnets*, p. 170.

[15] Raiding, especially for cattle, characterized non-European frontier societies. For instance, the population of Southern Africa in the early-modern period were mixed farmers, living in dispersed settlements, which were organized into warring chiefdoms where young men often indulged in cattle-raiding.

[16] C. Maxwell, ed., *Irish History from Contemporary Sources (1509–1610)* (London, 1923), p. 319.

grain, livestock, and whisky—in sustaining the Scottish clan system.[17] A chief collected grain into central storehouses to help ensure against crop failures and to increase mutual interdependence. Easy access to food also enabled him to maintain a body of fighting men and a large household of servants and to demonstrate his benevolence by hosting feasts. In other words, food—and the services which it could buy—served as 'part of the means whereby chiefs turned land into status'.[18] Similarly in Ireland, the importance of guesting (demanding hospitality from followers in a practice known as 'coshering') and feasting as a public display of a lord's power over his followers cannot be overstated. The description of a mighty banquet given by Brian O'Rourke, a County Leitrim chieftain, which was later translated from Irish and popularized by Jonathan Swift, captured the extravagance of the occasion: after devouring 140 cows and drinking 100 pails of whiskey, the guests danced, brawled, and then collapsed in a stupor on the floor. Though 'coshering' and providing victuals for these lavish feasts posed enormous burdens on followers, especially during times of dearth, these traditions enhanced a lord's standing and status within his domain in much the same way as did the maintaining of a large household of swordsmen, brehons (native Irish arbiters of Brehon law), hereditary physicians, harpists, bards, minstrels, ballad singers, and story-tellers ('seanchaidhean' in Scotland, 'seanchaidhthe' in Ireland). Though they hardly featured in the Northern Isles, these professional classes played an important role in the society and culture of Gaeldom and, to a lesser extent, along the Borders; and in return for rent-free farms and other privileges, they entertained and glorified local lords and their followers. As symbols of this 'feasting and fighting' culture, the removal of these 'tympanours, poets, story-tellers, babblers, rymours, harpers or any other Irish minstrels' became a priority for central government as it set out to civilize 'those rude parts'.[19]

'Civilizinge of those rude partes'

The fact that the political and social organization, the culture, and the economic practices of these frontier societies did not coincide with the norms of Lowland

[17] R. A. Dodgshon, '"Pretense of Blude" and "Place of Thair Duelling": The Nature of Scottish Clans, 1500–1745', in R. A. Houston and I. D. Whyte, eds., *Scottish Society, 1500–1800* (Cambridge, 1989), pp. 169–98. Like these lords, the Indian chieftain Powhatan, who held sway over 12,000 Indians (from thirty distinctive tribes), collected tribute (80% of the crops produced by his people), which acted as an insurance policy in times of dearth and as a means of demonstrating his power and influence at public functions. Rather than being evidence of his despotic tendencies, as the English maintained, this served as an important mechanism in storing and redistributing resources among Powhatan's people.

[18] R. A. Dodgshon, 'Pretense of Blude', p. 189.

[19] Edmund Curtis and R. B. McDowell, eds., *Irish Historical Documents, 1172–1922* (London, 1943), p. 55. Also see clause 8 of the Statutes of Iona, in Gordon Donaldson, ed., *Scottish Historical Documents* (Edinburgh, 1974), p. 175.

society left them open to scorn and led to comparisons with the Ancient Britons (whom the Romans had 'civilized') or with the Amerindians of the New World. Giraldus Cambrensis consistently referred to the Irish as 'a barbarous people', 'a rude people' with 'primitive habits' 'living themselves like beasts'.[20] In his description 'of the character, customs, and habits of this people' published in *The Topography of Ireland* (1188–89), he argued that Ireland's geographical isolation from the 'civilized nations' ensured that 'they learn nothing, and practice nothing but the barbarism in which they are born and bred, and which sticks to them like a second nature'.[21] Later observers appropriated this twelfth-century rhetoric. Fynes Moryson, secretary to Lord Mountjoy, travelled extensively throughout Europe, North Africa, the Middle East, and Turkey but saved his greatest scorn for the 'meere Irish', whom he regarded as filthy, rude, barbaric wild beasts and their women as drunken sluts. 'The Anatomy of Ireland' (1615) described the Irish as 'more barbarous and more brutish in ther costomes and demeanures then in any other parte of the world that is knowne'.[22] In *A Discovery of the True Causes why Ireland was never entirely subdued* (1612), the legal imperialist, Sir John Davies, portrayed the Irish as barbarians, murderers, and villains who behaved 'little better than Canniballes, who doe hunt one another, and hee that hath most strength and swiftnes doth eate and devoures all his fellowes'.[23] Like their Irish counterparts, the Highlanders and Islanders attracted similar derision. The late fourteenth-century Lowland chronicler, John of Fordun, depicted them as 'a savage and untamed nation, rude and independent...hostile to the English people and language...and exceedingly cruel'.[24] While he admitted that if well governed the inhabitants of the Borders could be loyal subjects, James VI nevertheless dubbed them 'godles, lawles, and disordered'.[25]

Contemporaries from the King down clearly regarded the Gaelic Irish and, to a lesser extent, the Highlanders and Borderers, both mentally and culturally as a lower form of humanity. They were savages and barbarians who had failed to progress, to farm for their food, or to inhabit an ordered polity regulated by the law and Christian morality.[26] Convictions of racial superiority critically shaped attitudes about how best these remote regions could be 'civilized'—how these unruly subjects could be reformed, their over-mighty lords tamed, thuggery and feuding replaced with law and order, and labour channelled into production

[20] Andrew Hadfield and John McVeagh, eds., *Strangers to that Land: British Perceptions of Ireland from the Reformation to the Famine* (Gerrards Cross, Buckinghamshire, 1994), p. 27.

[21] Ibid., p. 28. [22] Ibid., p. 47. [23] Ibid., p. 47.

[24] William F. Skene, ed., *John of Fordun's Chronicle of the Scottish Nation...*, 2 vols. (1872; Edinburgh, 1993), I, p. 38.

[25] *R[egister] [of the] P[rivy] C[ouncil of] S[cotland]*, First Series, VII, p. 706.

[26] Anthony Pagden, *The Fall of Natural Man: The American Indian and the Origins of Comparative Ethnology* (Cambridge, 1982), p. 26.

rather than destruction. Crown strategies ranged from annihilation to assimilation.[27] The militarized nature of frontier regions often forced the sovereign to resort to force; for as one Virginian settler quipped in the wake of the 1622 Indian massacre, which left a quarter of the Virginian settlement dead, 'Civility is not the way to win savages... Children are pleased with toys and awed with rods.'[28]

During the later decades of the sixteenth century a number of costly English campaigns not only completed the military conquest of Ireland and resulted in the exodus of thousands of ferine Irish swordsmen to the continental theatre of war, but also facilitated the colonization of Munster and Ulster. In Scotland James defeated the Earls of Huntly, Errol, and Angus in a series of royal campaigns in the north-east (1589–95) and launched five 'fire and sword' expeditions along the western seaboard between 1596 and 1608, expropriating where possible lands belonging to the insubordinate MacGregors, MacLeods, MacIains, and MacDonnells. While the English government contemplated colonizing the Borders and sending the 'notorious ill-livers and misbehaved persons to Virginia or to some other remote parts', after 1603 James VI and I adopted Draconian policies.[29] In an attempt to instil 'perfyte obedience and civilitie' along the Borders and to transform them into his 'Middle Shires', he executed thirty-two leading malcontents and empowered a Border Commission to subdue the region.[30] In addition, he singled out for particular persecution the troublesome Grahams of Eskdale; fifty were transplanted from Cumbria to Sir Ralph Sidney's estates in County Roscommon; while a further 2,000 unfortunates were despatched to fight in the Netherlands.[31]

Ultimately, inadequate financial and human resources ensured that central government generally favoured reforming initiatives which promoted the maintenance of law and order by attacking the military systems which underpinned lordship and clanship. However, the need both to tame over-mighty lords and to win the tacit co-operation of key members of the local élite was also central to any reform programme. Thus, along the English Border Marches Elizabeth I pursued conciliatory policies such as trying to win over local families with grants of land or pressuring leading lords to accept the authority of the Warden and to take

[27] For European comparisons see Mark Greengrass, ed., *Conquest and Coalescence: The Shaping of the State in Early Modern Europe* (London, 1991).

[28] Quoted in Sheehan, *Savagism and Civility*, p. 170.

[29] Quoted in S. J. Watts with Susan J. Watts, *From Border to Middle Shire: Northumberland, 1586–1625* (Leicester, 1975), p. 198.

[30] *RPCS*, First Series, VII, p. 702.

[31] Though the Roscommon colony proved a miserable failure as the luckless Grahams either returned home or dispersed throughout Ireland, other reivers prospered in Ireland. Some, such as Sir John Hume (of Fermanagh), came as undertakers; while the 'pull' of cheap land attracted many, especially from the Scottish West and Middle Marches, who quickly became the 'hard men' of frontier society.

responsibility for the actions of their followers. Like his predecessors, James VI skilfully twisted traditional Scottish baronial rivalries to his own advantage. In Orkney, after Earl Patrick's followers rebelled he allowed his arch-enemy, the equally vicious Earl of Caithness, to reduce the island and execute the leading insurgents. In the north-east he favoured the Gordons; while in the Western Isles royal power rested with the MacKenzies of Kintail (who replaced the troublesome MacLeods) and with the Campbells, Earls of Argyll, who, in the wake of the collapse of the lordship of the Isles after 1493, acquired vast estates stretching from Kintyre through the central Highlands to Cawdor in the north-east and acted as an effective (albeit self-interested) bulwark against the rebellious Clan Donald South.[32]

James VI also sought to make local lords directly responsible for the action of their kin, and in 1587 extended the 'General Band' (first applied to the Debatable Lands of the Borders in the 1520s) to the Highlands, requiring chiefs to find sureties for the peaceful conduct of their followers. The Statutes of Iona (1609), brokered by Andrew Knox, Bishop of the Isles, aimed to make the Highland chieftains agents of 'civilization' by requiring them to obey the King and to observe the laws and acts of the Scottish Parliament. More importantly, the Statutes, 'imbued with the cultural values of the Lowlands . . . commenced a sustained legislative offensive to modify, if not terminate, the disruptive aspects of clanship'.[33] Clauses such as those restricting the access to alcohol and its consumption, or controlling the size of a lord's household, aimed to undermine the culture of 'feasting'. Others sought to demilitarize the clans by ridding them of the 'buannachan' or 'idill men' and outlawing the exaction of 'conyie' (in Ireland known as 'coign'); while those 'found soirning, craveing meit, drink, or ony uther geir fra the tennentis and inhabitantis thairof' would be treated as thieves and face execution.[34]

Similarly in Ireland the government set out to weaken the military power-bases and to 'Anglicize' Irish lords. During the later sixteenth century a revitalization of central and provincial government occurred which facilitated the piecemeal reintroduction of English law—the critical prerequisite to the 'civilization' of Ireland.[35] For as Sir William Gerard, a lawyer and briefly Lord Chancellor, argued, 'sharpe lawes muste woorke the reform'; in a report of 1576 he asked, 'can the sword teache theim to speake Englishe, to use Englishe apparell, to restrayne theim from Irish axactions and extotions, and to shonne all the manners and orders of the

[32] E. J. Cowan, 'Fishers in Drumlie Waters: Clanship and Campbell Expansion', *Transactions of the Gaelic Society of Inverness*, LIV (1984–86), pp. 269–312.

[33] Macinnes, 'Crown, Clan and Fine', p. 38.

[34] Donaldson, ed., *Historical Documents*, p. 173.

[35] For further details see Ciaran Brady, *The Chief Governors: The Rise and Fall of Reform Government in Tudor Ireland, 1536–1588* (Cambridge, 1994), p. xi.

Irishe. Noe it is the rodd of justice that must scower out those blottes.'[36] Accordingly, legislation mandated that all lawsuits be settled by English common law and proscribed the collection of tribute, cattle-raiding, and the maintenance of armed retainers.

Since the frontiers within Britain and Ireland had first opened in the Middle Ages the English language had served, and was perceived, as an important instrument of empire.[37] The administration in Edinburgh held that 'the Irishe [Gaelic] language ... is one of the chief and principall causis of the continewance of barbaritie and incivilitie amongis the inhabitantis of the Ilis and Heylandis'.[38] Thus, the Statutes of Iona called for all gentlemen to educate their eldest son in 'the scuillis on the Lawland' so that they 'may be found able sufficientlie to speak, reid and wryte Inglishe'; while further legislation (1611) made attempts to abolish Gaelic.[39] In Ireland an Act of 1537 aimed to introduce 'a conformitie, concordance, and familiarity in language, tongue, in manners, order and apparel', and to cast aside 'the diversitie that is betwixt them [the English and Irish] in tongue, language, order and habite'.[40] To this end, many advocated the establishment of parochial and grammar schools, thereby ensuring, as Davies put it, 'that the next generation will in tongue and heart, and every way else, become English; so that there will be no difference or distinction, but the Irish sea betwixt us'.[41]

Closely linked to this drive to expose the young to the English language and culture was the desire to wean them from the subversiveness of popery, and by the mid-sixteenth century Protestantism had become a further key index of 'civilization'. Eager to tout their 'civility' and to promote the Reformed church, the Earls of Argyll used, with remarkable success, bardic poets to transmit the Protestant message to their largely illiterate, Gaelic-speaking followers.[42] In Ireland inadequate financial and human resources and the vibrancy of the Counter-Reformation, combined with the reluctance of the Catholic élite to conform (despite being deprived of government office for failing to do so), hampered the spread of

[36] Hadfield and McVeagh, eds., *Strangers to that Land*, p. 40.

[37] Quoted in P. Hulme, *Colonial Encounters: Europe and the Native Caribbean, 1492–1797* (London, 1986), p. 1.

[38] Donaldson, ed., *Historical Documents*, p. 178.

[39] Ibid., p. 174.

[40] *The Statutes at Large Passed in the Parliaments held in Ireland* ..., 8 vols. (Dublin), I, p. 120.

[41] John Davies, *A Discovery of the True Causes why Ireland was Never Entirely Subdued* (1612; London, 1968), p. 272.

[42] Jane Dawson, 'Calvinism and the Gaidhealtachd in Scotland', in A. Duke and others, eds., *Calvinism in Europe* (Cambridge, 1994), pp. 231–53. Also see Jane Dawson, 'Anglo-Scottish Protestant Culture and Integration in Sixteenth-Century Britain', in Steven G. Ellis and S. Barber, eds., *Conquest and Union: Fashioning a British State, 1485–1725* (London, 1995), pp. 87–114, and James Kirk, 'The Jacobean Church in the Highlands, 1567–1625', in M. MacLean, ed., *The Seventeenth Century in the Highlands* (Inverness, 1986), pp. 24–50.

Protestantism.[43] Yet on both sides of the North Channel, Protestant clergymen increasingly spearheaded Imperial initiatives. Wentworth's unpopular patriarch, John Bramhall, Bishop of Derry, behaved as an 'episcopal ogre' as he enforced canonical norms and recovered ecclesiastical patrimony in a bid to 'Anglicize' the Church of Ireland.[44] Similarly in Scotland, Bishop Law underpinned regal impulses in Orkney; while Andrew Knox, Bishop of the Isles, played a central role in tackling problems in the Highlands and Islands—little wonder that James sent him the following year, as Bishop of Raphoe, to tame the 'wild Irish' of Donegal.

Depending on local circumstances, the government supplemented these reforming, assimilationist policies with more-coercive measures: namely, expropriation and plantation. In his *Basilikon Doron*, James VI expressed the hope that the Isles would be tamed by planting 'colonies among them of answerable inland subjects, that within short time may reform and civilize the best inclined among them: rooting out or transporting the barbarous and stubborn sort, and planting civility in their rooms'.[45] Ultimately his plans came to nothing, and local hostility to the venture frustrated three attempts (1595–1602, 1605, and 1609) to settle the forfeited Isles of Lewis and Harris with adventurers from Fife. (Map 6.2) In stark contrast, the informal colonization of Orkney and Shetland by planters from Fife resulted in the successful—albeit unregulated—extension of Lowland practices to the Northern Isles (Map 6.1).

In Ireland demands for colonial enterprise and expropriation of native lands dated from the later Middle Ages. However, only after the Desmond rebellion of the 1570s did wholesale plantation win widespread acceptance. Further rebellions, especially the Nine Years War and the Confederate Wars (1641–52), focused attention on the treachery of the Irish in much the same way that wide-scale revolt (1568–70) among the Morisco population of Granada prompted the Habsburg government to transplant the bulk of this unassimilated racial minority to Castile and introduce in their place 50,000 'civilized' settlers from Galicia, Asturias, and León. (Interestingly, Sir John Davies later drew on the transplantation of the

[43] For further details see Nicholas Canny, 'Irish, Scottish and Welsh Responses to Centralisation, *c.*1530–*c.*1640: A Comparative Perspective', in A. Grant and K. J. Stringer, eds., *Uniting the Kingdom? The Making of British History* (London, 1995), pp. 148–57. In an attempt to demonstrate their loyalty and 'civility', members of the Irish Catholic élite, such as the Earls of Antrim, promoted the Protestant religion and rebuilt or refurbished churches (as at Clough or Dunluce in County Antrim) for their Protestant tenants.

[44] John McCafferty, 'John Bramhall and the Church of Ireland in the 1630s', in A. Ford, J. McGuire, and K. Milne, eds., *As by Law Established: The Church of Ireland since the Reformation* (Dublin, 1995), p. 104.

[45] W. C. Dickinson and G. Donaldson, eds., *A Source Book of Scottish History*, 3 vols. (Edinburgh, 1961), III, p. 261.

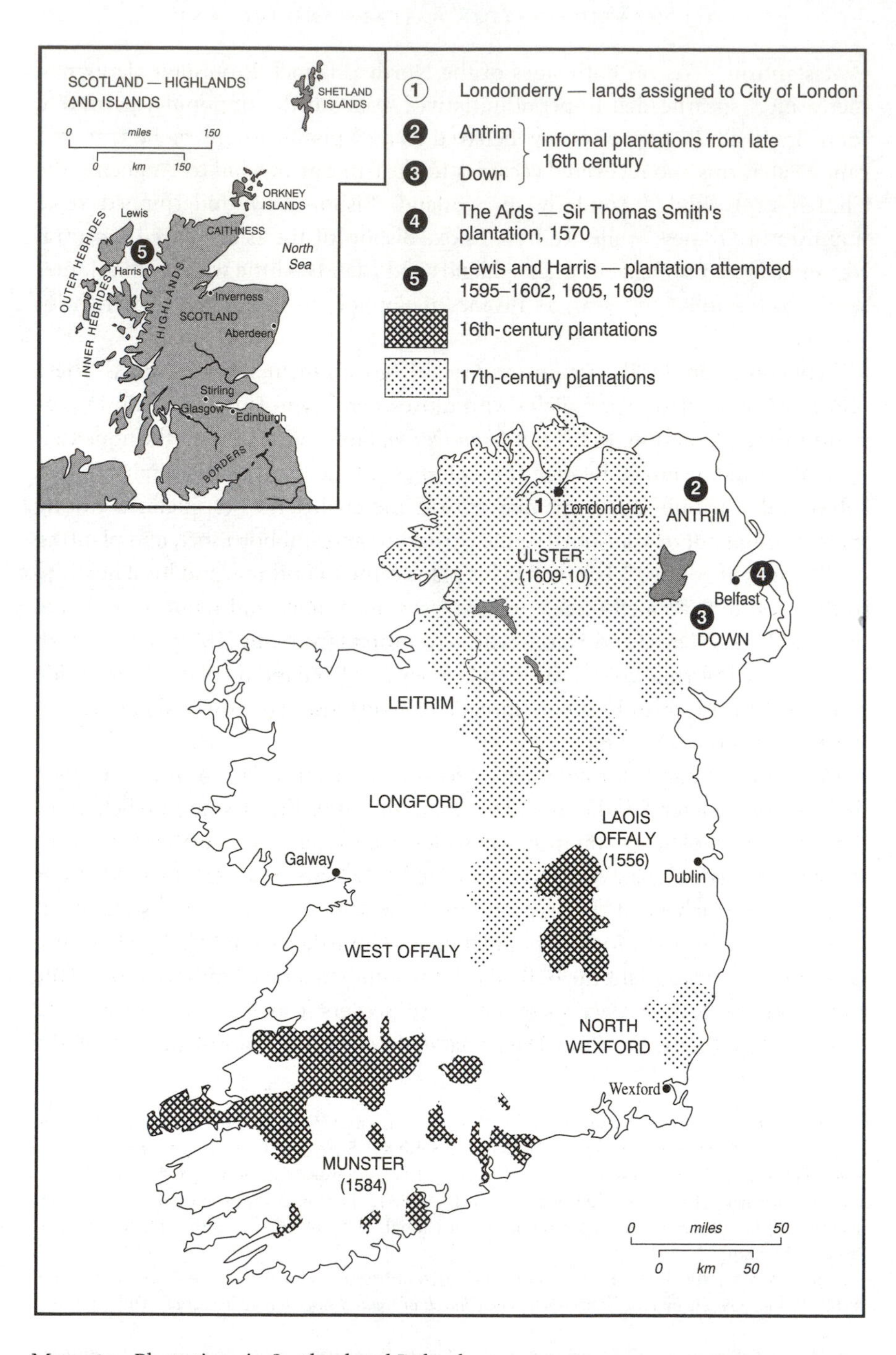

Map 6.2. Plantations in Scotland and Ireland

Moors and of the Grahams from the Borders in his justification of the Ulster plantation.[46]) Spenser, in *A View of the Present State of Ireland* (1596), called for the destruction of the existing Gaelic order and the systematic colonization of Ireland with English settlers who were to be made responsible for the erection of the political, economic, and social framework that was considered the necessary support of a civil life and the Protestant faith. The greatest seventeenth-century exponent of 'civilization' through conformity with the Church of England and, above all, plantation was Lord Deputy Thomas Wentworth, later Earl of Strafford. He believed that the settlement of English colonists remained the best means of enriching the English government and for 'civilizing . . . this people, or securing this kingdom under the dominion of your imperial Crown'. He continued that 'plantations must be the only means under God and your majesty to reform this subject as well in religion as manners'.[47]

Early attempts at plantation in Ireland failed on the lands belonging to the O'Connors, O'Mores, and O'Dempseys in Laois and Offaly or at Newry (see Map 6.2). Similarly in Ulster, efforts in 1571–72 by Sir Thomas Smith (in the Ards) and the Earl of Essex (in Clandeboye) to establish private military settlements, which would provide bulwarks against the destabilizing influences exerted by the MacDonnells, ended in disaster.[48] However, after the outbreak of the Munster rebellion, plantation became an instrument of royal policy and private enterprise was put to work for the purposes of state. In 1585, shortly after the first abortive English attempt to colonize the New World, the government announced an ambitious scheme which aimed to re-create the world of south-east England on the confiscated Munster estates of the Earl of Desmond. Grants of land, ranging from 4,000 to 12,000 acres, were awarded to thirty-five English landlords (and some 20,000 settlers), who vowed to introduce English colonists and to practise English-style agriculture based on grain-growing. By the end of the sixteenth century roughly 12,000 settlers were actively engaged in farming, and on the eve of the Irish rebellion, as one recent historian of the plantation has noted, 'The English visitor to Munster in 1640 would . . . have been faced with many familiar objects. As he moved about the province, using the passable roads, he would notice the number of enclosures, stone buildings and the occasional large house, surrounded by gardens and orchards.' Many inhabitants now wore shoes (rather than brogues),

[46] Sir John Davies, *Historical Tracts*, ed. George Chalmers (Dublin, 1787), p. 283.

[47] W. Knowler, ed., *The Earl of Strafforde's Letters and Despatches with an Essay towards his Life by Sir George Radcliffe . . .*, 2 vols. (London, 1739), I, p. 450. Also see Nicholas Canny, 'The Attempted Anglicisation of Ireland in the Seventeenth Century', in J. F. Merritt, ed., *The Political World of Thomas Wentworth, Earl of Strafford, 1621–1641* (Cambridge, 1996), pp. 157–86.

[48] Hiram Morgan, 'The Colonial Venture of Sir Thomas Smith in Ulster, 1571–5', *Historical Journal*, XXVIII (1987), pp. 261–78, and R. Dunlop, 'The Plantation of Leix and Offaly, 1556–1622', *English Historical Review*, VI (1891), pp. 61–96.

English caps, stockings, breeches, and jerkins, while an ever-increasing number of people spoke English.[49]

In the wake of English victory at the end of the Nine Years War, Ulster met a similar fate. The unexpected flight of leading Irish lords to the continent (1607) and the revolt of Sir Cahir O'Dogherty (1608) enabled the state to confiscate vast tracts of Ulster (encompassing present-day Counties Armagh, Tyrone, Fermanagh, Londonderry, Cavan, and Donegal). Influenced by the Munster experience and by his attempts to plant Harris and Lewis, James VI and I allocated land in relatively small parcels (ranging from 1,000 to 2,000 acres) to one hundred Scottish and English 'undertakers' and about fifty 'servitors' (largely English army officers who had settled at the end of the war) in the hope that they would create a British type of rural society. In addition, he set aside other acres to endow key 'civilizing' institutions—the church, towns, schools, and Trinity College, Dublin; while he obliged the City of London to take on the entire County of Londonderry in an effort to bring capital and economic prosperity to a commercial backwater. Finally, in the hope of creating a vested interest in the settlement and of 'civilizing' the native population, he allocated land to 300 'deserving' Irishmen. Predictably, the reality of the scheme failed to match the King's intentions. Many settler landlords did not construct the required number of buildings, or exploited their holdings for a quick return. Colonists such as John Rowley, initially chief agent for the Londoners, or Tristram Beresford, Mayor of Coleraine, illegally exported timber, illicitly felled trees for pipe-staves which they then sold, set up breweries, mills, and tanneries without licence, alienated church lands, and rented holdings at extortionate rates to native Irish tenants. More importantly from the government's perspective, the settlement did not generate much revenue, and during the reign of Charles I the wranglings over how the plantation in County Londonderry should be administered directly contributed to the outbreak of the 'Wars of the Three Kingdoms' (1638–52).[50]

Ironically, the unofficial and unregulated plantation of the non-escheated Counties of Down and Antrim, like that of the Northern Isles, proved to be much more successful. In 1605 Sir Hugh Montgomery, sixth Laird of Braidstone in Ayrshire, and another Scottish favourite of the King, James Hamilton, carved up the estates of Conn O'Neill, Lord of Upper Clandeboye and the Great Ards, in a tripartite agreement and attracted a significant number of settlers to the region. In County Antrim Sir Randal MacDonnell, later first Earl of Antrim, introduced

[49] Michael MacCarthy-Morrogh, 'The English Presence in Early Seventeenth Century Munster', in Ciaran Brady and Raymond Gillespie, eds., *Natives and Newcomers: The Making of Irish Colonial Society, 1534–1641* (Dublin, 1986), p. 188.

[50] Jane H. Ohlmeyer, 'Strafford, the "Londonderry Business" and the "New British History"', in Merritt, ed., *The Political World*, pp. 209–29.

many British Protestant settlers to his vast patrimony, and on numerous occasions the King thanked him for 'his services in improving those barren and uncultivated parts of the country, and planting a colony there'.[51] Randal would have been familiar with this concept because he had been fostered on the Scottish island of Arran (hence his name Randal Arranach) and thus exposed to James's unsuccessful attempts to 'plant' the troublesome Highlands with Scottish Lowlanders. In fact one recent scholar has suggested that Randal formed an important human link between the Irish and Scottish plantations.[52]

In addition to plantations, the Crown sought to tame 'those rude parts'—while at the same time enriching itself—by interfering in land titles. In 1598 James VI ordered leading Highland landowners to produce a legal deed to their holdings and to find sureties for the payment of royal dues. The comprehensive nature of the 1625 Act of Revocation may have aimed at recovering for the Crown Scottish ecclesiastical property and revenues, but the King's willingness to tamper with land titles rattled Scottish landowners who, in the words of the Privy Council, felt that 'nothing hes at ony tyme heirtofore occurrit whilk hes so far disquyted the myndis of your goode subjectis'.[53] More seriously, this directly contributed to the outbreak of civil war almost a decade later, in much the same way that the Edict of Restitution (1629), which aimed to recover church lands for the Emperor, alienated many German princes and helped to transform the Thirty Years War (1618–48) from a German religious war into an international struggle.[54] In Ireland the state's eagerness to question the validity of land titles antagonized Protestants and Catholics alike. In 1606 James established the Commission for the Remedy of Defective Titles which, on pain of fine or forfeiture, required all Irish landowners to prove their title to their land. Many failed, and this resulted in the redistribution of land in Counties Wexford, Leitrim, Longford, and other areas in the Midlands between 1610 and 1620; while after 1635 Wentworth challenged—unsuccessfully and with disastrous long-term results—land titles in Clare, in Connacht, and in the lordship of Ormond with a view to planting these areas with English colonists.

Whether government-sponsored or unregulated, the colonization of Ireland progressed at a faster pace than the settlement of North America. It appears that prior to 1641 100,000 people migrated to Ireland from Britain (30,000 Scots largely to Ulster and 70,000 Welsh or English migrants), which helps account for the

[51] Maxwell, ed., *Irish History*, p. 301.

[52] Lee, *Great Britain's Solomon*, p. 212.

[53] *RPCS*, Second Series, I, p. 193.

[54] For details see Geoffrey Parker, *The Thirty Years' War* (London, 1984), p. 98. Similarly, 'Reduktion' or land-resumption policies pursued by the Swedish Crown during the seventeenth century enabled it to claw back considerable chunks of land from the nobility: A. F. Upton, 'The Swedish Nobility, 1600–1772', in H. M. Scott, *The European Nobilities in the Seventeenth and Eighteenth Centuries*, 2 vols. (London, 1995), II, pp. 24–25.

presumed rise in the Irish population.[55] In stark contrast, the numbers of migrants crossing the Atlantic remained relatively small: *c.*6,000 settlers in Massachusetts by 1636 and *c.*8,000 in Virginia by 1640. Equally important, those colonists who settled in Ireland were more skilled and fared better than those who migrated to New England.[56]

On both sides of the Atlantic the planters registered their 'right' to the land and the permanent nature of their settlement by mapping *terrae incognitae* and then by building houses. From the later sixteenth century maps became an increasingly important 'tool of Empire' in the English colonial experience, especially in Ireland. In an effort to facilitate military conquest, administrative assimilation, and legal imperialism, late-Tudor bureaucrats (such as Lord Burghley or Sir George Carew) constantly commissioned new maps of the 'moving frontier' in Ireland and, prior to settling lands, the government ordered extensive surveys of Munster (1584), Ulster (1608), North Wexford (1609), Wicklow and the Midlands (1637–38), and Connacht (1636–40). As the estate maps of Sir Walter Ralegh's County Cork lands (1598) or those of the Essex estate in County Monaghan (1634) highlight, individual colonists were also keen to determine the boundaries of their patrimony. In addition, as extant surveys illustrate, planters in Ireland built English-style, stone and timber dwelling-houses and improved their holdings, either by fencing, draining, or planting a garden. This served as a symbolic barrier between the 'wild' world—where, as one anonymous critic noted, the Irish farmer 'never buildeth, repaire, or enclosethe the grownde'[57]—and the 'civilized' one they were creating.

Yet within a remarkably short period the native lords of the frontier—along the Anglo-Scottish border as well as in Ireland—began to accept the new commercial economic order inherent in this 'civilizing' and 'improving' ideology. Howard Lamar noted the speed with which even a small number of intruders could 'quickly initiate profound systematic changes in the indigenous society. The material goods they introduce may cause intense competition to control or monopolize them among segments of the local population and may damage the interests of the local people who previously made and exchanged goods that served equivalent purposes.'[58]

[55] The Irish population allegedly rose from *c.*1.4 million in 1600 to 2.1 million in 1641 (a growth of 1% per annum). During the same period *c.*40,000 Scots migrated to Poland and *c.*30,000 to Scandinavia; proportionately, the Scots migrated more than the English: T. C. Smout, N. C. Landsman, and T. M. Devine, 'Scottish Emigration in the Seventeenth and Eighteenth Centuries', in Nicholas Canny, ed., *Europeans on the Move: Studies On European Migration, 1500–1800* (Oxford, 1994), p. 79.

[56] Nicholas Canny, 'English Migration Into and Across the Atlantic during the Seventeenth and Eighteenth Centuries', in Canny, ed., *Europeans on the Move*, pp. 64–75.

[57] Hadfield and McVeagh, eds., *Strangers to that Land*, p. 64.

[58] Lamar and Thompson, eds., *The Frontier in History*, p. 9.

During the early seventeenth century the gradual conversion of customary tenures to leasehold occurred along the Borders as individual landlords, such as the ninth Earl of Northumberland, tried to restructure their estates by making long-term 'improving' leases which required tenants to enclose marginal and common land, build towns, and attract established farmers to their holdings. This, combined with nearly forty years of peace, ensured that rentals rose significantly; for instance, the rental of the Gray estate in the Till Valley in Northumberland soared from £1,000 in the 1590s to £7–8,000 by 1620. In the Western Isles increased contact with the more market-oriented economy of Lowland Scotland, combined with government encouragement, resulted in agricultural improvements, the widespread introduction of written leases, and the reorientation of estate management on a commercial basis.[59] The market towns of Campbeltown, Stornaway, and Gordonsburgh (now Fort William) became commercial centres in the early seventeenth century; while the Earl of Argyll's orchards and gardens at Inveraray probably date from the early seventeenth century.[60]

Similarly in Ireland, chieftains quickly realized that in order to survive and succeed in this 'civilizing' English world and to be considered 'worthy subjects', they had no alternative but to exploit the economic advantages of the English system of landlord–tenant relations and of a commercial economy. Surviving deeds from the estates of the first and second (Gaelic, Catholic) Earls of Antrim demonstrate their eagerness to become, and be perceived as, 'improving' landlords. Both encouraged English and Scottish Protestant tenants to settle on their lands, and by the late 1630s the Antrim estate could boast well over 300 'British' (or Protestant) families, while the town of Dunluce consisted 'of many tenements, after the fashion of the Pale, peopled for the most part with Scotsmen'.[61] In addition, they carved their estate into manageable units of around one or more townlands and offered long-term leases to men of substance, requiring them to invest time and capital in improving the property and to attract good tenants who were to enclose poor land, mark boundaries, build stone houses, plant trees, and pay their rents in cash rather than kind. The second Earl took some pride in reporting his own achievement to the Dublin government in 1637: 'I have compounded my affairs here with my tenants wherein I was not so inward to my [own] profit as to the general good and settlement by binding them to plant [trees] and

[59] Dodgshon, 'Pretense of Blude', p. 192.

[60] The seventh Earl (exiled after 1618) planted herb gardens and 'sundrie fruit trees verie prettilie sett', *Inventory of the Ancient Monuments of Argyll*, Vol. VII, *Mid Argyll and Cowal* (Edinburgh, 1992), p. 402.

[61] 'A Report of the Voluntary Works Done by Servitors . . . within the Counties of Downe, Antryme, and Monahan', P[ublic] R[ecord] O[ffice of] N[orthern] I[reland], T. 811/3, f. 13). Also see Jane H. Ohlmeyer, *Civil War and Restoration in the Three Stuart Kingdoms: The Career of Randal MacDonnell, Marquis of Antrim, 1609–1683* (Cambridge, 1993), pp. 24–26, 39–42.

husband their holdings so near as may be to the manner of England.'[62] This delighted Strafford and Charles I, just as the first Earl's initiatives had prompted James VI and I to laud 'his dutiful behaviour to the state and the example of his civil and orderly life endeavours very much of the reformation and civilizing of those rude parts . . . where he dwells'.[63]

In addition to reorganizing their estates, regional power-brokers increasingly adopted English dress and British architectural styles. In 1618 the fourth Earl of Clanricard spent £10,000 he could ill afford building a grand fortified house, with mullioned bay windows and an ornate interior, at Portumna, near Galway. During the 1630s the Earl of Kildare's hereditary seat at Maynooth was completely refurbished, at enormous cost. Though the outer buildings of the Earl of Antrim's principal seat at Dunluce remained defensive in character, the inner great house resembled an English manor house, with two-storied bay windows and leaded, diamond-shaped panes of glass. Likewise, Antrim's 'pleasant house' at Glenarm was built to impress both his followers and his peers and to demonstrate his 'Englishness'. Without doubt, these residences rivalled any of the other planter castles at Belfast, Carrickfergus, Mountjoy, or Donegal and were 'very richly furnished'—presumably according to the latest London fashions.[64] Even in yet more remote areas such as County Sligo, English fashions, architectural styles, and economic practices became increasingly widespread. Likewise, along the western seaboard of Scotland a large number of stately homes mushroomed during the first half of the seventeenth century; while local barons gentrified or added to their traditional strongholds. For instance, in 1623 Sir Rory MacLeod of Dunvegan overhauled and extended his medieval fortress at great expense; in 1614 Sir Duncan Campbell renovated Kilchurn Castle; while the Campbells of Cawdor and of Ardnamurchan remodelled their castles in the late 1630s.[65]

Building, combined with increased conspicuous expenditure (on furniture, clothing, education, legal expenses, living at court, and marriage), resulted in widespread indebtedness which not only disrupted the traditional redistributive economic order but created a breach within Gaeldom by reorienting Highland politics away from Ireland and towards the Lowlands. The example of the MacLeods of Dunvegan, who owned extensive estates on the islands of Skye and Harris, highlights this. While the payment of cash rents, combined with a rise in land values, ensured that the value of the estate rose tenfold (from £66 in 1600 to £675 in 1638), heavy expenditure on building and land, sumptuous clothing, trips to Edinburgh and to court in London, together with increased taxation and

[62] Antrim to Ormond[?], 2 Aug. 1637, Sheffield City Library, Strafford MSS, 17, f. 151.

[63] James I to Chichester, 3 May 1613, B[ritish] L[ibrary], Add[itional] MSS, 4794, f. 23.

[64] Earl of Clanricard to Earl of Essex, 14 Nov. 1629, BL, Add. MSS, 46188, f. 120.

[65] *Inventory*, VII, pp. 194, 230, 231, 238–39, 288.

escalating legal expenses, drove the family deep into debt. By his death in 1626 Sir Rory's debts exceeded £1,000, and within a generation these had more than quadrupled to £4,500 (the bulk of which were not settled until the early eighteenth century).[66] Extravagant spending between 1590 and 1633 left Simon Fraser, Lord Fraser of Lovat, heavily in debt; the acquisition of Islay and improvement to property caused Sir John Campbell of Cawdor to become deeply financially embarrassed; while liabilities accrued by the MacLeans of Duart during the 1630s ultimately contributed to their downfall in 1674. Mortgaging or 'wadsetting' land, especially in the Western Isles, became widespread and enabled the house of Argyll to expand further at the expense of the MacDonnells and other clans.[67]

Irish landlords sank deeply into debt. By the late 1630s the Earl of Antrim's debts hovered around £42,000 and pressure from his creditors for repayment forced him to mortgage nineteen properties on the Strand in London, together with the entire barony of Cary, the lordship of Ballycastle, and Rathlin Island. The majority of his Ulster neighbours, Catholic and Protestant alike—the Magennises of Iveagh, Sir Phelim O'Neill, the O'Neills of Edenduffcarrick, Sir William Brownlow, and Lords Clandeboye, Chichester, Cromwell, and Conway—were in a similar predicament, as were other prominent Irish figures such as the Earls of Ormond and of Clanricard. Though intimately linked to the 'civilizing' and colonizing policies of the 'core', the insidious financial and economic pressures proved, especially in the long term, more potent agents of change in those outlying areas than any parliamentary statute.

The Closing Frontier

If the frontier 'closes' when a single political authority emerges in the zone, when did the internal frontiers of the British monarchies finally solidify? Steven Ellis has argued that by 1640 the 'periphery' had been incorporated into the British political system.[68] Certainly by 1625, and the death of James VI and I, the Northern Isles and Borders ceased to enjoy the characteristics of frontier societies. The efficient administration of the Borders, under the watchful eyes of the Earls of Dunbar and of Dunfermline, combined with a series of good harvests between 1603 and 1611, facilitated the demilitarization process. Even though Charles I revived the Border Commission after 1635 to deal with outbursts of disorder and cattle-

[66] For details see R. C. MacLeod, ed., *The Book of Dunvegan, 1340–1700* (Aberdeen, 1938).

[67] Cowan, 'Fishers in Drumlie Waters', pp. 278, 304.

[68] Steven G. Ellis, '"Not mere English": The British Perspective, 1400–1650', *History Today*, XXXVIII (Dec. 1988), p. 48. More recently he argued that military conquest in 1603 'removed the final obstacles to centralised control', see Steven G. Ellis, 'Tudor State Formation and the Shaping of the British Isles', in Ellis and Barber, eds., *Conquest*, p. 62.

thieving, and during the 1640s lawlessness again became endemic as 'moss troopers' roamed the Borders, no restoration of the pre-1603 world order occurred. Without doubt, the pacification of the Borders—together with the fairly painless assimilation of the Northern Isles—ranks as one of the greatest achievements of the early Stuarts.

This occurred in part because of the character of James VI and I. While he never developed a comprehensive strategy for civilizing his kingdoms (indeed, it could be argued that his botched Highland initiatives ranked as one of the greatest disappointments of his reign), he nevertheless maximized fortuitous opportunities to demilitarize and to bring law and order to Ulster and the Borders. Equally important, he had a flair for appointing regional 'imperialists' who spearheaded with remarkable energy and effect government policy throughout the British monarchies. Yet even the combined efforts of the Stuart kings and 'imperialists' like Dunfermline, Strafford, Knox, or Bramhall failed to transform Irish and Scottish society into 'civilized', tax-paying, Protestant, English-speaking polities. In 1617, nearly a decade after the Statutes of Iona, the inhabitants of Islay complained that 'they ar verie havelie oppreist troublit and wrackit be a nomer of ydill men, vagabounds and sornairis who lyis upoun thame, consumis thair viveris and spoylis thame of thair goodis'.[69] By 1630, according to the Scottish Privy Council, the Highlands swarmed with 'nombers of brokin and lawlesse lymmars [thieves] . . . who . . . wer some yeers bygane reduced to the obedience of law and justice, hes now begun to renew thair . . . wicked trade of thift . . . and goe in sorning . . . ;'[70] and on the eve of the Bishops' Wars (1638–40) lawlessness in the Highlands had reached levels characteristic of the 1590s. The fact that nobles maintained their monopoly over the administration of justice in the localities, largely through baronial and regality courts, frustrated attempts by the Crown to replace their private authority and to introduce Justices of the Peace into Scotland (by 1625 less than a quarter of the Scottish shires had JPs). Therefore, despite the significance played by legislation like the Statutes of Iona in undermining the 'fighting and feasting' culture of the Western Isles, chiefs continued to maintain swordsmen, be delighted by harpists and bards, entertain on a grand scale, speak Gaelic, and retain large households. Highland chieftains may well have responded to changing models of landlordism by restructuring their estates and adopting a more commercially oriented economy, but it was not until the later seventeenth century that the Western Isles became relatively 'civilized', with violence and lawlessness limited to small bands of 'tories' and 'moss troopers' running small-scale protection

[69] Quoted in R. A. Dodgshon, 'West Highland Chiefdoms, 1500–1745: A Study of Redistributive Exchange', in Rosalind Mitchison and Peter Roebuck, eds., *Economy and Society in Scotland and Ireland, 1500–1939* (Edinburgh, 1988), p. 30.

[70] *RPCS*, Second Series, IV, p. 100.

rackets.[71] Even then the political frontier in the Highlands and Islands did not finally close until after the Jacobite rising of 1745, when the government outlawed Gaelic, disbanded the clans, and refused to tolerate lordly power.

What then of Ireland? On the eve of the Irish Rebellion of October 1641 English jurisdiction included Gaelic Ireland. Here too the frontier appeared to be closing. Nearly four decades of peace had facilitated the demilitarization of Irish lordships; the introduction of English legal, tenurial, and inheritance practices had effectively supplanted the system of 'coign and livery'; while the construction of towns, villages, churches, and manor houses had permanently transformed the physical landscape. The Irish economy also became increasingly commercialized as the growth in the wool- and cattle trades highlight (the number of live cattle exported from select Ulster ports increased tenfold). This was partly facilitated by the foundation of new market towns (between 1600 and 1649 over 500 grants were made authorizing the holding of markets) and the increased urbanization of Ireland. Even the professional classes appeared to adjust to the new world order. Bardic poets readily accepted grants of land in the plantation scheme; while bards on both sides of the North Channel modified the traditional themes of their poetry to meet the new circumstances and the changed priorities of their new patrons.[72]

Nevertheless, leading Irish lords, especially in Ulster and Connacht, continued to uphold traditional Gaelic values, maintain bards and swordsmen, practise transhumance, speak Irish, and, above all, practise the Catholic religion. For example, the Earls of Antrim may well have won royal acclaim for their 'improving' policies but they also publicly demonstrated their devotion to Rome by patronizing St Patrick's Purgatory at Lough Derg and by encouraging the Franciscans to maintain a friary at Bonamargy near Ballycastle, which became the headquarters from which they ministered to their tenants and set out on missions to the Western Isles. Customs such as booleying remained widespread, and throughout the 1640s semi-nomadic 'creaghts', with their large herds of cows, helped to maintain the confederate army of Ulster. Ultimately the onset of civil war in 1641—and again in 1688—delayed the implementation of effective political hegemony, and it was not until after 1690, and the completion of the Williamite conquest, that the Protestant interest finally closed the frontier in Ireland.

While James VI and I and his son never fully integrated Gaeldom into a greater Imperial polity, they nevertheless established a remarkable measure of control over the frontiers which had been sources of political instability since the Middle Ages

[71] For further details see Allan I. Macinnes, 'Repression and Conciliation: The Highland Dimension, 1660–1688', *Scottish Historical Review*, LXV (1986), pp. 167–95.

[72] B. Ó Buachalla, 'James our True King: The Ideology of Irish Royalism in the Seventeenth Century', in D. George Boyce and others, eds., *Political Thought in Ireland since the Seventeenth Century* (London, 1993), p. 10.

and thereby laid a foundation for the future development of a British Empire. Moreover, the ethnocentric mentalities which evolved, as the English flexed their muscles against the peoples of the British frontiers during the course of the sixteenth and seventeenth centuries, later characterized Imperial rule overseas whether in North America, Africa, or the Indian subcontinent. For instance, expansionists, such as Sir Walter Ralegh or Humphrey Gilbert, whose colonial exploits traversed the Atlantic, used their Irish experiences to confirm their assumptions of savagism, paganism, and barbarism and applied these 'to the indigenous population of the New World'.[73] In other words, Ireland, the Borders, and the Highlands and Islands all served to some degree or other as 'laboratories' of Empire. Moreover, the willingness of the Irish—and especially the Scots—to involve themselves in expansionist enterprise at home and later abroad helped to transform the English Imperial experience into a truly British one.

[73] Nicholas P. Canny, *The Elizabethan Conquest of Ireland: A Pattern Established, 1565–1576* (New York, 1976), p. 160.

Select Bibliography

K. R. Andrews, N. P. Canny, and P. E. H. Hair, eds., *The Westward Enterprise: English Activities in Ireland, the Atlantic and America, 1480–1650* (Liverpool, 1978).

K. M. Brown, *Bloodfeud in Scotland, 1573–1625: Violence, Justice and Politics in Early Modern Scotland* (Edinburgh, 1986).

Nicholas Canny, ed., *Europeans on the Move: Studies on European Migration, 1500–1800* (Oxford, 1994).

R. A. Dodgshon, 'West Highland Chiefdoms, 1500–1745: A Study of Redistributive Exchange', in Rosalind Mitchison and Peter Roebuck, eds., *Economy and Society in Scotland and Ireland, 1500–1939* (Edinburgh, 1988).

—— '"Pretense of Blude" and "Place of Thair Duelling"; the Nature of Scottish Clans, 1500–1745', in R. A. Houston and I. D. Whyte, eds., *Scottish Society, 1500–1800* (Cambridge, 1989).

Steven G. Ellis and Sarah Barber, eds., *Conquest and Union: Fashioning a British State, 1485–1725* (London, 1995), esp. chaps. by Steven Ellis, Jane Dawson, Micheál MacCraith, and Allan Macinnes.

Raymond Gillespie, *Colonial Ulster: The Settlement of East Ulster, 1600–1641* (Cork, 1985).

A. Grant and K. J. Stringer, eds., *Uniting the Kingdom? The Making of British History* (London, 1995), esp. chaps. by Nicholas Canny, Marcus Merriman, and Jenny Wormald.

Andrew Hadfield and John McVeagh, eds., *Strangers to that Land: British Perceptions of Ireland from the Reformation to the Famine* (Gerrards Cross, Buckinghamshire, 1994).

Maurice Lee, *Great Britain's Solomon: James VI and I in his Three Kingdoms* (Urbana, Ill., 1990).

Michael MacCarthy-Morrogh, *The Munster Plantation: English Migration to Southern Ireland, 1583–1641* (Oxford, 1986).

Allan I. Macinnes, 'Crown, Clan and Fine: The 'Civilising' of Scottish Gaeldom, 1587–1638', in *Northern Scotland*, XIII (1993).

—— *Clanship, Commerce and the House of Stuart, 1603–1788* (Edinburgh, 1996).

J. F. Merritt, ed., *The Political World of Thomas Wentworth, Earl of Strafford, 1621–1641* (Cambridge, 1996), esp. essays by Nicholas Canny, John McCafferty, and Jane Ohlmeyer.

Jane H. Ohlmeyer, *Civil War and Restoration in the Three Stuart Kingdoms: The Career of Randal MacDonnell, Marquis of Antrim, 1609–1683* (Cambridge, 1993).

M. Perceval-Maxwell, *The Scottish Migration to Ulster in the Reign of James I* (London, 1973).

Thomas I. Rae, *The Administration of the Scottish Frontier, 1513–1603* (Edinburgh, 1966).

Philip Robinson, *The Plantation of Ulster* (Dublin, 1984).

Ralph Robson, *The English Highland Clans: Tudor Responses to a Medieval Problem* (Edinburgh, 1989).

David B. Quinn, 'Ireland and Sixteenth Century European Expansion', in T. D. Williams, ed., *Historical Studies* (London, 1958).

7

England's New World and the Old, 1480s–1630s

NICHOLAS CANNY

The title of this chapter is adopted unashamedly from Sir John Elliott's *The Old World and the New.*[1] One of the more telling insights in that influential book was that Europeans of the sixteenth and seventeenth centuries remained largely indifferent to the encounter with the New World, because the range of exotic cultures reported on by European explorers appeared deficient to educated Europeans, whether measured against the civil standards of the ancient world or the moral code of Christianity. Many of the leads provided by Elliott have been pursued by others, but most scholars have drawn upon Spanish, French, and Portuguese experiences rather than that of the English.[2] This chapter seeks to make good the deficiency by considering how English people accommodated America and its inhabitants into their thinking during the century-and-a-half succeeding the first encounter—a subject that riveted the attention of earlier scholars but that has been strangely neglected by recent historians of England.

Those persisting in the established lines of enquiry have been primarily interested in trade, and few recent historians of early modern England have been concerned with the intellectual responses of English observers to foreign peoples and places. Historians of Colonial British America have been hardly more curious about early encounters, and Francis Jennings's thesis, that English people who became involved with America were bent upon an invasion of the land and the destruction of its peoples, has been but slightly modified. As the curiosity of historians has waned, literary scholars have become increasingly fascinated by English encounters with foreign peoples, and they have either relied on books such as Jennings's to provide a historical context for their interpretations, or have composed accounts of their own which rely principally on creative literature for their authority. This work by literary scholars has compounded the belief that

[1] J. H. Elliott, *The Old World and the New, 1492–1650* (Cambridge, 1970).

[2] Anthony Pagden, *The Fall of Natural Man: The American Indian and the Origins of Comparative Ethnology* (Cambridge, 1982) and *European Encounters with the New World* (New Haven, 1993); Stuart B. Schwartz, ed., *Implicit Understandings: Observing, Reporting, and Reflecting on the Encounters between Europeans and other Peoples in the Early Modern Period* (Cambridge, 1994); Karen Ordahl Kupperman, ed., *America in European Consciousness, 1493–1750* (Chapel Hill, NC, 1995).

English people were more blinkered than any other Europeans in their appraisal of alien cultures.[3]

This proposition has been advanced with scant regard for contemporary narratives, either those published close to the time by the two Richard Hakluyts and Samuel Purchas, or in modern editions, by such sponsors as the Hakluyt Society. Geographers and economic historians have been the academics most interested in these texts, but they have also attracted the popular audience that histories of Tudor and Stuart England once enjoyed. Prime testimony to this is the success of the five-volume *New American World*, a compilation which chronicles the endeavours of those involved with early English colonization.[4]

All surviving evidence shows that few English people were involved with overseas activity before the 1580s. These included fishermen who sailed regularly to Newfoundland, but fishermen had but scant interest in America and its inhabitants, and were more concerned to conceal their source of cod and whales from competitors than to broadcast their discoveries.[5] Others involved with long-distance voyaging were those seeking a route to Asia, either by a North-east Passage over Europe or a North-west Passage over America. Their quest proves that their sights were set on the Old World of Eurasia rather than the New World of America, but they were still

[3] Kenneth R. Andrews, *Elizabethan Privateering: English Privateering during the Spanish War, 1585–1603* (Cambridge, 1964), *Trade, Plunder and Settlement: Maritime Enterprise and the Genesis of the British Empire, 1480–1630* (Cambridge, 1984), and *Ships, Money and Politics: Seafaring and Naval Enterprise in the Reign of Charles I* (Cambridge, 1991); Robert Brenner, *Merchants and Revolution: Commercial Change, Political Conflict and London's Overseas Traders, 1550–1653* (Princeton, 1993); Karen Ordahl Kupperman, *Providence Island, 1630–1641: The Other Puritan Colony* (Cambridge, 1994). On the early encounter see Francis Jennings, *The Invasion of America: Indians, Colonialism and the Cant of Conquest* (Chapel Hill, NC, 1975); James Axtell, *The European and the Indian: Essays in the Ethnohistory of Colonial North America* (Oxford, 1981); Karen Ordahl Kupperman, *Settling with the Indians: The Meeting of English and Indian Cultures in America, 1580–1640* (Totowa, NJ, 1980); for the Native American's view see Neal Salisbury, *Manitou and Providence: The Making of New England 1500–1643* (Oxford, 1982); William Cronon, *Changes in the Land: Indians, Colonists and Ecology in New England* (New York, 1983); J. Frederick Fausz, 'Opechancanough: Indian Resistance Leader', in David Sweet and Gary B. Nash, eds., *Struggle and Survival in Colonial America* (Berkeley, 1981), pp. 21–37; Martin Quitt, 'Trade and Acculturation at Jamestown, 1607–09: The Limits of Understanding', *William and Mary Quarterly* (hereafter *WMQ*), Third Series, LII (1995), pp. 227–58; James Merrell, '"The Customes of Our Countrey": Indians and Colonists in Early America', in Bernard Bailyn and Philip D. Morgan, eds., *Strangers within the Realm Cultural Margins of the first British Empire* (Chapel Hill, NC, 1991), pp. 117–56. Influential works by literary scholars are Stephen Greenblatt, *Renaissance Self-Fashioning* (Chicago, 1980) and *Marvelous Possessions: The Wonder of the New World* (Oxford, 1991); Richard Helgerson, *Forms of Nationhood: The Elizabethan Writing of England* (Chicago, 1992).

[4] The spectacular editorial and scholarly achievements of David and Alison Quinn should be noted. David B. Quinn and others, eds., *New American World: A Documentary History of North America to 1612*, 5 vols. (New York, 1979) (hereafter *New American World*).

[5] *New American World*, I, pp. 91–120, 159–226; David B. Quinn, *England and the Discovery of America* (New York, 1974).

unable to ignite enthusiasm among their countrymen, other than when support was solicited by the monarch.[6] The limited extent to which these early English voyagers appreciated America as a New World was acknowledged in 1625 by Samuel Purchas when he stated that accounts of pre-1580 voyages were situated by him, in his multi-volume *Pilgrimes*, with texts relating to travel in the Old World because the navigators had then been 'sailing from and for Europe' and spent 'most of their time on the Asian and African coasts'.[7]

Englishmen also, up to then, were indifferent to the explorations of other Europeans, and a quickening of English interest in oceanic affairs was partly an extension into the Atlantic of developing European politico-religious animosities. Thus, the joint Anglo/French-Huguenot settlement of the 1570s on the coast of Florida was designed by Protestant enthusiasts as a base from which to attack the Spanish silver fleet, and it received extensive notice in England only when obliterated by the Spaniards. This venture also alerted some English officials to the benefits that Spain had derived from its New World possessions.[8] This consciousness was heightened in the 1580s when England and Spain became embroiled in hostilities that were to endure until 1604. This conflict created opportunities for privateering, while the exploits of more daring marauders made them folk heroes in England, thus strengthening the hand of those few statesmen who wished to emulate the Spaniards by supporting English colonization in North America.[9]

At this point accounts of earlier English-sponsored voyages suddenly became relevant, because they could help both to identify possible locations for settlement, and to legitimize English claims on grounds of precedent. Much surviving material was therefore published, and new works advocating settlement were commissioned by prominent politicians, particularly Sir Francis Walsingham, Secretary of State to Queen Elizabeth. There were two novel features to this literature. First, whether printed or in manuscript, it was dedicated to influential people; and second, the authors accepted America as a continent in its own right, and outlined the benefits that colonization there would bring to both English and Amerindian peoples.

The principal contributors to this new literature were the two Richard Hakluyts, Edward Hayes, and Christopher Carleill.[10] All were associated with Walsingham, and stressed England's sustained contact with North America since, and even

[6] *New American World*, I, pp. 159–78. See above, pp. 55–56.

[7] Samuel Purchas, *Hakluytus Posthumus or Purchas His Pilgrimes* (hereafter *Pilgrimes*), 20 vols. (Glasgow, 1905), I, p. xlv.

[8] *New American World*, II, pp. 277–471.

[9] See below, pp. 60–64; Andrews, *Trade, Plunder and Settlement.*

[10] *New American World*, III, pp. 1–176; David B. Quinn, ed., *The Hakluyt Handbook*, 2 vols. (London, 1974); Helgerson, *Forms of Nationhood*, pp. 151–91.

before, the Columbus voyage. To support this contention, and the associated claim to lands in North America, they tabulated the proceedings of earlier English voyagers in the Atlantic and so lent a coherence to these activities which they had never had. The four authors also contended that the English had an even greater moral responsibility than their continental rivals to bring civility and Christianity to America because theirs was the true religion. Even then they had little to say about indigenous society, and some who spoke of bringing Christianity to America meant no more than the settlement there of Europeans.[11]

Appraisals of the economic benefit of colonization were always cast in mercantilist terms, as propagandists for overseas ventures listed the raw materials which England had previously imported which might now be obtained, or produced, in colonial climates. Then as the commodities that would lead to this import-substitution were identified, so also were the unemployed artisans (and even petty criminals) in England who would find gainful employment in this new economic activity in the colonies, and as an added bonus, it was regularly insisted that the promotion of English transatlantic trade would consolidate England's interest in Ireland. Such prospects satisfied the younger Hakluyt in 1582 that this was England's moment to become engaged in colonization, because Providence had assigned 'a time for all men': thus, when experience showed 'the Portingales time to be out of date', and when Spain's tyrannical treatment of native Americans had been exposed by translations from the work of the Spanish missionary and theologian Bartolomé de Las Casas, it appeared: 'that the time approacheth and now is, that we of England may share and part stakes (if we will our selves), both with the Spaniards and the Portingale in part of America, and other regions as yet undiscovered'.[12]

Such sentiments were hyperbolic, and procedures for converting the Amerindians to Christianity were not even discussed. It was accepted that a way forward could only be devised when the English knew more of native societies, and the younger Hakluyt foraged for relevant information. Some was extracted from the accounts of earlier English explorers, but fresh information was also gleaned from continental sources investigated by the younger Hakluyt when he was posted, 1578–86, in France.[13] More important were the eye-witness descriptions of Amerindian life compiled after 1584 by English explorers. These too were collected by the Hakluyts and also by their disciple and rival Samuel Purchas, and published in fullest form in Purchas's *Pilgrimes*, based on 'a new way of eye-evidence'. Purchas

[11] *New American World*, III, pp. 70–123.

[12] Richard Hakluyt, *Divers Voyages* (1582; London, 1850), p. 8.

[13] David Armitage, 'The New World and British Historical Thought', in Kupperman, ed., *America in European Consciousness*, pp. 52–75.

established a standard of reporting by presenting his evidence 'in way of Discourse by each traveller relating what in that kind he hath seen'.[14]

The text that most complied with this standard was that by Thomas Hariot describing the natives on Roanoke Island. This was literally an eye-witness account because what Hariot described in print was given simultaneous visual depiction by the limner John White. Hariot's is arguably the most sympathetic portrayal by any European of any group of Amerindians during the early-modern period. Its particular merit is that it provided evidence that the Indians on Roanoke Island were an intelligent people who had devised a coherent, if primitive, civilization. He, like all European observers of that time, was especially curious about their religious beliefs and practices and condemned their priests as agents of Satan. None the less, Hariot was satisfied that these people understood some essential truths revealed in nature, and he believed they would, with time, effort, and catechizing in their own language, be made Christians.[15]

These assumptions were never put to the test, because the settlement on Roanoke became the famous 'lost' colony. Nevertheless, Hariot's views have been favourably regarded by scholars, and his attitude towards the Amerindians is frequently contrasted with that of his associate Ralph Lane, whose brusque behaviour and comments are considered more typically English. Hariot is therefore identified as the exception who proves the rule that English people never seriously contemplated the reform of the Amerindians but intended, from the outset, either to enslave them or deprive them of their lands.

This appraisal is crude. A reading of the evidence suggests that this negative response did not become dominant until after the Virginia massacre of 1622 or, in the case of New England, until the late 1630s or 1640s. The observations of most Englishmen who had direct dealings with Amerindians before those dates are sympathetic towards Native Americans and their cultures. Furthermore, it appears that English promoters of colonization wished to modify rather than destroy native cultures, although they, like all European observers, were still condescending towards native cultures which they presumed would wither away as Christianity and an English-dominated economy made headway. The texts composed during the years from 1584 through the 1630s, however, indicate that the English then made as genuine an effort as any Europeans to overcome their inherited

[14] *Pilgrimes*, I, pp. xxxvii, xl.

[15] Paul Hulton and David B. Quinn, *The American Drawings of John White*, 2 vols. (London, 1964); Paul Hulton, 'Images of the New World', in K. R. Andrews, N. P. Canny, and P. E. H. Hair, eds., *The Westward Enterprise: English Activities in Ireland, the Atlantic and America, 1480–1650* (hereafter *Westward Enterprise*) (Liverpool, 1978), pp. 195–214; J. H. Parry, 'Introduction', in *Westward Enterprise*, pp. 1–16; David B. Quinn, *Set Fair for Roanoke* (Chapel Hill, NC, 1985); J. W. Shirley, ed., *Thomas Hariot: Renaissance Scientist* (Oxford, 1974); *New American World*, III, pp. 139–55.

beliefs and prejudices and accommodate America and its peoples within their world view.

This implies that the opinions of Hariot were normative rather than exceptional. To say so is not to deny that Hariot *appears* more humane than any other commentator, but this can be attributed more to accidental rather than philosophical factors. Essentially Hariot was a scientist with a particular interest in natural history, and he therefore sought to represent the total context within which the Roanoke Indians lived. Hariot also had an advantage over other English observers because he had only to comment upon what he set John White to draw. The drawings then made it unnecessary for Hariot to devise pen-pictures of Amerindian life that would render his verbal descriptions intelligible in England. Others, forced to draw analogies, compared the dress, customs, and practices of the Indians with those of exotic peoples with whom English readers were already familiar, either through experience or reading, and the peoples most frequently alluded to were Turks, Ancient Britons, and Gaelic Irish. While Hariot's portrayal of the natives may have appeared humane because it required no such comparisons, it may also have been deliberately generous because, coinciding as it did with a spate of English criticism of Spanish treatment of Amerindians, Hariot may have wanted to demonstrate how fortunate were those Indians who had come under English rather than Spanish tutelage.[16]

While identifying pressures that made Hariot, and those English authors who followed him, portray Amerindians positively and explain how they might be reformed, we have also to allow that comparisons which today seem to reflect negatively on Native Americans were not necessarily so intended. For example, William Wood drew more frequent parallels than any other author between Irish and Amerindian modes, but he did so seemingly because he knew Ireland well rather than because he wished to denigrate Native Americans. Thus, when stating that the bear skins worn by the Indians were 'in form of an Irish mantle', and that 'in the wintertime the more aged of them wear leather drawers, in form like Irish trousers', Wood was conjuring up a meaningful image rather than slighting Americans. Even when he complained of their culinary practices and the loathsomeness of their 'unoatmealed broth, made thick with fishes, fowls and beasts', which he considered not half so good as Irish *bainne clábair* [coagulated milk], it was while praising the natives for their generosity in sharing communal meals with himself.[17]

When discerning the intent of English commentators we must also allow for the comparisons drawn between Indian and English practices. George Percy's

[16] W. S. Maltby, *The Black Legend in England* (Durham, NC, 1971).

[17] William Wood, *New England's Prospect* [1634], ed. Alden Vaughan (Amherst, Mass., 1977), pp. 84, 87–88.

description of Indians creeping animal-like upon the first party of English settlers in the Chesapeake is frequently cited, but not so his likening their gardens with 'the goodliest corn fields that ever was seen in any country'.[18] Similarly, Wood remarked that the Indians of New England 'in their planting of corn exceed our English husbandmen'.[19] Such praise was sometimes extended to manufacturing and hunting technologies of the Indians, and even to their recreations. Wood, in almost the same words as Hariot, admired the dexterity of the Indians in hunting, fishing, and making tools, and he detailed their skill in indoor and outdoor pursuits. He faulted them for spending 'half their days in gambling and lazing', but he praised their fortitude when accidentally hurt in games. He was fascinated by their wearing masks so that no injured player would know his assailant, but Wood still credited the Indians with exercising more restraint than the English

> at football (though they play never so fiercely to outward appearance. Yet angrier-boiling blood never streams in their cooler veins) if any may be thrown, he laughs out his foil. There is no seeking of revenge, no quarrelling, no bloody noses, scratched faces, black eyes, broken shins, no bruised members or crushed ribs, the lamentable effects of rage. But the goal being won, the goods on the one side lost, friends they are at the football and friends they must meet at the kettle.[20]

Similarly, Henry Spelman reported of the Indians with whom he had lived in the Chesapeake that their 'sports' were 'much like ours here in England', as also their 'dancing', which he found 'like our Derbyshire hornpipe'.[21]

When such commendations are weighed against negative comparisons it emerges that most English commentators believed that Indians were capable of being civilized. Allusions to Ancient Britons implied that the Amerindians were as the Britons had been when the Romans encountered them, but this also meant that the commentators accepted that they, like the Britons, could be reformed by an appropriate mixture of force and persuasion. William Strachey stated as much in a series of rhetorical questions relating to the Indians of Virginia: 'Can a leopard change his spots? Can a savage remaining a savage be civil? Were not we ourselves made and not born civil in our progenitors days? And were not Caesar's Britaines as brutish as Virginians? The Roman swords were best teachers of civility to this and other countries near us.'[22] When Strachey developed this theme, he cited Bede on the barbarism of the Ancient Britons and contended that, but for the Romans,

[18] Philip Barbour, ed., *The Jamestown Voyages under the First Charter, 1606–9*, 2 vols. (London, 1969), I, p. 137.

[19] Wood, *New England's Prospect*, p. 113.

[20] Ibid., pp. 92, 103–05.

[21] Henry Spelman, 'Relation of Virginea', in Edward Arber, ed., *The Works of Captain John Smith* (Birmingham, 1884), pp. ci–cxiv, esp. cxiv.

[22] William Strachey, 'A True Repertory of the Wreck . . .', in *Pilgrimes*, XIX, pp. 5–72, quotation p. 62, margin.

the inhabitants of England might 'yet have lived overgrown satyrs, rude and untutored in the woods, dwelling in caves, and hunting for our dinners . . . prostituting our daughters to strangers, sacrificing our children to our idols, nay eating our own children as did the Scots in these days as reciteth Thomas Cogan'. This imaginative flight rendered unanswerable Strachey's assertion that 'violence' was needed to bring to civility 'those (poor souls) who know not the good which they stand in need of'. Violence was all the more justified because the English strove to bring the Indians 'also to the knowledge (which the Romans could not give us) of that God who must save both them and us'. Therefore the force to be used was doubly justified, and Strachey recalled how 'Mr. Simonds preacher of St. Saviour's' had argued there was no more reason to criticize the methods of the English in bringing the Indians to civility than 'as if a father should be said to offer violence to his child when he beats him to bring him to goodness'.[23]

Such paternalistic analogies were employed by English commentators who accepted that the promotion of civility in all times and places had required some force. At the same time reporters were anxious to identify features of Amerindian life that could be adapted to civil conditions. Here Strachey acknowledged the influence of the Spanish Jesuit José de Acosta and, following him, he concluded that the Indians had a religious instinct, if not a religion, which might be put to good purpose. Already, from his experience in Virginia, Strachey described their child-like imitation of the English at Protestant service 'kneeling when we kneel, and lifting up their hands and eyes when we pray, not so docible as willing to receive our customs, herein like razed and unblotted tables apt to receive what form soever shall be first drawn thereon'. Consequently he believed they would be converted more readily than Turks, because they had 'less faith in a religion' and 'less power, either of reason or arms to defend it'.[24]

Few English commentators were as optimistic as Strachey, but all investigated Indian religions, both to discover what truths they had arrived at through the use of reason, and what elements of their religion were Satanic. On the positive side, Edward Winslow reported of Plymouth Plantation that the Indians there believed in one God, in an after-life, and in the Devil who they called upon in times of illness. While condemning their priests for invoking Satan and promoting sacrifice, Winslow credited them with cultivating a moral sexual climate.[25] Alexander Whitaker, the minister at Henrico in Virginia, spoke similarly of native religion, and sent to England 'one image of their God . . . which is painted upon

[23] William Strachey, *The Historie of Travell into Virginia Brittania* [1612], eds. L. B. Wright and Virginia Freund (London, 1953), pp. 23–25.

[24] Ibid., p. 18; and for references to Spain, pp. 20, 55, 90, 91, 93, 95, 106, 118; for analysis of Acosta's writings see Pagden, *Fall of Natural Man*, pp. 146–200.

[25] Edward Winslow, 'Good News from New England', in *Pilgrimes*, XIX, pp. 314–94, esp. 383–94.

one side of a toad stool'. Whitaker was, however, more condemnatory than Winslow of the malign influence of their priests who, like hermits and English witches, would have to be exterminated, being 'a generation of vipers, even of Satan's own brood'.[26] Thomas Morton, despite 'a common received opinion from Cicero that there is no people so barbarous but have some worship or other', found the natives of New England to be without an organized religion. None the less, he remained confident of their conversion, they being 'not altogether without knowledge of God'.[27]

These same observers also looked for coherent forms of government among the Indians. They corrected popular prejudice that all barbarians were alike by pointing to the diversity of tribes, languages, cultures, and physical attributes they had witnessed among the Indians, and most believed that each tribe had its individual government. Whitaker was satisfied:

> that the law of Nature dwelleth in them: for they have a rude kind of common-wealth and rough government wherein they both honour and obey their kings, parents and governors, both greater and less, they observe the limits of their own possessions, murder is scarcely heard of, adultery and other offences severely punished.[28]

Strachey concurred, and concluded that 'although the country people be very barbarous, yet have they amongst them such government, as that their magistrates for good commanding, and their people for due subjection and obeying excell many places that would be accounted civil'.[29] Such reportage became standard, and witnesses who did not follow the formula were sometimes questioned about what was missing from their accounts. Thus, Henry Spelman (who, as a boy, had spent some years with Chief Powhatan to learn Algonquian) remarked, as if under interrogation, that 'concerning their laws my years and understanding made me the less to look after because I thought that infidels were lawless'.[30] Since Spelman was writing in England his interrogators would have been advocates of colonization anxious to identify how Indian society could be absorbed into theirs.

The first requirement of all people in authority was that land for settlement should be purchased rather than plundered from the Indians. They also hoped that chiefs would submit to the English monarch, through the head of the various expeditions, thus making themselves vassals of the English Crown, and their subordinates Crown subjects. Accounts of these submissions were written after

[26] 'Part of a Tract . . . by Alex. Whitaker . . . 1613', in *Pilgrimes*, XIX, pp. 110–16.

[27] Thomas Morton, *New English Canaan* [1637], ed. C. F. Adams (New York, 1883), pp. 139–41, 167. Morton may have mocked his fellow Puritans by suggesting that Indians were more civil than they, but this does not counter the sincerity of his observations on the Indians.

[28] Whitaker in *Pilgrimes*, XIX, p. 111.

[29] Strachey, *Historie*, p. 87.

[30] Spelman, 'Relation', in Arber, ed., *Smith's Works*, p. cx.

they had failed to produce the desired result, but they still show that these pageants were carefully planned and sincerely undertaken by the English. In this respect they can be likened to surrender and re-grant negotiations with Gaelic chieftains conducted by Crown representatives in Ireland during the 1540s. Under these arrangements Gaelic lords, who had previously been regarded as the King's enemies living outside the law, were recognized as subjects, and granted titles of nobility and legal claim over their lordships, as a reward for the symbolic surrender of their estates and their political authority to the Crown. In similar fashion, the Indian chieftains on Roanoke Island gave 'themselves and their lands to the crown of England' and 'formally acknowledged Her Majesty as servants and homagers to her and under her to Sir W[alter] R[alegh]'. This allegedly established a precedent for what followed in Virginia, when 'Powhatan the chief lord of all the savages with thirty nine werowances [subsidiary lords] ... yielded to more than forms and circumstances of homage' when he accepted 'a copper crown as vassal to his majesty: which also he really performed for a time'.[31]

Powhatan's submission was initiated by the Virginia Company in London and managed by the Governor, Captain John Smith. On his second visit to Powhatan in 1608, Smith found him sitting 'upon a throne at the upper end of the house, with such a majesty as I cannot express, nor yet have often seen either in pagan or Christian'. More importantly, the respect was reciprocated, and Powhatan proclaimed Smith a 'werowance' (presumably under King James), and directed 'that all his subjects should so esteem us ... and that the corn, women and country should be to us as to his own people'.[32] At the ensuing ceremony, the suspicious Powhatan was presented with 'his basin, ewer, bed and furniture set up', and after he had been persuaded by an Anglicized Indian that 'they would do him no hurt', he donned 'his scarlet cloak and apparel (with much ado)'. Then, 'a foul trouble there was to make him kneel to receive his crown, he neither knowing the majesty nor meaning of a crown, nor bending of the knee'.

It was later alleged that 'this stately kind of soliciting made him so much overvalue himself' that Powhatan lost respect for the English.[33] But there can be no doubt that the intent of the planners in London was to make Powhatan a subject of King James. Nor was this the last of the pseudo-feudal ceremonies enacted in the Chesapeake. In 1614, when Sir Thomas Dale was Governor, some of

[31] 'Virginias Verger', in *Pilgrimes*, XIX, pp. 218–67, 228–30. I have chosen to refer to the chief as Powhatan (rather than Wahunsonacock), and to his daughter as Pocahontas because these are the names appearing in the quotations from English contemporary documents. Powhatan was really the name of the tribe. On Irish surrender and re-grant arrangements see Brendan Bradshaw, *The Irish Constitutional Revolution of the Sixteenth Century* (Cambridge, 1979).

[32] 'A True Relation', in Philip Barbour, ed., *The Complete Works of Captain John Smith*, 3 vols. (Chapel Hill, NC, 1986) (hereafter *Smith's Works*), I, pp. 65, 67.

[33] *Smith's Works*, I, pp. 233–37; II, pp. 181–89.

the Chickahominy tribe, who were rivals to Powhatan, petitioned to 'become not only our trusty friends, but even King James's subjects and tributaries', and to abandon their tribal name 'and take upon them, as they call us, the name of Tossantessas'. Dale concurred and they duly became 'Tossantessas, that is subjects of King James', and contracted to supply archers to the English 'against the Spaniards whose name is odious among them'.[34]

Such arrangements suggest that the intention of the English was, as with the Irish surrender and re-grant agreements, to win the co-operation of those who wielded influence in the native societies. As in Ireland, agreements usually came in the aftermath of a show of strength by the English, but the long-term hope was that those who had recognized the authority of the Crown would become agents for the reform of their peoples. We noted the contemporary claim that the ceremonies in Virginia were in direct succession to those enacted on Roanoke Island, and there were similar compacts negotiated with Indians by New England settlers during the early years.[35] There it was laid down that land should be purchased from the natives, and even then the terms did not satisfy the more scrupulous Puritans. To this extent, New England commanders, like their Chesapeake counterparts, were concerned to respect the political integrity of the native societies they encountered, and to effect conversion through persuasion and gradual assimilation rather than in the aftermath of war. It is therefore essential that such overtures be taken seriously rather than dismissed as hypocritical cant designed to cover the avarice of English colonists.[36]

Once allowance is made for this stratagem to promote reform, scholars might further accept that English colonists also entertained the hope that Amerindian society could be gradually assimilated into theirs through marriage alliances. This requires detailed documentation because of the notorious official English opposition, both before and after this time, to interracial marriages. One precedent that might have assisted the English in overcoming their inhibitions was that of the Spaniards in Mexico, whom the English admired as well as reviled. Strachey was especially impressed with Spanish management of indigenous society through the medium of *caciques* (local chiefs),[37] and the English in Virginia may have hoped to achieve equally useful linkages through marriage. The most celebrated of such marriages was that between John Rolfe and Pocahontas, a daughter of Powhatan. Pocahontas had associated with the English from the outset, and had been

[34] 'Letter of Dale, 1614', in *Pilgrimes*, XIX, pp. 102–08; *Smith's Works*, II, pp. 246–47.

[35] For Roanoke see 'Virginias Verger', in *Pilgrimes*, XIX, pp. 228–29; and see below, pp. 212–13.

[36] Jennings, *Invasion.*

[37] J. H. Elliott, *Britain and Spain in America: Colonists and Colonized*, The Stenton Lecture, University of Reading, 1994, pp. 8–12; Gary B. Nash, 'The Hidden History of Mestizo America', in *Journal of American History*, LXXXII (1995), pp. 941–64; Strachey, *Historie*, p. 93.

favoured by Captain John Smith, whose life she (allegedly) had saved from her father's wrath. She was subsequently reintegrated into Indian life, but in 1613 was captured by Captain Argall who, with his superior Sir Thomas Dale, hoped to exchange her for English hostages and weapons in Powhatan's possession. When negotiations failed, Pocahontas made herself at home with the English, initially at Jamestown and later at Henrico, where she received religious instruction from Alexander Whitaker. It was probably there she met Rolfe, 'an honest gentleman and of good behaviour', who, 'long before' the autumn of 1613, 'had been in love with Pochahontas and she with him'. Then Rolfe, in soliciting Dale's consent to a marriage, detailed the agony he had suffered before he satisfied himself that the union would enjoy God's blessing. Rolfe's letter is so heavily theological that it was possibly inspired by Whitaker, and he pronounced a desire to marry 'for the good of the plantation, the honour of our country, for the glory of God, for mine own salvation, and for the converting to the true knowledge of God and Jesus Christ an unbelieving creature, namely Pochahontas'.[38] Dale and Powhatan both gave their consent, and the marriage, celebrated at Jamestown in April 1614, fostered better trading relations with the natives. Rolfe was gratified by this outcome and later, after he had returned to Virginia from England (where Pocahontas had died after she had borne a son), he penned an idealized portrait of the state of Virginia, which he attributed to better relations with the native population, adding that he saw:

> no small hope by piety, clemency, courtesy and civil demeanour . . . to convert . . . 1000s of poor, wretched and misbelieving people, on whose faces a good Christian cannot look without sorrow, pity and commiseration seeing they bear the image of our heavenly creator and we and they come from one and the same mould.[39]

Such optimism was not unique, and Rolfe's was but one of several intermarriages contemplated. Again in 1614, soon after Pocahontas and Rolfe had departed for England, Governor Dale sought to marry Powhatan's youngest daughter, 'because being now one people and he [Dale] desirous for ever to dwell in his [Powhatan's] country he conceived there could not be a truer assistance of peace and friendship than in such a natural bond of an united union'.[40] This held no appeal for Powhatan, and the grand accommodation then cherished by Dale, Whitaker, and Rolfe was abandoned. Further evidence of what was intended comes from the reference to the two women who had accompanied Pocahontas to England. They had been sent there 'to be married to some [that] would have them, that after they were converted and had children they might be sent to their

[38] *Smith's Works*, II, pp. 245–46; the fullest version of Rolfe's letter is in the Bodleian Library, Ashmole MSS, 830.

[39] John Rolfe, 'A True Relation of the State of Virginia [1616 or 1617]', British Library, Royal MSS, 18. A xi, ff. 1–10.

[40] *Smith's Works*, II, pp. 248–50.

country and kindred to civilize them'. This came to nothing, and it was only in Bermuda, on the return voyage, that 'the marriage of one of the Virginia maids was consummated with a husband fit for her'.[41] If this was the final episode, attempts may have been under way from the moment of first contact in the Chesapeake to promote reform through intermarriage. This is suggested by the charge, denied by Captain Smith, that he had 'calculated he had the savages in such subjection, he would have made him[self] king by marrying Pochahontas'.[42]

Any such formal association—whether through treaty or marriage—between the societies of the natives and the newcomers would have been cultivated by the English as a preliminary to the gradual conversion of the Indians to English civil and religious standards. Another prerequisite to conversion was surmounting the language barrier, and this problem was also taken seriously by all English leaders of expeditions.

Early observers assumed that Amerindian and European languages stemmed from a common linguistic source, and that communication would become possible once the linguistic stemma of native languages was identified. Thus, Strachey speculated that Indians were a Britonic people because their language admitted 'much and many words, both of places and names of many creatures, which have the accents and Welsh significations'.[43] This notion was so widely shared that one Wynne, a Welshman, was in 1608 appointed interpreter for 'the people of Monacan', who 'spoke a far different language from the subjects of Powhatan, their pronunciations being very like Welsh'.[44] Settlers in New England detected residues of Greek and Latin in the language spoken by the natives there. While these did not tempt Thomas Morton to address Indians in Latin, they did encourage him to challenge the supposed Tartarian ancestry of the Indians and to posit 'that the originals of the natives of New England may be well conjectured to be from the scattered Trojans after such time as Brutus departed from Latium'.[45]

Once they accepted that there was no short cut to conversation between English and Indians, English colonizers took steps to train interpreters. The readiest expedient was to send boys to live among the Indians and thus learn to speak their language. Those selected seem, like Henry Spelman, to have resented being abandoned to Powhatan. However, Spelman proved himself an apt pupil and, despite a sojourn in Europe, he continued to serve as an interpreter for the colony until 1618.[46] When Spelman first went to live with Powhatan he found another English, Thomas Savage, already there, who like Spelman experienced difficulty in procuring his release, presumably because their expertise made interpreters

[41] Ibid., pp. 284–86. [42] Ibid., pp. 274–75. [43] Strachey, *Historie*, p. 11.
[44] Barbour, *Jamestown Voyages*, I, pp. 245–46. [45] Morton, *New England Canaan*, pp. 128–29.
[46] *Smith's Works*, II, p. 257.

equally valuable to the Indians and the English.[47] Savage was later killed by the Indians, but neither was he ever fully trusted by his own countrymen, possibly because, being able to mediate between two worlds, he was suspected of not owing his full loyalty to either. Perhaps it was to Savage that Captain Smith referred when he criticized the sending of 'boys amongst them to learn their language', both because 'they return worse than they went' and because he saw 'no probability by this course to draw them [the Indians] to goodness'.[48] Despite Smith's misgivings, the English continued to train interpreters, principally for commercial and political reasons, but also out of a concern to reform the natives. These efforts persisted in Virginia to the very eve of the 1622 massacre, when the Indians returned to 'his master' Captain Hamor one Browne, 'who then to learn the language lived among the Warrascoyacks'.[49]

Language acquisition was not a one-way process, and the English encouraged Amerindian pupils to live with them and learn English. Pocahontas and her maids presumably learnt English as well as religion from Whitaker, and such opportunities had been available to individual Indians from the earliest point of contact with the English in all settlements. It was reported from the Gosnold expedition of 1602 to the coast of New England that the Indians there 'pronounced our language with great facility', which suggests they were encouraged to speak English.[50] Some Amerindians were persuaded to accompany voyagers to England, while the unscrupulous kidnapped them. Such Indians were sometimes exhibited as curiosities, as, for example, Epenew who, 'being a man of so great a stature, he was showed up and down London for money as a wonder'. None the less, he mastered English, and used his knowledge to take revenge on his captors by spreading the news 'in Plymouth and the west' that he knew of the existence of gold in America, 'thus to get home, seeing they kept him a prisoner'.[51] Another Indian, Sakaweston, was captured by Captain Edward Harlow and 'lived many years in England' until he went as 'a soldier to the wars of Bohemia',[52] while another 'Pethagorian Indian', who had also fought in the Thirty Years War, became a settler in Ireland under the name John Fortune, and had the misfortune to be mistaken for an English Protestant by Irish Catholic insurgents in the rising of 1641.[53] Not all Indians who went to England were treated harshly. For example, John Slanie, a 'merchant in Cornhill', kept an Indian in his house and 'taught him English'.[54] We can even trace the political as well as the linguistic progress of an Indian in the story of Assocomoit who was on the *Richard*, under the captaincy of Henry Challon, when in 1606 it ran foul of the Spanish *flota*. Assocomoit was badly

[47] Ibid., p. 248.
[48] Ibid., p. 286.
[49] *Pilgrimes*, XI, p. 158.
[50] Ibid., XVIII, pp. 317–18.
[51] *Smith's Works*, II, p. 403.
[52] Ibid., p. 399.
[53] Trinity College, Dublin, MSS, 215, ff. 322, 358.
[54] *Pilgrimes*, XIX, p. 303.

injured when resisting the boarding but still shouted 'King James, King James, King James his ship', thus eliciting the wry comment of the narrator that this proved 'King James his name [was] little respected by Spaniards'.[55]

More plentiful opportunities were available to Native Americans to learn English within the white settlements of colonial British America. The 'praying Indians' of New England are the best known of those who converted to English ways, and we can presume that Alexander Whitaker and his associates in Virginia similarly invited Indians to live with them. We have already noted Strachey's description of Indians' attendance at religious services, and he mentioned one 'Kempis an Indian' who, after one year's residence at Jamestown, spoke English, went to church, and was 'made much of by the Lord General'.[56] Such associations continued to receive official encouragement in Virginia until 1622, and the Assembly of 1619 had specifically directed 'each town, city, borough and particular plantation' to 'obtain . . . by just means a certain number of the natives children to be educated by them in true religion and civil course of life'; this being 'a surer foundation of the conversion of the Indians to Christian religion'.[57] Many acquiesced and invited Indians among them, but this relaxed attitude was ultimately held responsible for the 1622 'massacre' in Virginia. Thereafter all such associations were prohibited in the Chesapeake, thus disregarding the fact that warning of the attack had been given by 'an infidel converted to Christianity' who 'belonged to one Perry', but was 'living in the house of one Pace' who 'had used him as a son'.[58]

Besides their efforts to have English and Indians trained as interpreters, the more educated colonists strove themselves to master the native languages, and to provide teaching aids for future settlers. Hariot, as always, led the way, and his example was followed by Captain Smith and Strachey.[59] What were initially word-lists of Algonquian speech were expanded to become mini-dictionaries, and some phrases that were likely to recur in everyday interactions with the Indians were also included in these compilations. In New England it was no different. A word-list was assembled by James Rosier, who was associated with Bartholomew Gosnold's expedition of 1605.[60] The 'small nomenclator' compiled by William Wood would have facilitated complex conversation because it included contextualized phrases as well as words, thus belying Wood's claim that it would appeal only to those

[55] David B. Quinn and Alison M. Quinn, eds., *The English New England Voyages* (hereafter *New England Voyages*) (London, 1983), p. 368.

[56] Strachey, *Historie*, p. 61.

[57] L. G. Tyler, ed., *Narratives of Early Virginia, 1606–25* (New York, 1907), p. 264.

[58] *Pilgrimes*, XIX, pp. 163, 167.

[59] *Smith's Works*, I, p. 139, n. 3; I, pp. 136–39; III, pp. 511–13; Strachey, *Historie*, pp. 174–207; David B. Quinn, ed., *The Roanoke Voyages, 1584–90*, 2 vols. (Cambridge, 1955), II, pp. 873–900.

[60] *New England Voyages*, pp. 481–93; see also Vivian Salmon, 'Missionary Linguistics in Seventeenth Century Ireland and a North American Analogy', *Historiographica Linguistica*, XII (1985), pp. 321–49.

wanting 'to hear some of the natives' language' as a guide to establishing 'to what language it is most inclining'.[61] Roger Williams's *A Key into the Language of America* was more ambitious and functional than anything previously published. He claimed originality for his *Key* because it concerned 'Native Language' as well as customs, and would consequently facilitate the preaching of the word and the conversion of those who would 'enjoy God's grace to true religion'. With his book colonists would be able 'to converse with thousands of natives all over the country', so 'by that converse it may please the Father of mercies to spread civility (and in his own most holy season) Christianity'.

Williams's method was to group words and phrases under headings that related to a particular cultural context, and in both his suggested conversations and descriptions of their life he indicated that he held the Indians in relatively high esteem. In the chapter devoted to religion, Williams identified points of doctrinal contention between natives and Christians, and constructed simple conversations suited to convincing Indians of the truth. Williams's *Key* might therefore be regarded both as a necessary aid to and a progression towards John Eliot's 1646 translation of the Bible. It was Williams's belief, and presumably also Eliot's, that once Indians were informed of the truth they would stand better hope of salvation than Jews, Turks, and 'the Christian false' who had persistently disregarded revealed truth.[62]

Historians have traditionally identified Puritans such as Williams and Eliot as exceptional figures, even freaks,[63] and have portrayed New England settlers as introverted seekers after personal salvation rather than missionaries concerned with the reform of Amerindians. Historians have also frequently contrasted the supposedly spiritually motivated New Englanders with the materialistic settlers of the Chesapeake who, they suggest, were indifferent to religion and had no moral scruples about destroying native institutions and peoples whenever these stood in the way of profit. The evidence now cited suggests that Eliot and Williams were doing no more than carrying the aims and ambitions of the promoters and propagandists of all English colonization to their culmination by seeking to accommodate the native population within an English spiritual and civil community. Recent publications on both New England and the Chesapeake also reject the polarity that was once thought to exist between the ambitions and actions of English settlers in these two areas, while some studies show that Puritan colonization could be driven as much by profit as that promoted by any other English

[61] Wood, *New England's Prospect*, pp. 116–28.

[62] Roger Williams, *A Key into the Language of America* [1643], ed. John Teunissen and Evelyn Hinz (Detroit, 1973), pp. 83–84, 99, 189–200.

[63] G. R. Elton, 'Contentment and Discontent on the Eve of Colonization', in David B. Quinn, ed., *Early Maryland in a Wider World* (Detroit, 1982), pp. 105–18.

colonists.[64] What we have seen here of the Chesapeake indicates that Whitaker was every bit as solicitous as Williams, Eliot, and Winslow for the spiritual and material welfare of Amerindians, and it is probable that Whitaker also proffered advice, that has not survived, on the reform of the natives. Whitaker was only one of several clergymen active in the Chesapeake during the early years of settlement, and the sincerity of the Virginia Company in recruiting suitable clergy for the colony was shown by their choice of Richard Hakluyt to serve there, even if Hakluyt nominated Robert Hunt as his proxy.[65]

In the Chesapeake these positive advances were interrupted by the 1622 massacre. Before then, the sponsors' concern had been to surpass the Spaniards, both in converting the Amerindians to Christianity and in facilitating the gradual assimilation of the people into civil society. The curiosity of the English about the cultures of Amerindians, and their expressed commitment to moderate reform, are all the more remarkable when we consider that these were the years (1580s–1630s) when English attitudes towards the Irish were most negative. In thus crediting the English organizers of colonization with a generous outlook, we must not suppose that all, or indeed many, English thought similarly about America or its population. The reality was that, before the 1630s, the English colonies in America hardly impinged upon the consciousness of most English people. The sermons that marked the launch of the Virginia Company are proof, not of widespread interest, but of the desperate need for publicity that would attract migrants and investment.[66] Moreover, it is significant that contemporaneous migration to and investment in Irish plantations probably exceeded that in all the American colonies combined,[67] yet there were few sermons and pamphlets employed to promote colonization there. Contrariwise, when British settlement in Ireland was challenged by native insurrection in 1641 there was a deluge of English printed propaganda decrying the event, while only a trickle of pamphlets condemned the various Indian attacks upon English colonists in America. Thus, while England's involvement with Ireland was of passive concern to most English people, it could be brought rapidly to the forefront of public attention when

[64] John Frederick Martin, *Profits in the Wilderness: Entrepreneurship and the Founding of New England Towns in the Seventeenth Century* (Chapel Hill, NC, 1992); James Horn, *Adapting to a New World: English Society in the Seventeenth-Century Chesapeake* (Chapel Hill, NC, 1994); Kupperman, *Providence Island*; Stephen Innes, *Creating the Commonwealth: The Economic Culture of Puritan New England* (New York, 1995).

[65] *Smith's Works*, III, p. 296.

[66] Extracts of sermons appear in Alexander Brown, *The Genesis of the United States*, 2 vols. (Boston, 1890), and are analysed in Loren Pennington, 'The Amerindian in English Promotional Literature, 1575–1625', and John Parker, 'Religion and the Virginia Colony, 1609–10', both in *Westward Enterprise*, pp. 175–94, 245–70; see also Strachey, *Historie*, p. 3.

[67] Nicholas Canny, 'English Migration', in Canny, ed., *Europeans on the Move: Studies on European Migration, 1500–1800* (Oxford, 1994), pp. 39–75.

England's interest there was challenged, and thousands of people, in Scotland as well as England, could be counted on to assist militarily or financially to restore authority there.[68] Colonies in America never enjoyed a similar surge of enthusiasm because most British people were ignorant of their existence or indifferent to their plight.

Another disappointment for English promoters of colonization in America was their failure to infuse those who did become involved with the missionary zeal of the sponsors. There is plentiful evidence from all English colonies that the recruits did not match the expectations of the promoters. Those in authority in the Chesapeake were shocked by the readiness with which their subordinates, women as well as men, would flee the settlement to live with the Amerindians.[69] There are fewer references from the northerly colonies of people 'going native', but there was much criticism of the unruliness of the common settlers in all areas, and their avarice and indiscipline was held responsible for provoking native attacks, thus defeating the moral purpose of colonization. Attacks brought counter-attacks, because the leaders of British settlement in all places, including Ireland, resolved that natives who rebelled bore full responsibility for their actions and that their societies would be destroyed: the first chilling example in New England being the English massacre of Pequot Indians in 1637. The ease with which English promoters of colonization could shift from being advocates of gradual assimilation to becoming angels of revenge is not surprising when we consider that the settlers must always have felt vulnerable because they were small in number in relation to the native population. Moreover, their accommodationist position ran counter to accepted English, and indeed European, opinion that civilization had first been achieved and subsequently sustained by force, so legitimations for stern action came readily to mind.[70]

Another fact which explains the rapidity with which the assimilationists' view could be abandoned is that their position had always been contested by pragmatists who valued North America because its resources could be exploited for England's benefit.[71] Some hoped that entrepreneurs from Scotland and Ireland might share the risks and the spoils, and these envisioned a British North Atlantic World that would rival New Spain. This vision too was bold and novel, but it offered no place for natives other than those who would become immediate participants in an English-

[68] John Wilson, ed., *Buckingham Contributions for Ireland, 1642* (Buckingham Record Society, No. 21, 1983).

[69] Nicholas Canny, 'The Permissive Frontier', in *Westward Enterprise*, pp. 17–44.

[70] This was repeatedly stated in the writings of Edmund Spenser, which have been analysed and contextualized in chap. 1 of Nicholas Canny, *Ireland in the English Colonial System* (Oxford, forthcoming); for sixteenth-century Spanish notions on the role of charismatic leaders in advancing primitive peoples towards civility, see Pagden, *Fall of Natural Man*, pp. 57–108, 140–43.

[71] Helgerson, *Forms of Nationhood*, pp. 151–91.

dominated Atlantic economy.[72] Like the Irish of this same period, the Amerindians would be forced to choose between becoming immediately Anglicized and Protestant or conceding control of their lands to settlers.

A shift from an accommodationist to a pragmatic attitude can be traced in the person of Henry Challon, who we last encountered in 1606 in the company of Assocomoit and another Indian who were to have guided him along the New England coast.[73] The boarding of his ship by Spaniards put an end to this prospect, and those crew who survived, including the two Indians, were brought to Spain, where several were executed. Challon procured his own release and broke bail,[74] later to appear as a consultant to the London companies contemplating investment in Irish plantations. He favoured an Irish investment, but his appraisal was based on the potential of the south-west coast rather than that of Ulster where a plantation was under way. The south-west attracted him because it lay on the English route to America, and Challon recommended the establishment of a strong fort and a series of interlinked corporate towns to supply England's military and naval requirements in both Ireland and the Atlantic. This base would also become an entrepôt from which to transport the food and textiles of Ireland to the various English settlements in the Atlantic, and through which the commodities of the Atlantic might be re-exported to England. This development, he contended, would rid the Atlantic of pirates who found shelter on that coast, would deprive the French of the Irish victuals and woollen goods which they exported to *Nova Francia* in exchange for such 'vain trifles' as 'wines, glasses, ornaments of pride and baby toys', and would provide a secure base for English 'sword men and ancient servitors of best spirits', who would displace the parasitic 'goose quill men' then dominating patronage and privilege. The soldiers, he expected, would prove their worth by challenging Spain's monopoly in the South Atlantic, thus opening the way for English merchants. The most compelling precedent cited by Challon was that of 'the Hollanders', who had grown rich and powerful through 'trade and navigation, by us neglected, although indeed it be the only means that truly enricheth all flourishing estates'.

Challon, therefore, had indeed absorbed the Atlantic into his world view, but no mention was made of Native Americans, despite Challon's earlier dependence upon two of them. Moreover, America was portrayed as a place open for exploitation by English merchants and soldiers, and English settlement was considered relevant only to the extent that it was necessary to a trading empire.[75] The ideas

[72] Nicholas Canny, *Kingdom and Colony: Ireland and the Atlantic World, 1566–1800* (Baltimore, 1988), pp. 31–68; Gillian Cell, *English Enterprise in Newfoundland* (Toronto, 1969); Joyce Lorimer, ed., *English and Irish Settlement on the River Amazon* (London, 1989).

[73] *New England Voyages*, p. 364.

[74] Ibid., pp. 355–75.

[75] Henery Challons, 'A View of the Irish Proceedings', Edinburgh, Scottish Record Office, RH 15/91/33.

adumbrated by Challon were to be further elaborated by subsequent writers and quickly became the dominant English view. These writings reveal how English people did, after a considerable interval, enlarge their geographic vision to take account of both the Atlantic Ocean and the American continent, but in doing so they narrowed their ethnographic vision to the point where they could ignore the existence of a native population and the moral problems they created.

This pragmatic view did not immediately become the dominant one, but the two coexisted uneasily until the sequence of Indian uprisings discredited the accommodationist view and made way for the ascendancy of its rival; the shift became easier after formal peace with Spain released Englishmen from moral competition with their Spanish rivals. Even then the promoters of English colonization in the Atlantic could not admit that their endeavours were without a reform purpose. The Puritan sponsors of the Providence Island Company convinced themselves that the natives of Nicaragua would immediately become Protestants once the English achieved victory over the hated Spaniards, and Cromwell's Western Design against the Spanish possessions in the Caribbean was partly justified by the belief that the attack was occurring at the moment assigned by God for the conversion of all humanity.[76] Subsequently, the leaders of all English colonial ventures advanced a reform purpose for their efforts in America, and English government officials could, when it suited their purpose (even in the eighteenth century), enter into political alliances with Amerindian tribes which were described as nations and their rulers as kings.[77] However, neither Puritans, nor Cromwell, nor later English colonizers and officials considered seriously how the conversion of Amerindians would be effected. Reform and conversion now usually became issues that concerned only exceptional divines, such as those in New England in the 1640s.

The endeavours of the early New England clergy as translators are remarkable; but they are also pathetic, because they had only just translated the Bible and supporting texts into a local Algonquian dialect, and trained a cohort of Indians to preach to the Indians in their own language, when the idea of conversion was discarded as irrelevant by their betters.[78] When they undertook their work of

[76] Kupperman, *Providence Island*, pp. 348–55; David Armitage, 'The Cromwellian Protectorate and the Languages of Empire', *Historical Journal*, XXXV (1992), pp. 531–55.

[77] I am grateful to Linda Colley for advice on this point, and see Eric Hinderaker, 'The "Four Indian Kings" and the Imaginative Construction of the First British Empire', in *WMQ*, Third Series, LII (1996), pp. 487–526.

[78] Besides the New and Old Testaments, John Eliot and his associates translated a catechism, and theological works by such authors as Lewis Bayly, Bishop of Bangor, and Richard Baxter; I consulted the extensive collection of this material at Yale University, Beinecke Library. See also Edward Winslow, *The Glorious Progress of the Gospel amongst the Indians* (London, 1649); John Eliot, *A Brief Narrative of the Progress of the Gospel... in New England... 1670* (London, 1671).

education and translation, John Eliot, Edward Winslow and others were satisfied that 'those poor Indians of America', crying out for the truth of the Gospel, were the lost tribes of Israel who 'afterwards filled that vast and long unknown country of America'.[79] They also expected that their work would be supported by the 'sachems' [chiefs], but, after exposure to European disease and English covetousness had taken their toll among the natives, they were forced to accept that they were welcome by the Indians only as protectors from rapacious English settlers. Their statements on the progress of reform are proof principally of their self-delusion, and they show that their converts were demoralized people who could endure economically only if given menial employment by the settlers. The most blatant acknowledgement of their failure to achieve the accommodation of a native society within an English-dominated world was included in the address to King Charles II in the 1663 edition of John Eliot's translation of the Bible. Here the King was congratulated on being the first European monarch to receive the Bible in a language 'from this American world, or from any parts so remote from Europe as these are', and, in a passage borrowed from Hakluyt, he was reminded that the souls that would be saved were altogether more valuable than the gold and silver which was the only 'fruit and end' of the 'discoveries and plantations' of the Spaniards. However, those to be converted were no longer represented as the noble, self-assured people of the early encounter, but rather:

> a lost people, as remote from knowledge and civility, much more from Christianity, as they were from all knowing civil and Christian nations; a people without law, without letters, without riches, or means to procure any such thing; a people that are deep in darkness, and in the shadow of death, as (we think) any since the creation.[80]

They were therefore a people destined to become victims of England's developing trading empire on the Atlantic, because they were superfluous to its requirements.

[79] Winslow, *Glorious Progress.*

[80] *The Holy Bible... Translated into the Indian Language and Ordered to be Printed by the Commissioners of the United Colonies in New England...* (Cambridge, 1663), preface to Charles II.

Select Bibliography

Charles M. Andrews, *The Colonial Period of American History*, 4 vols. (New Haven, 1934–38).

Kenneth R. Andrews, *Trade, Plunder and Settlement: Maritime Enterprise and the Genesis of the British Empire, 1480–1630* (Cambridge, 1984).

James Axtell, *The European and the Indian: Essays in the Ethnohistory of Colonial North America* (Oxford, 1981).

Philip L. Barbour, ed., *The Complete Works of Captain John Smith, 1580–1631*, 3 vols. (Chapel Hill, NC, 1986).

ROBERT BRENNER, *Merchants and Revolution: Commercial Change, Political Conflict, and London's Overseas Traders, 1550–1643* (Princeton, 1993).

NICHOLAS CANNY, ed., *Europeans on the Move: Studies on European Migration, 1500–1800* (Oxford, 1994).

J. H. ELLIOTT, *The Old World and the New, 1492–1650* (Cambridge, 1970).

STEPHEN GREENBLATT, *Marvelous Possessions: The Wonder of the New World* (Oxford, 1991).

RICHARD HAKLUYT [the younger], *The Principall Navigations, Voyages and Discoveries of the English Nation*, 12 vols. (1589; Glasgow, 1903–05).

JAMES HORN, *Adapting to a New World: English Society in the Seventeenth-Century Chesapeake* (Chapel Hill, NC, 1974).

PAUL HULTON and DAVID B. QUINN, *The American Drawings of John White*, 2 vols. (London, 1964).

FRANCIS JENNINGS, *The Invasion of America: Indians, Colonialism and the Cant of Conquest* (Chapel Hill, NC, 1975).

KAREN ORDAHL KUPPERMAN, *Providence Island, 1630–41: The Other Puritan Colony* (Cambridge, 1994).

PERRY MILLER, *The New England Mind: The Seventeenth Century* (Boston, 1939).

EDMUND S. MORGAN, *American Slavery: American Freedom: The Ordeal of Colonial Virginia* (New York, 1975).

SAMUEL ELIOT MORRISON, *The European Discovery of America: The Northern Voyages, A.D. 500–1600* (New York, 1971).

SAMUEL PURCHAS, *Hakluytus Posthumus or Purchas his Pilgrimes. Containing a History of the World in Sea Voyages and Land Travells by Englishmen and Others*, 20 vols. (Glasgow, 1905).

DAVID B. QUINN, *North America From Earliest Discovery to First Settlements: The Norse Voyages to 1612* (New York, 1977).

—— with the assistance of Alison Quinn and Susan Hillier, eds., *New American World: A Documentary History of North America to 1612*, 5 vols. (New York, 1979).

J. HOLLAND ROSE, A. P. NEWTON, and E. A. BENIANS, eds., *The Cambridge History of the British Empire*, Vol. I. (Cambridge, 1929).

8

Tobacco Colonies: The Shaping of English Society in the Seventeenth-Century Chesapeake

JAMES HORN

English society in the Chesapeake originated with the establishment of a fortified settlement at Jamestown, Virginia, in 1607 and, a generation later, the foundation of Lord Baltimore's colony at St Mary's City, Maryland, in 1634. Contemporaries were unimpressed by either. From controversies and scandals during the early years, complaints about over-dependence on the pernicious staple, tobacco, to attacks on the base character of settlers and absence of civil society, there was seemingly little to be said in favour of the tobacco colonies. Such were the 'odiums and cruell slanders cast on those two famous Countries of Virginia and Maryland', John Hammond wrote in 1656, that they 'are in danger to moulder away, and come in time to nothing . . .'[1] The failings of early Chesapeake society have been underscored by a series of comparisons with New England. Stable, consensual societies in the North have been contrasted to violent, chaotic societies in the South; long life and large families in New England to short lives and broken families in Virginia; the profound importance of religion in the Bible Commonwealth to irreligion and precocious secularism along the tobacco coast; small independent farmers relying on family labour in New England to plantation agriculture and slave labour along the Bay. Whereas the northern colonies in many important respects approximated Old World society in the New, the Chesapeake evolved as a grotesque imitation.

Recently historians have begun to revise this unflattering picture of life along the Bay. Partly as a consequence of intensive studies of local society and partly owing to shifts in perspective, the achievements of English colonists in adapting to uncertain conditions in the Chesapeake have received of late more attention than their shortcomings. Emphasis has been given to the remarkable development of Virginia and Maryland society after the difficult early years, in particular to the success of the tobacco industry, which secured the economic fortunes of the two

[1] 'Leah and Rachel, or, The Two Fruitfull Sisters Virginia and Mary-land, by John Hammond, 1656', in Clayton Colman Hall, ed., *Narratives of Early Maryland, 1633–1684* (New York, 1910), p. 283.

colonies, and to the adoption of a range of English institutions and procedures (suitably adapted) which established an acceptable basis for government at provincial and local levels.[2] In creating governing institutions, temporal and spiritual, in their efforts to establish orderly society at local and provincial levels, and in their assumptions about the proper relationship between rulers and ruled, settlers looked to England for guidance and inspiration. Conventional attitudes about the social order, the locus of political power, hierarchy, government, justice, property, marriage, the family, gender relations, and religion left immigrants in no doubt that they had arrived in 'English ground in America'.

First Contacts

The central natural feature of Virginia and Maryland is the Chesapeake Bay: a massive drowned river valley, 5 to 20 miles across and 195 miles long (Map 8.1), which provided a magnificent harbour for ocean-going vessels and was navigable nearly its whole length. Four major rivers—the James, York, Rappahannock, and Potomac—have carved the Western Shore into a series of peninsulas stretching into the Bay, while the entire region is characterized by innumerable tributaries, creeks, tidal marshes, and small islands strewn along the Bayside and Atlantic coast. Colonists were impressed by the scale and extensiveness of waterways. The James was described as 'one of the famousest Rivers that ever was found by any Christian, it ebbes and flowes a hundred and threescore miles where ships of great burthen may harbour in saftie'. Rivers and the long coastline opened up the region for settlement and allowed relatively quick, easy, and cheap transportation throughout the Tidewater, the potential benefits of which were not lost on settlers and merchants familiar with the advantages of river and coastal traffic in England.[3]

Aside from rivers and the Bay itself, the other natural feature frequently commented on by immigrants was the richness and diversity of woodlands. One traveller thought the Virginia shore looked 'like a forest standing in water', and the Revd Hugh Jones found Maryland 'Very Woody like one continued forest'. A rich variety of trees—pines, hickories, white oaks, cedars, cypress, poplars, black walnuts, and maples—spread over the land in a seemingly endless sweep of forest that stretched from the littoral to the Blue Ridge Mountains. Settlers entered a region of generally low relief, rarely above a few hundred feet, except in the interior where the coastal plain gradually rises to the higher elevations of the piedmont and mountains beyond. On the Western Shore, the ridges or 'necks' that form the

[2] The recent historiography of the early Chesapeake is summarized in Lois Green Carr, Philip D. Morgan, and Jean B. Russo, eds., *Colonial Chesapeake Society* (Chapel Hill, NC, 1988), pp. 1–46.

[3] Philip L. Barbour, ed., *The Jamestown Voyages under the First Charter, 1606–1609*, 2 vols. (London, 1969), I, p. 141.

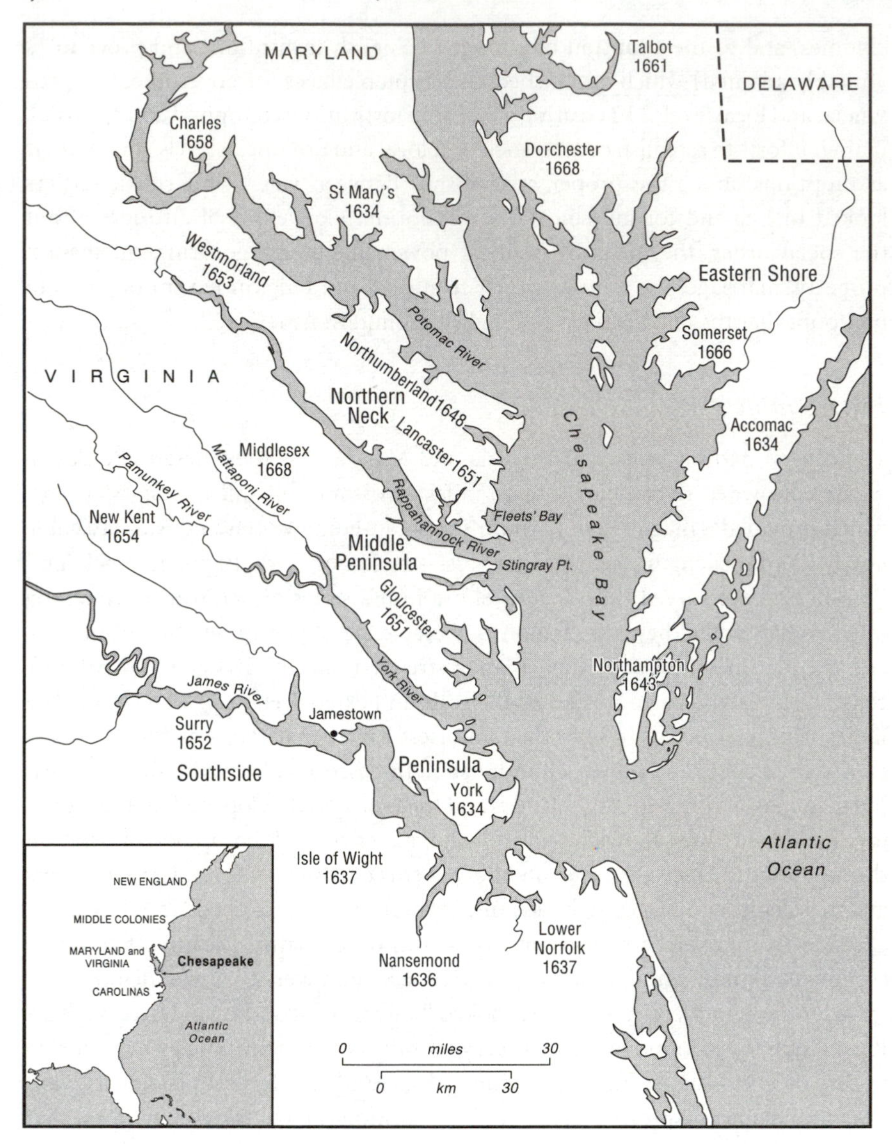

MAP 8.1. The Chesapeake in the Seventeenth Century

spines of peninsulas give the landscape a gently rolling quality of 'pleasant plaine hils and fertle valleyes', in contrast to the Eastern Shore which is mostly flat.[4]

[4] 'Report of the Journey of Francis Louis Michel from Berne, Switzerland to Virginia, October 2, 1701–December 1, 1702', *Virginia Magazine of History and Biography* (hereafter *VMHB*), XXIV (1916), p. 16; 'Part of a Letter from the Rev. Mr Hugh Jones to the Rev. Dr. Benjamin Woodruff, F.R.S., concerning

An initial response, frequently invoked in propaganda literature, was the emphasis given to abundance. A letter sent to the colony's sponsors in London two months after arrival expressed the belief, with fashionable exaggeration, that the 'land would Flowe with milke and honey so seconded by your carefull wisdomes and bountifull handes...' Alexander Whitaker considered Virginia 'a place beautified by God, with all the ornaments of nature, and enriched with his earthly treasures...' Meadows and woodlands abounded with game, rivers teemed with fish, and the skies darkened under huge flocks of birds. Abundance and plenty, a cornucopia of earthly delights, Virginia seemed to offer 'infinite riches', as in the first creation.[5]

But if the colony was latent with potential it nevertheless required, in the more sober judgement of Captain John Smith, to be 'inhabited by industrious people'.[6] The settlement was not intended as a temporary trading post, a conduit for trade with the interior, or merely as a strategic base of operations against Spanish shipping and possessions. In these respects, early Virginia was envisioned as a very different type of enterprise from those of commercial companies in Africa and Asia, where trade, not colonization, was the imperative. Following an abortive attempt to plant a colony at Roanoke (off the coast of present-day North Carolina) twenty years earlier, and in the context of the writings of a small group of influential men—Sir George Peckham, Christopher Carleill, and the two Richard Hakluyts—who emphasized the long-term benefits of colonization, Virginia was to be established as a permanent presence in the New World, peopled by English settlers whose endeavours would bring prosperity and honour to the colony and nation as well as handsome returns to investors.

These arguments were closely related to the theme of 'improvement', a trend in English political economy that developed in the second half of the sixteenth century but which was considerably more influential by the 1640s.[7] Improvement was a guiding principle behind English settlement in the early Chesapeake. Efforts to create a diversified economy in Virginia, based on the cultivation of a variety of new crops and the development of industries, were a direct consequence of similar economic experiments at home. Hemp and flax, dye crops, tobacco, vines, and mulberry trees for silk production, enthusiastically promoted by English projectors, had an equally enthusiastic reception amongst investors in colonial ventures. American colonies were testing grounds for all sorts of new projects being tried

Several Observables in Maryland', Jan. 23, 1698 [1699], LBC II (2), p. 247, Royal Society Archives, London; Philip L. Barbour, ed., *The Complete Works of Captain John Smith (1580–1631)*, 3 vols. (Chapel Hill, NC, 1986), I, p. 145.

[5] Barbour, ed., *Jamestown Voyages*, I, p. 79; Samuel Purchas, *Hakluytus Posthumus, or Purchas His Pilgrimes...*, 20 vols. (Glasgow, 1906), XIX, pp. 108, 112.

[6] Barbour, ed., *Complete Works*, II, p. 101. [7] See above, pp. 41–46.

simultaneously in the parent country. In addition, products traditionally imported into England from Europe and Asia could instead be procured at much lower cost from the colonies. Richard Hakluyt the younger considered that America 'will yelde unto us all the commodities of Europe, Affrica, and Asia, as far as wee were wonte to travell, and supply the wantes of all our decayed trades'. The northern parts would supply timber, masts, clapboard, pitch, tar, cordage, and naval supplies, and the southern parts wine, silk, fruits, oil, sugar, and salt.[8] From an English perspective, the entire eastern seaboard was perceived as a vast marginal expanse of forest and fen ripe for development.

If exploitation of natural riches was the ideal, the reality proved different. The initial phase of settlement, under the aegis of the Virginia Company of London, from first contact in 1607 to the mid-1620s, was a financial disaster. A combination of disease and 'meere famine' ravaged early settlers and brought the colony to the edge of extinction. Attempts to find a passage to the East and locate gold deposits were fruitless, and shipments of a range of exports—glass, pitch, tar, potash, clapboards, sassafras, and iron—were wholly inadequate to meet the costs of the colony. As losses of men and money mounted, factional disputes between leaders in Virginia, mirrored by struggles between financial backers in London, further weakened the colony. Sporadic Anglo-Indian hostilities led to a morale-sapping haemorrhage of colonists' already depleted resources and were a steady drain on colonists' material and human resources.[9] Unlike the Spanish *conquista* in Central and South America, English adventurers found little of apparent worth in their new world: no gold, silver, or precious minerals, no convenient access to the orient, and no advanced Indian civilizations which could be readily plundered.

Early explorations of the Bay confirmed the English had entered a populous land (see Map 15.1). Recent estimates suggest that approximately 13,000–22,000 Algonquian Indians lived in the Virginia Tidewater at the time of contact, scattered throughout the region in about 150 villages. In addition, the Susquehannocks were located along the river that bears their name in northern Maryland, and Iroquoian tribes (Nottoways and Meherrins) inhabited large areas of the Southside below the Appomattox River down to the Virginia–North Carolina border. Beyond the fall line, in the foothills of the mountains, were the powerful Siouan-speaking peoples of the Mannahoacs and Monacans, 'who owe no submission to Pawatan [Powhatan]'.[10]

[8] E. G. R. Taylor, ed., *The Original Writings and Correspondence of the Two Richard Hakluyts*, 2 vols. (London, 1935), II, pp. 211, 327–35, 347.

[9] Edmund S. Morgan, *American Slavery, American Freedom: The Ordeal of Colonial Virginia* (New York, 1975), pp. 71–91.

[10] Helen C. Rountree, *The Powhatan Indians of Virginia: Their Traditional Culture* (Norman, Okla., 1989), p. 15; for the names 'Powhatan' and 'Pocahontas', see above, p. 157, n. 31.

The reactions of English colonists to local tribes were shaped largely by an overwhelming sense of their own cultural superiority, mediated by the exigencies of conditions encountered. After an attempt to promote assimilation from a position of dominance,[11] stereotypes of Indians as savage, barbarous, uncivilized, and ungodly were called up. These derived from a reservoir of racial and cultural prejudice common throughout Europe, which could be readily employed and developed both to explain differences between the two races and to legitimize the conquest, dispossession, and enslavement of indigenous peoples in the Americas. Rationalizations for European possession of America had been developed by theorists of other nations long before the English arrived at Jamestown, and could be quickly summoned when circumstances dictated.[12]

In the light of English ethnocentrism and the chance arrival of colonists in the midst of one of the most powerful Indian alliances on the eastern seaboard, conflict between the two peoples was perhaps inevitable.[13] Wahunsonacock (Powhatan) had been steadily consolidating his influence throughout the Tidewater during the previous twenty years and controlled about thirty-two districts, occupying lands from south of the James River to the Potomac. Initially prepared to tolerate a small English contingent, believing it to be of no threat and possibly of benefit, the increasingly bellicose demands for corn and land by settlers persuaded him that the English were intent not on trade but aimed 'to invade my people, and possesse my Country'. Mindful of a prophecy that 'a Nation' would arise from the '*Chesapeack* Bay' and destroy his empire, Wahunsonacock precipitated hostilities which one recent historian has termed the first Anglo-Powhatan War of 1609–14. In a 'brutal and atrocity-ridden' conflict, the English, marching under the banner of King Jesus, destroyed entire villages, made off with provisions, and slaughtered men, women, and children.[14]

Land was the key. Once it became clear that the English were not so much interested in establishing a trading outpost as a permanent colony, the contest between two very different conceptions of possessing the land became increasingly evident. 'Our first worke', declared Sir Francis Wyatt shortly after the great Indian uprising of 1622 nearly wiped out the colony, 'is expulsion of the Salvages to gaine the free range of the countrey for encrease of Cattle, swine &c which will more then restore us, for it is infinitely better to have no heathen among us, who at best were

[11] See above, pp. 152–64.

[12] Gary B. Nash, 'The Image of the Indian in the Southern Colonial Mind', *William and Mary Quarterly* (hereafter *WMQ*), Third Series, XXIX (1972), pp. 197–230; Purchas, *Hakluytus Posthumus*, pp. 219, 229–30.

[13] See discussion below, pp. 336–37.

[14] Barbour, ed., *Complete Works*, I, pp. 246–47; J. Frederick Fausz, 'An "Abundance of Blood Shed on Both Sides": England's First Indian War, 1609–1614', *VMBH*, XCIII (1990), pp. 3–56.

but thornes in our sides, then to be at peace and league with them...'[15] The uprising, labelled by the English a 'barbarous Massacre', signalled the failure of the Powhatans to rid their territory of white interlopers, and justified to the settlers their abandonment of policies of accommodation in favour of further military action to expel Indians from the region.[16]

By the mid-1620s the survival of the English in Virginia was assured. The setbacks and disappointments of the early period obscured two achievements which laid the foundations of the colony's future. Anglo-Indian hostilities demonstrated that the English were capable of containing the threat posed by the Powhatans and their allies, and were able to prosecute offensive wars to their own advantage. From the point of view of the colony's sponsors, the first objective of securing the settlement and subduing the Indians had been realized. English possession of the land was in the long run unassailable, whether from the Powhatans or from European aggressors. As the immigrant population gradually increased and settlement expanded along the rivers, plans for a more orderly society were put in train and experiments with a variety of crops initiated. Besides 'winning of the Forrest', Governor Wyatt encouraged the 'planting [of] gardens and orchards for delight and health[,] setting vines and Mulberry trees for raising those two excellent comodities of wine and Silke...'[17] Rather than silk and wine, however, it was the introduction of a strain of tobacco, *Nicotiana tabacum*, imported from the West Indies, that was the key to the Chesapeake's prosperity. The resort to tobacco represented a radical departure from the vision of a mixed economy shared by Hakluyt and other promoters of colonial enterprise, but the relatively cheap production costs and prospect of a rapidly expanding market in Europe made its widespread cultivation irresistible. Here, at last, was a staple suited to local conditions which would reap handsome profits at home. With the introduction of tobacco the course of Chesapeake history was irrevocably altered, for English and Indians alike.

A Peculiar Society

Of the half-a-million people who left England in the seventeenth century for all transoceanic destinations, about four-fifths emigrated to America. Most went to colonies which produced the major staples of colonial trade, tobacco and sugar: some 200,000 went to the Caribbean, 120,000 to the Chesapeake, and the remainder to New England and Middle Colonies. The peak period of English emigration

[15] 'Letter of Sir Francis Wyatt, Governor of Virginia, 1621–1626', *WMQ*, Second Series, VI (1926), pp. 118–19.

[16] Ian K. Steele, *Warpaths: Invasions of North America* (Oxford, 1994), pp. 37–49.

[17] 'Letter of Sir Francis Wyatt', pp. 118–19.

occurred within a single generation, from 1630 to 1660, but the rapid growth of the tobacco industry created a continual demand for cheap labour in the Chesapeake throughout the century. During the 1630s and 1640s immigration averaged about 8,000–9,000 per decade and from 1650 to 1680 surged to 16,000–20,000 per decade. Highly sensitive to the social composition of new arrivals and closely attuned to demographic and social changes in the home country, Virginia and Maryland depended on large-scale emigration from English provinces to maintain their populations and support economic growth. Without sustained immigration they would have collapsed.[18]

Settlers came from a broad range of regions and communities: from London and the Home Counties, southern and central England, the West Country, and, in smaller numbers, from northern counties. At least half were from urban backgrounds: small market towns (little more than oversized villages), decayed county towns, growing provincial capitals, bustling ports, and great cities. London dominated colonial trade throughout the century, and the great majority of emigrants, rich and poor alike, began their long journey to the colonies from the city's busy docksides. Like Charles Parker from Staffordshire, who lived in Aldgate 'halfe a yeare' before emigrating in 1685, many migrants were not natives of the city but had moved to London a few months or years earlier. Emigration was typically a two-stage process, involving first the move to the city and subsequently the decision to take ship for the colonies. Consequently, large numbers of settlers had already experienced the upheaval of leaving their home parishes and settling in unfamiliar surroundings long before they moved to Virginia and Maryland.

Not less than 70 to 80 per cent of English immigrants arrived in the Chesapeake as indentured servants, and served usually four to five years in return for the cost of their passage, board and lodging, and various freedom dues. They were drawn principally from the impoverished and unemployed of urban slums, poor rural workers from southern and central England, women domestic servants, and men from semi-skilled and, in fewer cases, skilled trades who had decided that prospects were brighter in the colonies. Age at emigration confirms their relatively humble social standing. Most were between 15 and 24 (with 20 and 21 predominating), but servants who were not registered at their port of departure, and who consequently served according to the 'Custome of the Country' in the Chesapeake, were younger. About 90 per cent of those arriving without indentures in Lancaster County, Virginia, between 1662 and 1680 were less than 19 years old. The median age was 16. Generally, the youthfulness of servants implies that when they left

[18] Henry A. Gemery, 'Emigration from the British Isles to the New World: Inferences from Colonial Populations', *Research in Economic History*, V (1980), pp. 179–231; Russell R. Menard, 'British Migration to the Chesapeake Colonies in the Seventeenth Century', in Carr, Morgan, and Russo, eds., *Colonial Chesapeake Society*, pp. 99–132.

England they had little stake in society, little substance of their own, and, in many cases, little to lose by leaving home.[19]

Free emigrants, who paid their own passage, shared a number of similarities with servants. The majority were young, male, and single, and came predominantly from the same regions: London, the South-East, and a broad band of counties stretching from the Thames Valley to the West Country. They were a diverse group, ranging from men who had little more than the cost of their passage, fleeing from creditors or misfortune and hoping for better luck in the colonies, to wealthy merchants, gentry, and royal officials. The close connections that developed between merchants and mariners in the two major colonial ports, London and Bristol, and planter-merchants in the Chesapeake should be emphasized. Atlantic commerce, unrestricted by mercantile monopolies and regulated companies, allowed all sorts of petty traders—retailers, wholesale merchants, ship captains, seamen, and victuallers—to dabble in the tobacco trade. Small and middling traders, and mariners—such as James Turpin, a tobacconist of the Liberty of the Tower of London, who went to Virginia in 1675, and Edmund Goddard, citizen and cooper of London, originally from Suffolk—constituted the backbone of the planter-merchant class in the Chesapeake.[20]

Sons of gentlemen and minor gentry comprised another important category of free emigrants. Promoters of colonization and colonial leaders actively encouraged the gentry to move to the New World, believing them the natural rulers of society and finding it inconceivable that the colonies could be brought under orderly rule without persons of rank to govern them. With an eye to creating a Maryland aristocracy, Lord Baltimore offered lordships and manors, 'with all such royalties and priviledges' usual in England, to anyone transporting five or more men at their own expense. The *Relation of Maryland* of 1635 contained a list of 'Gentlemen adventurers that are gone in person to this Plantation', which was doubtless intended to encourage others to do the same.[21] The majority of gentry, however, did not emigrate with the ambition of becoming part of a permanent *officier* class in the colonies. Provincial politics was important, but more important was earning money from tobacco plantations, merchandizing, and other entrepreneurial activities. From this perspective, colonial gentry are hard to distinguish from merchants. County rulers, such as John Carter of Lancaster County and

[19] James Horn, 'Servant Emigration to the Chesapeake in the Seventeenth Century', in Thad W. Tate and David L. Ammerman, eds., *The Chesapeake in the Seventeenth Century: Essays on Anglo-American Society* (Chapel Hill, NC, 1979), pp. 54–87.

[20] James Horn, '"To Parts Beyond the Seas": Free Emigration to the Chesapeake in the Seventeenth Century', in Ida Altman and James Horn, eds., '*To Make America': European Emigration in the Early Modern Period* (Los Angeles, 1991), pp. 85–130.

[21] 'A Relation of Maryland, 1635', in Hall, ed., *Narratives of Early Maryland*, pp. 91, 101.

Thomas Willoughby of Lower Norfolk, Virginia, were both. Their gentle origins gave them an immediate introduction into the higher echelons of colonial society, yet first and foremost they were tobacco merchants and active managers of large plantations.

Black slaves from the Caribbean and Africa were a final category of immigrants, albeit reluctant ones. The size of the black population was initially small, no more than a few hundred before 1650, but from the 1680s, as the supply of indentured servants began to decline, numbers increased rapidly to about 13,000 by 1700 (13 per cent of the total population). Apart from emigrants from London or Bristol, most settlers probably encountered blacks for the first time in the Chesapeake, and in this context made the indelible connection between slavery and race. Yet the response to blacks on an everyday basis was more complex than the general framework of prejudice and the institution of slavery might imply. Especially in the early years of settlement, when numbers were small and blacks worked alongside servants and masters to bring in the tobacco crop, relations between the two races may have been relatively relaxed. Occasionally slaves were freed or purchased their liberty, and some acquired property and were able to live peaceably side-by-side with their white neighbours. The limited opportunities for blacks, slave or free, to improve their condition in this period should not be exaggerated, however. From the 1660s, when Virginia began legislating 'stringent racial laws' designed to regulate white–black relations, conditions for blacks began to deteriorate sharply. Mass shipments after 1680 and the changing origin of slaves (brought directly from Africa rather than from the Caribbean)[22] served to intensify discriminatory legislation and further debase the status of blacks.[23]

As the white population increased rapidly—from less than a thousand in 1620 to 8,000 in 1640, 25,000 in 1660, 60,000 in 1680, and 85,000 by 1700—so the spread of English settlement pushed back local Indian populations and opened up hundreds of thousands of acres for tobacco cultivation. By the mid-seventeenth century substantial migration had taken place northward beyond the York River to the Gloucester–Middlesex peninsula and the Northern Neck (Map 8.1). Large numbers of Virginia settlers crossed the Potomac into Maryland, the Chesapeake frontier of the 1650s and 1660s, moving up the Western Shore to Providence on the Severn River (Anne Arundel). The axis of population had shifted decisively from

[22] See in Vol. II pp. 451–52, Table 20.3; p. 456, Table 20.4.

[23] Alden T. Vaughan, 'The Origins Debate: Slavery and Racism in Seventeenth-Century Virginia', *VMHB*, XCVII (1989), pp. 344–54; Allan Kulikoff, *Tobacco and Slaves: The Development of Southern Cultures in the Chesapeake, 1680–1800* (Chapel Hill, NC, 1986), pp. 319–34; Lorena S. Walsh, 'Slave Life, Slave Society, and Tobacco Production in the Tidewater Chesapeake, 1620–1820', in Ira Berlin and Philip D. Morgan, eds., *Cultivation and Culture: Labor and the Shaping of Slave Life in the Americas* (Charlottesville, Va., 1993), pp. 170–79.

the older-settled region of the James River basin to the more northerly rivers of the York, Rappahannock, and Potomac, as well as across the Bay. Expansion came to halt about the same time as the flow of immigrants from England dried up, and by the beginning of the long tobacco depression (around 1680) settlement had virtually reached its seventeenth-century limits. In the rest of the century less desirable land was taken up in the interiors of established counties and there was a drift of population westwards across the fall line, foreshadowing the major impulse of the following century.[24]

The taking up of land and establishment of settlements were influenced by similar considerations throughout the Chesapeake: the quality of soils, convenience of access for shipping, trading links with English merchants, and the proximity of other households, particularly those of leading planter-merchants. Frequently, new lands were opened up by planters living in contiguous areas that themselves had been frontier settlements a few years earlier. Settlements along the York River and Mobjack Bay, Gloucester County, Virginia, for example, provided an excellent springboard for the exploration of lands along the Rappahannock River. Wealthy planters such as Colonel Richard Lee and captains William Brocas and Ralph Wormeley, all formerly of York County, Virginia, moved to the south side of the Rappahannock, near Rosegill Creek, in the mid-seventeenth century, and were joined by established planters from other parts of the colony. Together, they provided the new county (Lancaster) with capital and political leadership. By 1653, a few years after settlers first moved into the region, ninety-one households, scattered along both shores of the Rappahannock or clustered around numerous creeks and inlets, stretched forty-five miles from Stingray Point to the freshes upriver.

All along the tobacco coast, the formation of local societies was conditioned by the mixture of settlers from different parts of England coming into contact with one another, as well as, to varying degrees, with Indians, blacks, and other Europeans. Early settlers of York County came from London, Kent, Surrey, Essex, Middlesex, Bedfordshire, East Anglia, Wiltshire, Gloucestershire, Devon, Somerset, and Yorkshire. A group of colonists who settled in Westmoreland County, Virginia, in the middle years of the century came from Bristol, Plymouth, Somerset, Shropshire, Bedfordshire, Middlesex, and London. In a period when local customs and traditions were a vibrant force in shaping daily life and experience in England, the formation of communities in the Chesapeake, which suddenly brought together men and women from a multitude of different English backgrounds, constituted an abrupt break with the past. Unavoidably, much of the

[24] Richard L. Morton, *Colonial Virginia*, 2 vols. (Chapel Hill, NC, 1960), I, pp. 52, 58, 62–65, 122–30, 155–58, 163, 242.

particular richness of immigrants' own provincial backgrounds was lost, but contact with other English settlers and other peoples provided an equally rich source for forging a new regional culture.[25]

Given the cheapness of land and the nature of the economy, it made sense for planters to take up large tracts of land (by European standards) and seat themselves on or near convenient shipping routes. Water carriage not only provided the best means of transporting bulky tobacco leaf packed in hogsheads, but it was also favoured by English merchants who preferred to trade directly with individual producers: manufactured goods, liquor, and servants brought from London, Bristol, or other out-ports being exchanged on the spot for tobacco. An unfortunate consequence, as commentators never tired of pointing out, was that Chesapeake society failed to develop urban communities. 'Townes and Corporations have likewise been much hindered', Anthony Langston wrote of Virginia in the 1650s, 'by our manner of seating the Country; every man having Liberty... to take up Land (untaken before) and there seat, build, clear, & plant without any manner of restraint from the Government...'[26] Thirty years later the French Huguenot, Durand of Dauphine, commented that there was 'neither town nor village in the whole country, save one named Gemston [Jamestown], where the Council assembles. All the rest is made up of single houses, each on its own plantation.'[27]

In terms of first impressions, it is worth stressing that to English eyes what was missing in Virginia's and Maryland's landscape was as significant as what was present. Immigrants, whether from urban or rural backgrounds, were used to living in a society where there was a hierarchy of interdependent communities: village, market town, provincial capital, and city. Few people in England lived more than a few miles from a local town—an hour, if that, by road or across country. Along the tobacco coast, only the colonies' capitals resembled small towns and for most of the century even they were nearer in size, if not character, to English villages. Missing, too, was the bustle of fairs and market days, crowded taverns and inns (thick with the smell of smoke, ale, and stale bodies), and busy thoroughfares bringing people and goods to trade. Approximations existed, but nothing that could compare to the press of people and places familiar to English men and women in their native 'countries'.

Getting used to the absence of important aspects of daily life, taken for granted in England, posed one of the most difficult challenges to settlers adapting to

[25] James Horn, *Adapting to a New World: English Society in the Seventeenth-Century Chesapeake* (Chapel Hill, NC, 1994), pp. 164–87.

[26] 'Anthony Langston on Towns and Corporations; and on the Manufacture of Iron', *WMQ*, Second Series, I (1921), p. 102.

[27] Durand of Dauphine, *A Frenchman in Virginia, Being the Memoirs of a Huguenot Refugee in 1686*, trans. Fairfax Harrison ([Richmond, Va.] 1923), p. 90.

conditions along the Bay, but certain realities, faced by all colonists, proved equally challenging. Arriving in summer, they would have been struck by the heat (as 'hot as in Spaine'), humidity, and swarms of biting insects. 'The Natural Temperature of the Inha[bit]ed part of the Country', Robert Beverley remarked, 'is hot and moist.' Climate and health were closely related in the minds of colonists, and the heat and 'Moisture... occasion'd by the abundance of low Grounds, Marshes, Creeks, and Rivers' were believed harmful.[28] As early as the 1620s, the region was well known for its high mortality, and its insalubrious reputation persisted throughout the century. Colonists, George Gardyner opined, were subject to 'much sickness or death. For the air is exceeding unwholesome, insomuch as one of three scarcely liveth the first year at this time.'[29] Up to 40 per cent of new arrivals may have died in their first couple of years, commonly of a variety of ailments associated with malaria and intestinal disorders. Malaria occasionally reached epidemic proportions among settlers and frequently left survivors in poor health, easy prey to a variety of other diseases. Even if the outcome was not fatal, most immigrants experienced a period of sickness or 'seasoning' in their first year. Moving to Virginia and Maryland, like moving from the provinces to London, was risky and amounted to a calculated gamble on survival. For those who survived and lived long enough the rewards could be considerable, but that very success was predicated in part on a rapid turnover of population caused by the high death rate.[30]

Natural population growth was retarded also by the considerable sexual imbalance that existed throughout the century. Besides being an immigrant society, the Chesapeake was emphatically a male society. Responding to the demand of the tobacco industry for labourers, six times more men than women emigrated in the 1630s, and although greater numbers of females took ship after 1650, men continued to outnumber women by nearly three to one throughout the rest of the century. The highly skewed sex ratio restricted family formation, severely limited numbers of children per household, and dictated that as many as 20–30 per cent of men went to their graves unmarried. The problem was exacerbated by the relatively late age at which immigrant women married. Since the great majority of women (like men) arrived in the Chesapeake as indentured servants and were usually obliged to finish their term of service before marrying, they were unable to take a husband until their mid-twenties, which was about the same age they would have married in England. A shortage of women did not, therefore, lead to a lower age of marriage which would have increased their reproductive lives and the birth

[28] Robert Beverley, *The History and Present State of Virginia*, ed. Louis B. Wright (Chapel Hill, NC, 1947), pp. 296, 303–04.

[29] George Gardyner, *A Description of the New World* (London, 1650), pp. 99–100.

[30] Darrett B. Rutman and Anita H. Rutman, '"Of Agues and Fevers": Malaria in the Early Chesapeake', *WMQ*, Third Series, XXXIII (1976), pp. 31–60.

rate. Any one of these things—high rates of mortality and morbidity, sexual imbalance, and late age at first marriage—could have severely restricted natural increase, but acting in concert 'demographic failure along the tobacco coast was inevitable'. Not until the final years of the century did the white population of Virginia and Maryland become self-sustaining.[31]

'The Profit of the Country'

Little can be understood of the development of Chesapeake society without reference to the remarkable growth of the tobacco industry and expansion of plantation agriculture. From the early 1620s, when extensive production began, tobacco governed the character and pace of immigration, population growth, settlement patterns, husbandry, labour systems, transatlantic trade, the development of the home market, manufactures, opportunity, standards of living, and government policy. Settlers used leaf as local money, paid their taxes, extended credit, settled debts, and valued their goods in it. 'We have [no] trade at home and abroad', a contemporary stated, 'but that of Tobacco . . . [it] is our meat, drink, clothes, and monies.' The evolution of English society along the Bay was conditioned principally by the vicissitudes of tobacco.[32]

The advantages of tobacco were many: its yield per acre was high and its keeping qualities good; it fetched a higher price per pound than English grains, and the soils and climate of the Chesapeake were, for the most part, suitable for its cultivation. A plantation required relatively little capital to set up and a man's labour, or that of his family and a couple of servants, was sufficient to run it. Lastly, there were potentially expansive markets in England and Europe. An extraordinary growth of the industry took place during the century, when output rose from about 60,000 pounds (weight) in 1620 to 15 million pounds by the late 1660s and around 28 million by the mid-1680s. As production and marketing costs fell, merchants and planters were able to lower retail prices and further stimulate demand. The widespread appeal of tobacco in England was instant. Despite government fears that the 'health, manners and wealth' of the nation were at risk, by the early 1630s it was sold the length and breadth of the country and could be enjoyed by anyone with a few pence to spare for a smoke. The creation of a mass market was vital, since without it there would have been no significant expansion of output and no large-scale immigration to the Chesapeake.[33]

[31] Russell R. Menard, 'Immigrants and their Increase: The Process of Population Growth in Early Colonial Maryland', in Aubrey C. Land, Lois Green Carr, and Edward G. Papenfuse, eds., *Law, Society, and Politics in Early Maryland* (Baltimore, 1977), p. 97.

[32] Jones, 'Part of a Letter', pp. 250–53.

[33] Lois Green Carr, Russell R. Menard, and Lorena S. Walsh, *Robert Cole's World: Agriculture and Society in Early Maryland* (Chapel Hill, NC, 1991), chaps. 2–3; C[hancery] 66/2543, Pat. Roll, 6 Chas. I, pt. 11.

Plantation agriculture involved a form of husbandry and land-use altogether different from that generally practised in England. Plentiful cheap land allowed planters to take up tracts of several hundred acres at a time, a small proportion of which would be cleared immediately for tobacco and other crops and the rest held in reserve for future use and pasturing livestock. There was no necessity for the kind of intensive cultivation common in Europe, and nor was arable acreage limited by the numbers of livestock kept for fertilizing fields. Rather than expending time and money improving the same piece of land, most men cleared a fresh tract every few years and shifted their tobacco fields when the old land was exhausted. Old land could be used to raise maize, English cereals, other crops, or left fallow. 'Thus their Plantations', John Clayton wrote, with a touch of exaggeration, 'run over vast Tracts of ground, each [planter] ambitioning to engrosse as m[u]ch as they can, that they may be sure [to] have enough to plant, and for their Stocks and herds of cattle to range and feed in, that Plantations of 1000, 2000, or 3000 Acres are Common...' This form of husbandry may have elicited the contempt of commentators 'who delighted in the sprightly countrysides of England and the colonies northward', but with so much land available planters could afford to exploit its fertility to the utmost and then allow it to recuperate naturally.[34]

Tobacco, as the dominant cash crop, engaged the attention of most planters who depended on it for the bulk of their income, but there were other concerns. Planters were primarily farmers. As in English pasture-farming districts, cattle and swine were the most common animals found on Chesapeake plantations and comprised an extremely important element of the local economy. Cultivating orchards, like clearing land, fencing tobacco and corn fields, and building up livestock, represented a principal means of improving estates in the period.[35]

The long tobacco depression beginning in the 1680s underlined the enormous variability in the quality of soils and land and convenience of access to the main shipping routes. Planters were acutely aware of this, but while the price of leaf was high the economic impact of such variation was less apparent. Slumps affected everyone but hit men on marginal soils, in the interior or on the frontier, much harder than planters possessing the best land by the major rivers. While fluctuations in tobacco prices exerted a powerful influence on the Chesapeake economy as a whole, important differences in soils, location, timing of settlement, and links with English merchants distinguished regions and communities from one another and in large part determined how they would respond to contraction after 1680. In Virginia the best soils were to be found between the James and Rappahannock

[34] Edmund Berkeley and Dorothy Smith Berkeley, eds., *The Reverend John Clayton: A Parson with a Scientific Mind* (Charlottesville, Va., 1965), pp. 79–80.

[35] Gloria Main, *Tobacco Colony Life in Early Maryland* (Princeton, 1982), p. 62.

rivers, for example, in York and Middlesex counties, where the highly valued sweet-scented tobacco was grown mainly for the London market. In Maryland the lower Western Shore, particularly Anne Arundel County, was the prime tobacco area and produced the lower-priced oronocco. Mediocre or poor soils were found on the lower Eastern Shore and on the southern bank of the James in counties such as Surrey and Lower Norfolk (Map 8.1). Unsurprisingly, these were the first areas to move away from tobacco cultivation.[36]

Despite the tumbling price of leaf, and periodic slumps, an established market for tobacco remained. Whilst farm prices remained above a penny a pound a bare living could be made which, supplemented by the local sale of surplus food or undertaking casual work, was sufficient to ensure subsistence. The onset of the long depression after 1680, however, pushed many small producers in marginal areas to develop new sources of income. On Maryland's Eastern Shore planters gradually turned to the cultivation of English grains, notably wheat, for export and the manufacture of cheap coarse woollen cloth for domestic consumption. In Lower Norfolk County tobacco cultivation was replaced by the production of tar and the sale of livestock and foodstuffs to the West Indies. There was no rapid or wholesale switch to the sorts of commodities that Governor William Berkeley had in mind—silk, flax, hemp, pitch, potashes, iron, and wine—and large-scale manufacturing remained conspicuous by its absence. Yet, to critics of the Chesapeake's over-dependence on tobacco, it was a step in the right direction. Regional differentiation mitigated the worst effects of the tobacco depression of the late seventeenth century and produced an economic diversity along the tobacco coast absent two generations earlier. If salvation did not take the form of the silkworm, viticulture, or bar-iron, nevertheless important new sectors had been established which would play a leading role in the gradual transformation of the economy during the eighteenth and early nineteenth centuries.[37]

'English ground in America'

A common theme in accounts of the early Chesapeake is disorder. The scramble to make money, lack of community, high mortality rates, and élite factionalism, it is

[36] Lorena S. Walsh, 'Plantation Management in the Chesapeake, 1620–1820', *Journal of Economic History* (hereafter *JEcH*), XCIX (1989), pp. 393–400; Lois Green Carr and Russell R. Menard, 'Land, Labor, and Economics of Scale in Early Maryland: Some Limits to Growth in the Chesapeake System of Husbandry', *JEcH*, XCIX (1989), pp. 407–18.

[37] Joan de Lourdes Leonard, 'Operation Checkmate: The Birth and Death of a Virginia Blueprint for Progress, 1660–1676', *WMQ*, Third Series, XXIV (1967), pp. 44–74; William Berkeley, *A Discourse and View of Virginia* (London, 1663), pp. 2, 12; Lois Green Carr, 'Diversification in the Colonial Chesapeake: Somerset County, Maryland, in Comparative Perspective', in Carr, Morgan, and Russo, eds., *Colonial Chesapeake Society*, pp. 342–88.

argued, created a society disfigured by chaotic individualism and chronic political instability. If New Englanders lived in relative harmony, Virginians 'rioted and rebelled', and even during periods of apparent peace 'were haunted by the specter of social unrest'. Whereas society in the northern colonies 'allowed the acting out of the European fantasy—order, morality, stability... and a long life'—along the tobacco coast life was typically short, nasty, and brutish.[38]

The establishment of political authority and maintenance of social order were two of the most intractable problems which confronted Governors of Maryland and Virginia. Faced with an unfamiliar and at times hostile environment, and a diverse collection of settlers united by little other than a desire to make money, early rulers experimented with a variety of forms of governance to control the centrifugal forces that at times seemed to threaten the very existence of English settlement. There were several possibilities: a military-style government based on models of garrison rule developed in other English overseas possessions, corporate government organized along similar lines to boroughs in England, or a social order founded upon manorial principles. All were tried during the first twenty years with little success. Accordingly, in Virginia from the 1630s, and in Maryland after the collapse of Lord Baltimore's vision of manorialism in the 1640s, a new basis of polity emerged in the guise of adaptations of English local government.[39]

Following the creation of the eight original counties in Virginia in 1634, the 'shiring' of the Chesapeake recognized and gave official sanction to the creation of new communities as settlement rapidly spread throughout the region. The county court and Justice of the Peace became the keystone of local polity. Critical to the 'conservation of the peace and quiet government' was the recognition that everyone had a duty to maintain order. In Virginia and Maryland the English institution of magistracy was readily transferred, allowing the adoption of familiar local offices and functions which served to encourage social co-operation.[40] Settlers generally agreed that the agency of government which affected them most directly in their everyday affairs should be conducted by men who, although bearing the

[38] T. H. Breen, *Puritans and Adventurers: Change and Persistence in Early America* (Oxford, 1980), chaps. 6–8, esp. pp. 110–16; John J. Waters, 'The Traditional World of the New England Peasants: A View from Seventeenth-Century Barnstaple', *New England Historical and Genealogical Register*, CXXX (1976), p. 21.

[39] Philip Alexander Bruce, *Institutional History of Virginia in the Seventeenth Century: An Inquiry into the Religious, Moral, Educational, Legal, Military, and Political Condition of the People...*, 2 vols. (New York, 1910), II, pp. 229–522; Warren M. Billings, 'The Growth of Political Institutions in Virginia, 1634–1676', *WMQ*, Third Series, XXXI (1974), pp. 225–35; Lois Green Carr, 'The Foundations of Social Order: Local Government in Colonial Maryland', in Bruce C. Daniels, ed., *Town and County: Essays on the Structure of Local Government in the American Colonies* (Middletown, Conn., 1978), pp. 72–110.

[40] Carr, 'Foundations of Social Order', p. 99.

King's commission and usually of higher status, by and large shared their interests and were neighbours of those they judged. In a society deeply imbued with patriarchal values, county justices sought to assume the role of fathers of their communities, dispensing justice, regulating local business, and ensuring the continuance of 'the Amity, Confidence and Quiet that is between men'.[41]

Despite initial difficulties, by mid-century settlers had created governing institutions which reflected conventional assumptions about relationships between the rulers and the ruled. Colonial Assemblies were loosely modelled on Parliament and the county courts on English quarter and petty sessions. Justices were commanded to 'do justice as near as may be' to English precedent, and were granted similar extensive powers as their counterparts in English shires. County courts were empowered to decide criminal cases not involving loss of life and limb, and adjudicated all causes at common law and equity involving local parties. They also took on some of the powers of English church, manor, and admiralty courts in considering moral offences, testamentary business, orphans' estates, parochial affairs, poor relief, land grants, deeds, shipping, and salvage. Administrative duties ranged from the routine registering of cattle marks, licensing of taverns, and maintenance of highways to the more important tasks of setting and collecting the annual tithe, holding elections for burgesses, regulating Anglo-Indian relations, and enforcing acts passed by the provincial Assembly.[42]

In Virginia the most important subdivision below the county was the parish (the Anglican church was not established in Maryland until 1692). Early Governors were required by James I to ensure that 'the true word, and service of God and Christian faith be preached, planted, and used . . . according to the doctrine, rights, and religion now professed and established within our realme of England'. In 1619 Virginia's first Assembly, held in the 'Quire of the Church' in Jamestown, formally recognized the church's spiritual and temporal responsibilities by enacting a series of measures relating to the exercise of ministerial functions in conformity with 'the Ecclesiastical lawes and orders of the churche of Englande'. Five years later the Assembly reiterated its intention that 'there be an uniformity in our church as neere as may be to the canons in England; both in substance and circumstance, and that all persons yield readie obedience unto them under paine of censure'. Subsequently, the organization of the church and clerical duties were brought more closely into line with the mother church in England, with the result that two enduring principles were established in the colony: first was the primacy of Anglicanism and the liturgy of the Church of England, and

[41] Billings, 'Growth of Political Institutions', p. 227.

[42] Bruce, *Institutional History*, I, pp. 478–549; William Waller Hening, ed., *The Statutes at Large: Being a Collection of all the Laws of Virginia* . . . , 13 vols. (1809–23; Charlottesville, Va., 1969), I, pp. 125, 127, 132, 168–69, 224, 273.

second was an alliance between church and state to enforce social and moral discipline.[43]

Some idea of the range of responsibilities of the parish can be gained from the vestry minutes of Christ Church parish formed in 1666 on the south side of the Rappahannock River in what later became Middlesex County. At a meeting in early 1667 the fourteen vestrymen present ordered that John Blaike, 'a poore Decriped Man of This parish', be granted 1,000 pounds of tobacco 'Towards The Maintenance of his Wife and Family'. Mr Richard Morris was 'Dismist from being our Minister any longer', and Mr Gabriell Comberland was appointed as 'Reader' for the year: to 'read Divine Service Each Sabboth Day in ye fore-Noon' in the parish church 'till we can be provided of a Minister'. Major General Robert Smith and Henry Corbin Esq., both members of the vestry, were asked to write to Mr Richard Perrott, 'now in England to procure us a Minister to come over upon such Tearmes as they Shall Judge Convenient'. In 1672 the parish accounts reveal 16,000 pounds of tobacco paid to Mr John Shepherd, the minister, 10,000 to Mr William Dudley 'for Compleating ye Chappell', 200 for the nursing of 'a Bastard Childe', 500 to Robert Thompson, 'a poore Man', and 400 to David Barrick for two 'parish Children'. Payments were made also for communion wine, 'Cleaning ye Church Yard', and 'work done to ye Gleabe house'.[44]

The relationship between the vestry and local court was often close. Vestrymen commonly served as justices, sheriffs, and burgesses, and the court's authority was vital for the creation and recognition of the vestry. There was frequently a good deal of overlap in their respective duties. Whereas in England churchwardens' presentments were made to church courts (archdeaconry or consistory), in Virginia they were forwarded to the county court via the grand jury. Both detected and punished a variety of moral lapses, notably the 'heinous & odious sinne of fornicacion', bastardy, and defamation. Dual jurisdiction was reflected in punishments meted out to culprits. Offenders were often required to ask the forgiveness of the court and do penance in their parish church, but sometimes the punishment was more severe. Agnes Holmes of Lower Norfolk County was convicted of speaking 'certaine slanderous words tending to the great disparragement' of Captain Thomas Willoughby (one of the county's leading justices) shortly before Christmas 1646. Besides receiving fifteen lashes she was ordered by the court to

[43] William H. Seiler, 'The Anglican Parish in Virginia', in James Morton Smith, ed., *Seventeenth-Century America: Essays in Colonial History* (Chapel Hill, NC, 1959), pp. 121–23; Jon Butler, *Awash in a Sea of Faith: Christianizing the American People* (Cambridge, Mass., 1990), pp. 38–40; 'Proceedings of the Virginia Assembly' (1619), in Lyon Gardiner Tyler, ed., *Narratives of Early Virginia, 1606–1625* (New York, 1907), pp. 271–72; Hening, ed., *Statutes*, I, pp. 69, 123, 144, 155, 180, 240–43.

[44] C. G. Chamberlayne, ed., *The Vestry Book of Christ Church Parish, Middlesex County, Virginia, 1663–1767* (Richmond, Va., 1927), pp. 8–9, 20; Seiler, 'Anglican Parish', pp. 126–39.

'weare a paper upon her head with these words written in Capitall letters (vizt) for slandering Capt. Willoughby Esq.', and to stand for one hour in front of the congregations at Lynnhaven and Elizabeth River churches.[45]

Most Chesapeake settlers did not seek to build a 'City upon a Hill', but this does not imply that religion was unimportant in their lives or that they quickly shed their beliefs as irrelevant baggage. A dozen Anglican churches were established in Virginia by 1634 and another fifty by 1668 and, despite a shortage of clergy, rudimentary instruction was afforded in many parishes by lay readers. In addition, a small but important minority assuaged their spiritual needs by turning to Catholicism or Nonconformity. The latter established flourishing congregations in Lower Norfolk, Nansemond, Isle of Wight, Charles, and Anne Arundel counties, as well as along the Eastern Shore, areas that later became fertile ground for Quakerism. Catholics, Anglicans, Independents, Presbyterians, Anabaptists, and Quakers lived side-by-side in Maryland. The existence of a wide range of beliefs serves as a reminder that colonists had other imperatives besides the material concerns of earning a living and providing for their families. God and the devil, like corn and tobacco, had a real presence in the world.[46]

County and parish comprised an essential context for local political and religious organization, and provided links with the wider society as well as the setting in which colonists experienced the vital events of their everyday lives. The duties of courts and vestries, and the principles that underpinned them, would have been broadly familiar to English immigrants—reminiscent of the variety of jurisdictions in England. Most important—and this applies as much to Maryland as Virginia—local institutions instilled a sense of order and stability in societies where population turnover and mortality rates were high. Individuals might come and go but institutions remained and lent a degree of permanence to society.

Alongside familiar local institutions were familiar English attitudes towards the social order. Colonial society lacked the complexity and subtlety of European hierarchies, but the precept that political power followed economic power was generally acknowledged. As Chesapeake society matured in the second half of the century substantial wealth and inherited status became the usual criteria for entry into the squirearchy.[47] Gentry rule in the Chesapeake can be interpreted as an extension of gentry rule in England, and just as county rulers in England relied on the approbation and co-operation of those they governed, so did their counterparts in Maryland and Virginia.

[45] Lower Norfolk County, Virginia, Minute Book, I, ff. 5, 13, 37, 54, 69–70, 99–101, 137, 187; Wills and Deeds B, f. 15.

[46] Horn, *Adapting to a New World*, chap. 9.

[47] Billings, 'Growth of Political Institutions', pp. 236–38.

Notwithstanding the formidable problems posed by demographic disruption, family and household remained the bedrock of civil society. Family discipline and assumptions that governed family relations were little different to those prevalent in Europe. The family was a political as well as a social and economic unit, and orderly family life, it was believed, ensured an orderly society. Heads of household were held responsible for the conduct of the members of their family regarding religious observance, moral education of the young, and proper behaviour, and were empowered to exercise direct authority over wives, children, servants, and slaves.[48] Attitudes towards sex and marriage and expectations of the respective duties of husbands and wives were little different in the colonies compared to the parent country. Men were expected to provide economic support and to treat their partners with care and respect. Wives were expected to devote themselves primarily to raising children, keeping house, and supplementing the family income. A shortage of women in the Chesapeake does not appear to have undermined patriarchalism, either in regard to the theoretical basis of male dominance or to the somewhat more ambiguous relationship between men and women in practice.[49]

Family and household were the most intimate social contexts bounding the lives of individuals, but the local community was also of significance. Within the locality, friends and neighbours provided company and recreation, helped in periods of crisis, witnessed vital events in individual lives, kept watch and ward, mediated in local disputes, defined acceptable standards of behaviour, lent money and tools, exchanged crops and goods, participated in various communal activities, and carried out official duties. Individuals and families enmeshed, to one extent or another, in a complex web of interrelationships, acted first and foremost within the neighbourhood which also linked them to the larger world beyond.

Five to six miles was the usual extent of local communities, since daily interaction was difficult beyond this limit, but the most frequent contacts occurred within a shorter range, usually two to three miles, corresponding to the neighbourhood.[50] Of great importance in the daily lives of planters and their wives were visits, chance meetings, and occasional gatherings. When opportunities arose to escape from the drudgery of routine work, most men and women were ready to pass the time of day together, have a drink, and light a pipe. When a group of

[48] Carr, Menard, and Walsh, *Robert Cole's World*, pp. 142–50. Hening, ed., *Statutes*, I, pp. 286, 311–12, 358, 433, 525, 542; II, p. 103.

[49] Lorena S. Walsh, '"Till Death Us Do Part": Marriage and Family in Seventeenth Century Maryland', in Tate and Ammerman, eds., *Chesapeake in the Seventeenth-Century*, pp. 139–40; Kathleen Mary Brown, 'Gender and the Genesis of a Race and Class System in Virginia, 1630–1750', unpublished Ph.D. dissertation, Wisconsin, 1990, chaps. 2, 4, 7–8.

[50] James R. Perry, *The Formation of a Society on Virginia's Eastern Shore, 1615–1655* (Chapel Hill, NC, 1990), pp. 90–115; Lorena S. Walsh, 'Community Networks in the Early Chesapeake', in Carr, Morgan, and Russo, eds., *Colonial Chesapeake Society*, pp. 200–41.

friends arrived at Captain William Carver's house in Lower Norfolk County, Carver declared they should 'drinck a dram for hee was glad of their Comp[an]y'. Early in 1650 Royalists Sir Henry Chicheley and Sir Thomas Lunsford, who had recently arrived in Virginia, passed an evening 'feasting and carousing' with other gentlemen 'lately come from England', at Ralph Wormeley's plantation on the York River, where doubtless they discussed the recent turn of events in England. In Henrico County on a hot August afternoon, a group of freemen, servants, and 'Negroes' at work on the plantation of a local gentleman stopped to drink cider, and were joined by Katherine, the wife of a neighbour, who drank so much it 'turned her braines'.[51] Other visits were occasioned by the exchange of food, bartering local produce, or caring for sick neighbours. On the frontier, neighbouring families relied on each other for aid in times of distress, for borrowing essential supplies and tools, for helping with heavy work on the plantation or in the community, and for company and recreation.[52] Co-operation was vital for survival.

Traditional attitudes, inherited from their English backgrounds, powerfully influenced the way settlers thought about themselves, social relations, and the institutions of state and church they sought to establish. This is not to imply that inherited values were easily translated into accepted patterns of social and political behaviour as practised in England, or to underestimate the potential for periods of violence and disorder. The frontier was an unpredictable place. There was no ready-made template whereby English society could be inscribed on the New World, and the presence of Indians and Africans underlined a crucial difference between colonial and metropolitan society. Nevertheless, English society in Maryland and Virginia between the 1620s and 1690s had a distinctive quality. Most settlers were English by birth. They established an infrastructure based on English laws, government, and economic organization. They brought traditional English attitudes towards the social order and religion, and they maintained close commercial and social ties with home. Moving to America did not constitute a conscious desire to throw off old ways of thought or behaviour. English men and women who went to the Chesapeake in the seventeenth century saw themselves not as social outcasts exiled to a distant shore, or as a chosen people on God's errand, but as participants in a rich and expansive transatlantic world.

[51] Lower Norfolk County, Minute Book, I, ff. 180–81; Wills E, f. 127; Colonel [Henry] Norwood, 'A Voyage to Virginia' [1649], in Peter Force, ed., *Tracts and Other Papers Relating Principally to the Origin, Settlement, and Progress of the Colonies in America* . . . , 4 vols. (Gloucester, Mass., 1963), III, no. 10, p. 49.

[52] Walsh, 'Community Networks', p. 206.

Select Bibliography

WARREN M. BILLINGS, JOHN E. SELBY, and THAD W. TATE, *Colonial Virginia: A History* (White Plains, NY, 1986).

T. H. BREEN and STEPHEN INNES, *'Myne Own Ground': Race and Freedom on Virginia's Eastern Shore, 1640–1676* (Oxford, 1980).

KATHLEEN M. BROWN, *Good Wives, Nasty Wenches, and Anxious Patriarchs: Gender, Race, and Power in Colonial Virginia* (Chapel Hill, NC, 1996).

LOIS GREEN CARR, RUSSELL PHILIP D. MORGAN, and JEAN B. RUSSO, eds., *Colonial Chesapeake Society* (Chapel Hill, NC, 1988).

——, RUSSELL R. MENARD, and LORENA S. WALSH, *Robert Cole's World: Agriculture and Society in Early Maryland* (Chapel Hill, NC, 1991).

PAUL G. E. CLEMENS, *The Atlantic Economy and Colonial Maryland's Eastern Shore: From Tobacco to Grain* (Ithaca, NY, 1980).

WESLEY FRANK CRAVEN, *The Southern Colonies in the Seventeenth Century, 1607–1689* (Baton Rouge, La., 1970).

J. FREDERICK FAUSZ, 'Indians, Colonialism, and the Conquest of Cant: A Review Essay on Anglo-American Relations in the Chesapeake', *Virginia Magazine of History and Biography*, 95 (1987), pp. 133–56.

JAMES HORN, *Adapting to a New World: English Society in the Seventeenth-Century Chesapeake* (Chapel Hill, NC, 1994).

ALLAN KULIKOFF, *Tobacco and Slaves: The Development of Southern Cultures in the Chesapeake, 1680–1800* (Chapel Hill, NC, 1986).

AUBREY C. LAND, LOIS GREEN CARR, and EDWARD C. PAPENFUSE, eds., *Law, Society, and Politics in Early Maryland* (Baltimore, 1977).

GLORIA L. MAIN, *Tobacco Colony: Life in Early Maryland, 1650–1720* (Princeton, 1982).

RUSSELL R. MENARD, 'The Tobacco Industry in the Chesapeake Colonies, 1617–1730: An Interpretation', *Research in Economic History*, V (1980), pp. 109–77.

EDMUND S. MORGAN, *American Slavery, American Freedom: The Ordeal of Colonial Virginia* (New York, 1975).

JAMES R. PERRY, *The Formation of a Society on Virginia's Eastern Shore, 1615–1655* (Chapel Hill, NC, 1990).

HELEN C. ROUNTREE, *The Powhatan Indians of Virginia: Their Traditional Culture* (Norman, Okla., 1989).

DARRETT B. RUTMAN and ANITA H. RUTMAN, *A Place in Time: Middlesex County, Virginia, 1650–1750* (New York, 1984).

TIMOTHY SILVER, *A New Face on the Countryside: Indians, Colonists, and Slaves in South Atlantic Forests, 1500–1800* (Cambridge, 1990).

THAD W. TATE and DAVID L. AMMERMAN, eds., *The Chesapeake in the Seventeenth Century: Essays on Anglo-American Society* (Chapel Hill, NC, 1979).

ALDEN T. VAUGHAN, 'The Origins Debate: Slavery and Racism in Seventeenth-Century Virginia', *Virginia Magazine of History and Biography*, XCVII (1989), pp. 311–54.

LORENA S. WALSH, 'Slave Life, Slave Society, and Tobacco Production in the Tidewater Chesapeake, 1620–1820', in Ira Berlin and Philip D. Morgan, eds., *Cultivation and Culture: Labor and the Shaping of Slave Life in the Americas* (Charlottesville, Va., 1993), pp. 170–99.

9

New England in the Seventeenth Century

VIRGINIA DEJOHN ANDERSON

Of all the places English explorers visited in North America, New England seemed perhaps the least promising site for a colony. Its dense forests and stony soils looked discouraging to prospective farmers, and the winters were so notoriously hard that Oliver Cromwell dismissed New England as a 'poor, cold, and useless' place.[1] Whatever his other talents, the Puritan general proved to be a poor prophet. The thousands of English settlers who flocked to the north-eastern coastline of the continent of North America during the early seventeenth century established a flourishing society which so closely resembled that of the mother country that it alone, of the many English outposts erected on the far side of the Atlantic, could reasonably be known as New England.

Although New England's town-based settlement, diversified economy, and family labour system corresponded broadly to English patterns, colonial society differed in important ways. New Englanders interacted—sometimes peacefully, sometimes violently—with Indian peoples. The established Puritan religion of all New England colonies except Rhode Island constituted religious dissent in England, where for much of the century its adherents were subject to persecution and legal disabilities. The availability of land in New England gave its inhabitants a degree of economic independence that Englishmen could only envy.

Indeed, New Englanders occasionally acted as if they were virtually independent of England. When John Endecott cut the cross out of the royal flag in 1635, claiming that it was a popish symbol, Massachusetts magistrates reprimanded him not for having affronted the King, but for making it seem as if the rest of them 'would suffer idolatry'.[2] New Englanders valued the colonial charters that granted them extraordinarily broad powers of self-government precisely because these documents offered King and Parliament little role in their affairs. Their principal economic connection was not to England itself, but to the West Indies. The ties

[1] Quoted in Alan Heimert and Andrew Delbanco, eds., *The Puritans in America: A Narrative Anthology* (Cambridge, Mass., 1985), p. 7.

[2] John Winthrop, *The History of New England from 1630 to 1649*, ed. James Savage, 2 vols. (Boston, 1825), I, p. 158.

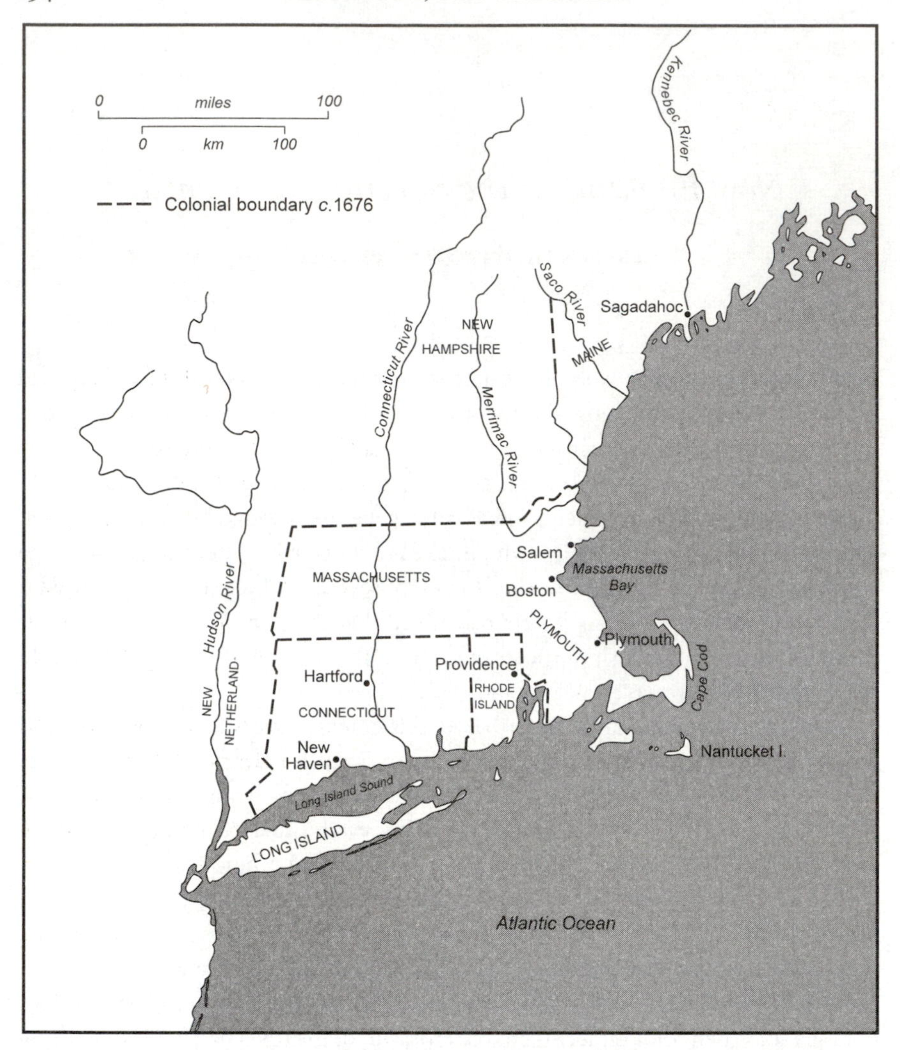

MAP 9.1. New England in the Seventeenth Century

that bound New England to the mother country in the seventeenth century were not institutionally robust so much as functional and emotional. Near the end of the century, however, the nature of that relationship would change.

Patterns of Settlement

The first attempt to colonize New England gave little indication of future success. In 1606 a group of West Country Englishmen formed a joint-stock company with royal permission to plant a colony anywhere between the Potomac and Kennebec rivers. These efforts produced an abortive settlement in 1607 at Sagadahoc in Maine, which succumbed within a year due to financial troubles and conflict with the Indians.[3] Twelve years passed before the English tried again. The next ventures—Plymouth Colony in 1620 and Massachusetts Bay Colony in 1630—succeeded handsomely. These colonies owed their existence less to the profit-seeking impulses of gentlemen backers (although their founders hoped for some financial gain) than to a desire to create refuges for English people beset by religious, economic, and political woes at home.

Many prospective emigrants saw recent events as portents of England's imminent destruction. Puritans viewed with alarm the Anglican church's turn toward Arminianism, the anti-predestinarian doctrine they believed heralded a return to Catholicism. Economic troubles, bad harvests, and a decline in the textile industry brought hardship and seemed to be signs of divine displeasure. Charles I's suspension of Parliament in 1629 deprived its members of legitimate channels to express their political concerns. These problems festered until the nation eventually dissolved into civil war; meanwhile, they induced thousands of English people to flee to the New World.[4]

The Puritan founders of Plymouth and Massachusetts nurtured a strong ideological commitment to their colonies, soliciting funds and recruiting settlers from among their co-religionists. Although some settlers did not share the founders' religious views, a sense of common purpose generally characterized both colonies. Their success also depended on the fact that the first colonists encountered a sharply diminished native population.

Between Sagadahoc's abandonment in 1608 and the founding of Plymouth in 1620, a majority—perhaps 90 per cent—of New England's natives died of such European diseases as smallpox, plague, and measles, against which they lacked

[3] Charles M. Andrews, *The Colonial Period of American History*, 4 vols. (New Haven, 1934–38), I, pp. 90–94; Neal Salisbury, *Manitou and Providence: Indians, Europeans, and the Making of New England, 1500–1643* (New York, 1982), pp. 92–94.

[4] Historians disagree about the relative importance of these motives for New England emigration. For interpretations stressing religious motivation, see Virginia DeJohn Anderson, 'Migrants and Motives: Religion and the Settlement of New England, 1630–1640', *New England Quarterly* (hereafter *NEQ*), LVIII (1985), pp. 339–83; Nellis M. Crouse, 'Causes of the Great Migration, 1630–1640', *NEQ*, V (1932), pp. 3–36; N. C. P. Tyack, 'The Humbler Puritans of East Anglia and the New England Movement: Evidence from the Court Records of the 1630s', *New England Historical and Genealogical Register*, CXXXVIII (1984), pp. 79–106. For arguments emphasizing a mix of religious, economic, social, and political factors, see T. H. Breen and Stephen Foster, 'Moving to the New World: The Character of Early Massachusetts Immigration', *William and Mary Quarterly* (hereafter *WMQ*), Third Series, XXX (1973), pp. 189–222; David Grayson Allen, *In English Ways: The Movement of Societies and the Transferal of English Local Law and Custom to Massachusetts in the Seventeenth Century* (Chapel Hill, NC, 1981), pp. 163–204; David Cressy, *Coming Over: Migration and Communication between England and New England in the Seventeenth Century* (Cambridge, 1987), chap. 3.

adequate immune responses. Indians who survived the epidemics witnessed an unprecedented disruption of their way of life and struggled to understand the meaning of the sudden catastrophe. The colonists, by contrast, concluded that God had providentially cleared the land of its inhabitants to accommodate His chosen people.[5]

Both Plymouth and Massachusetts attracted settlers convinced that God favoured their emigration, but the colonies differed in important ways. Separatists, who established Plymouth (the smaller and weaker of the two), believed that the Church of England was too corrupt to be salvaged. This extreme view placed them in a perilous position in England, where they survived by avoiding public attention and denying that their rejection of the Anglican church implied a rejection of the monarch who headed it. One group, the Pilgrim church of Scrooby, Nottinghamshire, left England for the Netherlands, where they worshipped in obscurity for more than a decade.

In Holland, however, these people found limited economic opportunities and feared that their children were adopting the worldly manners of the Dutch. Seizing on the Virginia Company of London's offer of inducements for American settlement, the Pilgrim leaders decided to cross the Atlantic. They travelled first to England, where they were joined by some London Separatists and a number of 'strangers' who wanted to emigrate but lacked the Separatists' religious convictions. Then they chartered two ships for the voyage: the *Speedwell*, which leaked so badly that it turned back; and the *Mayflower*, which made it to America after a difficult eleven-week passage.[6]

The *Mayflower* landed 200 miles north-east of its intended destination of northern Virginia. Some passengers, concluding that the royal patent authorizing their settlement was no longer valid, opposed the civil authority established by that document. In response, Pilgrim leaders drew up the Mayflower Compact for all the free adult male passengers to sign. This agreement created a body politic among the settlers, who promised to obey laws created by men of their own choosing, and who acknowledged John Carver as their elected Governor. With the framework for self-government in place, the emigrants spent a month looking for a suitable location for their settlement.[7]

They chose Plymouth because it had fresh water, cleared land, and no Indians. Ironically, they owed their survival to the Indians who had died shortly before. Native farmers had made the clearings so recently that the forest had not yet

[5] Salisbury, *Manitou and Providence*, pp. 101–06, 175–77.

[6] George D. Langdon, Jr., *Pilgrim Colony: A History of New Plymouth, 1620–1691* (New Haven, 1966), chap. 1.

[7] Ibid., pp. 14–15; William Bradford, *Of Plymouth Plantation, 1620–1647*, ed. Samuel Eliot Morison (New York, 1975), pp. 75–76.

returned; the Pilgrims thus could plant crops in the spring of 1621 without laborious preparations. Meanwhile, they survived their first New England winter by living off caches of Indian corn, buried by natives who had not lived to use them. When an English-speaking native arrived the next spring to show the Pilgrims how to plant corn and to serve as an interpreter, the colonists thanked God for this sign of His favour. The Indian, Squanto, doubtless understood the encounter differently. Kidnapped years earlier by an English sea captain, Squanto had returned home to find that he was the last of the Patuxet people.[8]

Nearly half of the Pilgrims died of disease and exposure during the first winter, but the survivors submitted themselves to what they believed to be God's will and persisted. They planted crops and began to pay off their debts to English investors by cutting timber and trading with Indians for furs. John Carver negotiated a treaty of friendship with Massasoit, sachem (or chief) of the Wampanoags. In the autumn of 1621 colonists joined with Indians in celebrating the harvest feast that descendants commemorated as the first Thanksgiving. The colony's legal status improved when the *Fortune* arrived with a new land patent from the Council for New England.[9]

As the first permanent English colony in New England, Plymouth's historical reputation exceeds its contemporary importance. Massachusetts Bay Colony soon overshadowed it demographically: whereas Plymouth's population never exceeded 7,500, more than 13,000 people moved to Massachusetts in its first decade alone.[10] Economically, Plymouth remained insignificant. Its farmers wrung a modest subsistence from the land, but produced little for export. The fact that the settlers finally repaid their English creditors in 1642 testified more to persistence than prosperity.

The Pilgrims' utopian vision, not their worldly success, makes Plymouth memorable. Fleeing England's corruption, they hoped to establish pure churches of visible saints. This corporatist impulse initially shaped political and economic life as well. The Mayflower Compact created a government founded on the consent of the governed. Settlers held all property in common and shared the products of their labours until 1627, when they ended their increasingly inefficient experiment in communism and divided up the common stock for private ownership.[11] Plymouth's reputation as a place of peace and co-operation rested, however, less on its communalism than on its contrast with Massachusetts, a different kind of Puritan colony.

[8] Bradford, *Plymouth Plantation*, pp. 64–66, 79–80; Salisbury, *Manitou and Providence*, pp. 107–08.

[9] Langdon, *Pilgrim Colony*, pp. 16–17; Bradford, *Plymouth Plantation*, pp. 80–81, 90.

[10] Henry A. Gemery, 'Emigration from the British Isles to the New World, 1630–1700: Inferences from Colonial Populations', *Research in Economic History*, V (1980), p. 212; Langdon, *Pilgrim Colony*, p. 55.

[11] Edmund S. Morgan, *Visible Saints: The History of a Puritan Idea* (Ithaca, NY, 1963), pp. 58–62; Langdon, *Pilgrim Colony*, pp. 29–31.

Although they shared other beliefs with the Pilgrims, most Massachusetts emigrants rejected Separatism and argued that the Church of England could be reformed. Their more aggressive approach to settlement grew from this position, for instead of avoiding public attention, Bay colonists offered their venture as a model for Puritan reform. It was no accident that several prominent ministers, having tested their ideas in New England, recrossed the Atlantic during the 1640s to apply that experience to a war-torn Britain and Ireland suddenly ripe for the imposition of godly order.[12]

The Massachusetts Bay Company, formed in 1629, attracted investments from London merchants who saw an opportunity to further the Puritan cause and make money. The Company recruited John Winthrop, a prosperous Suffolk lawyer, to lead the enterprise. By the spring of 1630 Winthrop and other East Anglian Puritans gathered 700 emigrants from among their relatives, friends, and neighbours. In April seven vessels set sail, arriving nine weeks later in Cape Ann harbour. Over a thousand emigrants a year—mostly family groups of middling economic status—followed them for the next decade, an exodus that ended when civil war erupted in England.[13]

Most trading companies involved in colonization kept their headquarters in London, where royal officials could observe their activities. But the Massachusetts Bay Company's charter stipulated no location, and when Company leaders decided to meet in America, they effectively transformed a commercial charter into an instrument of government. The Governor and General Court of the Company became, respectively, the Governor and legislature of the colony, with virtually autonomous control over an enterprise 3,000 miles away from royal oversight.[14]

Like Plymouth's settlers, Bay colonists shared a corporatist vision, which they projected on society through the instrument of the covenant. Derived from the Puritans' understanding of the contractual nature of the relationship between God and humans, covenants governed religious and social relations. Massachusetts law required each town to have a church organized along congregational lines. Members signed a covenant that committed them to peaceful worship and fellowship. Town governments similarly used covenants to bind their inhabitants to live in harmony. Even if these agreements were frequently broken, they none the less expressed a genuine desire for co-operation.[15]

[12] On the remigration of ministers, see Andrew Delbanco, 'Looking Homeward, Going Home: The Lure of England for the Founders of New England', *NEQ*, LIX (1986), pp. 358–86.

[13] Andrews, *Colonial Period*, I, chaps. 17 and 18.

[14] Edmund S. Morgan, *The Puritan Dilemma: The Story of John Winthrop* (Boston, 1958), pp. 84–86.

[15] Morgan, *Puritan Dilemma*, pp. 69–83, 93–95; Kenneth A. Lockridge, *A New England Town: The First Hundred Years* (New York, 1970), chaps. 1 and 2. The most eloquent expression of covenantal ideals in New England is John Winthrop's lay sermon, 'A Model of Christian Charity', in *The Winthrop Papers*, ed. Allyn B. Forbes and others, 6 vols. (Boston, 1929–92), II, pp. 282–95.

Covenants linked inhabitants within towns but not between them, contributing to the development of a powerful localism. Towns seldom encountered interference from a central government that often encouraged local autonomy. So long as none of their activities violated colony law, townsmen could make whatever political arrangements they desired. This freedom fostered diverse patterns of local administration. Settlers from various parts of England attempted either to replicate former practices or to compromise with fellow townsmen of different backgrounds.[16] Yet broad similarities eventually emerged within the colony. Most towns elected a committee (usually called the board of 'selectmen') to manage town finances, execute local ordinances, and resolve disputes. They also called town meetings, usually at least twice a year. Townsmen met each spring to elect a representative to the General Court; they could, however, meet at any time to debate issues too important—or too divisive—to leave to the selectmen's discretion.[17]

Towns also controlled local land policy. The General Court granted land to towns as corporate entities, leaving allocation to the inhabitants. They generally avoided complex English systems of land tenure in favour of freeholdership, which conferred outright ownership and the freedom to sell or bequeath land at will. Town grants were typically large, but colonists rarely divided up a whole tract at once, if only because few families could clear more than a couple of acres each year. Most households began with holdings of ten to fifty acres, distributed by selectmen on the basis of each householder's social rank and responsibilities. This ensured that no family declined in social standing because of emigration and yet gave even poor families enough property to support themselves. Towns retained as 'common' those lands not initially divided among the inhabitants, distributing them as the need arose among the grantees (called 'proprietors') or their descendants. Most farmers eventually accumulated estates of 100 or 200 acres.[18]

Townsmen jealously guarded local privileges and occasionally clashed with colony magistrates over the interpretation of the Company charter that had become the colony's instrument of government. The charter placed governing power in the hands of shareholders (called 'freemen'), who comprised the General

[16] David Grayson Allen argues that local differences based on diverse English experience endured for at least a generation; see *In English Ways*, *passim*; see also Sumner Chilton Powell, *Puritan Village: The Formation of a New England Town* (Middletown, Conn., 1963), chaps. 2 and 3.

[17] John Fairfield Sly, *Town Government in Massachusetts (1620–1930)* (Cambridge, Mass., 1930), chap. 2; Kenneth A. Lockridge and Alan Kreider, 'The Evolution of Massachusetts Town Government, 1640 to 1740', *WMQ*, Third Series, XXIII (1966), pp. 54, 74.

[18] Virginia DeJohn Anderson, *New England's Generation: The Great Migration and the Formation of Society and Culture in the Seventeenth Century* (New York, 1991), pp. 92–100. For an interpretation that stresses entrepreneurialism over communalism, see John Frederick Martin, *Profits in the Wilderness: Entrepreneurship and the Founding of New England Towns in the Seventeenth Century* (Chapel Hill, NC, 1991).

Court. But this group included only a minority of the adult male colonists. When the General Court first met in October 1630, many men attended who technically had no political role. The Court extended freemanship to all adult male landowners, later stipulating that they also be church members. After further disputes with Winthrop and other magistrates, the freemen appropriated the right to elect the Governor and Deputy Governor, as well as to choose representatives to the two houses (the Court of Assistants and the General Court) of the legislature. This system of representative government lasted until the end of the century.[19]

By 1650 New England contained over forty towns and nearly 23,000 colonists.[20] Land policy stimulated the proliferation of towns by awarding special advantages to proprietors. Proprietors, as the earliest settlers, divided the best farmland among themselves, located their house lots near the town centre, chose the town minister, often served as selectmen, and held rights to future divisions of common land. Later arrivals, denied such benefits, often chose to move on and found other towns.[21]

This expansion of settlement soon created new colonies. Settlers leaving Massachusetts for various religious, economic, and political reasons established Connecticut, New Hampshire, Rhode Island, and New Haven, replicating the intense localism of Massachusetts along with some version of its representative government. But each new colony also acquired a distinctive character because of the motives that inspired its founders to leave the Bay Colony.

As early as the mid-1630s, some Bay colonists began to complain of overcrowding. Since they frequently specified a shortage of pasture, the problem seems to have arisen more from an increase in livestock rather than the human population. Settlers headed for the rich meadows of the Connecticut River Valley in 1634, founding towns at Wethersfield, Windsor, and Hartford. The exodus gained momentum in 1636 when the Revd Thomas Hooker took part of his Cambridge congregation to Hartford. Good farmland doubtless attracted Hooker, who had a large family, but some contemporaries suspected that he wanted to put distance between himself and Boston's leading minister, John Cotton, with whom he disagreed on several doctrinal points.[22]

The Massachusetts government claimed jurisdiction over the new towns, although they were far from Boston and the Bay Colony had no legal title to the region. New Netherlands and Plymouth Colony already had trading posts near

[19] Morgan, *Puritan Dilemma*, pp. 90–92, 107–14.

[20] John J. McCusker and Russell R. Menard, *The Economy of British America, 1607–1789* (Chapel Hill, NC, 1985), Table 5.1, p. 103.

[21] Anderson, *New England's Generation*, chap. 3.

[22] Andrews, *Colonial Period*, II, chap. 3; Frank Shuffelton, *Thomas Hooker, 1586–1647* (Princeton, 1977), pp. 208–09.

Hartford and protested the settlers' intrusion. Late in 1635 Massachusetts's claim lost force when a group of English peers obtained a patent to Connecticut lands from the Council for New England and sent John Winthrop, Jr., to set up a colony. Ironically, only the Pequot Indians welcomed the settlers, for they hoped to make them military allies. This diplomatic overture, however, failed once it was apparent that the price of an alliance was Pequot subjugation to English authority.[23]

The Pequots, beset by Indian foes and confronting belligerent colonists, set aside their long-standing enmity toward the Narragansetts and invited them to join a pan-Indian union against the settlers. The plan failed and the Narragansetts, who would have preferred neutrality, became allies of the English. War began in 1637 with a series of Pequot raids on the river towns; the English (with Indian allies) responded in kind. The violence culminated in May 1637 with the massacre of several hundred Pequots—mainly women, children, and old men—in a village near the Mystic River. Afterwards, English soldiers rounded up the remaining Pequots, executing most of the men and selling the women and children into slavery.[24] (Map 15.1)

The war destroyed Pequot power and demonstrated the high cost of opposing English soldiers. Some Indian groups, such as the Mohegans, submitted to English dominance; others, such as the Narragansetts, struggled to preserve their independence. The settlers viewed the war as a religious as well as a military triumph, providing incontrovertible evidence of divine favour. Their victory also solved the problem of Connecticut's political and legal status.

During the conflict a commission jointly appointed by John Winthrop, Jr., and the Massachusetts General Court ostensibly governed Connecticut. Problems with managing and financing the colony's defence, however, revealed the commission's ineffectiveness. In response, Connecticut's inhabitants created their own General Court, composed of committees chosen by the towns and magistrates elected by the committees. After the war, in 1639, they drew up a compact called the Fundamental Orders, which created a system for the election of a Governor, magistracy, and representative Assembly similar to that in Massachusetts, with the one difference that Connecticut's freemen did not have to be church members. The Fundamental Orders remained in force until 1662, when Connecticut received a royal charter that ratified its provisions.[25]

Connecticut's society closely resembled that of Massachusetts, with townsmen controlling local affairs, churches, and land distribution. Early demographic differences—more single men and fewer women in Connecticut—soon disappeared. As in Massachusetts, rapid population growth encouraged geographical

[23] Andrews, *Colonial Period*, II, pp. 75–92; Salisbury, *Manitou and Providence*, pp. 210–11.

[24] Salisbury, *Manitou and Providence*, pp. 211–26.

[25] Andrews, *Colonial Period*, II, chap. 4.

expansion. By 1675 settlers occupied the entire coastal region and most of the river valley, and had founded towns on Long Island—much to the dismay of the Dutch, who claimed it as theirs. The principal difference between Connecticut and Massachusetts testified to the early settlers' accurate perceptions. Better land and a slightly longer growing season gave Connecticut's farmers a generally higher standard of living.[26]

Like Connecticut, New Hampshire began as an extension of Massachusetts. In 1622 two members of the Council for New England, Sir Ferdinando Gorges and Captain John Mason, acquired title to lands along the Piscataqua and Merrimack rivers, hoping for profits from fishing and the Indian trade. Gorges also contemplated founding an Anglican colony. They sent colonists who built three settlements; only two—Strawberry Bank (later Portsmouth) and the Isles of Shoals—survived. New Hampshire began to grow only when Massachusetts settlers moved there in the 1630s.

Some new arrivals sought farms; others moved for political or religious reasons. A few were enemies of John Winthrop and his allies, and some were Anglicans unwelcome in the Puritan colony. Still others—including the Revd John Wheelwright, brother-in-law of Anne Hutchinson—were exiles, banished from Massachusetts after the Antinomian Controversy in 1637 (discussed below). When Massachusetts asserted control over the new settlements, the heirs of Mason and Gorges sued to recover their inheritance. The dispute dragged on until 1679, when English officials finally made New Hampshire a royal colony with an appointed Governor—thus setting it apart from all other New England colonies.[27]

The first settlers of Rhode Island and New Haven also arrived by way of Massachusetts. They shared religious motives for leaving the Bay Colony, but disagreed completely on the reason: Rhode Islanders chafed under the rule of the dominant religious establishment, while New Haven's founders believed that Massachusetts's churches were insufficiently orthodox. In each case, the founders' distinctive religious visions shaped colonial development.

English settlement of Rhode Island began in 1635 with the arrival of Roger Williams, a radical Separatist banished from the Bay Colony. Williams called Massachusetts's churches impure because they had neither rejected the Church of England nor instituted criteria for membership stringent enough to exclude the unregenerate. He also contended that the English King had no right to grant Indian lands to settlers and that the civil government could not legitimately

[26] Jackson Turner Main, *Society and Economy in Colonial Connecticut* (Princeton, 1985), chaps. 1 and 3.

[27] David E. Van Deventer, *The Emergence of Provincial New Hampshire, 1623–1741* (Baltimore, 1976), chaps. 1 and 3.

enforce the first four of the Ten Commandments. Such ideas led to charges of sedition, and Williams was ordered back to England.[28]

Fleeing to Rhode Island, Williams and a few followers established the village of Providence on land purchased from the Indians. Soon other settlers, most of whom also sought asylum, moved there. The most notorious was Anne Hutchinson, another exile from Massachusetts. Soon after arriving in Boston in 1636, she had acquired a following as an interpreter of John Cotton's sermons. The magistrates, alarmed by her radical insistence on grace, accused her of antinomianism, the view that the Elect were exempt from moral law. Her position was not as extreme as that, but during her trial she claimed to receive direct revelations from God. Her judges banished her as a blasphemer in 1637, along with many of her adherents. Hutchinson eventually moved to Long Island, but others in her company stayed in Rhode Island.

Rhode Island remained a loose confederation of towns united only when threatened by other colonies' claims to their land. To counter these moves, Roger Williams returned to England in 1644 to get a charter from the Puritan Parliament—repeating this mission in 1663, when the restoration of Charles II invalidated the earlier document. The charter established the colony's boundaries and instituted a government similar to those of its neighbours, with an elected Governor and bicameral legislature. The similarity ended there, however. Rhode Island remained an outcast society, lacking the internal cohesion of its neighbours and deliberately excluded from the Confederation of New England, formed in 1643 to manage regional defence. Williams's insistence on religious toleration only sealed the colony's contemporary reputation as a blot on the otherwise godly map of New England.[29]

New Haven was the last New England colony to be founded and the first to disappear. A group of intensely rigorous Puritans, led by the Revd John Davenport and Theophilus Eaton, a wealthy London merchant, arrived in Boston in the midst of the Antinomian Controversy. Horrified by the turmoil in Boston, they moved to Quinnipiac on Long Island Sound where they planned to improve on Massachusetts's evidently imperfect example of a holy commonwealth. But New Haven also fell victim to contention, as Davenport and Eaton struggled for control and colonists fought among themselves. The commercial aspirations of the founders—many of them merchants—were frustrated by an inferior harbour and competition from Connecticut and New Netherland. Connecticut, emerging from the Pequot War with ambitions for regional dominance, and recognizing

[28] Morgan, *Puritan Dilemma*, chap. 9.

[29] For Rhode Island's beginnings, see Sydney V. James, *Colonial Rhode Island: A History* (New York, 1975).

that New Haven's lack of a charter made it vulnerable, mounted an aggressive campaign to take over its weaker neighbour. It succeeded in annexing New Haven in 1665.[30]

Religious Culture

The prominence of religion as a motive for emigration from England—and of religious dissent as an incentive for migration within New England—ensured that spiritual concerns would strongly influence the region's development. Puritanism both shaped local culture and fostered connections between New England and other parts of the Empire. New England ministers exchanged letters with English Puritans; John Cotton corresponded with Oliver Cromwell. Puritan merchants in London provided New Englanders with credit for goods and capital for enterprises such as ironworks. Colonists solicited funds from their co-religionists in England for Indian missions. Both John Winthrop and Emmanuel Downing maintained contact with their relatives who had settled in Ireland, while they also hoped to draw recruits from among the Scots Calvinists who became ever more numerous in Ulster. They also familiarized themselves with other Puritan groups in America, whether in the Chesapeake or the West Indies, and they paid particularly close attention to the short-lived Puritan settlement of Providence Island, off the coast of Nicaragua. Some New Englanders even moved there.[31]

It was in New England itself, however, where Puritanism exerted its greatest influence. Although no colony allowed religious leaders to wield civil power directly, secular and spiritual authority were mutually supportive. The alliance between magistrates and ministers emerged most clearly in Massachusetts. Each town had to have a church, and the inhabitants—whether members or not—had to attend services and pay taxes to support the minister. The colony's legal code, the Body of Liberties of 1641, drew upon Scripture as well as English practice in defining the bounds of acceptable behaviour—specifying, for example, twelve capital offences, of which eleven (including idolatry, blasphemy, and adultery) followed Old Testament precedent. Ministers preached special sermons on election days and official days of fasting or thanksgiving. The founding of Harvard College in 1636, and a 1647 law requiring towns with at least fifty families to hire a schoolmaster, were as much religious as educational measures. Harvard supplied a

[30] Isabel MacBeath Calder, *The New Haven Colony* (New Haven, 1934).

[31] Francis J. Bremer, *Congregational Communion: Clerical Friendship in the Anglo-American Puritan Community, 1610–1692* (Boston, 1994); Bernard Bailyn, *The New England Merchants in the Seventeenth Century* (Cambridge, Mass., 1955), pp. 34–38, 62–63; William Kellaway, *The New England Company, 1649–1776: Missionary Society to the American Indians* (London, 1961), chaps. 1–5; Karen Ordahl Kupperman, *Providence Island, 1630–1641: The Other Puritan Colony* (New York, 1993), p. 325.

trained ministry, while the schoolmasters aimed to create a laity capable of reading the Bible.[32]

Puritan emigrants intent on creating a godly 'city on a hill' in Massachusetts undertook a remarkable experiment to prevent the unregenerate from joining their churches or exercising political power. By the mid-1630s Massachusetts churches required prospective members to convince the minister and existing membership that they had experienced conversion. Surviving narratives of these examinations attest to the intensity of the experience and the participants' scrupulousness in evaluating its authenticity.[33] Successful candidates completed an extraordinary rite of passage to full participation in a society that restricted the franchise, as well as church membership, to the Saints, or God's converted.

This public piety rested upon a foundation of private devotion. Families and neighbours gathered to read and discuss the Bible, offering women and children opportunities for participation denied them in public worship. Some colonists followed rigorous courses of private study and prayer. Book ownership was more widespread in New England than anywhere else in the English colonies; the predominance of Bibles and religious tracts in probate inventories attests to an impressive level of lay piety. Private devotions enhanced understanding of Sabbath sermons, the cornerstone of Puritan worship. Over his or her lifetime, the average churchgoer listened to perhaps 7,000 sermons, each of two or more hours' duration. The message varied little from pulpit to pulpit as ministers drew upon a common sequence of Scriptural texts. Preachers, with few rivals as authority figures in early New England, helped to shape a remarkably consistent religious culture.[34]

Certain tensions strained this impressive religious culture. Puritans who gravitated towards Congregationalism were always—except during the years of the Interregnum—identified as nonconformists in England. Their efforts to establish their beliefs as an established faith in New England left many of their followers struggling to come to terms with this transformation. The churches' effort to

[32] Theodore Dwight Bozeman, *To Live Ancient Lives: The Primitivist Dimension in Puritanism* (Chapel Hill, NC, 1988), chap. 5; Stephen Foster, *Their Solitary Way: The Puritan Social Ethic in the First Century of Settlement in New England* (New Haven, 1971), chap. 3; Harry S. Stout, *The New England Soul: Preaching and Religious Culture in Colonial New England* (New York, 1986), pp. 23–31; Nathaniel B. Shurtleff, ed., *Records of the Governor and Company of the Massachusetts Bay in New England*, 5 vols. (Boston, 1853–54), I, p. 183; II, p. 203.

[33] Morgan, *Visible Saints*, chap. 3; George Selement and Bruce C. Woolley, eds., 'Thomas Shepard's Confessions', *Colonial Society of Massachusetts Publications*, LVIII (Boston, 1981).

[34] Charles E. Hambrick-Stowe, *The Practice of Piety: Puritan Devotional Disciplines in Seventeenth-Century New England* (Chapel Hill, NC, 1982); David D. Hall, *Worlds of Wonder, Days of Judgment: Popular Religious Belief in Early New England* (New York, 1989), chap. 1; Stout, *New England Soul*, p. 4, chap. 2; Charles Lloyd Cohen, *God's Caress: The Psychology of Puritan Religious Experience* (New York, 1986).

create new criteria for membership manifested this process in one way; contention between clergy and laity showed it in another. Lay control had typified English Puritanism, and New Englanders expected to continue exercising authority in their churches. But New England ministers began to stress their indispensable functions as preachers and administrators of the sacraments. Some claimed that their authority came from Christ through their ordinations, and not through the congregation's call to office. Ministers even met in synods, threatening the cherished ideal of congregational independence.[35]

The struggle between clergy and laity emerged most clearly in 1662, when a synod addressed the problem of shrinking church membership. Together with the region's rapid population growth, strict scrutiny of prospective members' conversion narratives was opening a huge gap between church members and the population as a whole by the early 1660s. As the children of the Saints awaited their conversions, they did not hesitate to marry, but as non-members of their congregations they could not claim the privilege of baptism for their offspring. The ministers proposed to modify the requirements so that church members' adult children—baptized by virtue of their parents' membership but lacking the conversion experience necessary for full membership—could have their own children baptized. Thus second- and third-generation colonists would be brought under the authority of the clergy but could not take communion or vote in church affairs until they demonstrated an experience of saving grace. Derided by its opponents as the Half-Way Covenant (which polluted congregations with 'half-way' Christians), the proposal was overwhelmingly rejected by the churches to which it was submitted for approval. Only towards the end of the century did many churches adopt the measure that their ministers had long espoused.[36]

Rejection of the Covenant showed that ministers had done their job only too well: they had instructed their congregations so assiduously in the perils of seeking membership without assurance of grace that worshippers feared the consequences of lowering admission standards. Throughout the seventeenth century ordinary people listened to the preachers' message and interpreted it to fit with their own experience. Some colonists, however, differed too profoundly with orthodox views to remain within the fold of fellowship.

The range of acceptable differences of opinion was limited. The Newbury, Massachusetts, church adopted Presbyterian practices without arousing concern, but most variations were rooted out. Even Particular Baptists—predestinarian Calvinists who denied the efficacy of infant baptism—were unwelcome. Far more

[35] David D. Hall, *The Faithful Shepherd: A History of the New England Ministry in the Seventeenth Century* (Chapel Hill, NC, 1972).

[36] Robert G. Pope, *The Half-Way Covenant: Church Membership in Puritan New England* (Princeton, 1969).

disturbing were extreme Separatists such as Roger Williams and antinomians such as Anne Hutchinson, whose beliefs threatened civil and religious disorder. When Quakers appeared in Massachusetts in the 1650s, proclaiming their radical ideas (including rejection of sacraments and an ordained ministry, and a belief in direct divine revelation), magistrates banished them. (Four Quakers were hanged in Boston between 1659 and 1661 for returning after banishment.) Vigilant magistrates could not eliminate dissent in New England, but drove it to the margins of settlement, including Rhode Island, parts of Plymouth Colony and New Hampshire, and Nantucket.[37]

Puritans would not tolerate heresy, but allowed certain popular religious beliefs. As providentialists, they discerned supernatural meanings in temporal events, sometimes in ways indistinguishable from superstition. Settlers mingled Christian and folk interpretations of such 'remarkable providences' as eclipses, sudden deaths, and 'monstrous births', and kept almanacs with astrological tables alongside their Bibles and religious tracts. Even as orthodox a Puritan as John Winthrop, Jr., dabbled in alchemy. Problems emerged, however, when such relatively innocuous activities gave way to consorting with the devil.[38]

Puritans, like almost all Christians of that time, believed in the existence of witches—humans who acted as Satan's agents. They identified witches by their exercise of special powers, by which they inflicted pain or property loss on their enemies. Connecticut executed New England's first accused witch in 1647; more than a dozen were hanged in the next few decades. Many more were accused of witchcraft and exonerated—free to sue their accusers for slander. But witchcraft remained only a small part of New England life until the winter of 1691–92, when several children and young women in Salem, Massachusetts, made accusations that launched the largest witch-hunt in New England history. Several hundred people were named as suspects, including the Governor's wife; in the end, nineteen women and men were convicted and hanged.

Salem's witch-hunt was notable for its size, but not its pattern of development. Witch-hunting was primarily a religious activity, sanctioned by ministers and inspired by a belief in Satan's malign influence in the world. It also sparked intense human dramas that set neighbour against neighbour and revealed troubled social relationships. Salem's crisis occurred against a backdrop of economic tension as some inhabitants seemed to prosper at the expense of others. More significantly, witch-hunting, in Salem and elsewhere, exposed a normally submerged suspicion of women. Far more women than men were accused—and convicted—of

[37] Philip F. Gura, *A Glimpse of Sion's Glory: Puritan Radicalism in New England, 1620–1660* (Middletown, Conn., 1984); Jonathan M. Chu, *Neighbors, Friends, or Madmen: The Puritan Adjustment to Quakerism in Seventeenth-Century Massachusetts Bay* (Westport, Conn., 1985).

[38] Hall, *Worlds of Wonder*, chap. 2.

witchcraft. This pattern probably arose from fears of female sexuality and maternal authority, since witches were thought especially to threaten infants and children. Most accused were comparatively poor, over 40 years old, and reputedly quarrelsome—characteristics that suggest other strains as well. Though poor, many accused witches were economically independent (often widows) in a society where men controlled property; that they were often cantankerous also hurt them in a culture founded upon co-operative ideals.[39]

The Salem crisis, though sometimes seen as the end of Puritanism, marked a shift in religious culture that occurred as New England's founding generation died off. New leaders, awed by the achievements of their parents, dismayed by social change, and beset by crises that included not only witchcraft but a terrifying Indian war and the royal confiscation of colonial charters (discussed below), lamented their inadequacy even as they proved themselves capable of guiding New England toward the new century. The religious fervour of the early years moderated, but a culture founded upon Puritan beliefs endured. Townsmen ritually renewed the covenants of the founders, hoping to reinvigorate a sense of communal purpose. A new generation of writers composed providentialist histories that, while unsparing in their criticism of errors, still proclaimed New Englanders to be a chosen people.[40]

Economy and Society

Although second-generation New Englanders worried that worldly success might overshadow religious ideals, their region generated far less wealth than the Chesapeake or Caribbean plantation colonies. Lacking a staple crop such as tobacco or sugar, the economy relied on capital brought by settlers until immigration ceased in 1641 and a severe depression ensued. The Massachusetts General Court offered bounties and other incentives to encourage local production of goods that otherwise had to be imported from England. Shortages of capital and labour thwarted these efforts, but the region's economy gradually improved as settlers learned to exploit local resources. By 1700 they had created a diversified economy far less prone to cyclical disruption than were the staple-crop colonies and developed patterns of trade that linked New England to the transatlantic commercial Empire.

[39] The vast literature on New England witchcraft has produced much disagreement about its causes and social implications. Influential works include: Paul Boyer and Stephen Nissenbaum, *Salem Possessed: The Social Origins of Witchcraft* (Cambridge, Mass., 1974), which links witchcraft to social and economic tensions in Salem; John Putnam Demos, *Entertaining Satan: Witchcraft and the Culture of Early New England* (New York, 1982), which examines witchcraft incidents prior to the Salem outbreak in their social and psychological contexts; and Carol F. Karlsen, *The Devil in the Shape of a Woman: Witchcraft in Colonial New England* (New York, 1987), which situates witchcraft within the context of gender relations.

[40] Anderson, *New England's Generation*, chap. 5; Stout, *New England Soul*, chap. 6.

Their greatest success came from the sea. New Englanders soon dominated the North Atlantic cod fishery. As early as 1645 the value of fish exports reached £10,000, and these profits spawned ventures in shipbuilding and commerce. Using wood from their seemingly limitless forests, colonists constructed hundreds of vessels, and many coastal villagers earned substantial portions of their income from shipbuilding and related crafts. By 1660 New England fishermen obtained nearly all of their boats locally; by the end of the century colonial shipbuilders supplied the English market as well.[41]

Colonial merchants expanded from marketing of fish into broader trade networks. Wine received in exchange for fish in the Wine Islands (Madeira, the Canaries, and the Azores), for instance, was sold in English and colonial markets. New England produced little that England could use, but its trade with the West Indies ensured its economic vitality. With most of their land planted in sugar cane, the islanders needed the livestock, preserved meat and fish, corn, and wooden staves (for making barrels) that New Englanders brought to exchange for sugar, molasses, and other tropical products. Because its food exports fed Caribbean slaves, New England—although too poor to import many slaves of its own—depended upon slavery to sustain its economy. Meanwhile, other correlates of trade, including freight charges, insurance, and the extension of commercial credit, enriched the region. By 1676 English merchants complained that New England had supplanted the mother country as 'the great Mart and Staple' of the Atlantic world.[42]

Maritime industries led the seventeenth-century economy, but most colonists made their living through agriculture. Even artisans and professionals—including ministers—farmed in addition to their other activities. Efforts to reproduce English agricultural practices in New England met with only partial success. Many settlers came from England's wood-pasture regions, where farmers raised both crops and livestock, and they followed a similar agricultural regime in New England. But instead of wheat (which proved vulnerable to black stem-rust fungus), colonists grew maize as their main crop, learning about its use and cultivation from Indians. Settlers transplanted English animals more successfully than grains. Livestock-raising suited a society short on labour. Swine and cattle populations grew rapidly, providing sustenance for settlers and a major item of export to the West Indies.[43]

Most colonial farmers prospered modestly, raising food for their families and small surpluses for local exchange. Their goal was 'competency'—a comfortable

[41] McCusker and Menard, *Economy of British America*, pp. 99–101.

[42] Ibid., pp. 100–01; quotation on p. 84; see below p. 222.

[43] Anderson, *New England's Generation*, pp. 137–57; Howard S. Russell, *A Long, Deep Furrow: Three Centuries of Farming in New England* (Hanover, NH, 1976), chaps. 1–4.

household independence. Rooted in freehold ownership of land, it was a goal that most colonists—unlike most English people—achieved and passed on to their descendants.[44] This economic success reinforced certain distinctive characteristics of New England society.

Because most emigrants were of middling economic status, social stratification was limited in early New England; it remained limited because colonists succeeded in attaining competencies. The policy of granting free land to townsmen guaranteed that few colonists would live in poverty, even as the scarcity of capital compressed the spectrum of wealth. The lack of a staple crop—which might have encouraged heavy investment in bound labour, as in the Chesapeake and Caribbean colonies—likewise fostered relative equality. New England competencies were gained through the labour of family members, not indentured servants or slaves. Yet because no farm, however prosperous, was completely self-sufficient, networks of local exchange developed that complemented the region's ideological commitment to communalism. Neighbours traded goods and services, maintaining accounts of mutual obligations to the same people with whom they had pledged co-operation in town and church covenants.[45]

In New England, as in England, adult males controlled economic resources, monopolized political and legal authority, and ruled their families. Women lacked legal identities apart from their fathers and, in adulthood, their husbands; only widows enjoyed some independence. The relationship between men and women was thus unequal, yet men did not exercise unlimited power. They were expected to provide for their families and rule benevolently over wives and children. New Englanders largely replicated English patterns, yet Puritan ideals and economic conditions caused certain changes in the character of patriarchal authority.

By emphasizing fathers' roles as spiritual, as well as secular, heads of their families, Puritanism added a new dimension to patriarchalism. Colonists took the fourth commandment seriously—even prescribing the death penalty, never enforced, for children convicted of unprovoked verbal or physical assault on their parents. Religious and legal injunctions, however, did less to enforce deference than fathers' control of economic resources. With enough land to provide farms for all of their sons, but too little labour to develop it without their help, fathers enforced prolonged dependency on sons until they permitted them to marry, usually in their mid-twenties. Even then, some fathers refused to transfer title to

[44] Anderson, *New England's Generation*, chap. 4; Daniel Vickers, 'Competency and Competition: Economic Culture in Early America', *WMQ*, Third Series, XLVII (1990), pp. 3–29.

[45] Daniel Vickers, 'Working the Fields in a Developing Economy: Essex County, Massachusetts, 1630–1675', in Stephen Innes, ed., *Work and Labor in Early America* (Chapel Hill, NC, 1988), pp. 49–69; Laurel Thatcher Ulrich, *Good Wives: Image and Reality in the Lives of Women in Northern New England, 1650–1750* (New York, 1982), chap. 3.

real property except in their wills—thus demonstrating the strength of paternal authority, but also revealing their reliance on their sons' labour.[46]

Women's lives also changed after emigration, although the results resist characterization as either improvement or deterioration. Puritanism emphasized the individual's relationship with God irrespective of gender; women were as likely as men to be numbered among the elect, and indeed comprised the majority of church members. Male and female equality before God, however, had few practical consequences. Although full members, women could not vote or otherwise manage church affairs. One Puritan reform—the transformation of marriage from sacrament to civil contract—did help some women by making divorce easier to obtain in cases of desertion or adultery.[47]

Women's labour was indispensable for the attainment of family competencies. They did housework, cared for children, prepared and preserved foods, tended gardens, and produced such marketable items as textiles, butter, eggs, and cheese. Although men technically owned the family's property, women informally owned the products of their own labour, trading them and their services with neighbouring wives in a distinct 'female economy'. Custom sanctioned the notion of female inferiority, but in practice women often performed the duties, if only temporarily, of absent or indisposed husbands in managing farms and shops. In the early years of settlement men may have especially valued women's contributions. Most husbands trusted their wives' managerial skills sufficiently to make them executors of their estates, a practice that diminished in the eighteenth century.[48]

Women devoted much of their lives to bearing and rearing children, fuelling New England's remarkable demographic expansion. The non-Indian population increased from about 14,000 in 1640 to nearly 23,000 a decade later; by 1700 it surpassed 90,000.[49] Virtually all growth after 1640 came from natural increase. The comparatively even sex ratio among the first settlers, with perhaps six men for every four women (compared to four or five men per woman in the early Chesapeake) started population growth early, and the tendency of New Englanders to marry earlier than their English counterparts—at about 22 on average for women and 25 for men—helped sustain it at high levels thereafter. Women typically bore seven or eight children, six or seven of whom survived to produce

[46] Philip Greven, *The Protestant Temperament: Patterns of Child-Rearing, Religious Experience, and the Self in Early America* (New York, 1977), pp. 32–55; John Demos, *A Little Commonwealth: Family Life in Plymouth Colony* (New York, 1970), chap. 6; Philip Greven, *Four Generations: Population, Land, and Family in Colonial Andover, Massachusetts* (Ithaca, NY, 1970), chaps. 3–4.

[47] Cohen, *God's Caress*, pp. 240–41; Edmund S. Morgan, *The Puritan Family: Religion and Domestic Relations in Seventeenth-Century New England*, revised edn. (New York, 1966), pp. 34–38.

[48] Ulrich, *Good Wives*, chaps. 1–3; Carole Shammas, Marylynn Salmon, and Michel Dahlin, *Inheritance in America: From Colonial Times to the Present* (New Brunswick, NJ, 1987), pp. 59–60.

[49] McCusker and Menard, *Economy of British America*, p. 103.

their own large families. Settlers enjoyed unusually long lives for the seventeenth century, with perhaps half surviving to age 70 or more.[50]

The creation of large, healthy families and the longevity of adults promoted social stability, not least by fostering the steady accumulation of family property and its orderly transfer from one generation to the next. The same conditions that favoured the colonists, however, threatened New England's Indians. A burgeoning population of settlers intent on securing land-based competencies confronted a shrinking population of Indians determined to preserve their territory and way of life. By the end of the century conflict between the two groups was all but inevitable.

Anglo-Indian Relations

Colonists' interactions with Indians dramatically shaped New England's development. The settlers could not have occupied the land so rapidly without the demographic disasters that preceded colonization. Epidemics of European diseases (smallpox, measles, influenza) swept through coastal Algonquian societies between 1616 and 1618, spreading inland in the 1630s. By 1700 only about 10 per cent of the pre-contact native population remained alive. The remarkable healthfulness and fecundity of the English population filled lands left vacant, while the cultural damage of the epidemics—the loss of native leaders, disruption of kinship networks, and discrediting of native religious systems—often rendered Indian survivors incapable of resistance.[51]

Colonists marvelled at the way God had 'cleared the land' for settlement; they were less able to grasp the positive contributions the Indians made to their survival. Plymouth's settlers would not have made it through their first winter had they not found supplies of Indian corn; for at least three more years they depended upon the Wampanoags for food. Furs trapped by native hunters helped Plymouth pay off its debts to English investors.[52] Indians initially assumed that they could incorporate the English into established networks of exchange, using trade to cement bonds of mutual protection as well as profit. But the natives' vision of reciprocal relations among equals was not shared by the colonists, or at least not for long.

The English desired dominance over the Indians, not equality with them. They could have achieved that through population growth alone: by 1633 settlers already outnumbered Indians in the Massachusetts Bay area. But they insisted on formal

[50] Anderson, *New England's Generation*, pp. 20–21, 180–83, 223, 225–26; Demos, *A Little Commonwealth*, pp. 192–93; Greven, *Four Generations*, pp. 26, 30.

[51] Salisbury, *Manitou and Providence*, pp. 101–09.

[52] Langdon, *Pilgrim Colony*, pp. 13, 33.

submission, making treaties like the 1621 agreement between the Wampanoag leader Massasoit and Plymouth that, in theory, subjected the Indians to the English King and the colony government. Similarly, the English sought advantage, not mutual benefit, through trade, disrupting native networks of exchange. Such aggressiveness helped spark the Pequot War in 1637, when English (and Dutch) traders rejected the Pequots' monopoly of the trade in European goods to the Connecticut interior.[53]

In the Bay Colony, the few surviving Massachusett Indians encountered English dominion in another form. Beginning in 1644, the Revd John Eliot endeavoured to convert them to Christianity—a process, he believed, that required the Indians first to give up their 'savage' ways and live like the 'civilized' English. With the sanction of the Bay Colony government, Eliot established fourteen 'praying towns' where Indians would learn to live and worship as the English did. Some natives, disoriented by disease and cultural disintegration, responded to Eliot's message; others remained sceptical. The praying towns never included more than a minority of Indians, and their inhabitants never fully abandoned native ways.[54]

Although relations between Indians and settlers remained tense after the Pequot War and violence broke out at times, peace prevailed for over three decades because the English could not afford to alienate the powerful Narragansetts (see Map 15.1), upon whom they depended for wampum. Wampum beads, made of purple and white shells of small whelks found along the coast of Long Island Sound, functioned as a critical item of exchange in a complex trade network. The Narragansetts and their allies produced the beads, using steel drills obtained from the English, and traded them to colonists for cloth, metal tools, and glass beads. The English in turn traded wampum with northern Indians for furs, and used the beads among themselves as currency. This trade relationship, of course, depended on a steady English demand for wampum. But by the 1660s New England Indians had few furs to trade and an influx of English specie induced colonists to abandon wampum as legal tender. The one remaining Indian possession that Englishmen coveted was land.[55]

[53] Salisbury, *Manitou and Providence*, chaps. 4, 5, 7; Ian K. Steele, *Warpaths: Invasions of North America* (New York, 1994), pp. 86–94.

[54] James Axtell, *The Invasion Within: The Contest of Cultures in Colonial North America* (New York, 1985), chap. 7; Neal Salisbury, 'Red Puritans: The "Praying Indians" of Massachusetts Bay and John Eliot', *WMQ*, Third Series, XXXI (1974), pp. 27–54; Harold W. Van Lonkhuyzen, 'A Reappraisal of the Praying Indians: Acculturation, Conversion, and Identity at Natick, Massachusetts, 1646–1730', *NEQ*, LXIII (1990), pp. 396–428. See above, pp. 167–68.

[55] Salisbury, *Manitou and Providence*, pp. 147–52; Salisbury, 'Indians and Colonists in Southern New England after the Pequot War: An Uneasy Balance', in Laurence M. Hauptman and James D. Wherry, eds., *The Pequots in Southern New England: The Fall and Rise of an American Indian Nation* (Norman, Okla., 1990), pp. 90–91.

The settlers' land hunger intensified after 1660 as a new generation sought farms. Colonists settled closer to native villages, and problems of their livestock trespassing in Indian cornfields worsened. Colony governments initially ordered livestock owners to compensate native farmers for damage, but this practice decreased as the balance of population and power shifted in favour of the English. Indians forced to live on diminishing territory could not ignore the incursions either of the animals or their owners, but lacked ways to defend themselves against the pressures of land-hungry colonists. Faced with the prospects of being forced to move away or to live as servants or labourers in English households, Indians by 1675 concluded that war—despite its risks—was perhaps their only hope of survival.[56]

In that year Wampanoag warriors launched a series of raids on Plymouth towns. Massasoit's son, Metacom (known to the English as King Philip), assumed leadership of a war begun in retaliation for decades of abuses at the hands of colonists. What began as Wampanoag raids blossomed into a larger conflict as virtually all of New England's Algonquian peoples strove to drive the English away. In proportion to the populations involved, King Philip's War remains the most destructive conflict in American history. Indians attacked more than half of all New England towns and destroyed a dozen. By the winter of 1675–76, however, English soldiers who had failed to defeat Indian warriors or even to defend English towns began to destroy Indian food supplies. Hunger and disease weakened Philip and his forces, while in western New England they were attacked by the Mohawks, a nation that stood to gain by helping the English. Soon after Philip's death in August 1676—shot by a Christian Indian—the war ended, and with it Indian political autonomy in New England.[57]

Many of Philip's followers were either executed or sold into slavery; even some Indian allies of the settlers fled to Canada or New York. Indians who stayed in settled areas of New England occupied marginal positions in English towns or isolated themselves in praying towns, which became, in effect, reservations. The settlers understood the war as a chastisement, but the victory as a sign of God's renewed favour. Instead of weakening their faith, the war strengthened it. Church membership reached unprecedented levels. New England had been tested and had survived; now it could expand, since the Lord had subdued its enemies.[58]

[56] Virginia DeJohn Anderson, 'King Philip's Herds: Indians, Colonists, and the Problem of Livestock in Early New England', *WMQ*, Third Series, LI (1994), pp. 601–24.

[57] Douglas Edward Leach, *Flintlock and Tomahawk: New England in King Philip's War* (New York, 1958); Russell Bourne, *The Red King's Rebellion: Racial Politics in New England, 1675–1678* (New York, 1990). Francis Jennings, *The Invasion of America: Indians, Colonialism, and the Cant of Conquest* (Chapel Hill, NC, 1975), chap. 17, emphasizes English aggression.

[58] On Puritan interpretations of victory, see Stout, *New England Soul*, pp. 77–85.

The colonists also rejoiced that victory had been achieved without help from England, interpreting this as an affirmation of their long-standing autonomy within the Empire. Neither the King nor his councillors concurred. In June 1676 the Lords of Trade—the Privy Council committee responsible for colonial affairs—sent Edward Randolph to Boston to gather evidence of Massachusetts's lax observance of Imperial directives. The war was not yet over. Randolph's observations of the devastation convinced him that the time was ripe to bring New England under royal control.[59]

Complaints had simmered for years about New Englanders' evasion of trade regulations, reluctance to recognize parliamentary authority, and refusal (mainly in Massachusetts) to permit Anglican worship. In 1684 the Court of Chancery annulled Massachusetts's charter to curb the settlers' overweening notions of independence. The following year James II announced his plan to combine the New England colonies with New York and New Jersey into a single unit called the Dominion of New England. It seemed as though New Englanders had conquered an internal foe only to be threatened by an unexpected adversary from across the sea.[60]

James's Dominion proved to be a short-lived experiment that ended in 1688 with his overthrow and exile from England and a rebellion in Massachusetts against his agent, Sir Edmund Andros. The end of the crisis did not, however, bring a return to previous arrangements. Connecticut and Rhode Island retained their elective governorships, but Massachusetts received a new charter in 1691 making it a royal colony with a Crown-appointed Governor. The charter eliminated church membership as a prerequisite for the franchise, altered procedures for land grants in such a way as to promote speculation, and guaranteed liberty of conscience for all Protestant Christians. It also confirmed Massachusetts's annexation of Plymouth Colony and its jurisdiction over Maine.[61] At this point New England's phase as a set of exclusively Puritan colonies was over, but the experiment was already being imitated by other religious groups in England—notably the Quakers—who strove to achieve an ideal society in this world. Moreover, the New England Puritan quest was destined to serve as an inspiration for religious enthusiasts through the long history of England's involvement with Empire.

By the close of the seventeenth century the six original New England colonies had been reduced to four, and the survivors were enmeshed in a web of Imperial connections as never before. England no longer ignored the 'poor, cold, and

[59] Richard R. Johnson, *Adjustment to Empire: The New England Colonies, 1675–1715* (Leicester, 1981), pp. 28–29, 45–46. Randolph's report on the war is in Nathaniel Bouton and others, eds., *Provincial Papers: Documents and Records Relating to the Province of New-Hampshire*, 40 vols. (Concord, NH, 1867–1943), I, p. 344.

[60] Johnson, *Adjustment to Empire*, chap. 2.

[61] See below, pp. 456–62.

useless' region whose shipping industry and West Indies trade made it a vital part of the Imperial economy. The creation of the Board of Trade in 1696 and of royal governorships in Massachusetts and New Hampshire ensured a measure of English oversight of colonial activities. More than these institutional developments, however, new ties of sentiment bound New England to the mother country. With the founding generation dead and religious toleration (at least for Protestants) enforced, the old connections of family and Puritanism gave way to new-forged links of political allegiance. In Boston as in London, Englishmen celebrated a common heritage of rights and liberties that had been vindicated in the Glorious Revolution. The descendants of Winthrop and Endecott happily proclaimed themselves loyal and obedient subjects of the King—until, that is, the King gave them reason to think otherwise.[62]

[62] Richard L. Bushman, *King and People in Provincial Massachusetts* (Chapel Hill, NC, 1985).

Select Bibliography

VIRGINIA DEJOHN ANDERSON, *New England's Generation: The Great Migration and the Formation of Society and Culture in the Seventeenth Century* (New York, 1991).

CHARLES M. ANDREWS, *The Colonial Period of American History*, 4 vols. (New Haven, 1934–38).

BERNARD BAILYN, *The New England Merchants in the Seventeenth Century* (Cambridge, Mass., 1955).

WILLIAM BRADFORD, *Of Plymouth Plantation, 1620–1647*, ed. Samuel Eliot Morison (New York, 1975).

T. H. BREEN, *Puritans and Adventurers: Change and Persistence in Early America* (New York, 1980).

WILLIAM CRONON, *Changes in the Land: Indians, Colonists, and the Ecology of New England* (New York, 1983).

JOHN DEMOS, *Entertaining Satan: Witchcraft and the Culture of Early New England* (New York, 1982).

STEPHEN FOSTER, *The Long Argument: English Puritanism and the Shaping of New England Culture, 1570–1700* (Chapel Hill, NC, 1991).

PHILIP J. GREVEN, Jr., *Four Generations: Population, Land, and Family in Colonial Andover, Massachusetts* (Ithaca, NY, 1970).

DAVID D. HALL, *Worlds of Wonder, Days of Judgment: Popular Religious Belief in Early New England* (New York, 1989).

—— and DAVID GRAYSON ALLEN, eds., *Seventeenth-Century New England: The Colonial Society of Massachusetts Publications*, LXIII (Boston, 1984).

STEPHEN INNES, *Creating the Commonwealth: The Economic Culture of Puritan New England* (New York, 1995).

JOHN FREDERICK MARTIN, *Profits in the Wilderness: Entrepreneurship and the Founding of New England Towns in the Seventeenth Century* (Chapel Hill, NC, 1991).

EDMUND S. MORGAN, *The Puritan Dilemma: The Story of John Winthrop* (Boston, 1958).

—— *Visible Saints: The History of a Puritan Idea* (Ithaca, NY, 1963).

NEAL SALISBURY, *Manitou and Providence: Indians, Europeans, and the Making of New England, 1500–1643* (New York, 1982).
HARRY STOUT, *The New England Soul: Preaching and Religious Culture in Colonial New England* (New York, 1986).
LAUREL THATCHER ULRICH, *Good Wives: Image and Reality in the Lives of Women in Northern New England, 1650–1750* (New York, 1982).
DANIEL VICKERS, *Farmers and Fishermen: Two Centuries of Work in Essex County, Massachusetts, 1630–1830* (Chapel Hill, NC, 1994).
JOHN WINTHROP, *The History of New England from 1630 to 1649*, ed. James Savage, 2 vols. (Boston, 1825).

10

The 'Hub of Empire': The Caribbean and Britain in the Seventeenth Century

HILARY McD. BECKLES

Eric Williams, the historian who became the Prime Minister of Trinidad and Tobago, described the West Indian islands as 'the hub of Empire'.[1] Certainly by the end of the seventeenth century commentators on Empire such as Charles Davenant, Josiah Child, and Dalby Thomas judged the West Indian islands to be Britain's most profitable overseas investment. Eighteenth-century analysts of colonial trade and economic growth developed this argument in relation to profitability in the sugar plantation economy. For Adam Smith, the place of sugar among colonial produce was clear: 'the profits of a sugar plantation in any of our West Indian colonies are generally much greater than those of any other cultivation that is known either in Europe or America'.[2] 'The Sugar colonies', noted Arthur Young, 'added above three million [pounds] a year to the wealth of Britain.'[3] In our own time, however, there has been widespread agreement that the sugar colonies were dismal social failures.[4]

In 1600 England's interests in these 'small scraps of land' seemed 'more an opposition program' characterized by erratic, but violent, assault upon Spanish settlements and trade than the projection of a clearly defined policy of colonization.[5] Raiding and plundering became the norm, and represented what seemed to be the extent of English capabilities, attracting considerable capital from the investing community. English merchants thus proved themselves ready to invest in long-distance projects, even in politically volatile areas, once the returns were good.

During the twenty years of war with Spain, 1585–1604, there was 'no peace beyond the line', and the value of prize money brought to England from the

[1] Eric Williams, *Capitalism and Slavery* (1944; London, 1964), p. 52.

[2] Adam Smith, *The Wealth of Nations* (1776; New York, 1937), p. 538.

[3] Arthur Young, 'An Inquiry into the Situation of the Kingdom on the Conclusion of the Late Treaty', in *Annals of Agriculture and Other Useful Arts*, 14 vols. (London, 1784), I, p. 13.

[4] John J. McCusker and Russell R. Menard, *The Economy of British America, 1607–1789* (Chapel Hill, NC, 1985), pp. 144–45.

[5] K. G. Davies, *The North Atlantic World in the Seventeenth Century: Europe and the World in the Age of Expansion* (Minneapolis, 1974), p. 60.

Caribbean ranged between £100,000 and £200,000 per year.[6] Privateering, linked directly to contraband trades, continued to be important well into the century. It had an impact on everyday life in Jamaica (which came into English possession following Cromwell's Western Design of 1655–56 on Spanish possessions in the West Indies), especially as returns contributed to local financing of the agricultural economy.[7] The Elizabethan state, for tactical political reasons, had not wished publicly to support such Caribbean operations, but individual adventurers were confident that they had the means to solve any problem which might be encountered in the Americas, and they could call on financially experienced courtiers and gentlemen to organize and invest in these ventures.[8]

In these approaches to colonization, the English followed the Dutch, who had formulated ground-plans to trade and settle in the Caribbean. The Guiana coasts, located between Spanish settlements on the Orinoco and Portuguese possessions on the Amazon, attracted English as well as Dutch attention. In 1604, nine years after Ralegh's effort, Charles Leigh attempted a settlement on the Wiapoco. There were others: Harcourt's attempt (1609–13), Ralegh's (1617–18), and Roger North's (1619–21). An important outcome of these operations was the opportunity to survey the Windward and Leeward Islands, which the Spanish had left neglected and undefended.[9]

The Spanish had attached little economic value to the Lesser Antilles because the islands could not yield large quantities of precious metals, and the English who first became involved in individual islands also encountered determined opposition from the Kalinagos (Caribs) similar to that which had discouraged the Spaniards. The turning-point was Thomas Warner's visit to St Christopher (St Kitts) in 1622. Warner was a participant in North's Guiana project, and considered St Christopher ideally suited for the establishment of tobacco plantations. A group of mariners, led by John Powell, touched at Barbados in 1625 *en route* from the Guianas, and made similar observations. Warner and Powell returned to England to seek financial backing for a novel type of English colonizing activity (see Map 10.1).

Failed attempts at a Guiana settlement marked the beginning of a new approach by England to Caribbean colonization. The financial collapse of the Virginia Company in 1624 had resulted in a management takeover by the Crown which

[6] McCusker and Menard, *Economy of British America*, p. 147; see above, pp. 67–68.

[7] Nuala Zahedieh, 'Trade, Plunder, and Economic Development in Early English Jamaica', *Economic History Review*, XXXVIII (1986), pp. 205–22; 'The Merchants of Port Royal, Jamaica, and the Spanish Contraband Trade, 1655–1692', *William and Mary Quarterly* (hereafter *WMQ*), Third Series, XLIII (1986), pp. 570–93; '"A Frugal, Prudential and Hopeful Trade": Privateering in Jamaica, 1655–89', *Journal of Imperial and Commonwealth History*, XVIII (1990), pp. 145–68.

[8] Robert M. Bliss, *Revolution and Empire: English Politics and the American Colonies in the Seventeenth Century* (Manchester, 1990), p. 9; Davies, *North Atlantic World*, p. 61.

[9] J. H. Parry and P. Sherlock, *A Short History of the West Indies*, 3rd edn. (London, 1971), p. 48.

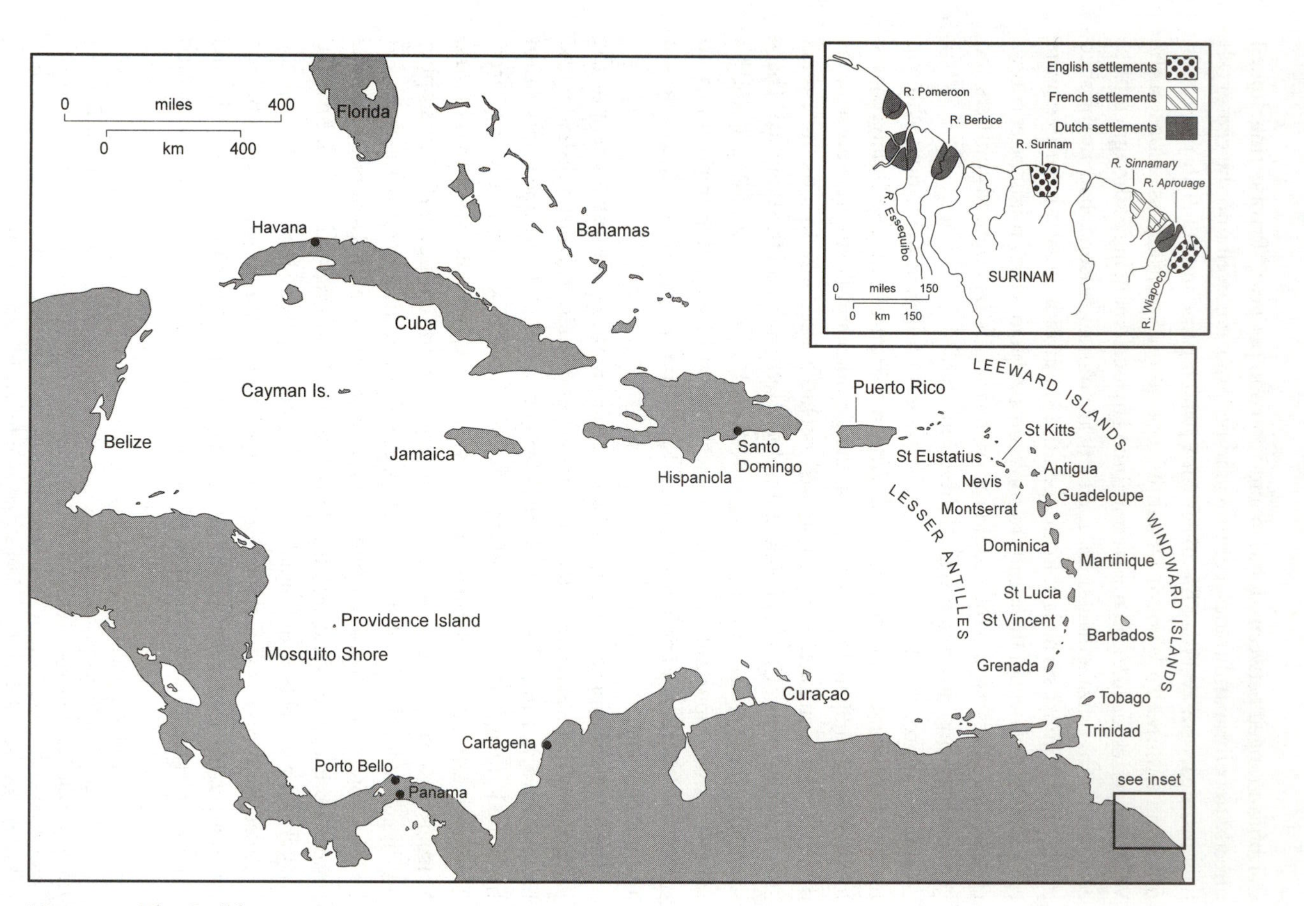

MAP 10.1. The Caribbean

signalled a greater determination to convert commercial enterprises into permanent settlement. The furthering of agricultural settlements financed by joint-stock companies, syndicates, and individuals symbolized the beginning of a conceptual triumph over the long-standing tradition of piracy. At the same time, it brought to the centre of the colonizing mission powerful groups of nobles and gentry who saw this as a new arena in which to compete for royal patronage, and some became participants in a 'patent war' for control of overseas territories. For example, on 2 July 1625 James Hay, Earl of Carlisle, was issued a grant by Charles I of the 'Caribbean Islands', and on 25 February 1628 the Earl of Pembroke obtained a grant from the King for the same territories. A violent and bloody struggle ensued between settlement parties despatched to the islands by both nobles, and it was only further royal intervention which settled the conflict in favour of Carlisle.[10]

In the next decade the Caribbean islands experienced a veritable 'swarming of the English' as more settlers established themselves in the West Indies than in any single mainland colony. This was in spite of the political and constitutional chaos which resulted from clashes between rival patents. What survived these conflicts, significantly, were the three principles that constituted the legacy of the failed Virginia Company: the option of a permanently settled community; the production for export of agricultural crops; and the idea that propertied Englishmen in far-flung colonies had an inalienable right to self-government. The aggressive promotion and defence of this legacy made the islands a place which held out greater prospects of glamour, excitement, danger, and quick profit than any mainland colony.[11]

Given the opportunity, these earliest English colonial sponsors would probably have followed their Spanish enemies into establishing some sort of feudal system, by subjecting the aboriginal population and establishing themselves as lords living on tributes, as they preferred the search for gold and silver to agricultural production for the export trade.[12] By the 1620s these opportunities were no longer available. Hopes of easy gold and the myth of Ralegh's El Dorado had subsided. It was clear that successful colonization in the Caribbean would be based on agriculture and trade.

The English established colonies at St Christopher in 1624, Barbados in 1627, Nevis in 1628, and Montserrat and Antigua in 1632. Previous to the campaign of 1655–56, when Oliver Cromwell added Jamaica to the list of English possessions, these small islands were the backbone of England's seaborne Empire, and the

[10] Davies, *North Atlantic World*, pp. 60, 61.

[11] McCusker and Menard, *Economy of British America*, p. 148.

[12] John H. Parry, 'The English in the New World', in K. R. Andrews, N. P. Canny, and P. E. H. Hair, eds., *The Westward Enterprise: English Activities in Ireland, the Atlantic and America, 1480–1650* (Liverpool, 1978), p. 2.

primary location of capital accumulation in the Americas. The economic importance of these islands far surpassed that of Puritan New England, but that is not to say that Puritans were not interested in the West Indies. Individual Puritans, including members of the prominent Winthrop and Downing families, spent some time in the West Indies, but collectively Puritans never attained the political power necessary to promote the West Indies as a location for New Jerusalem evangelism.[13] Even at Providence Island, off the coast of Nicaragua, where they financed a settlement and secured political control, the culture of piracy and smuggling, as well as cruel exploitation of unfree labour, transcended considerations of building a religious utopia and rendered their community indistinguishable from those of other European settlers in neighbouring islands.[14]

By 1640 the English had gained a demographic advantage in the Caribbean over other European nations. The islands attracted more settlers than mainland colonies up to 1660, which suggests that they were perceived as the destinations that held the best prospects for material and social advancement.[15] The white population grew rapidly up to about 1660 when it reached 47,000, constituting some 40 per cent of all the whites in Britain's transatlantic colonies. Gemery's estimates suggest that of the total of 378,000 white emigrants to America between 1630 and 1700, 223,000 (about 60 per cent) went to the colonies in the wider Caribbean.[16]

Economic depression and political turmoil of the 1620s and early 1630s, and the effective marketing of the colonies as places of opportunity for all classes, constituted a winning formula for pro-emigration agents. The population of Barbados in particular rose sharply during the 1630s, advancing sevenfold between 1635 and 1639. No other colony rivalled Barbados as a destination for settlers during this period. The West Indies also forged ahead of the mainland colonies in the expansion of economic activities. Investment and trade increased in direct relation to population growth, and West Indian capitalists were able to secure in the early years the greater share of labourers leaving both Ireland and Britain for America.

The organization of staple production—tobacco and cotton—in the formative years depended upon the labour of thousands of British indentured labourers.

[13] Jack P. Greene, *The Intellectual Construction of America* (Chapel Hill, NC, 1993), p. 55.

[14] Karen Ordahl Kupperman, *Providence Island, 1630–1641: The Other Puritan Colony* (Cambridge, 1993), chaps. 7 and 8.

[15] Davies, *North Atlantic World*, pp. 72–96.

[16] McCusker and Menard, *Economy of British America*, p. 154; Henry A. Gemery, 'Emigration from the British Isles to the New World', *Research in Economic History*, V (1980), pp. 179–231; 'Markets for Migrants: English Indentured Servitude and Emigration in the Seventeenth and Eighteenth Centuries', in P. C. Emmer, ed., *Colonialism and Migration: Indentured Labour before and after Slavery* (Dordrecht, 1986), pp. 33–54; Nicholas Canny, 'English Migration into and across the Atlantic during the Seventeenth and Eighteenth Centuries', in Canny, ed., *Europeans on the Move: Studies on European Migration, 1500–1800* (Oxford, 1994), pp. 39–75, esp. 64.

Unlike the islands acquired by the Spanish in the Greater Antilles, the Lesser Antilles lacked a large indigenous population which could be reduced to servitude. In the absence of a native labour force such as had been exploited by the Spaniards in Mexico and Peru, the obvious alternative supply of workers was found through the importation of indentured servants. This meant—as it also did in the Chesapeake—that the producer who commanded most servants was the individual most likely to succeed.[17]

Promoters of Empire in the first half of the seventeenth century published many polemical works, largely on demographic issues. Two main themes can be identified in these writings: the need to develop a labour market in the colonies which would rid England (and also Ireland and Scotland) of potential trouble-makers; and the need to ensure colonial dependence upon the mother country. Both themes were central to the notion of England and her colonies as 'one great body'. Such arguments should be understood in relation to the pervasive and narrow English nationalism which informed political and economic thinking. Each labourer, it was argued, had a duty to work as part of his moral obligation to society, and if work was not available then the community had a right to find work for him.[18] These ideologies, together with the views of statisticians that the home country was greatly over-populated, provided the conceptual basis for the legitimation of colonial indentured labour, and as the requirement for labour became more acute with the introduction of sugar production in the West Indies during the 1640s, the question of labour supply for the colonies became the subject of debate even in the House of Lords. Here, the Lords noted how indentured servants were 'hailed with delight by planters who wanted cheap labour' in their feverish 'desire to make quick fortunes'.[19]

During the seventeenth century more than half of all white immigrants in the English colonies south of New England were indentured servants. In addition, nearly half of the total white immigration to the West Indian colonies during the century was by indenture. Jamaica, for example, attracted more servants than the Chesapeake in the 1680s and more than any other colony up to 1700.[20]

[17] Winthrop Jordan, 'Unthinking Decision: Enslavement of Negroes in America to 1700', in T. H. Breen, ed., *Shaping Southern Society: The Colonial Experience* (New York, 1976), p. 100; see above, pp. 176–79, and Edmund S. Morgan, 'The First American Boom: Virginia, 1618–30', *WMQ*, Third Series, XXVIII (1971), pp. 178–79.

[18] See E. Lipson, *The Economic History of England*, 3 vols. (London, 1943), III, p. 164; E. Furniss, *The Position of the Laborer in a System of Nationalism* (New York, 1957), pp. 15–40.

[19] Cited in Leo F. Stock, ed., *Proceedings and Debates of the British Parliament Respecting North America, 1542–1739*, 4 vols. (Washington, 1924), I, pp. 185–86; see above, pp. 19–20.

[20] David Galenson, *White Servitude in Colonial America: An Economic Analysis* (London, 1981), pp. 3–19; and Galenson, *Traders, Planters, and Slaves: Market Behavior in Early English America* (New York, 1986), p. 137.

TABLE 10.1. *Population of the English West Indies, 1655–1715*

Barbados			*Jamaica*			*Leeward Islands*		
Year	White	Black	Year	White	Black	Year	White	Black
1655	23,000	20,000	*1660*	3,000	500	*1660*	8,000	2,000
1673	21,309	33,184	*1661*	2,956	3,479	*1670*	8,000	3,000
1684	19,568	46,502	*1673*	7,768	9,504	*1678*	10,408	8,449
1696	—	42,000	*1690*	10,000	30,000	*1690*	10,000	15,000
1715	16,888	—	*1713*	7,000	55,000	*1708*	7,311	23,500

Sources: For Barbados for 1655 see Vincent T. Harlow, *History of Barbados, 1625–1685* (Oxford, 1926), p. 338; for 1673, *Calendar of State Papers, Colonial Series [CSPC], 1669–1674*, no. 1101; for 1684, B[ritish] L[ibrary] Sloane MSS, 2441; for 1696, CO 318/2, f. 115; and for 1715, CO 28/16. The rounded figures for Jamaica in 1690 and 1713 and the Leewards in 1660, 1670, and 1690 are Dunn's estimates: Richard Dunn, *Sugar and Slaves* (see below, n. 22) p. 312. For Jamaica in 1673 see *Journal of the House of Assembly of Jamaica, 1663–1826*, I, p. 20. The Leeward figures for 1678 and 1708 are from CO 1/42, f. 193–243, and *CSPC, 1706–1708*, nos. 1383 and 1396. For other population estimates see David Galenson, *Traders, Planters and Slaves: Market Behaviour in Early English America* (Cambridge, 1986), pp. 4–5; John J. McCusker, 'The Rum Trade and the Balance of Payments of the Thirteen Continental Colonies, 1650–1775', unpublished Ph.D. dissertation, University of Pittsburgh, 1970, pp. 691–1775; and Robert V. Wells, *The Population of the British Colonies in America Before 1776: A Survey of Census Data* (Princeton, 1975), pp. 195–96, 238–39.

It is frequently alleged that these white workers were misled or duped into emigrating to a place that proved hazardous to their health, but it has also to be borne in mind that many found in the indenture contract a credit mechanism by which they could borrow against the future returns of their labour. Servants transported to the colony repaid the cost of passage and resettlement to their sponsor with labour. It was, therefore, a flexible and mutually attractive instrument that provided access to the West Indies for people without capital. 'Everyone knows', stated the historian A. E. Smith in a pungent description, that the colonial world 'was a haven for the godly', 'a refuge for the oppressed', 'a challenge to the adventurous', and 'the last resort of scoundrels'.[21]

Barbados developed the largest labour market in the West Indies during the century. This was because it led the way into large-scale sugar production. The opportunity to switch from tobacco and cotton production was open to planters in Barbados because sugar prices on the European market rose in the 1640s on account of production dislocations caused by civil war in Portuguese Brazil, previously the principal supplier. The more venturesome of the British planters in Barbados, with considerable Dutch financial and technological support, moved in and captured a significant market share. By the early 1650s Barbados produced an annual crop valued at over £3 million and was described as the richest spot in

[21] A. E. Smith, *Colonists in Bondage: White Servitude and Convict Labor in America, 1607–1776* (Chapel Hill, NC, 1947), p. 5.

the New World; the island's value, in terms of trade and capital generation, was greater than that of all the other English colonies put together. Barbados had replaced Hispaniola as the 'sugar centre' of the Caribbean, and the French islands lagged behind the English even though their production of sugar also rose steadily over the century. Richard Ligon captured the nature of this economic explosion in terms of the planters' expectations. He related the case of his friend Colonel Thomas Modyford, son of the Mayor of Exeter, who arrived on the island in 1645. Modyford bought a plantation of 500 acres and provided it with a labour force of twenty-eight English servants and a larger number of slaves. He took 'a resolution to himself not to set face in England, till he had made his voyage and employment there worth him a hundred thousand pounds sterling; and all by this sugar plant'. Modyford's optimism was, indeed, justified; by 1647 he had made a fortune and was made Governor in 1660. In the 1660s he expanded his interests into newly acquired Jamaica and became Governor of that island in 1664. At his death, in 1679, he owned one of the largest plantations in the West Indies, with over 600 slaves and servants.[22]

Reports from the West Indies during the second half of the century indicate the steady advance of sugar cultivation, although sugar monoculture was certainly not the case in these islands. Contests for the best lands in Jamaica between sugar farmers, cash-crop producers, and cattlemen remained as intense as that between agriculturalists and contraband traders for control of official policy with respect to the colony's development. Piracy and contraband also remained attractive in Jamaica as a means of wealth accumulation, despite the ascendancy of the agricultural trades which the mercantilist intellectuals considered to be the only sustainable source of wealth. The cultivation of cacao, which had been pursued on Jamaica by the Spaniards, was persisted in by some English planters, and it was the profits made from cacao that made it possible for some of them to become involved with sugar production. Efforts were also made to cultivate sugar on the four Leeward islands of Antigua, Montserrat, Nevis, and St Christopher, but none of these became a major sugar producer in the seventeenth century despite the fact that the planters in all these areas were lured by the Barbados model. Less suitable agricultural terrain, and the high cost of constructing the mill, the boiling house, and the curing house that was necessary on every sugar plantation, go some way towards explaining the limited advance of sugar production into the Lesser Antilles. The more weighty disincentive, however, would have been the close location of these islands to the Caribbean settlements of other European powers. Their consequent exposure to attack by European rivals made them altogether

[22] Richard Ligon, *A True and Exact History of the Island of Barbados* (London, 1657), pp. 69, 86, 93–96; Richard S. Dunn, *Sugar and Slaves: The Rise of the Planter Class in the English West Indies, 1624–1713* (London, 1973), pp. 68–69, 81–82, 154–55.

more risky places for the high capital investment that sugar required than Barbados and Jamaica. Instead of the monocrop production of sugar that came to characterize Barbados after the 1650s, the Lesser Antilles persisted with more mixed economic activity that included the production of indigo, tobacco, ginger, cotton, domesticated cattle, and fish as well as sugar.[23]

The reorganization of economic activity in Barbados and the Leewards is generally referred to as 'The Sugar Revolution'.[24] The cultivation of sugar cane on large plantations on Barbados steadily displaced the growing of tobacco, cotton, and indigo on smaller farms, and supplemented these activities on the other islands. Sugar planting, with its larger labour- and capital-equipment needs, stimulated demand for bigger units. Landowners enclosed on tenants, and small freeholders were bought out, and pushed off. As a result, land prices escalated and there was a rapid reduction in the size and output of non-sugar producers. In most islands some small-scale farmers continued to occupy prime lands, maintaining a cash-crop culture on the margins of plantations. But small farmers found it difficult to compete as tobacco and cotton prices fell and their operations often proved unprofitable. By the 1680s the 'sugar islands' had lost their reputation as hospitable places for propertyless European migrants, while the progress of sugar cultivation on the island of Barbados effected a more rapid and more total manipulation of the natural environment than occurred anywhere else in the Atlantic that came under English control during the course of the seventeenth century.[25]

Economic transformation had considerable implications for the social structure and political life of West Indian society. The emergence of a planter élite, considered the richest colonists in America, distinguished the 'sugar islands' and set them apart. In most colonies, successive generations of men from élite families dominated political institutions, legislatures, and judiciaries, and these were responsible for constructing mansions on the island of Barbados that matched those of comfortable English gentry families, as well as port towns and churches that gave a superficial English appearance to all these tropical islands. On the negative side, the more successful planters, especially on Barbados and Jamaica, used systems of exclusion such as property qualifications, membership of professional bodies,

[23] Dunn, *Sugar and Slaves*, esp. pp. 117–87; Jack P. Greene, 'Changing Identity in the British Caribbean: Barbados as a Case Study', in Nicholas Canny and Anthony Pagden, eds., *Colonial Identity in the Atlantic World, 1500–1800* (Princeton, 1987), pp. 213–66; R.B., *The English Empire in America* (London, 1685), pp. 167–209.

[24] By 1700 the English West Indies were producing about 40% of Europe's sugar (of which Barbados 40%, Jamaica 30%, and the Leewards 30%). See below, pp. 410–11.

[25] The question of environmental change in Barbados is touched upon in Dunn, *Sugar and Slaves*, pp. 44–116; and for a point of comparison see William Cronon, *Changes in the Land: Indians, Colonists and the Ecology of New England* (New York, 1983).

and possession of university degrees, which helped them to dominate colonial society at the expense of middling and smaller planters, as well as all non-whites. They also played prominent leadership roles in further colonial expansion. The sponsorship of Caribbean settlements in Jamaica, the Windwards, and the Guianas, as well as in Virginia and the Carolinas on the mainland, benefited in large measure from the migration and investments of Barbadian families.

Sugar meant slaves, and in the Lesser Antilles, as in Hispaniola and Brazil, it meant African slaves. Those acquainted with sugar production in Brazil would have known that the work regime was so severe that it would not be endured by any free labour force, and that planters had resorted to slaves imported from Africa. The work associated with sugar production was unusually burdensome because it involved a considerable manufacturing input on the plantation as well as harsh agricultural labour. Workers were required not only to clear the ground of lush natural vegetation and to sow, tend, and harvest the sugar cane in the tropical sun, but also immediately to crush the juice from the cane in a sugar mill, and then to boil the juice in cauldrons before it had time to ferment. Work on a sugar plantation was arduous and labour-intensive throughout the year, but was particularly onerous at harvest time when the sugar works operated incessantly, with the workers organized in shifts to keep the operation going.[26] Large profits in sugar during the mid-century meant that the more successful sugar planters could absorb the high labour cost associated with slavery and, as they rapidly dispensed with indentured servitude as unsuitable for sugar production, they established the islands as the greatest British colonial market for slaves. The capital and credit needed to revolutionize the market for unfree labour were available. English as well as Dutch merchants and financiers were eager to do business with sugar planters. By 1660 the African slave trade was the 'life line' of the Caribbean economy. In 1645, some two years after the beginning of sugar production, Barbados had only 5,680 slaves; in 1698 it had 42,000 slaves. Jamaica followed Barbados into 'sugar and slavery' towards the end of the century. In 1656 the colony had 1,410 slaves; in 1698 it had over 41,000.[27] The mortality of these slaves was high. Overwork, malnutrition, resistance, all contributed to this. The planters therefore needed an annual input of fresh slaves to keep up their stock. In 1688 it was estimated that Jamaica needed 10,000 slaves, the Leewards 6,000, and Barbados 4,000 to maintain existing stocks. The combination of the sugar trade and slave trade represents a dual economic system upon which the Caribbean depended.

Barbadian planters were to experience the pressing need to regularize the relations between slaves, servants, and masters. In 1661 legislators settled both

[26] Dunn, *Sugar and Slaves*, pp. 188–223.

[27] See Richard S. Sheridan, *Sugar and Slavery: An Economic History of the British West Indies, 1623–1775* (Bridgetown, 1973), pp. 234–60; Dunn, *Sugar and Slaves*, pp. 224–63.

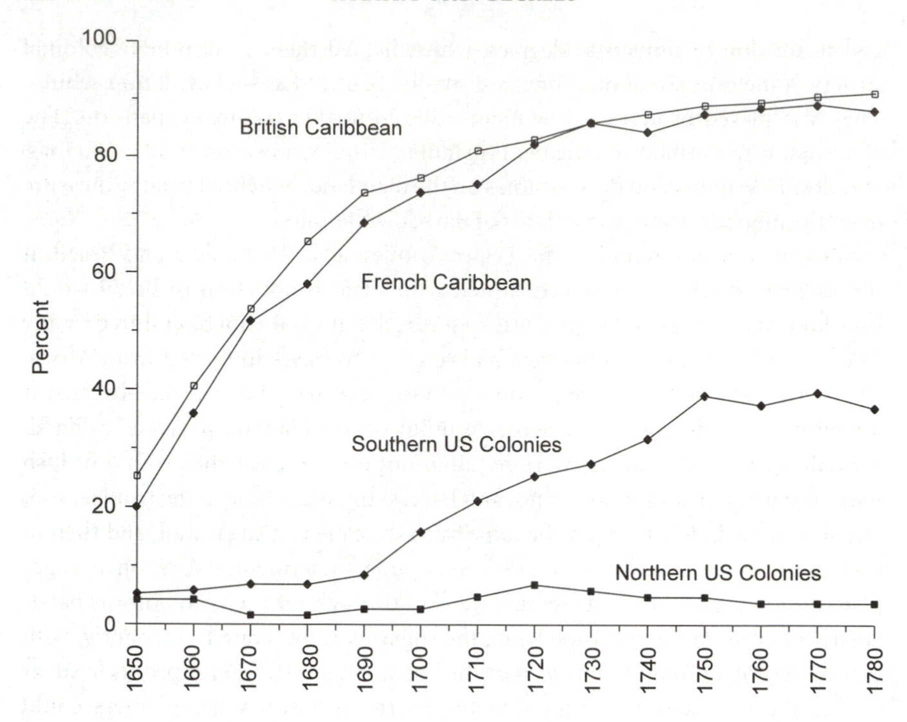

FIG. 10.1. *Blacks as a percentage of the total population in four regions*
Sources: Robert William Fogel and Stanley L. Engerman, *Time on the Cross: The Economics of Negro Slavery* (Boston, 1974), p. 21.

matters with two separate codes. The slave code, 'An Act for the Better Ordering and Governing of Negroes', sanctioned rigid segregation.[28] It formed the legal basis of slave–master relations, and represented an attempt legally to constitute the social order. It was amended in 1676, 1682, and 1688. It maintained that masters were responsible for the feeding, sheltering, and clothing of slaves, who were described as 'heathenish', 'brutish', and 'dangerous'.[29]

Similar attitudes towards white servants were reflected in the ideas and language that shaped the 1661 Servant Code by which previous 'customs', 'Orders of Council', and 'Acts of the Assembly' were consolidated. Legislators stated explicitly that the purposes of the Code were to protect masters' investments in servants, facilitate their social and political suppression, and at the same time protect them, as chattels, from the excesses of brutal masters. Entitled 'An Act for the Good Governing of Servants, and Ordaining the Rights between Masters and Servants',

[28] Dunn, *Sugar and Slaves*, p. 246.
[29] Richard Hall, *Acts Passed in the Island of Barbados, 1643–1762* (London, 1764), No. 42, pp. 112–13.

the law was passed at the time when slaves and servants worked in gangs on the sugar estates and the racial division of labour was not yet a noticeable social development.[30] Planters believed that legislation was necessary to strengthen their hand while servants expressed dissatisfaction with social and working conditions by violent rebellion, running away, and seeking unilateral termination of their contracts. The discovery of planned servant revolts in 1634 and 1647, and the need to suppress bands of runaway slaves (known as Maroons) during the 1650s, informed the political and ideological contexts of the Code.

In 1670 the legislature at Montserrat explicitly stated that slaves and servants should be subject to the same coercive and regulatory instrument. This thinking was embodied in the 'Act for Restraining the Liberty of Negroes and to Prevent the Running Away of Christian Servants'. The protective approach to servant care, however, could be seen in an Act passed in the same year to prohibit 'the turning away of Christian servants in sickness by their masters'. The Lords of Trade and Plantations confronted the Jamaican legislature in 1676 after reading the draft of an 'Act for the Good Governing of Christian Servants'. They objected in particular to the use of the term 'servitude' on the grounds that it was understood as 'a mark of bondage and slavery'. The word 'service' was proposed to the Jamaicans, who were reminded by the Lords that 'servants were not slaves' but 'only apprentices for years'.[31]

The Legislative Council of the Leewards, constituted by a core of men who had made fortunes in Barbados, was greatly influenced by the Barbadian model. The legal organization of unfree labour on the islands' sugar plantations indicated the extent to which Barbadian planters had ushered in a legislative, managerial, and labour culture which was accepted as an ideal type. Sugar planters in Antigua were closest to Barbadians in terms of their entry into large-scale sugar plantation production, and were the first to produce a code for the governance of master–servant relations that spoke directly to local conditions. Their 1669 Act, unlike that of Jamaica in 1664, specified terms of service that reflected concern with the wider issues of community relations, economic growth, and political conflict. Legislatures on the mainland followed. Comprehensive master and servant codes were enacted, for example, in Maryland (1676, 1692, 1699, 1704, and 1715). Collectively, these legislative instruments constituted an edifice designed to manage interests seemingly in conflict—the property rights and class rule of masters and the social aspirations of propertyless migrants.[32]

[30] Manuscripts Laws of Barbados, C[olonial] O[ffice] 30/1 No. 30.

[31] 'An Act for Restraining the Liberties of Negroes and to Prevent the Running Away of Christian Slaves', *C[alendar of] S[tate] P[apers] C[olonial] [Series], 1669–74*, No. 372; see also *CSPC, 1669–74*, No. 374; *CSPC, 1675–76*, No. 927.

[32] Smith, *Colonists*, pp. 228–29.

English masters in the Caribbean were also suspicious of Irish servants who bulked large in their labour force, and legislatures targeted them for special consideration. In Barbados, following widespread suspicion of Irish involvement in the aborted slave revolt of 1692, planters adamantly refused to accept them as servants. Instead, between 1693 and 1696, they petitioned, in vain, for Scottish servants to strengthen their militia forces. In 1697, when the home authorities made an offer of Irish servants, the legislature made its position explicit: '[W]e desire no Irish rebels may be sent to us: for we want not labourers of that colour to work for us, but men in whom we may confide, to strengthen us.'[33] Nevis was first among the Leewards to take legislative action to limit the numbers and activities of Irish inhabitants. In 1701 the Legislative Council passed an Act to prevent 'papists' and 'reputed papists' from settling in the island and to bar those already settled from public office. This was repealed following criticism from London. Montserrat also debated similar 'Protestant Bills' aimed at excluding Irishmen from public service, including militia duties. The Barbadians, however, who had not passed legislation removing Irish civil liberties, merely imposed oaths of abjuration in order to vote or to hold public office.

The daily lives of servants on the estates, then, were regulated in ways not too dissimilar from those governing slaves. Servants during their indentures were at the absolute disposal of their masters. The use of legislation to regulate indentured labour shows that the planters viewed the status of an indentured servant as that of a chattel. The degree of 'unfreedom' between the slave and the servant, however, though important and reflected in differentiated material consumption and social expectations, did not preclude common references to servants as 'white slaves' in everyday language.[34]

Against this background, on the evening of 24 March 1659, two petitions, 'which leaped over the heads of about four score others', were presented to the House of Commons Grand Committee of Grievances on behalf of seventy-three political prisoners 'sold into slavery in Barbados' by the Cromwellian authorities after a disturbance at Salisbury in March 1654. One petition was tabled on behalf of M. Rivers and O. Foyle and seventy others; the other by Rowland Thomas, all sold in Barbados as the 'goods and chattel' of leading West Indian merchant Martin Noell—under the Lord Protector's instructions. The petition of Foyle and Rivers

[33] Minutes of the Barbados Council, 1697, *CSPC, 1696–97*, No. 1108; *Journal of the Council of Trade and Plantations*, 28 Dec. 1696, *CSPC, 1696–97*, No. 535. See also Hilary Beckles, 'A "Riotous and Unruly Lot": Irish Indentured Servants and Freemen in the English West Indies, 1644–1713', *WMQ*, Third Series, XLVII (1990), pp. 503–22, and L. M. Cullen, 'The Irish Diaspora of the Seventeenth and the Eighteenth Centuries', in Canny, ed., *Europeans on the Move*, pp. 112–49.

[34] C. S. Higham, *The Development of the Leeward Islands Under the Restoration, 1660–1668: A Study of the Foundations of the Old Colonial System* (Cambridge, 1921), p. 176; Smith, *Colonists*, p. 233. Hilary McD. Beckles, *White Servitude and Black Slavery in Barbados, 1627–1715* (Knoxville, Tenn., 1989), pp. 59–79.

was published as a pamphlet in 1659 to obtain popular support against the arbitrary shipping of the defenceless poor to the sugar colonies. For the first time politicians discussed the experiences of English labourers in the West Indies. The views of many back-benchers on black slavery, the embryonic concept of 'human rights', the limitations of party-political conflict, and the need for white solidarity at the colonial frontier were articulated. Parliamentarians responded to the evidence in different ways, and the debate gives glimpses into the views of politicians on enforced labour at this juncture of English colonization.[35]

The question being raised was whether it was proper that the Wars of the Three Kingdoms (1638–52) should have produced a flow of 'white slaves' to the 'sugar machine of the Indies'. Thomas Carlyle, in his biographical study of Oliver Cromwell, was to note that the very name of Barbados was transformed into an active verb, when to be 'Barbadosed' replaced the word 'transported' in popular usage. It was estimated that Barbados alone received and employed some 12,000 political prisoners, many of them Irish and Scots, between 1649 and 1655. What the petitioners wanted to know was, 'by what authority so great a breach is made upon the free people of England . . . by merchants that deal in slaves and souls of men?'

Martin Noell, who owned significant property in the islands, was called to give evidence concerning this trade. Noell was defensive, and constructed an apologetic image for West Indian servitude. He told the House of Commons: 'I abhor the thought of setting £100 upon any man's person. It is false and scandalous . . . the work is hard but . . . not so hard as is represented to you; it [Barbados] is a place as grateful to you for trade as any part of the world . . .' Parliament was not convinced by Noell's account. Most members took the view that they should be careful in dealing with Cavaliers, for in the final instance they were Englishmen, and one justification for the Wars of the Three Kingdoms in its English dimension was to defend the 'human rights' of all Englishmen. Discussion focused on 'the freeborn people of England'. Sir Henry Vane was firm in his conviction that the issue of 'white slavery' transcended party politics, and was basically one of 'human rights' and individual liberty. Mr Boscaven placed before the Commons the underlying principle of ethnic relations within the Empire: 'I am as much against the Cavalier party as any man in these walls . . . but you have Paul's case before you. A Roman ought not to be beaten . . . or our lives will be as cheap as those of negroes.'

The debate marked a fundamental shift that was taking place in colonial economic interest and trends. Between 1659 and 1662 the Commons supported plans to sponsor an African trading company. This was established in 1663 as the

[35] M. Rivers and O. Foyle, *England's Slavery or Barbados Merchandize, Represented in a Petition to the High Court of Parliament* (London, 1659); the Parliamentary debate is recorded in Thomas Burton, MP, *Parliamentary Diary, 1656–59*, 8 vols. (London, 1828), IV, pp. 252–307, and Stock, ed., *Proceedings*, I, pp. 247–73.

'Company of Royal Adventurers Trading into Africa'. When this company went bankrupt, the Commons supported plans to establish another company, which was formed in 1672 as the Royal African Company.[36]

In the 1660s significant changes took place in West Indian servant and slave markets. These changes were sufficient to give slave labour a clear price advantage over servant labour. The decade was marked by a powerful anti-emigration campaign, led by prominent mercantile theoreticians who moved from the previous position that had justified indenture servitude and argued instead that England was under-populated and that its potential for agricultural and commercial expansion lay in its having the largest possible store of labour. While demographers provided evidence of a downturn in the growth of population, it was evident that in many parts of England real wages were rising. Labourers and artisans, for the first time in the century, experienced significant increases in real wages over an extended period and held expectations about future improvements in living standards. Within this context workers seemed less keen to emigrate. The sugar colonies were criticized as drawing upon the domestic labour market at a level hostile to the national interest. Sir William Petty, for example, noted that the future power of England depended upon the size of its population, while Roger Coke insisted that 'a ruinous number of men daily flock to the plantations . . . to the weakening of the nation'.[37]

This campaign, supported by the state, had the effect of further diminishing emigration. The rise of South Carolina and the expansion of Virginia and Maryland placed West Indian planters in an uncompetitive position for attracting settlers. Colonial Assemblies responded to reduced levels of immigration by cutting the length of servitude by between 55 and 60 per cent. It was hoped that this would attract a larger number of settlers. But with market prices stabilized at around £12 for a healthy male servant, this reduction in effect meant the doubling of prices for servant labour. Against this background great steps were taken towards increasing the West African slave supply. In 1664 the Company of Royal Adventurers Trading into Africa supplied slaves at prices between £14 and £22 per head. By 1675 the average price of slaves in the West Indies had fallen by 25–30 per cent, and the supply had increased by over 200 per cent.[38]

English planters quickly became experienced in slave organization, and their management policies were brutal. They kept slaves subordinated by an effective

[36] K. G. Davies, *The Royal African Company* (London, 1957).

[37] C. H. Hull, ed., *The Economic Writings of Sir William Petty*, 2 vols. (Cambridge, 1899), I, pp. 21, 34; R. Coke, *A Discourse on Trade* (London, 1670), pp. 12–13.

[38] See Hilary Beckles, 'The Economic Origins of Black Slavery in the British West Indies, 1640–1680: A Tentative Analysis of the Barbados Model', *Journal of Caribbean History* (1982), XVI, pp. 52–53; Hilary Beckles and Andrew Downes, 'The Economics of Transition to the Black Labor System in Barbados', *Journal of Interdisciplinary History* (1987), XVIII, pp. 225–47.

deployment of militia regiments, supported by government troops. Legal instruments were designed to regulate slaves' social behaviour, within and outside the production process, as well as to police their daily movements. For crimes of a public nature, such as rebellion, slaves were subject to capital punishment. In such cases, the island's Treasurer compensated slave-owners for their loss of capital. In addition, slaves were declared to be 'real estate' as opposed to mere chattel; this meant that slaves were legally tied to plantations, and could not easily be alienated from them in probate settlements. No legal provisions were made for the Christianization of slaves; they were generally regarded by the established Anglican church as intellectually unable to comprehend the concept of the faith and the Christian vision.

Slave Codes covered almost every area of the slave's social existence. They provided that no planter should give a slave permission to leave the estate without a signed ticket stating the time set for return. Any white person who found an authorized slave on his property without such a ticket and did not make an apprehension was liable to forfeit a sum of money to the Treasurer, some of which was paid to the informant.[39] Codes also stated that slaves were not lawfully allowed to 'beat drums, blow horns, or use other loud instruments', and their houses were to be 'diligently searched' from time to time. Any white who entertained a 'strange' Negro, upon conviction, was to forfeit a sum of money. A series of punishments was provided for slaves who traded in stolen goods, struck Christians, ran away, burnt sugar canes, or stole provisions. In addition, whites were liable to fines for improper policing of slaves, assisting them to escape, murdering them, or exposing them to seditious doctrines. However, slaves received some limited legal protection, as the laws recognized the need to 'guard them from the cruelties and insolence of themselves, and other ill-tempered people or owners'.[40]

Slaves were real estate and, therefore, could not own property—the basis of social mobility. Blacks were not permitted to give evidence in court against whites until the early nineteenth century, and whites rarely came to the legal assistance of blacks. If a master wilfully killed the slave of another, he was fined upon conviction. It was not until the nineteenth century that the murder of a slave by a white became a capital felony in the West Indies. On the other hand, slaves could be punished by death for striking or threatening a white person, or stealing property. These were the essential features of social relations with slaves established by the English in Barbados, Jamaica, and the Leeward Islands.

Within the Caribbean world, however, the Windward Islands remained a frontier area for the English. The success of the Kalinagos in holding on to a

[39] See Elsa Goveia, *The West Indian Slave Laws of the Eighteenth Century* (Bridgetown, 1970), pp. 16–34.

[40] Ibid.

significant portion of this territory, and their attacks on plantation settlements in the Leewards, fuelled the determination of the English to destroy them. By the mid-century English merchants, planters, and colonial officials agreed that the Kalinagos 'were a barbarous and cruel set of savages beyond reason or persuasion and must therefore be eliminated'. By this time, it was also clear that the slave-based plantation system demanded an 'absolute monopoly' of the Caribbean, and tolerated no 'alternative system'. Kalinago independence and self-reliance constituted a major contradiction to the internal logic of capitalist accumulation within the plantation economy. As a result, the plantocracy was determined to bring the contradiction to a speedy resolution by any means necessary.[41]

The Kalinagos had been able to resist the small-scale military expeditions that were sent against them in the 1630s and, having taken advantage of the differences that arose between the European powers during the 1650s and 1660s, they were able to provide assistance to the French and the Dutch on occasion in order to consolidate their own position against the English.[42] While this might have served their short-term purpose it ultimately steeled the English in their resolve to be rid of them, and successive English officials sought first to implant themselves within the territories held by the Kalinagos, then to enter into compacts with them, and finally (whenever the Kalinagos broke with their terms of submission) to strive for their expulsion by fair means or foul. The thrust of the onslaught which, at different times, drew upon the resources of London merchants, the English state, and the British settler population in the islands, was pursued intermittently between 1666 and 1700. It never achieved a complete success because the Kalinagos were able to cling on tenaciously in Dominica, where they were aided by the French, who feared that English settlement on that island would sever connections between Martinique and Guadeloupe in time of war. However, most of the islands—St Vincent, St Lucia, Tobago, and Grenada—were later brought into English possession.

The security issues, apart from fear of attack from other European powers, that preoccupied English settlers and colonial administrators throughout the seventeenth century were the control of unruly indentured servants and rebellious slaves, and the eradication of resisting natives. It is critical to take account of these issues because the pacification of these social groups had a considerable

[41] Gordon Lewis, *Main Currents in Caribbean Thought: The Historical Evolution of Caribbean Society in its Ideological Aspects, 1492–1980* (Kingston, 1983), pp. 104–05; Dunn, *Sugar and Slaves*, p. 246.

[42] Vere Langford Oliver, *The History of the Island of Antigua*, 3 vols. (London, 1984), I, pp. xix, xxv; Sheridan, *Sugar and Slavery*, p. 87; Petition of Major John Scott to King, 1667, *CSPC, 1661–68*, No. 1788; Governor William Willoughby to King, 11 Feb. 1668, *CSPC, 1661–68*, No. 547; Henry Willoughby to William Willoughby, 15 June 1667, *CSPC, 1661–68*, No. 1498; David Watts, *The West Indies: Patterns to Development, Culture and Environmental Change since 1492* (Cambridge, 1987), pp. 242–43.

influence upon the shaping of colonial policy and society. These conflicts, and the search for solutions, however, did not overshadow political controversies that emerged between the powerful, wealthy planter-merchant élite and government authority in London. Both tensions were endemic to West Indian society, and tended towards the destabilization of the colonial enterprise.

The English state, like its European counterparts, insisted upon the regulation of trade and settlement in order to create order from the uncertainty that resulted from military conquest. To this end, it developed elaborate administrative concepts and structures designed to shape and govern colonial relations. Over time these were adjusted to meet the peculiarities of local circumstances, but the objectives of ownership and control remained largely unchanged. In narrow terms, policies were designed to ensure that the hard-won resources of the Caribbean were not siphoned off by contesting colonial powers, and vigilance and authoritarianism surfaced as two obvious themes.

English settlements were usually financed and organized by private enterprise—the settlement of Jamaica was exceptional because it originated, in 1655–56, in the seizure of the island from Spain by Cromwell's Republican army, and the colony was therefore established as a state enterprise. The general economic principle of early English colonization, though, was private enterprise, and representative government took shape within the framework of constitutional royal authority.[43] English law and customs made clear provision for individual colonies to be granted or leased by the monarch to prominent people. These individuals were designated Lords Proprietor and were given royal authority to appoint colonial Governors to manage the affairs of colonies. Colonists, then, were under the indirect jurisdiction of the Crown since, theoretically at least, the proprietor or his Governor could be removed by royal authority. Governors were given rights to allocate colonial lands and appoint officials on behalf of the proprietors. In most colonies proprietors also gave them authority to interpret the law. Governors, therefore, had extensive powers in colonial affairs.

The granting of territories by the English Crown was part of the feudal legacy of the seventeenth century. Once grants were confirmed, grantees were free to do as they wished with the land. Colonists were required to pay dues on land obtained from Governors who collected them on the proprietor's behalf. Since land was initially held at the proprietor's pleasure, colonists quickly began to press for legally recognized rights to freehold ownership. By the mid-seventeenth century this concession was granted by proprietors to colonists, and private property rights in land became an important feature of English colonization.

[43] Dunn, *Sugar and Slaves*, esp. chaps. 2–3; Vincent T. Harlow, *A History of Barbados, 1625–1685* (Oxford, 1926), pp. 48–97.

It was during the mid-seventeenth century that the English state, like that of the French, considered the control of colonies to be slack, and took measures to strengthen its authority and bring colonists under more direct metropolitan rule, such as the Spanish crown had enjoyed from the early sixteenth century. Economic policies were proposed and reflected mercantile doctrine that explained the achievement of national wealth and power in terms of the nation's exclusive control over its colonial trades. National interest was, therefore, conceived in terms of the exclusion of foreigners, and the establishment of strict legal control over the economic activities of colonies.

The Cromwellian government took the first step in 1650, restricting the trade in sugar by legally excluding foreign merchants from all West Indian commerce. The first of the Navigation Acts was passed in 1651. It provided that, as a rule, colonial goods could be imported to the mother country, to Ireland, or to other colonies only by English or colonial- owned and –manned ships. This Act was clearly directed against the Dutch, who were now declared economic enemies by the Cromwellian state. In 1660 Charles II expanded restrictive trade laws and navigation regulations, in addition to terminating proprietary rule of grantees. The 1660 Navigation Act sought to ensure that valuable colonial products were first imported to England before they could be re-exported to foreign countries. This law applied to the principal West Indian crops—sugar, tobacco, cotton-wool, ginger, and indigo. The following year Parliament passed the Tariff Act, which provided English colonial sugar with preferential treatment in English markets; a duty of 1*s.* 5*d.* per hundredweight was imposed on English sugar compared with 35*s.* 10*d.* on foreign sugar. Collectively, navigation laws, including the Staple Act of 1663, sought to protect and expand the vital customs revenues on sugar and other colonial produce. The collection of these revenues provided a critical justification for colonial activity. They enabled the state to project nationalist grandeur and command a political advantage at a time of competitive imperialist expansion.

Between 1650 and 1665, then, a policy aimed at bringing the plantations more completely under the domination of the state was relentlessly pursued. Newly created offices were subsequently empowered to police the application of economic policies, and to secure the compliance of colonial administrators. In 1675 a committee, under the control of the Lords of Trade and Plantations, was formed with the objective of imposing Crown rule on all colonies, directing their trade, and creating the English 'exclusif'. These formal restrictive structures, which were also designed to facilitate the commercial links between mainland and island colonies, could not fully prevent illicit intercolonial trade nor discourage colonists from seeking greater political autonomy. Free traders and interlopers succeeded in undermining monopoly companies in particular, most of which collapsed into bankruptcy and disorganization. As a result, the English abandoned some monopoly policies. In 1698 they opened the slave trade to all suppliers. While colonists sought free trade in slaves and other colonial imports, they none the less insisted upon the preservation of a protected metropolitan market for their produce.

Generally, English colonists obtained a high degree of internal autonomy and came close to establishing an acceptable political and constitutional arrangement with the metropolitan government. This was partly due to the proprietorial nature of the early colonial government and the extent to which private enterprise was the dominant motive force of colonization. Such a legal and economic framework was conducive to the development of a democratic spirit among property-holders. It was to be expected, therefore, that the planter élite would show themselves determined to enjoy the political rights and freedoms which wealthy Englishmen already enjoyed within the metropolitan political culture.

Following the lead of the Virginians and colonists at Bermuda, the Barbadians took the initiative among West Indian sugar planters in 1639 and established an elected Assembly to represent local interests and defend them against incursions from England. Parishioner freeholders won the right to elect representatives to the Assembly, which was vested with powers to initiate and legislate money bills and control taxation. The Barbadian model was developed elsewhere in the English Caribbean, so that by mid-century the principle of representative government had been assumed by the planting élite. Though Governors and their Councils maintained the right to veto and oppose the Assembly, Assemblymen reacted strongly to such actions and could prove truculent. Indeed, the tradition of Assemblymen treating Governors as figureheads developed in the seventeenth century.

The overriding principle within the English colonial political culture was the Assembly's right to rule with minimal interference from London. This political arrangement became known as the Old Representative System, and from its beginnings in the mid-century elected Assemblies sought to resist supervisory control by not voting money for projects and by insisting on the use of Committees and Boards to carry them through. Elected Assemblies with legislative and fiscal powers were regarded as a right which property conferred.

From the 1640s the plantocracy, strengthened by the massive accumulation of capital generated by the sugar industry, began to conceive its economic interests in class terms. In general it was not prepared to allow political disputes in England to undermine its authority and interests. The planters would not tolerate proprietary powers undermining their perceived right to manage colonial affairs in a manner that suited them. They were determined to ensure that the colonies enjoyed a maximum degree of self-government within a broader colonial structure. This meant the adoption of a neutral position over the conflict between King and Parliament. The colonies had prospered under a free-trade policy which facilitated trade with Dutch merchants, and they were prepared to pursue that line in spite of

English opposition. Indeed, it was evident during the 1640s that some prominent planters, in Barbados at least, would rather push for home rule and independence than relinquish their freedom of trade and their rights to self-government. In this period no colony was as forthright as Barbados in confronting the power of Parliament in order to preserve its economic autonomy.[44]

News of the execution of Charles I by Parliament in January 1649 threw the West Indian plantocracy into disarray. They had managed to maintain a policy of non-interference for nearly a decade and had not split their communities with Cavalier–Roundhead conflict. No one was prepared to see the colonies' self-government subjected to rule by Imperial parliamentary decree. In Barbados, Royalist sympathizers expressed their opposition to parliamentary authority, and advocated that colonists should reject the mercantile principles of Cromwell and practise free trade as formerly. As Royalist opinion among the plantocracy moved in favour of 'independence' from the Commonwealth, few expressed the principle of the King's right to rule. Parliament considered the political stance of the Royalist planter faction offensive and resorted to a military operation to subdue the colony. Planters, both Roundheads and Cavaliers, were described by Parliament as insurrectionists who had to be crushed.

On 7 May 1650 the General Assembly of Barbados voted to receive Francis, Lord Willoughby, as Governor, a move which confirmed that Cavaliers had succeeded in breaking Roundhead political power. The Willoughby government wasted no time in deporting many Roundheads from the colony and in confiscating their properties. Parliament was distressed by these developments and despatched a fleet under the command of Sir George Asycue to subdue the colony. For three months Asycue blockaded Barbados as his force of 860 men lacked the military power to defeat the Royalists' militia. Finally, on 11 January 1652, the colonists, feeling the pressures of commercial isolation, agreed to accept the terms of Asycue's delegation.

Barbadians considered the terms of agreement favourable to themselves. They agreed to recognize the rule of Parliament and its nominated Governor in return for continued self-government, free trade, and a restoration of confiscated properties. With this agreement, planters got back to their task of producing sugar, even though it was clear to many that Parliament had no intention of honouring the agreement to allow them free trade with the Dutch. This agreement, known as the Charter of Barbados, represented for the planters formal recognition by England of their right to rule themselves in local affairs, and a confirmation that propertied Englishmen were entitled to the same political freedoms that they enjoyed at

[44] Jack P. Greene, *Peripheries and Centers: Constitutional Development in the Extended Polities of the British Empire and the United States, 1607–1788* (Athens, Ga., 1986), pp. 19, 25; also, 'Legislative Turnover in British America, 1696–1775: A Quantitative Analysis', *WMQ*, Third Series, XXXVIII (1981), pp. 442–63.

home. At the Restoration both Barbados and the Leewards made the same bargain with Charles II. In exchange for royal government and the continuation of land titles, the island Assemblies in 1664 consented to a 4.5 per cent duty on commodities exported from the isles.

Englishmen had entered the Caribbean rather tentatively, but by the beginning of the eighteenth century they were confident and in effective control. The first enemy, the Spanish, had early become reconciled to the English presence in the Lesser Antilles, and later surrendered Jamaica without much of a fight. The Dutch had consolidated a considerable commercial empire after 1621, when their West India Company was formed and 'parented' pioneering English settlers. By 1650 the English, now feeling secure and ambitious, bit the Dutch hand that had fed them, first in 1652–54 and then in a series of trade wars in 1665–67 and 1672–74. Turning to the French, the English assaulted settlers and harassed traders in the wars of 1666–67 and 1689–97. Finally, in 1713 they succeeded in crushing French resistance and captured the prime prize: the *Asiento* contract to supply slaves to the Spanish colonies.[45]

The English developed the islands as major economies in their own right, but also as part of the Atlantic trading system. The islands were valuable to the economic viability of the mainland colonies, with commodity trade between the two being of vital importance to English merchants. Trading connections in rum, foodstuffs, construction materials, sugar, and slaves contributed to the perception of the islands as the 'hub of Empire'. While English merchants had established global trading networks, the West Indies were central to their operations, and were represented as such in the first depictions of what came to be called 'the English [after 1707, the British] empire in America'.[46] The islands absorbed more slaves over time, and produced a more lucrative commodity than any other region in colonial America. The Atlantic system, as an economic order centred on the slave-plantation complex, was therefore revolutionized in the seventeenth century. The sugar estate was the hub of this network in the movements of labour, capital, and management. The West Indies thus occupied a special place in the development of what ultimately became the British Empire.

[45] See below, [Israel], pp. 423–44.

[46] P. F. Campbell, 'The Merchants and Traders of Barbados', *Journal of the Barbados Museum and Historical Society*, XXXIV (1972), No. 1, pp. 85–98; and XXXIV (1974), No. 2, pp. 166–86; R.B., *The English Empire in America*; John Oldmixon, *The British Empire in America*, 2 vols. (London, 1708).

Select Bibliography

Kenneth R. Andrews, *The Spanish Caribbean: Trade and Plunder, 1530–1630* (New Haven, 1978).

—— *Ships, Money, and Politics: Seafaring and Naval Enterprises in the Reign of Charles I* (Cambridge, 1991).

Joyce Appleby, *Economic Thought and Ideology in Seventeenth-Century England* (Princeton, 1978).

Hilary McD. Beckles, *White Servitude and Black Slavery in Barbados, 1627–1715* (Knoxville, Tenn., 1989).

Ralph Paul Bierber, 'The British Plantation Councils of 1674', *English Historical Review*, CLVII, 40 (1925), pp. 93–106.

Robert Bliss, *Revolution and Empire: English Politics and the American Colonies in the Seventeenth Century* (Manchester, 1990).

Robert Brenner, *Merchants and Revolutionaries: Commercial Change, Political Conflict and London Overseas Traders, 1550–1653* (Cambridge, 1993).

Nicholas P. Canny, 'The Ideology of English Colonisation: From Ireland to America', *William and Mary Quarterly*, Third Series, XXX (1973), pp. 575–98.

Ralph Davis, *The Rise of the English Shipping Industry in the Seventeenth and Eighteenth Centuries* (Newton Abbot, 1971).

Richard S. Dunn, *Sugar and Slaves: The Rise of the Planter Class in the English West Indies, 1624–1713* (New York, 1972).

David W. Galenson, *White Servitude in Colonial America: An Economic Analysis* (London, 1981).

Jack P. Greene, *Peripheries and Centers: Constitutional Development in the Extended Polities of the British Empire and the United States, 1607–1788* (Athens, Ga., 1986).

—— and J. R. Pole, eds., *Colonial British America: Essays in the New History of the Early Modern Period* (London, 1984).

Lawrence A. Harper, *The English Navigation Laws* (New York, 1939).

Gordon Lewis, *Main Currents in Caribbean Thought: The Historical Revolution of Caribbean Society in its Ideological Aspects, 1492–1980* (Baltimore, 1983).

Anthony McFarlane, *The British in the Americas, 1480–1815* (London, 1994).

Richard Middleton, *Colonial America: A History, 1607–1760* (Oxford, 1992).

G. V. Scammell, *The First Imperial Age: European Overseas Expansion, c.1400–1715* (London, 1989).

Eric Williams, *Capitalism and Slavery* (1944; London, 1964).

Nuala Zahedieh, 'Trade, Plunder and Economic Development in Early English Jamaica', *Economic History Review*, Second Series, XXXVIII (1986), pp. 570–93.

11

The English in Western Africa to 1700

P. E. H. HAIR AND ROBIN LAW

'Western Africa' is the 3,000-mile coastline between the southern end of the Sahara Desert and the northern end of the Kalahari Desert, together with its hinterland. The first two-thirds of the coast, running largely west–east, came to be called, by Europeans of the period, 'Guinea'; the final third, running north–south, comprised mainly the region known as 'Angola'.

Five centuries ago the population of western Africa was sparse, but at intervals along the coastal region, especially in Guinea, denser nodes existed. Peasant farmers cultivating long-established food crops by long-established methods predominated, but their necessary exchanges and additional requirements had produced local fairs, traders, and trade-routes—even a number of long-distance routes, in part to involve seaside fishermen and salt-makers. Goods were exchanged, generally overland, though some traffic existed on rivers and in coastal waters, using mainly canoes. But the ocean was not attempted, hence the further offshore islands were not settled. Economic circumstances had also produced a stratum of specialized artisans and craftsmen. Metals were worked and textiles widely produced, yet in each case the technology limited output, creating an unsatisfied consumer demand. When the region developed external commerce, just as Africans required no training in profitable exchange, so the trade commodities were largely within the categories of those already exchanged internally. From a distant past, import–export exchanges across the Sahara had occurred and had even affected the coast in a few localities, though the trade was inevitably on a small scale. However, this trade between West and North Africa had been sufficient to alert Mediterranean Europe to a distant source of gold, pepper, and slaves.

Like many other parts of the world before 1700, western Africa was linguistically and ethnically fragmented. In consequence, it had multiple polities of varying size, structure, and potential.[1] Within units, blood ties vied with limited economic

[1] Most recent research on early Afro-European trade has focused on particular societies or regions, rather than treating western Africa as a whole; although of varying approach, balance, and value, such local studies serve usefully to illustrate the variety of the African experience, as well as the variable level and character of English involvement; examples include (from west to east along the coast): Walter Rodney, *A History of the Upper Guinea Coast, 1545–1800* (Oxford, 1970); Kwame Yeboa Daaku, *Trade and Politics on the Gold Coast, 1600–1720* (Oxford, 1970); Robin Law, *The Slave Coast of West Africa, 1550–1750*

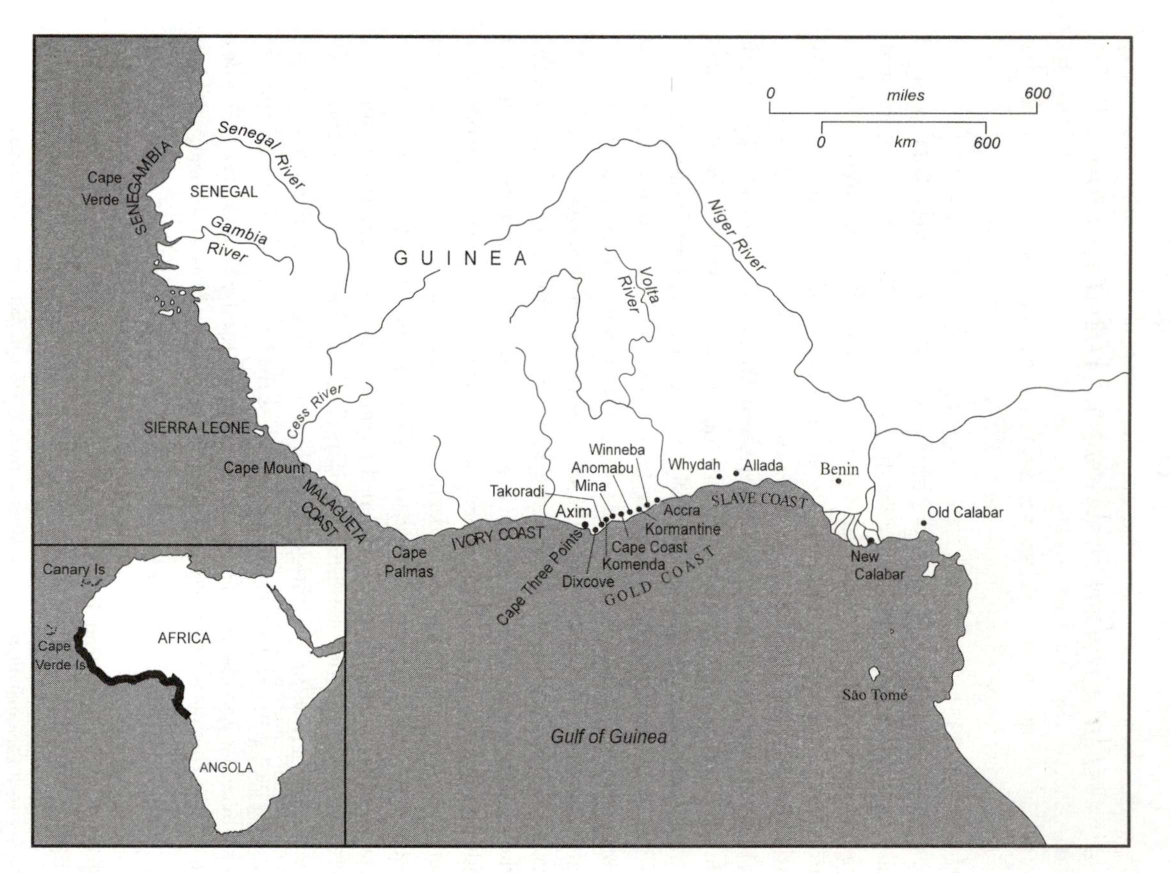

MAP 11.1. English Trade with Western Africa

stratification as agents of social stability and development. Societies were in general pre-literate but rich in oral discourse, religions localized and polytheistic. Through the spread of Islam the culture of parts of the northern hinterland was tenuously linked to that of the Maghrib and Middle East, but the coastal region east of Senegal was almost wholly untouched by Islamic influence. Hence, for most of coastal western Africa the arrival of aliens bringing trade by sea, the Europeans, brought a new direction in cultural and political transformation, a process that, although slow, unequally diffused, and seldom revolutionary yet at points traumatic, still operates today.

At the end of the twentieth century the greater part of the population of western Africa is to be found in states which have English as their official language of government and education; in the first half of the century almost all these particular territories were part of the British Empire, and between 1750 and 1950 the maritime export–import trade of the whole region was dominated by British merchants and shipping. In sharp contrast to these later developments, the English were very late arrivals among the Europeans who impinged on western Africa.[2]

The Portuguese reached Guinea in the 1440s and by the end of the fifteenth century had established trading relations along most sections of the coast of western Africa, as well as settling the offshore islands.[3] Although a glimmer of interest in direct trade with Guinea appeared in English ports in the 1480s, the earliest recorded English voyages to Guinea, numbering perhaps five or six, were made only at uncertain dates between 1530 and 1540; and these appear to have been essentially exploratory voyages to Brazil, only touching Africa *en route*.[4] A gap of a

(Oxford, 1991); A. F. C. Ryder, *Benin and the Europeans, 1485–1897* (London, 1969); A. J. H. Latham, *Old Calabar, 1600–1891* (Oxford, 1973); David Birmingham, *Trade and Conflict in Angola* (Oxford, 1966).

[2] Two Scottish companies for trade in Guinea existed in the seventeenth century but both were ephemeral, and Scottish influence was negligible in the region throughout the period—hence 'English' rather than 'British'.

[3] The most comprehensive account of the first period of European penetration into Guinea remains John W. Blake, *European Beginnings in West Africa, 1454–1578* (London, 1937), enlarged and retitled *West Africa: Quest for God and Gold, 1454–1578* (London, 1977); for documentation of both Portuguese and English enterprise, see John W. Blake, *Europeans in West Africa (1450–1560)*, 2 vols. (Hakluyt Society, London, 1942). There is no equally comprehensive account or set of documentation covering the later sixteenth century, but see Rodney, *History of the Upper Guinea Coast*, esp. chaps. 3–4; Kenneth R. Andrews, *Trade, Plunder and Settlement: Maritime Enterprise and the Genesis of the British Empire, 1480–1630* (Cambridge, 1984), chap. 5. For the Portuguese background, see Avelino Teixeira da Mota, *Aspects of Portuguese Colonisation and Sea Trade in West Africa in the 15th and 16th Centuries* (Bloomington, Ind., 1978); and generally, Vitorino Magalhães Godinho, *L'Économie de l'empire portugais au XVe et XVIe siècles* (Paris, 1969).

[4] These voyages are very poorly documented. The earliest reference in print was Richard Hakluyt, *Principall Navigations* (London, 1589), p. 520; the archive material can be found in J. A. Williamson, *John Hawkins* (London, 1927), pp. 9–15, 2nd edn. entitled *Hawkins of Plymouth* (London, 1949), pp. 27–33.

decade or more then intervened before the English resumed contact with Guinea, this time, more significantly, with a dozen trading voyages solely to Africa, made almost annually between 1553 and 1567.[5]

Why were the English so slow to be active in western Africa? They were, after all, in the same period taking some economic interest, albeit a limited one, in the North Atlantic. Even to the south, on the road to Guinea, minor initiatives were taken. Traditional Anglo-Iberian trading led to occasional contacts with Morocco, the earliest in the 1470s; while by the 1500s at least one estate in the Spanish Canaries was owned by English businessmen. Yet Guinea remained beyond reach. It was not that the Portuguese discovery and exploitation of the region passed unnoticed. England and Portugal had a long history of commercial exchange and, from the start, among the goods conveyed to Guinea by the Portuguese were English woollens.[6] The crews of Portuguese vessels often included men of other nationalities, and although no record of any English sailor is known, it is not inconceivable that it was a Portuguese vessel that brought the first Englishman to Guinea. Information about the islands off Guinea discovered by the Portuguese up to the 1460s was circulating at Bristol by the 1480s.[7] The products of the Portuguese out-thrust to the south soon reached England. In 1454, not long after the Portuguese settlement of Madeira, a cargo of sugar from that island arrived at Bristol, and it is likely that similar cargoes were soon being carried in English bottoms.[8] A complaint about the English seizure of Portuguese ships carrying sugar from the Guinea island of São Tomé made in the 1560s included references to such seizures in the 1530s; we can safely assume that sugar ships from Guinea were piratically seized much earlier.[9] In the 1480s, shortly after the Portuguese reached the 'Malagueta Coast' (in modern Liberia), the Portuguese crown awarded the monopoly of dealing in malagueta pepper across part of northern Europe to Duarte Brandão, alias Sir Edward Brampton, a Jewish businessman who served in the royal councils of both Portugal and England.[10] The

[5] The most recent and fullest study of these voyages is A. Teixeira da Mota and P. E. H. Hair, *East of Mina: Afro-European Relations on the Gold Coast in the 1550s and 1560s* (Madison, 1988); see also P. E. H. Hair and J. D. Alsop, *English Seamen and Traders in Guinea, 1553–1565* (Lewiston-Lampeter, 1992).

[6] D. Escudier, *Voyage d'Eustache Delafosse* (Paris, 1992), p. 38; J. M. da Silva Marques, *Descobrimentos Portuguesas*, 3 vols. in 5 pts. (Lisbon, 1944–71), III, p. 157.

[7] A. Z. Cortesão, *History of Portuguese Cartography*, 2 vols. (Lisbon, 1971), II, pp. 142–48; R. A. Skelton, 'English Knowledge of Portuguese Discoveries in the 15th Century: A New Document', *Congreso Internacional de História dos Descobrimentos, Lisbon 1960* (Lisbon, 1960), t. II, pp. 365–74.

[8] Magalhães Godinho, *L'Économie de l'empire portugais*, pp. 437–38, 440.

[9] Hair and Alsop, *English Seamen*, p. 51, n. 9.

[10] C. Roth, 'Sir Edward Brampton', *Transactions of the Jewish History Society of England*, XVI (1952), pp. 121–27; Marquês de São Paio, 'Um aventureiro português na guerra das duas rosas: Duarte Brandão, senhor de Buarcos', *Anais, Academia Portuguesa de História*, Second Series, VI (1955), pp. 143–65; Luís de Albuquerque and M. E. Madeira Santos, eds., *Portugaliae Monumenta Africana*, 2 vols. (Lisbon, 1993, 1995), I, documents 161, 187.

value of the Guinea export trade became even more apparent after the Portuguese in the 1470s tapped the gold trade of 'Mina' (the later 'Gold Coast'), as signalled by the founding of the fort of São Jorge da Mina (later miscalled Elmina) in 1482. While England dallied, other nations reacted. The Castilians were bought off by the Portuguese in 1480, but from the 1520s the French challenged the Portuguese in Guinea.

Diplomatic tradition and dynastic connection seem to have been among the factors accounting for the English inaction. In 1396 the Treaty of Windsor had established between England and Portugal what was to be eventually described as Britain's 'oldest alliance'. The two royal houses of the early fifteenth century, Avis and Lancaster, were linked by marriage; the Infante Dom Henrique ('Henry the Navigator') was a nephew of Henry IV of England. It may therefore be significant that the first flicker of interest in Guinea to appear among the English occurred only after Lancaster had been overthrown by York. In 1481 Edward IV sought permission from the Pope to 'exchange baser merchandise for nobler' in Africa, apparently a discreet request to be allowed to break into the Mina gold trade. The year before, certain unnamed 'English merchants seeking pilots for Guinea' were ordered to be expelled from Seville, presumably as a result of Portuguese pressure. The Portuguese crown followed this up by sending envoys to England, to protest, 'in terms of the ancient league', against an intended English voyage to Guinea, allegedly in association with an Iberian grandee. The English apparently gave way. A few years later, when a Portuguese nobleman in exile thought of organizing an expedition to Guinea from England, envoys were again sent and Henry VII obliged Portugal by imprisoning the nobleman. The English Crown appears to have accepted the Portuguese claim to Guinea monopoly for a further half-century.[11]

From the 1540s the English made fairly regular voyages to 'Barbary', that is, Atlantic Morocco, and this probably encouraged ventures further south.[12] The dozen trading voyages to Guinea of the mid-sixteenth century brought home pepper and gold, mainly from the 'Gold Coast' (with one voyage further east to Benin, in modern Nigeria), but projects of building a fort on the coast came to nothing, and losses of ships and men led to the enterprise petering out.[13] In the

[11] Hakluyt, *Principall Navigations*, pp. 80–81; Rui de Pina, *Crónica de El-Rei D. João II*, ed. Alberto Martins de Carvalho (Coimbra, 1950), cap. 33; Blake, *Europeans in West Africa*, pp. 264–65. Of these episodes, the fullest account remains that in Blake, *European Beginnings*, pp. 60–63, slightly corrected in P. E. H. Hair, *The Founding of the Castelo de São Jorge da Mina* (Madison, 1994), p. 63, n. 56.

[12] J. A. Williamson, 'England and the Opening of the Atlantic', in J. Holland Rose, A. P. Newton, and E. A. Benians, eds., *Cambridge History of the British Empire*, 9 vols. (Cambridge, 1929), I, esp. p. 42; Blake, *Europeans in West Africa*, p. 250; T. S. Willan, *Studies in Elizabethan Foreign Trade* (Manchester, 1959), p. 100.

[13] That Queen Elizabeth gave way to Portuguese complaints and forbade the trade (as stated in Williamson, 'England and the Opening of the Atlantic', p. 42) is a misreading of a 1572 treaty, which

1570s and 1580s a handful of multi-continental English voyages made brief calls at the Sierra Leone estuary, but trading voyages to Guinea were resumed only in the late 1580s. Two voyages to Benin for pepper were not great successes, and were not repeated.[14] More significant for the future were a number of voyages after 1587 to Senegambia, trading for hides and wax, at first notionally in alliance with the Portuguese émigré Pretender, Dom António.[15] These voyages were not very profitable in themselves, but partly represented a preliminary reconnaissance of the interior gold trade which the Portuguese tapped via the River Gambia. During their desultory approach to Guinea in the sixteenth century, the English had acted in the shadow of Afro-European trading relations established very much earlier by Portuguese activity, both official and non-official.

Set apart from this limited English concern for direct trade with Guinea during the first century of Anglo-African relations—a concern so limited that it seemed to portend no particular quest for empire in that region—was a set of dramatic but exceptional Guinea episodes. The three Hawkins voyages of 1564–69 slaved in Africa, then sailed to Spanish America, while the disaster of the final voyage had significant international consequences. In each aspect exceptional, the voyages nevertheless did not entirely ignore the normal pattern of Anglo-African relations. The English being greenhorns as slavers, Hawkins first attempted to obtain slaves by raiding. When this proved a fiasco, he thereafter traded for slaves with backwoods Portuguese merchants (who later told the authorities, wisely but probably untruly, that they had been coerced); and further, by lending men as mercenaries to an African polity engaged in attacking its neighbour, he received in return a share of the prisoners taken.[16] Yet, in contrast to the dramatic features of the Hawkins procedure, the other twenty-five or so English voyages in Guinea in the sixteenth century, and also the vast majority of all those up to *c.*1640, did not deal

merely promised that she would frown on trade to 'the conquests' of Portugal, *C[alendar] [of] S[tate] P[apers] Foreign 1571*, item 2191; *1572–4*, items 66, 108, 689. The English refused to accept that all of Guinea and its seas was a Portuguese 'conquest'.

[14] Hakluyt, *Principall Navigations*, pp. 818–19; Richard Hakluyt, *Principal Navigations*, 3 vols. (London, 1598–1600), II, 2, pp. 126–33; Ryder, *Benin and the Europeans*, esp. pp. 339–43 (references to a proposed earlier voyage). These voyages probably brought back to England the earliest extant African artefact in British collections, a carved tusk, with a later inscription in English; see W. A. Hart, 'A Rediscovered Afro-Portuguese Horn in the British Museum', *African Arts*, XXVI, 4 (1993), pp. 70–71, 87–88; 'A Reconsideration of the Rediscovered "Afro-Portuguese" Horn', ibid., XXVII, 1 (1994), pp. 92–93.

[15] Hakluyt, *Principal Navigations*, II, 2, pp. 189–92; John W. Blake, 'English Trade with the Portuguese Empire in West Africa, 1581–1629', *Quarto Congresso do Mundo Português*, VI, 1 (1940), pp. 314–33; Mario Alberto Nunes Costa, 'D. António e o trato Inglês da Guiné', *Boletim Cultural da Guiné Portuguesa*, VIII (1953), pp. 683–797.

[16] Williamson, 'England and the Opening of the Atlantic', pp. 48–49; and for more recent discussions of the Guinea aspects of the Hawkins voyages, see P. E. H. Hair, 'Protestants as Pirates, Slavers and Proto-Missionaries: Sierra Leone 1568 and 1582', *Journal of Ecclesiastical History*, XXI (1970), pp. 203–24; Andrews, *Trade, Plunder and Settlement*, pp. 112–13.

in slaves (and therefore did not sail to America). Given that long before the 1640s the Portuguese had traded extensively in African slaves, and the Spaniards, French, and Dutch had all at times joined in the trade, the English abstinence from slaving probably testifies less to moral compunction than to the low level of English involvement in western Africa and the Caribbean.

The limitations of the first period of English intervention in the region, contrasting with the British role in later periods, can be further indicated.[17] While the African gold brought home *c.*1555 may have had some momentary significance for the English Treasury and coinage, the contribution of Guinea trade throughout the period to the national economy cannot have been much more than trifling. The earlier voyages were forced to use renegade Portuguese pilots and Portuguese charts, although navigational experience was fairly soon obtained.[18] While the English traders faced bitter official Portuguese hostility (and hence never visited the settled Portuguese islands), they generally traded within the interstices of the current Afro-Portuguese trading network, often in fact dealing with those Portuguese traders who resented official restrictions on trade with foreigners, or with Portuguese who had gone further and become 'run-aways' (*lançados*). After the forced union of the crowns of Portugal and Spain in 1580, the English alliance with the Portuguese Pretender led to minor contributions both to the eventually defeated Antonine cause in the Azores and to an unsuccessful Franco-Antonine descent on the Cape Verde Islands.[19] At intervals thereafter English fleets devastatingly raided the latter islands, now firmly under the control of King Philip. Whereas this land assault weakened the Portuguese position in western Guinea, increasing English captures of Portuguese vessels returning to Europe with tropical products diminished the overall value of Guinea to the Portuguese crown.[20] The Portuguese on the coast, divided in their loyalties, remained ambivalent about

[17] In 1929 Williamson claimed too much for the mid-century voyages: 'the Guinea traffic of this period is one of the fundamental transactions of British expansion . . . it produced an oceanic war with Portugal, the first English war of its kind [presumably outside Europe] . . .' ('England and the Opening of the Atlantic', p. 44).

[18] See John W. Blake, 'Diogo Homem, Portuguese Cartographer', *Mariner's Mirror*, XXVIII (1942), pp. 148–60; Luiz de Sousa, *Annaes de ElRei Dom João Terceiro* (Lisbon, 1844), p. 438; Manoel de Andrada Castel Blanco, *To Defend your Empire and the Faith: Advice Offered to Philip, King of Spain and Portugal, c. 1590*, ed. P. E. H. Hair (Liverpool, 1990), p. 191, n. 3; David B. Quinn, 'Simão Fernandes, a Portuguese Pilot in the English Service, circa 1573–1588', *Actas, Congreso Internacional de História dos Descobrimentos* (Lisbon, 1961), t. III, pp. 449–56.

[19] For a slight English attempt to assist D. António in the Azores, see David B. Quinn, 'England and the Azores, 1581–1583: Three Letters', *Revista da Universidade de Coimbra*, XXVII (1979), pp. 205–17 (also série separatas 123, Centro de Estudos de Cartografia Antiga, Lisbon, 1979). The failed attack on the Cape Verde Islands appears to have produced neither a contemporary account nor a modern study, but see *CSP Foreign, 1583*, item 160; Andrada, *To Defend your Empire*, p. 71, n. 12.

[20] Hakluyt, *Principal Navigations*, III, pp. 599–600; Mary Frear Keeler, *Sir Francis Drake's West Indian Voyage, 1585–86* (Hakluyt Society, London, 1981), esp. pp. 134–50, 225–35.

the lure of trade with the heretical English, and commerce between the two continued to be conducted largely *sub rosa*.[21]

The organization of the sixteenth-century voyages is poorly recorded. The mid-century voyages were individually organized and financed, collective continuity being limited to the occasional use of the same ships and seamen, and to the financing of ships and goods being undertaken by similar groups of merchants drawn from the small pool of capital-providers that financed other overseas ventures. On the voyages individual merchants were represented by separate agents. Despite diplomatic protests from Portugal, the Crown was mildly involved, at least after Elizabeth succeeded Mary, albeit more covertly than openly, by lending or hiring out royal vessels.[22] Continuing collective efforts comparable to those of the Muscovy and Levant Companies can only be detected from the late 1580s, when the Senegambian trade was begun by a group of London and West Country merchants. A royal ten-year licence for this trade was issued in 1588, followed by another for the Sierra Leone trade in 1592—the latter trade seems not to have taken off. The Senegambian enterprise was double-headed inasmuch as the promoters, or some of them, also held a licence from Dom António, the Portuguese Pretender, and this led to furious quarrels and litigation, it being difficult to decide which voyages were licensed and which interloping. The licence for trade in Senegambia was renewed in 1598 but given to two courtiers; it is not clear whether they acted on it. This was therefore a small and uncertain step towards the more formal organization of the Guinea trade in the following century.[23]

The first Guinea voyages were recorded in print by Richard Eden in 1555, being in fact the very first English intercontinental voyages to be so recorded in any detail.[24] With slight exceptions, the later sixteenth-century voyages were only recorded in print when accounts of them were gathered up by Richard Hakluyt and published in his editions of 1589 and 1598–1600.[25] While Hakluyt only chose to publish, or was only able to procure, accounts of a proportion of the twenty-five or so direct trading voyages, he published accounts of all three Hawkins slaving voyages. This imbalance, inasmuch as it was deliberate, was doubtless due to the

[21] Hair, 'Protestants as Pirates', p. 210; P. E. H. Hair, 'Sources on Early Sierra Leone: (14) English accounts of 1582', *Africana Research Bulletin* (Freetown), IX (1978), pp. 82–90.

[22] Hair and Alsop, *Seamen and Traders*, esp. pp. 105–57; J. D. Alsop, 'The Career of William Towerson, Guinea Trader', *International Journal of Maritime History*, IV, 2 (1992), pp. 48–82.

[23] Contrary to a 1929 view: 'supported by royal patronage, the organisation of the African trade advanced rapidly' (Eveline C. Martin, 'The English Slave Trade and the African Settlements', in *Cambridge History of the British Empire*, I, p. 438).

[24] Richard Eden, *The Decades of the Newe Worlde* (London, 1555), ff. 343–60.

[25] For details, see P. E. H. Hair, 'Guinea', in David B. Quinn, ed., *The Hakluyt Handbook*, 2 vols., single pag. (Hakluyt Society, London, 1974), pp. 190–96.

predominantly American content of the Hawkins accounts and their more sensational nature. However, the later English reader of Hakluyt was tempted to consider regular English involvement in the slave trade as dating from the mid-sixteenth century, about a century too early. Nevertheless, it seems unlikely that before 1600—and perhaps even before 1700—the reading of accounts of Guinea voyages by a tiny literate minority was a major generator of a widespread English view that Black Africans were a particularly inferior set of non-English, and even less likely that there existed a literary campaign to degrade Africans, motivated by a desire to justify slave-trading.[26]

Writing in the time of Philip and Mary, Eden, in his introduction to the 1555 volume, was tactfully respectful of Spanish claims to the Americas, but fiercely challenged Portuguese claims to a trading monopoly in Guinea, a nationalistic view subsequently pressed by Elizabeth in diplomatic jousts with Lisbon in the 1560s and 1570s.[27] While these were minor diplomatic engagements, and while England was merely copying an intellectual assault on Iberian overseas monopoly begun by France, the arguments put forward by the English in relation to western Africa went some way towards the evolving international law doctrines of 'open seas' and 'effective occupation'.[28]

During the first half of the seventeenth century English interest in the African trade grew. The context for this was the weakening of Portuguese dominance in Guinea, which in turn arose in large part out of the war of independence of the Netherlands against Spain. Since Spain until 1640 was in a regal union with Portugal, the latter's overseas trade and possessions, in Africa and elsewhere, became subject to Dutch attack.[29] The Dutch entered the African trade only in the 1590s, but then very quickly outstripped the Portuguese. The Dutch challenge took a more aggressive form with the formation in 1621 of the West India

[26] Winthrop D. Jordan, *White over Black: American Attitudes Towards the Negro, 1550–1812* (Chapel Hill, NC, 1968); among the many studies which derive from Jordan's analysis are Elliott M. Tokson, *The Popular Image of the Black Man in English Drama, 1550–1688* (Boston, 1982), and Anthony Gerard Barthelemy, *Black Face, Maligned Race: The Representation of Blacks in English Drama from Shakespeare to Southerne* (Baton Rouge, La., 1987). For a critique of this approach, see P. E. H. Hair, 'Attitudes to Africans in English Primary Sources on Guinea up to 1650', in P. D. Harvey, ed., *Rethinking Cultural Encounter: The Diversity of English Experience, 1500–1700* (forthcoming 1998).

[27] The documents, with commentary, are in Visconde de Santarem, *Quadro elementar dos relações diplomaticas de Portugal*, 18 vols. (Paris, 1841–1860), XV (1854), and scattered throughout the 1560–75 volumes of *CSP Foreign*. This aspect is usefully discussed in Williamson, 'England and the Opening of the Atlantic', pp. 45–47.

[28] Cf. Williamson, 'England and the Opening of the Atlantic', p. 44.

[29] For the rise of Dutch trade and naval power in the Atlantic, see Ernst van den Boogaart, Pieter C. Emmer, Peter Klein, and Kees Zandvliet, *La Expansión Holandesa en el Atlántico, 1580–1800* (Madrid, 1992); and generally, Jonathan I. Israel, *Dutch Primacy in World Trade, 1585–1740* (Oxford, 1989).

Company, which launched a systematic assault on the Portuguese position, culminating in the capture of the Portuguese headquarters at São Jorge da Mina in 1637. Portugal (having seceded from its union with Spain in 1640) made a truce with the Netherlands in 1641, recognizing Dutch possession of the former Portuguese sphere in Guinea. Thereafter, the Dutch considered themselves as having inherited the monopoly rights in the Guinea trade formerly claimed by Portugal.

England was initially (down to 1604, and again in 1625–30) allied with the Netherlands against Spain and Portugal. But with the Dutch triumph in the 1630s, the Dutch West India Company took the place of Portugal as the established power which other nations interested in the Guinea trade would have to challenge. There followed a complicated struggle for commercial and naval dominance on the Guinea coast, in which the Dutch position was challenged by French, Swedish, Danish, and Courlander (from the Baltic Duchy), as well as English interests.[30] By the mid-seventeenth century the English had emerged as the principal rivals to the Dutch in the Guinea trade, creating tensions which culminated in the Second Anglo-Dutch War of 1665–67, which began with fighting in Africa.

In the negotiations for peace with Spain in 1604 the English pressed for freedom of trade with Guinea and other overseas Spanish dominions; the Spanish refused to concede the point, but the treaty incorporated an ambiguous formula which the English interpreted as giving them access to the South Atlantic.[31] Anglo-Spanish hostilities, in the form of reciprocal privateering, persisted in Guinea (as elsewhere 'beyond the Line') after 1604, but at the same time peaceful trade increased. Initially, English commercial interest remained concentrated on the extreme western portion of the coast, from the River Senegal to Sierra Leone. The voyages further east, to the Gold Coast and Benin, which had been intermittently undertaken in the second half of the sixteenth century, were not followed up until the 1630s. It does not appear that this trade was conducted under the licences issued in 1588–98, which seem to have lapsed; as far as the evidence goes, English trade with Africa was now, for the moment, free. Increasingly, the trade was now dominated by businessmen from London, to the exclusion of the West Country merchants who had participated in earlier ventures.

English trade with Senegambia, initiated from 1587, is poorly documented from English sources after 1604, but was clearly significant. A Dutch trader visiting the Senegal area in 1606, for example, found four English ships trading at Portudal; and another English ship joined with the Dutch to attack a Portuguese ship at

[30] The best detailed account of European rivalries in West Africa in this period remains unpublished: Robert Porter, 'European Activity on the Gold Coast, 1620–1667', unpublished D.Litt. thesis, University of South Africa, 1975.

[31] Andrews, *Trade, Plunder and Settlement*, pp. 254–55.

Jual.[32] The trade in this area was mainly for hides, gum arabic (used for sizing cloth) and wax; some gold, brought down the rivers from the interior, was also available, but this was not yet a significant article of trade for the English.

Further south-east along the coast, in Sierra Leone, the principal trade was for redwood (used for dyeing cloth). Although a licence for trade here had been issued in 1592, it is not clear how soon this was taken up. A significant English trade for African redwood did develop, however, from the 1600s, the principal pioneer being John Davies (d. 1626), a London merchant who had earlier been involved in financing privateering against Spanish shipping.[33] Davies engaged in the redwood trade from *c.*1607 onwards, and in 1614 unsuccessfully petitioned the Privy Council for a monopoly of it. By 1611 he had a factor resident on the Guinea Coast, presumably in the Sierra Leone area, for this trade—this being, as far as the evidence goes, the earliest English establishment anywhere on the western African coast, though it was perhaps only ephemeral.[34]

The efforts of Davies and others culminated in the formation of the Company of Adventurers of London Trading to the Parts of Africa (more commonly called the 'Guinea Company'), which was granted a monopoly of trade in this area 'for ever hereafter' by King James I in 1618—the first genuinely joint-stock company for English trade with Africa.[35] The geographical scope of the grant is specified as 'Gynney and Bynney', that is, Guinea and Benin, a formula which implicitly encompassed the whole of the West African coast from Senegal to what is today Nigeria. In practice, however, the Company restricted its activities to the areas of established English interest—Senegambia and Sierra Leone. The wording of the charter excluded foreigners, as well as English subjects, from the Company's sphere, evidently in imitation of earlier Portuguese pretensions, though how seriously this was intended is doubtful.

The principal effort of the Company was initially directed towards the trade in gold, and more especially to the River Gambia, by which it was thought possible to penetrate to the source of the gold in the interior. Three voyages were despatched to the Gambia between 1618 and 1621—the third (1620/21) commanded by Richard

[32] K. Ratelband, ed., *Reizen naar West-Afrika van Pieter van den Broecke, 1605–1614* (The Hague, 1950), pp. 6, 10–12.

[33] Blake, 'English Trade with the Portuguese Empire', pp. 327–28.

[34] In 1650 the Guinea Company claimed that, prior to its own activities in the 1630s, the only previous English factory in Africa had been established at the Gambia by the first Guinea Company (chartered 1618) 'about 35 years since'—evidently referring imprecisely to the latter's Gambia expedition of 1618/19: *CSP Colonial 1574–1660*, p. 339. Davies's earlier factory was perhaps ignored as being a private venture.

[35] The only substantial account, itself frequently neglected, remains John W. Blake, 'The English Guinea Company, 1618–1660', *Proceedings of the Belfast Natural History and Philosophical Society*, III, 1 (1945/46), pp. 14–27.

Jobson, who published an account of it.[36] Although making some contribution to geographical knowledge, commercially the Gambia venture was a disaster, the three voyages incurring an accumulated loss of over £5,600. What trade was done, moreover, was not in gold but in hides, wax, and ambergris. Although a trading station was established up the Gambia River, this was evidently abandoned after 1621.

A more profitable trade continued to be done in the Sierra Leone area, for redwood. John Davies in 1620 secured from the Company a grant of the monopoly of trade at the Sierra Leone River, which he presumably exercised until his death in 1626. Other members of the Company, however, were able to trade at the River Sherbro, further east along the coast, where a factory for the redwood trade was established by 1628; since this trade post (unlike earlier ventures) appears to have been maintained continuously thereafter, its establishment can perhaps be more validly regarded as marking the beginnings of an English presence on the western African coast.[37] The Company was not, however, able in practice to monopolize the Sierra Leone trade, but faced competition from English interlopers operating in breach of its monopoly. Its difficulties in defending its rights were compounded by its political vulnerability at home, due to its dependence on royal favour; in 1624 its monopoly was declared a grievance by Parliament.

The Company's difficulties led to its takeover by Nicholas Crispe (1598–1666), a London merchant, who invested in the Company from 1625 and bought a controlling interest in 1628.[38] Although Crispe continued the Sierra Leone redwood trade, he also sought to reorient the Company's interest to the Gold Coast, which was the principal source of African gold, and where Portuguese dominance was crumbling in the face of the continuing challenge by the Dutch. His efforts to reinvigorate the Company were only partially successful; its debts were exacerbated by the failure of some shareholders to pay their subscriptions, and compounded by losses of shipping in the Anglo-French War of 1627–29. In 1631 a new charter was granted to a body called the Company of Merchants Trading to Guinea, given a monopoly for thirty-one years of trade from Cape Blanco to the Cape of Good Hope (that is, now including Angola, as well as Guinea). Although the wording of the charter implies that this was an entirely new Company, distinct from that chartered in 1618, this has been shown to be misleading, since those involved were those who now dominated the existing Company, including especially Nicholas Crispe.[39] Apart from reorganization, the purpose of the new

[36] Richard Jobson, *The Golden Trade, or a Discovery of the River Gambra* (1623; repr. London, 1932).

[37] Blake, 'English Guinea Company', pp. 25–26.

[38] Robert Porter, 'The Crispe Family and the African Trade in the Seventeenth Century', *Journal of African History*, IX (1968), pp. 57–77.

[39] John W. Blake, 'The Farm of the Guinea Trade in 1631', in H. A. Crone, T. W. Moody, and David B. Quinn, eds., *Essays in British and Irish History in Honour of James Eadie Todd* (London, 1949), pp. 86–106.

charter was to underline its claim to the whole western African trade, with a view to extending its operations east of Sierra Leone. The new charter asserted territorial, as well as purely commercial, rights, and promised government support against foreign competitors. The challenge was no longer against Portugal, England having again made a separate peace with Spain and Portugal in 1630, but rather, explicitly, against the now-dominant Dutch.

To assert the Company's claims, Crispe employed a renegade from the Dutch West India Company, Arent de Groot, who sailed to Africa in 1632 and established factories on the Gold Coast, first at Komenda, and later at Kormantin and Winneba. Other factories were subsequently established at Anomabu (1639), Takoradi (1645), and Cabo Corso (Cape Coast) (1650). Kormantin became the Company's local headquarters, and was fortified from 1638. In addition to trading on the Gold Coast, the Company's agents sent yachts east along the coast to Benin (mainly to buy locally made cloth, which in turn could be exchanged on the Gold Coast for gold), where a trade station was maintained in the 1640s; and also to the Portuguese island of São Tomé, to purchase sugar. (Despite the scope of the charter, no serious attempt was yet made to trade to Angola.) The Company's main concern was now gold; Crispe later claimed to have imported gold to a total value of £500,000, probably over the period of twelve years, 1633–44.[40]

Despite its successful establishment on the Gold Coast, the Guinea Company proved ultimately ineffective in challenging the dominance of the Dutch West India Company. Like its predecessor, the new Company also faced difficulties in enforcing its monopoly against English interlopers. In 1634 a Scottish 'Guinea Company' was also chartered, which sent at least two ships to trade for gold on the Gold Coast in 1636–37 (though only one of these got back home, the other being seized by the Portuguese at São Tomé).[41] The English company also suffered political difficulties in England, from the challenge to royal authority culminating in the Civil War, through Crispe's identification with the Royalist cause. In 1640 he was ordered by Parliament to surrender his patent for the monopoly of the Guinea trade, and in 1644 his shares in the Company were confiscated in lieu of a debt owed to the state. Control of the Company then passed to merchants who supported the Parliamentarian cause, some of whom had earlier been interlopers in the Guinea trade, notably Maurice Thompson (also prominent in the East India Company).[42]

[40] Porter, 'Crispe Family', p. 66.

[41] Robin Law, 'The First Scottish Guinea Company, 1634–9', *Scottish Historical Review* (1997).

[42] Kenneth R. Andrews, *Ships, Money and Politics: Seafaring and Naval Enterprise in the Reign of Charles I* (Cambridge, 1991), pp. 57–61; also Robert Brenner, *Merchants and Revolutionaries: Commercial Change, Political Conflict and London's Overseas Traders, 1550–1663* (Cambridge, 1993); see below pp. 276–77.

The Company's difficulties with English interlopers came to a head in the late 1640s, when its position on the Gold Coast was challenged by a group of merchants led by Samuel Vassall, whose agents ousted the Company's merchants from their lodge at Winneba in 1648. Petitions and counter-petitions between the Company and Vassall's group led to a Committee of Trade inquiry in 1650–51, which found the trade in a disastrous state, due to competition from the Dutch and others, the Company having lost £100,000 up to that date. Although the Company's monopoly was extended for a further fourteen years, it was now geographically restricted to an area twenty leagues either side of its two principal trading centres, at Sherbro in Sierra Leone and Kormantin on the Gold Coast; in effect, this meant that it retained a monopoly of the redwood and gold trades, but the trade further east, mainly in slaves, became free.

Although Vassall now joined the Company, its fortunes did not improve, since it faced further challenges locally in Guinea. It suffered severe financial losses from the depredations of the Royalist fleet under Prince Rupert, which attacked Company vessels at the Gambia in 1652; in conflicts on the Gold Coast, where its factory at Cape Coast was seized by the Swedes in 1652; and from further losses of shipping in the Anglo-Dutch War of 1652–54. By the mid-1650s the Guinea Company had ceased to function as an effective trading body, though it retained its fort at Kormantin and other stations on the Gold Coast. In 1657 it leased its rights and factories to the East India Company, which was seeking gold and ivory for the Indian market.[43] Like the Guinea Company earlier, the East India Company also traded along the coast to Benin, where it re-established a factory in 1661, for cloth which could be sold for gold on the Gold Coast.

Down to the mid-seventeenth century English trade with western Africa was mainly in commodities other than slaves. In 1620, when Jobson on the Gambia was offered slaves, he replied that 'We were a people who did not deale in any such commodities, neither did wee buy or sell one another, or any that had our owne shapes'.[44] This was not entirely accurate, since there were certainly at least occasional English slaving ventures in the early seventeenth century. The English ship which joined the Dutch in attacking the Portuguese ship at Jual in 1606, for example, claimed the slaves on board as its share of the booty, though it is not specified where it intended to sell them. The Guinea Company itself seems initially to have played little role in slaving; the charter of 1631 stresses trade in gold, and makes no mention of slaves. In 1637 the

[43] Margaret Makepeace, 'English Traders on the Guinea Coast, 1657–1668: An Analysis of the East India Company Archive', *History in Africa*, XVI (1989), pp. 285–310; and original documentation in Makepeace, ed., *Trade on the Guinea Coast, 1657–1666: The Correspondence of the English East India Company* (Madison, 1991).

[44] Jobson, *Golden Trade*, p. 120.

Company intervened to prevent a projected interloping voyage, which reportedly intended to sail to Guinea to take 'nigers' and 'carry them to foreign parts', presumably to Spain or Spanish America; but whether this implies that it sought to trade in slaves itself is doubtful.[45]

A significant English slave trade emerged only with the introduction of sugar cultivation on Barbados in the early 1640s, which for the first time created a substantial demand for African slaves within the English Empire. It then, however, developed rapidly, challenging the dominance of the Dutch.[46] The trade was mainly conducted by illicit traders operating in breach of the Guinea Company's monopoly. The main focus of slaving activity was east of the Gold Coast, initially at New Calabar (Nigeria) and subsequently also at Allada (Republic of Benin); though Vassall's agents in the late 1640s purchased slaves on the Gold Coast itself. In the debates of 1650–51 the Company was criticized for its failure to supply slaves to English colonies; and it did undertake slaving voyages subsequently. But the geographical restriction of its monopoly in 1651 left the principal slaving ports, Allada and Calabar, outside its privileged sphere, and freely open to all English merchants.[47] The East India Company, which took over the Gold Coast trading stations in 1657, was not interested in the slave trade, and in 1660 it further forbade its agents from trading in slaves on their own account. Slaving by other English merchants continued, however, illegally on the Gold Coast and legally further east.

The Restoration of 1660 enabled a group of courtiers, led by Prince Rupert and James, Duke of York, to form a new Company of Royal Adventurers into Africa, which was given monopoly trading rights in western Africa for 1,000 years.[48] Initially, because of the need to negotiate over the pre-existing rights of the Guinea and East India Companies, the new Company's activities were restricted to the Gambia. Its first decisive act was to despatch a naval expedition to Africa, under Sir Robert Holmes, which established a fort on James Island in the Gambia (1661). The new Company was definitively re-chartered (as the Company of Royal Adventurers of England Trading into Africa, but commonly called the Royal African Company) in 1663, when it took over the English factories on the Gold Coast. James, Duke of York, was elected Governor of the Company.

[45] *CSP Colonial, 1574–1660*, pp. 259–60.

[46] Larry Gragg, '"To Procure Negroes": The English Slave Trade to Barbados, 1627–60', *Slavery and Abolition*, XVI, 1 (1995), pp. 65–84.

[47] For documentation of English slaving ventures in this period, see John C. Appleby, 'A Guinea Venture, *c.*1657: A Note on the Early English Slave Trade', *Mariner's Mirror*, LXXIX, 1 (1993), pp. 84–87; '"A Business of Much Difficulty": A London Slaving Venture, 1651–1654', ibid., LXXXI, 1 (1995), pp. 3–14.

[48] The principal account remains George Frederick Zook, *The Company of Royal Adventurers Trading into Africa* (New York, 1919).

Although the charter of 1660 mentioned specifically only trade in gold, the terms of its monopoly also encompassed the supply of slaves to the West Indian colonies, which had previously been handled mainly by private traders. The Company therefore came under pressure, either to allow a free trade in slaves or to supply slaves itself, and in 1662 it undertook to supply 3,000 slaves annually to the West Indian colonies.[49] This shift of emphasis was confirmed in the new charter of 1663, which for the first time explicitly mentioned the slave trade among the Company's interests. In consequence, the Company extended its activities east of the Gold Coast, into the area which was becoming known as the 'Slave Coast', where it established a trading station at Allada in 1663; slaving voyages were also undertaken to New and Old Calabar, further east. The suggestion that the slave trade had now become the Company's 'main pursuit' is, however, unwarranted.[50] Gold remained the main object of trade; in 1665 the Company estimated its annual revenue from gold sales at £200,000, as against only £100,000 from the delivery of slaves to English colonies, with a further £100,000 from other commodities (ivory, wax, hides, dyewoods, and pepper).[51] African gold was coined in 'guineas', stamped with an elephant as the Company's symbol, from 1663 onwards.

The Company made an ambitious start, claiming to have established (or re-established) eighteen factories in Africa and despatched over forty ships to trade there in the first year of its operation. But it then became embroiled in conflict with the Dutch, with clashes on the Guinea coast leading to the Second Anglo-Dutch War (not formally declared until March 1665). The Dutch regarded Holmes's establishment at the Gambia as an intrusion into their own monopoly sphere; and in 1661–62 they seized several of the Company's ships trading in Guinea and obstructed trade with its factories. The Company mounted a naval expedition, again commanded by Holmes, to assert its rights in 1663–64, which took several Dutch factories, including Cape Coast (which had now passed from Swedish into Dutch hands). However, the decision was reversed by Admiral de Ruyter's expedition in 1664–65, which captured or recaptured most of the English-held factories on the Gold Coast, including the Company's headquarters at Kormantin. The Company retained only Cape Coast, which consequently now replaced Kormantin as the English headquarters in Guinea.

The losses sustained at de Ruyter's hands ruined the Company, which did little trade after 1665. The Company licensed private traders from 1667, leased the

[49] The Company also undertook, in 1663, to supply 3,500 slaves annually for the contract (*Asiento*) for Spanish America, but few were actually delivered.

[50] Martin, 'English Slave Trade', p. 440.

[51] *CSP Domestic, 1661–68*, item 903. These are estimates of the trade the Company would have done, but for Dutch intervention, rather than actually achieved; it also projected earnings of a further £86,000 per year from sales of slaves to Spanish America, but this scheme was almost wholly abortive.

Gambia trade to a separate company of Gambia Adventurers in 1669, and was liquidated and replaced by a new Royal African Company in 1672.[52] Initially the Gambia Adventurers maintained their rights, but in 1678 they were bought out by the Royal African Company. By comparison with the Royal Adventurers, the new Company was dominated by merchants rather than courtiers, though James, Duke of York (and later as King), remained titular Governor.

The Royal African Company, in contrast to its predecessors, traded mainly for slaves; in 1674 it undertook to supply 5,600 slaves annually to the West Indies and Virginia (though this total was not, in practice, attained).[53] It also continued, however, to purchase gold and other commodities, such as dye-woods and ivory; sales of African goods still accounted for around two-fifths of its income.[54] Trading posts were maintained at the Gambia and in Sierra Leone, mainly for the commodity trade. The main centre of the Company's activities remained the Gold Coast, which increasingly became a source of slaves as well as of gold. The principal centre of the slave trade, however, was the 'Slave Coast' to the east, where a trading post was re-established in Allada in 1674 (and transferred to neighbouring Whydah in 1682). Further east, the Company initially maintained a factory at Benin, to purchase cloth for the Gold Coast market, but this trade was abandoned by the end of the century.[55] Ships also went to the Calabars and Angola for slaves, but no trading stations were maintained in these regions.

The Royal African Company benefited from the decline of Dutch trade after the Third Anglo-Dutch War of 1672–74. Although there was competition also from French, Danish, and, after 1680, Brandenburger companies, the English now became the leading traders in Guinea: by the 1690s the Dutch still had the largest share of the gold trade,[56] but the English were shipping the most slaves. Like its predecessors, however, the Company had difficulties in maintaining its position against competition from English intruders. Between 1679 and 1682, for example, at least thirty-two interloping ships delivered slaves to the West Indies, as against around seventy of the Company's.[57] Some English ships also bought slaves

[52] See esp. K. G. Davies, *The Royal African Company* (London, 1957).

[53] Minutes of Court of Assistants of Royal African Company, 12 May 1674, T[reasury] 70/76; for actual deliveries (which exceeded 5,000 annually only in 1684–8), see Davies, *Royal African Company*, pp. 361–64. But for an upward revision of Davies's figures, see David Eltis, 'The Volume and West African Origins of the British Slave Trade before 1714', *Cahiers d'Études Africaines*, XXXV (1995), pp. 617–27.

[54] Davies, *Royal African Company*, pp. 179–82.

[55] Ryder, *Benin and the Europeans*, p. 124.

[56] Total exports from the Gold Coast were estimated at 7,000 marks annually, of which the Dutch were taking 3,000 and the English (Royal African Company and interlopers combined) 2,500: William Bosman, *A New and Accurate Description of the Coast of Guinea* (London, 1705), pp. 88–89.

[57] Davies, *Royal African Company*, pp. 113–14.

from Madagascar in East Africa, which was outside the limits of the Company's monopoly.

Although the Company at first appeared to be profitable, paying regular dividends down through the 1680s, it was simultaneously incurring significant debts. By the early 1690s its accumulated debt, around £150,000, was roughly equivalent to the total it had paid out in dividends; in effect, the Company had been borrowing money to pay dividends.[58] It was solvent only on paper, its debts being secured against assets which were either of doubtful value (such as payments outstanding for slaves delivered to the West Indies) or (in the case of its establishments in Africa) realizable only through the Company's own liquidation. In the 1690s its tenuous position was exposed.

The Royal African Company's difficulties were compounded by the Anglo-French War of 1689–97, which again involved fighting in Africa, with the English briefly occupying the French fort of St Louis on the Senegal (1692–93), and the French in turn taking Fort James on the Gambia from the English in 1695 (but restoring it under the Peace of 1697). More critically, the Company suffered severe financial losses from French privateering, around a quarter of its ships trading to Africa during the war being taken. There was also unofficial fighting with the Dutch West India Company; although in Europe the Netherlands and England were allied against France, their local agents in Africa pursued their commercial competition to the point of military means, normally through the financing and incitement of African allies, but at times also in overt intra-European violence.

At the same time, the Royal African Company's political position within England was undermined by the Revolution of 1688.[59] Although the Bill of Rights did not mention monopolies, the Company's opponents maintained that monopolies based on royal grants had been invalidated, and the African trade was now free. Certainly, the actual policing of the Company's monopoly became politically impossible, and it abandoned attempts to pursue legal actions against interlopers. The Company also faced competition from a new Scottish company, the Company of Scotland Trading to Africa and the Indies, formed in 1695. This originated, in part, in an attempt by a group of London-based merchants to find a legal basis for breaking into the monopolies of the English Royal African and East India Companies; but it was re-formed in 1696 as a more genuinely Scottish venture. The Company is best known for its abortive attempt to establish a Scottish colony on the Darien Isthmus in Central America; but it also sent at least two ships to trade in Africa in 1699–1700—one to the Gold Coast

[58] Ibid., pp. 77–79.

[59] Ann M. Carlos and Jamie Brown Kruse, 'The Decline of the Royal African Company: Fringe Firms and the Role of the Charter', *Economic History Review*, XLIX (1996), pp. 291–313.

for gold and one to Madagascar for slaves, though the second was taken by pirates.[60]

The Revolution was followed by a debate about the organization of the African trade, as the Royal African Company and its rivals, the 'separate traders', appealed to Parliament to legislate in their interests. This debate had a geographical, as well as a purely organizational, aspect, with merchants in the colonies and in English 'outports' such as Bristol demanding freedom to compete with the London-based company. It also involved West Indian sugar planters and English manufacturers who sold part of their output into the African trade (especially woollen manufacturers), who both supported free trade. The debate concerned not only the issue of monopoly versus free trade, but also whether the maintenance of trading stations and forts on the African coast was necessary for the trade, and if so, how this might best be arranged.

The ultimate outcome was a compromise. An Act of 1698 ended the Royal African Company's monopoly, opening the African trade to all English merchants, but on payment of a 10 per cent levy on goods exported to Africa to subsidize the Company's operations. Forced to compete, the Company was quickly swamped by the separate traders: in 1708 it was estimated that the latter had imported around 75,000 slaves into English colonies since 1698, as against only about 18,000 by the Company.[61] Free trade delivered larger numbers of slaves, though increased competition also brought substantial increases in prices. The 1698 Act was valid for only thirteen years, and with its expiry in 1712 the trade became totally free. By 1730 the Company had ceased to function as a trading company, but was then granted a government subsidy in order to maintain its African factories, in the interests of English trade in general. The opening of the African trade after 1698 stimulated a shift of its main centre away from London towards Bristol and other 'outports'.[62]

The significance of seventeenth-century English enterprise in western Africa for the English economy is difficult to assess. The Royal African Company in 1680 maintained that it had promoted 'the exportation of our native woollen and other manufactures in great abundance... whereby the wooll of this nation is much more consumed and spent then formerly; and many thousand of the poor people

[60] George Pratt Insh, *The Company of Scotland Trading to Africa and the Indies* (London, 1932). The dissolution of the Company was stipulated in the Act of Union of 1707.

[61] Davies, *Royal African Company*, p. 143.

[62] David Richardson, *Bristol, Africa and the Eighteenth-Century Slave Trade to America*, Vol. I, *The Years of Expansion, 1698–1729* (Bristol Record Society, 1986); Nigel Tattersfield, *The Forgotten Trade, Comprising the Log of the Daniel and Henry of 1700 and Accounts of the Slave Trade from the Minor Ports of England, 1698–1725* (London, 1991).

employed'.[63] The Company had indeed from 1677 arranged for the copying in England of certain textiles for the African trade which had previously been imported from the Netherlands. But it is clear that the African market was of very limited significance, even at the end of the century accounting for under 3 per cent of total English exports.[64] Nearly half of the goods sold in Africa, moreover, consisted not of English manufactures but of re-exports, including goods from India—especially textiles, but also cowrie shells, used as currency in much of western Africa—as well as from Europe. Even African gold was less important than the rhetoric of those interested in the trade implied; between 1677 and 1689 the Company supplied only 7 per cent of gold coined in the Royal Mint.[65] Africa's principal contribution was clearly not to the metropolitan economy directly, but rather to the American colonies, especially in the Caribbean, for which it supplied the labour upon which sugar production depended.

The longer-term significance of seventeenth-century English enterprise in the African trade for the growth of the British 'Empire' is also problematical. The project of asserting monopoly trading rights against rival European nations, to the point of making war against them, may be considered a form of 'Empire', albeit of a maritime rather than a territorial form. But this project was never, in fact, realized, and was seriously attempted on only one occasion, by the Company of Royal Adventurers in its conflict with the Dutch in 1661–65. Early English involvement in the African trade also involved the beginnings of 'Empire' in the sense of the establishment of settlements on the coast. When the slave trade was abolished in 1807 some of these were abandoned (e.g. that at Whydah), but others were retained. These can be regarded as the beginnings of what became the British colonies of Gambia, Sierra Leone, and the Gold Coast, at least in the sense that physical occupation was more or less continuous from the seventeenth century, though the extension of British rule over the interior did not occur until the nineteenth century.[66] There was no such continuity of occupation, however, in the case of the fourth British colony in West Africa, Nigeria, which had to be re-established from scratch, beginning in 1861.

In any case, it is misleading to treat these establishments in their earlier phases as 'colonies'. They were merely trading posts, which did not develop significant agricultural capacity. Although there were some projects of establishing planta-

[63] *Certain Considerations Relating to the Royal African Company of England* (1680), extract in Elizabeth Donnan, ed., *Documents Illustrative of the Slave Trade to America*, 4 vols. (Washington, 1930–35), I, p. 267.

[64] On the relative importance of English-African trade, see below, pp. 403–04.

[65] Davies, *Royal African Company*, p. 181.

[66] In Sierra Leone occupation was chronologically overlapping at various sites, rather than strictly continuous at any one.

tions in Guinea, using African slaves locally to produce tropical crops such as indigo and cotton, from the late seventeenth century onwards these were limited in scale and ultimately abortive, and the idea was abandoned by the mid-eighteenth century.[67] Legally, moreover, the African settlements were not held of sovereign right, but by agreement with the indigenous authorities, to whom rent or tribute was paid for some of them, including the Royal African Company's headquarters, Cape Coast Castle. As the Board of Trade observed in 1752, 'in Africa we were only tenants of the soil which we held at the goodwill of the natives'.[68]

The more important factories were fortified and defended by cannon: besides James Fort on the Gambia and Cape Coast Castle, fortified from the 1660s, additional forts were built on the Gold Coast at Accra and Anomabu in 1679, and at Komenda, Dixcove, and Winneba (and also at Whydah on the Slave Coast) in the 1690s.[69] These forts were not, however, intended to assert military control over African localities, but rather to defend shipping against rival European nations (and their main batteries accordingly pointed out to sea rather than inland). Although the more substantial forts could normally defend themselves against African attack (as Cape Coast Castle, for example, defied a siege in 1688), lesser stations were militarily vulnerable; the Company factory at Winneba was destroyed by local forces in 1679, and that at Sekondi in 1694. The military superiority which Europeans initially enjoyed over the Africans through their possession of firearms was undermined during the second half of the seventeenth century, when European traders began selling guns locally—a development initiated by English interlopers in the 1640s and necessarily, given the competitive character of the African trade, followed by traders of other nations, both interlopers and official companies. European traders in the seventeenth century did not normally, as Hawkins had initially attempted in the 1560s, enslave Africans by direct force, but purchased captives taken in intra-African wars.

European powers, including the English, did exercise a degree of political influence over African societies on the coast, less through direct military intervention than by supplying firearms and finance for the hiring of mercenaries, both in intra-African conflicts and against other Europeans. The English, for example, supported Komenda in a prolonged war with the Dutch in 1694–99. On one notorious occasion, when the King of Komenda had made peace with the Dutch he was assassinated by the English on a visit to Cape Coast Castle—though as a means of securing a friendly regime in Komenda this proved counter-productive,

[67] Robin Law, 'King Agaja of Dahomey, the Slave Trade, and the Question of West African Plantations: The Mission of Bulfinch Lambe and Adomo Tomo to England, 1726–32', *Journal of Imperial and Commonwealth History*, XIX, 2 (1991), pp. 138–63.

[68] *Journal of the Commissioners for Trade and the Plantations*, 14 Feb. 1752.

[69] A. W. Lawrence, *Fortified Trade-Posts: The English in West Africa, 1645–1822* (London, 1969).

provoking a violent anti-English reaction.[70] The English and other Europeans on the Gold Coast might perhaps be regarded as exercising a form of 'informal empire' over the African communities allied to them; but it might equally be argued that it was the Africans who were exploiting European support, and playing off rival Europeans against each other, rather than vice versa. The degree of political influence which Europeans enjoyed on the Gold Coast was in any case exceptional, due to the relative strength of their military presence and the political fragmentation of the local African societies. On the Slave Coast, faced with a single African power in the kingdom of Whydah, Europeans had to defer to indigenous authority, as seen most obviously in recurrent deportations of those who offended the local rulers, including two chief factors of the Royal African Company in 1682 and 1692; as a Company employee observed on the latter occasion, 'Here is no resisting the country'.[71]

Down to the late seventeenth century, the European impact on western Africa remained limited, and the specifically English impact less significant than that of the Portuguese and Dutch. In Guinea, in contrast to Portuguese Angola, direct influence was restricted to the immediate coastal area; Europeans, including the English, rarely penetrated the interior.[72] The impact of their trade was felt more widely, with slaves in particular sometimes being brought from considerable distances inland. In the longer run, the growth of slave exports, together with imports of firearms, would have a profound effect in at least some areas of the interior, provoking dramatic political upheavals and stimulating the militarization of social structures; but only the beginnings of this process were visible by 1700.[73]

[70] Daaku, *Trade and Politics on the Gold Coast*, pp. 83–88.

[71] Robin Law, '"Here is No Resisting the Country": The Realities of Power in Afro-European Relations on the West African "Slave Coast"', *Itinerario*, XVIII, 2 (1994), pp. 50–64.

[72] Exceptional penetrations inland were those of the French up the River Senegal, *c.*1680, and of an agent of the English Royal African Company into the hinterland of the Gambia in 1689–90: for the latter, see Thora G. Stone, 'The Journey of Cornelius Hodges in Senegambia, 1689–90', *English Historical Review*, XXXIX (1924), pp. 89–95.

[73] Ray A. Kea, *Settlements, Trade and Polities in the Seventeenth-Century Gold Coast* (Baltimore, 1982).

Select Bibliography

KENNETH R. ANDREWS, *Trade, Plunder and Settlement: Maritime Enterprise and the Genesis of the British Empire, 1480–1630* (Cambridge, 1984).

JOHN C. APPLEBY, '"A Business of Much Difficulty": A London Slaving Venture, 1651–1654', *The Mariner's Mirror*, LXXI, 1 (1995), pp. 3–14.

JOHN W. BLAKE, *European Beginnings in West Africa, 1454–1578* (London, 1937); revised edn., *West Africa: Quest for God and Gold, 1454–1578* (London, 1977).

—— 'English Trade with the Portuguese Empire in West Africa, 1581–1629', *Quarto Congreso do Mundo Português*, VI, 1 (1940), pp. 313–41.

—— *Europeans in West Africa (1450–1560)*, 2 vols. [Hakluyt Society] (London, 1942).

—— 'The English Guinea Company, 1618–1660: An Early Example of the Chartered Company in Colonial Development', *Proceedings of the Belfast Natural History and Philosophical Society*, III, 1 (1945/46), pp. 14–27.

—— 'The Farm of the Guinea Trade in 1631', in H. A. Crone, T. W. Moody, and David B. Quinn, eds., *Essays in British and Irish History in Honour of James Eadie Todd* (London, 1949), pp. 86–106.

ANN M. CARLOS and JAMIE BROWN KRUSE, 'The Decline of the Royal African Company: Fringe Firms and the Role of the Charter', *Economic History Review*, XLIX (1996), pp. 291–313.

K. G. DAVIES, *The Royal African Company* (London, 1957).

ELIZABETH DONNAN, ed., *Documents Illustrative of the Slave Trade to America*, 4 vols. (Washington, 1930–35).

P. E. H. HAIR, 'Protestants as Pirates, Slavers and Proto-Missionaries: Sierra Leone 1568 and 1582', *Journal of Ecclesiastical History*, XXI (1970), pp. 203–24; also in *Africa Encountered: European Contacts and Evidence, 1450–1700* (Aldershot, 1997).

—— and J. D. ALSOP, *English Seamen and Traders in Guinea, 1553–1565: The New Evidence of their Wills* (Lewiston/Lampeter, 1992).

A. W. LAWRENCE, *Trade Castles and Forts of West Africa* (London, 1963); revised edn., *Fortified Trade-Posts: The English in West Africa, 1645–1822* (London, 1969).

MARGARET MAKEPEACE, 'English Traders on the Guinea Coast, 1657–1668: An Analysis of the East India Company Archive', *History in Africa*, XVI (1989), pp. 285–310.

—— ed., *Trade on the Guinea Coast, 1657–1666: The Correspondence of the English East India Company* (Madison, 1991).

ROBERT PORTER, 'The Crispe Family and the African Trade in the Seventeenth Century', *Journal of African History*, IX, 1 (1968), pp. 57–77.

—— 'European Activity on the Gold Coast, 1620–1667', unpublished D.Litt. thesis, University of South Africa, 1975.

A. TEIXEIRA DA MOTA and P. E. H. HAIR, *East of Mina: Afro-European Relations on the Gold Coast in the 1550s and 1560s* (Madison, 1988).

J. A. WILLIAMSON, *John Hawkins* (London, 1927); revised edn., *Hawkins of Plymouth* (London, 1949).

GEORGE FREDERICK ZOOK, *The Company of Royal Adventurers Trading into Africa* (1919; repr. New York, 1969).

12

The English in Asia to 1700

P. J. MARSHALL

During the sixteenth and seventeenth centuries an ancient pattern of long-distance trade between Asia and Europe grew greatly in scale. As had been the case since Roman times, this trade was built on European demand for certain Asian crops, above all for pepper and spices, and for the silk and cotton textiles, porcelain, and other products of Asian artisans. At the end of the fifteenth century Europe's supply of Asian spices and pepper through Venice has been estimated at about 3,500,000 pounds a year.[1] In the 1620s Europe's annual consumption of Asian goods has been put at 5 million pounds of pepper, approximately 1 million pounds of the rarer spices, that is, cloves, nutmeg, and mace, more than 350,000 pounds of indigo, and 500,000 pounds of silk.[2] By the end of the seventeenth century an annual average of over a million pieces of cotton calicoes or muslins had been added to the other commodities.[3]

This spectacular growth in intercontinental trade was the consequence of a number of developments that began to take effect from the end of the fifteenth century. The demand for Asian imports, especially in western Europe, grew with increased purchasing power among certain sections of the population. New supplies of bullion from America gave European merchants the means with which to buy more Asian goods. The opening up of the route round the Cape of Good Hope enabled an ever-increasing volume of Asian goods to be transported to Europe at reduced cost and with a reasonable reliability. Finally, commercial organizations evolved which proved themselves capable of effectively transacting trade on a large scale over great distances. The English East India Company was one of these organizations. At the end of the seventeenth century it was set to become the most successful of the European traders operating in Asia.

[1] F. C. Lane, 'Venetian Shipping during the Commercial Revolution', in *Venice in History* (Baltimore, 1966), p. 13.

[2] Niels Steensgaard, *Carracks, Caravans and Companies: The Structural Crisis in the European–Asian Trade in the Early 17th Century* (Copenhagen, 1973), pp. 155–62.

[3] Niels Steensgaard, 'The Growth and Composition of the Long-distance Trade of England and the Dutch Republic before 1750', in James D. Tracy, ed., *The Rise of the Merchant Empires: Long-Distance Trade in the Early Modern World, 1350–1750* (Cambridge, 1990), p. 126.

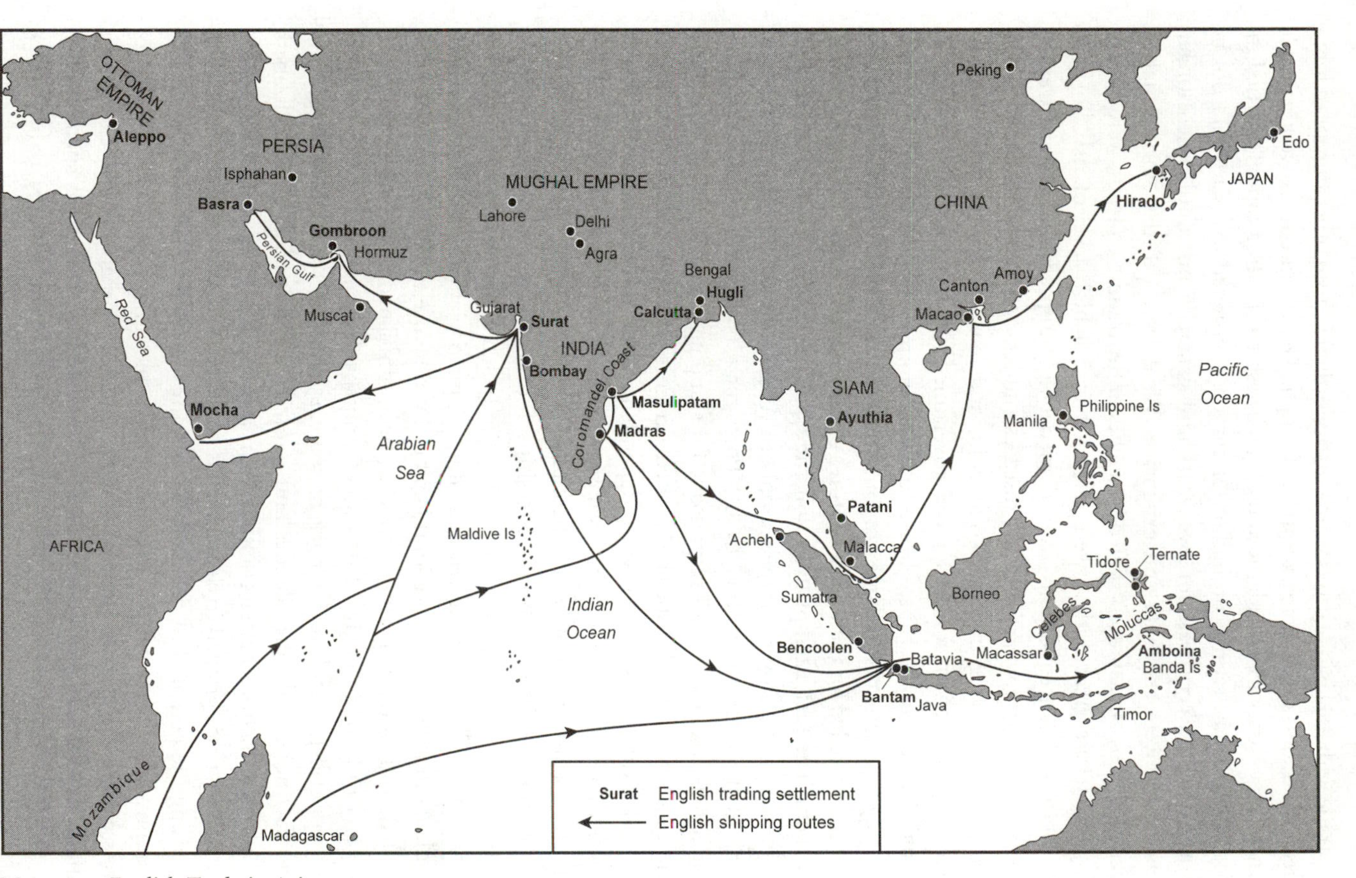

MAP 12.1. English Trade in Asia

Trade with Asia had features which distinguished it from other European long-distance trades. Costs were exceptionally high. The commodities were valuable ones. They were carried in large and expensive ships. Trading capital was tied up for long periods: returns on bullion or cargoes consigned to Asia would not be realized at the very least for two years and generally not until much longer. Overheads were elaborate and expensive. What were called factories, that is, permanent trading stations staffed by agents of the trading concern, were needed in Asia. These great outlays were attended with a high level of risk. To most Europeans, Asian conditions seemed menacingly unpredictable. Ships were at the mercy of typhoons, unknown diseases suddenly carried off men, wars and famines could bring trade to a standstill, and merchants were believed to be harried by capricious and tyrannical governments. Sales of Asian commodities could also be badly disrupted by war or civil commotion in Europe.

Only governments or large combinations of merchants could mobilize the resources needed for these great ventures or could afford to run the risks involved in them. The first attempt to exploit the Cape route in order to attain a commanding position over Europe's supply of Asian goods was made at the beginning of the sixteenth century by the Portuguese crown through its *Estado da India*, a department of state responsible for shipping out cargoes to Asia, obtaining Asian goods, and disposing of them in Europe. At the end of the century groups of merchants in the newly independent Netherlands began to defy Portuguese claims to exclusive rights to navigation beyond the Cape of Good Hope. In 1595 a consortium of Dutch merchants sent out two fleets of ships. In 1598 five companies fitted out twenty-two ships, four of which returned the following year with very valuable cargoes. In 1602 the Dutch government encouraged the union of the various ventures in a single United Netherlands Chartered East India Company with a large joint capital. Even before the creation of the great united Company, English merchants had been stimulated by the successful Dutch voyages to form an English East India Company. In September 1599 a group of 101 subscribers established a stock of some £30,000 to 'set forthe a vyage... to the Est Indies and other ilandes and cuntries therabouts', if Queen Elizabeth would give them a charter granting them a monopoly of English Asian trade.[4] The charter was granted in September 1600. There were formidable obstacles to realizing the potential of the trade. Large sums of money had to be raised and committed for long periods from an English money market that for much of the century had only a limited capacity. Those who managed the Company's affairs in England had to learn how to direct complex operations spanning two continents. They also had to be politically astute. From the first request for a

[4] William Foster, *England's Quest of Eastern Trade* (London, 1933), p. 146.

charter, the Company revealed its dependence on the national government. That support had to be maintained in often turbulent conditions. The Company had to recruit agents for its Asian service who could be trusted with its concerns and who would be able to acquire the expertise needed to deal with Asian merchants and governments in circumstances that varied greatly from port to port. Both at home and in Asia the Company faced fierce competition. Other groups of English merchants attempted to break into its privileges, while in Asia both the Portuguese and the Dutch tried to restrict English activities and thus to curb the growth of London as a rival market for Asian goods to Lisbon or Amsterdam.

The extent of the problems facing the East India Company is reflected by the sharp fluctuations in its fortunes over its first hundred years. Its first ventures, if small by Dutch standards, achieved real success in buoyant commercial conditions up to the 1620s. Thereafter the Company entered a period of contraction and difficulty that was to last through the English Civil War into the 1660s. In the later seventeenth century the East India Company recovered and prospered with the growth of the English economy. It had to contend with a rival company after the Glorious Revolution of 1688, but by the end of the century the two companies were coming together; the prospects for the eighteenth century were for prosperous growth.

During the sixteenth century Asian commodities reached England, as they had done for centuries, either overland through the Middle East to the eastern Mediterranean ports where they were mostly handled by the Venetians, or from Portuguese shipments round the Cape. In the 1570s English ships began to trade with Turkish ports where Asian pepper, spices, and silks were still arriving in large quantities by the overland route, in spite of Portuguese activities in the Indian Ocean. In 1581 a group of merchants trading to Turkey formed themselves into a company which became the Levant Company in 1592.

The Levant Company had a very important influence on the East India Company. It provided much of its leadership and an important segment of its initial capital. The Turkey merchants, as merchants trading to Russia had done, even experimented with making direct contacts overland with Persia and India. In 1583 a group of English merchants travelled through Syria to the Persian Gulf and on to India. One of them, Ralph Fitch, reached Burma and Malacca before returning to England in 1591. Within a few years, however, ventures overland to Asia from the eastern Mediterranean were rendered insignificant by the success of the Dutch ships in going round the Cape, and by the threat that Dutch domination of Asian trade would shortly follow from the despatch of twenty-two ships. As one of the Company's agents observed in 1599, 'This trading to the Indies' by the Dutch 'have clean overthrown our dealings to Aleppo.'[5] English Levant merchants felt that they had no alternative to following the Dutch round the Cape and therefore backed the launching of the East India Company.

From the outset the East India Company acted as a joint-stock concern. As the founder members put it in their petition, ventures 'so farre remote from hence cannot be traded but by a joint and unyted stock'.[6] Funds were to be subscribed and placed under the management of directors, called the Court of Committees, initially to finance single voyages, later for set periods, and only after 1657 for a permanent joint stock of the kind used by the Dutch company from its origins. Although the Company attracted the support of a considerable part of the mercantile élite of London, the sums subscribed were still limited and lack of resources imposed severe restraints on what it could undertake. Investors in the early voyages were reluctant to pay their subscriptions in full and expected a quick distribution of profits. It was only after the success of the first voyages that relatively plentiful funds became available, although investors were still wary of committing them for long periods. Conditions of financial stringency recurred in the 1620s.

The East India Company quickly became by far the largest of the English chartered companies operating overseas, raising nearly £3 million in its first thirty years. Whereas much of the exploitation of the Atlantic was based on West Country ports, trade with Asia was managed exclusively from London and overwhelmingly financed by the investments of the London merchant community. In its early years the affairs of the East India Company were directed by great entrepreneurs, who often played a leading role in other companies, as well as having a stake in royal finance, such as customs farming. Such people frequently held high office in the hierarchy of the City: half the Aldermen in 1640 were members of the East India or the Levant Company. Through them the Company became a strong force in London politics, arousing antagonism from those who resented its privileges. Analysis of the mass of investors in the Company suggests that the great majority of them were merchants, with fewer of the courtiers or gentry who joined the Virginia Company in large numbers. East India Company members usually had investments in other companies as well.[7]

During its first twenty years the Company experimented with a variety of commercial strategies. Contemporary doctrines about the role of foreign trade

[5] K. N. Chaudhuri, *The English East India Company: The Study of an Early Joint-Stock Company, 1600–1640* (London, 1965), p. 11.

[6] Foster, *England's Quest*, p. 147.

[7] For membership of the Company, see Theodore K. Rabb, *Enterprise and Empire: Merchant and Gentry Investment in the Expansion of England, 1575–1630* (Cambridge, Mass., 1967); Robert Brenner, *Merchants and Revolution: Commercial Change, Political Conflict and London's Overseas Traders, 1550–1653* (Princeton, 1993), pp. 21–23, 77–79.

made it politic for the East India Company to promise that it would promote the export of English manufactured goods. In fact the demand for woollens or other English goods was limited in most parts of Asia where the Company established its trade. English exports were made even more difficult to sell by the differential in the price of silver between Europe and Asia. The high price of silver in Asia was a strong inducement to export bullion rather than goods. Although the practice exposed the Company to repeated attacks for depriving the realm of gold and silver, there was no practical alternative to loading ships for Asia with bullion. In its first twenty-three years the Company exported bullion worth £753,336 and only £351,236 worth of goods.[8]

The immediate incentive for English voyages direct to Asia was to purchase at source the pepper and spices which had been available in the eastern Mediterranean. Pepper was grown along the south-west or Malabar coast of India, and in Sumatra, Java, and southern Borneo. Large quantities of pepper were available at ports over which the Portuguese had no control, such as Bantam in western Java or Acheh in northern Sumatra. The rarer spices, cloves, nutmeg, and mace, were grown on small Molucca islands further east, Ternate and Tidore, Amboina, and the Banda islands.

The islands of the Indonesian archipelago with their spices and pepper were the natural first objectives for English voyages, but the East India Company quickly extended its operations into other areas. The Asian regions that engaged in seaborne trade interlocked with one another in a complex pattern. The Company's agents discovered that spices and pepper could best be secured by bartering commodities from other regions for them. Some of these commodities could also be shipped to England to diversify a trade that was dangerously dependent on pepper and spices. Moreover, trade from one part of Asia to another could be a source of profit in itself. In the sixteenth century the Portuguese took large quantities of silk as freight on their ships in a lucrative carrying trade between China and Japan. The English East India Company wished to follow their example and to use their ships to earn freight by carrying the goods of Asian merchants. This was the origin of what came to be known as the 'country trade', whereby the trade from Asia to Europe was supplemented by a trade from one Asian port to another. The needs of the spice and pepper trade, the search for additional exports to England, and the desire to participate in inter-Asian trade all meant that in the early seventeenth century English trade fanned out from the spice and pepper ports and quickly extended from the Red Sea to Japan.

India and the Indonesian islands were very closely linked commercially. Indian merchants carried a considerable proportion of the spices and pepper destined for

[8] Chaudhuri, *East India Company*, p. 117.

Europe by the overland route to their own ports and then transhipped them on to the Red Sea or the Persian Gulf. In return they supplied the islands with Indian cotton and silk. Two Indian regions were heavily involved in this trade: Gujarat on the west coast and the Coromandel coast of the south-east, which specialized in producing cotton cloth for the island markets. The East India Company was soon despatching ships both to Gujarat and to the Coromandel coast. Gujarat was closely linked not only with South-East Asia but also to the westward with the Persian Gulf and the Red Sea. The Company was attracted to both these areas. Through the Persian Gulf the English hoped to get access to supplies of Persian silk, one of the traditional staples of the overland trade to the eastern Mediterranean, which had so far been largely unaffected by the rise of the Cape route.

From the ports of the Indonesian archipelago the English were drawn into a network of Far Eastern trade. Apart from a Portuguese concession at Macao, Chinese ports were closed to Europeans, but the junks of southern China came to South-East Asia and Japan, bringing gold, silk, and porcelain with which to buy silver and spices. As well as trying to trade with the junks in the archipelago, the English set up factories through which to trade with China in Siam, the Malay peninsula, and Japan. Trade with Japan had its own attractions. In the early seventeenth century Japan was a major producer of silver. Selling goods in Japan for silver would therefore reduce the quantities of bullion that had to be exported from Europe to pay for cargoes from other parts of Asia.

For all the wide dispersal of its operations across Asia, the Company's trade in the first decades of the seventeenth century was mainly focused on two areas: the Indonesian archipelago and India. By the 1620s the Company was encountering serious difficulties in the archipelago, although it still maintained its trade there. In India English trade gained a firm foothold.

The Company's first voyage, consisting of four ships under the command of James Lancaster, set out in 1601, going first to Acheh in Sumatra, where pepper was obtained, then to Bantam in Java for more pepper. Agents were left at Bantam to establish a factory. All the ships were back by 1603, having made what proved to be a profitable voyage. The second voyage went straight to Bantam, with two ships going on to try to obtain spices from the Moluccas. From the third voyage of 1607 ships began to be sent to Surat, the main port in Gujarat, which became a focal point of English operations, and to other destinations outside South-East Asia, but the Bantam factory and pepper remained central to the Company's trade.

Attempts to obtain spices brought the English into conflict with the Dutch. The Dutch Company imposed treaties on the rulers of the Molucca islands which stipulated that the entire crop should be handed over to them. To enforce their treaties the Dutch began in 1609 to drive English ships away from the islands. The East India Company responded by petitioning the Crown to seek redress on their behalf and later by launching their own armed retaliation in Asia. In 1618 the English attacked Dutch ships and settlements on the Java coast, eventually suffering heavy losses of ships all over Asia, which left them with no option but to agree to peace on the terms of a treaty negotiated in Europe in 1619. This stipulated that the English Company would pay contributions to the cost of enforcing controls over spice production in return for one-third of the crop. The Dutch continued to obstruct English attempts to trade in Moluccan spices, while the large outlays required to meet their share of the costs made the trade unprofitable for the English. In 1622 they had decided to withdraw from the Moluccas, but before this decision could be carried out they were eliminated by force. On the pretext that they were planning an armed coup, ten English merchants at the Amboina factory were put to death in 1623.

The Amboina 'massacre' became a legendary and long-cherished grievance against the Dutch. At the time, however, it does not seem to have had the significance once attributed to it. It did not, for instance, bring about a realignment in English trade from the archipelago to India. The Bantam factory continued to play an important role in the Company's trade until the Dutch closed it down in 1682. Even then, the English maintained factories to buy pepper in Sumatra. Pepper remained a major item in the Company's trade until late in the seventeenth century.[9] Nor did the Amboina massacre end English participation in the spice trade. The decision to withdraw from the Moluccas had been taken before the massacre, but Dutch control over the produce of the islands, however ruthlessly applied, remained imperfect. Asian ships still took spices to English factories, especially to Macassar in the Celebes. In the 1630s the English at Macassar received a larger proportion of Amboina cloves than the Dutch were able to collect on the spot. The English stake in the trade of the Indonesian archipelago was only effectively confined to western Sumatra towards the end of the seventeenth century, after a prolonged series of wars had enabled the Dutch to close independent ports such as Bantam and Macassar.

A ship of the third voyage was the first one belonging to the East India Company to enter an Indian port. In 1608 the *Hector* anchored off Surat. Trade there was fraught with political difficulties. In the first place, Surat was under the direct administration of the Mughal empire, which controlled most of northern India and was extending its authority into the peninsula. Permission to establish a trade there would require diplomatic negotiations with Mughal officials and ultimately with the Emperor in person. Secondly, the Portuguese were well established along the western coast of India and would resist intrusion by other Europeans.

[9] K. N. Chaudhuri, *The Trading World of Asia and the English East India Company, 1660–1760* (Cambridge, 1978), p. 529.

William Hawkins, commander of the *Hector*, was told that permission to establish a factory depended on the consent of the Emperor Jahangir, to whom he delivered letters from James I when he was received at Agra in 1609. Other emissaries trod the same path. In 1615 Sir Thomas Roe, sent to India as ambassador from the King of England, arrived at the imperial court and remained there until 1618. In 1613 the English had been given a grant of protection and the right to trade at Surat. They still hoped for a formal confirmation of privileges to be embodied in a treaty between the Emperor and James I. While the Mughal government was concerned to promote the trade of Surat and to ensure that foreigners did not disrupt it and the route out of it to the Holy Places of Islam through the Red Sea, it is most unlikely that the Emperor himself had any interest in treaties about commercial matters with a remote European king. No treaty was forthcoming. Jahangir was, however, attracted by European art and skills, valued appropriate presents, and may have been curious about religious diversity. The Englishmen who visited his court were made welcome. Roe, although he was apparently not aware of the significance of what had happened, was even made a personal disciple of the Emperor.[10]

The curiosity which the Emperor showed about his English envoys was at best partially reciprocated. Before the eighteenth century Englishmen contributed little to Europe's knowledge of Asian cultures by comparison, for instance, with the achievement of Jesuit missionaries in China. Access to the Mughal court, however, enabled Englishmen of sophistication, like Roe or his chaplain Edward Terry, to record their impressions of a rich and cultivated court. Versions of what they wrote were published by Samuel Purchas in his *Pilgrimes* of 1625[11] and circulated widely. They played a part in the very slow replacement of English beliefs in an India of marvels, still dominant in Elizabethan literature, by an awareness of an India based on recorded observation, albeit observation heavily coloured by the prejudices of the beholders. Roe and Terry saw Mughal India with strong convictions of European superiority. Both accepted that the Emperor was one of the richest and most powerful monarchs in the world, but in the last resort his regime was that of a 'barbarian'. It was an unregulated tyranny. Roe was disappointed by the court: 'anciently magnificent' buildings were in decay and there were 'almost no civill arts, but such as straggling Christians have lately taught'.[12]

The Portuguese resentment of English intrusion into the trade of western India led to attacks on the Company's ships off Surat, which were beaten off in 1612 and

[10] John F. Richards, *The New Cambridge History of India*, I. 5, *The Mughal Empire* (Cambridge, 1993), pp. 104–05.

[11] Samuel Purchas, *Hakluytus Posthumus or Purchas his Pilgrimes*, 20 vols. (1625; Glasgow, 1905–07), III, IV, and IX, pp. 1–54.

[12] William Foster, ed., *The Embassy of Sir Thomas Roe to India* (London, 1926), pp. 102, 116.

1615. When the English moved into the Persian Gulf to trade in silk, they were again opposed by the Portuguese. In 1622, somewhat reluctantly, the Company committed its ships to support a Persian attack on the Portuguese base at Hormuz. The capture of the base gave the English privileged access to Persian ports. In 1635 the East India Company and the Portuguese came to a formal agreement to end hostilities in Asia.

Through negotiations with Mughal officials and passages of arms with the Portuguese the English established themselves at Surat on a permanent footing. But they did not dominate or radically change the trade of the port; rather, they were gradually absorbed into 'the traditional structure of Gujarat's maritime trade'.[13] Surat in the seventeenth century was administered by officials directly appointed by the Mughal Emperor. The agents of the English and later the Dutch, like leading Asian merchants, built their houses in the inner city, around the Mughal castle. The servants of the English Company lived in considerable comfort as a largely self-contained community following their own customs, including Christian worship. From Surat the English set up subordinate factories in the main commercial centres of Gujarat and in north Indian cities, such as Lahore and Agra. In addition to cotton cloth, at first largely for the Indonesian market but increasingly shipped to London, the inland factories provided indigo, the blue dye for textiles, which became the most valuable of Surat's exports to England in the early seventeenth century.

In 1611 an East India Company ship was sent directly to the Coromandel Coast. A factory was established at Masulipatam, the port of the kingdom of Golconda, chiefly to supply Bantam with cotton cloth. Trading contacts were also made with the ports of the small Hindu states serving the textile areas to the south. One of these ports was to grow into the English settlement of Madras.

By comparison with trade with the archipelago or with India, English contacts with mainland South-East Asia and the Far East in the early seventeenth century were limited and short-lived. No direct access to China was attempted. Factories were, however, established at Ayuthia in Siam, Patani on the Malay peninsula, and at Hirado in Japan, ports of call for the Chinese junks, where it was hoped that gold and silk could be obtained from them. None of the Far Eastern factories fulfilled expectations and all three were abandoned as an economy measure in 1623. The Japanese venture did, however, give Englishmen brief contact with another great Asian court, that of the Tokugawa Shoguns, short accounts of which were also published in Purchas's *Pilgrimes*. John Saris, who brought the first English ship to Japan in 1613, was taken to the Shogun's court by Will Adams, an Englishman already in Japan in Dutch service. His accounts of the ceremonial

[13] Ashin Das Gupta, *Indian Merchants and the Decline of Surat, c.1700–1750* (Wiesbaden, 1979), p. 90.

of the court and of the 'glorious appearance' of rich, densely populated but spaciously laid out cities, like Edo (Tokyo), Miako (Kyoto), or Osaka, appeared in print together with some letters from Adams and other English merchants.[14] Saris also shipped back 'Some Japan wares, as ritch Scritoires: Trunckes, Beoubes [screens], Cupps and Dishes of all sortes, and of a most excellent varnish'.[15]

During the 1620s the East India Company tried to reduce its outlays in Asia by abandoning outlying factories and concentrating its efforts on the Indonesian archipelago and on India. It was entering into a period of contraction and difficulty that was to last into the 1660s. The twelve separate voyages sent out between 1601 and 1612 had made handsome returns, but those who contributed to the second joint stock of £1,629,040 between 1617 and 1632 consistently lost money. When a third joint stock was launched in 1631, it too returned poor results.[16]

The English presence in the archipelago survived the disastrous war with the Dutch and the Amboina massacre. Dutch competition, however, became increasingly formidable. Deploying much greater resources than the English could ever hope to do, the Dutch tightened their grip on the spice-producing islands of the Moluccas and eliminated independent Asian ports to which spices had been 'smuggled'. While the deployment by the Dutch of naval power that the English could not match was making it increasingly difficult for the East India Company to obtain spices and even pepper by the mid-seventeenth century, the incentive for the Company to concentrate on these trades was diminishing. By comparison with some other tropical commodities, most notably sugar, the demand in Europe for pepper and spices was relatively inelastic. Greater shipments by the Dutch meant a fall in price. This encouraged the English Company to look for other items to import.

The most promising alternatives to pepper and spices seemed to be Persian silk, indigo, or calicoes from Surat, and calicoes from the Coromandel Coast of India, after 1639 mostly shipped out of the fortified settlement established at Madras. While Persian silk rarely proved to be profitable and indigo was vulnerable to competition from cheaper sources in the Americas, Indian cotton cloth had no rival in Europe until late in the eighteenth century. The Company's future lay with textiles generally and above all with calico.

Indian calicoes became a new item of mass consumption throughout Europe and beyond in European colonies by the end of the seventeenth century. Very high quality printed cottons or chintzes had been admired by European connoisseurs

[14] Purchas, *Pilgrimes*, II, pp. 326–46, III, pp. 442–77.

[15] Oliver Impey, *Chinoiserie: The Impact of Oriental Styles on Western Art and Decoration* (London, 1977), p. 112.

[16] Chaudhuri, *East India Company*, pp. 215–23.

for their colours and designs for centuries. What the seventeenth-century East India companies, led by the English, were able to do was to import huge quantities of relatively cheap cloth, either coloured in India by painting or printing or white cloth which could be coloured in Europe. This meant that those who could not afford linen or silk, the only previous alternatives to wool, now had a light, washable material for hangings, underclothes, shirts, or dresses, affordable for large sections of the population. During the boom in imports in the late seventeenth century it was said that 'now few think themselves well dresst till they are made up in Calicoes, both men and women, Calico shirts, Neckcloths, Cuffs, Pocket-handkerchiefs for the former, Headdresses, Nightroyls, Hoods, Sleeves, Aprons, Gowns, Petticoats, and what not for the latter, besides India-stockings for both Sexes'.[17] Imports by the Company began on a significant scale in 1613. Most of the early shipments seem to have been intended for re-export to the Levant and North Africa, areas already supplied with Indian cloth overland. By 1625, however, when over 220,000 pieces of Indian cotton cloth were brought in by the Company, sales at home were evidently on a significant scale.[18] The trade was badly hit by the famine in Gujarat in the 1630s which devastated weaving districts. This encouraged the Company to import Coromandel cloth and to turn their attention to Bengal, which was to be so important in the future. In the 1640s and 1650s all the Company's Asian trade was severely restricted by shortage of funds caused by the disruptions of the Civil War, which meant that the factories were starved of shipments of bullion or goods from England. From the 1660s, however, growth in calico shipments was to be spectacular.

Growth without shortages in supply or sharp rises in price indicated that Indian textile production could easily accommodate new European demands, which probably only amounted to a small proportion of the domestic and Asian demand. Cotton weaving was very widely diffused. Certain areas were already specializing in long-distance internal trade or in producing cloth for export by sea to other Asian markets. In these areas there were merchants capable of handling large orders from Europeans, while weavers showed considerable adaptability in working to new patterns when required.

After the abandonment of the factories in 1623, English activities in the Far East were limited. English ships did, however, reach China for the first time. In 1635 an English ship from Surat was allowed to call at Macao by the Portuguese. In 1637 four ships, not belonging to the East India Company, forced their way into Canton against Chinese opposition and brought away a small cargo. Although regular

[17] Cited by John E. Willis, 'European Consumption and Asian Production in the Seventeenth and Eighteenth Centuries', in John Brewer and Roy Porter, eds., *Consumption and the World of Goods* (London, 1993), p. 136.

[18] Chaudhuri, *East India Company*, p. 193.

trade did not begin until the end of the century, Chinese items, especially blue-and-white porcelain, began to reach England, either from very large shipments made by the Dutch or from English purchases in other Asian ports.

While the East India Company in Asia was beginning to concentrate its trade on India and on textiles, it was being severely buffeted at home. In the 1620s economic recession adversely affected the Company's domestic sales and its re-exports to Europe. At the same time its relations with the English state deteriorated.

The Company's dependence on the state for its grants of privileges, above all for its sole right to import Asian goods, and for diplomatic support, however limited, against the Portuguese and the Dutch was self-evident. From the state's point of view, confining Asian trade to a single body also had advantages. It greatly facilitated the collection of customs and other dues. A monopoly company was also a potential source of direct financial support to the Crown. The Company could be expected to pay for the maintenance of its privileges. This could involve direct payments or loans to the Exchequer as well as personal payments (bribes, to put the matter crudely) to king or ministers. The support of the Crown was indispensable, but the Crown was an unreliable ally against many potential enemies.

Monopoly grants were often in themselves unpopular and open to attack, while there was no lack of competitors who wished to gain access to Asian trade. Once the infrastructure of the Company's Asian factories had come into existence, others wished to use it. Neither James I nor Charles I could resist the lure of selling permission to trade against the Company's monopoly or of making grants at its expense. Charles's grants were particularly threatening to the Company, since under them English ships appeared in Asian waters with the aim of transferring to Asia the privateering which had been so lucrative in the Atlantic. Asian ships in the western Indian Ocean were their prey. The consequences of such depredations could be very serious. The Mughal authorities at Surat demanded satisfaction for the loss of ships belonging to the port from the East India Company on pain of seizing the Company's assets. In 1637 Sir William Courteen obtained a licence from the King to fit out a large expedition to the Indian Ocean and another expedition was permitted to try to establish a base off the island of Madagascar. Courteen's grant was taken over in the 1640s by a group of London merchants led by Maurice Thompson, already well known as one of London's most aggressive entrepreneurs in Atlantic trade and colonization. These men took up the Madagascar project. They were highly critical of what they saw as the Company's limited ambitions and believed that colonies of English settlement could be established on Madagascar on West Indian lines, to grow new crops, as well as to create a base for inter-Asian trade and no doubt for piracy. They formed themselves into an Assada Company, named after an island off Madagascar, which they tried to settle in 1645 and 1649.

The coming of the Civil War created serious problems for the Company. War made it difficult to raise money for trade and disrupted the sale of the Company's cargoes. It also exposed the Company to new political threats. The King had shown little regard for its privileges for some years and in 1640 the Company felt obliged to lend him £50,000. Under the parliamentary regimes, the Company was exposed to the attacks of merchant groups who resented the privileges that it had enjoyed for so long and were now well placed to try to dismember it.[19]

The Company continued to operate, but others were allowed to compete with it. Thomson's syndicate, which had taken over the King's concession to Courteen, enjoyed a free hand to send ships to Asia. Eventually the Council of State of the Interregnum insisted that the old Company and its competitors join together to form a new joint stock in 1650, which was to take up Thompson's Assada project and his grandiose designs 'to build forts, plant garrisons, and settle factories, colonies and jurisdictions of their own', regardless of grants from Asian rulers.[20] In 1653 the new joint stock ran out and private voyages were resumed, while the Company waited on the pleasure of Oliver Cromwell, the Lord Protector. At one point Cromwell appears to have contemplated a grand partition of the world with the Dutch, the English abandoning all their Asian projects in return for a Dutch renunciation of all concerns in the Americas, but he also professed his desire to maintain a 'national interest' in the East. Thomson and his friends pressed strongly for the creation of what would have been a regulated company, that is, a body whose members were free to trade on their own account under common rules, but the Protectorate decided in 1657 to establish another joint stock to be managed as a single body enjoying a monopoly of English trade with Asia. This joint stock was to be a permanent one, not wound up until the demise of the Company in 1858. Under Cromwell the Company had regained the privileges it had been given by Elizabeth. A joint stock enjoying a monopoly was evidently judged to be the most reliable mechanism for successful Asian trade, on which a number of important state interests depended.

During the prosperous years of the later seventeenth century the Company's Asian operations remained set in the pattern that had evolved in the period of contraction from the 1620s. India became even more prominent, while trade with the Indonesian islands declined further. The factories in the Far East were not

[19] Brenner, *Merchants and Revolution*, pp. 374–81, sees the Company as a supporter of the Royalist cause in the 1640s, by contrast to Robert Ashton who argues that it was not closely identified; see his *The City and the Court, 1603–1643* (Cambridge, 1979), pp. 139–41, 202.

[20] Cited in Derek Massarella, '"A World Elsewhere": Aspects of the Expansionist Mood of the 1650s', in Colin Jones, Malyn Newitt, and Stephen Roberts, eds., *Politics and People in Revolutionary England* (Oxford, 1986), p. 155. For Thompson's involvement in African trade see above, p. 253.

re-established, although at the end of the century the Company was gaining direct access to China and was beginning to import tea, a commodity that was to play so prominent a part in the Company's future. There was no return to complex inter-Asian trading through a far-flung network of factories. The majority of ships were sent directly to Indian ports, loaded for the most part with bullion, and returned as quickly as possible with cargoes of textiles.

Within India a change of emphasis was becoming apparent by the end of the century: Surat and western India began to play a diminishing role, while Bengal assumed the dominant one. The political stability, so beneficial for trade, which the Mughals had been able to maintain throughout the first half of the seventeenth century, eventually broke down in western India, as the Marathas of the Deccan threw off imperial authority. In 1664 and 1670 the Marathas forced their way into Surat and plundered it, although Surat was not cut off from its hinterland until the Marathas occupied Gujarat permanently in the early eighteenth century. So long as Surat remained an effectively functioning port, the development of Bombay, the new English acquisition in western India, would be restricted. Bombay was ceded by the Portuguese to the English Crown in 1661 as part of Charles II's marriage settlement. In 1668 the Company took it over. This gave them full sovereignty over an island base that could be fortified and which had a fine harbour. Bombay was, however, far removed from the areas that produced textiles or from other trading centres. In spite of inducements offered to them by the English, merchant communities, such as the Parsis, were slow to move their businesses away from Surat or other ports in Gujarat. Bombay long remained an underdeveloped settlement.

On the Coromandel Coast the new English settlement at Madras prospered as the Mughal armies moved south into Golconda, bringing war that disrupted the trade of Masulipatam and the other northern ports along the coast. Unlike Bombay, Madras was extremely successful in attracting Indian merchants to move under British protection. Madras too was fortified, and a 'white town' of European settlement grew up around Fort St George separate from the 'black town' of Indian merchants and artisans. At the height of a trading season at the beginning of the eighteenth century, the Governor of Madras could boast that there could be 'fifty sayle of ships in the roade, besides small craft at least 200; ... the place, when I left it, was not onely admired but in favour of all the kings and princes in those parts; a regular and peaceable government within ourselves, and continued friendship of all about us'.[21]

English traders from the Coromandel Coast established their first factory in the new Mughal province of Bengal in 1651 at the port of Hugli. Other factories followed,

[21] *Historical Manuscripts Commission Thirteenth Report*, pt. III, *Manuscripts of J. B. Fortescue* (1892), I, p. 45.

some far inland. As well as being an abundant source of cotton cloth, Bengal provided much raw silk, poorer in quality but cheaper than Persian silk, and silk cloth 'taffetas'. These proved very popular, as did the plain white cotton muslins. As the shipments of Indian calico by the Company climbed from 250,000 pieces in the 1660s to around 1 million pieces in the early 1680s,[22] the role of Bengal in English trade began to match that of Gujarat and Coromandel. The Company sought a more secure base for their operations and, after an unsuccessful use of force against the Mughals from 1686 to 1689, settled on a relatively new site, Calcutta. In 1696 the English took the opportunity of a local rebellion to gain permission to build a fort at its new settlement. In the early eighteenth century a considerable town, like Madras, roughly segregated between black and white towns, grew up around Fort William.

The textile trade from Gujarat, Coromandel, and Bengal was the basis of the Company's commercial success in the late seventeenth century. Not only were Indian cotton and silk supplying a growing domestic market, but great quantities were being re-exported from London. Although the Dutch also imported textiles from Indian factories, English sales were markedly higher.[23] The East India Company was clearly winning the competition for European markets. So successful was the Company that it provoked bitter opposition from the textile industry at home. The silk weavers objected to the import of silk cloth, rather than raw silk to be worked up in England, while woollen manufacturers protested that the sale of Indian textiles was making serious inroads into their markets and creating unemployment. The Company's opponents were able to get an Act of Parliament passed in 1700 that laid down that silk cloth and coloured calicoes could only be brought into England for re-export, but not be sold for the home market. Imports of white cloth, which would provide employment for cotton printers in England, were permitted. These restrictions seem to have made very little difference to the volume of the Company's trade in textiles.

Bombay, Madras, and Calcutta, English settlements in which many Indians lived, were quite different kinds of places from Surat, Masulipatam, or Hugli, Indian towns in which the English had factories. The growth of Madras and Calcutta in particular is evidence of the size of the business transacted by the Company with Indians as it obtained its cargoes for England. But it is also evident that these towns had become major centres of inter-Asian trade as well. That development owed much more to the private enterprise of Englishmen than it did to the Company's activities. Early in the century the English Company had been actively engaged in shipping goods from one Asian port to another, most obviously, for instance, in taking Indian textiles from Surat or the Coromandel

[22] Chaudhuri, *Trading World*, p. 547.

[23] Steensgaard, 'Trade of England and the Dutch', pp. 123–28.

Coast to Bantam. In mid-century, however, as an economy measure, the Company had largely renounced its role in the inter-Asian 'country trade', concentrating its ships on trading to and from England. Instead, it allowed its servants and other Englishmen living in Asia to trade from port to port in their own ships. This was in fact legalizing what private Englishmen had already been doing for some time against the Company's regulations. Large personal fortunes were said to have been made this way. Virtually all the senior Company servants in Asia traded by sea, either carrying their own goods or those of Asian merchants for freight, on ships mostly built in India and crewed by Indian seamen with a few European officers. At the end of the century Madras had the largest fleet of private ships, ten or twelve of which made long-distance voyages to the Red Sea and the Persian Gulf in the west and to the Philippines or southern China to the east, as well as many smaller ones making shorter journeys. Private country trade was to be a very important part of the British presence in Asia during the eighteenth century.

Another distinctive feature of the new English settlements in Asia is that they were fortified and garrisoned by small contingents of soldiers. Trade was being backed by limited force. The official policy of the East India Company had, however, generally been to renounce the use of force as involving expense for which there could be no commercial justification. The English liked to contrast their own reliance on the protection of Asian rulers, on negotiated trading contracts, and on open competition with Asian or other European merchants with the violent coercion and enforced monopolies allegedly practised by the Portuguese and the Dutch. In 1685 the English Company asked whether the Dutch have not 'killed thousands of *Indians* for one that ever dyed by the *English* hands'.[24]

Resort to armed force on a large scale had its advocates. Critics of the Company, such as those who backed the Assada projects of the 1640s, proposed to imitate the Dutch by establishing armed bases, which would pay for themselves by customs duties levied on Indian shipping and by taxing the local populations. This became official policy in the 1680s when the Company was dominated by Sir Josiah Child, one of its most forceful and ambitious chairmen. Child believed that the Company could only operate effectively from secure fortified settlements, outside the control of any Asian ruler, and sustained by their own revenues. He proposed to build up Madras and Bombay into such settlements and to take a suitable base in Bengal by force. To achieve this, an expedition including royal troops was despatched in 1686, but failed ignominiously against the Mughal defences. The English waged war against the Mughal empire in 1688–89 by seizing ships off western India, only to have the Surat factory closed and Bombay blockaded. Peace and a restoration of trading rights on the Emperor's terms had to be sought.

[24] *An Impartial Vindication of the English East India Company* (London, 1688), pp. 118–19.

A policy of open war in Asia was not to be repeated until the mid-eighteenth century. It seems likely, however, that what kept armed action by the Company within limits was not any principled rejection of war as an instrument of trade, still less any doctrinaire commitment to free trade, but a realistic calculation of costs and benefits. The strategy that the Company was forced to adopt from the 1620s—a restricted number of factories, with shipping concentrated on voyages to and from England—was intended to limit expenditure in Asia. Once India became the main focus of its operations, there was little temptation to embark on expensive wars. Even supposing that such wars could be won, the textile production of India, unlike Moluccan spices, could never be brought under the control of a single European power. This strategy of limited commitment paid off in economic terms. While trading in textiles with low overheads was making the English Company increasingly profitable in the later seventeenth century, the cost of the network of bases set up by the Dutch for inter-Asian trade and to control the output of pepper and spices was plunging their Company into deficits in Asia from which it was never to recover.[25] The scale of Child's wars may have been an aberration, but to take every advantage of the weakening of political authority on the fringes of the Mughal empire, and thus to turn Bombay, Madras, and Calcutta into places where the Company no longer had to rely on the goodwill of Asian powers, was compatible with a policy of carefully regulating expenditure to likely benefits.

Outside India the Company made no deployment of military power. Indeed, the Bantam factory, so long the centre of its South-East Asian trade, was closed down by the Dutch in 1682. The Company continued, however, to trade in pepper, establishing settlements on the west coast of Sumatra. In the later seventeenth century interest in Far Eastern trade revived. A ship even reached Japan in 1672, but was immediately turned away. By contrast, the new Ch'ing regime in China was for a time less rigid. In 1676 the Company was allowed to station agents in the port of Amoy. In 1699 English operations shifted their operations to Canton, which in the eighteenth century was to become the sole European point of access to China. Silk goods were the main item shipped out of China, together with porcelain and small quantities of tea. Tea had been brought back from Asia to present to the royal family in the 1660s. At the very end of the century tea drinking began to become widely fashionable. In 1701 120,000 pounds of tea were imported; within twenty years the total was to be over a million pounds.[26]

Under the restored monarchy after 1660, the Company soon recovered the support of the English state. This ensured that its charter and its monopoly were

[25] F. S. Gaastra, 'The Shifting Balance of Trade of the Dutch East India Company', in Leonard Blussé and F. S. Gaastra, eds., *Companies and Trade: Essays on Overseas Trading Companies during the Ancien Régime* (The Hague, 1981), pp. 61–64.

[26] Chaudhuri, *Trading World*, p. 538.

regularly renewed. Increased powers were given to the Company, such as the right to make war on non-Christian peoples and to administer justice within their settlements. Help that was urgently needed since the trade had been effectively opened to all comers during the Interregnum was given in prosecuting 'interlopers', that is, private ships going to Asia in defiance of the Company's monopoly. The price of support was close identification with the government and large payments or loans on favourable terms, together with personal acknowledgements to members of the royal family. Links with the Crown became especially close in the 1680s. This was the period of Josiah Child's supremacy. He was able to use royal support to beat off a challenge to his leadership in 1683, but he and the Company were very vulnerable indeed when James II fled in 1688.

By then the Company had acquired many enemies. For most of the period the Company gave every outward sign of prosperity: it paid high dividends and the selling price of its stock was greatly enhanced in value.[27] The beneficiaries of this largess were, however, limited. The working capital of the Company was raised by borrowing sums of up to £1 million short-term on bonds at low rates of interest rather than by increasing the quantity of stock, which remained at the very low level of £369,000 fixed in 1657. It was being alleged, with some reason, that the Company was run by an oligarchy for its own benefit. By 1691 some 70 per cent of the stock was held in large blocks of £2,000 or more, while Child's personal holding amounted to £51,000.[28]

The Company's critics argued that its trading strategies were far too restricted to take advantage of all the opportunities of Asian trade. Its stock should be widened or others should be allowed to send their own ships to Asia. Interloping ships in defiance of the monopoly began to be sent out by syndicates of merchants who felt themselves excluded from the trade. By the 1680s the huge influx of Indian textiles was adding English silk and woollen interests to the Company's assailants. Child's personal links with James II also gave it many political opponents.

The Glorious Revolution, combined with the failure of the campaigns in India, forced the Company on to the defensive. It had to fight a prolonged rearguard action against moves either to abolish the monopoly altogether or to admit other groups to a share in it. By political skills, which included liberal payment of bribes, the Company won a limited renewal of its charter in 1693, but it appeared finally to have lost when a New East India Company was given a charter by Act of Parliament in 1698 in return for a loan of £2 million to the government. The new Company was backed by those who had already been trying to trade to Asia

[27] Ibid., pp. 415–33.

[28] K. G. Davies, 'Joint Stock Investment in the later Seventeenth Century', *Economic History Review*, Second Series, IV (1952), pp. 283–301; D. C. Coleman, *Sir John Banks, Baronet and Businessman: A Study of Business, Politics and Society in Later Stuart England* (Oxford, 1963), p. 87.

independently as well as by other merchants, such as those shipping wine from the Mediterranean, whose activities had been curtailed by the European war of the 1690s and who were looking for alternative outlets for their funds.[29]

The Old Company was given time in which to wind up its affairs, so that for some years two English companies traded in Asia. In practice it proved impossible to eliminate the Old Company. It had bought part of the New Company's stock, and the expertise and facilities built up by its servants in Asia proved to be indispensable for successful trade. Negotiations for a merger led to agreement in 1702 and the formation of a United East India Company in 1709.

The Old Company had been forced to widen its membership and take in its competitors and critics, but the character of the East India Company had not fundamentally changed. It was still by far the most prestigious and solidly based of the overseas trading ventures. The American colonizing companies had long since disappeared, leaving the North American and West Indian trades to a mass of individual merchants and partnerships, many of whom 'participated in a very small way'.[30] The more recent Royal African Company was in terminal decline and its monopoly was proving to be unenforceable.

As it had been able to do since early in the century, the East India Company could draw on the funds of the London business community. Very large investments were made by what have been called 'the cosmopolitan mercantile plutocracy', while much of the rest of the stock was held in substantial blocks by City merchants. The relative security of East India stock was increasingly attracting non-mercantile people, professional men, landowners, and even widows and trustees. East India stock and bonds were an important element in the emerging London stock market of the 1690s, when the Company had a significant role in mobilizing funds for the floating of the national debt.[31] The Company had become a pillar of the new structure of public finance as well as being a great trading body.

By the end of the seventeenth century the role that Asian trade would play in English overseas expansion was clear. Through the East India Company's pepper, then its textiles, and later its tea, Asia began to contribute a significant proportion of England's imports and of its re-exports. In 1700–01 the value of imports from Asia was comparable to those from the West Indies and twice those from North America.[32] Re-exported goods from Asia were among the most important items

[29] D. W. Jones, *War and Economy in the Age of William III and Marlborough* (Oxford, 1988), pp. 286–307.

[30] See below, pp. 403–05.

[31] Davies, 'Joint Stock Investment'; P. G. M. Dickson, *The Financial Revolution in England, 1688–1756* (London, 1967).

[32] See Vol. II, p. 101.

traded on the African coast for slaves.[33] The wealth generated by Asian trade was, however, more narrowly concentrated than that which flowed from the Atlantic. London was the sole port engaged in Asian trade and London naturally received most of its benefits. Relatively few manufactured goods were exported and small numbers of ships were used, even if they were the biggest merchant ships in the world. The dividends from the trade, together with opportunities for making capital gains from the stock, were confined for the most part to a limited body of shareholders who invested in large blocks of stock. Asia did not draw out waves of British migrants. Instead, a small number of seamen and factors went there in the service of the Company, amongst whom there was a high mortality, even if a few spectacular fortunes were already being made through private trade around the Indian Ocean.

If direct experience of Asia was uncommon by comparison with the huge numbers who crossed the Atlantic, wide sections of the English population had still been affected by Asian trade. The Company had introduced one item of mass consumption, calicoes, and it was about to introduce another, tea. Direct shipments by the East India Company from the Yemen also began to increase the amount of coffee reaching England. Calicoes, tea, and coffee became thoroughly domesticated to English tastes, but they also retained something of the exotic. Although the Company tried to teach Indian weavers and colourers of textiles to conform to European fashion, they were also aware of the appeal of what seemed to be alien; 'whatever is new gawdy or unusual will always find a good price at our Candle' [auctions].[34] Tea was drunk out of teacups. For the rich these might be Chinese porcelain; for the less affluent they were likely to be European earthenware, perhaps decorated with what were thought to be appropriate Chinese motifs. 'Chinoiserie' styles of what was deemed to be 'Oriental' had evolved in Europe in the sixteenth century and had even been exported to Asia for craftsmen to imitate on articles intended for European markets. Chinoiserie designs on textiles, lacquered furniture, wallpapers, porcelain, or earthenware may have been far removed from any Asian original but their availability through the East India trade gave English consumers some intimations of Asian worlds different from their own.

[33] See above pp. 256–57.

[34] Cited in John Irwin and P. R. Schwartz, *Studies in Indo-European Textile History* (Ahmedabad, 1966), p. 46.

Select Bibliography

D. K. Bassett, 'The Factory of the English East India Company at Bantam', unpublished Ph.D. thesis, London, 1955.

—— 'Early English Trade and Settlement in Asia, 1602–1690', J. S. Bromley and E. H. Kossman, eds., *Britain and the Netherlands in Europe and Asia* (London, 1968), pp. 83–109.

Robert Brenner, *Merchants and Revolution: Commercial Change, Political Conflict, and London's Overseas Traders, 1550–1653* (Princeton, 1993).

K. N. Chaudhuri, *The English East India Company: The Study of an Early Joint-Stock Company, 1600–1640* (London, 1965).

—— *The Trading World of Asia and the English East India Company, 1660–1760* (Cambridge, 1978).

Susil Chaudhury, *Trade and Commercial Organization in Bengal, 1650–1720* (Calcutta, 1975).

Ashin Das Gupta and M. N. Pearson, eds., *India and the Indian Ocean, 1500–1800* (Calcutta, 1987).

William Foster, *England's Quest of Eastern Trade* (London, 1933).

Holden Furber, *Rival Empires of Trade in the Orient, 1600 to 1800* (Minneapolis, 1976).

Oliver Impey, *Chinoiserie: The Impact of Oriental Styles on Western Art and Decoration* (London, 1977).

John Irwin and P. R. Schwartz, *Studies in Indo-European Textile History* (Ahmedabad, 1966).

Philip Lawson, *The East India Company: A History* (London, 1993).

Bruce P. Lenman, 'The East India Company and the Emperor Aurangzeb', *History Today*, XXXVII (Feb. 1987), pp. 23–29.

P. J. Marshall, 'Taming the Exotic: The British and India in the Seventeenth and Eighteenth Centuries', in G. S. Rousseau and Roy Porter, eds., *Exoticism in the Enlightenment* (Manchester, 1990), pp. 46–65.

Derek Massarella, *A World Elsewhere: Europe's Encounter with Japan in the Sixteenth and Seventeenth Centuries* (New Haven, 1990).

Earl H. Pritchard, *Anglo-Chinese Relations during the Seventeenth and Eighteenth Centuries* (Urbana, Ill., 1929).

W. R. Scott, *The Constitution and Finance of the English, Scottish, and Irish Joint-Stock Companies to 1720*, 3 vols. (Cambridge, 1910–12).

Niels Steensgaard, *Carracks, Caravans and Companies: The Structural Crisis in the European–Asian Trade in the Early 17th Century* (Copenhagen, 1973).

13

The English Government, War, Trade, and Settlement, 1625–1688

MICHAEL J. BRADDICK

It is a commonplace of the historiography of early modern England that the national government was weak. Lacking a bureaucracy and armed forces, and the financial means with which to acquire these things, it delegated responsibilities to subordinate bodies. This was even more striking in relation to government activity further afield. During the seventeenth century the 'overseas activities' of government—trade, war, and settlement—were undertaken by means of an administrative repertoire of delegation and 'government by licence'. On the other hand, both at home and overseas, the seventeenth century saw an increasing amount of administrative activity taken on more directly by national government. Such developments were not necessarily driven by overseas activities, still less by an Imperial vision, but they had implications for, and were affected by, the external commitments of the English government. This chapter examines the increasingly direct responsibility for war, trade, and colonization assumed by the national government and considers issues relating to 'Imperial policy' only in this more general context.

England was at war quite regularly during this period, with varying degrees of success. An expedition to fight for Frederick of Bohemia (James I's son-in-law) against the Spanish was prepared under the command of the German mercenary Mansfeld in 1625, and further expeditions were sent to Cadiz (1625) and the Île de Rhé (1627) (Map 3.2). English forces fought against the Scots in 1639–40 (the Bishops' Wars), the Irish in 1642, and major expeditions were launched against both Scotland and Ireland in 1649–52. War with Spain in the late 1650s led to the capture of Jamaica (1655), and there were three wars against the Dutch in the later seventeenth century (1652–54, 1665–67, and 1672–74). The largest military commitment of this period, and the most significant motor behind fiscal and military reform, however, was the Civil War, in which perhaps one in ten adult males in England were combatants at any given time. Of the foreign campaigns, only some were clear military successes. The expeditions of the 1620s were, notoriously, humiliating. Of the three Dutch wars the English could only really claim victory in the first, and the Spanish war of the 1650s was at best a measured success. Clearly, however, the Cromwellian conquests of Scotland and Ireland were militarily successful and noteworthy: many previous English governments might have envied such military ascendancy throughout Britain and Ireland.

This record was not one of unalloyed success, then, but there was a striking change in the underlying military capacity of government. The fleet for service at Rhé was crewed by 4,000 men. In 1653 19,254 men were put to sea, and during the Restoration up to 20,000 men could be mobilized in wartime. In so far as the English monarchy can be said to have maintained a standing army before the 1640s it was employed in Ireland, and even that force had been greatly reduced in size by the closing years of the reign of James I. By 1653, however, the Instrument of Government, the written constitution, could call for a permanent land force of 30,000, and in the face of invasion in 1688 James II could mobilize 40,000 men quite quickly.[1] But it was not just the size of the armed forces that was changing, it was also their nature. This period saw the creation of both a state owned- and -funded navy and of a standing army.

Elizabethan naval effort had depended on an alliance between the Crown and the owners of armed merchant ships. By the 1620s, though, there were tensions in this relationship and a greater reluctance to lend ships to Crown service, partly because there were, increasingly, more lucrative prospects than warfare for armed merchant ships. During the sixteenth century a royal bounty was paid to those who built ships of over 100 tons, in return for some obligation to serve the Crown in wartime. In 1618 payment of the bounty was suspended, probably as part of a programme of retrenchment prompted by publicity about inefficiencies of naval administration, and although it was revived in 1625 it applied to fewer and fewer ships. By the Restoration period only the largest East Indiamen benefited, and it was finally abandoned in the early eighteenth century, 'testimony to the professionalization of the navy' at that point. This separation of Merchant and Royal Navy was also prompted by changes in ship design which increasingly encouraged specialization of function.[2] The result was a general trend towards the creation of specialized military ships, a trend graphically demonstrated by Table 13.1.

The creation of a national navy, fully owned by the national government, required the development of new fiscal resources. The ship-money levies of the 1630s went some way towards providing this, supporting a modest shipbuilding

[1] For fuller reference see M. J. Braddick, 'An English Military Revolution?', *Historical Journal* (hereafter *HJ*), XXXVI, 4 (1993), pp. 965–75, and *The Nerves of State: Taxation and the Financing of the English State, 1558–1714* (Manchester, 1996), pp. 27–34, 190–92.

[2] Brian Dietz, 'The Royal Bounty and English Shipping in the Sixteenth and Seventeenth Centuries', *Mariner's Mirror*, LXXVII (1991), pp. 5–20; see above, pp. 96–97

TABLE 13.1. *Composition of English naval forces, 1625–1688*

		Royal ships	*Private vessels*
1625	Cadiz	14	30
1627	Île de Rhé	10	90
1635	Ship Money	19	6
1636	Ship Money	24	3
1637	Ship Money	19	9
1638	Ship Money	24	7
1639	Ship Money	28	11
1641	Summer Guard	15	10
1642	Summer Guard	16	16
1643	Summer Guard	24	23
1644	Summer Guard	30	55
1645	Summer Guard	36	16
1646	Summer Guard	25	4
1652	Mobilization	39	0
1653	Gabbard	25	15
1666	Four Days Battle	31	1
1672	Sole Bay	32	0
1673	Schoonveldt	49	0
1688	Dartmouth's Fleet	35	0

Source: Richard Harding, *The Evolution of the Sailing Navy, 1509–1815* (Basingstoke, 1995), p. 152. The figure for private ships in service at Rhé includes transports.

programme and regular patrols of the Channel. The English navy, however, continued to lose ground against other European navies, a fact symbolized by the experience of John Pennington in November 1639. Charged with providing a squadron to protect Spanish troops *en route* for Flanders, Pennington was forced to stand by and watch a Dutch attack, securing only a token acknowledgement of the sovereignty of English waters. During the 1640s Parliament took control of the navy, with the result that the command structure changed, but the use of merchantmen alongside the government's ships persisted (Table 13.1). Many of the hired ships were part-owned by naval commanders, and privateering remained a significant element of naval activity.[3]

The most dramatic changes were achieved between 1649 and 1660, when 216 ships were added to the navy, half as prizes and about half newly built.[4] The effectiveness of this new fleet was impressive. It resulted, for example, in consider-

[3] Andrew Thrush, 'Naval Finance and the Origins and Development of Ship Money', in Mark Charles Fissel, ed., *War and Government in Britain, 1598–1650* (Manchester, 1991), pp. 133–62; Richard Harding, *The Evolution of the Sailing Navy, 1509–1815* (Basingstoke, 1995).

[4] Bernard Capp, *Cromwell's Navy: The Fleet and the English Revolution, 1648–1660* (Oxford, 1989), pp. 4–5, 6–9.

able successes against the Dutch and greatly assisted the capture of Jamaica (although not the original objective, Hispaniola). State ships were subsequently committed to the defence of trade, eventually taking over this role from the merchants themselves. The Republican and Restoration navies were increasingly professionally supplied, crewed, and officered, and the reliability of naval convoying in the Mediterranean clearly contributed to the growing importance of English shipping in those trades in the Restoration period. Although privateering continued it was of reduced military significance, and by 1660 'the divorce between the state's military fleet and the merchant marine was . . . clearly established'.[5]

The principal military resource of the early Stuarts was the militia, in theory composed of all able-bodied men aged between 16 and 60, mustered on a county basis each year. This process was directed by a Lord-Lieutenant responsible for one or more counties. From this potential was drawn a more select group, the trained bands. The militia and trained bands, however, were defensive forces, reluctant even to serve outside their home county, let alone abroad. Expeditionary forces could be mobilized in a variety of ways—mercenaries were sometimes hired or troops raised by noblemen or other individuals under commission from the Crown—but increasingly recruitment depended on pressing men for service. This was done through the machinery of the militia, using the Lieutenancy and the muster books. It was not usually the trained men who were chosen, however, because they were thought too valuable to lose. Instead, impressment usually produced men of low status and non-existent training.[6]

The effectiveness of both the militia and expeditionary forces depended to some extent on the capacity of government to equip, train, feed, and pay its soldiers. It is in this respect that the seventeenth century saw improvements in military capacity. In seeking to achieve this improvement the government faced a problem of mobilizing consent. Consistent pressure was applied to Lieutenants to improve the militia in the decades before the Civil War. However, improving militia equipment, mustering, and training required, for example, the imposition of local rates and the enforcement of attendance at musters, and this caused tensions in local society.[7] The same problem of participation was posed by the raising of expeditionary forces, which required, among other things, impressment, clothing, and transport of the troops out of the county in which they had been raised. In

[5] J. D. Davies, *Gentlemen and Tarpaulins: The Officers and Men of the Restoration Navy* (Oxford, 1991); Sari R. Hornstein, *The Restoration Navy and English Foreign Trade, 1674–1688: A Study in the Peacetime Use of Sea Power* (Aldershot, 1991); Harding, *Sailing Navy*, quotation at p. 82.

[6] For a concise summary of sixteenth-century developments, see Penry Williams, *The Tudor Regime* (Oxford, 1979), pp. 109–35.

[7] Anthony Fletcher, *Reform in the Provinces: The Government of Stuart England* (New Haven, 1986), pp. 282–316.

1624, for example, in raising men prior to Mansfeld's expedition, constables 'quickly exhausted the supply of village bad-boys, marginal cottagers, and unemployed labourers'. The English campaigns in the Bishops' Wars were similarly handicapped by the problem of securing consent.[8] These difficulties were exacerbated by those of supply. Before 1640 Parliamentary revenues had proven insufficient to sustain major campaigns, and in wartime the Ordnance Office struggled to equip and supply the troops.[9]

During the Civil War new forms of taxation and improved techniques of borrowing enabled more regular supply and pay for troops, and this played an important part in the success of the Parliamentary war effort. The advantages of the new pay-and-supply system were subsequently demonstrated in Ireland and Scotland, where Cromwell achieved a military dominance that had eluded previous English armies.[10] Similar fiscal resources sustained a small standing army after the Restoration, and although it was not well-disciplined, its mutinies were only rarely about pay and many of its men were volunteers. In February 1685 there were about 8,900 men in the English army at home and abroad, and a further 9,700 in the Irish and Scottish armies.[11]

Behind this military change lay successful fiscal reform: it has been estimated that the proportion of national wealth that could be mobilized by government for war probably doubled in the 1640s before doubling again in the 1690s, and these increases came after centuries of rough parity.[12] We have already noted the relationship between the creation of a Royal Navy and fiscal reform in the case of the ship-money fleets. After 1640 fiscal reform depended both on revitalizing old institutions and creating new ones, but much of this intensification of government depended on participation.[13] For example, the proportion of total revenues granted and controlled by Parliament increased dramatically after 1640 (a change confirmed at the Restoration), and direct taxation remained in the hands of local

[8] Thomas Garden Barnes, 'Deputies not Principals, Lieutenants not Captains: The Institutional Failure of the Lieutenancy in the 1620s', in Fissel, ed., *War and Government*, pp. 58–86, quotation at p. 61; Mark Charles Fissel, *The Bishops' Wars: Charles I's Campaigns against Scotland, 1638–1640* (Cambridge, 1994).

[9] Richard W. Stewart, 'Arms and Expeditions: The Ordnance Office and the Assaults on Cadiz (1625) and the Isle of Rhé (1627)', in Fissel, ed., *War and Government*, pp. 112–32.

[10] Ian Gentles, *The New Model Army in England, Ireland and Scotland, 1645–1653* (Oxford, 1992); James Scott Wheeler, 'Logistics and Supply in Cromwell's Conquest of Ireland', in Fissel, ed., *War and Government*, pp. 38–56, and 'The Logistics of the Cromwellian Conquest of Scotland, 1650–1651', *War and Society*, X (1992), pp. 1–18.

[11] John Childs, *The Army of Charles II* (London, 1976), chap. 2, p. 216, and *The Army, James II, and the Glorious Revolution* (Manchester, 1980), pp. 1–2, 5.

[12] P. K. O'Brien and P. A. Hunt, 'The Rise of a Fiscal State in England, 1485–1815', *Historical Research*, LXVI (1993), pp. 129–76, esp. pp. 148–155.

[13] For the following see Braddick, *Nerves of State.*

commissioners acting voluntarily. Reform of direct taxation took the form of limiting the freedom of action of such office-holders by asking them to apportion a fixed quota of taxation, rather than to assess the wealth of their neighbours as the principal pre-war direct tax (the subsidy) had done. Office-holders had acted as assessors reluctantly and inaccurately, often pursuing personal grudges or acting as good neighbours rather than conscientious servants of the Crown. Faced with a quota (by no means an innovatory administrative strategy in the seventeenth century), they could, and did, continue to use tax administration in this way, but the discipline of the quota ensured that it was no longer at the expense of national coffers. Such quota taxation remained the most productive single source of wartime revenue well into the eighteenth century.

At the same time reform of the customs administration ensured that the yield of the duties kept pace with the expansion of revenues generally, and allowed the government to profit from the expansion of overseas trade. Alongside the customs an entirely new form of indirect taxation, the excise, was established. Like the customs, this was collected by specialized agents of government. In this sense, the increasing effectiveness of mobilization rested not just on improved administration by office-holders but also, and increasingly, on the assumption of more direct responsibility for the revenues by specialized agents. In effect, government in the core of the territories of the Stuart Crown was intensified by means both of limiting the discretion of agents of delegated authority such as local office-holders and by instituting more direct forms of government. These changes provided the basis for further expansion of the revenues during the 1690s, in a period of intensive European war. In that decade the sources of revenue were broadly the same and the changes were mainly quantitative, although there were notable changes in the capacity of the government to secure long-term credit.

Whereas European mobilization in the 1690s created mainly quantitative improvements and, aside from techniques of long-term borrowing, limited qualitative change, the period 1640–60 had seen both. This transformation represented an intensification of government that rested both on the creation of new institutions and on the revitalization of old ones, such as the militia. As the regular army took over the militia's military functions, the militia increasingly became an instrument for securing civil and social order. In this role, and backed by clear statutory powers, the effectiveness of its administration improved dramatically while remaining in the hands of local commissioners.[14]

Overall, the capacity to mobilize for all military purposes was transformed in the period 1625–88. From the mid-1630s, but particularly after 1650, the government was taking more direct responsibility for naval activity. Its power at sea

[14] Fletcher, *Reform in the Provinces*, pp. 316–32.

provided a tool for the protection of trade and the promotion of diplomatic interests, and from the 1640s onwards the government also commanded notable military resources on land. This was not an Imperial phenomenon but one of European competition and, decisively, of civil war, but it did, clearly, affect Imperial and trading interests. For example, English naval protection was a considerable help to English merchants in the lucrative Mediterranean trades after 1670. Moreover, the changes of this period were a prelude to further quantitative change in the 1690s. The Civil War and associated conflicts forced both a quantitative and qualitative change in the fiscal and military resources of the state. Qualitatively, military mobilization involved increasingly direct governmental responsibility for these functions: a more specialized navy; a more effectively supplied and regular army; and specialized administration of indirect taxation. Older forms of government were also revitalized: Parliament granted, and office-holders collected, huge sums of direct taxation; commissioners implemented militia measures more effectively; and standards of administration were probably improving in other established institutions. On the whole, the capacity for warfare increased and this was partly associated with the assumption of more direct responsibility by national government.

The range of trading interests of English merchants changed dramatically during the seventeenth century, in what is known as the commercial revolution. There was a marked decline in the proportion of English exports made up of raw materials and semi-finished products, and a corresponding rise in the value of exported manufactures. The importance of foreign merchants in English trade and of Antwerp as an entrepôt for English imports and exports declined. London became a centre of world trade, drawing in and re-exporting colonial goods in addition to those from across Europe. Crucial to this development was the increasing sophistication of English financial and shipping interests. A corollary of these changes was that, whereas in the mid-sixteenth century English trade was overwhelmingly north European, by the later seventeenth century it was global. This is usually said to have been a phenomenon of the seventeenth century, and in particular of the period after 1640, but its roots lay in the later sixteenth century.[15]

In entering new and long-distance trades English merchants encountered non-commercial risks. First, they were cutting into the established interests of European rivals, notably the Spanish, Portuguese, and Dutch. For example, the reason for the doggedness with which English explorers sought a northern passage to the East Indies was that they would thereby gain access to the trade without interfering

[15] Robert Brenner, *Merchants and Revolution: Commercial Change, Political Conflict, and London's Overseas Traders, 1550–1653* (Cambridge, 1993), chap. 1, and see chap. by Nuala Zahedieh.

with the established Portuguese monopoly of the southern route. The tensions caused by their presence in the East Indies in the seventeenth century are perhaps best illustrated by the 'massacre' at Amboina in 1623. Secondly, such long-distance trade often also brought English traders into contact with societies that were little understood—Mughal India, for example. As a result, trade and military action were closely related. The Crown could not always provide the military and diplomatic shell within which trading activity could be carried on by private, civilian, commercial interests. The amalgam of private and public that we have observed in Elizabethan naval warfare was equally characteristic of long-distance trade, as trading companies took on these military and diplomatic functions.

Early chartered companies had negotiated trading concessions, represented the interests of their members at home and abroad, regulated access to the trade, and controlled the commercial aspects of it, such as price, quality, and quantity. In a sense, then, they acted as guild organizations but they also had diplomatic functions. Investment in a new trade could be encouraged by a government charter and monopoly, which enabled a company to provide the necessary diplomatic and military protection. Thus, although the government could not provide protection, it could encourage new trades by chartering companies which were able to cover these costs by exercising a monopoly and taking levies from members. The expansion of trade in the sixteenth century had been fostered in part by such chartered companies—to Barbary, Venice, Turkey, Spain, and the Baltic (the Eastland trade). Of course, these privileges may have been granted for less far-sighted reasons too, in return, for example, for political or financial favours. In so far as it was a strategy for the promotion of trade, however, the chartering of companies reflects the weakness of the government in providing military and diplomatic protection for trade.

Such chartered companies were often 'regulated', using monopoly and charter privileges to protect and promote trade without cost to the government. Another form of risk-limitation was the joint-stock company, also often protected by charter and monopoly. Such companies were established to trade with, for example, Guinea, Muscovy, the Levant, Virginia, the East Indies, West Africa, and Hudson Bay, spreading the risk of failed voyages and thus helping to mobilize capital. Not only were these trades hazardous, but their nature was often only vaguely understood. For example, early voyagers to the East Indies had only the haziest notion of the 'East' and what commodities might be sold there.[16] In practice, the distinction between joint-stock and regulated companies was fluid. The East India Company did not have continuous joint stock until 1657, for example, and the Muscovy Company evolved from a joint-stock into a regulated

[16] Philip Lawson, *The East India Company: A History* (London, 1993), pp. 1–5; on the Amboina 'massacre', see above pp. 270–71.

company.[17] The important point for our purposes was that the government was acting to promote trade (along with other less lofty aims) by proxy—licensing corporations to undertake the military and diplomatic protection of merchants and their goods.

Such monopolies were unpopular, however, and as the military and diplomatic reach of the English government increased, their justification became less obvious. The monopoly granted to merchants opening up the Eastland trade, for example, became less justifiable as that trade became established and routine, and as the capacity of the government to provide military and diplomatic protection in the Baltic increased. As the arguments for corporate privilege became less convincing, those against it acquired extra force. Crudely stated, these monopolies had a limited life-span: in the Barbary, Levant, and Muscovy trades something similar had happened earlier, in part because the trades had become relatively securely established earlier.[18]

The Navigation Act of 1651 marked an important change in the regulation of trade because it made blanket provision for foreign trade unmediated by privileged corporate bodies. It aimed at the promotion of English shipping, inevitably at the expense of Dutch merchants who dominated the carrying trade. Although it was not primarily a measure of colonial government, it has enjoyed some prominence in accounts of the relationship between the colonies and England, being interpreted as a sign of a more coherent level of government regulation.[19] The main lines of this legislation were confirmed in the 1660 Navigation Act, and the Staple Act of 1663 completed the legislated monopoly of the colonial carrying trade. The significance of these measures was limited by the problems of enforcement, but this was equally true of the regulation of trade through chartered companies, which had always suffered competition from illegal and interloping merchants. The increased naval capacity of the government resulted in decreased reliance on licensed agents, and underpinned the development of the navigation system which speeded their demise in some trades. The navigation system depended on naval power and growing fiscal competence. In this way the increasing fiscal and military power of the national government allowed it to take on a more direct role in relation to trade.

[17] T. S. Willan, *The Early History of the Russia Company, 1553–1603* (Manchester, 1956), pp. 271–73.

[18] R. W. K. Hinton, *The Eastland Trade and the Common Weal in the Seventeenth Century* (Cambridge, 1959); Willan, *Early History of the Russia Company*, and *Studies in Elizabethan Foreign Trade* (Manchester, 1959), chap. 4.

[19] Robert M. Bliss, *Revolution and Empire: English Politics and the American Colonies in the Seventeenth Century* (Manchester, 1990), pp. 58–60. For the provisions of these Acts see chap. by Nuala Zahedieh. There were precedents for seeking to exclude foreigners from colonial trade, albeit by different means: Brenner, *Merchants and Revolution*, p. 585.

The enforcement of the Navigation Acts rested largely on the customs service (with help from excise officers, and the army and navy), and by the late seventeenth century the range of regulatory statutes being enforced in the colonies added considerably to the complexities of the work of a customs officer.[20] Another indication of the way in which the customs service had become an arm of directly administered, legislative commercial policies was in tariff policy. Parliament took control of the duties in 1640, and as they became a legislative matter they also acquired a more marked function in the regulation of trade. Generally speaking, tariffs have both fiscal purposes and economic consequences, and as Parliamentary control over the tariffs was established these economic consequences seem to have been more consciously manipulated. Elizabethan and early Stuart tariff revisions did not follow any particular pattern except to increase revenues: there was no correlation between high rates and the protection of domestic production or between low rates and the encouragement of exports. During the Interregnum the weight of duties was adjusted with other purposes in mind, and this became even more marked after 1660. Throughout the Restoration period the Commons tended to push for revisions in the interests of protecting domestic production and encouraging exports while the Crown applied consistent pressure to maximize revenue. There had always been duties which were not primarily intended to raise revenue, of course, but manipulations of the duties seem to have been of increasing significance.[21]

Direct government responsibility for trade was not, however, adopted comprehensively. The East India Company retained its quasi-governmental powers well into the eighteenth century, and the Levant Company also retained influence over the embassy at Constantinople: it was only the appointment of Sir William Trumball in 1687 that 'transformed a commercial agent masquerading as an ambassador into a servant of the Crown sent primarily for political and diplomatic business'.[22] The Company retained nominal control over the embassy long after our period. These were long-distance trades to societies with complex political structures, where the purchase of increased English military power was more limited. But it was not just that privilege continued: it was created in other trades. Charters were granted to merchants trading in Africa (1660, 1663, and 1672) and Hudson Bay (1670). Here, again, the necessary protection from European rivals and, in Africa, from potentially powerful and hostile local populations could not be provided by the English government.

[20] Thomas C. Barrow, *Trade and Empire: The British Customs Service in Colonial America, 1660–1775* (Cambridge, Mass., 1967); Elizabeth Evelynola Hoon, *The Organization of the English Customs System, 1696–1786* (New York, 1938).

[21] Braddick, *Nerves of State*, pp. 120–23.

[22] A. C. Wood, 'The English Embassy at Constantinople, 1660–1762', *English Historical Review* (hereafter *EHR*), XL (1925), pp. 533–61.

None the less, from around 1650 the English government legislated for trade as a whole and the justification for monopoly trading privileges was accepted only for rather exceptional trades. This has tempted some historians to regard the Navigation Acts as the cornerstone of an Imperial vision, an issue to which we will return later. It is also true, however, that both privateering and chartered companies retained an important place in English trade. Thus, although the English government did take much more responsibility for the regulation and protection of trade, government by licence remained of considerable significance in some trades.

The territorial area subject to the authority of the Stuart Crown expanded in this period, notably in the decisive conquest of Ireland. Direct rule had a limited geographical compass but its radius was increasing. The military outposts of English rule in the later seventeenth century were dramatically further away than they had been in Elizabeth's day—Tangier and Bombay. But rule in these places at a great distance, already densely populated by societies with impressive capacities for political and military organization, was not accompanied by sustained attempts at settlement. These outposts remained fairly forlorn garrisons, were poorly supplied, and were maintained essentially as adjuncts to the private interests of the semi-public trading companies and merchants involved in long-distance trade.[23] Other settlements of this kind, in Africa and Asia, for example, were undertaken and protected by trading companies themselves.[24]

Settlement in the Americas was a special case. It became apparent that the potential riches of these areas lay in agriculture rather than in commodities produced by the local populations, or minerals, although privateering offered valuable early capital in Jamaica. The principal threat to English trading interests came from other European powers, not the local population. Hence, settlement was undertaken neither as a means of controlling the local population, as in Ireland, nor as a means of supporting trading interests, as in Africa and Asia.[25] It became increasingly clear, then, that this was a particular kind of territorial expansion, with peculiar problems. Once again, however, we can discern the development of more direct rule from London. This process is evident in two ways: the local arrangements for the regulation of the affairs of these places;

[23] E. Routh, 'The English Occupation of Tangier (1661–1683)', *Transactions of the Royal Historical Society*, Second Series, XIX (1905), pp. 61–78; Hornstein, *Restoration Navy, passim.*

[24] K. G. Davies, *The Royal African Company* (London, 1957), pp. 240–64; Lawson, *East India Company*, pp. 46–49.

[25] Many of these points are made by Jack P. Greene, *Peripheries and Center: Constitutional Development in the Extended Polities of the British Empire and the United States, 1607–1788* (Athens, Ga., 1986), chap. 1, and *Negotiated Authorities, Essays in Colonial Political and Constitutional History* (Charlottesville, Va., 1994), chap. 1.

and the administrative arrangements made at the centre in order to co-ordinate the local governments.

Early settlements in Virginia and Massachusetts were undertaken by chartered companies, but their record, particularly that of the Virginia Company, was far from exemplary. Settlement continued in Hudson Bay, Asia, and Africa to be undertaken by companies for reasons outlined above, and perhaps also because it was an adjunct to trade, not a prelude to agricultural self-sufficiency. Other settlements were established on an entirely different basis. The Maryland charter (1632) was expressly based on the palatine charters granted to the Bishops of Durham to govern the English borderlands in the fourteenth century. It created the heirs of the Lord Baltimore lords and proprietors, and as such they enjoyed remarkable powers to create titles, grant lands with manorial rights, incorporate towns, create ports, raise revenues, and license religious worship. This was to be done with the advice and assent of free men, but it was, none the less, feudal in tone: in return for these powers the proprietor had to deliver two arrows to the monarch each year as a sign of fealty. Similar proprietary settlements were established in the Carolinas in 1663, in New York in 1664, following its capture from the Dutch, and in William Penn's settlements in 1681. This feudal tone was not restricted to the proprietary colonies either—in return for its generous charter powers the Hudson's Bay Company was bound to supply the King, his heirs, and successors with two elks and two black beavers if they visited the region.[26] Thus, as the range of direct rule increased, so too did the range of indirect rule. Territorial accretion continued in familiar ways, new lands being brought under Crown authority by means of licensed agencies.

A third general form of colonial government was direct royal rule. Jamaica, captured from the Spanish in 1655 and governed by the military commander for the rest of the 1650s, was more or less taken over on those terms by the restored monarchy in 1660. The Governor-General became a royal appointee, but retained the military, civil, and economic powers enjoyed under the Protectorate. This form of direct government had also been implemented in Virginia after the failure of Company government in 1625, when it was declared that the purpose of the settlement was 'for the propagation of the Christian Religion, the increase of trade, and the enlarging of [the King's] Royal empire'.[27]

Virginia's history exemplifies another problem in generalizing about colonial government during the seventeenth century—it varied significantly over time. The exact nature of the warrant by which settlement in Connecticut and Rhode Island was justified was by no means clear, and in the latter cases the relationship

[26] E. E. Rich, *Hudson's Bay Company, 1670–1860*, Vol. I, *1670–1763* (New York, 1961), p. 52.

[27] Quoted in Richard Middleton, *Colonial America: A History, 1607–1760* (Oxford, 1992), p. 37.

between the settlers and their nearest chartered authorities was not at all comfortable. All colonies exercised dubious authority during the Interregnum, of course, and the authority of the New England settlements in particular was questioned during the 1680s. The most spectacular result of this was the revocation of the Massachusetts Bay charter and the imposition of Dominion government on the whole of New England in 1685 (New Hampshire had already been declared a royal province in 1679).

Oversight of these chartered and royal bodies was equally haphazard. Whatever the nature of the charter, the right to settle and govern these colonies derived from the Crown. Their regulation therefore depended on the King-in-Council and in practice on subcommittees and boards of the Privy Council, not on Parliament. At various times fairly permanent-looking bodies took responsibility for the plantations, and this interest was increasingly conflated with that of trade in general. These developments, however, were by no means smooth. For example, in 1625 a commission of trade was established as a subcommittee of the Privy Council while at the same time a committee of the Privy Council was established to deal with special questions of trade, but 'Neither of these bodies appear to have had more than a temporary existence . . .'. More-permanent bodies were created in the 1630s and 1640s, notably a Commission for the Plantations established in 1634, recommissioned in 1636, and in continuous existence until at least 1641. During the same period a Committee of Trade with a regular membership and time of meeting had been active, but the importance of these early boards has generally been discounted. In part this is because they did not do what historians think they should have done; for example, they were concerned with political and religious regulation, not simply with commercial matters,[28] or their practical interest in the internal affairs of the colonies was limited.

A Council of Trade with regular membership and a paid secretary, Benjamin Worsley, was active between 1650 and 1653, and was succeeded by a number of relatively assiduous committees of the Council of State. These bodies generally attract more favourable comment and their activities are often seen as an extension of the intent demonstrated by the Navigation Act. However, many of them were short-lived and more recently greater emphasis has been placed on the Restoration bodies. There was a Council for Trade and Plantations from 1660 to 1665 and a new Council of Trade established in 1668. In 1670 a new Council for Plantations was created and the two Councils were amalgamated in 1672. This combined Council, in existence for two years, is seen by many as the crucial one in the evolution of Imperial administration. There were plans for a special building

[28] Charles M. Andrews, 'British Committees, Commissions, and Councils of Trade and Plantations, 1622–1675', *Johns Hopkins University Studies in Historical and Political Science*, series 26, nos. 1–3 (1908), quotation at p. 13.

to house it and its annual budget of £7,400 included £6,400 for salaries, a modest but none the less significant sum. Benjamin Worsley was employed once again.[29] Its instructions were similar to those of the Lords of Trade, who were responsible for trade and colonial affairs from 1675 to 1696, and their successor, the Board of Trade (1696–1782). There is, thus, a strong case for arguing that by the 1670s (and possibly the 1650s) an administrative structure was in place with which to co-ordinate the nascent Empire.

Historians have tended to discern in these arrangements an index of the seriousness of English commitment to colonial control. Royal colonies, it is presumed, were bound more tightly into the Imperial system, and coherent Privy Council oversight was a necessary prerequisite for tight administration. On the other hand, lapses in Privy Council oversight and the concession of proprietary government or generous charters are presumed to signify more relaxed government from the centre. A further indicator is the internal arrangements of the colonies. Most colonies evolved a tripartite system of government consisting of a Governor and bicameral legislature. This was not the product of a metropolitan blueprint but of local political development drawing on Old World traditions in the light of New World conditions.[30] Attempts to increase the authority of London, however, took the form of strengthening the hand of Governors against their legislatures. For example, following Bacon's rebellion in Virginia in 1676 an aspect of the restoration of royal authority and good governance was to require the royal Governor to seek a permanent revenue that would free him from dependence on the legislature. Similar efforts to increase the authority of Governors were made in other royal colonies at the same time: Jamaica, Barbados, and the Leeward Islands. In the later 1670s the Lords of Trade also investigated the possibility of extending Poynings' Law (which required the prior consent of the English Privy Council before the passage of legislation in Ireland) to Jamaica and Virginia, which would have further curbed the independence of colonial Assemblies.

Using such a typology, historians of colonial America have argued for a decisive turning-point in relations with England in the 1670s. The measures noted previously coincided with others of a similar kind. New Hampshire was made a royal colony and the private charters of Massachusetts Bay and Bermuda were questioned (the former eventually being recalled and replaced by direct government of the Dominion of New England). All this, it has been argued, amounted to a more vigorous Empire, to which some adjustment was necessary.[31]

[29] Ralph Paul Bieber, 'The British Plantation Councils of 1670–74', *EHR*, XL (1925), pp. 93–106.

[30] Yunlong Man, 'English Colonization and the Formation of Anglo-American Polities, 1606–1664', unpublished Ph.D. dissertation, The Johns Hopkins University, 1994.

[31] Bliss, *Revolution and Empire*, esp. pp. 176–89.

Clearly these changes were important in the history of the American colonies, but such structures were not without precedent. Neither were they applied to all overseas territories. In America there were previous statements of intent to govern more directly. For example, the commitment to good government made by the Virginia Company in its Great Charter in 1618 was echoed in Charles I's proclamation in 1625 establishing Virginia as a royal colony.[32] The Massachusetts Bay charter (1629) suggests, however, a lack of commitment on this score. It failed to stipulate a place of meeting for the company and thereby allowed it to establish its base in America, thus creating, effectively, an independent colonial government. The 1650s furnish further examples of an intention to take responsibility for the colonies in the Navigation Act and the Council of Trade and its successors. After 1660, however, proprietary charters continued to be granted—to New York and the Carolinas, as we have seen, and to the Bahamas, which were added to the territories of the Carolinas. The importance of these earlier commitments was qualified, therefore, but so too was that of the 1670s. Proprietary government was established in Pennsylvania in 1681 and a chartered company controlled trade and settlement in Hudson Bay.

The English government was clearly adopting a more direct role in the governing of some of its overseas territories and interests throughout the seventeenth century. But this was geographically variable and the chronology is complex. By the 1670s close oversight by the Privy Council and a persistent desire to control colonial government was manifest in relation to America and the Caribbean. This was matched by the domination achieved in Ireland. But both can be traced to the 1650s at least: to the committees of the Council of State, the intent of the Navigation Act, and to the military changes achieved by the revolutionary regime. In fact, the desire to govern the Americas well can be seen as early as 1625. On the other hand, privateering persisted beyond 1700, and at the same time trading companies continued to take responsibility for the military diplomatic defence of important trades. Indeed, in 1668 the East India Company took over a royal possession (Bombay) which it was better able to protect.[33]

Just as there was a life-span for chartered companies there might have been one for colonies, where proprietary or company charters remained the preferred means of establishing a colony, as in Hudson Bay or Pennsylvania.[34] Once a settlement reached a particular level of sophistication, however, as in Virginia, New England, and the Caribbean by the mid- or late-seventeenth century, more-

[32] Ibid., pp. 11–13, 18–21. [33] Lawson, *East India Company*, p. 47.

[34] Rich, *Hudson's Bay Company*, p. 12, suggests that this was the accepted 'form of organization for colonial settlement and trade' in 1670.

direct government of the King's subjects became appropriate.[35] Part of the equation was, no doubt, revenue potential. Colonies producing valuable cash crops, such as the Caribbean islands and Virginia, offered potential income to government as they became 'more sophisticated'. Similarly, the English government collected more revenue through the Navigation Acts than it had through the concession of trading charters in return for political and financial favours in the early seventeenth century. In terms of this life-cycle, then, Hudson Bay and Africa are more like sixteenth-century charters such as the Eastland Company's than the contemporary measures being taken in relation to established American colonies. Where more direct government was appropriate, the details of its form was a political issue on which agreement was by no means guaranteed, as we will see. None the less, overall the English government was by 1688 taking more direct responsibility not just for overseas trade but also for overseas settlement.

The reach of English government increased in this period. In the core areas government intensified, not least in the extraction of fiscal and military resources. More established trades and settlements were subject to more-direct forms of government and the extent of 'government by licence' also increased. This growth, extensive and intensive, took place largely within an established repertoire of direct, delegated, and licensed authority, but there was a significant expansion of specialized public agencies such as the armed forces, the customs, and the excise services. We have noted the complexities of this process geographically and the difficulty of isolating a particular turning-point appropriate to trades and settlements in each of which there was a life-cycle and particular local conditions. In fiscal-military terms, the Civil War and Revolution were important, while the period after 1675 was of particular significance for well-established colonies in America and the Caribbean. This tangled chronology makes it difficult to infer a coherent Imperial vision. This is further complicated by the way in which these overseas interests intersected with domestic politics.

There is not space here to consider whether or not there was a 'mercantilist' blueprint for these policies, or to consider in detail whether commercial policy reflected the growing influence of particular interest groups.[36] It has been argued, however, that as a result of the commercial revolution an influential group of 'new

[35] Jack P. Greene and J. R. Pole, 'Reconstructing British–American Colonial History: An Introduction', in Greene and Pole, eds., *Colonial British America: Essays in the New History of the Early Modern Era* (Baltimore, 1984), pp. 1–17.

[36] There is a large literature on this subject. For mercantilism, see Charles Wilson, *Profit and Power: A Study of England and the Dutch Wars* (London, 1957), and *Mercantilism* (London, 1958). Joyce Oldham Appleby, *Economic Thought and Ideology in Seventeenth-Century England* (Princeton, 1978), offers a different view.

merchants' emerged in England who were not dependent on Crown privileges for their economic well-being. These men were influential in opposition to the Crown during the seventeenth century, making common cause with landowners concerned about property rights, and they secured considerable political influence during the 1640s and particularly after 1649. Thus, for example, the interests of these new merchants were important to the naval build-up, the institution of the navigation system, and the outbreak of hostilities with the Dutch. It is difficult to prove beyond doubt, however, that all of these men are best characterized as new merchants, that their politics flowed primarily from their economic interests, or that they took the lead in policy-making.[37] Moreover, the naval build-up had other roots, clearly, in long-standing aspirations to improve naval strength and in response to changes in ship design. The passage of the Navigation Acts and the wars with the Dutch were also responses to a variety of interests, among which were, pretty clearly, non-economic concerns. In general, the complexity of decisions to go to war, the passage of the Navigation Acts, and of the interests at stake in the administration of the colonies make it difficult to demonstrate the existence of a coherent trade or Imperial policy.

The passage of the first Navigation Act was uncontroversial and so there is little documentation with which to appraise whether or not it reflected the interests of particular merchant groups. However, it is possible to view it, and the programme of which it was a part, as reflective of 'a pervasive and time-honoured concept of the proper relationship between trade and the public interest'. The confidence to challenge Dutch interests, though, was probably bolstered 'by the growing diplomatic confidence, commercial assertiveness and naval strength of the Commonwealth', naval strength which was not commercial in origin.[38] Anglo-Dutch politics in this period clearly have a non-mercantile context which displays continuities with the foreign-policy concerns of the early Stuart period. There is more to foreign policy than going to war, of course, but explaining decisions to go to war does cast light on the priorities of government and the pressures on decision-makers. Tariffs increasingly reflected a concern for broader economic questions and it has also been claimed that war became a tool of economic policy, that the period saw a fundamental shift away from religious and dynastic war, such as the wars of the 1620s, for example, towards trade wars of which the Anglo-Dutch Wars are said to be examples.

Religious concerns were clearly of central importance to the foreign policy of the 1620s. The failure of the Spanish match, between Charles and the Spanish

[37] Brenner, *Merchants and Revolution.* For a critique see John Morrill, 'Conflict Probable or Inevitable?', *New Left Review,* CCVII (1994), pp. 113–23.

[38] Blair Worden, *The Rump Parliament* (Cambridge, 1974), pp. 257–58, 299; Brenner, *Merchants and Revolution,* pp. 580–84.

Infanta, signalled the collapse of attempts to protect Protestantism and the dynastic interests of Frederick of the Palatinate by diplomatic means. It was followed by a 'blessed revolution' in foreign affairs, as English policy turned away from pro-Spanish diplomacy towards war. Charles and the Duke of Buckingham, having been humiliated in Madrid, were intent on defending personal and national honour, and they provided the nucleus for a factional realignment at court. These 'patriots' found support in Parliament and the country against their pro-Spanish opponents. The change of policy appealed to a zealous Protestant nationalism intent on reliving the glories of the Elizabethan wars with Spain, the defence of Protestantism abroad being for many a corollary of support for the true religion at home.[39] Among other things, this entailed thwarting the plans of the Spanish monarch for a universal monarchy, the temporal equivalent of the pretensions of the papacy.

In the conduct of routine diplomacy the domestic political stakes were rarely as high, but when it came to war broad coalitions of domestic support were formed, and it was such coalitions that allowed the mobilization to go forward—money from Parliament and troops from local office-holders, for example. The wishes of the monarch were crucial, of course, as were factional politics at court, but so too was the political support of broader sections of the population. Recent work has shown how this broader political context makes it difficult to represent the Anglo-Dutch Wars as 'trade wars'. Protestant nationalism remained of crucial importance, but it was reinterpreted in the light of new European and colonial developments. The wars against the Dutch were as much domestic, European, and religious as they were Imperial or commercial. For example, the 1651 Navigation Act was passed in a mood of outrage at the public affronts and political evasions that had met the embassy of the new English Republic. The Navigation Act did not lead directly to war, but the hostility expressed in print about the Dutch, who were said to have been corrupted by the pursuit of wealth and were apparently retreating from their condition of republican purity, made peace difficult to secure. Although trading issues were embroiled in this image, the war was not 'about' trade, and the peace terms at the end of the war do not reflect a desire to secure commercial ends. Instead, the war reflected the interests of a Protestant alliance, intent on chastising the Dutch who had become, in some eyes, allies of the Whore of Babylon.[40]

[39] Thomas Cogswell, *The Blessed Revolution: English Politics and the Coming of War, 1621–1624* (Cambridge, 1989).

[40] Steven C. A. Pincus, *Protestantism and Patriotism: Ideologies and the Making of English Foreign Policy* (Cambridge, 1996). Compare with Wilson's verdict that 'though other factors, notably political, assisted, the period of gestation of both wars [1652–54, 1665–67] was one of economic depression peculiarly favourable to war hysteria', *Profit and Power*, p. 151; for the diplomatic background to the struggle see chap. by Jonathan I. Israel.

The restored regime also went to war with the Dutch and, of course, trade was an important issue, but again there were also important domestic dimensions to this commitment. In 1663–64 many felt that the stability of the Restoration regime was threatened, and an influential body of 'Anglican Royalist' opinion held that this threat came from religious nonconformists and republicans. These people managed to seize the initiative in domestic and foreign affairs, claiming that it was the Dutch who aspired to create a universal monarchy. They were said to be engrossing trade to this end and their Presbyterian religion was just another kind of popery—here interpreted as religion damaging to the interests of kings. The Crown more or less solicited anti-Dutch complaints from a Parliamentary committee on trade, but those merchants who complied did so not because it was in their economic interest in the short term (most knew that it was not, or that the Dutch were not their biggest problem), but because they were sympathetic to the broader Anglican Royalist programme.[41] This view was not consensual, however, and it lost ground during the Second Dutch War. For example, the Great Fire of London was, on the whole, blamed on papists and the French rather than Nonconformists and the Dutch. The view that the French were the most serious aspirants to universal monarchy did not win out until midway through the third war. It was then that the Dutch turned their backs on republicanism and that French international ambition and duplicity were most convincingly revealed. Thus a majority came to fear that it was the French who posed the most serious threat to English church and state.[42]

These are complicated episodes and they do not represent the full range of foreign or commercial policy. However, the first Navigation Act and all three Dutch wars were, obviously, emanations of domestic as much as economic or Imperial interests. Trade was involved in these disputes because it was important to European powers, but war was not a 'tool of economic policy'. European politics were interpreted in a sophisticated way by English people, and the idea of a universal monarchy was a flexible one. It came to embrace trading rivalries and also the possibility that universal monarchy could be pursued by bad Protestants as well as by Catholics. As a vision of national interest, though, it was religious and constitutional rather than commercial, and it is difficult to find a definition of Imperial that would embrace it. In the light of such complexities, it is not easy to demonstrate the existence of an overall policy, or the decisive and sustained influence of any particular group.

[41] Paul Seaward, 'The House of Commons Committee of Trade and the Origins of the Second Anglo-Dutch War, 1664', *HJ*, XXX (1987), pp. 437–52; Steven C. A. Pincus, 'Popery, Trade and Universal Monarchy: The Ideological Context of the Outbreak of the Second Anglo-Dutch War', *EHR*, CVII (1992), pp. 1–29.

[42] Steven C. A. Pincus, 'From Butter Boxes to Wooden Shoes: The Shift in English Popular Sentiment from Anti-Dutch to Anti-French in the 1670s', *HJ*, XXXVIII (1995), pp. 333–61.

The regularization of colonial government was also related to domestic politics. There is an influential consensus that Imperial history starts after 1650, and in particular during the 1670s, but there is a debate about how or why the English government sought it. In part this is because of the inconsistency of arrangements for colonial government throughout the seventeenth century. The key to these complexities perhaps lies more in English than Imperial politics. It has been suggested that there was a consensus by 1625 that the colonies should be governed well. The nature of good government was, of course, contentious in seventeenth-century England. Before 1649 all forms of colonial government were varieties of government by licence, whether company or proprietary charter, or self-government under a royal Governor. After 1649 this 'contractual empire' began to give way to the 'legislative empire'. The continued preference for contractual arrangements in some circumstances after the Restoration should not obscure the importance of increasingly direct forms of government, but at the same time it points up some of the continuities in the aspirations of the Crown which can be traced back to 1625. Thus, variations in form do not necessarily reflect variations in intent. The discourse of government was constant in relation to the colonies, which were recognized to be extensions of the English polity early on: it was the nature of good government that was contested. Thus, the return to government by contract and licence after the Restoration can be harmonized with the domestic, conservative instincts of that regime. The changes were not a result of changes in the Imperial policy—that was reasonably constant—but of changes in perceptions of what constituted good and appropriate government.[43]

Alongside this discourse of government there were others, of course. Trade and martial interest were present in the Elizabethan experience of trade, plunder, and settlement, and both remained significant to visions of government in the colonies and government responsibilities for trade. It used to be argued, in fact, that the English Empire in America was commercial in origin and that these commercial interests contrasted with Empire properly understood—government, territorial control, centralization, and domination.[44] There is much to recommend such a view: the origins of settlement in commercial ventures; the close relationship between the English presence in the West Indies and privateering; the navigation system; and wars against the Dutch that clearly related to commercial interest, for example. There was a pretty continuously expressed desire, however, to bring good order to the colonies, and it no longer seems appropriate to term the Dutch wars commercial in a pure sense. Commerce clearly took its place alongside other interests in the development of the Empire.

[43] Bliss, *Revolution and Empire*, chaps. 5–6.

[44] Charles M. Andrews, *The Colonial Background of the American Revolution: Four Essays in American Colonial History* (New Haven, 1931). See above, pp. 55–78.

One other such interest was undoubtedly military. A military interest has been shown to have been present at the inception of settlement and to have been of crucial importance at key moments in colonial history, as in the career of John Smith in Virginia. The presence of the military can be documented throughout the period, in Ireland in the late sixteenth and mid-seventeenth century, in England and Scotland in the mid-seventeenth, and in Jamaica in the 1650s. It has been suggested that it became the dominant element in the nascent Empire in the later seventeenth century, in the aftermath of rebellion in Virginia. Thereafter military men were prominent among colonial Governors and the military presence in the colonies was heavy. Clearly this military interest was important, but it was not the sole motive force behind the government of the Empire, running as it did alongside commercial concerns.[45] It is also plain that alongside this military domination ran a process of co-option. Even in Ireland, often taken to be the exemplar of expansion by conquest, there is plenty of evidence of the way in which local interests could be reconciled with English rule. Recent work has emphasized this, and suggested that rebellion there did not always reflect nationalist rejection of alien rule. As the political and social life of the colonies became more complex, and as the interest of the metropolitan government in colonial affairs increased, a similar pattern of coalition-building emerged, between interests in societies of similar levels of complexity.[46]

In the formation of policy, debates about trade, government, and military order were all present, but historians have tended to try to isolate one as the bottom line. To contemporaries, however, these goals were not necessarily alternatives. For men such as Benjamin Worsley, for example, godliness, commercial success, social order, good government, and fruitful agriculture were complementary ideals.[47] The appeal of measures such as the Navigation Acts was presumably exactly that they achieved so many laudable aims at once. If particular policies could be successfully promoted as achieving these things, it is no wonder that they could be enacted and enforced. The difficulty was making that case. Between the 1650s and the 1670s it seems to have been possible on crucial occasions to persuade a coalition of interests that the Navigation Acts and war with the Dutch served these ends. After the 1670s competition with the French seems to have been a more convincing argument.

[45] Stephen Saunders Webb, *The Governors-General: The English Army and the Definition of the Empire, 1569–1681* (Chapel Hill, NC, 1979). See also the debate with Richard R. Johnson, *William and Mary Quarterly*, Third Series, XLIII (1986), pp. 408–59.

[46] See, for example, Nicholas Canny, 'Irish Resistance to Empire? 1641, 1690 and 1798', in Lawrence Stone, ed., *An Imperial State at War: Britain From 1689 to 1815* (London, 1994), pp. 288–321. For America, see Greene and Pole, 'Reconstructing British–American Colonial History'.

[47] Charles Webster, *The Great Instauration: Science, Medicine and Reform, 1626–1660* (London, 1975), *passim*.

Behind many of these debates lies an essential problem: that is, whether this government was capable of 'policy' as distinct from 'decisions'. The decision to go to war in any particular case has a complex history in Whitehall, Parliament, and the country, and any policy decision was backed by a coalition of interests. It is possible to discern an Imperial policy, if one 'construes policy from actions, especially those that entailed predictable fiscal and political costs', thereby stripping out extraneous proposals and debate. Other historians, faced with such qualifications, are more sceptical.[48] If by 'policy' we mean a tendency for decisions, when taken, to fall in a particular way, it is possible to see some changes in this period. Government by licence was pushed to more distant peripheries—Africa, Asia, and the far north of America—as the power of English government, the regularization of trade and diplomatic contacts, and the increasing sophistication of the social and political life of the earliest colonies made more-direct government possible. In fact, as the political life of the colonies became more sophisticated, so the usefulness of metropolitan authority to the colonists increased: London was often invited in. The form of metropolitan authority also varied in response to the degree of competition from European rivals and the nature of the local society. Moreover, trades and settlements had life-cycles which affected their relationship with English government.

There was, thus, some consistency in the strategies adopted in the face of comparable combinations of these variables between, for example, the creation of trading companies in the mid-sixteenth and late seventeenth centuries. But there is also a further complication—such decisions were affected by English disagreements about what constituted appropriate government action: what constituted good government was a product not just of circumstance but of ideology. Intervention in the government of New England in the 1680s was an extension of current visions of domestic government which was defeated before the fall of the domestic regime of which it was an extension. The Navigation Acts and Dutch Wars are similarly to be understood in a domestic as well as an international context.

The English government took more-direct responsibility for more areas of overseas activity during the seventeenth century. In part this was to do with a transformation of its structure. More intensive government in the core (reflected in an increased capacity for military mobilization) underwrote more-direct forms of government in the peripheries and pushed less-direct forms to more-distant corners of the globe. But this experience was not uniform and, ultimately, it derived as much from the necessities of civil war as it did from Imperial ambition. The variety of local experience gives the lie to any claim for a very coherent

[48] Daniel Baugh, 'Maritime Strength and Atlantic Commerce: The Uses of "a Grand Marine Empire"', in Stone, ed., *Imperial State at War*, pp. 185–223, quotation at p. 188. Jeremy Black, *A System of Ambition? British Foreign Policy, 1660–1793* (London, 1991), is more sceptical.

Imperial policy, and the content of such a policy was also varied. It contained a concern for trade and for domination of territory, but this was modulated according to the nature of the trade or settlement. It was further modulated by domestic issues: governance of the colonies and decisions to go to war were evidently perceived as closely related to domestic politics. The transformation of the military and fiscal capacity of the state and the commercial revolution created new interests, new possibilities, and new ambitions, but in the end they took their place alongside existing ones.

Select Bibliography

JEREMY BLACK, *A System of Ambition? British Foreign Policy, 1660–1793* (London, 1991).

ROBERT M. BLISS, *Revolution and Empire: English Politics and the American Colonies in the Seventeenth Century* (Manchester, 1990).

MICHAEL J. BRADDICK, *The Nerves of State: Taxation and the Financing of the English State, 1558–1714* (Manchester, 1996).

ROBERT BRENNER, *Merchants and Revolution: Commercial Change, Political Conflict, and London's Overseas Traders, 1550–1653* (Cambridge, 1993).

BERNARD CAPP, *Cromwell's Navy: The Fleet and the English Revolution, 1638–1660* (Oxford, 1989).

JOHN CHILDS, *The Army of Charles II* (London, 1976).

—— *The Army, James II and Glorious Revolution* (Manchester, 1980).

THOMAS COGSWELL, *The Blessed Revolution: English Politics and the Coming of War, 1621–1624* (Cambridge, 1989).

J. D. DAVIES, *Gentlemen and Tarpaulins: The Officers and Men of the Restoration Navy* (Oxford, 1991).

MARK CHARLES FISSEL, ed., *War and Government in Britain, 1598–1650* (Manchester, 1991).

ANTHONY FLETCHER, *Reform in the Provinces: The Government of Stuart England* (New Haven, 1986).

IAN GENTLES, *The New Model Army in England, Ireland and Scotland, 1645–1653* (Oxford, 1992).

JACK P. GREENE, *Peripheries and Center: Constitutional Development in the Extended Polities of the British Empire and the United States, 1607–1788* (Athens, Ga., 1986).

—— *Negotiated Authorities: Essays in Colonial Political and Constitutional History* (Charlottesville, Va., 1994).

—— and J. R. POLE, eds., *Colonial British America: Essays in the New History of the Early Modern Era* (Baltimore, 1984).

PHILIP LAWSON, *The East India Company: A History* (London, 1993).

ANTHONY MCFARLANE, *The British in the Americas, 1480–1815* (London, 1994).

STEVEN C. A. PINCUS, *Protestantism and Patriotism: Ideologies and the Making of English Foreign Policy* (Cambridge, 1996).

STEPHEN SAUNDERS WEBB, *The Governors-General: The English Army and the Definition of the Empire, 1519–1681* (Chapel Hill, NC, 1979).

—— *1676: The End of American Independence* (New York, 1984).

14

New Opportunities for British Settlement: Ireland, 1650–1700

T. C. BARNARD

In 1673 an opportunist pamphleteer described Ireland as 'one of the chiefest members of the British empire'. He went on to celebrate (though not to explain) how the island had been transformed recently from 'a grave to bury our best men and a gulf to swallow our greatest treasure' into 'an orderly commonwealth, civil in itself and in time like to prove profitable to the prince, and at all times a good additional strength to the British Empire'.[1] The novelty of this analysis lay not in its sunny predictions, since commentary on Ireland invariably veered between optimism and dejection, nor in the nostrums which would complete Irish assimilation to England and usher in prosperity. Rather, it lay in the concept of empire, and Ireland's unexpected place in it. Such thinking, however, proved precocious in the later seventeenth century. It expressed ideas of empire circulating in England, not in Ireland. The thoughtful Irish regarded their country as 'a separate and distinct kingdom from England', annexed to the English sovereign and so subject to his prerogative.[2] Uncertainties about how best this sovereignty should be exercised ruffled the relationship. The English monarch, his entourage, or (worst of all) the Westminster Parliament dealt out Irish lands and offices, regulated trade, and in 1691 decided Ireland's rulers (William and Mary). Nevertheless, there persisted the comforting idea of Ireland as a sister kingdom to England. Hibernia, to be sure, was Britannia's younger sister, or, varying the analogy to the most popular biblical one, an Eve to England's Old Adam.[3]

Ireland's unwillingness simply to obey England prompted interference which culminated in the dramatic reconquests of 1649–52 and 1689–91. New English victories opened Ireland to enforced settlement from Britain, rather than the

[1] Anon, *The Present State of Ireland* (London, 1673), sig. A2^{v}–3, pp. 78–79. On English concepts of Empire see above, pp. 1–2 and 103–04.

[2] William Domville, 'Disquisition', *c.*1660, N[ational] L[ibrary] [of] I[reland], Dublin, MSS, 40, f. 4.

[3] E. Borlase, *The Reduction of Ireland to the Crown of England* (London, 1675), sig. [a6^{v}]; T. C. Barnard, 'The Protestant Interest', in Jane H. Ohlmeyer, ed., *Ireland: From Independence to Occupation, 1641–1660* (Cambridge, 1995), p. 238.

gentler infiltration which had been bringing immigrants for generations. In early modern Ireland land abounded; people, especially with capital or specialized skills, were scarce. After prolonged warfare, the population reduced by famine and disease, many of the indigenes dead, exiled, or marked down for expropriation and resettlement, opportunities beckoned to new British settlers. Yet fewer than hoped came. It is that gap between the official aim and how Ireland developed in the later seventeenth century which has to be described and explained.

Given the ferocity and duration of the uprising after 1641, it was perhaps surprising that the English victors reverted to the traditional policy of sponsored plantations to pacify and Anglicize their troublesome dependency. The feebleness of the settlements before 1641, together with the manifold failings of the settlers, much criticized by contemporaries, seemed to explain both why the revolt had happened and why it had been so hard to suppress. Flaws in the earlier enterprises were identified, but these simply warned the architects and overseers of any future scheme to avoid them. The wars of the 1640s and 1689–91 also revealed the resilience of Catholic power, notwithstanding the systematic erosion of its economic and political foundations in the intervening years. Those bloodied by the resurgent Irish Catholics vowed that the latter, when defeated, should be permanently emasculated. Protestants already settled in Ireland besmirched their local rivals and lobbied unscrupulously in Dublin and London to advance themselves. Because the incumbent Protestants won so much in the subsequent redistribution and had so blatantly exaggerated the misdeeds of their adversaries, they were accused of having engineered, or even of inventing, the turmoil. In 1689 an excited Protestant welcomed the fresh opportunity to defeat the Catholics, because 'the protestants who have estates will add to 'em, and they who have none, will get some'.[4] Yet, whatever gains opportunists expected, the insurrections overstretched the military capabilities of Irish Protestants. Despite a much-bruited prowess in the field, they were saved only by expeditionary forces from England, Scotland, and (in 1690) Europe. Those who had recaptured Ireland extorted their price. In the 1640s 1,533 'adventurers' had subscribed cash for the campaigns. Between 30,000 and 35,000 soldiers had fought them. Again in the 1690s, a now smaller stock of confiscated property would be used by William III to reward his helpers.[5]

In the early 1650s the English Parliament proposed to bring approximately 36,000 new owners to Ireland. Initially they would be concentrated in ten counties, stretching in an arc from Antrim, Down, and Armagh in north-east Ulster, through the midland counties of Meath, Westmeath, King's, Queen's, and Tip-

[4] *The Declaration of the Protestant Nobility and Gentry of the Province of Munster* (London, 1689).

[5] K. S. Bottigheimer, *English Money and Irish Land: The 'Adventurers' in the Cromwellian Settlement of Ireland* (Oxford, 1971), pp. 140–41; J. G. Simms, *The Williamite Confiscation in Ireland, 1690–1703* (London, 1956), pp. 148–57, 194.

perary, to the south-west (Limerick) and south-east (Waterford). However, because the defeated property-owners were more generally to be dispossessed (by some calculations, 80,000 in all), much land and housing throughout the towns and countryside would be on offer. This policy created an administrative and technical task of daunting scale and complexity. It dominated and destabilized Irish life for the next fifty years. The procedures, adjudicating the guilt of the old owners, identifying and measuring, allocating and gaining possession of these portions, made work which in itself drew some to Ireland.

The majority of those who were to receive lands in the 1650s—private soldiers and junior officers from England, Wales, and Scotland and the civilian investors absent in England—grew impatient. Some, sceptical that their grants would amount to no more than a tract of bog and scrub in a townland whose name they could not find on any map or even pronounce, cashed in their entitlements. The patient and those with ample purses bought up these debentures (the certificates of qualification).[6] Even some speculators repented of their gamble as the baffling details of the Cromwellian arrangements became the impenetrable uncertainties of the Restoration settlement. Lawyers, predictably, flourished as they interpreted and advised. In 1670, when the formal process was declared to be ended (soon it would be reopened), the authorities took stock. About 8,000 individuals had their holdings confirmed. Thus, a projected influx of 36,000 had dwindled to about 8,000. The civilian adventurers had dropped from 1,533 to approximately 500; the military to perhaps 7,500. This infusion, certainly useful, would make only a limited impact in a Protestant population, which was thought in the 1670s to number between 200,000 and 300,000.[7] Furthermore, even some who had persevered to the end lived in England and simply rented out their distant Irish holdings.[8]

The use of Irish lands to pay off an English army, apart from neatly solving an otherwise awesome puzzle, was attractive because it would bring to Ireland the skills as well as the numbers that it lacked. The disbanded soldiers, endowed with Irish farms or houses, were expected to return to their civilian callings as farmers, tradesmen, craftsmen, or labourers. At the same time they would keep those martial skills necessary to intimidate the unruly locals. A problem in the 1650s was that the demobbed soldiers who already possessed skills, capital, and contacts useful to trade and agriculture were most eager to resume interrupted lives in England. Those who lacked the strong incentive to sail back often adjusted only

[6] Conveyances of debentures to Lt Charles Odell, 1656–57, Chatsworth House, Derbyshire, Lismore MSS, 28/51–62, 71–72, 75–78, 80–81; sales of debentures to William Waring, 1656, P[ublic] R[ecord] O[ffice] [of] N[orthern] I[reland], Belfast, D 695/114, 117, 120, 122.

[7] Bottigheimer, *English Money and Irish Land*, pp. 140–41.

[8] N. Jones to G. Legge, 18 April 1671, 20 Jan. 1670[1], 12 April 1672, Staffordshire County Record Office, Stafford, Dartmouth MSS, D (W) 1778/I/i, 308, 311, 319; B[ritish] L[ibrary], Egerton MSS, 2649, ff. 114, 145, 156, 162, 194, 267.

slowly to the travails of farming and dealing in the uncertain conditions of Ireland in the later 1650s. Wartime habits were hard to shed, especially in a landscape alive with those very Irish whom the Protestants had been taught to fear and despise. Moreover, the newcomers, if they were to thrive, needed not just luck and fortitude, but additional cash with which to stock and improve their properties or buy materials and tools. Often, too, they lacked a firm nexus of local connections through which services, credit, and both practical and psychological support could be delivered. It was at these levels particularly that their rivals, familiar with the terrain and its inhabitants—the dispossessed Irish Catholics and the Protestants settled there before 1641—could either aid or trouble the lately arrived.

An impression of the disappointing results of the grandiose project of the 1650s is conveyed by the dwindling of the expected 36,000 new owners to perhaps a quarter of this number. The national picture, to be sure, displayed a dramatic change. The proportion of land owned by Catholics fell from 61 per cent in 1641 to 22 per cent in 1688 and a mere 14 per cent by 1704.[9] The weight seemed to have shifted decisively from the older Catholic to the newer Protestant interest. The list towards the latter was accentuated by other official measures which debarred Catholics from the upper reaches of government and office. But behind the screen which supposedly hid the drudging Irish papists, destined now to be hewers of wood and drawers of water, from their privileged Protestant mistresses and masters, a more complicated situation obtained. Local studies have revealed much variation in the fortunes of landed Catholics. A few, well-connected and loyal to the Stuarts, such as Antrim, Carlingford, Clancarty, and Richard Talbot, the future Tyrconnell and Lord-Deputy under James II, held on. Their large holdings, coupled with those of other fortunate Catholics, meant that in County Dublin, for example, ninety-seven Catholic proprietors survived in 1669, between them owning 35 per cent of the total acreage.[10] In some districts only the additional Williamite seizures extinguished the guttering flame of a Catholic gentry. Thus, in County Kilkenny, where earlier the interest and obligations of the Duke of Ormonde had protected his kinsfolk and clients even when Catholic, by 1715 the Catholic proportion of land had dwindled to a paltry 8 per cent and the local Protestants had established their ascendancy over the area.[11] Similarly, in County Cork, the delayed breakup of the Clancarty estate left Catholics (in practice about fifteen survivors) with only 8 per cent of the land.[12] Districts where Catholics kept

[9] Simms, *Williamite Confiscation*, p. 195.

[10] L. J. Arnold, *The Restoration Land Settlement in County Dublin, 1660–1688* (Dublin, 1993), pp. 109, 138–39, 141–45.

[11] M. Brennan, 'The Changing Composition of Kilkenny Landowners, 1641–1700', in W. Nolan and K. Whelan, eds., *Kilkenny: History and Society* (Dublin, 1990), pp. 169, 174–75.

[12] D. Dickson, 'An Economic History of the Cork Region in the Eighteenth Century', unpublished Ph.D. thesis, Trinity College, Dublin, 1977, I, pp. 65–67.

a significant proportion of the acreage, such as Louth, Galway, or Antrim, were the exception by the early eighteenth century, and often involved the survival of a single large proprietor.[13] Yet, if this result realized the intention behind the Cromwellian and Williamite policies, the corollary, that the old Catholic élites would be dispersed or disintegrate, had not always followed. Ingenious and adaptable, Catholics hung on as tenants, squatters, or householders, pushed into humbler dwellings, infertile districts, and uncongenial activities. Through a variety of stratagems former owners kept their old status and connections, if not the prosperity which had previously attached to them.[14]

The confiscations of the 1650s, trumpeted as the greatest opportunity to participate in and profit from Ireland, yielded disappointing results partly because Catholics could not be, and were not, cleared from the projected plantations. Their presence, first as labourers and artificers, soon as tenants, was necessary to any successful enterprise. For some settlers, isolated among a strange and potentially unfriendly population, the press of Catholics added to their disinclination to root themselves in the Irish hinterland. Others copied their predecessors by adapting to the ways of their Catholic neighbours, learning that sometimes their odd methods and implements better suited the locale, and even by intermarrying. In the 1670s, for example, the widow of the Protestant Bishop of Clogher was 'vehemently suspected' to have remarried and turned papist.[15]

Above all, the grandiose plan of the 1650s yielded ambiguous results because Irish land had lost much of its magnetism. Estates, the bait to hook immigrants, disillusioned their holders. Contrary to what many of the brochures had promised, even in the 1650s lands did not lie empty and untenanted, awaiting only the kiss of the energetic stranger to blossom into paradisical plenty. Instead, wet, sour, and inaccessible, alive with shadowy and seemingly sinister wraiths, although tilled and tenanted, they hardly repaid the effort. Holdings of the extent easily to be had in seventeenth-century Ireland would bestow considerable standing and wealth in lowland England and Wales. In Ireland, by contrast, while the possessors were accorded the styles of esquire or gentleman congruent with their large estates, ran their counties, and sat in the Dublin Parliament, they lacked the income to buy a fitting style of life. The low value and return of much Irish land was further

[13] Jane H. Ohlmeyer, *Civil War and Restoration in Three Stuart Kingdoms: The Career of Randal MacDonnell, Marquis of Antrim, 1609–1683* (Cambridge, 1993), pp. 258–77; H. O'Sullivan, 'Landownership Changes in the County of Louth in the Seventeenth Century', unpublished Ph.D. thesis, Trinity College, Dublin, 1992, I, pp. 333, 372–74.

[14] L. M. Cullen, 'Catholics under the Penal Laws', *Eighteenth-Century Ireland*, I (1986), pp. 23–36; Cullen, 'Catholic Social Classes under the Penal Laws', in T. Power and K. Whelan, eds., *Endurance and Emergence: Catholics in Ireland in the Eighteenth Century* (Dublin, 1990), pp. 57–84.

[15] 'State of the Case between James Leslie and Nicola Conyngham', after 1673, PRONI, D 3406/D/2/1C.

depressed when fighting disrupted, devastated, and depopulated it. On widely separated estates—of the Brownlows around Lurgan in the Lagan valley, of Lady Huntingdon in Fermanagh and Tyrone, of Thomond in Counties Carlow and Clare, and of the Percevals in County Cork—receipts crept back to their pre-war levels only in the later 1670s and 1680s, and then, in some cases, plummeted with the new warfare in the early 1690s.[16] These difficulties aggravated but hardly caused the slowness with which rents improved before the 1740s.

Landowners caught in this trap reacted variously. Some increased rentals by snapping up extra land whenever it became available. Existing proprietors, therefore, interested themselves deeply in the redistributions of the 1650s and 1690s. Already on the spot, apprised of the quality and potential of particular parcels and with friends on the panels which apportioned the grants, they were suspected to have done well. Careful investigation of who gained what in the Cromwellian resettlement of the three west Ulster counties of Donegal, Londonderry, and Tyrone shows that a startling 91 per cent of the land intended for new planters fell to those already settled before 1641.[17] The attributes of superior local links and better access to cash or credit, vital to worsting interlopers in the Interregnum, again assisted the established in the 1690s. Then, with a smaller stock to be distributed—no more than 457 substantial estates—the settlement involved fewer.[18] Some choice lands which the envious had long coveted, notably those of the Marquess of Antrim, still eluded the predators.[19] Others, such as Clancarty's in County Cork, fell to the greedy. Well-placed and affluent locals digested what they had been eyeing for generations. Even so, large purchasers needed the additions of marriage portions, a soldier's pay, or earnings from the law, trade, or office, to fund their acquisitions.[20]

Officials in London and Dublin, keen to entice over more of substance to undertake the onerous and costly duties of landownership, encouraged the legend that a sizeable Irish estate represented the jackpot in a colossal lottery. Accordingly, the progress of the early-seventeenth-century buccaneer, Richard Boyle, from obscurity to an Irish fortune worth about £18,000 per annum by 1641 and the

[16] T. C. Barnard, 'Land and the Limits of Loyalty: The Second Earl of Cork and First Earl of Burlington (1612–1698)', in T. C. Barnard and J. Clark, eds., *Lord Burlington: Architecture, Art and Life* (London, 1995), pp. 172, 188; Raymond Gillespie, 'The Irish Economy at War, 1641–52', in Ohlmeyer, *From Independence to Occupation*, p. 178; Raymond Gillespie, ed., *Settlement and Survival on an Ulster Estate: The Brownlow Lease Book, 1667–1711* (Belfast, 1988), p. lix.

[17] K. McKenny, 'The Seventeenth-Century Land Settlement in Ireland: Towards a Statistical Interpretation', in Ohlmeyer, *From Independence to Occupation*, pp. 198–99.

[18] Simms, *Williamite Confiscation*, pp. 177–92.

[19] Entries for 27 Jan. 1690[1], 12 Feb. 1690[1], Minute Book of Londonderry Municipal Corporation, 1688–1704, PRONI, LA 79/2A/2.

[20] Dickson, 'Cork Region in the Eighteenth Century', I, pp. 68–72.

earldom of Cork, which he chose to regard as the just reward of providence, publicly proclaimed Ireland as the kingdom of untrammelled opportunities.[21] In the later seventeenth century the exemplary tale of Cork would be coupled with that of Sir William Petty, enriched by the upheavals of the 1650s. These examples of a rise, if not from rags then at least from Irish frieze to riches, continued with that of the most spectacular profiteer from the redistributions of the 1690s: the Donegal attorney William Conolly, who by the 1720s ruled as Speaker of the Irish House of Commons and was rumoured to be worth over £15,000 per annum.[22] Common to each, as the admiring and jealous agreed, was the chance offered to the forceful to hoist himself to eminence and wealth through Irish confiscations. Also integral to each story, as was widely perceived, were the corners cut, officials suborned, laws and regulations flouted, and rivals intimidated. The authorities did not advertise, because it was too well known, the latitude allowed the freebooter in Ireland. Nor did the publicists for Irish enterprises ponder the exasperation expressed by many as they grappled with the impediments strewn in their paths by the government. Petty, the testy virtuoso who had expected his large Irish rents—over £5,000 per annum—to underpin a public and scientific career, after a decade of distracting entanglements raged: 'Our estates here are mere visions and delusions and require more attendance than a retail shop.'[23]

The absent or inattentive, delegating oversight of estates to underlings, soon discovered how those on the spot stole a march. Petty had wearily concluded that an Irish estate 'cannot subsist without the owner's daily presence and inspection'.[24] However, as Petty's own case demonstrated, absenteeism and devolution were inevitable, since the holdings of the most considerable proprietors were seldom consolidated in a single county let alone in one barony. Furthermore, even the resident, though they might convert the demesne overlooked by their houses into an experimental station where new crops and techniques were tested, saw their lands as means to other ends. The public duties and sociable recreations, not the drudgery of daily inspection, were what lands should support. In order to free themselves for their wider civic responsibilities landlords needed to maximize revenue by employing trustworthy agents, attracting industrious and solvent

[21] Nicholas Canny, *The Upstart Earl: A Study of the Social and Mental World of Richard Boyle, First Earl of Cork, 1566–1634* (Cambridge, 1982).

[22] O. Gallagher to O. St George, 4 Nov. 1729, London, C[hancery] 110/46/733; Jane Bulkeley to Jane Bonnell, 18 June 1728, NLI, PC 435/15; L. Boylan, 'The Conollys of Castletown: A Family History', *Quarterly Bulletin of the Irish Georgian Society*, XI (1968), pp. 1–12.

[23] T. C. Barnard, 'Sir William Petty, Irish Landowner', in H. Lloyd-Jones, V. Pearl, and B. Worden, eds., *History and Imagination: Essays in Honour of H. R. Trevor-Roper* (London, 1981), p. 214.

[24] Ibid., p. 214.

tenants, and settling proficient craftsmen and tradespeople. These requirements offered openings for new settlers, but increasingly could be supplied from within the existing population.

As in England when the agricultural boom of the sixteenth century slackened, so in Ireland, through a much longer period of static or falling rents and receipts, the laborious and costly work of agrarian improvement and innovation attracted less notice than the more sensational schemes, many of which, like Jonah's gourd, collapsed overnight. Tenants, like trout, had to be tickled and, once netted, kept. Projects, as in England, abounded. Rural industries, such as fishing and iron-making, were developed to supplement seasonal agriculture and its uncertain returns. One who invested in the tackle and vessels needed for fishing justified his expenditure, 'forasmuch it will be an employment of the people who otherwise would be troubled to pay rent'.[25] In this spirit, even the appearance of the Lord-Lieutenant at horse-races on the Curragh in County Kildare, pleasant refreshment after the stench of Dublin, contributed to the public good since it would stimulate selective breeding and raise the prices that horses fetched both as exports and essentials in daily life.[26]

These designs, the dotty as well as the solid, drew in merchants and investors, particularly from England, but also from the United Provinces. The Irish market, long known to specialists, with its sizeable and prospering clientele clamouring for novelties, tempted those looking for diversification. Trial cargoes were shipped into Irish ports to see how they sold. A growing trade, striking by the 1680s, benefited producers, agents, factors, and merchants in Ireland. Quakers, first established in Ireland during the Interregnum, lured over more of their kind, particularly from north-western England. Thanks to an intricate filigree of kinship and commerce, notably in cloth, they became a distinctive presence. Travelling regularly to their religious meetings within and beyond Ireland, the Friends simultaneously attended to their trade.[27] Others with specialized skills now urgently wanted in Ireland were prevailed upon to immigrate. Hammermen, finers, and forgeworkers lured away from the Severn Valley or Dutch and Flemish experts in the fishing and textile industries were prized. Those few who stayed long were poached by competitors and moved rapidly from site to site, sometimes perhaps diffusing their skills. These ventures, despite the *brouhaha* they raised,

[25] T. C. Barnard, 'Fishing in Seventeenth-Century Ireland: The Experience of Sir William Petty', *Journal of the Kerry Archaeological and Historical Society*, XIV (1981), p. 24.

[26] Lord Essex to C. Harbord, 11 April 1674, Bodleian Library, Oxford, MSS, Add. C. 34, f. 81; Lord Massareene to R. Newdegate, 8 Nov. 1683, Warwickshire County Record Office, Newdegate MSS, CR 136/B 285; Sir William Temple, 'An Essay upon the Advancement of Trade in Ireland', in W. Temple, *Miscellanea* (London, 1680), pp. 132–35.

[27] Journal of Joseph Gill, 1674–1741, Friends' Historical Library, Dublin.

generally affected only the immediate locality and the wealth of their patrons—often adversely.[28]

More than a marginal and usually localized effect could be attributed to only one manufacture: textiles. With food, drink, shelter, and fuel, and not forgetting the new addiction to tobacco, clothing was a necessity. Moreover, since the settlers in Ireland were to differentiate themselves both from one another and, more importantly, from the Irish Catholics through dress, sumptuary ideology complicated need and vanity. Vigorous proprietors sought alternatives to the pastoralism of their tenants. A better-developed Irish textile industry might cure 'that lazy, sleepy, easy way of getting so much money as will just buy them brogues and sneezing and strong beer, and put them on other ways that by trades and manufactures would improve and enrich and beautify' Ireland.[29] To strengthen the stirrings of activity the grandees of Restoration Dublin vowed to buy and wear only Irish. Kitted out in their bulky suits of Irish frieze, they aimed to popularize the fashion at court. The vogue did not sweep smart London and proved a passing fad in Dublin (though it would be revived regularly at moments of patriotic or economic stress).[30] Nevertheless, the steadier demand for staples sustained the textile industry.

As was the custom of the age, the important claimed, or were given, credit for what had been achieved. Close to the viceregal bolt-hole of Chapelizod the then Lord-Lieutenant Ormonde encouraged a former Cromwellian officer to open a factory for linen, tapestry, woollen cloth, and stuffs, employing 300 workers. A Dutch expert toured England and Flanders in a quest for artificers and the tricks of the trade. The works, though subsidized by the state and awarded contracts to supply the army, may never have woven the intended broadcloths, Turkey-work carpets, and upholstery for chairs. After eleven years the venture had lost between £2,000 and £3,000.[31] More promising were the works in populous Munster towns such as Bandon, Tallow, and Kinsale in the 1680s and 1690s. Using local capital and labour, together with well-developed networks for distribution and sale, each withered as it flowered. First the political instability of James II's reign and then the naval warfare, embargoes, and finally a ban by the English Parliament stifled them. English intervention, which had earlier in the 1660s banned the export of livestock, enraged the articulate in Ireland. They were reminded painfully of how,

[28] T. C. Barnard, 'An Anglo-Irish Industrial Enterprise: Iron-making at Enniscorthy, Co. Wexford, 1657–92', *Proceedings of the Royal Irish Academy*, LXXXV, C (1985), pp. 4–44; Barnard, 'Sir William Petty as Kerry Ironmaster', ibid., LXXXII, C (1982), pp. 1–32.

[29] Lord Roscommon to Lord Cork, 23 Jan. 1665[6], BL, Althorp MSS, B.5.

[30] D. Johnson to ? E. Pilsworth, 1671, Birr Castle, Co. Offaly, Rosse MSS, A/16; Lord Broghill to Lord Dorset, 19 Jan. 1665[6], Kent Archives Office, Maidstone, Sackville MSS, U 269/C18/2.

[31] Submissions of Richard Lawrence, May–Oct. 1668, Bodleian, Carte MSS, 35, f. 861; 36, f. 521; 66, ff. 303, 323; Reports of Alex. van Fornenbergh, 1668, ibid., 36, ff. 347–48, 497–98.

when powerful sectional interests captured the Westminster Parliament, Ireland, owing to its dependence, furnished an easy sacrifice.[32] At such moments the English government forgot its professed aim of making Ireland a laboratory of useful skills and innovations. While those in Ireland shrieked, they also quietly redoubled their exertions to supply more of their domestic needs through home manufacture and to perfect an industry better suited to Irish weather and soils. Accordingly, they cultivated flax and made linen.

In the spread of the linen manufacture, as in the encouragement of woollens, the conspicuous few—in the 1660s Ormonde, Orrery, or Richard Lawrence; later, the Huguenot Crommelin—have sometimes been seized upon to explain the success of an industry which hardly required that kind of fillip. With wool, the shadowy traders in Clonmel, Cork, Kilkenny, New Ross, Waterford, and Youghal passed the packs along the chains between suppliers and customers. Linen, customarily made on a small scale for domestic and local use, attracted the interest of interconnected groups of Ulster landlords and merchants and Dublin traders, and was rapidly hailed by gregarious and imitative gentlemen as the solution to their own and their tenants' difficulties. For the most part, despite allegations to the contrary, this distinctive development, so vital to the character and structure of Irish Protestant society, arose from within rather than being introduced from outside.[33]

A final device to persuade the talented and industrious to try Ireland, which the new possessors of Irish property were expected to patronize, was the town. Towns, supposedly unknown in Gaelic Ireland, had become the redoubts of the English and (more recently) the Protestant interest, as the Anglo-Norman and later settlers had taken over the Viking ports around the coast and created others of their own. Emptied of their Catholic property-owners during the 1650s, the towns, together with their government and trade, were entrusted to the Protestants. In some boroughs already well populated but not controlled by Protestants in 1641, such as the Munster towns of Cork, Kinsale, and Youghal, these upheavals did not shatter all existing commercial links. In others, especially those outside the denser Protestant settlements, such as Galway, Limerick, Waterford, and Wexford, the substitutes of the 1650s were either too poor or too few quickly to drive the old trade.[34] Towns, designed for a pivotal role in the new Ireland, received special attention. As in earlier plantations, they would serve as nurseries in which the

[32] P. H. Kelly, 'The Irish Woollen Export Prohibition Act of 1699: Kearney Revisited', *Irish Economic and Social History* (hereafter *IEcSH*), VII (1980), pp. 22–44.

[33] W. H. Crawford, 'Drapers and Bleachers in the Early Ulster Linen Industry', in L. M. Cullen and P. Butel, eds., *Négoce et industrie en France et en Irlande aux XVIIIe et XIXe siècles* (Paris, 1980), pp. 113–19; Crawford, 'The Evolution of the Linen Trade of Ulster before Industrialization', *IEcSH*, XV (1988), pp. 42–45.

[34] T. C. Barnard, *Cromwellian Ireland: English Government and Reform in Ireland, 1649–1660* (Oxford, 1975), pp. 62–71.

ingenious and active would be concentrated and whither they could retreat if ever again affairs in the countryside turned ugly.

In some respects the towns of later seventeenth-century Ireland fulfilled these hopes. In the 1670s Petty believed that at best 20 per cent of Ireland's population was Protestant, but guessed that of those that dwelt in the towns half were Protestants.[35] Perhaps, too, they did function as the reception centres for the desired and desirable immigrants. Some who subsequently thrived as merchants first appeared in the towns shortly after the Cromwellians had taken over: William Hovell, originally of Kinsale later of Cork, Edward Hoare in Cork, or Edward Lawndy at Youghal.[36] However, this does not prove that they had arrived in the Interregnum. Without detailed records of apprenticeship or prosopographies of urban élites it is possible only to speculate how much these newly Protestant towns lured over newcomers or merely advanced the established. In Kinsale, its main owner, Robert Southwell, took whatever openings appeared. In turn he victualled Prince Rupert's privateers, the Cromwellian, and the Stuart navies. Southwell had been flexing his muscles in the 1630s in Kinsale, but came to full power only after 1649. Eastwards along the coast, at Youghal, Owen Silver bought the posts of town clerk and recorder for life and acquired valuable urban and rural properties. He, unlike Southwell, had arrived in the Cromwellian army.[37]

Stray examples catch the eye, as they did in the seventeenth century, but may or may not illustrate larger trends. The physical as well as social mobility of Ireland probably produced highly unstable urban populations. Even without the interruptions of warfare and the official changes which twice, in the 1650s and 1690s, replaced papists with Protestants, craftsmen and traders moved in and out of occupations and localities with bewildering alacrity. Robert Clarke, admittedly rather an odd denizen of Kinsale in the 1680s, had tried various callings from shoemaker to mariner which took him from Bantry in the south-west to Athlone in the midlands and thence to Antigua, where he was alleged to have sold two of the ship's crew into slavery, and back to Hamburg with a cargo of tobacco.[38] The eccentric circuit he described by land and sea was probably not exceptional among his neighbours in the busy port. At a more elevated pitch, Lionel Beecher had been

[35] W. Petty, *The Political Anatomy of Ireland* (London, 1691), p. 8.

[36] T. C. Barnard, 'The Political, Material and Mental Culture of the Cork Settlers, *c.*1650–1700', in P. O'Flanagan and C. G. Buttimer, eds., *Cork: History and Society* (Dublin, 1993), pp. 347, 350; R. Caulfield, ed., *The Council Book of the Corporation of Youghal* (Guildford, 1878), pp. 295, 302; Dickson, 'Cork Region in the Eighteenth Century', I, p. 46; II, p. 423; C. M. Tenison, 'The Private Bankers of Cork and the South of Ireland', *Journal of the Cork Historical and Archaeological Society*, I (1892), pp. 221–22.

[37] Lease to O. Silver, 29 Sept. 1664, Cork Archives Institute, Youghal Corporation Records, U 138/C7; Barnard, 'Cork Settlers', pp. 339–40.

[38] Depositions of Mary Rawlins, John Story, etc., Kinsale, 28 April 1686, Cork University College Library, Kinsale Manorial Papers, 1676–92, U 55.

driven by the fighting of the 1640s from Youghal back to north Devon. Once peace returned to County Cork, so did he. As well as pressing a claim for twelve ships said to have been sunk during the earlier hostilities, he tapped the congeries of kin and patrons to accumulate varied posts. A trader on his own account, Beecher also served as customs official in the local port and agent and seneschal of a leading notable.[39] Another who reveals both the chances and the mobility encouraged by Irish towns is Thomas Parsons. Apprenticed originally in the cloth trade in Devon, Parsons applied his expertise to promoting the woollen industry of southern Ireland. Back in England during the Jacobite *revanche* of the late 1680s, he renewed his West Country links. These he exploited when in the 1690s, now in Dublin and a brewer and maltster, he solicited the agency of Somerset clothiers keen to buy good Irish wool.[40]

Towns, with their thicker mesh of markets and Protestant residents, multiplied the profitable sidelines through which the canny could shift from subsistence to comfort or at least avoid immiseration. They also organized and accelerated the traffic in people and goods across the Irish Sea. These functions added to the reasons to increase their number. Self-interest and public spirit combined to recommend this work to the settlers favoured with generous grants of land. Charters of incorporation showered down on the undertakers in early seventeenth-century Ulster and Munster. The patents, carrying rights to parliamentary representation and the hierarchical government of boroughs, enlarged the patronage of the owner and guaranteed a Protestant majority in the Irish House of Commons. These creations, with their classic configurations of Protestant church, regular plan with market-place, and buildings of some pretension to house magistrates, town council, and other functionaries, embodied the English vision for Ireland. Many remained names on vellum unless they attracted trade. After 1660 the government continued to incorporate boroughs and authorize new markets and fairs (the last two not necessarily in towns), but at a slower pace than earlier in the century.[41] The slackening tempo of town creation hinted at an island now well-, even over-stocked with such centres. The newly rich found it harder to slot in their own creations among the many dotted across the island. Coming late to the game, Sir Richard Cox, beneficiary of law and office, was pushed into the wilder uplands of County Cork to establish his town, Dunmanway, in 1693. If, quickly enough, it took on the characteristic physical form, Cox had not judged it worth 'the trouble and charge' to have it created a borough. Nor,

[39] Barnard, 'Cork Settlers', p. 341.

[40] Petition of Thomas Parsons to Orrery, *c.*1668, Petworth House, West Sussex, Orrery MSS, general series, 10; Parsons to R. Drake, 17 March 1696[7], C 104/12, box 1.

[41] P. O'Flanagan, 'Settlement, Development and Trading in Ireland, 1600–1800', in T. M. Devine and D. Dickson, eds., *Ireland and Scotland, 1600–1850* (Edinburgh, 1983), pp. 146–50.

so his heir later grumbled, had he bothered greatly as to how the inhabitants would live.[42]

The cult of the town as prestigious and costly toy rather than economic dynamo was exemplified by the Lord Chancellor in the early 1660s. Sir Maurice Eustace wanted his County Wicklow manor of Baltinglass elevated into a borough. Eustace, himself of Old English ancestry and with many relations still Catholics, subscribed wholeheartedly to the dogma of urbanity. As blandishments to new settlers of the right calibre he proposed to construct a parish church and school, and promised to settle £100 per annum on the incumbent and £40 on the master. On the look-out for skilled textile workers, he proffered a stock of 300 stone of wool, houses of timber and brick rent free for three years, and a loan of £20 to each family which settled. In 1662 he reported the arrival of some, mostly English, and desired 'only to have more of the same to join them'.[43] The ability of notables who founded towns after the Restoration, such as Orrery at Charleville and Castlemartyr, Archbishop Boyle at Blessington, or Sir George Lane at Lanesborough, to draw in skilled craftsmen and workers, often exaggerated for effect, may nevertheless have had some foundation. Similarly, the owners of existing towns, such as Ormonde at Kilkenny, Carrick-on-Suir, and Clonmel, the Southwells at Kinsale, or the Boyles in Bandon, Tallow, Dungarvan, and Youghal, exploited their contacts or estates in England to speed the interchange of personnel and techniques.

Proprietors at a loss to invigorate sluggish settlements turned to the opportunities which providentially opened as first the Huguenots and then the Protestants of the Palatinate were expelled from their homes. A County Wicklow landowner saw the chance to help the endangered Protestant interest both locally and internationally, as earlier Ormonde and Orrery had and as later Sir Thomas Southwell would in County Limerick. Sir Richard Bulkeley sent to hesitant Huguenots a bright prospectus of what they would enjoy if they settled with him at Dunlavan. Two annual fairs, a weekly market, river transport from Waterford, subsidized plots and a church and pastor of their own, and a variety of vegetables on sale—roots, pulses, artichokes, leeks, and potatoes—were bound to ensnare the French.[44] If the Huguenots rejected Bulkeley's baits, the inhabitants of established towns might also spurn the efforts of their creators. Birr, the County Offaly borough remade by its new owners, the Parsons, in the 1620s, had been loaded with the benefits that well-placed agents could procure. Yet it was reported in 1687

[42] R. Cox to E. Southwell, 6 Feb. 1713[14], BL, Add. MSS, 38157, f. 65; R. Cox, *A Letter from Sir Richard Cox, Bart, to Thomas Prior, Esq.* (Dublin, 1749), pp. 4–7.

[43] F. W. X. Fincham, ed., 'Letters Concerning Sir Maurice Eustace, Lord Chancellor of Ireland', *English Historical Review*, XXX (1920), pp. 257–58; *Calendar of State Papers, Ireland, 1663–5*, p. 4.

[44] Proposal of Sir Richard Bulkeley, *c.*1690, Nottingham University Library, Portland MSS, Pw A 2333.

that the townspeople 'are not only ungrateful but seemingly still beggars, notwithstanding that they were seldom . . . without a troop or company [of soldiers] who paid particularly for what they have had'. In procuring public meetings, the assizes, and sessions for the town, the patron's own profit intertwined with that of the general welfare. The Parsons drew about three-quarters of their annual revenues of £1,000 from Birr.[45]

So far this account has dwelt on the gap between intention and achievement in later seventeenth-century Ireland. Contemporary wisdom expected the powerful, notably the newly estated, to draw others after them. Later explanations of the undoubted but jerky growth, though not indifferent to the numbers and skills of the settlers, have uncovered the hidden forces which animated agriculture and trade. At the time observers noticed how the ebb and flow of distant wars stimulated or depressed demand, how fashion popularized new commodities—notoriously tobacco, but also cheaper and brightly patterned fabrics—or how frosts, floods, murrains, and local disasters suddenly blighted prospects. The recently ensconced Protestants regularly gave way to introspection or dismay in the face of Catholic resurgence, English discrimination, and international recession. Putative settlers from Britain were alternately encouraged and repelled. Some would contend that the appeal of Ireland itself mattered less than conditions elsewhere. By the mid-seventeenth century England's population had stabilized, easing the pressure on the limited stocks of land, food, and work, and so fewer were inclined to take ship for a new life in Ireland. Moreover, in the leaflets which sold Ireland to speculators and settlers in Britain, the strange and menacing had always vied for attention with evocations of an adjacent El Dorado. During the vicious fighting of the 1640s and, to a lesser extent, in the late 1680s, propagandists expatiated on the danger and barbarism of rebellious Ireland. For those unfamiliar with the kingdom, indeed for some who knew it intimately, such images lingered subliminally after the peace had been concluded. So, it would seem, only where harsh economic, social, political, or religious conditions prevailed, notably in western Scotland and northern England, were many still pushed across the narrow channel to seek a livelihood.

The permanent and transient migrants, it is clear, often followed well-worn routes of travel and trade. Movement within an already defined sphere, such as the littoral of the Irish Sea, quickened and slackened in response to hidden motors. An ancient port like Youghal had long pulsed to these rhythms. In the 1660s the inhabitants of Minehead and its environs thought little of sailing over to be touched by the healer, Valentine Greatorex, a few miles up river from Youghal,

[45] H. Oxburgh to Sir Laurence Parsons, 10 Oct. 1687, Birr Castle, Rosse MSS, A/1/149; List of refugees from Ireland and their incomes, 1689, Trinity College, Dublin, MSS, 847.

after his cures had been publicized in England.[46] A similarly easy passage between County Down and Scotland ferried over those beguiled by the talk of better economic and religious conditions first in one, then in the other kingdom.[47] What impelled so many from the north country to come—economic hardship, religious scruples, or restless ambition—has yet to be demonstrated.

The great planned settlement of the second half of the century never occurred. Instead, Ireland witnessed the piecemeal enlargement of established plantations and the foundation of relatively few new ones. Yet, although official largess, so prodigal with Irish land, did not swell numbers greatly, the Protestant population rose. By 1687 Ireland's inhabitants probably totalled nearly 2 million. Protestants were thought to constitute about 20 or 25 per cent.[48] Those who had arrived since the later sixteenth century were usually synonymous with Protestants, although some earlier settlers had conformed and newcomers defected to Catholicism. A Protestant population of the magnitude of 400,000 or 500,000 is not immediately visible in later seventeenth-century Ireland. The dense settlements in Ulster, Munster, and Dublin, and the other towns, now bastions of the Protestant interest, are the most likely locations (see Map 6.2). By 1641 the planted districts of Munster were thought to contain 22,000, recovering and increasing after the Restoration to 30,000.[49] Ulster in the 1630s attracted at least 15,000 British settlers: a total which may have doubled already by 1660.[50] Dublin, a magnet for the ambitious and impoverished from within and beyond Ireland, grew rapidly from the mid-1650s. It quickly overcame the losses of war, expulsion, and plague, so that by 1685 it contained maybe 45,000 people; by 1706 this had grown to 62,000. Perhaps 70 per cent of those who lived in the capital were Protestants: 44,000 by the early eighteenth century.[51] Of other Irish towns only Cork was large: its population perhaps 6,000 in 1660 and nearly 18,000 by 1706. Protestants, though a strong presence, were not preponderant: between 33 and 40 per cent.[52] The remaining

[46] *A Brief Account of Mr. Valentine Greatraks* (London, 1666), pp. 36–37.

[47] T. C. Barnard, 'Scotland and Ireland in the Later Stewart Monarchy', in Steven G. Ellis and Sarah Barber, eds., *Conquest and Union: Fashioning a British State, 1485–1725* (London, 1995), p. 261.

[48] D. Dickson, C. Ó' Gráda, and S. Daultrey, 'Hearth Tax, Household Size and Irish Population Change, 1672–1821', *Proceedings of the Royal Irish Academy*, LXXXII, C (1982), pp. 154–55; Petty, *Political Anatomy*, p. 8.

[49] Barnard, 'Cork Settlers', p. 315; M. MacCarthy-Morrogh, *The Munster Plantation: English Migration to Southern Ireland, 1583–1641* (Oxford, 1985), p. 260.

[50] L. M. Cullen, 'Population Trends in Seventeenth-Century Ireland', *Economic and Social Review*, VI (1975), pp. 149, 154; Raymond Gillespie, *Colonial Ulster: The Settlement of East Ulster, 1600–1641* (Cork, 1985), pp. 54–56; Gillespie, *The Transformation of the Irish Economy, 1550–1700* (Dundalk, 1991), p. 14; P. Robinson, *The Plantation of Ulster* (Dublin, 1984), pp. 104–08.

[51] D. Dickson, 'The Demographic Implications of Dublin's Growth', in R. Lawton and R. Lee, eds., *Urban Population Development in Western Europe from the Late-Eighteenth to the Early-Twentieth Century* (Liverpool, 1989), p. 180.

[52] Dickson, 'Cork Region in the Eighteenth Century', II, p. 420.

towns were small and, outside the planted regions of Munster and Ulster, smaller still in their percentage of privileged Protestants—nowhere more than a quarter of the total, sometimes only one-eighth. Even when aggregated, the Protestants of more than one hundred boroughs, many of them no better than a cluster of cabins at a crossroads, constitute a fragment of the 400,000 or 500,000.

The large figure of Protestants in later seventeenth-century Ireland signifies success for the English design at variance with the generally discouraging picture which has been sketched. The total, if not grossly inflated (which it may have been), can be explained by two factors for which there is solid, albeit very limited, evidence. Ulster, although parts of it were fought over in the 1640s and 1689–90, quickly attracted immigrants, sometimes even before peace had returned as Scottish soldiers and their followers campaigned there. The province continued to draw newcomers from Scotland and northern England until the early eighteenth century, when some of the Protestant strength flowed away to North America. Estimates of how many had come varied and often betrayed the anxieties of those alarmed at the influx. The totals proposed for the new arrivals after 1690 were 50,000, or even 80,000.[53] Other indicators, the size and trade of Belfast and Lisburn, the vitality and more complex organization of the Presbyterian church, divided by 1659 into five presbyteries and in 1688 into 100 separate congregations, displayed the growth.[54] Moreover, the sharper pressure on once abundant resources pushed the immigrants further west and south into the borderlands of Westmeath, Cavan, and Sligo. Official glee at this thriving plantation was muted by the religious nonconformity of much of the new population. The old problem of Catholic primitivism had not been superseded but was simply complicated by that of a cohesive Ulster Scots Presbyterianism.

This vigorous interest in Ulster, prone still to reverses, fuelled itself. The practical toleration allowed to Presbyterian worship, occasionally rescinded, contrasted with the more systematic repression in Scotland under John Maitland, Duke of Lauderdale, in the 1670s, and forced more, at least temporarily, over the Northern Channel.[55] These impulses seconded the other force which was strengthening the settler population: natural increase. In the south Antrim parish of Blaris, coinciding partly with Lisburn, between 1661 and 1700 baptisms averaged an

[53] Bp. John Evans to Abp. Wake, 30 April 1717, Christ Church, Oxford, Wake MSS, XII, f. 149^{v}; W. Macafee and V. Morgan, 'Population in Ulster, 1660–1760', in P. Roebuck, ed., *Plantation to Partition: Essays in Ulster History in Honour of J. L. McCracken* (Belfast, 1981), p. 58; T. C. Smout, N. C. Landsman, and T. M. Devine, 'Scottish Emigration in the Seventeenth and Eighteenth Centuries', in Nicholas Canny, ed., *Europeans on the Move: Studies on European Migration, 1500–1800* (Oxford, 1994), p. 88.

[54] Raymond Gillespie, 'The Presbyterian Revolution in Ulster, 1660–1690', in W. J. Shiels and D. Wood, eds., *The Churches, Ireland and the Irish, Studies in Church History*, XXV (1989), p. 159; J. S. Reid, *History of the Presbyterian Church in Ireland* (Belfast, 1867), ed. W. D. Killen, II, pp. 380–81, 589–91.

[55] Barnard, 'Scotland and Ireland in the Later Stewart Monarchy', p. 261.

annual 150.2 and burials only 55.2. Furthermore, a low age at marriage, thanks to the relative ease of household and family formation, encouraged the population to grow.[56] By 1733, when enquiries ascertained the confessional balance of Ireland's inhabitants, Ulster recorded 62,624 Protestant families, containing perhaps 300,000 people, about 60 per cent of the Protestants of Ireland.[57] This remarkable increase since the 1630s, if built partly on foundations laid then, testified to the continuing power of natural impulses to draw immigrants into Ireland. Even so, this influx, apparently unique to Ulster, created an imbalance. The Irish Protestant interest, always held in uneasy equilibrium between competing territorial, ethnic, and confessional groups, was now shifting decisively in Ulster's favour. The demographic process had a more visible counterpart in the speed and success with which a mafia from north-western Ulster colonized the institutions of the Irish Protestant state and even the London business and banking worlds after 1690. During the revolution of the 1650s the supple Munster Protestants had used Cromwell's presence and their own intimacy with the conquerors to secure favours.[58] In and after 1690 Ulster Protestants, to the fore in resisting Catholic aggression, celebrated for their heroism at Derry and Enniskillen, and at Carrickfergus the hosts of William of Orange, rallied quickly and wholeheartedly to their Protestant deliverer. Over the next decades they rewarded themselves and utilized the contacts already offered by the London trading companies, owners of substantial tracts of Ulster, to move into city life.[59]

New immigrants, arriving after 1650, precisely because they were late-comers took their place alongside the longer established. Often they waited their turn, unless especially favoured and thrusting, while the descendants of the Elizabethan and early Stuart settlers collected peerages and the other rewards for long and loyal service. In the geology of Protestant Ireland the Cromwellian and later settlers could still be distinguished as a recent and distinctive stratum, and one which was integral to the cliff-face of the Protestant Ascendancy. This latest deposit took time to be accommodated within the already complicated structure of Protestant Ireland, and longer still into the sophisticated society of the whole kingdom. The attention that it attracted, both at the time and subsequently, has given it an

[56] W. H. Crawford, 'Landlord–Tenant Relations in Ulster, 1609–1820', *IEcSH*, II (1975), p. 10; Gillespie, *Settlement and Survival*, p. xix; V. Morgan, 'A Case Study of Population Change over Two Centuries: Blaris, Lisburn, 1661–1848', *IEcSH*, III (1976), pp. 8–15.

[57] *An Abstract of the Number of Protestant and Popish Families* (Dublin, 1734), p. 6.

[58] T. C. Barnard, 'Irish Images of Cromwell', in R. C. Richardson, ed., *Images of Oliver Cromwell: Essays for and by Roger Howell* (Manchester, 1993), pp. 190–91.

[59] J. Bonnell to H. Conyngham [*c*.1693–98], NLI, Ainsworth Report, no. 381, p. 2716; W. Conolly to W. Crookshanks, 30 April 1692, PRONI, D 1449/2/15; L. M. Cullen, 'Landlords, Bankers and Merchants: the Early Irish Banking World, 1700–1820', *Hermathena*, CXXXV (1983), pp. 28, 31–32; Alexander Nesbitt, *History of the Family of Nisbet or Nesbitt in Scotland and Ireland* (Torquay, 1898), pp. 37–40.

importance in the history of Ireland that neither its numbers nor its impact really deserve. The fresh settlement, decreed by an English state trapped in outmoded thinking, coincided only loosely with the economic and social imperatives which had powered earlier migrations to Ireland. Protestants, refugees from continental persecutions or the footloose seeking betterment, arrived, but in small numbers. In the absence of a numerous soldiery and affluent adventurers, this final phase of forcible resettlement benefited those already in Ireland or the immigrants into Ulster.

English misapprehensions about what was appropriate and possible in Ireland were encapsulated by the Lord-Lieutenant in 1674. The kingdom, he believed, after a few months of grappling with its intractability, had to be treated 'as a plantation (for in reality it is little other)'.[60] Such an opinion persisted among those charged with the making and implementation of English policy. Generally, however, it did not long survive immersion in the divided but sophisticated society. Greater realism was exhibited by the next viceroy, Ormonde, who, in 1679, concluded that projects often failed in Ireland because their directors assumed 'this place to be as desert as the unplanted parts of America and that they should have land for nothing'.[61] Ormonde, as head of the greatest lineage which negotiated the transition from the older systems of kinship and custom to the new brutalism, was one of many, acutely aware of ancestry and responsibilities as 'the English of Ireland', who corrected English crassness. Mid-seventeenth-century Ireland, notwithstanding victory, pillage, and clearances, never resembled 'a white paper' on which immigrants could inscribe whatever they pleased. The residue from the past settlements stained the supposedly clean sheet, so that the crude geometry of the new plantation, when not obliterated, was blurred as the earlier configurations showed through.

[60] Lord Essex to C. Harbord, 28 March 1674, Bodleian, Add. MSS, C. 34, f. 71; F. Brewster, *Essays on Trade and Navigation* (London, 1695), pp. 13–14.

[61] Ormonde to C. Wyche, 17 Feb. 1678[9], National Archives, Dublin, Wyche MSS, 1/1/28.

Select Bibliography

J. Agnew, *Belfast Merchant Families in the Seventeenth Century* (Dublin, 1996).

L. J. Arnold, *The Restoration Land Settlement in County Dublin, 1660–1688* (Dublin, 1993).

T. C. Barnard, *Cromwellian Ireland: English Government and Reform in Ireland* (Oxford, 1975).

—— 'The Political, Material and Mental Culture of the Cork Settlers, *c.*1650–1700', in P. O'Flanagan and C. G. Buttimer, eds., *Cork: History and Society* (Dublin, 1993).

—— 'Land and the Limits of Loyalty: The Second Earl of Cork and First Earl of Burlington, 1612–1698', in T. Barnard and J. Clark, eds., *Lord Burlington: Architecture, Art and Life* (London, 1995).

K. S. Bottigheimer, *English Money and Irish Land: The 'Adventurers' in the Cromwellian Settlement of Ireland, 1690–1703* (Oxford, 1971).
—— 'The Restoration Land Settlement in Ireland: A Structural View', *Irish Historical Studies*, XVIII (1972).
S. J. Connolly, *Religion, Law and Power: The Making of Protestant Ireland, 1660–1760* (Oxford, 1992).
L. M. Cullen, *The Emergence of Modern Ireland, 1600–1900* (London, 1981).
—— 'The Irish Diaspora of the Seventeenth and Eighteenth Centuries', in Nicholas Canny, ed., *Europeans on the Move: Studies on European Migration, 1500–1800* (Oxford, 1994).
David Dickson, C. Ó. Gráda, and S. Daultrey, 'Hearth Tax, Household Size and Irish Population Change, 1672–1821', in *Proceedings of the Royal Irish Academy*, LXXXII, 100 (1982).
Raymond Gillespie, 'The Presbyterian Revolution in Ulster, 1660–1690', in W. J. Shiels and D. Wood, eds., *The Churches, Ireland and the Irish: Studies in Church History*, XXV (1989).
D. W. Hayton, 'From Barbarian to Burlesque: English Images of the Irish, *c.*1660–1750', *Irish Economic and Social History*, XV (1988).
S. Pender, ed., *A Census of Ireland, circa 1659* (Dublin, 1939).
R. C. Simington, ed., *The Civil Survey, A.D. 1654–56*, 10 vols. (Dublin, 1931–61).
—— ed., *Books of Survey and Distribution*, 4 vols. (Dublin, 1944–67).
—— ed., *The Transplantation to Connacht, 1654–58* (Dublin, 1970).
J. G. Simms, *The Williamite Confiscation in Ireland, 1690–1703* (London, 1956).
—— *Jacobite Ireland, 1685–91* (London, 1969).
—— *War and Politics in Ireland, 1649–1730*, ed. D. W. Hayton and G. O'Brien (London, 1986).

15

Native Americans and Europeans in English America, 1500–1700

PETER C. MANCALL

The much-studied encounter between the group of settlers led by Thomas Hariot and the Indians on Roanoke Island encapsulates the dilemma that would confront all English colonizers, and indeed all Europeans, in their dealings with Native Americans over the next hundred years. Hariot conveyed the reassuring news that future colonists would have no reason to be uneasy about the 'naturall inhabitants' of that region, for 'in respect of troubling our inhabiting and planting', the Indians 'shall have cause both to feare and love us, that shall inhabite with them'.[1] At the time that he wrote, Hariot knew a great deal about the particular Indians he had met on Roanoke Island, but he can have had only the vaguest notion of the number and variety of native societies that then inhabited the continent of North America; he could not have imagined the scale and nature of settlement that would soon be attempted by his countrymen and other Europeans along the coastline of North America. Yet his appraisal of likely contacts between the two peoples was prophetic; sustained contact between English settlers and Indians often bred distrust which flared into major conflagrations in different areas in the 1620s, 1630s, 1640s, and 1670s. But in spite of these violent outbursts natives and newcomers repeatedly made efforts to maintain peace and trading relations.

In 1500 perhaps 560,000 Indians lived in the territory that became the principal theatre of European colonization efforts (Table 15.1). Most of the indigenous peoples, especially those south of the Saco-Kennebec watershed (in modern-day Maine), concentrated on agriculture and hunting for their subsistence; those to the north relied more heavily on hunting alone. Native economies were generally gender-segregated, with women farming while men hunted and fished. Each group had its own political system designed to maintain internal order and negotiate with outsiders, as well as its own set of religious beliefs. Groups also differed in appearance. The Aberginians (probably Passaconaways, Penacooks, or another group to the north of Massachusetts Bay) were 'between five or six foot

[1] T. Hariot, *A Briefe and True Report of the New Found Land of Virginia* (1590; New York, 1972), p. 24.

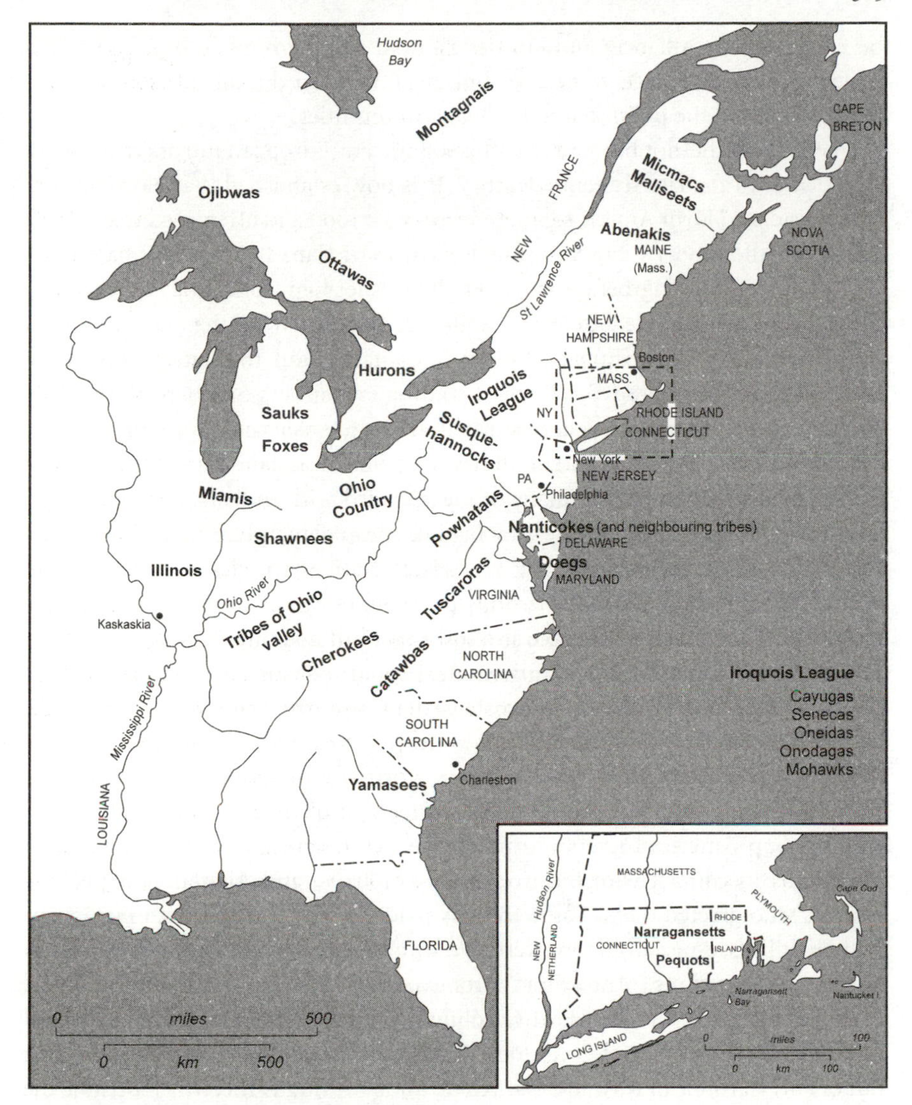

MAP 15.1. Native Americans in Eastern North America

high' according to one observer, while the Susquehannocks, by contrast, 'seemed like Giants to the English'. Native groups' desire for contact with Europeans also varied; Tomahittans, who inhabited the mountains of Virginia, had little contact with colonists as late as 1670 even though other Indians had by that time had long experience of the English.[2] Finally, politics throughout Indian country tended to

[2] William Wood, *New England's Prospect* [London, 1634], ed. Alden Vaughan (Amherst, Mass., 1977), p. 82; John Smith, 'A Map of Virginia' [London, 1612], in Philip Barbour, ed., *The Complete Works of*

be village-based. Alliances and kin ties allowed some groups to organize themselves beyond the village, to be sure, but even the most durable of these associations hinged on the politics of individual communities.

The English did not become the most significant European intruders in North America until the late sixteenth century. It is now established that Norse adventurers reached North America sometime after AD 1000 and attempted to establish 'Vinland' (the modern-day Maritime Provinces of Canada), but they had abandoned this effort long before 1500.[3] English fishermen, following or preceding John Cabot who landed in Newfoundland in 1497, were the next group of Europeans to make an impact, but their contacts with the native population were sporadic and were typically brief trading encounters on board the English ships or on the shore.[4] French, Spanish, and Basque fishermen were more active than the English in quest of cod off the coast of Newfoundland during the first half of the sixteenth century, and many of these traded with Indians, particularly for beaver and marten to supply the growing European demand for furs. Continental Europeans soon became familiar to coastal Native Americans ranging from Florida to Canada, and inland groups perched along major rivers such as the Susquehanna and the St Lawrence also soon encountered travellers eager to barter manufactured goods for pelts. Promotional propaganda for such ventures, such as the stories circulated about Jacques Cartier's dealings with the St Lawrence Iroquois, stressed the Indians' willingness to treat visitors with kindness.

European efforts to find the ever-elusive North-west Passage and a quick water route to the great Asian market on the other side of their world led still more explorers up American rivers during the sixteenth century. Such ventures kept Europeans in contact with the Iroquoian-, Siouan-, and Algonquian-speaking peoples who greeted them. Some Indians paid for their contact with Europeans with their lives, especially if they were sold into slavery or carted around Europe to entertain the curious.[5] And some Europeans remained in North America. The French established a post at Fort Caroline, in modern-day Florida, in 1562, and immediately began to trade with local Timucuas. The Spanish forced the French out of Fort Caroline in 1565, and that year founded St Augustine, which became the

Captain John Smith, 3 vols. (Chapel Hill, NC, 1986), I, p. 149; James H. Merrell, '"The Customes of Our Countrey": Indians and Colonists in Early America', in Bernard Bailyn and Philip D. Morgan, eds., *Strangers Within the Realm: Cultural Margins of the First British Empire* (Chapel Hill, NC, 1991), p. 119.

[3] See Alfred Crosby, *Ecological Imperialism: The Biological Expansion of Europe, 900–1900* (Cambridge, 1986), pp. 44–56.

[4] James A. Williamson, *The Cabot Voyages and Bristol Discovery Under Henry VII*, Hakluyt Society, Second Series, CXX (Cambridge, 1962), pp. 91–92; James Axtell, 'At the Water's Edge: Trading in the Sixteenth Century', in Axtell, ed., *After Columbus: Essays in the Ethnohistory of Colonial North America* (New York, 1988), p. 171.

[5] Axtell, 'At the Water's Edge', pp. 145–81; and see above, p. 161.

most important European settlement in the south-east until the founding of Charles Town in 1670. Like the French, the Spanish eagerly traded with Indians, though they used the settlement as a base for missionary activities as well. Elsewhere in New Spain (in modern-day New Mexico) Spanish traders had obtained the hides of bison and antelope; in Florida they got mostly deerskins. They sent skins directly to Europe, but also to Cuba, where Dutch traders bought them for the leather market in Amsterdam.[6]

In 1565 John Hawkins, captain of the *Jesus of Lübeck*, led an English expedition to the Florida coast, and in describing the natural resources and inhabitants of the region he concluded that 'the commodities of this land are more than are yet known to any man'. These, however, did not include gold and silver, such as had made the Spanish rich, and therefore did not encourage Hawkins to settle.[7]

Wherever Europeans arrived—whether they were Spanish in the south-east or smaller numbers of French, Dutch, and English in territory stretching from Delaware Bay to Canada—they brought Old World epidemic diseases. The first explorers unwittingly transported pathogens across the Atlantic Ocean, thereby beginning a demographic catastrophe that increased in intensity during the seventeenth century. The Indian population of eastern North America fell by 59,000 over the course of the sixteenth century, a loss of approximately 10.5 per cent (Table 15.1).

TABLE 15.1. *Indian and colonist demography, 1500–1700*

	1500	1600	1700
Indians			
North-east	357,700	345,700	149,360
South-east	204,400	157,400	105,125
TOTAL	562,100	503,100	254,485
Colonists			
North-east	—	—	145,900
Chesapeake & South-east	—	300*	114,500
TOTAL	—	300	260,400

Note: *Figure for 1610.

Sources: Douglas H. Ubelaker, 'North American Indian Population Size: Changing Perspectives', in John W. Verano and Douglas H. Ubelaker, eds., *Disease and Demography in the Americas* (Washington, 1992), p. 172; John J. McCusker and Russell R. Menard, *Economy of British America* (Chapel Hill, NC, 1985), pp. 103, 136, 173, 203.

[6] Gregory A. Waselkov, 'Seventeenth-Century Trade in the Colonial Southeast', *Southeastern Archaeology*, VIII (1989), pp. 117–18.

[7] 'The Voyage Made by Master John Hawkins . . .', in Richard Hakluyt, *Principall Navigations* (1589), reprinted in Louis B. Wright, ed., *The Elizabethans' America* (Cambridge, Mass., 1966), pp. 36–45, quotations at 41, 45.

It is difficult to trace sixteenth-century epidemics with any precision since Indians did not need sustained contact with Europeans to become ill. Hernando de Soto's rapid sixteenth-century *entrada* quite possibly spread Old World pathogens in the south-east.[8] More likely, diseases moved inland from the coast, and from one Indian group to another along traditional paths earlier travelled by native traders, warriors, and diplomats. Diseases that rarely killed the Europeans who had brought them (most of whom had encountered these illnesses as children and thus gained immunities to them) became lethal when unleashed among Indians during 'virgin soil' epidemics. Influenza made its first appearance among Indians in 1559 in the south-east and struck the north-east in 1647. Smallpox, the deadliest disease, apparently raced through much of North America in the early 1520s, and the Great Lakes region and New France experienced another epidemic in the early 1590s. By the mid-seventeenth century measles, scarlet fever (though not yet identified), and diphtheria had probably all taken their toll.[9]

At the same time that Eurasian diseases undermined native communities, European goods transformed Indians' material culture. Native Americans welcomed trade with colonists, since Europeans offered goods that natives soon adapted to customary practices; newcomers were likewise eager to accept the goods offered by Indians. Native Americans often controlled the exchange of goods, and Europeans realized that trading sessions needed to be festive occasions, filled with music and socializing rather than hard bargaining. Metal tools, such as axes and fish-hooks, which could replace indigenous wares; kettles, which could be cut up and used for jewellery; woven coats and shirts; and a variety of goods such as glass beads, mirrors, mouth-organs, and combs soon became common in native villages.[10] Some European goods, notably glassware and copper products, were quickly integrated into sacred rites since Indians believed these commodities were similar to indigenous copper, shells, and rare stones already used in rituals.[11]

Many Indians reoriented their lives to pursue the new goods. Some groups in modern New York were so interested in trade that they abandoned their earlier migratory ways and within decades of contact settled near the shore, where they could more easily participate in trade as both consumers of European goods and producers of wampum, strings of beads made from shells harvested on Atlantic

[8] See Ann F. Ramenofsky, *Vectors of Death: The Archaeology of European Contact* (Albuquerque, N. Mex., 1987), p. 71.

[9] Henry F. Dobyns, *Their Number Become Thinned: Native American Population Dynamics in Eastern North America* (Knoxville, Tenn., 1983), pp. 11–16; see also Alfred W. Crosby, *The Columbian Exchange: Biological and Cultural Consequences of 1492* (Westport, Conn., 1972), pp. 35–63, and *Ecological Imperialism*, pp. 195–216.

[10] Axtell, 'At the Water's Edge', pp. 154–61.

[11] Christopher L. Miller and George R. Hammell, 'A New Perspective on Indian–White Contact: Cultural Symbols and Colonial Trade', *Journal of American History*, LXXIII (1986), pp. 311–28.

beaches that were used as currency.[12] From the Gulf of Maine to the south-east, native groups tried to integrate themselves into trade relations with Europeans.[13]

Although Europeans stayed near the shore, their goods almost immediately penetrated the interior, carried along aboriginal trade routes. European wares appeared in Iroquoia (modern-day New York State) by the middle of the sixteenth century, long before Indians there had extensive contact with colonists. In Iroquoia as elsewhere, natives who adopted European goods often used these commodities for religious as well as utilitarian purposes. In particular, they incorporated European products into the parcels of goods buried in rituals designed to prepare the dead for the afterlife.[14] On the sites of former Seneca villages in western New York, archaeologists have found pieces of delftware, a silver wine taster apparently made in London in 1576, and a brass mirror box adorned with an image of the mid-sixteenth-century Dutch leader William of Orange (William the Silent), on horseback.[15]

It is impossible to separate the effects of disease and trade, at least in terms of relations between Europeans and Native Americans. Each had political and diplomatic consequences. Desire for European goods and negotiating advantage led groups of Indians to establish confederacies. It is no coincidence that the sixteenth century witnessed the rise of the Huron confederacy in southern Ontario, the Powhatan confederacy near Chesapeake Bay, and the final development of the Iroquois confederacy in territory lying between the Great Lakes and the Hudson River. To gain the best terms with Europeans, and the better to defend themselves against enemies (European and Indian), these natives created political alliances to strengthen their internal cohesion and thereby increase their numbers in an age of demographic collapse. During the seventeenth century these alliances shaped much of the emerging economic and diplomatic culture of eastern North America.[16]

During the 1580s a few determined and far-sighted people in England wanted to move beyond simple trade with the Indians to establish permanent colonies in

[12] Lynn Ceci, 'The Effect of European Contact and Trade on the Settlement Pattern of Indians in Coastal New York, 1524–1665', Ph.D. dissertation, City University of New York, 1977 (pub. New York, 1990), esp. pp. 277–83.

[13] Bruce J. Bourque and Ruth H. Whitehead, 'Tarrentines and the Introduction of European Trade Goods in the Gulf of Maine', *Ethnohistory*, XXXII (1985), pp. 327–41; Waselkov, 'Seventeenth-Century Trade', pp. 118–19.

[14] Daniel K. Richter, *The Ordeal of the Longhouse: The Peoples of the Iroquois League in the Era of European Colonization* (Chapel Hill, NC, 1992), p. 52.

[15] Charles F. Wray and Harry L. Schoff, 'A Preliminary Report on the Seneca Sequence in Western New York, 1550–1687', *Pennsylvania Archaeologist*, XXIII (1953), pp. 53–63; see also Donald A. Rumrill, 'An Interpretation and Analysis of the Seventeenth Century Mohawk Nation: Its Chronology and Movements', *Bulletin and Journal of Archaeology for New York State*, XC (1985), p. 26.

[16] Axtell, 'At the Water's Edge', pp. 180–81.

North America which would rival, and perhaps overthrow, those settlements established by the Iberians in Central and South America. The first serious effort at colonization in North America was the attempt by Hariot on Roanoke Island. The more astute colonizers recognized that the essential key to success, at least in the short term, was the establishment of peaceful relations with the natives. Consistent with this hope was the observation made in 1584 by Arthur Barlowe, an associate of Sir Walter Ralegh, that the people were 'most gentle, loving, and faithfull, void of all guile and treason, and such as lived after the manner of the golden age'. To sustain his point Barlowe marvelled how 'the earth bringeth foorth all things in aboundance as in the first creation, without toile or labour'.[17]

Such reports encouraged English settlement in 1585, and the most influential tract of the age, Thomas Hariot's *A Briefe and True Report of the New Found Land of Virginia*, first published in 1588, described the Roanoke encounter. Hariot was an ideal chronicler of North America's resources and peoples; he possessed a keen eye and an abiding interest in the natural world and he also knew some Carolina Algonquian, which he learned from Manteo and Wanchese, two Indians who had been taken captive and transported to England in 1584.[18]

Hariot used his linguistic skill to give one of the most accurate ethnographic accounts of any Native American group. With John White, whose paintings of early North Carolina were engraved by Theodor de Bry and appeared in the 1590 edition of the *Report*, Hariot gave the early modern English their first in-depth look at America's peoples. The Indians in the *Report* were civil with each other, inhabited orderly towns, and maintained an economic system resembling, in some ways, that of an English village. Hariot paid particular attention to the Indians' appearance, abodes, and religious beliefs. 'Some religion they have alreadie,' he wrote, 'which although it be farre from the truth, yet beyng [as] it is, there is hope it may bee the easier and sooner reformed.'[19]

But not all English colonizers shared Hariot's hopes. Ralph Lane, the Governor of Roanoke during 1585–86, feared that Indians once willing to accept Christianity had begun 'to blaspheme, and flatly to say, that our Lord God was not God, since hee suffered us to sustaine much hunger. . . .'. Lane feared that the natives 'woulde have knocked out my braynes' and possessed 'villanous purposes against us'; he therefore responded to an apparent Algonquian plot to kill the colonists by killing several Indian leaders, including the headman, Wingina. With this memory still

[17] Barlowe, 'The First Voyage Made to the Coasts of America . . .', in Richard Hakluyt, *The Principall Navigations, Voiages and Discoveries of the English Nation*, 2 vols. (1589; Cambridge, 1965), II, p. 731; also on Roanoke see above, pp. 152–53.

[18] Karen Ordahl Kupperman, *Roanoke: The Abandoned Colony* (Savage, Md., 1984), p. 17; see above, pp. 162–63.

[19] Hariot, *A Briefe and True Report*, pp. 25–26.

fresh when he returned to England, Lane saw little purpose in any further colonization of the area unless Europeans discovered profitable mines there or perhaps 'a passage to the Southsea'.[20]

In the end, neither Hariot's optimism nor Lane's pessimism mattered much to the migrants: the Roanoke colonists vanished by the end of the 1580s, thereby bringing a mysterious end to the first sustained English contacts with American natives. Yet, although other colonization efforts also went awry—including English hopes for a colony in the Amazon and Sir Walter Ralegh's ill-fated effort to establish an English presence in Guiana—the colonizing impetus was not deterred by failure.[21]

Descriptions of America and its peoples that circulated in England after the decline of Roanoke at times suggested the positive ties that colonists could make with natives. Of particular importance were reports of English sailors who encountered natives in the Caribbean basin, including the dreaded Caribs who were, the English had earlier believed, always eager to devour the flesh of Europeans. Time and again during the late sixteenth century English writers noted that Indians in the West Indies wanted to trade with them. The English were the beneficiaries in these transactions; they received necessary food as well as tobacco and other goods, including light fabric that protected them from mosquitoes.[22] Even the sailors on the ill-fated *Olive Branch*, most of whom were killed by Caribs on St Lucia, traded with Indians before and, remarkably, after the natives assaulted them. English sailors were on the verge of starvation after an attack when the natives brought food to trade. As John Nicholl recalled, the English then gave 'prayse to God (thus miraculously) for to feede us, for wee had no meanes of our selves to get any'.[23]

If even the bloodthirsty Caribs wanted to trade, the English realized, then the potential for establishing positive relations with any group of Indians was there. Indians needed to be 'reduced' to civilization, to be sure, to be tamed and made less haughty; English missionaries in the seventeenth century sought nothing less than the reformation of Indian societies on the mainland and in the Caribbean. But however culturally inferior America's native peoples were thought to be in

[20] David B. Quinn, ed., *The Roanoke Voyages, 1584–1590*, 2 vols. (1955; New York, 1991), I, pp. 277, 286, 288, 273; Edmund S. Morgan, *American Slavery, American Freedom: The Ordeal of Colonial Virginia* (New York, 1975), pp. 40–41.

[21] For the hopes for the Amazon, see Joyce Lorimer, ed., *English and Irish Settlement on the River Amazon, 1550–1646*, Hakluyt Society, Second Series, CLXXI (1989); for Ralegh, see Kupperman, *Roanoke*, pp. 150–58.

[22] See the reports of Sir Francis Drake, Robert Davies, and George Clifford (the Earl of Cumberland) from the 1590s, in Peter Hulme and Neil L. Whitehead, eds., *Wild Majesty: Encounters with Caribs from Columbus to the Present Day* (Oxford, 1992), pp. 54, 55–56, 58–59.

[23] Nicholl, *An Hour Glass of Indian Newes*... [London, 1607], in Hulme and Whitehead, eds., *Wild Majesty*, pp. 68–69, 72, 78; see also the report of William Turner on the same expedition in *Wild Majesty*, pp. 63–64.

1600, Elizabethans recognized that Indians could become vital diplomatic and commercial allies in any effort to colonize eastern North America.

When English colonists finally attempted to establish themselves on mainland America (at Jamestown in 1607 and Plymouth in 1620), they recognized that their survival depended upon their ability to establish trading relations with the Indians they encountered. This was necessary because settlers could not, during the early years of settlement, grow sufficient food to meet their requirements and they relied on the Indians to supply them with their surplus. The Indians, for their part, were attracted to the metal and manufactured goods offered them by the Europeans in exchange for food, and the ensuing trade made it possible for the settlers in both Jamestown and Plymouth to endure their initial travails. Endurance meant expansion, and the survival of Plymouth opened the way for the 'Great Migration' of Puritans during the 1630s which led to the founding of Massachusetts Bay. These crucial early experiences in both areas proved that natives and newcomers could coexist, but tensions also arose which suggested that relations would be plagued by destructive misunderstandings and deadly encounters.

When discussing Jamestown it is important to bear in mind that this was only one settlement among many established by Europeans during the first decade of the seventeenth century. This decade also marked the starting-point for French colonization in Canada, initiated by Samuel de Champlain in 1603 and consolidated by him when he founded Quebec in 1608. In the same period, Dutch colonization in North America began with the voyage of Henry Hudson up the river that still bears his name. When these incursions are added to Spanish expansion in Florida, it appears that the straggling settlements of the English were relatively inconsequential, and there is no reason to imagine they would have appeared more significant to Native Americans than any other European settlement.

Yet, though it needs to be set in context, the Jamestown experience is important because it foreshadowed the sorts of relationships that often brought English and Indians together—and drove them apart—over the course of the seventeenth century. The Virginia Company explicitly ordered its servants 'to have great care not to offend' the Indians, and also instructed them to trade for food. The Powhatans who controlled the area seemingly welcomed the newcomers, and their recently elected *werowance* (headman), Powhatan (Wahunsonacock) seems to have sensed that access to English trade-goods would place him in a position to redistribute them among his subordinates and would thus strengthen his control over the loose confederacy of perhaps thirty groups who inhabited the Virginia Tidewater.[24]

[24] James Axtell, 'The Rise and Fall of the Powhatan Empire', in Axtell, ed., *After Columbus*, pp. 183–87; Martin H. Quitt, 'Trade and Acculturation at Jamestown, 1607–1609: The Limits of Understanding', *William and Mary Quarterly* (hereafter *WMQ*), Third Series, LII (1995), pp. 227–58.

Indians and colonists therefore looked opportunistically across the cultural divide. Hence, the first meeting between the leaders of the settlement and Powhatan went well: Powhatan offered some of his own clothing—a fur mantle—to Captain Christopher Newport, who proffered English metal and glass in exchange, and they celebrated their encounter in typical English fashion with a toast.[25] However, English mismanagement kept settlers near the James River where the water gave them dysentery and typhoid, and they were subject to malaria. In the words of George Percy, eighth son of the eighth Earl of Northampton, '[t]here were never Englishmen left in a forreigne countrey in such miserie as wee were in this new discovered Virginia'.[26] Colonists who survived these diseases suffered from apathy induced by malnutrition and from irritability as a result of drinking salt water. As a result, they neglected to grow their own food.[27]

The insatiable demand of the English for food exhausted the patience of the Indians, who by 1609 had come to recognize that these were no transitory visitors. Their demand for greater parity in exchange with the colonists in turn annoyed Captain John Smith, and led eventually to the first 'Anglo-Powhatan' War. These sporadic hostilities were ended only in 1614 through the capture of Powhatan's daughter and her marriage to John Rolfe.[28] That marriage points to the willingness of some influential colonists of that time to contemplate converting the Indians to English ways,[29] but few other interracial marriages followed, and the English discovery of the economic potential of growing tobacco meant that they now began to covet Indian land as well as food. The ensuing tensions might have been resolved by Powhatan and the more scrupulous leaders of the colony, but the chief had died in 1618 and, by the early 1620s, the confederacy had come under the nominal control of Opechancanough. He at first had allowed the English to use Powhatan lands for their tobacco fields, and had so impressed the English with his co-operation that one colonist remarked that there were 'more motiones of religione in him then Coulde be ymagined'. However, experience with the English exhausted his patience also, and in March 1622 he led the attack which was intended by the Indians to end the English intrusion into their world and which resulted in the death of 347 colonists.[30]

[25] Axtell, 'Rise and Fall of the Powhatan Empire', pp. 191–93.

[26] Percy, 'A Discourse of the Plantation of the Southern Colonie in Virginia', in David B. Quinn and Alison O. Quinn, eds., *New American World*, 5 vols. (New York, 1979), III, pp. 273–74.

[27] Carville Earle, 'Environment, Disease, and Mortality in Early Virginia', in Thad Tate and David Ammerman, eds., *The Chesapeake in the Seventeenth Century* (Chapel Hill, NC, 1979), pp. 96–125; Karen Ordahl Kupperman, 'Apathy and Death in Early Jamestown', *Journal of American History*, LXVI (1979), pp. 24–40.

[28] Quitt, 'Trade and Acculturation at Jamestown', pp. 244–58. See above, pp. 175–76.

[29] See above, pp. 158–60.

[30] Morgan, *American Slavery, American Freedom*, pp. 97–99.

Though some of the English grasped that the Indian attack was motivated by the fear that the newcomers 'would dispossesse them of this country', most interpreted the natives assault as a betrayal of trust which justified revenge by every possible means. The events of 1622 therefore mark a decisive shift in English–Indian relations, and thenceforth the English believed that even the most friendly Indian was a potential killer. The colonists avenged the death of their comrades by giving poisoned wine to 200 Indians, by ambushing another fifty in 1623, and by killing 800 in battle in July 1624.

The economic collapse of the Virginia Company did not slow down the colonization of the Chesapeake. Rather, the prospect of making money on tobacco lured more settlers, and the population-base of the colony became more stable after the 1620s. Natives did not give way everywhere to newcomers, and groups such as the Piscataways in Maryland survived by adapting their culture to that of the now dominant English.[31] However, the Powhatans experienced difficulty in maintaining a presence in the area they had so recently controlled, as each incoming English ship brought young men (and some young women) whose arrival as a labour force meant further land under cultivation. The Powhatans under Opechancanough planned one desperate effort to recover their lost power and rose in rebellion on 18 April 1644, perhaps the bloodiest day for the English in seventeenth-century America. However, the assault did not stop the growth of the colony, which had already reached a population figure of 10,000 by 1644. The futility of the last Powhatan effort to resist encroachment was symbolized by the capture of Opechancanough and by his humiliating incarceration in Jamestown, where one guard took matters into his own hands and shot him in the back.[32]

To the north, developments took a different course. The Algonquian-speaking Indians who inhabited coastal New England had, by the early seventeenth century, long-standing contact with Europeans, though not much contact with English colonizers. Instead, these Indians had been trading with the French and, to a lesser extent, the Dutch, for most of the sixteenth century. In 1602 Bartholomew Gosnold, who had the support of the Earl of Southampton, led an expedition to New England to establish the first English settlement in North America since Roanoke. When they arrived, the English discovered that the Indians already possessed European trade goods. Further, as Gabriel Archer reported, the Indians also spoke 'divers Christian words, and seemed to understand much more than we, for want of Language could comprehend'. Gosnold knew that the way to establish ties with the Indians was through trade, and he and his crew offered

[31] James H. Merrell, 'Cultural Continuity among the Piscataway Indians of Colonial Maryland', *WMQ*, Third Series, XXXVI (1979), pp. 548–70.

[32] Axtell, 'Rise and Fall of the Powhatan Empire', pp. 215–21; Ian K. Steele, *Warpaths: Invasions of North America* (New York, 1994), pp. 46–49.

goods in exchange for the natives' tobacco and food. But Gosnold did not understand the protocols necessary for sustaining alliances, and when he prevented Indians from entering a hastily constructed English fort on an island off Cape Cod, and added to this insult by then cutting off trade, the natives of the region drove the settlers out. In subsequent years the English remained unable to establish long-lasting ties to any particular coastal group. Their failure rested, at least in part, on their inability to grasp the central role that trade played in the maintenance of peaceful relations. Into the mid-1610s English explorers in New England gathered information about the regional environment and peoples, but they rarely sustained contacts with any Native American group.[33]

The 1610s proved as decisive in New England as they had been along the shores of the James River, but for different reasons. Between 1616 and 1618 an unknown epidemic, perhaps plague, struck New England, decimating the Algonquians who inhabited coastal regions. Travelling through New England in 1622, Thomas Morton could barely contain his shock at the carnage. The 'bones and skulls' of the unburied corpses 'made such a spectacle' that 'it seemed to me a new found Golgatha'. The Massachusetts and Pokanokets lost perhaps 90 per cent of their numbers in the epidemics.[34]

Soon after, the first large group of Puritans arrived at Plymouth, hoping to create a Bible commonwealth free of the persecutions they had experienced in England. To do so, the Puritan leaders recognized that they would have to make alliances with the surviving Indians in the region. But unlike earlier explorers, whose relations with the natives were limited to trade, the Puritans wanted to transform the Indians into Protestants. Their reading of scripture demanded not only that they try to extend their religion to Native Americans; the Bible also taught them that any who stood in their way must be subdued. John Winthrop, Governor of the Massachusetts Bay Company, justified the Puritans' stance in 1629, arguing that local Indians were not using the land as God had intended. '[F]or the Natives in New England they inclose noe land neither have any setled habitation nor any tame cattle to improve the land by,' Winthrop declared, '& soe have noe other but a naturall right to those countries Soe as if wee leave them sufficient for their use wee may lawfully take the rest, there being more then enough for them & us.' Winthrop even offered proof that he was right: God had already consumed 'the Natives wth a great plague in those parts soe as there be few inhabitants left'.[35]

[33] Neal Salisbury, *Manitou and Providence: Indians, Europeans, and the Making of New England, 1500–1643* (New York, 1980), pp. 85–96.

[34] Ibid., pp. 101–05.

[35] Winthrop, 'Reasons to Be Considered for Justifying the Undertakers of the Intended Plantation in New England and for Encouraging Such Whose Hearts God Shall Move to Join with Them in It', *Massachusetts Historical Society Proceedings*, VIII (1864–65), pp. 420–25. See above, pp. 42–43, 212.

With such an ideological arsenal in place, Puritans were poised to remake the landscape of New England. Forests needed to be cleared; residents had to establish year-round dwellings; fences had to demarcate property boundaries and rein in the livestock brought across the ocean by the English. The colonists had no understanding of how north-eastern Algonquians used the land. They never grasped the important role that forests and edge habitats played in regulating game or the logic of seasonal migrations to increase food supplies with minimal labour.[36] None of this mattered to the Puritans. They believed that God had a single vision for the proper ordering of an economy. Although the Almighty might be inscrutable, the message from the Lord was consistent: the Puritans were the servants of God and were doing God's work by creating their new society in New England; anyone who objected would suffer divine retribution. Still, although the Puritans' theology suggested specific and rigid plans for Indians, some migrants in the 1630s held out the hope that natives and immigrants could live as neighbours; William Wood's *New England's Prospect* (1634), for example, offered a systematic description of local Indian cultures and included a brief grammar for communicating with natives.

To survive in New England, colonists needed more than peaceful coexistence with local Indians; they also needed furs to pay off their creditors in London. To achieve their ends, the Puritans created ties to the Narragansetts and Pequots, who obtained shells used for wampum in Narragansett Bay and Long Island Sound and sold them to the Puritans. The colonists then used the shells in their dealings with Abenakis and other inland Indians who inhabited territory with larger populations of beaver. Wampum, which had flowed much more slowly and intermittently along aboriginal trade routes before the colonial period, became a major commodity in the emerging economy of New England. The English soon controlled this economy, and used the new trade system to gain peltry and solidify their ties to different Indian groups.[37]

But two events in the 1630s revealed the weakness of the system, as well as the power of the Puritans' vision. The first was a 1634 smallpox epidemic which, with the epidemic of 1616–19, reduced north-eastern Indian populations to somewhere between 5 and 15 per cent of the pre-1616 levels.[38] The epidemic was frightful, Plymouth's Governor William Bradford recalled, since 'they that have this disease have them in abundance, and for want of bedding and linen and other helps they fall into a lamentable condition as they lie on their hard mats, the pox breaking

[36] See William Cronon, *Changes in the Land: Indians, Colonists, and the Ecology of New England* (New York, 1983).

[37] Salisbury, *Manitou and Providence*, pp. 149–52.

[38] Dean R. Snow and Kim M. Lamphear, 'European Contact and Indian Depopulation in the Northeast: The Timing of the First Epidemics', *Ethnohistory*, XXXV (1988), p. 28.

and mattering and running one into another, their skin cleaving by reason thereof to the mats they lie on'. But, he wrote, 'by the marvelous goodness and providence of God, not one of the English was so much as sick or in the least measure tainted with this disease, though they daily' cared for the Indians.[39] This episode seemed to tell the Puritans that they had been right all along. By reshaping the ecology of New England to serve their own purposes—and in the process making it impossible for the natives to continue their traditional economic practices—the migrants were doing what God had intended.

Three years later the English received final confirmation that their policies toward Native Americans had divine favour. In 1637 Puritans worried that their pre-eminent position in the region might be threatened. In particular, they feared an alliance between the Pequots and the Narragansetts that could have cut off their supply of wampum and threatened their lives. A series of skirmishes between colonists and Pequots made the leaders of Plymouth and Connecticut wary. The English, Bradford recalled, realized that they 'could not long subsist but they would either be starved with hunger or be forced to forsake the country'. Fortunately for the English, the Narragansetts, seemingly concerned that the Pequots' supposed plans would threaten their own access to English goods, decided to reaffirm their alliance with the Puritans. Soon after, a group of Puritans and Narragansetts surrounded a large Pequot village on the Connecticut River before dawn, launched burning arrows into the compound, and then proceeded to shoot the Pequots who tried to escape. 'It was conceived they thus destroyed about 400 at this time,' Bradford wrote:

> It was a fearful sight to see them thus frying in the fire and the streams of blood quenching the same, and horrible was the stink and scent thereof; but the victory seemed a sweet sacrifice, and they gave the praise thereof to God, who had wrought so wonderfully for them, thus to enclose their enemies in their hands and give them so speedy a victory over so proud and insulting an enemy.[40]

Colonists captured some of the surviving Pequots, shipping them as far away as Providence Island to be slaves. By the end of the century hundreds of other Indians, most of them captured in battle, would also be sold into slavery.[41]

By 1637, then, Puritans came to believe that God had selected some Indians for destruction while other natives, who remained friendly to the English (especially those who hunted beaver or gathered shells for wampum), should remain commercial partners. The Puritans did not murder the doomed for no reason, nor did

[39] Bradford, *Of Plymouth Plantation*, ed. Samuel Eliot Morison (New York, 1952), pp. 270–71.

[40] Ibid., pp. 294–96.

[41] Karen Ordahl Kupperman, *Providence Island, 1630–1641: The Other Puritan Colony* (Cambridge, 1993), p. 172; Margaret E. Newell, '"The Drove of Adam's Degenerate Seed": Indian Slavery in Seventeenth-Century New England', paper presented at the First Annual Conference of the Institute for Early American History and Culture, June 1995.

the Pequot War, however horrific, signal the adoption of a genocidal programme to eliminate all Indians. Many Pequots, perhaps three-quarters, survived the conflict and resettled with other Indians or created new, identifiably Pequot, communities. Yet by reducing the Pequots and by consolidating their alliance with the Narragansetts, the Puritans in 1637 demonstrated their continued ability to distinguish between Indian allies and Indian enemies. Even more important, the events of 1637 also revealed that Indians in southern New England did not all share animosity toward the English. Like the colonists, Algonquians continued to make alliances that they believed were in their best interest.[42]

After 1637 colonists transformed the landscape of southern New England more rapidly. Their settlements spread into lands once controlled by Pequots, but Puritans also moved on to lands needed by Narragansetts and other coastal Algonquians. The political ties that had helped Puritans in 1637 ended up doing little for the Narragansetts, who witnessed the growth of the colonial population with increasing dismay. In 1642 Miantonomo, a Narragansett sachem (chief), described what had happened. '[Y]ou know our fathers had plenty of deer and skins, our plains were full of deer, as also our woods, and of turkies, and our coves full of fish and fowl,' he declared. 'But these English having gotten our land, they with scythes cut down the grass, and with axes fell the trees; their cows and horses eat the grass, and their hogs spoil our clam banks, and we shall all be starved.' Ecological abundance for one people had disappeared in little more than a generation. The economy of the colonists would thereafter prevail, and there was little any Indian group could do to shift its course.[43]

Still, the Pequot War of 1637 and the suppression of the Powhatans' uprising in 1644 did not eradicate trade between English colonists and Native Americans. During the middle of the century New England Indians adopted a greater variety of colonial goods and incorporated Old World livestock purchased from colonists into their economies. Many colonists, for their part, also sought to secure their relations with the indigenous peoples of the region. In 1643 Roger Williams published *A Key to the Language of America*, a tract intended to facilitate reasoned discussion between the peoples of New England.[44] But alliances made to increase access to European trade goods had proved double-edged for natives. Although some Indians got the goods, the growing numbers of colonists threatened the livelihood of any nearby Indian village.

[42] See Steven Katz, 'The Pequot War Reconsidered', *New England Quarterly* (hereafter *NEQ*) (1991), pp. 206–24.

[43] Salisbury, *Manitou and Providence*, p. 13; Cronon, *Changes in the Land*, pp. 159–70.

[44] Roger Williams, *A Key into the Language of America, or an Help to the Language of the Natives in that Part of America called New England* (orig. pub. London, 1643), in *Collections of the Rhode-Island Historical Society*, I (1827); see above, pp. 163–64.

From 1650 to the end of the century relations between the peoples of eastern North America were often even more fractious than they had been between 1500 and 1650, especially during the 1670s. Yet those tensions did not lead to a permanent rift between Indians and the growing numbers of English colonists in their midst. Missionary activities, already evident from the north-east to the West Indies, increased during the second half of the century; the founding of Pennsylvania, with the Quakers' attempt to establish positive relations with local Indians, suggested that many English colonizers remained more interested in reforming Native Americans than eliminating them. The latter decades of the century also witnessed the emergence of the liquor trade, a commerce that often poisoned any surviving goodwill between Indians and colonists.

The most dramatic moments in Indian–colonist relations took place in the Chesapeake and New England. The violence in Virginia in the 1670s was symptomatic of simmering hostilities between Indians who had survived the first wave of English population growth and colonists who felt bolder in dealing with Native Americans. The conflict, which would soon escalate into the uprising known as Bacon's Rebellion, began in July 1675 when some Doegs, who then inhabited territory in Maryland, stole some hogs from a colonist in Virginia, claiming that he owed them money. The settler disagreed, and fighting between local colonists and the Indians led to deaths on both sides, fuelling animosity among other colonists who, in separate incidents, killed eleven Doegs and fourteen Susquehannocks, perhaps believing they were responsible for the initial violence. The Susquehannocks then launched retaliatory raids, from an abandoned Piscataway fort in Maryland, on colonists in Virginia. Not all Indians took up arms against the English; the Occaneechees initially helped Nathaniel Bacon, the backcountry organizer of the rebellion, to capture the Susquehannocks. Yet after Bacon killed the captives, his forces then turned on the Occaneechees and murdered them.

Such hostility fits the prevailing mood of late seventeenth-century Virginia. After all, Governor William Berkeley himself had recently noted that Indians were conspiring to wipe out colonists 'in all the western parts of America'. After Bacon's assault on the Occaneechees, Berkeley wrote that all Indians were in league with the Susquehannocks; he urged his subordinates 'to spare none that has the name of an Indian for they are now all our Enemies'. Though Bacon's Rebellion unleashed a wave of hostility against Indians in Virginia, even here Indians and colonists later formed alliances.[45]

In New England, violence too broke out in the mid-1670s, on a scale even greater than in Virginia. But the origins of the conflict there were more complicated, and stemmed in part from changes in Indian–colonist relations since the Pequot War.

[45] Morgan, *American Slavery, American Freedom*, pp. 250–70, quotations at 256 and 260.

After that earlier fighting, some Puritan missionaries, most notably John Eliot, had made strenuous efforts to convert the Indians of southern New England to English ways. To do so, the missionaries had to teach the Indians Christianity. They also had to get Native Americans to abandon their annual migrations and adopt sedentary agriculture. Although the task was enormous, Eliot and other missionaries discovered that many natives welcomed the changes and agreed to abide by the colonists' rules. Whatever their reasons for changing their ways, perhaps 1,100 'Praying Indians' came to inhabit the new settlements, the largest being at Natick, Massachusetts. Although some Indians, such as the Wampanoag sachem Metacom (King Philip to the English), rejected Eliot's call for conversion, they too adopted aspects of English material culture, notably the raising of livestock, even though the changes often entailed altering traditional life-styles.[46]

But not all natives adopted English livestock, and many came to believe that the praying Indians' acceptance of cattle and hogs, as well as of missionaries, signalled dangerous inroads into customary practices. Not surprisingly, conflicts erupted between Indians and colonists when free-ranging livestock consumed foodstuffs (crops, nuts, even clams) that Indians needed. Some Native Americans sought compensation from colonial authorities, but often found the legal system frustrating. Not receiving the satisfaction they sought, they took matters into their own hands, often stealing or killing colonists' cows and hogs. Further, colonial population growth led settlers to seek ever more Indian land.

By the mid-1670s accumulated grievances on both sides fuelled hostilities that erupted in King Philip's War, the most widespread violence between Indians and colonists in New England. During the war, animosity toward Indians—all Indians, even those who had converted to English ways and resided in praying towns—was so intense that surviving Native Americans at Natick, who had supported colonists in 1675, were captured and sent to Deer Island in Boston Harbour, where they endured horrific conditions for two years until they could return to their community.[47] By the time the war ended in 1677 losses were staggering. Hundreds of natives and colonists died in the deadliest war (in terms of the proportion of casualties to the population) in American history.[48]

In the decades after King Philip's War (also known as Metacom's War), English colonists celebrated their triumph over New England's Indians. Though some

[46] Harold W. Van Lonkhuyzen, 'A Reappraisal of the Praying Indians: Acculturation, Conversion, and Identity at Natick, Massachusetts, 1646–1730', *NEQ* (1990), pp. 399–419; Virginia DeJohn Anderson, 'King Philip's Herds: Indians, Colonists, and the Problem of Livestock in Early New England', *WMQ*, Third Series, LI (1994), pp. 612–13.

[47] Anderson, 'King Philip's Herds', pp. 601–24; Philip Ranlet, 'Another Look at the Causes of King Philip's War', *NEQ* (1988), pp. 79–100; Van Lonkhuyzen, 'A Reappraisal of the Praying Indians', pp. 420–21.

[48] Richard Slotkin and James K. Folsom, eds., *So Dreadfull a Judgment: Puritan Responses to King Philip's War, 1676–1677* (Middletown, Conn., 1978), pp. 3–4; Steele, *Warpaths*, pp. 107–08.

Indians continued to inhabit southern New England, and some communities of praying Indians survived well beyond 1700, hostility dominated the region. Indeed, the conflict spawned the development of what became the most popular literary genre in early America: captivity narratives, most of them recounting the horrors suffered by colonists at the hands of Native Americans. The tales often followed specific thematic lines and contained lurid depictions of Indian assaults on colonial families. Such accounts did little to improve relations between one-time antagonists. Still, not all Puritans abandoned the desire to convert Indians to English ways and to Protestantism. Increase Mather, who published his *Brief History of the Warr with the Indians in New England* in 1676, even before the conflict had ended, reminded his readers about the importance of bringing proper ideas about Christianity to Indians who would otherwise fall under the thrall of Catholic missionaries.[49] But the cause of conversion must have meant far less to colonists who witnessed families torn apart in the war or read accounts of alleged Indian atrocities. New England Indians, for their part, also continued to feel aggrieved after the conflict. The Western Abenakis, for example, long harboured resentment toward the English after the spread of the war into their territory in the Green Mountains. When King William's War (the War of the League of Augsburg, 1689–97) spread to New England, the French found willing allies among the Abenakis.[50]

While relations between English colonists and New England Indians deteriorated even further during the later decades of the century, not all natives and colonists eyed each other with murderous animosity. Indeed, the development of English colonies in New York and Pennsylvania brought the English into extensive contact with the natives of Iroquoia and the Susquehanna and Delaware Valleys, and in the south the development of Carolina and its trading post at Charles Town (Charleston after 1783) led to the creation of extensive ties to southeastern Indians. Although violence flared in these regions—especially in New York, where Indians had battled with Europeans sporadically during the entire century—natives and newcomers still tended to work together, when possible, to create profitable trade alliances and stable diplomatic networks.

Pennsylvania's early history presents perhaps the best example of Indians and colonists trying to smooth over differences and create peaceful ties. Native Americans in that region, notably the Delawares, had had contact with Europeans since the 1620s, when Swedish and Dutch migrants travelled to the Delaware Valley. Though the number of migrants remained small, these Europeans, like others, apparently unleashed deadly epidemics among the Indians. But they never made

[49] Mather, *A Brief History of the Warr with the Indians in New-England* [Boston, 1676], in Slotkin and Folsom, eds., *So Dreadfull a Judgment*, pp. 82–84.

[50] Colin G. Calloway, *The Western Abenakis of Vermont, 1600–1800: War, Migration, and the Survival of an Indian People* (Norman, Okla., 1990), pp. 92–97.

serious efforts to colonize the region; their combined population was less than 1,000 at its highest point in the 1650s. When William Penn arrived in 1681 he sought to treat natives fairly, as had earlier colonists in the region. But, like other colonists, Penn and his associates believed that the Indians had their faults and needed to be converted to English ways.[51]

For all his peaceful intentions, Penn's ability to attract migrants from Europe put pressure on the Delawares, many of whom moved westward to seek new lands. Though the settling of Penn's colony lacked the outbreaks of violence which characterized other regions, here too epidemic diseases and growing numbers of colonists combined to reduce the power of the indigenous peoples.[52] When Pennsylvania became known across the Atlantic as 'the best poor man's country' in the eighteenth century, it was because even open-minded attempts at co-existence led to Indian removal; Penn's promise of a profitable life was meant primarily for Europeans.

Despite the losses in their numbers and the amount of land under their control, Indians were not meek witnesses to European colonization in Pennsylvania or elsewhere. Many were able to negotiate with the newcomers, creating commercial and diplomatic alliances that preserved much of their world. Not surprisingly, the Indians who benefited most from ties to Europeans inhabited the interior and thus had less contact with land-hungry migrants than the coastal peoples. Among these natives, the Iroquois, a confederation of five tribes—the Senecas, Cayugas, Onondagas, Oneidas, and Mohawks—until the Tuscaroras joined them in the early eighteenth century, were perhaps the Indians best able to survive the expansion of European colonies in North America. In part, the Iroquois were beneficiaries of the policies of Europeans that placed colonizers to the north, south, and east of Iroquoia; situated between the French, Dutch, and English, the Iroquois soon established relations with all of them. Perhaps more important, the Iroquois were often skilled diplomats; their Haudenosaunee ('the whole house') or Great League of Peace had provided the foundation of their confederacy long before Europeans arrived in North America.[53]

Yet the rise of the Iroquois occurred at least in part because the confederacy could take advantage of other changes in the north-east that reduced the strength of their neighbours. Desire for peltry had led the Mohawks (the easternmost group in the confederacy) to battle with the Mahicans from 1624 to 1628, and the entire confederacy, seeking new members as well as furs, contributed to the victory over

[51] Penn to the Free Society of Traders [16 Aug. 1683], in Richard S. Dunn and Mary Maples Dunn, eds., *The Papers of William Penn*, 5 vols. (Philadelphia, 1981–87), II, pp. 453–54.

[52] Thomas J. Sugrue, 'The Peopling and Depeopling of Early Pennsylvania: Indians and Colonists, 1680–1720', *Pennsylvania Magazine of History and Biography*, CXVI (1992), pp. 12–15.

[53] See Richter, *Ordeal of the Longhouse*, pp. 30–49.

the Hurons in the so-called 'Beaver Wars' of the 1640s. By the 1670s the Iroquois also claimed suzerainty over the Susquehanna Valley, territory lying almost vacant after the virtual disappearance of the Susquehannocks (themselves notable victims of European colonization).[54]

But even though the Iroquois could, for a time, survive the incursions of Europeans, the forces that swept eastern North America eventually moved through Iroquoia as well. A series of epidemics during the seventeenth century made the Iroquois more vulnerable to colonial incursions. As their numbers decreased, many Iroquois became more willing to establish stronger ties to the English, whose numbers continued to grow, especially after the Dutch lost control of New Netherland in the 1660s. During the 1670s, while the French remained on the northern boundaries of Iroquoia and while Jesuits established missions competing with Protestants for Iroquois souls, leaders of the League established the so-called Covenant Chain, an alliance with English colonists. Yet even subsequent treaties with the French and English could not provide the stability the Iroquois once possessed.[55]

In the south-east, the latter decades of the seventeenth century also brought change for colonists and Indians. As with the Iroquois, the engine of change was commerce, though European diseases and the growth in the colonial population added to pressures felt in many Indian communities. Although trade first took place along the shore, Native Americans soon created networks to haul goods from inland villages to the coast and European goods into the interior. By the 1680s the English knew of Indian trails leading deep into the interior, facilitating trade between Europeans clustered at the shoreline and natives who wanted European goods. For these Indians, many of them forming new communities after disease had ravaged their numbers, political alliances within the region allowed them to withstand some of the devastating forces of colonization until long after 1700.[56]

While Indians throughout eastern North America struggled to survive after mid-century, the European introduction of alcohol, especially distilled spirits produced from West Indies sugar, further undermined their communities. Although Indians did not receive sufficient alcohol to suffer from debilitating physiological illness, binge drinking led to fighting and even murders within villages. Growing Indian demand for liquor also encouraged many young men to over-hunt fur-bearing animals, thereby threatening long-standing economies

[54] Ibid., pp. 55–66; Peter C. Mancall, *Valley of Opportunity: Economic Culture Along the Upper Susquehanna, 1700–1800* (Ithaca, NY, 1991), pp. 30–32.

[55] Richter, *Ordeal of the Longhouse*, pp. 133–42, 215–16.

[56] Waselkov, 'Seventeenth-Century Trade', pp. 118–19; James H. Merrell, *The Indians' New World: Catawbas and Their Neighbors from European Contact Through the Era of Removal* (Chapel Hill, NC, 1989).

based at least in part on the annual hunting of these animals. Despite the efforts of colonial legislators to outlaw the liquor trade by the end of the century—the Rhode Island Assembly termed the commerce an 'abominable filthyness'—too many colonists saw profits in it. Over time, the trade poisoned relations between Indian leaders who also wanted to end the business and colonists who either supported it or simply could not stop the trafficking in what one Delaware religious leader later called a 'deadly medicine'.[57]

In 1697 Cotton Mather, perhaps the leading cleric in New England, published *Humiliations Followed With Deliverances*, including in an appendix the narrative of the capture and redemption of Hannah Dustan. Dustan was a great heroine to Mather and other colonists because she and two other colonists slew ten Indian captors in 1676, scalping them before escaping. For her efforts, she received fame—the Governor of Maryland sent her 'a very generous token of his favor'—and a reward of £50 from the colonial government.[58] Six years later another prominent minister, Solomon Stoddard of Northampton, Massachusetts, wrote to the Governor of the colony with a cure for the recurring problem of Indians capturing colonists. Stoddard suggested that dogs be trained to hunt Indians, thereby reducing the threat to colonists. 'They act like wolves', he declared, 'and are to be dealt withal as wolves.'[59]

The animosity toward Indians evident in such clerical writings reflected the poisoning of relations between Europeans and Native Americans that had taken place in North America since the 1580s. The English concocted no plan to extirpate Indians. The native peoples in the interior of the continent, especially in the Great Lakes region, where diplomatic relations consisted mostly of alliances between villages and French colonizers, knew that colonists still needed them to procure pelts and furs.[60] By 1700 English colonists had not gained political control of eastern North America. Although epidemics had raced through coastal communities and forced many Indians to migrate inland, Indians remained in the eastern woodlands.

In the end, as in the beginning, local circumstances dictated relations between Indians and colonists. Warfare between groups of Indians and colonists did not necessarily signal broader hostility between all Indians and all Europeans. As the

[57] Peter C. Mancall, *Deadly Medicine: Indians and Alcohol in Early America* (Ithaca, NY, 1995).

[58] Mather, 'A Narrative of Hannah Dustan's Notable Deliverance from Captivity', in Alden T. Vaughan and Edward W. Clark, eds., *Puritans Among the Indians: Accounts of Captivity and Redemption, 1676–1724* (Cambridge, Mass., 1981), pp. 161–64.

[59] Stoddard to Governor Joseph Dudley, 22 Oct. 1703, in Demos, ed., *Remarkable Providences* (1972; rev. edn., Boston, 1991), pp. 373–74.

[60] Richard White, *The Middle Ground: Indians, Empires, and Republics in the Great Lakes Region, 1650–1815* (Cambridge, 1991), pp. 1–185.

experience of the peoples of southern New England made clear, particular groups of Native Americans and colonists could create alliances even after destructive warfare. Indians might have organized themselves into confederacies, and colonists might have been emissaries of a nation-state, but such trans-regional allegiances still tended to matter less than relations between leaders of particular Indian villages and specific colonies.

At the dawn of the eighteenth century, with the numbers of Indians and colonists near parity in eastern North America, the inhabitants of what had become English America often eyed each other with suspicion and hostility. Yet, while the opportunism that had characterized relations between Indians and Europeans since the early sixteenth century was weakened, its passing was not entirely evident in 1700. For at that moment, with goods still changing hands at a fevered pace in trade posts scattered the length of the Atlantic coast, many Native Americans could still hope that maintaining ties with colonists would be to their benefit.

To the Indians' misfortune, colonists increasingly devoted their attention to agriculture and the production of staple exports for the Atlantic commercial world. The shift led to ever greater demand for natives' lands and declining interest in Indians as trading partners. By contrast, the French in New France and the Spanish in New Mexico and Florida, unable to attract large numbers of migrants from Europe, remained more interested in saving native souls and obtaining natives' goods.

The English had once needed Native Americans to survive in North America. By 1700 Indians had plenty of reason to fear these Europeans, as Hariot had hoped, but few colonists would have shared his vision that many natives 'loved us, that shall inhabite with them'.

Select Bibliography

Virginia DeJohn Anderson, 'King Philip's Herds: Indians, Colonists, and the Problem of Livestock in Early New England', *William and Mary Quarterly*, Third Series, LI (1994), 601–24.

James Axtell, *The Invasion Within: The Contest of Cultures in Colonial North America* (New York, 1985).

Philip L. Barbour, ed., *The Complete Works of Captain John Smith*, 3 vols. (Chapel Hill, NC, 1986).

Colin G. Calloway, *The Western Abenakis of Vermont, 1600–1800: War, Migration, and the Survival of an Indian People* (Norman, Okla., 1990).

William Cronon, *Changes in the Land: Indians, Colonists, and the Ecology of New England* (New York, 1983).

Alfred Crosby, *Ecological Imperialism: The Biological Expansion of Europe, 900–1900* (Cambridge, 1986).

THOMAS HARIOT, *A Briefe and True Report of the New Found Land of Virginia* (1590; New York, 1972).

PETER HULME and NEAL WHITEHEAD, eds., *Wild Majesty: Encounters with Caribs from Columbus to the Present Day* (Oxford, 1992).

KAREN ORDAHL KUPPERMAN, *Roanoke: The Abandoned Colony* (Savage, Md., 1984).

PETER C. MANCALL, *Deadly Medicine: Indians and Alcohol in Early America* (Ithaca, NY, 1995).

JAMES H. MERRELL, *The Indians' New World: Catawbas and Their Neighbors from European Contact through the Era of Removal* (Chapel Hill, NC, 1989).

CHRISTOPHER L. MILLER and GEORGE R. HAMELL, 'A New Perspective on Indian–White Contact: Cultural Symbols and Colonial Trade', *Journal of American History*, LXXIII (1986), 311–28.

EDMUND S. MORGAN, *American Slavery, American Freedom: The Ordeal of Colonial Virginia* (New York, 1975).

DAVID BEERS QUINN, ed., *The Roanoke Voyages, 1584–1590*, 2 vols. (1955; New York, 1991).

MARTIN H. QUITT, 'Trade and Acculturation at Jamestown, 1607–1609: The Limits of Understanding', *William and Mary Quarterly*, Third Series, LII (1995), 227–58.

DANIEL K. RICHTER, *The Ordeal of the Longhouse: The Peoples of the Iroquois League in the Era of European Colonization* (Chapel Hill, NC, 1992).

NEAL SALISBURY, *Manitou and Providence: Indians, Europeans, and the Making of New England, 1500–1643* (New York, 1980).

GREGORY A. WASELKOV, 'Seventeenth-Century Trade in the Colonial Southeast', *Southeastern Archaeology*, VIII (1989), 117–33.

RICHARD WHITE, *The Middle Ground: Indians, Empires, and Republics in the Great Lakes Region, 1650–1815* (Cambridge, 1991).

WILLIAM WOOD, *New England's Prospect* (1634; Amherst, Mass., 1977).

16

The Middle Colonies: New Opportunities for Settlement, 1660–1700

NED C. LANDSMAN

Among the principal regions of extensive English settlement in North America during the seventeenth century, that which became the Middle Colonies was the last to experience a concerted effort at English settlement. While New England, the Chesapeake, and several West Indian islands all attracted substantial immigration before 1660, and Carolina a decade after that, England only asserted its rights to the mid-Atlantic coastline in 1664; its first significant settlement commenced more than a decade later. The fact of late settlement within an already well-established English colonial world was of major significance in the development of the region. Moreover, the existence of neighbouring English settlements gave the region a well-defined role within the English colonial system and affected the character of mid-Atlantic society.[1]

Historical understanding of the Middle Colonies has been strongly shaped by a focus upon its most prominent founder, the Pennsylvania proprietor William Penn, and his co-religionists among the Society of Friends. Penn's 'liberal' settlement plan and powerful vision of toleration and peaceful relations with the native inhabitants have rightly been seen as important influences upon the region, leading to the principal social characteristics for which it became renowned: the expansive pattern of settlement, extensive commercial development, the emergence of a factious and popular form of politics, religious and ethnic diversity, and an early form of cultural pluralism.[2]

While it would be impossible to discuss the early history of the mid-Atlantic without devoting substantial attention to Penn and the Quakers, his stature should not be allowed to obscure the other structural factors that affected the evolution of

[1] A useful survey of early American regions is Jack P. Greene, *Pursuits of Happiness: The Social Development of Early Modern British Colonies and the Formation of American Culture* (Chapel Hill, NC, 1988).

[2] A recent historiographical summary is Wayne Bodle, 'Themes and Directions in Middle Colonies Historiography', *William and Mary Quarterly* (hereafter *WMQ*), Third Series, LI (1994), pp. 355–88, which updates Douglas Greenberg, 'The Middle Colonies in Recent American Historiography', *WMQ*, Third Series, XXXVI (1979), pp. 396–427.

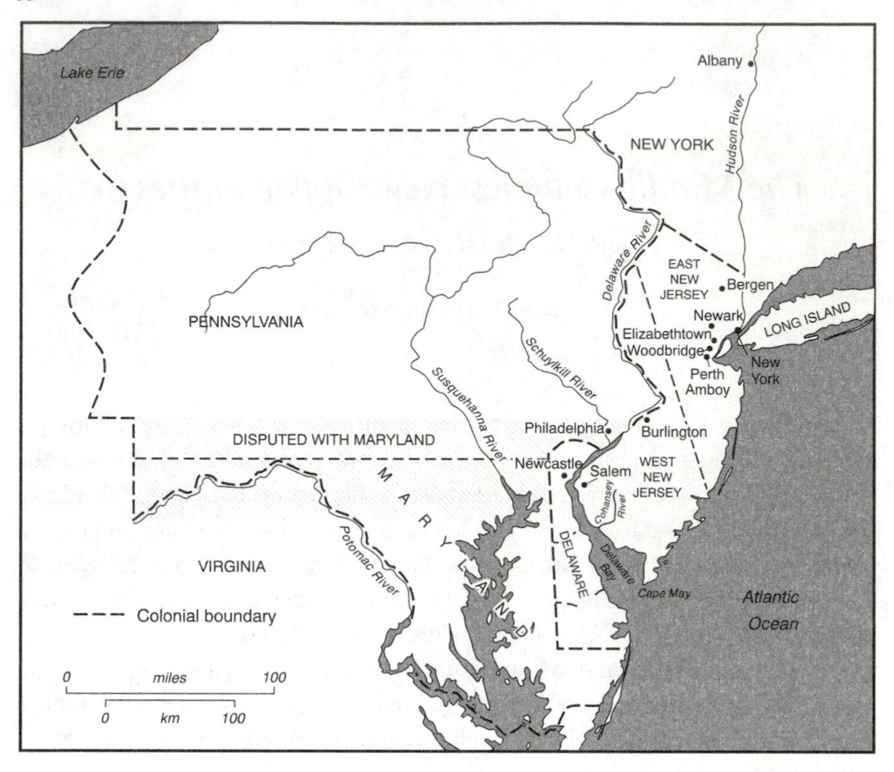

Map 16.1. The Middle Colonies

the region. Those included its physical and human environments, its place within the English colonial system, and the particular historical circumstances that surrounded its development. The English presence there certainly did not begin with Penn: there was already a substantial English undertaking in New York, under the authority of the Duke of York, another important figure in the development of the region, whose proprietary claim originally encompassed virtually the whole of what became the Middle Colonies. Even Quakers had already established a noteworthy presence in the mid-Atlantic before the founding of Pennsylvania, and in a manner rather different from that which we associate with the Quaker proprietor.

Even before Penn's involvement—in some respects even before 1660—some of the patterns that would characterize the Middle Colonies can be discerned. The region already contained an unusual degree of human diversity, native as well as European, that cut across its shifting and conflicting national and imperial claims. The need for settlers, and the difficulty almost every European nation but the English had in attracting colonists in the seventeenth century, led to a *de facto* system of limited toleration. There existed already the outlines of the characteristic bifurcation of the region along lines created by the trading networks that followed the two principal rivers—the Delaware and the Hudson—as well as the long-lasting economic differentiation between upriver and down. Fort Orange, in the vicinity of what would become Albany, had already emerged as a focal point for international commerce and diplomacy, with ramifications that would extend throughout the region.

It is only against that background that Penn's influence can be comprehended. To a considerable degree, those same factors made his highly original colonial experiment possible. The Restoration era provided some markedly new kinds of opportunities for settlement in the New World, and the mid-Atlantic colonies that emerged during that period filled a distinct niche within the developing British colonial system. Indeed, in attracting the involvement of proprietors and settlers to the mid-Atlantic from beyond the bounds of England, the colonization of the Middle Colonies did much to add a truly British dimension to what had been England's overseas empire.

The Mid-Atlantic Region

The area commonly referred to as the Middle Colonies encompasses what became the three-colony region of New York, New Jersey, and Pennsylvania; the last of those originally claimed what became Delaware as well. From an English colonial perspective, it constituted a middle area already by 1660, lying between the Chesapeake settlements to the south and New England to the north. Much of the land within the region is low-lying and arable, especially suitable for the cultivation of grain. The region also contained excellent natural harbours and navigable rivers, including the Hudson, the Delaware, and—farther inland—the Susquehanna. The combination allowed for rapid commercial penetration well into the interior before 1660.

Long before the advent of English settlement, the mid-Atlantic already was a land of many peoples. The native inhabitants included a variety of Algonquian tribes in coastal areas, the Five Nations or Iroquois across the Mohawk Valley through much of what would become upper New York, and the Algonquian-speaking Lenni Lenape or Delaware and the Iroquoian Susquehannocks along the rivers to the south and west. The region also housed a variety of European groups. At New Amsterdam, the Dutch West India Company established a colony as early as 1624, along with numerous other settlements in the Hudson and Delaware Valleys. By 1664 the city on the Hudson contained perhaps 1,500 persons; the European population of the colony was probably three or four times that number.[3]

[3] Oliver A. Rink, *Holland on the Hudson: An Economic and Social History of Dutch New York* (Ithaca, NY, 1986). For further consideration of Indians, see above, pp. 328–30.

Long Island held Dutch settlements in the west and migrants from New England in the east, the latter claiming allegiance to the government of Connecticut. The Delaware Valley included outposts of both New Netherland and New Sweden until the latter colony, about 400 strong, was conquered by the Dutch in 1655.

Each of those colonies was a good deal more diverse than their labels suggest. To populate their settlements, the fledgling mid-Atlantic colonies accepted migrants of varied backgrounds, resulting in *de facto* policies of toleration. Thus New Netherland, sponsored by one of the most heterogeneous national states in Europe, contained a mixed population of Dutch, German-speakers, French Huguenots, French-speaking Walloons, Scandinavians of several sorts, Africans, and Jews, among others. The largest element in the population of New Sweden was probably Finnish. Long Island housed significant settlements of Dutch Reformed, New English Congregationalists, and English Quakers. The varying cross-currents involved in those settlements was apparent from the outset. The Dutch claim to New Netherland rested on the discoveries of the English sea captain Henry Hudson. New Sweden's colonial effort was promoted by a number of Dutch merchants; its leading venturer was Peter Minuet, a previous Governor of New Netherland.[4]

All of those settlements were intended primarily as commercial ventures. New Netherland, under the sponsorship of the Dutch West India Company, was an outpost of a far-flung Dutch commercial empire in the seventeenth century, with New Amsterdam and Albany well situated to promote Dutch interests within the north-eastern fur trade. New Sweden was established as a trading outpost on the Delaware with similar commercial aims. Even the New English outposts on eastern Long Island were sited principally along the coast, where maritime occupations would long constitute one of the area's principal employments.

The combination of a central location and commercial pursuit involved the mid-Atlantic region early on within the intricate web of international trade and diplomacy. Already by 1660 the site of Albany constituted the principal place for Dutch commerce and negotiation with the Five Nations. New Amsterdam had already garnered an important place within the West Indian provisioning trade. New Sweden found itself entangled in triangular diplomacy among the Delaware and the Dutch. On Long Island were such experienced soldiers as Lyon Gardiner and John Underhill; the latter would play a key role in the complicated battles among Indians, English, and Dutch.[5]

[4] David Cohen, 'How Dutch were the Dutch of New Netherland?', *New York History*, LXII (1981), pp. 43–60; C. A. Weslager, *Dutch Explorers, Traders and Settlers in the Delaware Valley, 1609–1664* (Philadelphia, 1961), chaps. 6–7.

[5] Mildred Murphy DeRiggi, 'Quakerism on Long Island: The First Fifty Years, 1657–1707', unpublished Ph.D. dissertation, State University of New York at Stony Brook, 1994, pp. 78–102.

Conquest and Colonization

Although scattered groups of English colonists were to be found within New Sweden and New Netherland, as well as on Long Island, formal English involvement along the mid-Atlantic coast began in 1664, when a small fleet under the command of Richard Nicolls arrived at Gravesend Bay on Long Island, within striking distance of New Amsterdam, and demanded its surrender. The colony was in poor shape to resist, and conquest was accomplished without a shot being fired. Both the city and the colony were renamed 'New York', the province encompassing a territory that extended from east of the Hudson River to the southern reaches of Delaware Bay.

The name New York was no idle compliment. The moving force behind the conquest was James Stuart, Duke of York, Lord High Admiral of England, brother of Charles II and later his successor to the Crowns of England and Scotland. In the world of Restoration politics James cut a substantial figure. Unlike his elder brother, James was no trimmer. While throughout Charles's reign rumours circulated of the King's secret conversion to the Church of Rome, James boldly proclaimed his Catholic allegiance. That, combined with aggressive assertions of the King's prerogative, made him a widely feared figure within much of the English Protestant community.

James displayed his assertiveness not only in the seizure of territory but in the structuring of the colony. The charter he received had fewer restrictions than that of almost any other colony. It provided for no representative Assembly; instead, the proprietor was free to establish laws and control trade. In 1665 Nicolls issued what became known as the 'Duke's Laws', which established an elective Council in the place of a legislature but offered few other concessions to the inhabitants until the granting of a short-lived 'Charter of Libertyes and Priviledges' nearly two decades later. The principal concession offered was religious toleration, a carry-over from the Dutch period and amenable to the needs of the old inhabitants. It was very much in keeping with James's long-standing preferences as well, at least in part because toleration legitimized Catholic forms of worship and the holding of political office by adherents of the Church of Rome in a colony inhabited largely by Protestant settlers.[6]

For decades thereafter, New York displayed characteristics of a conquered society. The majority of the European inhabitants were still hold-overs from the Dutch period, but their allegiance was considerably divided. At the upper levels of society, some began to seek an accommodation with the conquerors that would lead to the eventual creation of an Anglo-Dutch merchant élite. Elsewhere,

[6] Robert C. Ritchie, *The Duke's Province: A Study of New York Politics and Society, 1664–1691* (Chapel Hill, NC, 1977).

Dutch-speaking families often retreated into local enclaves, maintaining a considerable degree of isolation from the newcomers; the town of Albany, for example, would long retain a decidedly Dutch character and a notoriously independent spirit. Within some such communities, the inhabitants became more uniformly Dutch in language, religion, and kinship than they had been before.[7]

Contributing to that isolation was the peculiar topography, which helped to render land within the new colony, or at least land for ownership, relatively inaccessible. North of New York City the bulk of arable land was confined to the broad expanse of the Hudson Valley; settlement further west was impeded by the Catskill Mountains. Moreover, much of the Valley was already distributed in the form of the vast 'Patroonships' that the Dutch Company had granted to its most aggressive or politic promoters. Rather than abandoning that system, the English government chose to further it, granting large manors to its favourites, from the Livingston and Cortland Manors in the north to the Manors of Sagtikos and St George on southern Long Island.[8]

The diversity of the colony offered dramatic possibilities for opportunistic interlopers. None was more successful than Robert Livingston, son of a Scottish Presbyterian minister, who arrived in Albany in 1674 and embarked upon a long career of self-advancement. Livingston benefited from a cosmopolitan and commercial upbringing. Having fled Scotland with his family in 1663 after the Restoration of the Scottish Episcopal church, Livingston spent his adolescent years among the Scottish traders of Rotterdam, where he learned the arts of commerce and personal connection, along with the Dutch language. In 1673 he embarked for Massachusetts, but the newer colony to the west seemed to hold prospects better suited to his background. The following year he moved on to Albany.

From small beginnings, Livingston utilized his varied experience and connections to put himself at the centre of a vast commercial web. In Albany he became the English secretary to Nicholas van Rensselaer of Rensselaerswyck Manor, whose wealthy widow he married upon the death of his patron. He established a partnership with the Scottish merchant James Graham of New York. He used his linguistic and negotiating skills to get himself appointed Secretary to the Board of Indian Affairs. In the process, Livingston became one of the principal conduits of the fur

[7] A. G. Roeber, '"The Origin of Whatever Is Not English Among Us": The Dutch-speaking and the German-speaking Peoples of Colonial British America', in Bernard Bailyn and Philip D. Morgan, eds., *Strangers within the Realm: Cultural Margins of the First British Empire* (Chapel Hill, NC, 1991), pp. 220–83; also Donna Merwick, *Possessing Albany, 1630–1710: The Dutch and English Experiences* (New York, 1990).

[8] Sung Bok Kim, *Landlord and Tenant in Colonial New York: Manorial Society, 1664–1775* (Chapel Hill, NC, 1978); Michael Kammen, *Colonial New York: A History* (White Plains, NY, 1975), pp. 79–81, 140, *passim.*

trade. At the same time his ability to work within that trade, and to mobilize resources, would make the Scotsman indispensable to the functioning of government and commerce. Over the years he was able to obtain land and offices from Governors of all political persuasions, who needed his particular skills to make New York work.[9]

New Jersey began as an offshoot of New York. In June of 1664, even before the conquest of New Netherland was complete, James severed New Jersey from his colony and granted it to Lord John Berkeley and Sir John Carteret, two Stuart loyalists and prominent Restoration figures. They in turn issued 'Concessions and Agreements' designed to attract settlers from other English settlements to their colony. The proprietors divided the colony in 1676, shortly after Berkeley had sold his share, which became the western half, to a London-based group of English Quakers. Carteret retained the eastern section until 1682, when he sold it to another group of Quaker proprietors.

The West Jersey proprietary constituted the first organized Quaker foray into the region. It began almost by accident; the colony was purchased by the English Quaker merchant Edward Byllinge and an associate, John Fenwick, in an effort to repair the former's shaky finances. Byllinge's impending failure eventually drew in several prominent Quaker leaders, including William Penn, in an effort to put things right. The initial imperative of managing the estate expanded into an active colonial enterprise, and the Quaker proprietary was soon divided into more than a hundred shares.[10]

Quaker settlement began in 1675, with the arrival of about a hundred colonists at Salem in West Jersey in a separate undertaking sponsored by John Fenwick called 'Fenwick's Colony'. The larger movement to what remained of Byllinge's interest began two years later, promoted by Penn and others. Within five years more than 1,400 Quakers had migrated to West Jersey.

East Jersey would follow a markedly different course of development. Carteret planned no colonization ventures of his own, seeking instead to use liberal terms to attract settlers from existing colonies. From the start, East Jersey was less homogeneous than its western neighbour. Under Carteret's proprietorship, diverse groups of settlers from Long Island and New England began to settle to the south and west of New York City. There they established six New England-style townships from Newark to Woodbridge. Together with the Dutch settlers in and

[9] Lawrence H. Leder, *Robert Livingston, 1654–1728, and the Politics of Colonial New York* (Chapel Hill, NC, 1961).

[10] John E. Pomfret, *The Province of West New Jersey, 1609–1702* (Princeton, 1956); Gary B. Nash, *Quakers and Politics: Pennsylvania, 1681–1726* (Princeton, 1968), pp. 4–8.

around Bergen they totalled perhaps 3,000 persons; those would long form two of the larger population groups in East Jersey.[11]

The original Quaker proprietary of 1682 added little to the population, since Friends by that time were devoting most of their attention to the other two colonies of West Jersey and Pennsylvania. Instead, the twelve original proprietors took on an additional twelve partners, six of whom were Scots, led by the prominent Scottish Quaker Robert Barclay, another Restoration figure with ties to the Stuart court. They in turn divided their shares among a much larger group, mostly Scots. That Scottish proprietary group soon grew to over a hundred members and became the most active promoters of the colony.[12]

The Scots plan for the colony was ambitious and distinct. Over the next several years they organized four expeditions to East Jersey and sent close to 700 settlers. Rather than interspersing their settlements among their English neighbours, the proprietors arranged to have their lands allocated together within separate Scottish settlements, creating a colony within a colony. Those they organized into neighbourhoods of large estates of 2,000 acres or more, modelled on the hierarchical society of rural Scotland. At the same time they discouraged land sales in units of less than 500 acres. They also set out to challenge the land patents of several of the older English towns in the colony.

The Scottish effort was substantially influenced by the divisions of the Restoration. The proprietary group was closely connected to the upper reaches of Scottish society. The highest-ranking proprietors were James Drummond, Earl of Perth, and his brother John, Lord Melfort, both important Restoration politicians. Even Barclay had close ties to the Duke of York, although that had not prevented a stay in prison for his adherence to the Quaker faith. On the other side, a few active purchasers were Presbyterian dissenters, who during the 1680s found themselves fined, imprisoned, and exiled from Scotland during the height of the 'killing times'.

As in New York, the effort to establish a society based upon manorial estates generated modest population growth. After the initial flush of settlement, emigration from Scotland tailed off in the 1690s. Instead, East Jersey continued to attract a slow but steady flow of immigrants both from across the Atlantic and, more importantly, from neighbouring colonies. By 1700 perhaps 6,000–7,000 European settlers resided across the whole of East Jersey, up to a thousand of them Scots, concentrated in a narrow band of Middlesex and Monmouth Counties. A substantial Dutch contingent remained in Bergen County.

[11] John E. Pomfret, *The Province of East New Jersey, 1609–1702: The Rebellious Proprietary* (Princeton, 1962).

[12] The following discussion draws upon Ned C. Landsman, *Scotland and its First American Colony, 1683–1765* (Princeton, 1985).

Thus English settlement in the mid-Atlantic, as well as Quaker involvement in that settlement, were well under way before the founding of Pennsylvania. That venture built upon the earlier settlements: William Penn's first American involvement had been a modest engagement with West Jersey, where he had witnessed the interest the colony attracted among Friends. Moreover, he, like Byllinge before him, thought of using colonial investment to fortify his own unsettled fortune.

Penn was a devout Quaker and probably the most renowned member of that despised sect. The Society of Friends had originated in Civil War England, as one of a number of radical groups that sprang up in those troubled times. Most of the early Quakers had been people of marginal status, many from remote areas of northern and western England, with little social standing and correspondingly little respect for social rank. Instead, Friends made a point of defying hierarchy, refusing to doff their hats or show respect towards their social superiors. Early Quakers were disorderly in the extreme, one of the principal reasons for their persecution by authorities.[13]

At the heart of those Quaker attitudes was the concept of the Inner Light—the internal voice of God. In that respect Friends differed from their Puritan predecessors, who believed that truth was revealed in Scripture, and that true godliness was confined to an elected few; the Inner Light was in everyone. Not everyone attended to that voice, of course, and Quakers worked to spread the message, or 'convince' those around them. Such ideas led to an opposition to priests and hierarchies and a belief in spiritual equality, as well as an emphasis upon persuasion or 'tender dealings' as the means to convincement.

By Penn's generation the character of the Society of Friends had altered considerably. With the advent of persons of greater standing, such as William Penn, some of its radicalism was muted. Penn—like his East Jersey counterpart Robert Barclay—was well born and well connected at court. His claim to the colony depended on a debt owed by the King to Penn's father, Sir William Penn, an Admiral in the Royal Navy and member of the Restoration Privy Council. The younger William Penn's conversion to the Quaker faith subdued some of his courtly attitudes, but not all: he continued to spend his income as lavishly as a courtier and, as events in Pennsylvania would show, he continued to believe in his own entitlement to rule. He also maintained his relations with James. Penn's life thus required an extraordinary effort to reconcile seemingly contradictory impulses, as would appear in his efforts to plan and promote the colony.

One of the seeming oppositions that Penn sought to balance was the rights of the proprietor and the liberties of his subjects. This he set out to accomplish

[13] Richard T. Vann, *The Social Development of English Quakerism, 1655–1755* (Cambridge, Mass., 1969).

through the careful construction of a constitution, an interest he shared with many liberal thinkers of the day; all of the Restoration colonies except New York would have detailed constitutional plans. Penn and several associates devoted an enormous effort to drafting a constitution for his colony. Among the surviving Penn Papers are to be found twelve full or fragmentary drafts of what became *The Frame of Government of the Province of Pennsylvania in America*, three outlines, two drafts of a variant plan, the 'Fundamentall Constitutions of Pensilvania', and three written commentaries upon those plans by friends and advisers.[14]

The *Frame of Government* suggests some of the balancing that Penn attempted. Compared to the Duke's Laws or the Scottish Proprietors' plan for East Jersey, the *Frame* was liberal in its guarantee of an elected Assembly, its allocation of suffrage, and its unusually strong guarantee of religious liberty. Yet in reality that was not so far removed from established practice within the region, where *de facto* toleration existed almost everywhere. Moreover, the *Frame of Government* was clearly less liberal in its political structure than the corresponding Concessions and Agreements of West Jersey, which had consolidated legislative powers in a powerful and elected one-house legislature. In Pennsylvania, by contrast, most legislative power was located in an élite upper house, which served also as a Governor's council, while the popularly elected lower house could do little but assent to the laws.

The difference was deliberate. During the drafting of the *Frame of Government* Penn and his lawyers worked gradually from earlier, more liberal plans of government towards a final version that deliberately secured the powers of the prominent and powerful. The purpose was partly to attract the participation of wealthy purchasers, which was necessary both for the success of the venture and the repair of Penn's fortune. None the less, the changes drew sharp criticism from some of the more liberal colleagues in Penn's circle.[15]

The Pennsylvania colonization was the most concentrated colonial venture since the Puritan 'Great Migration' to New England of half-a-century before. In 1682 Penn sent some 2,000 settlers aboard twenty-three ships; another 6,000 followed within three years of that. By the end of the century Pennsylvania had as many as 18,000 colonists, Quaker and non-Quaker alike.[16]

[14] Mary Maples Dunn and Richard S. Dunn, eds., *The Papers of William Penn*, 4 vols. (Philadelphia, 1981–86), II, pp. 135–238. For constitutional comparisons, see below, pp. 379–82.

[15] 'Benjamin Furly's Criticism of the Frame of Government', in Dunn and Dunn, eds., *Papers of William Penn*, II, pp. 229–38; Gary B. Nash, 'The Framing of Government in Pennsylvania: Ideas in Contact with Reality', *WMQ*, Third Series, XXIII (1966), pp. 183–209; and Ned C. Landsman, '"Of the Grand Assembly or Parliament": Thomas Rudyard's Critique of an Early Draft of the Frame of Government of Pennsylvania', *Pennsylvania Magazine of History and Biography*, CV (1981), pp. 469–81.

[16] Richard T. Vann has argued that only a small minority of the early immigrants to Pennsylvania had been Friends in good standing; see 'Quakerism: Made in America?', in Richard S. Dunn and Mary Maples Dunn, eds., *The World of William Penn* (Philadelphia, 1986), pp. 157–70.

Penn recruited widely. In addition to English Friends, he engaged Quakers from Ireland, Wales, and Holland in the venture and had attempted to involve Scottish Friends before their decision to pursue East Jersey. Yet although the proprietor was planning a Quaker colony, he wanted it to be profitable and populous as well, and Pennsylvania promoters advertised also among German Lutheran, Reformed, and sectarian groups. Each of these would establish a substantial presence in the colony. From an early date, Pennsylvania, like East Jersey, had separate national groups inhabiting distinct areas of settlement, in such places as Germantown and the Welsh Tract.

Much of the attraction was land. Compared to his fellow proprietors in New York and East Jersey, Penn adopted a liberal land policy designed to spur settlement. Pennsylvania was not without manors and other large properties, but Penn did not attempt to shape society along such lines but permitted the sale of small farming units as well. That would make Pennsylvania more appealing than its neighbours to many prospective settlers.

Unlike the immigrants to the southern plantation colonies, who sought their fortunes largely as individuals, Pennsylvania's early settlers contained a large proportion of families. The land in the colony was well suited to family farming and the production of grain, and Pennsylvania farmers quickly began to thrive by growing wheat. This would hardly have been feasible half-a-century earlier, when there was only a limited market for European cereal crops; those early New Englanders who had engaged in tillage did so mostly to provide for the needs of their own settler communities. By the late seventeenth century new arrivals found a ready market for grain in the earlier plantation colonies to the south, and particularly in the West Indies; the high profits of sugar discouraged Barbadian planters in particular from devoting any of their plantation lands to food crops. After the English conquest of Jamaica in 1655, and with the placing of restrictions upon imports from outside the Empire in the first Navigation Act, the prospects for colonial grain-farmers were more than ample.[17]

Pennsylvanians were well placed to take advantage of growing southern markets for their produce. They did not pioneer new markets but they successfully entered the provisioning trade for the English West Indies that had been developed by merchants in New Netherland and New York. That colony, with its Dutch commercial connections, developed an additional trade route through the Dutch West Indies to the plantation colonies of Portugal and Spain.

Pennsylvania thus had a marked appeal to potential farming families, especially because toleration allowed prospective colonists of varying religious persuasions

[17] John J. McCusker and Russell R. Menard, *The Economy of British America, 1607–1789; Needs and Opportunities for Study* (Chapel Hill, NC, 1985), pp. 191–94.

to conduct their affairs without interference. Moreover, while some Pennsylvanians raised other crops, such as tobacco, or other products, such as lumber, grain farming proved especially well suited to the aspirations of Friends. Such farms provided at once a stable income and the means to support strong and stable familial relationships, allowing farming families to secure property and independence for their lineal descendants while moulding their tender consciences in the ways of true religion. The result was a prominent focus upon child-rearing and the development of surprisingly modern, affectionate families. Indeed, a recent historian has described the Quakers as pioneers of modern families, in which affection and nurture were utilized to cultivate the spiritual potential of individuals.[18]

With the establishment of such families upon the land, rural Pennsylvanians soon spread themselves out into dispersed country neighbourhoods, with only occasional ethnic pockets of concentrated German or Welsh settlement. There were few attempts to create central villages other than market centres, although Penn's plan had included them. In that fashion the spiritual independence of the Friends imposed itself upon the landscape.[19]

Pennsylvanians were not unique in developing such a tradition of single-family farms, which were found interspersed even among the manors of East Jersey and New York in ever-increasing numbers, encouraged by the commercial opportunities and the *de facto* toleration that prevailed throughout the region. It was long assumed that population growth in New York and East Jersey was stunted by the presence of such manors, but recent research suggests that their effect was modest, and that those colonies grew at a substantial rate in the latter years of the seventeenth century.[20]

The other distinguishing feature of the Pennsylvania landscape was the commercial city of Philadelphia, which grew to about 2,000 souls within the first two decades, stretched out narrowly along the banks of the Delaware River. Much of that growth was attributable to the commercial success of Quaker merchants, who aggressively established their place within the Atlantic trading world, trading directly with fellow Quakers in London, Bristol, Barbados, and wherever else Friends already had established commercial footholds. Similarly concentrated

[18] Barry Levy, *Quakers and the American Family: British Settlement in the Delaware Valley* (New York, 1988); James A. Henretta, 'Families and Farms: *Mentalité* in Pre-Industrial America', *WMQ*, Third Series, XXXV (1978), pp. 3–32.

[19] James T. Lemon, *The Best Poor Man's Country: A Geographical Study of Early Southeastern Pennsylvania* (Baltimore, 1972).

[20] McCusker and Menard, *Economy of British America*, pp. 202–08; Menard, 'Was There a "Middle Colonies Demographic Regime"?' and Robert V. Wells, 'The Demography of a Region: Historical Reality or Historian's Creation?', in Susan E. Klepp, ed., *Symposium on the Demographic History of the Philadelphia Region, 1600–1860*, Proceedings of the American Philosophical Society, CIII (1989), pp. 215–22.

trading networks would be employed by Dutch merchants in New York and, after the turn of the century, Scottish traders in both cities.[21]

From the wealth those merchants generated, and from their ties to the West Indian trade, Pennsylvanians began to invest in slaves for their households, shops, and estates. Slavery was not part of Penn's formal plan, but there was certainly no prohibition on the institution either, and slaves were employed on Penn's manor from the early days. By 1700 Pennsylvanians owned in excess of 3,000 slaves. Slavery played a significant role throughout the region. The Dutch merchants of New Netherland, with their West Indian ties, had started that province on a course of slave-holding that, by the turn of the century, exceeded that of Pennsylvania and even several southern colonies.[22]

The ability of Pennsylvanians to take advantage of the West Indian market was an indication of the growing interdependence of England's American colonies; the character of Middle Colony society was owing in no small measure to its relatively late date of settlement and the existence from the beginning of well-established colonial societies nearby. Mid-Atlantic grain farmers depended not only upon the presence of ready markets to the south, but also upon the relative state of peace maintained with the local Indian nations. In part, that was a product of Penn's policy of peace in his relations with his Indian neighbours and the alliance he forged with the local Delawares. Also significant, and an important factor in the ability of Pennsylvania to maintain a policy of peace, was the complicated series of alliances involving the English and Indian inhabitants of the mid-Atlantic from before the time the Quakers arrived, extending from Virginia as far north as New York and the Five Nations. Indian relations within the various colonies were strongly interrelated; in 1675, for example, the ability of New Englanders to withstand King Philip's assault in western Massachusetts was in part the result of pressure put on Philip's forces by New York's Mohawk allies. The potential animosity of the Susquehannocks of what became central Pennsylvania was muted by their precarious location between the sometimes hostile forces of Iroquois Indians and Maryland settlers.[23]

The most important element in Imperial diplomacy throughout the region was an evolving and wide-ranging set of oral and written agreements between Imperial

[21] Frederick B. Tolles, *Quakers and the Atlantic Culture* (New York, 1960).

[22] Jean R. Soderlund, *Quakers and Slavery: A Divided Spirit* (Princeton, 1985); McCusker and Menard, *Economy of British America*, pp. 203, 221–24.

[23] Francis Jennings, *The Invasion of America: Indians, Colonialism, and the Cant of Conquest* (Chapel Hill, NC, 1975), chaps. 17–18; Stephen Saunders Webb, *1676: The End of American Independence* (New York, 1984), pp. 221–44. In *The Ambiguous Iroquois Empire: The Covenant Chain Confederation of Indian Tribes With English Colonies* (New York, 1984), Francis Jennings attributes to Penn's successors responsibility for subverting his more equitable Indian policy and augmenting the power of both the Iroquois and of aggressive mid-Atlantic settlers. On King Philip's War, see above, pp. 214–15; more generally on Indians see chap. by Peter C. Mancall.

authorities in New York and the Five Nations known as the 'Covenant Chain'. The Chain is hard to describe, in part because it was interpreted variously by different sides. In that sense, it was both less and more than a formal alliance. It was less than an alliance in that it was neither fully comprehensive nor precise. Thus, specific agreements negotiated between the parties could never be fully binding on all of their allies; for example, a pact of non-aggression between the government of New York and the Mohawks could not guarantee the peaceable conduct of far-flung bands of Seneca Indians or rampaging colonists from Maryland. Moreover, the terms of the Covenant Chain were almost always metaphorical, left to interpretation by peoples possessing very different cultural assumptions.[24]

The Covenant Chain was more than a treaty of alliance as well. It was not restricted to a few specific terms but was intended to signify an ongoing process of mutual accord. The very lack of precision and centralization allowed it to survive occasional infringements; if neither the Five Nations nor the English government could control the actions of all of their allies, they could validly disclaim responsibility for individual violations and maintain at least an effort at negotiation. The Covenant evolved over time and would influence the behaviour of Indians and colonists who were not directly involved in its initiation. The effects of the Chain thus reached far beyond the immediate vicinity of New York. During the latter part of the seventeenth century, Middle Colony settlers maintained more peaceful relations with their Indian neighbours than did the settlers of the other principal mainland regions.

Diversity and Disruption

The mid-Atlantic colonies remained closely connected to their Restoration origins. Hence, the political and religious conflicts that plagued Restoration England and Scotland had their effects within the region as well, augmented by the myriad religious and national divisions that were present there, and inherent conflicts between proprietary ambition and popular aspiration. By 1700 each of the colonies had experienced a substantial period of disruption, linked in part to the troubles overseas. The result in every case was persistent factional conflict, a substantial diminution of proprietary authority, and the development of an increasingly popular political style.[25]

[24] Jennings, *Ambiguous Iroquois Empire*; Daniel K. Richter and James H. Merrell, *Beyond the Covenant Chain: The Iroquois and their Neighbors in Indian North America, 1600–1800* (Syracuse, NY, 1987).

[25] Alan Tully, *Forming American Politics: Ideals, Interests, and Institutions in Colonial New York and Pennsylvania* (Baltimore, 1994), chaps. 1–2.

In New York, the imposition of English authority upon a largely Dutch-speaking population created the potential for instability. Even the ease of the English conquest failed fully to settle the disposition of the colony; New York was reconquered by the Dutch in 1673 during the Third Anglo-Dutch War, before a final reversion to English control the following year. More disruptive were the events of 1688; the removal of James from the throne and his replacement by William and Mary in the 'Glorious Revolution' set off a chain of reaction in the colonies, as militant Protestant groups in several colonies seized their governments from regimes loyal to King James, proclaiming allegiance to William and Mary and to the Protestant succession.

No colony experienced a greater disruption than New York, where the conflict was intensified by several circumstances: the general level of ethnic contention between Dutch and English within the colony, commercial rivalries between the merchants of Albany and New York, and the fact that James, the deposed monarch, had also been proprietor of the colony. Religious divisions were particularly acute, as James's government included prominent Catholics. To add to the symbolism of the event, William of Orange, who with his wife Mary succeeded James, was himself a Dutch Prince. Thus the fault-lines of local politics in New York everywhere overlapped Imperial divisions. New York also suffered from antagonism towards aggressive proprietary claims and the recent incorporation of their colony into an enlarged Dominion of New England.

The conflict in New York began in 1689, after New Yorkers received word of the Revolution in England and of the rebellion against the Dominion's Governor, Edmund Andros, in Boston. A succession of towns began to rebel against the Dominion, joined soon after by the New York militia which eventually coalesced under the authority of the merchant Jacobus Leisler, proclaiming William and Mary and the Protestant religion. Leisler was a veteran of the Dutch colony, and with a group consisting principally of Dutch-speakers controlled the province for nearly two years, albeit with considerable opposition from merchant élites both in New York and in Albany.[26]

Leisler's demise came swiftly. Early in 1691 Captain Richard Ingoldsby arrived at New York and demanded its surrender on behalf of the newly appointed Governor, Henry Sloughter. Leisler refused to give way until he had seen the Captain's commission, which Ingoldsby did not have. When Sloughter himself arrived late one March day, Leisler still delayed until the following morning. For those offences he was arrested and, with the backing of those whose power he had threatened, quickly tried for treason. He and his associate and son-in-law Jacob Milborne were subjected to a gruesome traitor's execution.

[26] David William Voorhees, 'The "Fervent Zeale" of Jacob Leisler', *WMQ*, Third Series, LI (1994), pp. 447–72, and see below, pp. 456–60.

The hanging of Leisler did nothing to end the contentions. Some of Leisler's Dutch supporters dispersed to New Jersey. Others retreated into their local communities. Still others joined in opposition to the government; over the next several decades they helped establish a tradition of factious politics. The actual revenge extracted by the Leislerians when they took power was modest, consisting chiefly of the exhuming of Leisler and Milborne in 1695 for proper burial, as well as the condemnation, but not the execution, of one of their adversaries.[27]

Pennsylvania and the Jerseys avoided overt rebellion in 1689, although East Jersey came close thereafter. Yet all suffered from acute political contention accentuated by religious and ethnic antagonisms. The disruptions in New Jersey followed the principal social divisions; in the words of Colonel Robert Quarry in a 1703 letter to the Board of Trade: 'The Contests of West Jersey have always been betwixt the Quakers and her majesty's subjects that are no Quakers . . . The contest in East Jersey is of a different nature, whether the country shall be a Scotch settlement or an English settlement.'[28] In Pennsylvania, the dominance of the Quakers ensured formal peace with the proprietary within the uncontested bounds of the colony. Yet even there a peaceful relationship was far from an unconflicted one.

In East Jersey the lines of contention parallelled ethnic divisions, aggravated by the particular character of its Scottish proprietary group. Their close court connections left the group severely weakened by the Revolution. The two most prominent leaders, the Earl of Perth and Lord Melfort, fled Scotland for the Continent, and few proprietors devoted much attention to the colony thereafter. Instead, control of the province devolved upon a different group, the resident proprietors, who lacked the wealth or authority of the proprietors in Scotland but continued to pursue proprietary claims.[29]

Their principal adversaries in East Jersey were the inhabitants of the older English towns in the colony. Not only did the townspeople have little desire to defer to the authority of the proprietors; the proprietary claims threatened the security of their land titles as well. In response, they made common cause with a succession of ambitious office-seekers of various sorts who were willing to take an anti-proprietary stance in return for popular support.

A good example of such an official was the sometime Anabaptist minister Jeremiah Basse, a supporter of England's Surveyor-General of Customs, Edward

[27] Adrian Howe, 'The Bayard Treason Trial: Dramatizing Anglo-Dutch Politics in Early Eighteenth-Century New York City', *WMQ*, Third Series, XLVII (1990), pp. 57–89; Randall H. Balmer, *A Perfect Babel of Confusion: Dutch Religion and English Culture in the Middle Colonies* (New York, 1989).

[28] Robert Quarry to the Lords of Trade, 16 June 1703, quoted in *Documents Relating to the Colonial History of the State of New Jersey* (Newark, Trenton, etc., 1880–), II, p. 544.

[29] Landsman, *Scotland and its First American Colony*, pp. 122–26.

Randolph, and an opponent of the Scottish proprietors. When the passage of the Navigation Act of 1696 threw into question the legitimacy of Scottish office-holding in the colonies, the proprietors appointed Basse as Governor. They soon realized their mistake, as Basse set out to curb the power of the proprietors by accusing the Scots of smuggling and piracy. When the proprietors removed Basse, he enlisted the townspeople of Elizabethtown in an anti-proprietary campaign to free the colony of its 'Scotch yoak'. By 1700 Middlesex County had descended to riots and jailbreaks, leading the proprietors to petition the Crown to take over the government of the colony. Proprietary rule, though not proprietary ownership of the land, was at an end.[30]

Anti-proprietary sentiment in West Jersey was less widespread, but no less aggressive. There also Basse managed to put himself at the centre of contention, first as agent for the West Jersey Society, where he represented a London-based organization of non-Quaker investors, as Governor for a brief period, and as a principal member of an emerging anti-Quaker faction. The largely Quaker colony maintained the peace longer than its eastern neighbour but, with Basse fomenting opposition, that colony too descended into disorder and riot. As in East Jersey, the surrender of the government to the Crown seemed the only remedy.[31]

The larger size of the Pennsylvania colony led to a compounding of difficulties. Like the East Jersey proprietors, Penn laid claim to a territory that already had numerous European settlers, in his case the remnants of the New Sweden settlements in the 'lower counties' along the Delaware, occupied also by numerous English settlers who had come into the region with patents either from the Duke of York or from Lord Baltimore's colony to the south. In his eagerness to establish government by consent, Penn allowed those settlers representation in the Assembly, where they held nearly half of the seats. At best those settlers tolerated Quaker domination, but rarely supported it. Their votes contributed to the rejection of Penn's original *Frame of Government*, along with other measures designed for a Quaker colony. When the Glorious Revolution in England severed the proprietor's ties to the court, the Lower Counties, aided and abetted by Baltimore's agents, began to move toward outright rebellion.[32]

Not all opposition came from non-Quakers. The independent spirit that characterized members of the Society of Friends, coupled with their persistent drive for land and independence, soon pushed them into conflict with proprietary

[30] Ibid., pp. 167–69; and *Documents Relating to the Colonial History of the State of New Jersey*, III, pp. 198–204; IV, pp. 8–10.

[31] Pomfret, *Province of West New Jersey*, pp. 206–15.

[32] Nash, *Quakers and Politics*; much of the primary material is in Dunn and Dunn, eds., *Papers of William Penn*.

authority. Well before the end of the century Pennsylvania Friends would experience unforeseen contentions both within the government and within the meeting.

Part of the contention arose from an inherent tension within the proprietor's vision for the colony: Pennsylvania was to provide an international homeland for Quakers, but it was to do so in a way that would profit the proprietor. 'Though I desire to extend religious freedom,' Penn wrote, 'yet I want some recompense for my trouble.'[33] It was partly the relatively high prices Penn set for Pennsylvania lands that persuaded the Scottish Quaker proprietors to choose East Jersey instead. As the leader, Robert Barclay, remarked to Penn at the time: 'Thou has land enough, so need not be a churle if thou intend to advance thy plantation.'[34]

Once in Pennsylvania, some purchasers thought that Penn had reserved too much for himself. While 'First Purchasers' had been promised a dividend of land in the commercial city of Philadelphia as an inducement to buy shares, they soon discovered that they were not receiving the choicest waterfront lots but rather lands on the outskirts of the city. They were even less pleased when, just two years after the founding, the proprietor began to pursue his claims for quitrents upon the land.

Another source of contention arose from within Quakerism itself, in the principles and personal styles that characterized the Society of Friends. The Quaker insistence upon liberty within the spiritual realm carried over into the political. Friends in Pennsylvania, like their fellows elsewhere, were sensitive to anything that suggested an infringement of their liberties, even at the hands of a Quaker proprietor. Thus the *Frame of Government* was challenged by some right from the beginning, and was voted down in the Pennsylvania Assembly when a group of Quaker assemblymen made common cause with the representatives of the lower counties. Over the succeeding decade-and-a-half proprietary authority in Pennsylvania was continually challenged by a faction of leading Friends promoting the cause of provincial autonomy. That led Penn to plead with his co-religionists to 'be not so governmentish'.[35]

Towards the end of the century Pennsylvania politics took a different turn. Where political opposition during the first decade had sprung largely from prominent Friends dissatisfied with proprietary greed, by the later years the principal source of dissent was not the wealthier Quakers but lesser members, who would coalesce within the Assembly behind the figure of David Lloyd, who had originally gone to Pennsylvania to serve as Penn's Attorney-General. Once in the colony Lloyd took to opposition, heading an anti-proprietary faction within

[33] William Penn to ——, July 1681, quoted in Nash, *Quakers and Politics*, p. 10.

[34] Robert Barclay to William Penn, 19 Nov. 1681, in Dunn and Dunn, eds., *Papers of William Penn*, II, p. 132.

[35] Penn to Council, 19 Aug. 1685, quoted in Nash, *Quakers and Politics*, p. 49.

the Assembly that opposed the prerogatives of proprietors and Governors. In the process, Lloyd appealed for support among country delegates and persons of middling position in attacking the powers of proprietors and élites. The result would be a gradual popularization of political proceedings in Pennsylvania.[36]

Factionalism within the political realm was amplified by religious conflict. In the last decade of the century the Society of Friends divided, in a dispute that reverberated throughout the region. At the centre of controversy was the Scots Quaker George Keith, an associate of Robert Barclay and an intimate of important figures of the early Enlightenment. Keith came to East Jersey in 1685 to work as surveyor for the Scottish proprietors. From there he moved on to Philadelphia, where he soon began to quarrel with that city's Quaker establishment.[37]

At the heart of the dispute were some significant changes that were taking place within the Society of Friends. While the first generation of Quakers had been noted for a radical spiritualism that made them seem among the most disruptive groups in mid-seventeenth-century England, with the conversion of such prominent individuals as Penn and Barclay the Society began to change. Under the leadership of George Fox, some of the radically individualist aspects of Quakerism were muted by a countervailing emphasis upon organization through an orderly hierarchy of local, monthly, quarterly, and yearly meetings, dominated by evermore selective groups of Friends. If Quakers still looked to the inner light, the light was increasingly identified through the sense of the meeting and the authority of weighty Friends.

In Pennsylvania, where Friends were in actual possession of a colony, the drive towards organization was particularly acute. Prominent Friends in Pennsylvania worked to solidify their supervisory authority within the meeting in their role as travelling ministers or Public Friends. In so doing, they came to differ considerably from the practice of the Quaker meetings on Long Island and New Jersey that were founded before the Philadelphia Meeting and lay outside of its immediate influence. Quakers in those meetings probably remained closer to the spiritual egalitarianism of the early Quakers.

Into that division stepped George Keith, who brought with him a reputation as one of the most learned members of the Society of Friends. Keith hailed from Aberdeen, the primary home of Scottish Quakerism but also a university town. Scottish Quakers in general were known to have a greater concern for theology and learning than did other Friends, and Keith was no exception. After arriving in Philadelphia and listening to the pronouncements of leading Quakers in that city, Keith decided that Friends there needed to pay closer attention to the Bible and

[36] Ibid., pp. 287–305.

[37] Ethyn Kirby, *George Keith, 1638–1716* (New York, 1942).

Christian theology rather than relying so heavily upon the authority of the quarterly and yearly meetings. That suggestion proved unacceptable to Quaker leaders.[38]

The Keithian schism divided the Society of Friends. On the whole, Keith's appeal was greatest among marginal groups of Friends. In Philadelphia, the majority of Quakers remained with the Meeting, especially among the more prominent Friends. Keith did gain considerable support among the tradesmen and the middling sorts, who seemed to share his concerns about the authority of more highly placed Quakers. A critical follower was William Bradford, the city's only printer, who helped to publicize Keith's cause. In East Jersey, most of the Scots joined with Keith, along with many of their neighbours, and whole meetings severed their connection with the Philadelphia Meeting. On Long Island, some joined with Keith, while others, adhering to the initial individualist tendencies among Friends, broke away in still more radical directions. Some allied with the Rhode Island Meeting; others would further subdivide into such radical branches as the Singing Quakers, or would abandon the Society to become Baptists.[39]

The Keithian dispute overlapped other issues of spirituality and authority among Friends. One of those was slavery. The same well-to-do merchants who claimed authority within the quarterly and yearly Meetings were also among the leading Quaker slave-holders. Yet from the very beginning some Friends questioned that trade. As early as 1676 the English Quaker William Edmundson, then in Newport, Rhode Island, recorded the first such attack on slavery, among the very first anti-slavery statements to appear in English America. The first such pronouncement in Pennsylvania appeared in 1688, signed by four Germantown Friends, on the grounds that slavery violated the Golden Rule ('do unto others as you would that they should do unto you'), encouraged sinful rather than Christian behaviour, and was founded upon violence.[40]

Quaker attacks upon the institution of slavery occurred sporadically over the succeeding decades, often—although not always—offered by members of marginal position. One such statement appeared in 1693, issued by a group of Keithians recently separated from the Meeting. Another Keithian, John Hepburn of East Jersey, published an extensive anti-slavery tract in the second decade of the eighteenth century. Moreover, opposition to slave-holding would continue to

[38] Jon Butler, '"Gospel Order Improved": The Keithian Schism and the Exercise of Quaker Ministerial Authority in Pennsylvania', *WMQ*, Third Series, XXXI (1974), pp. 431–52.

[39] Nash, *Quakers and Politics*, pp. 152–61; Landsman, *Scotland and its First American Colony*, pp. 169–73; DeRiggi, 'Quakerism on Long Island', pp. 128–32, 219–24; Edgar L. Pennington, 'Journal of the Reverend George Keith', *Historical Magazine of the Protestant Episcopal Church*, XV (1951), pp. 343–487; Jon Butler, 'Into Pennsylvania's Spiritual Abyss: The Rise and Fall of the Later Keithians, 1693–1703', *Pennsylvania Magazine of History and Biography* (hereafter *PMHB*), CI (1977), pp. 151–70.

[40] Soderlund, *Quakers and Slavery*, pp. 17–31.

grow among a number of local Meetings, many in peripheral areas where Keithians and radical Friends still had considerable support. Yet within the Philadelphia Yearly Meeting anti-slavery expression was often suppressed by the actions of weighty Friends. Not until the second half of the eighteenth century, following a considerable change in membership in the Meeting, would it take a formal stand against the institution.[41]

Did the Middle Colonies Exist?

If the Middle Colonies were the last group of English colonies to be opened to English settlement during the seventeenth century, the region was also the last to be designated. Lacking the obvious religious coherence of New England or the unifying plantation cultures of the West Indies, the Chesapeake, or Carolina, what we know as the Middle Colonies simply represented what lay in between. Not until the next century would observers begin to think of a middle region, as in the Anglican missionary Andrew Burnaby's account of a 1759 tour through the 'middle settlements'.[42] Thereafter, observers would increasingly refer to a middle section or 'middle provinces'; even that would remain less fixed as a geographical designation than 'New England' or 'the Chesapeake' or the 'southern plantation colonies'.

The Middle Colonies possessed a number of common characteristics. All contained populations diverse in nationality and religion, alongside substantial toleration. All developed prosperous family farms served by well-developed commercial sectors; in each, one could see evidence of the establishment of characteristic 'liberal' values of family, property, and independence. All were established as proprietary colonies, and the leading proprietors of each had close ties to the Restoration Court. The troubles that this association caused between proprietors and discontented settlers led to the development everywhere of heightened popular political participation and a distinctly factious politics.[43]

Despite those similarities, some have questioned whether the mid-Atlantic colonies really constituted a single geographic region. The region lacked a particular founding moment comparable to the 'Great Migration' to New England in the 1630s or the Virginia Company settlement at Jamestown; European nationalities there experienced a diverse series of 'foundings' between 1620 and 1680. While

[41] Ibid., pp. 32–53.

[42] Andrew Burnaby, *Travels through the Middle Settlements in North-America*, 2nd edn. (London, 1775).

[43] On the typicality of the Middle Colonies, see Michael Zuckerman, 'Introduction: Puritans, Cavaliers, and the Motley Middle', in *Friends and Neighbors: Group Life in America's First Plural Society* (Philadelphia, 1982), pp. 3–25.

all of the Middle Colonies were ethnically diverse, the populations of the colonies, and even the patterns of diversity, differed considerably from one to another. New York, despite the almost bewildering variety of population in its Dutch antecedent, increasingly became divided into distinct Dutch and English factions. The Quaker colony of Pennsylvania, in contrast, developed ever-greater religious variety. The population of the Jerseys, as usual, differed from the other two and from each other. And while all of the colonies displayed a considerable sphere of toleration, the motivations behind it differed greatly; from New York, where it existed in practice to a much greater extent than it did in theory, to Pennsylvania, where toleration ranked as the first principle of the 'Fundamentall Constitutions'.

In several respects, the commercial centres at New York and Philadelphia represented two poles pulling the region in opposite directions in commerce and in culture; a number of historians have suggested that each constituted the centre of a distinct 'migration field'.[44] East Jersey resembled New York in having a prominent proprietary group and pronounced ethnic divisions and was tied to the latter colony in trade; there was a considerable overlap also between the New York and East Jersey élites. West Jersey was more like Pennsylvania in its Quaker origin, its looser proprietary control, and a pattern of diversity that did not automatically translate into division.

And yet colonies established as late as those of the Middle Colonies could not have been anything but interdependent. From the time of the English conquest in 1664, English-sponsored settlement proceeded to fill in the coastal plain of the mid-Atlantic region that linked English colonies to the north and to the south, creating a contiguous zone of settlement along the Atlantic seaboard from New England to Carolina. The ports of Philadelphia and New York served not only their respective colonies but also an expanding commercial network that extended across the Atlantic. Within the interior of New Jersey, merchants would develop a string of roads and ferries across the central corridor that connected those two commercial centres across fluid provincial borders. And at the international diplomatic centre at Albany, Imperial negotiators helped secure a zone of settlement for English or British colonies along much of the Atlantic coastline.

The colonies were linked in function as well. Within each colony, religious or ethnic merchant communities were able to use their overseas connections to develop a vital presence within the provisioning trade, carrying the produce of mid-Atlantic farms. The result was the substantial economic diversification of what would become a truly British colonial world. In the process, the Middle Colonies provided homes for mobile and ambitious European farming families

[44] Wells, 'The Demography of a Region', in Klepp, ed., *Symposium on the Demographic History*, pp. 219–22; also Robert J. Gough, 'The Myth of the Middle Colonies: An Analysis of Regionalization in Early America', *PMHB*, CIII (1983), pp. 392–419.

under the twin promises of pluralism and prosperity, drawing a vastly expanded network of potential migrants into the web of the emerging British Empire. They were the home as well of a liberal ethic of individual achievement, later refined and popularized by such representative figures as Benjamin Franklin, whose maxims in the persona of 'Poor Richard' suggested rather emphatically that individual aspiration represented the overall key to social improvement.

The emergence of the Middle Colonies thus represented a distinct phase in British colonial settlement, the time in which disparate English colonial outposts on the North American mainland were drawn together into a contiguous and interdependent line of increasingly British colonies. In the middle was a society in which the aspiration for land to provide for families led to a steady course of extended development. Perhaps the most articulate spokesman for that society would be still another mid-Atlantic resident of the eighteenth century, the French-born J. Hector St John de Crèvecœur, who, while residing in New York, would write in the guise of a Pennsylvanian presenting himself to the world as the 'American Farmer'. To Crèvecœur, as to many voices of the European Enlightenment, the Pennsylvanian was the American, a mixed race of people bred from all of the nations of western Europe. To the Farmer, Pennsylvania was famous for both toleration and prosperity, and the two were closely linked. Henceforth, the toleration and pluralism that characterized British provincial and later American society would be justified by their contribution to the ever-expanding progression of settlement.[45]

[45] J. Hector St. John Crèvecœur, *Letters from an American Farmer and Sketches of Eighteenth-Century America* (1782; New York, 1981), esp. pp. 74–75; also Milton M. Klein, ed., *The Independent Reflector or Weekly Essays on Sundry Important Subjects More Particularly Adapted to the Province of New York by William Livingstone and Others* (Cambridge, Mass., 1963), p. 183, for another mid-Atlantic example.

Select Bibliography

RANDALL H. BALMER, *A Perfect Babel of Confusion: Dutch Religion and English Culture in the Middle Colonies* (New York, 1989).

WAYNE BODLE, 'Themes and Directions in Middle Colonies Historiography', *William and Mary Quarterly*, Third Series, LI (1994), pp. 355–88.

PATRICIA U. BONOMI, *A Factious People: Politics and Society in Colonial New York* (New York, 1971).

MARY MAPLES DUNN and RICHARD S. DUNN, eds., *The Papers of William Penn*, 4 vols. (Philadelphia, 1981–86).

JOYCE D. GOODFRIEND, *Before the Melting Pot: Society and Culture in Colonial New York City, 1664–1730* (Princeton, 1992).

FRANCIS JENNINGS, *The Ambiguous Iroquois Empire: The Covenant Chain Confederation of Indian Tribes With English Colonies From its Beginnings to the Lancaster Treaty of 1744* (New York, 1984).

MICHAEL KAMMEN, *Colonial New York: A History* (White Plains, NY, 1975).
NED C. LANDSMAN, *Scotland and its First American Colony, 1683–1765* (Princeton, 1985).
JAMES T. LEMON, *The Best Poor Man's Country: A Geographical Study of Early South-eastern Pennsylvania* (Baltimore, 1973).
BARRY LEVY, *Quakers and the American Family: British Settlement in the Delaware Valley* (New York, 1988).
DONNA MERWICK, *Possessing Albany, 1630–1710: The Dutch and English Experiences* (New York, 1990).
GARY B. NASH, *Quakers and Politics: Pennsylvania, 1681–1726* (Princeton, 1968).
EDWARD B. O'CALLAGHAN and BERTHOLD FERNOW, eds., *Documents Relative to the Colonial History of the State of New York*, 15 vols. (Albany, 1853–87).
OLIVER A. RINK, *Holland on the Hudson: An Economic and Social History of Dutch New York* (Ithaca, NY, 1986).
DANIEL K. RICHTER, *The Ordeal of the Longhouse: The Peoples of the Iroquois League in the Era of European Colonization* (Chapel Hill, NC, 1992).
ROBERT C. RITCHIE, *The Duke's Province: A Study of New York Politics and Society, 1664–1691* (Chapel Hill, NC, 1977).
JEAN R. SODERLUND, *Quakers and Slavery: A Divided Spirit* (Princeton, 1985).
FREDERICK B. TOLLES, *Meeting House and Counting House: The Quaker Merchants of Colonial Philadelphia, 1682–1763* (Chapel Hill, NC, 1948).
ALAN TULLY, *Forming American Politics: Ideals, Interests, and Institutions in Colonial New York and Pennsylvania* (Baltimore, 1994).
MICHAEL ZUCKERMAN, ed., *Friends and Neighbors: Group Life in America's First Plural Society* (Philadelphia, 1982).

17

'Shaftesbury's Darling': British Settlement in The Carolinas at the Close of the Seventeenth Century

ROBERT M. WEIR

Carolina, lying between Virginia and Spanish Florida, appeared to be a particularly inviting area for English colonization after the Restoration of the monarchy in 1660. Native Americans inhabited the region, but most of the coastal groups were not particularly powerful. The French had tried to establish a settlement at Port Royal Sound in the 1560s, but abandoned the effort; and the Spanish, who held tenuous claims and isolated missionary outposts, had withdrawn from their once-substantial settlement at Port Royal. Moreover, the English capture of Jamaica in 1655 revealed that Spain was no longer capable of defending all of its possessions in the New World.

A number of well-placed Englishmen hoping to profit from a settlement on the south-eastern coast of North America requested that Charles II recognize them as the Lords Proprietor of Carolina and grant them title to a large area. Being indebted to some of them pecuniarily as well as politically, the King complied in 1663. Though reluctant to make the gift, Charles II seems to have hoped that the grant would prove an efficient way to establish tractable colonies, and he was to follow similar procedures when approving colonization along the mid-Atlantic coastline of North America. Unimpressed with the often unruly colonies that had been founded during the first half of the century, the Proprietors of the Restoration colonies had plans to promote the development of orderly, obedient, and profitable settlements. Although none would be entirely satisfied with the results, their efforts led to the establishment of several successful but very different colonies. Of these, Carolina proved to be perhaps the most unusual, partly because its Proprietors devised an elaborate plan for a hierarchical society, but more importantly, because some settlers attempted to reconstitute on the malarial lowlands the social conditions they had known in Barbados, where a small number of whites dominated a large black labour force. To understand this development one must examine the origins of colonial society in Carolina.[1]

[1] For the Carolinas in this period, see Converse D. Clowse, *Economic Beginnings in Colonial South Carolina, 1670–1730* (Columbia, SC, 1971); William S. Powell, *North Carolina through Four Centuries*

Barbadian Problems and the Attractions of Carolina

The problems and the promise of Barbados provided the impetus for the settlement of Carolina. During the 1640s planters in Barbados had switched from tobacco to sugar, which became the most lucrative of all colonial exports. The resulting boom produced fabulous wealth for some and abject poverty for others, who were described by contemporaries as 'poor men that are just permitted to live . . . derided by the Negroes, and branded with the Epithite of white slaves'.[2] The rapid increase of Africans as well as whites soon made the island one of the most densely populated places in the English-speaking world. Land became so scarce that not even wealthy planters could provide a sufficient inheritance for their younger sons, and no one wanted to divert land that was suitable for sugar cane to less lucrative food crops. Casting about for better opportunities elsewhere, some Barbadians went to Jamaica in the 1660s and 1670s. Others found Carolina more attractive.

The magnificent sound at Port Royal, South Carolina, which sixteenth-century French seamen had considered sufficient to hold 'all the shippes in the worlde', provided the best harbour on the south-eastern coast of North America and the one closest to the West Indies (Map 17.1). Captain William Hilton, sent to explore the area by a group of Barbadians in 1663, praised its anchorage and the good soil.[3] Three years later, Robert Sandford, also reconnoitering for Barbadians, reached the same area and was favourably impressed with the fertility and commodiousness of the Sea Islands.[4] Farther north, the shores of Albemarle Sound appeared equally promising. Following his expedition of 1580, Arthur Barlowe reported that the area was another Eden where 'The earth bringeth foorth all things in aboundance, as in the first creation, without toile or labour'.[5] More experience in the New World disabused Englishmen of their illusions about the labour requirements but not about the possibilities, for their dreams were often merely the penumbra of reality. An account of Virginia published in 1650, when Virginians began penetrating the Albemarle Sound area, paid special attention to the 'South parts'

(Chapel Hill, NC, 1989); M. Eugene Sirmans, *Colonial South Carolina: A Political History, 1663–1763* (Chapel Hill, NC, 1966); David Duncan Wallace, *History of South Carolina*, 4 vols. (New York, 1934–35), I; and Robert M. Weir, *Colonial South Carolina: A History* (1983; Columbia, SC, 1997).

[2] Quoted in Carl and Roberta Bridenbaugh, *No Peace Beyond the Line: The English in the Caribbean, 1624–1690* (New York, 1972), p. 215.

[3] Jean Ribault, 'The True Discoverie of Terra Florida' [1563], in David B. Quinn and others, eds., *New American World: A Documentary History of North America to 1612*, 5 vols. (New York, 1979), II, p. 293; William Hilton, 'A Relation of a Discovery' [1664], in Alexander S. Salley, Jr., ed., *Narratives of Early Carolina, 1650–1708* (1911; New York, 1939), p. 44. See above, pp. 226–27.

[4] Robert Sandford, 'A Relation of a Voyage on the Coast of the Province of Carolina', 1666, in Salley, ed., *Narratives*, p. 101.

[5] 'Arthur Barlowe on the First Virginia Voyage' [1584], in David B. Quinn and others, eds., *New American World*, III, p. 280.

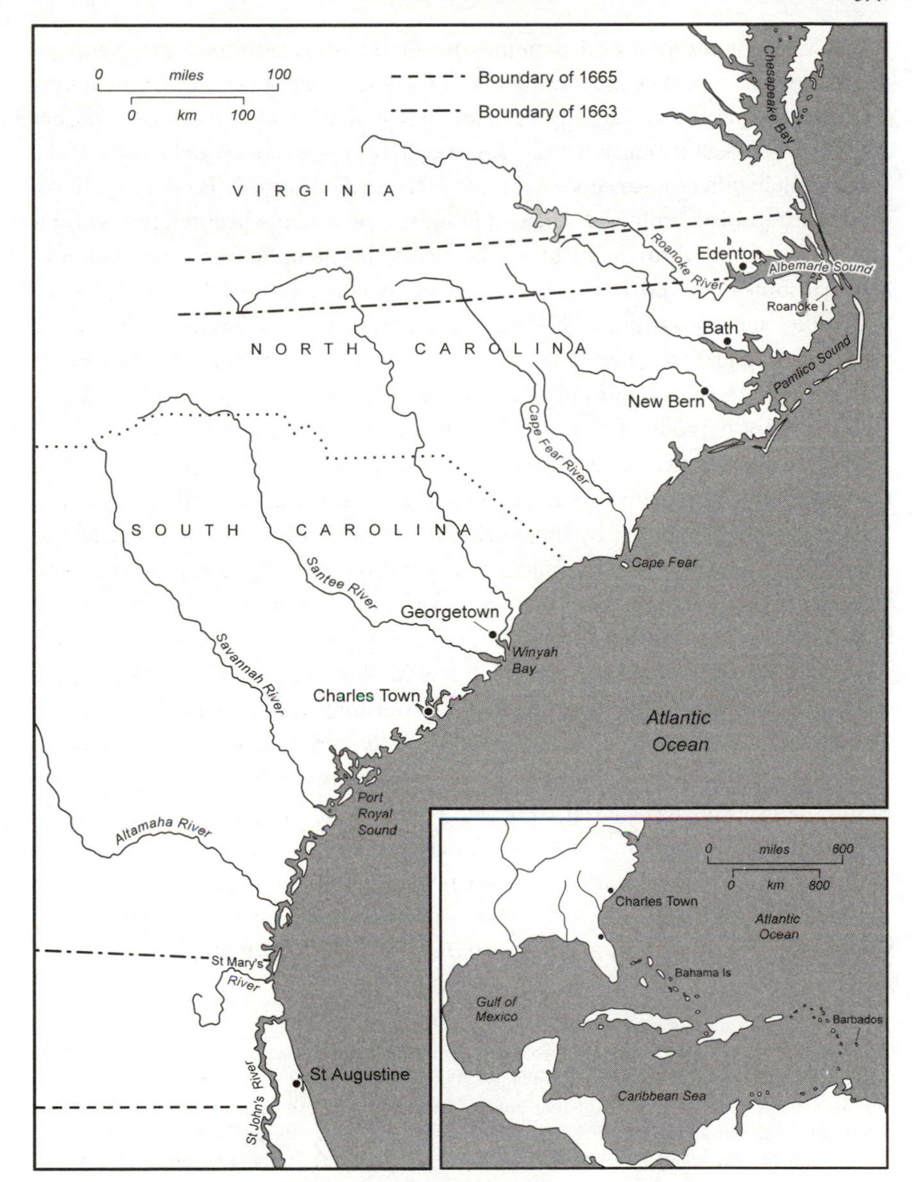

MAP 17.1. The Carolinas in the Seventeenth Century

thereof, which had been 'a long neglected Virgin' awaiting those who might recognize her worth.[6]

[6] Edward Williams, *Virgo Triumphans; or, VIRGINIA in Generall, but the South part therof in particular: Including the fertile CAROLANA*... (London, 1650), n. p.

These early accounts sounded themes that later writers amplified; its advantages made Carolina a land of enchantment and the logical place from which to supply Barbados. Some found magic in the glow of the fireflies at night, while another reporter remarked prosaically that 'you may have five successive Harvests of the same grain in different seasons'.[7] An ox, another writer claimed, 'is raised at almost as little expense in Carolina, as a hen is in England', while hogs proliferated 'without any charge or trouble to the Planter'. The result, this pamphleteer claimed in 1682, was that some men who 'have never a Servant' own 'two or three hundred Hogs of which they make great profit; Barbadoes, Jamaica and New England, affording a constant good price for their Pork'.[8] There was, others maintained, 'no Place in the Continent of *America*, where People can transport themselves to greater Advantage'. At the very least, 'moderate Industry' would ensure 'all the Necessaries of Life'.[9]

Nor would the Native Americans interfere. We do not know the population of the Carolinas before 1670 with any precision but it seems to have been well over 20,000.[10] Settlers were not daunted by these numbers because they assumed that Native Americans would be either friendly or incapable of opposing European weapons. Experience exposed the error of these assumptions, but some writers still persisted with the view that the Indians of Carolina were 'of a mild nature and neither able nor disposed to hurt the *English*; they being few in Number, and disunited amongst themselves by their Broils'.[11] John Archdale, Governor of Carolina during the 1690s, elaborated: 'the Hand of God' had been 'eminently seen in thinning the *Indians*, to make room for the *English*', thereby sparing Englishmen much of the 'Bloody Work' of the Spanish who, he believed, were better suited to it. Thus, pamphleteers could still argue that the presence of Native Americans was an attraction rather than a deterrent. Being 'great Hunters', the Indians were 'serviceable to kill Dear, &c. for to procure Skins for Trade with us'.[12] Furthermore, a contemporary observed that 'The English Traders are seldom without an *Indian* Female for his Bed-fellow.'[13]

[7] T. A. Gent, 'Carolina: or a Description of the Present State of that Country, and the Natural Excellencies Thereof' [1682], in B. R. Carroll, ed., *Historical Collections of South Carolina*, 2 vols. (New York, 1836), II, p. 74; Williams, *Virgo Triumphans*, p. 3.

[8] Samuel Wilson, 'An Account of the Province of Carolina, in America' [1682], in Carroll, ed., *Historical Collections*, II, pp. 29, 30.

[9] Thomas Nairne, 'A Letter from South Carolina' [1710], in Jack P. Greene, ed., *Selling a New World: Two Colonial South Carolina Promotional Pamphlets* (Columbia, SC, 1989), pp. 35, 38.

[10] Peter H. Wood, 'The Changing Population of the Colonial South: An Overview by Race and Region, 1685–1790', in Peter H. Wood, Gregory A. Waselkov, and M. Thomas Hatley, eds., *Powhatan's Mantle: Indians in the Colonial Southeast* (Lincoln, Nebr., 1989), p. 38.

[11] Peter Heylyn, *Cosmography in Four Books* (London, 1703), p. 961.

[12] John Archdale, 'A New Description of that Fertile and Pleasant Province of Carolina' [1707], in Carroll, ed., *Historical Collections*, II, pp. 88, 94.

[13] John Lawson, *A New Voyage to Carolina* [1709], ed. Hugh Talmage Lefler (Chapel Hill, NC, 1967), p. 35.

Settlement and Politics

The attractions of the mainland and the problems of Barbados made a propitious combination for the Proprietors of Carolina. Perhaps the first Barbadian to act upon the possibilities was Sir John Colleton. A Royalist who had fought for Charles I, he had fled to Barbados and became a planter. In London to claim his reward for faithful service after the Restoration of the monarchy in 1660, he sought help from John, Baron Berkeley of Stratton, and Lord Berkeley's brother, William Berkeley, Governor of Virginia. Through the Berkeley connections the group won the support of the Duke of York and through him of Sir George Carteret (soon to share with John, Lord Berkeley, a gift of New Jersey from the Duke of York). Colleton himself was connected with the powerful Duke of Albemarle, who also became involved. This group (Colleton, the two Berkeleys, Carteret, and Albemarle) was soon to be joined by three others: William, Lord Craven; Edward Hyde, Lord Clarendon; and Anthony Ashley Cooper, later Lord Shaftesbury. Their combined influence persuaded the King in 1663 to cancel the grant of 'Carolana' made, in 1629, by his father to the Attorney-General, Sir Robert Heath—a grant that had produced much litigation but no settlement—and to bestow 'Carolina' on the eight Lords Proprietor. Their possessions would include 'ALL that Territory or Tract of ground' from the Virginia border southward to Spanish Florida and westward 'as far as the South Seas'.

Two years later Charles issued another charter extending the boundaries of the colony to encompass everything between latitudes 29° and 36° 30′ north, thereby including Spanish St Augustine as well as some existing English settlements on Albemarle Sound. Designed in part to pressure Spain, this enlarged grant gave the Carolina Proprietors title to the upper Gulf Coast. Alarmed, Spanish authorities responded in the Treaty of Madrid by agreeing to recognize England's claim to the area that it effectively occupied north of modern Charleston. What effective occupation meant remained debatable for many years, and the Spaniards in Florida tried to make the best of the doubt for much of the next century. In other essentials, the two Carolina charters were virtually the same. Like the document granting Maryland to Lord Baltimore a generation earlier, they conferred governmental as well as property rights. The Proprietors could make laws with the 'advice, assent, and approbation of the Freemen', establish courts, maintain military forces, bestow titles of nobility (as long as they were different from those prevailing in England) and, among other things, provide such religious toleration as they believed to be 'fit and reasonable'.[14]

[14] For the 1663 and 1665 charters, see Mattie E. E. Parker, ed., *North Carolina Charters and Constitutions, 1578–1698* (Raleigh, NC, 1963). Quotations from pp. 76–77, 94, 104.

Equipped with these broad powers, the grantees sought to generate income by attracting settlers who would pay for their use of the land. Impressed by the Puritans' ability to create towns in New England, the Proprietors welcomed a group from Massachusetts which settled on the Cape Fear River in 1663. These settlers abandoned Carolina within a few months, and the liberal Concessions and Agreements of 1665 were subsequently issued by the Proprietors, possibly to salvage the reputation of the colony. This document (which Berkeley and Carteret later reused with little modification in New Jersey) promised settlers virtually complete self-government through an elected Assembly having the exclusive right to tax inhabitants, freedom of religion, and nearly free land under a headright system that would give the first arrivals up to 150 acres for each member of a family. In return, the Proprietors retained the power to veto legislation and to charge a quitrent of a halfpenny per acre per year.

Meanwhile, several Barbadians planned to settle the area. One group, calling themselves the 'Barbadian Adventurers', despatched William Hilton on an exploring voyage, but they failed to come to terms with the Proprietors. Some of them then established a second settlement at Cape Fear, also without completing formal arrangements with the Proprietors. In the interim, however, negotiations between the original group of Barbadians and the Proprietors produced an agreement and the choice of Sir John Yeamans as Governor. Accordingly, in 1665 he and some others joined the settlers already at Cape Fear, but within two years they abandoned the post and scrapped plans for a second settlement at Port Royal. Trouble with Indians, bad luck, and poor leadership were chiefly responsible for the failure.

Up to this time the Proprietors themselves had done little to promote the settlement of Carolina. They probably believed their involvement to be unnecessary, and the Great Plague and the Fire of London, as well as war with Holland and France, certainly commanded attention between 1665 and 1667. In 1669, however, Anthony Ashley Cooper prevailed upon his colleagues to contribute the necessary funds, and he organized the expedition that succeeded in establishing the first permanent settlement in South Carolina. The expedition left England in August 1669, stopped briefly in Ireland and Barbados, and after the loss of two vessels reached the vicinity of modern Charleston on 15 March 1670. Then, to comply with the Proprietors' instructions, the settlers continued to Port Royal Sound, but they quickly recognized that this situation was dangerously close to the Spanish in Florida. Accordingly, they adopted the suggestion of a local Indian and moved north to what is now the confluence of the Ashley and the Cooper Rivers. There, a short way up the Ashley River at Albemarle Point, they constructed an outpost. In August the Spanish attacked from St Augustine but failed to drive the English out. In 1679 the Proprietors ordered the Carolinians to move to a site on the peninsula between the two rivers, where they established Charles Town (incorporated as Charleston in 1783).

European settlement of North Carolina proceeded independently. Squatters from Virginia, who moved into the nearby area around Albemarle Sound perhaps as early as 1653, were the first settlers. Recognizing their presence, the Proprietors established a county in the area and named William Drummond, a Scot then living in Virginia, as its Governor. The Barbadian settlement on the Cape Fear River was to be the nucleus of another county, Clarendon, but its abandonment put 300 miles of wilderness between the northern settlement and the focus of the Proprietors' main interest on the Ashley River. Isolated as it was, the Albemarle outpost grew slowly, and Bath, the first town in North Carolina, was not established until 1706.

Political Development

To establish 'the interest of the Lords Proprietors with Equality, and without confusion', and make the form of government 'most agreeable' to the 'Monarchy under which we live', Shaftesbury and his secretary, John Locke (later to become famous as a philosopher), drew up the Fundamental Constitutions of Carolina.[15] That Shaftesbury later called the colony 'my Darling' suggests that he had an emotional as well as financial investment in the project, and he was the one ultimately responsible for the document.[16] Locke, however, probably contributed some ideas. Like the other Proprietors, both men wished to 'avoid erecting a numerous Democracy'. Doubtless they were familiar with James Harrington's *Oceana*, which maintained that political power should be distributed in proportion to property-holdings. The Fundamental Constitutions accordingly made land the foundation of the hierarchical society envisioned for Carolina. Landgraves (a German title that Locke may have picked up on a recent trip to Cleves) and *cassiques* (cacique—a Spanish designation for an Indian chief) constituted the local nobility; each of the former would receive baronies totalling 48,000 acres, the latter 24,000. Collectively, the aristocracy would control two-fifths of the land; the people would have three-fifths. Each of the Proprietors was to head one of eight administrative courts; they and the subordinate members of these bodies would make up the Grand Council, which was to propose legislation. A unicameral Parliament, composed of the Proprietors, the nobility, and elected representatives of the freeholders, could merely approve or disapprove these proposals.

[15] 'Fundamental Constitutions' [1669], in Parker, ed., *N.C. Charters*, p. 132. On Locke see above, pp. 42–43.

[16] K. H. D. Haley, *The First Earl of Shaftesbury* (Oxford, 1968), p. 252.

The whole arrangement, which was somewhat analogous to the situation in Ireland where the Irish Parliament could only consider legislation previously approved by the English Privy Council, now appears anachronistic and cumbersome, but it was designed to distribute and balance power so as to protect everyone. Despite the aristocratic elements of the plan, Shaftesbury was able to maintain that even the Proprietors' own power was insufficient to harm the 'meanest' or most insignificant man in the province.[17] Moreover, the constitutions included some extraordinarily liberal provisions, including wide religious toleration and use of the secret ballot.

The Fundamental Constitutions influenced later developments in the Carolinas—the Proprietors granted some baronies, for example—but the document never became law. An appointed Governor and Council, meeting with a few representatives elected by the freemen, governed from Charleston. Objecting to some provisions in the Fundamental Constitutions, this group rejected the document; later, Carolinians refused to approve revised versions on the grounds that so changeable a document could not be a fundamental constitution. During the 1690s, following English precedents, the elected representatives began meeting separately and calling themselves the Commons House of Assembly. North Carolinians took a separate but similar path. Originally, the Proprietors had expected that they would elect representatives to the Assembly at Charleston, but the distance made this impractical. As in South Carolina, a unicameral body composed of a Deputy Governor and his appointed Council, joined by elected representatives, governed until the mid-1690s, when the North Carolina representatives also began meeting separately. Accepting the inevitable, the Proprietors officially appointed a separate Governor for North Carolina in 1712, and later events confirmed this division. In the interim, different practices developed in the two colonies. In South Carolina, for instance, counties became little more than paper categories used to designate the location of land grants; the fundamental unit of local government, as in Barbados, was the parish. Charleston, however, remained the centre of real power. In North Carolina, on the other hand, Virginia provided the model, and counties became functioning entities.

Despite such institutional differences, turbulent and factional politics characterized both Carolinas during the early years. Some of the same individuals caused trouble in both areas. One of them, John Culpeper, served as Surveyor-General in the southern settlement during 1671–72, but he and a few confederates attempted to defect from the colony. Local authorities seized their vessel, but they escaped.

[17] 'Fundamental Constitutions', 1669, in Parker, ed., *N.C. Charters*, p. 132; Lord Shaftesbury to Maurice Mathews, 20 June 1672, in 'The Shaftesbury Papers and Other Records Relating to Carolina', in Langdon Cheves, ed., *Collections of the South Carolina Historical Society*, V (1897), p. 399. For examples of other colonial constitutions devised at this time, see above, pp. 359–60.

Culpeper then turned up in the Albemarle region, where he became involved in what came to be known as Culpeper's Rebellion, though he was not the leading figure in the local faction that opposed the Proprietors' attempts to enforce the English Navigation Acts. Nevertheless, he helped to organize the armed group that in December 1677 imprisoned several men, including the acting Governor, who had himself been arresting others arbitrarily. The insurgents took over the government, which they continued to operate 'by their owne authority & according to their owne modell',[18] and elected an Assembly. When some of the prisoners eluded their captors and fled to England, the rebels sent Culpeper to London to explain the situation. Tried for treason, he was acquitted after Shaftesbury, testifying on his behalf, downplayed the seriousness of the whole affair lest the Crown deem it a sufficient reason to vacate the Proprietors' charter. Historians, however, have considered 'Culpeper's Rebellion' one of the earliest popular upheavals in the colonies.

The Proprietors' next two choices for Governor also encountered disturbances; the first, Seth Sothel, who had purchased one of the proprietary shares, in fact proved to be the chief author of his own difficulties. Assuming his duties in the Albemarle area in 1683, Sothel seized both the persons and property of his opponents. By the end of the decade local residents lost patience with him, and in 1689 the Assembly banished him from the area. Sothel then went to Charleston where, being a Proprietor, he was able to claim the governorship. But his conduct of the office once again caused trouble, and in 1691 the Proprietors replaced him. Meanwhile, their choice to succeed Sothel in the Albemarle area, Philip Ludwell, faced another rebellion led by John Gibbs, who claimed the governorship for himself. But the latter realized that he lacked sufficient forces and fled to Virginia.

Ludwell's administration began a period of stable government that lasted for about a decade before religious divisions contributed to its breakdown. Many immigrants were dissenters from the Church of England, and Quakers dominated some of the elected Assemblies. Thus, various attempts to establish the Anglican church produced increasingly serious friction. By 1708 the governorship had competing claimants and the Assembly rival delegations from each county. Resolved to end the chaos, the Proprietors appointed Edward Hyde, a distant kinsman of Queen Anne, as Governor. His first Assembly met in March 1711 and voided all laws passed under his predecessor, Thomas Cary, whose ship then fired on the house in which the Governor and his associates had gathered. But Cary's vessel soon ran aground and the rebels fled to Virginia. Four years later the legislature managed to pass a number of acts that established the Church of

[18] Case Between Thomas Miller[,] Collector of His Majesty's Customs[,] & Capt. Zachariah Gilham[,] Culpeper..., endorsed Recd. from Sir P. Colleton, 9 Feb. 1679–80, in William L. Saunders, ed., *The Colonial Records of North Carolina*, Vol. I, *1662–1712* (Raleigh, NC, 1886), p. 288.

England, regularized governmental procedures, fostered internal improvements, and contributed to increasing political stability.

Early South Carolinians were nearly as fractious as their North Carolina counterparts. The Barbadians, some of whom lived along a tributary of the Cooper River that gave them the sobriquet 'Goose Creek Men', proved to be especially assertive. Their highest hope for Carolina, Shaftesbury scornfully observed, was to make it subservient 'to the Interest of Barbados'. The Proprietors had better things in mind. The oath prescribed for members of the Council revealed their aspirations: the incumbents, who also acted as judges, were to swear to 'doe equall right to the rich and to the poore'; and not offer 'Councill for favor or affection, in any difference or quarrell depending before you', but to behave themselves 'as to equity and justice appertaines'.[19]

The Proprietors expected the conduct of Indian affairs to be equally enlightened. Their own behaviour in taking possession of the Native Americans' land, they assumed, was entirely justified. In a much-quoted and now famous phrase, Locke would later write that in 'the beginning all the World was *America*'—by which he meant that America was still in a state of nature, where title to property belonged only to the individual who had appropriated it by his immediate labour; Native American governments had not developed the institutional forms that conferred collective ownership of raw land.[20] That such notions ignored Indian concepts of property and served as convenient rationalizations for the Proprietors' actions does not necessarily mean that they were being hypocritical. In many areas they clearly tried to treat Native Americans fairly. Observing that the 'natives of that place, who will be concerned in our Plantations, are utterly Strangers to Christianity, whose Idolatry, Ignorance, or mistake gives us no right to expel or use them ill', the Proprietors stipulated that anyone—including Native Americans—who professed a God that they publicly worshipped should be accorded religious toleration.[21] Renaming two sons of a local Indian chief 'Honest' and 'Just', they arranged for the young men to be brought to England. After an audience with the Crown, the 'Indian princes' set sail for home and, perhaps as a harbinger of things to come, disappeared from the historical record.[22]

[19] Proprietors to Governor and Council, 18 May 1674, in 'The Shaftesbury Papers', in Cheves, ed., *Collections*, V, p. 436; William J. Rivers, *A Sketch of the History of South Carolina to the Close of the Proprietary Government by the Revolution of 1719* (Charleston, 1856), p. 370.

[20] This is a condensation of Locke's complex argument. For an illuminating discussion of his reasoning, see James Tully, *An Approach to Political Philosophy: Locke in Contexts* (Cambridge, 1993), pp. 137–76, and see above, pp. 42–47.

[21] 'Fundamental Constitutions', 1669, in Parker, ed., *N.C. Charters*, p. 148.

[22] Julien R. Childs, 'Honest and Just at the Court of Charles II', *South Carolina Historical Magazine*, LXIV (1963), p. 27; quotation from 'The Shaftesbury Papers', in Cheves, ed., *Collections*, p. 476 n.

The settlers quickly subverted many of the Proprietors' best intentions. One of the first Governors at Charleston, Sir John Yeamans, apparently arranged the murder of a rival in Barbados and a few weeks later married his widow. Presumably the Proprietors remained ignorant of these details, but some of them soon lost their illusions about him. 'If to convert all things to his present private profitt be the marke of able parts', Shaftesbury concluded, 'Sir John is without doubt a very judicious man.'[23] Self-interest seemed to be the general rule. Indeed, the Proprietors sought to recoup their expenses in settling the colony by granting themselves exclusive rights to commerce with the nearby Westo Indians. Local traders broke that monopoly by the simple expedient of fomenting a war, which virtually exterminated the tribe.

To circumvent the Goose Creek Men, who came originally from Barbados, the Proprietors encouraged the efforts of Lord Cardross and his Scottish followers to establish themselves at Port Royal in 1684. But within two years disease and a Spanish attack wiped out Stuart's Town. Meanwhile, the Proprietors recruited French Huguenots and English Dissenters. Both groups sent sizeable contingents to South Carolina, but the new arrivals failed to undermine the power of the Goose Creek Men; instead, their presence increased the religious dimensions of political conflict since most of the Barbadians were Anglican. Hoping that one of the Barbadians might be able to deal with his own ilk, the Proprietors then appointed James Colleton as Governor. But in 1690 the local governing body ousted and banished him. Sothel succeeded him. Five more years elapsed before John Archdale, a Quaker who had purchased a proprietary share, assumed the governorship and managed to achieve some political order and harmony. Still, chicanery facilitated passage of the Act that established the Anglican church in 1706, and factionalism continued to roil local politics for several decades.

None of these upheavals in either of the two Carolinas had much to do with the Glorious Revolution. To be sure, some issues—such as enforcement of the Navigation Acts and establishment of the Church of England—would not have arisen had the Carolinas not been colonies, but during the early days of these settlements Imperial concerns drove local politics only intermittently; the pursuit of power, booty, and the perquisites of office figured more routinely. Other considerations eventually assumed more important roles, but avaricious factionalism persisted longer in North Carolina, partly because its economy offered few attractive alternatives and it was militarily less vulnerable than its southern neighbour. In South Carolina, on the other hand, internal divisiveness threatened to become a fatal luxury after 1689, when the accession of William III brought England into the

[23] Lord Shaftesbury to Sir Peter Colleton, 27 Nov. 1672, in 'The Shaftesbury Papers', in Cheves, ed., *Collections*, p. 416.

continental coalition against France, and the southern frontier became a hotly contested area.

Perhaps because France had not yet established outposts on the Gulf Coast (the first, Biloxi, dated from 1699), little real fighting occurred in the area during King William's War (the War of the League of Augsburg, 1689–97). Queen Anne's War (the War of the Spanish Succession, 1702–13) involved more serious local conflict. Governor James Moore of South Carolina attacked France's Spanish allies at St Augustine in 1702 but failed to capture its fort; two years later he led a second expedition that destroyed the missions in northern Florida. Indian auxiliaries accompanied him, but Native Americans soon became apprehensive about the increasing white population of the Carolinas. After German and Swiss settlers established New Bern, North Carolina, in 1710, the Tuscarora Indians devastated much of the colony. South Carolina sent help in 1711, and a force of Yamasee Indians and whites defeated the Tuscaroras, many of whom soon departed for New York where they joined the Iroquois. Four years later the Yamasees themselves made war on South Carolina. Many contemporaries blamed the French and Spanish for instigating these hostilities, but depletion of the game by white encroachment on their hunting grounds and abuses in the deerskin trade provided sufficient cause for the Indians' resentment. Most of the southern tribes sided with the Yamasee, and at one point South Carolinians were able to defend only Charleston and the immediately surrounding territory. The Cherokees, however, initially remained neutral and eventually provided aid. Carolinians accordingly prevailed, but the Yamasees continued sporadic raids from Florida for the next fifteen years.

These conflicts, which depopulated the Port Royal area of South Carolina, contributed to the overthrow of the proprietary government. When rumour of an impending Spanish attack reached Charleston in 1719, the Assembly proclaimed itself to be a convention of the people and chose James Moore (son of the Governor of the same name) to replace the Proprietors' executive, Robert Johnson; it then requested that the King take over the local government. The Crown responded by appointing a provisional Governor for South Carolina. In North Carolina the Proprietors' representative remained in place until ensuing negotiations between royal authorities and the Proprietors culminated in 1729 with the Crown's purchase of seven of the eight proprietary shares. The eighth Proprietor, Sir George Carteret, continued to hold title to the northern half of North Carolina, known as the Granville District, until the Revolution. That this area was comparatively secure militarily is significant. Numerous issues had contributed to the revolt against the Proprietors, but the central problem was their inability to provide for the defence of the colony. Indeed, South Carolina's military weakness and exposed position on the southern frontier remained a continuing concern throughout much of the eighteenth century.

The Economy

Despite military weakness, royal control, increasing political stability, and somewhat better military security—especially after the establishment of Georgia in the 1730s—contributed to greater prosperity, particularly in South Carolina. By the mid-eighteenth century visitors often remarked about the wealth evident in and around Charleston, but seventeenth-century Carolinians had not been so fortunate. Like the other mainland colonies, South Carolina offered abundant land. 'But', as an early promotional pamphlet noted, 'a rational man will certainly inquire, When I have Land, what shall I doe with it?'[24] Satisfactory answers were not immediately forthcoming, although the Proprietors encouraged various experimental plantings. Given its latitude, they thought that South Carolina might produce oranges, lemons, olives, silk, and wines, but none of these worked out. Indigo and cotton would later become important crops, but early attempts to grow and process both proved discouraging.

Barbadians, we know, arrived intending to supply the Sugar Islands with foodstuffs and lumber, and Carolinians were soon shipping corn, peas, and meat to the West Indies. This trade continued throughout the entire colonial period, but it never proved especially lucrative. It did, however, foster development of a livestock industry that was ideally adapted to local conditions, where hogs and cattle could forage through the woods and open savannahs. Round-ups, branding, cow pens, and cattle drives accordingly presaged techniques later associated with the western plains. Not surprisingly, ranching was most important to the economy during the early years. The Yamasee War destroyed much of the industry, and it never recovered its former position.

Although some men made money raising livestock, not many acquired fortunes this way or, indeed, in any manner during the seventeenth century. The few who prospered usually did so by aggressively pursuing multiple opportunities. Provisioning pirates, pursuing the perquisites of office, and trading with the Indians were among the more remunerative activities, albeit not always the most edifying. Carolinians were also heavily involved in commerce in Indian slaves. These were captured by Native Americans as well as Europeans. The traders found a ready local market for women and children who were considered tractable, while the men were often killed or sent as slave labourers to the West Indies or elsewhere. This trade was profitable as long as there were Indians available who might be enslaved, but the dwindling supply, restive captives, and opposition from the Proprietors limited the business.

Other kinds of trade with Native Americans endured longer. Beavers were too scarce locally to fulfil early hope for furs, but deer were abundant. There was also

[24] Wilson, 'An Account of the Province of Carolina' [1682], in Salley, ed., *Narratives*, p. 174.

considerable European demand for buckskin. Consequently, by *c*.1700 approximately 200 traders were annually acquiring thousands of deerskins from the Indians. Between 1699 and 1715 Carolinians sent, on average, more than 53,000 hides—worth perhaps £30,000—to England each year, and deerskins were, for a time, the most valuable single export. Exploring as far west as the Arkansas River, Carolinians who traded in these commodities advocated British control of the entire lower Mississippi Valley. But the Yamasees killed some traders and disrupted the trade. The subsequent rise of other commodities relegated the deerskin trade to a subordinate place in the economy.

More valuable commodities surpassed deerskins after the turn of the century. Pitch and tar used to caulk ships and waterproof cordage were among the new products. Englishmen traditionally obtained these naval stores from Scandinavia, but the French wars interfered with the supply. British officials and merchants therefore turned to the colonies. Surveying the situation in 1699, a royal official maintained that Carolina was 'the only [or best] place for such commodities upon the Continent of America'.[25] In 1705 Parliament placed naval stores on the list of enumerated products—thereby restricting their exportation to the Empire—and granted bounties for production in the colonies. South Carolinians in turn made the colony the largest producer of naval stores in America. By 1717 exports reached 44,000 barrels a year, and the volume soon glutted the market.

Carolinians responded to the Imperial incentives with such alacrity because the returns were initially good. Slaves and others roamed the woods collecting the resinous heartwood of dead pine trees, which was then heated in a kiln to produce tar; further distillation yielded pitch. Twelve men working approximately 2,000 acres, it was estimated in 1705, could produce commodities worth £500. Unfortunately, however, English ropemakers believed that tar made from dead trees, as in Carolina, 'scorched' or weakened cordage; they therefore preferred the Swedish product derived from green wood. Discovering that Americans were loath to adopt more labour-intensive live-tree methods, Imperial authorities let the bounty expire in 1724, and the Carolina industry collapsed. British merchants and American colonists then sought help from Parliament, which passed a new act in 1729 that was periodically renewed for the remainder of the colonial period. It provided lower bounties for pitch and tar made by the American method and higher premiums for that produced by the Swedish process. North Carolinians, who lacked many lucrative alternatives, became the leading producers of naval stores; South Carolinians turned to more profitable pursuits.

During the early eighteenth century rice became the leading export. It had been among early experimental plantings, but making it a commercial success required

[25] Edward Randolph to the Board of Trade, 16 March 1698/1699, in Salley, ed., *Narratives*, p. 208.

more skill and experience. Around 1690 mariners acquired improved varieties of the grain from Madagascar and the East Indies, and newly imported slaves from some areas of Africa were familiar with its cultivation. Perhaps as a result, planters soon switched from dry-land cultivation to using freshwater swamps. Planting occurred in April and May; periodic flooding of the fields to irrigate the crop and control weeds followed during the summer; harvesting in September and October. Threshing and 'pounding out', or removing the husk of the grain with a wooden mortar and pestle, completed the seasonal cycle. Thus it was usually December or later before most rice was ready for market. By the turn of the century Carolinians had become familiar with the routine, and they were exporting nearly 270,000 pounds per year. During the next few years exports grew by more than 20 per cent per year as planters imported slaves and brought more land into production. In 1722 1.16 million acres appeared on the tax rolls; during the next two decades the amount approximately doubled. Slave labour made this possible.

A Slave Society

To attract Barbadians and other slave-holders, the Proprietors made slavery legal from the outset, and Sir John Yeamans was one of the first to import a substantial number of slaves. But the demand remained limited until planters developed an export. Not being very numerous, slaves initially inspired little fear, and the contrast with Barbados, where blacks substantially outnumbered whites, was such that Carolinians failed to enact a comprehensive slave code until 1696, when they adopted Barbadian statutes. Meanwhile, blacks had considerable autonomy in the frontier settlement, where men valued their woodcraft skills. Ironically, the archetypal figures of the era therefore include both Yeamans, the exploitative planter, and the slave cowboy who ranged the woods alone. In fact the latter may account for the term 'cowboy' itself.

Black cowboys persisted throughout the colonial period, but conditions changed for most slaves as their numbers increased. Whether the rapid rise in the slave population first depended on naval stores or rice is not clear, but it is certain that the simultaneous increase in the production of both produced an extraordinary demand for slave labour. As one ambitious planter observed in 1701, the timber growing on his land was alone worth more than £10,000, 'but I can make little advantage of it till I can compass a good gang of Negroes'.[26] Increased demand in Carolina and elsewhere, as well as lobbying by merchants who wanted to share the market, induced Parliament in 1698 to revoke the Royal African Company's

[26] Edward Hyrne to Burrell Massingberd, 19 Jan. 1701, in H. Roy Merrens, ed., *The Colonial South Carolina Scene: Contemporary Views, 1697–1774* (Columbia, SC, 1977), p. 18.

monopoly and permit all English vessels to engage in the slave trade. Partly as a result, the local slave population, which had stood at 1,500 in 1690, reached 4,100 by 1710. Half the population, not counting Indians, was black by 1708. By 1720 the figure was two-thirds, and in some rice-producing areas slaves outnumbered whites by as much as eight to one. Some fifty years later whites coming into the upcountry restored the racial balance in the colony as a whole, but this migration failed to alter the ratio in the lowcountry, which continued to resemble the West Indies. Numerically preponderant blacks were able to retain many African cultural traits, and their presence constantly reminded whites of their own precarious position in the event of a slave revolt. Indeed, in 1732 a newly arrived European observed that Carolina appeared 'more like a negro country than like a country settled by white people'.[27] This was the result of the increasing black population and the failure of other ethnic groups to keep pace.

The Native American population fell precipitously. From approximately 10,000 in each of the Carolinas east of the Appalachian Mountains in 1685, it declined to about 15,000 in both by 1700. Fifteen years later the total was down to 8,100.[28] Although the Tuscaroras of North Carolina and the Yamasees of South Carolina retained sufficient strength to wage war against the white settlers during the early eighteenth century, many of the Indians in the lowcountry had already departed, died out, or been enslaved. Indian slaves, of which there were 1,400, in fact constituted nearly 15 per cent of the 9,580 people reported to be living in South Carolina in 1708.[29] Some free Native Americans, like those purported to hunt game for whites, also continued to live close to white settlements. But the fate of most of these Indian communities was sealed. By the end of the colonial period an acting Governor of South Carolina would observe that, of the myriads of Indians once 'swarming' over the area, nothing then remained 'but their names' on the land.[30]

On the other hand, the white population grew slowly during the seventeenth century although for several decades it remained small. Despite their unreliability, early population figures provide a reasonable indication of the general trend. Approximately 200 settlers established the first outpost at Albemarle Point; ten years later perhaps 1,000 lived in and around Charleston. Promotional efforts by the Proprietors added perhaps another 1,000 during the next few years, and, despite the fiasco at Stuart's Town, the total number of whites reached 3,800 before 1700. But Queen Anne's War deterred immigration and the Yamasee War inflicted

[27] Samuel Dyssli to His Mother, Brothers and Friends, 3 Dec. 1737, in R. W. Kelsey, 'Swiss Settlers in South Carolina', *South Carolina Historical and Genealogical Magazine*, XXIII (1922), p. 90.

[28] Wood, *Powhatan's Mantle*, p. 38.

[29] A Report of the Governor and Council, 1708, in Merrens, ed., *Colonial S.C. Scene*, p. 32.

[30] Governor William Bull, Representation of the Colony, 1770, in Merrens, ed., *Colonial S.C. Scene*, p. 268.

heavy losses. Consequently, the figure had still not reached 10,000 by 1730. (North Carolina stood at 27,300 by this time.) Sixty years later, however, South Carolina, though still small, had become one of the fastest-growing areas in the United States.[31]

The population explosion in the late eighteenth century prompts the question why such growth was so late. The explanation lies in both an imbalanced sex ratio during the early period and the endemic diseases of the lowcountry or coastal environment. Almost 83 per cent (76 out of 92) of the passengers on one of the first vessels to arrive in 1670, the *Carolina*, were men; and only about 200 of the approximately 680 settlers known to have been in South Carolina during the next ten years were women.[32] Although the proportion of women rose in the eighteenth century as more women immigrated and a larger percentage of the population was born locally, a considerable imbalance persisted. According to a Governor's report in 1708, the colony contained 1,420 white men and only 960 white women; the ratio, therefore, still remained at about 1.5 to 1.[33]

Because creoles had greater resistance to endemic diseases than migrants and native-born women might have given birth earlier, the coming-of-age of a creole generation presumably should have led to more natural increase. But custom may have dictated traditionally late marriages—though this does not appear to have been the case in the Albemarle Sound area of North Carolina—and diseases continued to kill even the native-born.[34] The low-lying coastal areas of South Carolina in particular turned out to be a death-trap after the first few years. Slaves brought virulent African forms of malaria and yellow fever to which they, but not whites, had partial immunity. The resulting devastation prompted many sayings during the eighteenth century to the effect that 'they who want to die quickly, go to Carolina', which was 'in the spring a paradise, in the summer a hell, and in the autumn a hospital'. Residents who survived bore the sallow complexions jocularly known as the 'Carolina Phiz' or physiognomy of sufferers from chronic malaria.[35] These diseases helped to account for the extremely high rate of childhood

[31] Wood, *Powhatan's Mantle*, p. 38.

[32] Agnes Leland Baldwin, *First Settlers of South Carolina, 1670–1680* (Columbia, SC, 1969), like her enlarged volume, *First Settlers of South Carolina, 1670–1700* (Easley, SC, 1985), provides very valuable lists of names but contains enough errors to call for caution.

[33] A Report of the Governor and Council, 1708, in Merrens, ed., *Colonial S.C. Scene*, p. 32.

[34] In the period before 1700, the average age at first marriage for women varied between 18.65 and 22.45. James M. Gallman, 'Determinants of Age at Marriage in Colonial Perquimans County, North Carolina', *William and Mary Quarterly* (hereafter *WMQ*), Third Series, XXXIX (1982), p. 179.

[35] H. Roy Merrens, 'The Physical Environment of Early America: Images and Image Makers in Colonial South Carolina', *Geographical Review*, LIX (1969), p. 535; Johann David Schoepf, *Travels in the Confederation [1783–1784]*, ed. Alfred J. Morrison, 2 vols. (New York, 1968), II, p. 172; Henry Laurens to James Wright, 7 Aug. 1768, in George C. Rogers, Jr. and David R. Chesnutt, eds., *The Papers of Henry Laurens*, 14 vols., VI, *1768–1769* (Columbia, SC, 1978), p. 51.

mortality, which reached 86 per cent in some regions of the lowcountry until well into the eighteenth century. Thus, in 1726 the 108 white families in one coastal parish were reported to have only 266 children, or roughly 2.5 per family.[36] Obviously they, and presumably their white neighbours in the lowcountry as a whole, were still barely reproducing themselves. Immigrants therefore accounted for almost all of the white population increase.

These immigrants represented a heterogeneous assortment of people. Interestingly enough, Barbadians were conspicuous by their absence in 1670; perhaps their earlier failures in trying to settle Carolina prompted them to await the outcome of the current venture. They began to arrive in force, however, in 1671; during the next decade about half of those whose place of emigration is identifiable were from Barbados. All social classes contributed to the flow. Senior members of the most influential families tended to remain behind, though some of them acquired land grants in Carolina, while younger sons migrated. Probably half of the immigrants were small planters or farmers who had owned ten acres or less. A few were merchants. And of the 117 known immigrants embarking from Barbados during the first ten years, twenty-two were indentured servants.[37]

Some of those who arrived from Barbados had been transients on the island; others had been resident longer, but like most immigrants to Carolina during the century, both groups were predominantly of English stock. Thus the lowcountry remained mostly African-American and English throughout the colonial period. But the Proprietors' attempts to dilute the early Barbadian influence did produce some ethnic and more religious diversity. Few, if any, of the Scots from Stuart's Town remained in the colony after its destruction in 1686, but most of the 500 Huguenots did. Some resided in Charleston; larger numbers lived along the 'French' Santee River north of the city, where many continued to speak French. Although most of the Huguenots soon became Anglicans, they initially increased the proportion of religious Dissenters. Moreover, the Proprietors' recruiting efforts in England—which, a contemporary noted, made Carolina as well as Pennsylvania 'the refuge of the sectaries'—added another 500 or so people during

[36] H. Roy Merrens and George D. Terry, 'Dying in Paradise: Malaria, Mortality, and the Perceptual Environment in Colonial South Carolina', *Journal of Southern History*, L (1984), p. 542; Frank J. Klingberg, *An Appraisal of the Negro in Colonial South Carolina* (1941; Philadelphia, 1975), pp. 58–60.

[37] Richard Waterhouse, *A New World Gentry: The Making of a Merchant and Planter Class in South Carolina, 1670–1770* (New York, 1989), pp. 9–15. See also Aaron M. Shatzman, *Servants into Planters: The Origin of an American Image: Land Acquisition and Status Mobility in Seventeenth-Century South Carolina* (New York, 1989), *passim*. Both Shatzman and Waterhouse have done meticulous work, but some of their conclusions are based on questionable data from Baldwin's *First Settlers*. Some Carolinians who have been identified as Barbadians were probably transients. See Kinloch Bull, 'Barbadian Settlers in Early Carolina: Historiographical Notes', *South Carolina Historical Magazine*, XCVI (1995), pp. 329–39. This finding does not necessarily militate against the role of Barbados as the cultural hearth for Carolina.

the 1680s.[38] In North Carolina both the immigration of Dissenters and the conversion of local residents had a similar effect. Quakers predominated in the Albemarle area. South Carolina also attracted numerous Friends, and by 1710 contemporaries believed that Quakers constituted nearly 2.5 per cent of the population. Presbyterians were the largest group (45 per cent), with Anglicans right behind at 42.5 per cent. One in ten residents was a Baptist.[39]

During the early years many individuals, whatever their religious affiliation, came as indentured servants, though the Carolinas were well down the list of preferred destinations. One recent study found 241 servants among the approximately 680 identifiable whites who arrived in South Carolina prior to 1680. At first, as we have seen, some of them came from Barbados, but the Governor of South Carolina soon requested that the Proprietors send Englishmen, for 'wee find that one of our Servants wee brought out of England is worth 2 of ye Barbadians, for they are soe much addicted to Rum, yet they will doe little but whilst the bottle is at their nose'. Accordingly, during the first decade 65 per cent of the known servants arrived directly from England. More than half for whom the data is available could sign their names, which suggests that they may have possessed other skills as well.[40] Perhaps they were responding to promotional pamphlets like the one that specifically invited 'all Artificers, [such] as *Carpenters, Wheel-rights, Joyners, Coopers, Bricklayers, Smiths*, or diligent Husbandmen and Labourers, that are willing to advance their fortunes' in a fine place 'where Artificers are of high esteem, and used with all Civility and Courtesie imaginable' to take ship for Carolina.[41]

To assess how these immigrants fared, one needs to know their expectations as well as their fate. Not many, however, were explicit about their motivations. Cases as clear as that of John Barnwell are rare. Despite good prospects at home, he left Dublin for Carolina, a contemporary observed, for no other reason but 'a humor to goe to travel'.[42] One has to infer that he satisfied his wanderlust, since he remained in the colony. To judge from promotional pamphlets, however, most immigrants wished to attain at least 'that State of Life which many People reckon the happiest, a moderate Subsistance, without the Vexation of Dependance'. That attained, they might aspire to 'advance themselves in Riches, Honour, and good

[38] Christopher Jeaffreson, *A Young Squire of the Seventeenth Century* [1683], quoted in David W. Galenson, *White Servitude in Colonial America: An Economic Analysis* (Cambridge, 1981), p. 110.

[39] James Glen, 'A Description of South Carolina' [1761], in Chapman J. Milling, ed., *Colonial South Carolina: Two Contemporary Descriptions* (Columbia, SC, 1951), pp. 66, 87.

[40] Gov. Joseph West to Lord Ashley, &c., 21 March 1670/1671, in 'The Shaftesbury Papers', in Cheves, ed., *Collections*, V, p. 299; Shatzman, *Servants into Planters*, pp. 154, 70.

[41] Robert Horne, 'A Brief Description of the Province of Carolina' [1666], in Carroll, ed., *Historical Collections*, II, p. 17.

[42] John Page to John Harleston, 1 Dec. 1708, quoted in A. S. Salley, Jr., 'Barnwell of South Carolina', *South Carolina Historical and Genealogical Magazine*, II (1901), p. 47 n.

Repute'.[43] Upward social mobility depended on land, and the opportunity to acquire a headright proved to be a powerful lure. Affluent men may have bought indentured servants as much for their headrights (which accrued to their owners) as for their labour, while poor people indentured themselves to acquire the second headright that would be part of their freedom dues at the expiration of their terms. Among the men who arrived before 1680 and can later be identified as free, the average term of service was about 3.6 years, and 85 per cent (83 individuals) ultimately acquired measurable amounts of land. The initial grant averaged 102.8 acres, and the average estate at death was 369 acres. These figures indicate that the indentured servants who survived—and the qualification is obviously an important one—did somewhat better in Carolina than their contemporary counterparts in the Chesapeake. Some ex-indentured servants were very successful in South Carolina. Four who were once bound men became members of the local representative Assembly.[44]

As their upward mobility suggests, disparities in wealth were comparatively small and society remained relatively open during the century. Status and wealth counted, of course, and men from prominent families did especially well. The James Colleton who served as Governor in the 1690s was the youngest son of Sir John, the Proprietor. Robert and Thomas Gibbes, younger sons of a substantial Barbadian planter who left his plantation to their elder brother, arrived in South Carolina in 1678; Robert eventually became Governor (1710–12). Moreover, prominent families tended to retain their position over time. Merchants who arrived around 1700 to take advantage of the rice trade, as well as other newcomers with capital, did not displace but joined the older élite. This pattern, which contrasts with that of Virginia, helped to consolidate the position of the existing upper class and reflected a society in which there was a scarcity of individuals to fill positions of power and prestige. An attempt to elect the first Parliament in South Carolina failed when it was discovered that there were not enough freemen to compose it. In short, the concentration of wealth in the hands of the relatively few, which became characteristic after the wholesale adoption of slave labour, had not progressed far by the turn of the century.

Being less prosperous, North Carolina was even less stratified. In Perquimans County between Virginia and Albemarle Sound, the median landholding was 150 acres in the mid-1690s, and it remained a relatively modest 400 acres as late as 1716, though the wealthiest 10 per cent of the residents owned about a third of the land. Few of the nearly 15,000 whites in the entire colony owned slaves, and the total number of blacks was only 1,800 in 1715.[45] William Byrd's famous *The History of the*

[43] Nairne, 'A Letter from South Carolina' [1710], and John Norris, 'Profitable Advice for Rich and Poor in a Dialogue' [1712], in Greene, ed., *Selling a New World*, pp. 66, 81.

[44] Shatzman, *Servants into Planters*, pp. 147, 172–76, 181.

[45] Gallman, 'Determinants of Age at Marriage', *WMQ*, p. 177; Wood, *Powhatan's Mantle*, p. 38.

Dividing Line (1728) between Virginia and North Carolina similarly depicted a society in which most people had the essentials but few of the amenities of life. Describing one of the principal coastal towns, Edenton (incorporated in 1722), Byrd noted that it contained '40 or 50 Houses, most of them Small, and built without Expense. A Citizen here is counted Extravagant, if he has Ambition enough to aspire to a Brick-chimney.' Nothing was costly except 'Law, Physick, and Strong Drink, which are all bad in their Kind, and the last they get with so much Difficulty, that they are never guilty of the Sin of Suffering it to Sour upon their Hands'.[46] Despite his humorous exaggerations, Byrd was correct about the generally modest standard of living. Nevertheless, his remarks suggest—and the landholding data confirm—that some men had begun to outdistance their neighbours. By the 1730s the process was perhaps most evident along the lower Cape Fear River, where a number of men, including some South Carolinians, established rice plantations.

During the eighteenth century the increasing levels of wealth and the accompanying social stratification in both Carolinas—but especially in South Carolina—made these colonies seem something more like England and less like precarious outposts in the wilderness. But the high attrition rate among the populace, the increasing number of black slaves, and the knowledge that their own economic opportunities were greater than if they had not immigrated doubtless made most white inhabitants realize that they lived in a 'Strange Country',[47] replete with perils and promise. Their world was neither England nor Barbados, though it embodied elements of both. Carolinians never committed themselves to one crop as exclusively as Barbadians did, but they did create an exploitative society in which free whites prospered on black slave labour. Their model was Barbados, and they succeeded in re-creating it closely enough that South Carolina became in turn the pattern for parts of North Carolina and Georgia. The inhabitants of these areas seldom called their colonies 'home', for they reserved that term for England, but they increasingly termed their surroundings 'my Country'.

Their use of these terms suggests that they were becoming acclimatized to their surroundings, psychologically as well as physiologically, and that they had passed through the first of what have been identified as the three principal stages in the socio-cultural development of most colonies: simplification, elaboration, and replication.[48] Migration to Carolina and early experiences there simplified the

[46] William Byrd, *Histories of the Dividing Line Betwixt Virginia and North Carolina* [1728], ed. Percy G. Adams (New York, 1967), p. 96.

[47] Norris, 'Profitable Advice for Rich and Poor' [1712], in Greene, ed., *Selling a New World*, p. 83.

[48] Jack P. Greene, *Pursuits of Happiness: The Social Development of Early Modern British Colonies and the Formation of American Culture* (Chapel Hill, NC, 1988), *passim*, but esp. pp. 166–69.

social and institutional structure that settlers had been accustomed to in their homelands. The relatively egalitarian social structure lacked the hierarchical organization of its English counterpart, let alone the elaborate arrangements envisioned in the Fundamental Constitutions. But as the population and the economy grew, local institutions became more complex and elaborate. The local Assemblies developed their own precedents. Increased wealth widened gaps in the social structure; and, particularly in South Carolina, the presence of more slaves enlarged the gulf between men who were—or would become—free and those who were not. At the same time the racial division masked the increasing complexity of white society. These and other differences from England made local society unique, but numerous ties bound Carolinians to the Empire. Distance, it is true, weakened royal authority, while time and the declining proportion of Englishmen in the population eroded family links. People nevertheless realized that the Imperial trading system promoted prosperity and that the Crown provided vital protection against internal slave insurrections as well as external enemies. Gratitude therefore augmented loyalty to a community that they considered to be the freest in the world. No wonder South Carolinians were, in the words of one contemporary, fond of British manners and customs 'even to excess'.[49] Emulation of English norms also reassured local inhabitants that they had not degenerated in the provincial environment. But the trajectory of local development had been such that they had virtually no chance to reshape their society on the English model, while the composition of their own white population increasingly entitled them to assert claim to being British rather than English.

Metropolitan scorn for American efforts to be English, and the increasing realization that they must inevitably fail, led Carolinians to rationalize a situation that they could not change and affirm their own identity. As an advertisement for *The History of Carolina, from the Date of our Charter in 1663, to the Year 1721* strongly implied, Carolinians were what they were thanks to the 'Resolution, Firmness, and Intrepidity' of their ancestors on 'the most trying Occasions'.[50] They, a judge told a South Carolina grand jury in 1769, 'arrived in this country when it was a dreary wilderness, inhabited only by wild beasts, and great numbers of savages . . . ; and notwithstanding the great hazard they ran of losing their lives, and the many hardships and disadvantages they labored under, . . . yet they bravely maintained their ground'. Since then, he continued, Carolinians 'by their great industry' have 'improved and cultivated the colony to so great maturity, that it is become the land of plenty, as well as of liberty, and fruitful, like the land of

[49] David Ramsay, *The History of the Revolution of South Carolina from a British Province to an Independent State*, 2 vols. (Trenton, NJ, 1785), I, p. 7.

[50] *South Carolina Gazette and Country Journal* (Charleston), 18 Feb. 1766.

Egypt'.[51] And almost as different from home, some visitors from England might have added.

[51] Robert Pringle, Charge to the Grand Jury, 1769, printed in John Belton O'Neall, *Biographical Sketches of the Bench and Bar of South Carolina*, 2 vols. (Charleston, 1859), I, pp. 393, 394.

Select Bibliography

J. E. BUCHANAN, 'The Colleton Family and the Early History of South Carolina and Barbados, 1646–1775', unpublished Ph.D. thesis, Edinburgh, 1989.

CONVERSE D. CLOWSE, *Economic Beginnings in Colonial South Carolina, 1670–1730* (Columbia, SC, 1971).

PETER A. COCLANIS, *The Shadow of a Dream: Economic Life and Death in the South Carolina Low Country, 1670–1920* (New York, 1989).

VERNER W. CRANE, *The Southern Frontier, 1670–1732* (1929; New York, 1981).

RICHARD S. DUNN, 'The English Sugar Islands and the Founding of South Carolina', *South Carolina Historical Magazine*, LXXII (1971), pp. 81–93.

A. ROGER EKIRCH, *'Poor Carolina': Politics and Society in Colonial North Carolina, 1729–1776* (Chapel Hill, NC, 1981).

DANIEL W. FAGG, Jr., 'Carolina, 1663–1683: The Founding of a Proprietary', unpublished Ph.D. dissertation, Emory University, 1970.

JACK P. GREENE, 'Colonial South Carolina and the Caribbean Connection', in *Imperatives, Behaviors, and Identities: Essays in Early American Cultural History* (Charlottesville, Va., 1992).

RICHARD L. HAAN, 'The "Trade Do's Not Flourish as Formerly": The Ecological Origins of the Yamassee War of 1715', *Ethnohistory*, XXVIII (1981), pp. 341–58.

CHARLES M. HUDSON, *The Southeastern Indians* (Knoxville, Tenn., 1976).

LAWRENCE LEE, *The Lower Cape Fear in Colonial Days* (Chapel Hill, NC, 1965).

CHARLES H. LESSER, *South Carolina Begins: The Records of a Proprietary Colony, 1663–1721* (Columbia, SC, 1995).

JAMES H. MERRELL, *The Indians' New World: Catawbas and their Neighbors from European Contact through the Era of Removal* (Chapel Hill, NC, 1989).

HARRY ROY MERRENS, *Colonial North Carolina in the Eighteenth Century: A Study in Historical Geography* (Chapel Hill, NC, 1964).

JOHN ALEXANDER MOORE, 'Royalizing South Carolina: The Revolution of 1719 and the Evolution of Early South Carolina Government', unpublished Ph.D. dissertation, South Carolina, 1991.

R. C. NASH, 'South Carolina and the Atlantic Economy in the Late Seventeenth and Eighteenth Centuries', *Economic History Review*, XLV (1992), pp. 677–702.

WILLIAM S. POWELL, *North Carolina through Four Centuries* (Chapel Hill, NC, 1989).

M. EUGENE SIRMANS, *Colonial South Carolina: A Political History, 1663–1763* (Chapel Hill, NC, 1966).

ROBERT M. WEIR, *Colonial South Carolina: A History* (1983; Columbia, SC, 1997).

PETER H. WOOD, *Black Majority: Negroes in Colonial South Carolina from 1670 through the Stono Rebellion* (New York, 1974).

18

Overseas Expansion and Trade in the Seventeenth Century

NUALA ZAHEDIEH

In the late fifteenth century the European 'discoveries' of 'new' lands and sea routes, combined with improvements in shipping technology and navigational skill, opened up a wealth of commercial opportunities. In the sixteenth century a few Englishmen began to exploit these opportunities in a direct fashion: fishing, raiding, and trading in the Americas, making faltering forays to the East. But most were content to rely on the monopoly distribution networks constructed by the peninsular powers (which had borne the major costs and risks of expansion and expected to reap the major rewards) until, at the end of the century, war threw the system, centred on Seville, Lisbon, and Antwerp, into disarray. Direct access to distant markets and sources of supply, whether by force or by agreement, became much more attractive and led to a surge in privateering and trading ventures.[1] These bore fruit in the seventeenth century. It was after the establishment of the East India Company in 1600 and the first successful English settlement in Virginia in 1607 that English trade and enterprise underwent truly radical change, acquired a thoroughly intercontinental character, and laid the foundation of Empire. This chapter will outline the development of English transoceanic commerce during these expansionary times, and consider its impact on the economy of the mother country.

A survey of commerce in any period should begin by providing a firm statistical foundation. As William Petty argued in the 1660s, 'comparative and superlative arguments' are less appropriate than expressions in terms of 'number, weight and measure'.[2] Ironically, despite the rise of a new spirit of scientific enquiry, the seventeenth century is renowned as an age of statistical darkness. There is no continuous series of trade statistics between 1603 and 1696 when, under pressure of financing war, the King appointed an Inspector-General of the Customs and there begins a

[1] Kenneth R. Andrews, *Trade, Plunder and Settlement: Maritime Enterprise and the Genesis of the British Empire, 1480–1630* (Cambridge, 1984); G. V. Scammell, *The First Imperial Age: European Overseas Expansion, c.1400–1715* (London, 1989).

[2] William Petty, 'Political Arithmetick', in *Several Essays in Political Arithmetick* (London, 1699), Preface.

permanent series of customs ledgers, detailing trade by country and commodity. Trade figures for the previous nine decades are fragmentary and obscure. The scrappy nature of the available evidence makes estimates of value dubious and comparisons between years precarious, but none the less, although the figures do not have precision, the broad conclusions about a revolution in trade outlined by Fisher and Davis still seem secure. Overall trade did not grow particularly fast—estimates suggest that between 1600 and 1699–1700 imports grew sixfold from under £1 million and exports (including re-exports) grew from about £1 million to around £6.5 million. However, there was a major shift in the nature of trade: a change in markets and merchandise. Trade with Europe was becoming less important and England became increasingly involved with the world beyond. While trade with traditional markets stagnated in the early seventeenth century, trade with Spanish, African, and Mediterranean ports—doorways to American and Asian markets—expanded, accounting for as large a share of London's exports as Germany and the Low Countries by the 1640s. In the second half of the seventeenth century Englishmen increasingly became directly involved with transoceanic commerce, and trade with the plantations and India accounted for over 30 per cent of imports and 15 per cent of exports by the end of the century (Table 18.1). Linked with this was a diversification in the product mix. Sugar, tobacco, and calicoes were becoming prominent among imports; miscellaneous manufactures added variety to traditional woollen exports; and re-exports were another novel feature.[3]

TABLE 18.1. *English transoceanic trade in the late seventeenth century* (£000)

	1663/69 London	1699–1701 London	1699–1701 England
	Value (%)	Value (%)	Value (%)
Imports			
Plantations	421 (12)	863 (18)	1,107 (19)
East India	409 (12)	756 (16)	756 (13)
TOTAL	3,495 (100)	4,667 (100)	5,849 (100)
Exports			
Plantations	163 (8)	410 (15)	539 (12)
East India	30 (1)	122 (4)	122 (3)
TOTAL	2,039 (100)	2,773 (100)	4,433 (100)
Re-exports			
Plantations	—	254 (15)	312 (16)
East India	—	14 (1)	14 (1)
TOTAL	—	1,677 (100)	1,986 (100)

Source: Ralph Davis, 'English Foreign Trade, 1660–1700' (see below note 3).

[3] F. J. Fisher, 'London's Export Trade in the Early Seventeenth Century', *Economic History Review* (hereafter *EcHR*), Second Series, III (1950), pp. 151–61; Ralph Davis, 'English Foreign Trade, 1660–1700',

Direct purchase and sale in distant markets substituted one transaction for many. For example, Eastern spices which had previously been carried through the Middle East and the Mediterranean in short stages, passing through many hands, and frequently breaking bulk, could now be brought to their English distribution point in a single, unbroken voyage. However, while direct trade promised reduced transactions costs it also entailed high initial outlays, huge risks, and slow returns, presenting a major organizational challenge which was resolved in rather different ways in the East and West.

The English East India Company, based in London, chartered by the Crown in 1600 and granted a monopoly of English East India commerce, was a trading company pure and simple, which bought and sold goods and did not engage in production. As such, it drew on precedent and was in many ways merely a grander version of familiar forms. The joint-stock capitalization was a well-established way for high-cost enterprises to spread risk and draw on a pool of capital from beyond those involved in active management. Collective trading was commonly believed to enhance merchants' strength in negotiations with powerful local rulers and facilitated defence of shipping and trading bases. Both the English and the Dutch were convinced that the threat of force was essential in persuading either the Portuguese or local rulers to allow them to trade. Finally, company organization was a familiar vehicle for obtaining a monopoly and other privileges from the Crown: merchants benefited from being able to limit competition and enhance prices in return for using part of the profits to provide loans and gifts to the state as well as political support.[4] However, the formula was not entirely successful, for after a profitable beginning the Company undertook a number of losing voyages after the 1620s, was

TABLE 18.2. *East India Company's trade, 1660–89 (annual average value, £ sterling)*

	Imports	*Exports*
1660–69	82,472	112,985
1670–79	268,784	324,088
1680–89	403,717	447,663

Source: Chaudhuri, *Trading World of Asia*, pp. 507–08 (see below note 5).

EcHR, Second Series, VI (1954), pp. 150–66; W. E. Minchinton, ed., *The Growth of English Overseas Trade in the Seventeenth and Eighteenth Centuries* (London, 1969).

[4] For a comprehensive survey of the chartered companies in the context of overseas expansion, see E. L. J. Coornaert, 'European Economic Institutions and the New World: The Chartered Companies', in E. E. Rich and C. H. Wilson, eds., *The Cambridge Economic History of Europe*, 8 vols. (Cambridge, 1967), IV, pp. 223–74. For a more recent revisionist perspective, see L. Blussé and F. Gaastra, eds., *Companies and Trade: Essays on Overseas Trading Companies during the Ancien Regime* (The Hague, 1981).

short of capital, not always supported by the Crown, and looked to be in a parlous state by the time of the Civil War. But the charter was renewed in 1657 and reaffirmed at the Restoration, and the Company entered a buoyant phase with a fourfold increase in trade between the 1660s and 1680s (Table 18.2).

Interloping was widespread, as was private trade by Company employees. In 1661 the Company withdrew ships from the country trade between regions and opened this to its employees in 1674, accepting that it might as well bow to the inevitable. It would have been difficult to persuade Englishmen to accept the privations and risks of life in the East without a real prospect of enrichment. But even so, the monopoly of this lucrative trade caused increasing resentment. Pressure mounted to persuade the government to open the trade to private merchants and to enlarge the membership of the original Company, which limited shares to enhance dividends. The Company responded by granting large annual gifts to the Crown, thus becoming firmly linked with the Stuart monarchy, and its position became increasingly precarious after the Glorious Revolution. In 1698 a rival New East India Company was chartered, beginning a final period of uncertainty until the two were fused into a United Company in 1709.

From the start the Company had two main trading arenas: Indonesia and the Indian subcontinent. Attempts to trade with Japan in the 1620s ended in failure, but successful links were formed with China towards the end of the century. The better-capitalized and better-organized Dutch company was determined to secure a monopoly of the spice trade and, although it did not succeed entirely, it was able to limit the English presence in South-East Asia. Meanwhile, the English Company had negotiated with the Mughals to secure bases in India, Surat being the most important until mid-century, after which the focus shifted south to Madras and north to Bengal. Although there was trade in pepper, indigo, and saltpetre, the major attraction of India proved to be its well-organized textile industry, producing calicoes in a range of stunning colours and designs which proved hugely popular in European and American markets and accounted for about two-thirds of Company imports in the later seventeenth century. Cotton goods achieved a lasting impact on European trade and fashion which ultimately led to efforts at copying and successful import substitution. The major embarrassment for the Company was that the East never showed similar enthusiasm for European goods and between 70 and 90 per cent of returns were made in bullion. This was, of course, obtained mainly in America, linking traders with East and West in an interlocking, mutually dependent system.[5]

[5] K. N. Chaudhuri, *The English East India Company: A Study of an Early Joint Stock Company, 1600–1640* (London, 1965), and *The Trading World of Asia and the English East India Company, 1660–1760* (Cambridge, 1978). See chap. by P. J. Marshall.

TABLE 18.3. *Chief English ports in colonial trade, 1686*

	West Indies			*North America*		
	No. of ships		*Average tonnage*	*No. of ships*		*Average tonnage*
	In	*Out*		*In*	*Out*	
London	225	161	179	110	114	115
Bristol	42	56	110	31	17	94
Liverpool	8	2	110	13	13	94

Source: Davis, *Shipping Industry*, pp. 298–99 (see below note 16).

While the East India Company, based entirely in London, relied on the principle of exclusive rights and joint-stock capitalization to cope with the costs and risks of long-distance trade, those engaged in the Atlantic trade, which was shared by London and the outports (Table 18.3), demonstrated a spirit of innovation which was reflected in major changes in the conduct of commerce.

Joint-stock companies on similar lines to the East India Company were established to undertake American colonization, but they proved singularly inappropriate for what was not merely a trading project. The native economy was not organized on lines which could provide Europeans with regular supplies of desired commodities (except perhaps furs), but native society was such that Europeans were able to appropriate territory and, after a number of failed attempts, the plantation established in Virginia in 1607 laid the foundations of successful English settlement in America. By the end of the century about 350,000 Englishmen had crossed the ocean, relieving their country of the supposed burden of 'overgreat' and 'superfluous' multitudes by taking advantage of what they perceived as 'free' land across the Atlantic, and had established permanent colonies from Maine to South Carolina on the mainland and in Barbados, the Bahamas, the Leewards, and Jamaica in the Caribbean.[6] The success of the enterprises relied on the slow, hard work of clearing land and creating the entire physical fabric of new communities, which required not only a very large investment but also close, careful supervision to secure a profit. Progress was most rapid when those overseeing improvement had proprietary rights. Absentee management by English merchants proved ill suited to the task.[7]

[6] On the contemporary perception of over-population, see M. Campbell, 'Of People Either too Few or too Many', in W. A. Aitken and B. O. Henning, eds., *Conflict in Stuart England: Essays in Honour of Wallace Notestein* (London, 1960), pp. 169–201. The most recent estimate of migration levels is given by Nicholas Canny, 'English Migration into and across the Atlantic during the Seventeenth and Eighteenth Centuries', in Canny, ed., *Europeans on the Move: Studies on European Migration, 1500–1800* (Oxford, 1994), pp. 39–75.

[7] For discussion of the difficulties faced by a joint-stock company attempting to extract a profit from a distant plantation, see Edmund S. Morgan, *American Slavery, American Freedom: The Ordeal of*

The organization of production and the provision of finance was, in fact, left largely to those on the spot and, after experimentation, those in different regions pursued different strategies suited to their climate and topography. The American settlers all depended to some extent on European manufactured goods, and the first requirement of a successful plantation was to find a way to pay for them. The southern colonies did so by producing valuable cash crops: tobacco in the Chesapeake; sugar in the Caribbean from the 1640s, as well as indigo, ginger, cotton, and dyestuffs. The northern colonies earned their living and assisted the specialization in the plantation south by furnishing food, timber, ships, and shipping services which drew Davenant to conclude 'that southward and northward colonies having such a mutual dependance upon each other all circumstances considered are almost equally important'.[8]

The business of shipping American commodities grown by a large number of competing producers was organized in various ways. At first much was sold to ships' captains or travelling supercargoes visiting the colonies, but as the staple trades became firmly established this opportunistic system soon declined. It became increasingly common for produce to be shipped on the planters' own account, to be sold on commission in England or by merchants in colonial ports operating on their own or a correspondent's behalf.[9] It is not possible to estimate the relative importance of the different methods, but it is clear that the trading system was not amenable to regulation and restricted entry in the manner of the East India trade. The Atlantic trades (apart from trade with Hudson Bay, and the slave trade which was, until 1689, the monopoly of the Royal African Company chartered in 1663 and 1672) quickly became open to all and, as has been shown for London and for Bristol, large numbers participated (Tables 18.4 and 18.5), including manufacturers, retailers, gentlemen, and widows: an opportunity for all.[10]

Colonial Virginia (New York, 1975); W. F. Craven, *The Dissolution of the Virginia Company: The Failure of a Colonial Experiment* (New York, 1932). Other infant settlements faced similar difficulties.

[8] C. Davenant, *Discourse on the Plantation Trade* (London, 1698), p. 24.

[9] Jacob M. Price, *Perry of London: A Family and a Firm on the Seaborne Frontier, 1615–1753* (Cambridge, Mass., 1992); K. G. Davies, 'The Origins of the Commission System in the West India Trade', *Transactions of the Royal Historical Society*, Fifth Series (1952), pp. 89–107.

[10] Robert Brenner, *Merchants and Revolutionaries: Commercial Change, Political Conflict and London's Overseas Traders, 1550–1653* (Cambridge, 1993); David Harris Sacks, *The Widening Gate: Bristol and the Atlantic Economy* (Berkeley and Los Angeles, 1991). The two exceptional companies form the basis of a recent group of articles presenting an optimistic view of the efficiency of chartered joint-stock companies. Political factors are ignored. The most important are: A. M. Carlos and S. Nicholas, 'Giants of an Earlier Capitalism: The Chartered Trading Companies as Modern Multinationals', *Business History Review*, LXII (1988), pp. 398–419, and 'Theory and History: Seventeenth-Century Joint Stock Trading Companies', *Journal of Economic History* (hereafter *JEcH*), LVI (1996), pp. 916–24. For critique, see S. R. H. Jones and S. Ville, 'Efficient Transactors or Rent-seeking Monopolies? The Rationale for Early Joint Stock Companies', *JEcH*, LVI (1996), pp. 898–915.

TABLE 18.4. *Merchants in London's colonial export trade, 1686*

Value of trade (£ sterl.)	0–99	100–999	1,000–4,999	5,000–9,999	Total
West Indies					
Number of merchants	521	166	20	2	702
Value of trade (£)	14,355	54,393	31,303	11,341	111,392
% of total	12.8	48.8	28.2	10.2	100
North America					
Number of merchants	476	176	18	1	691
Value of trade (£)	13,379	51,500	29,780	5,881	100,541
% of total	13.3	51.3	29.6	5.9	100

Source: London Port Books, E190/139/1; 141/5; 136/4. Values are taken from official valuations assembled by D. W. Jones from the Inspector General's Ledgers.

TABLE 18.5. *Merchants in London's colonial import trade, 1686*

Value of trade (£ sterl.)	0–99	100–999	1,000–4,999	5,000–9,999	10,000+	Total
West Indies						
Number of merchants	742	427	86	15	13	1,283
Value of trade, (£)	25,845	101,847	187,533	118,104	217,186	674,518
% of total	3.8	20.0	28.0	17.5	32.0	100
North America						
Number of merchants	339	172	38	5	2	626
Value of trade, (£)	10,972	57,923	77,078	32,992	28,166	100
% of total	5	28	37	16	14	100

Source: London Port Books, E190/143/1; 137/2. Values as in Table 18.4.

But although the broad participation gave the Atlantic trades an appearance of openness, most participated in a very small way. About 60 per cent of those people consigning goods to either North America or the West Indies exported goods worth less than £50, and over two-fifths imported less than £50-worth. Profits could be high, but this reflected high risks: bad weather, war, pirates, the vagaries of the market, and above all dishonest or incompetent agents were only some of the more common causes of grief. Given the high risks, it is not surprising that, as has been shown for the Chesapeake tobacco trade, the colonial trade in general quickly became concentrated in relatively few hands.[11] In 1686 twenty-two merchants exported goods worth over £1,000 to the West Indies and nineteen to North America. In the import trade twenty-eight merchants received over £5,000 from the West Indies, accounting for almost 50 per cent of total value, and seven from

[11] Jacob M. Price and P. G. E. Clemens, 'A Revolution of Scale in Overseas Trade: British Firms in the Chesapeake Trade, 1675–1775', *JEcH*, XLVII (1987), pp. 1–43.

North America (nearly 30 per cent). All the same, the presence of a very large number of small traders did mean that, unlike the East India trade (with quarterly auctions at India House), there was no central market-place. The Royal African Company, which was the largest importer, held about six auctions a year at Africa House but this accounted for about 5 per cent of total imports in 1686.[12] The remaining 95 per cent of West Indian and American goods were sold privately, with much haggling and bargaining, and the large numbers of small traders obstructed efforts at price fixing.

Not surprisingly, there were small groups of merchants who attempted to establish exclusive companies in different branches of Atlantic trade but, apart from the slave trade, these did not obtain state support.[13] The state saw no merit in a policy which might enable merchants to restrict supplies to increase prices. The state's interests lay in maximizing imports as they levied high duties on tobacco, sugar, and other colonial commodities as well as a 4.5 per cent tax on Barbados and the Leewards' produce from 1661.[14] However, the state did have an interest in ensuring that as much as possible of colonial trade was carried in English ships (stimulating the shipping and shipbuilding industries and hence national security), and as much as possible passed through English ports, so facilitating taxation. The state was thus receptive to suggestions that everything possible should be done to exclude foreign merchants and shipping, particularly the Dutch, who were believed to have taken advantage of English weakness during the Civil and Spanish wars to assume an important role in England's Atlantic carrying trade. The policy was justified by contemporaries such as John Cary, who argued in 1695 that as England had provided the manpower for settlement and bore the costs of colonial administration and defence it was fair that it should reap the rewards:

> This was the first design of settling plantations abroad that the people of England might better maintain a commerce and trade among themselves, the chief profit whereof was to redound to the centre; and therefore laws were made [so that] England would become the centre of trade and standing like the sun in the midst of its plantations would not only refresh them but also draw profits from them; and indeed it's a matter of exact justice it should be so, for from hence it is fleets of ships or regiments of soldiers are frequently sent for their defence, at the charge of the inhabitants of this Kingdom.[15]

It took some years of trial and error before a workable system for protecting trade was designed, but this was securely in place by the end of the century. The Navigation Act of 1651 proved too sweeping in its provisions, and impossible to

[12] K. G. Davies, *The Royal African Company* (London, 1957), pp. 179–81.

[13] B[ritish] L[ibrary], Egerton MSS, 2395, ff. 88–90.

[14] C. D. Chandaman, *The English Public Revenue, 1660–88* (Oxford, 1975), pp. 9–36; A. P. Thornton, *West India Policy Under the Restoration* (Oxford, 1956), pp. 258–59.

[15] John Cary, *An Essay on the State of England in Relation to its Trade* (Bristol, 1695), pp. 68–70.

enforce, but the legislation was re-enacted and improved after the Restoration. The principal provisions of the Act of 1660 were as follows: all goods carried to and from the colonies were to be carried in English or colonial ships; masters and three-quarters of the crew were to be English; no tobacco, sugar, indigo, ginger, fustick, or other dye-wood produced in English colonies was to be exported to any place other than England, Ireland, or an English possession (these were the so-called enumerated commodities and the list was changed from time to time); a wide range of goods, including nearly all the principal products of the Mediterranean and Baltic (except iron), and all produce of the Russian and Turkish empires were to be imported into England, Ireland, or Wales in English ships or those belonging to the country of origin or first shipment. Foreign goods imported by English-built and English-manned ships were to be brought only from the place of origin or first shipment. In so far as the Act could be enforced, the Dutch were eliminated from English carrying trade.

Succeeding measures refined the detailed workings of the Act, and the Staple Act of 1663 required that European goods intended for sale in English colonies should be laden in England or Wales and carried directly to the colonies, with the exception of salt for the Newfoundland fisheries, Madeira and Azores wine, and horses and provisions from Scotland and Ireland. An Act of 1673 placed duties on goods sent from one colony to another to prevent New Englanders, in particular, shipping enumerated goods to Europe and undercutting English merchants. An Act of 1696 codified the legislation, which remained essentially intact until 1849.[16]

The laws were enforced with as much vigour as the administration could muster, which meant that there were probably few infringements in England but many in the colonies and Ireland—which relied on Governors, naval officers, and the fairly thin naval presence to police the system. It is clear that many decided the benefits of disregarding the law outweighed the risk of penalty—confiscation of ship and goods or a heavy fine in lieu.[17] But it is also clear that a substantial number of traders, colonial as well as English, preferred not to take risks and

[16] For detailed accounts of the legislation, see L. A. Harper, *The English Navigation Laws: A Seventeenth Century Experiment in Social Engineering* (New York, 1939); G. L. Beer, *The Origins of the British Colonial System, 1578–1660* (New York, 1908). For a brief summary, see Ralph Davis, *The Rise of the English Shipping Industry in the Seventeenth and Eighteenth Centuries* (Newton Abbot, 1962), pp. 306–10.

[17] Evasion of the laws was widespread in a number of areas, notably in trade between New England and Europe where it was commonplace to hide cargoes of sugar with a thin layer of fish. 'Case of *Olive Branch*' [1686], BL Add. MSS, 29800, f. 758. Ireland, which provided substantial quantities of foodstuffs particularly for the West Indies, was another 'back door' for European manufacturers, as was Newfoundland. Commissioners of Revenue in Ireland to the Lord-Lieutenant, 15 Feb. 1686, in J. W. Fortescue, ed., *C[alendar] [of] S[tate] P[apers], Colonial Series, America and the West Indies, 1685–1688* (London, 1899), pp. 152–53; R. C. Nash, 'Irish Atlantic Trade in the Seventeenth and Eighteenth Centuries', *William and Mary Quarterly* (hereafter *WMQ*), Third Series, XLII (1985), pp. 329–56.

perceived mutual benefits in Imperial protection. Their compliance dealt a heavy blow to Dutch competition.

The rapid growth of England's transoceanic trade, particularly in the period after the Restoration, had important repercussions for the economy. It stimulated expansion of shipping, shipbuilding, and port facilities; it created employment in manufacturing, processing, and refining industries; it encouraged growth of occupational and regional specialization; it promoted innovation and refinement of financial instruments, credit, banking, and insurance services. All in all, colonial commerce generated innumerable multiplier, feedback, and spin-off effects which will be discussed under four main headings, shipping, imports, exports, and commercial developments.

Shipping

The first requirement of overseas trade was, of course, the provision of adequate shipping, and this was determined by the volume of goods and length of voyages. A ship trading between London and Dieppe might make eight or ten return voyages per year, whereas a round trip to America or the Indies would engage a ship for a year or more. Furthermore, the cargoes of sugar, tobacco, pepper, and other exotic commodities were bulky and needed a high volume of space for the value. As a result, the increase in transoceanic trade proved a more important stimulus to the expansion of shipping than the increase in the value of the trade might suggest. According to Davis, England's merchant shipping tonnage increased from a pre-Civil War peak of about 150,000 tons in 1640 to about 340,000 tons in 1686,[18] and the transoceanic trade played a major role in the expansion, increasing from virtually nothing in the early seventeenth century to over 40 per cent of overseas trading tonnage in 1686 (Table 18.6).

TABLE 18.6. *Tonnage of shipping required to serve England's overseas trades (000 tons)*

	1663		1686	
	000 tons	%	000 tons	%
Northern Europe	13	10	28	15
Nearby Europe, Scotland, and Ireland	39	31	41	22
Southern Europe and Mediterranean	30	24	39	21
America and West Indies	36	29	70	37
East India	8	6	12	6

Source: Davis, *Shipping Industry*, p. 17.

[18] Davis, *Shipping Industry*, p. 15.

The increased employment for shipping in turn stimulated a large demand for shipwrights, carpenters, carvers, blacksmiths, glaziers, sail-makers, gunmakers, instrument-makers, and other craftsmen needed for the annual refitting of several hundred ships, as well as the more fundamental task of initial building. It is significant that England would have been unlikely to increase her fleet sufficiently to be able to exclude the Dutch from her carrying trade if she had not had the resources of the American frontier to assist her. The Navigation Acts permitted plantation-built ships to participate in colonial trade on equal terms with those built in England. New England, in particular, took advantage of this opportunity. At least half the ships entering London from New England in 1686 were colonial-built and owned, and many were sold in England. By the end of the seventeenth century one in three adult males in Boston had money in shipping, and the town's fleet matched that of Bristol, England's second port.[19] But given the abundance of high-quality timber in America, the presence of skilled workmen in the ports, and the fairly low capital requirements (a typical ship of 130 tons, the *President*, which was built in New England in 1685 cost £1,000), it is not surprising that building not only coastal craft but also transatlantic vessels was fairly ubiquitous.[20]

Apart from stimulating demand for shipbuilding skills, increased plantation trade required expansion of other port-related facilities; the number of quays and wharves in London increased by 30 per cent in the 1670s and 1680s and there was a similar expansion in Bristol;[21] unloading and loading the ships required fleets of small boats, porters, and car-men; storing the goods needed warehouses;[22] seamen needed lodging and entertainment in port; victualling the ships for the long voyages was big business—in 1686 the 300 or so ships clearing London for the American plantations needed provisions for over 9,000 men (larger than the population of all but six or seven towns in England)[23] for two to three months. Ships' accounts show expenditure of sixteen or seventeen shillings per month on common seamen, who were given a fairly nasty diet of bread—often full of weevils—peas, a little salt-pork, stockfish, cheese, and beer, but additional food was taken on board for officers and quality passengers.[24] Expenditure for London's plantation

[19] Bernard Bailyn and Lotte Bailyn, *Massachusetts Shipping, 1697–1714: A Statistical Study* (Cambridge, Mass., 1959).

[20] Articles of Agreement between Thomas Hunt and Arthur Tanner, 30 July 1685, M[assachusetts] H[istorical] S[ociety], Jeffries Papers, Vol. VI, pp. 10, 12, 13. For details of ship construction, see E. Bushnell, *The Compleat Shipwright* (London, 1664).

[21] Henry Roseveare, '"Wiggins' Key" Revisited: Trade and Shipping in the Later Seventeenth-Century Port of London', *Journal of Transport History* (1995), pp. 1–20; David Harris Sacks, *The Widening Gate*.

[22] H.N., *The Compleat Tradesman* (London, 1684), pp. 5, 11, 43–44, 90–99.

[23] E. Anthony Wrigley, 'Urban Growth and Agricultural Change: England and the Continent in the Early Modern Period', in Robert I. Kotberg and Theodore K. Rabb, eds., *Population and Economy: Population and History from the Traditional to the Modern World* (Cambridge, 1986), pp. 123–68.

[24] Basil Lubbock, ed., *Journal of Edward Barlow* (London, 1934).

trade alone in 1686 would have been in excess of £25,000. Bulk demands made of fishmongers, butchers, brewers, and bakers all served as powerful positive stimuli to the commercialization of food production and distribution.[25]

In its early years the East India Company owned two shipyards on the Thames in which it built its own ships. But the Company soon began to show a preference for charter, which transferred risks of ships lying idle or losses at sea to the owner. Blackwell Yard was sold in 1654, and although part of Deptford Yard was retained for repairs, by the time the Company was reorganized in 1657 it depended almost entirely on hire for its activities.

Most ships were owned by partnerships. Active partners in shipping were usually merchants whose business required them to cultivate networks of correspondents abroad and familiarize themselves with overseas markets, making an investment in shipping an attractive way to take additional advantage of these connections as well as to ensure that their own goods were freighted at reasonable rates. Apart from providing the capital of £2,000–3,000 to build, fit, and victual the vessels, the most important task of the partnerships was to hire a master who would earn a good return on their investment. A master needed navigational competence and management skills to supervise the crew and stores, and, in the case of the plantation trade, for securing freight and disposing of it at the journey's end. Above all, he needed to be hard-working, reliable, and trustworthy. The importance of the master was reflected in fairly high pay (£6 per month and perquisites), which gave access to modest gentility for sons of affluent artisans, merchants, and even gentlemen.[26]

Finally, the merchant fleet needed ordinary sailors, and the high mortality rates and defence needs of long-distance trade required high manning levels. It has been calculated that ships in plantation trade required one man for every 8 to 10 tons, whereas in north European trade the ratio was as much as one to 20 tons.[27] Using the figures in Table 18.6, transoceanic trade probably employed over 10,000 men in the 1680s; a considerable satisfaction to the state which, increasingly wedded to a 'blue water' strategy, regarded the merchant fleet as a recruitment pool for the navy in wartime.[28] In the merchant Josiah Child's words, 'this kingdom being an island, it is our interest, as well for our preservation as our profit to have many sea-men'.[29]

[25] In 1674 the fishmongers Goffe and Kent supplied 1,000 stockfish to the *Henry and Sarah* for £20. H[igh] C[ourt] [of] A[dmiralty] 15/12. The trade described in *Reasons Humbly Offered to the Consideration of Parliament why Stock Fish and Live Eels should be Imported into England* (London, 1695).

[26] Deposition of Francis Neight, 1684, HCA 13/79; Davis, *Shipping Industry*, pp. 116–20.

[27] Davis, *Shipping Industry*, pp. 59–61.

[28] Daniel A. Baugh, 'Maritime Strength and Atlantic Commerce: The Uses of "A Grand Marine Empire"', in Lawrence Stone, ed., *An Imperial State at War: Britain from 1689 to 1815* (London, 1994), pp. 185–223.

[29] Josiah Child, *A New Discourse of Trade* (London, 1692), p. 91.

Imports

In 1686 the English in America were shipping commodities worth almost £900,000 to London alone (Table 18.7). The West Indies accounted for almost 80 per cent of the total (justifying their reputation as the most valuable of the plantations), and island produce was heavily dominated by sugar. England had depended on Iberian supplies until the 1640s, when the crop was introduced to Barbados and the high profits encouraged a rapid spread of production. Annual imports of this 'king of sweets' more than doubled, from about 150,000 hundredweights to about 370,000 hundredweights between 1663–69 and 1699–1701 (years of stable population), and an accompanying decline in the retail price from 1.25 shillings per pound in the 1630s to below 0.5 shillings in the 1680s stimulated increasingly widespread use.[30] Sugar was used for elaborate decoration in displays of status; as a spice in a wide variety of savoury dishes; as a vital ingredient in the range of puddings and pies for which England was renowned by the late seventeenth century; and as a sweetener of wines, punches, and the newly popular caffeine drinks.[31] Imports amounted to about 4 pounds per head in 1700, which was a long way short of the 24 pounds per head needed for the whole population regularly to sweeten food or drink (that level was reached in the 1790s), but it was enough to

TABLE 18.7. *Imports to London from the plantations, 1686*

	West Indies		*North America*	
	£ sterl.	%	£ sterl.	%
Dye-woods	9,754	2	1,982	1
Molasses	—	—	20,171	10
Skins/hides	3,997	1	20,588	10
Sugar	586,528	87	16,675	8
Tobacco	7,548	1	141,606	68
Other	66,693	9	6,109	3
TOTAL	674,518	100	207,131	100

Source: London Port Books, E190/143/1; 136/4; 137/2. Values as in Table 18.4.

[30] 'There is no one commodity that doth so much encourage navigation, advance the King's customs and our land and is at the same time of so great a universal use, virtue and advantage as this king of sweets', Thomas Tryon, *Tryon's Letters, Domestick and Foreign to Several Persons of Quality Occasionally Distributed in Subjects* (London, 1700), p. 221. For sugar imports, see Davis, 'English Foreign Trade', p. 81, and for a recent reworking of certain figures, David Eltis, 'New Estimates of Exports from Barbados and Jamaica, 1665–1701', *WMQ*, Third Series, LII (1995), pp. 631–48. For prices, see J. T. Rogers, *A History of Agriculture and Prices in England*, 7 vols. (Oxford, 1886–1902), VI, pp. 41–48.

[31] Sidney W. Mintz, *Sweetness and Power: The Place of Sugar in Modern History* (New York, 1985), chap. 3.

indicate that sugar was a significant presence in the lives of a large number of Englishmen.[32]

Tobacco from the Chesapeake was the most important North American import and the increase in London's declared tobacco imports from 173,000 pounds in 1620 to 1.25 million pounds in 1640, 9 million in 1660, and 11 million in 1676, with the price falling to below a penny a pound, reflected another major change in consumption patterns.[33] While in the 1620s only gentlemen had taken tobacco, and that in moderation, it had by the 1690s become 'a custom, the fashion, all the mode—so that every plow-man had his pipe'.[34]

About a third of the sugar and two-thirds of the tobacco imported into England in 1686 was re-exported and exchanged for European goods. This re-export trade did little to stimulate English manufacturing but did generate profits for English shipping, ports, and merchants in the form of freight, commission, and handling charges.[35]

Grocers, who were also sometimes importers, distributed considerable quantities of the retained sugar in its semi-processed state. However, a large part was certainly sold to the growing number of sugar refiners in the city. This important industry seems to have been introduced into England from Antwerp in the 1550s and was encouraged by large influxes of prize sugar during the period of active privateering against Spain in the late sixteenth century.[36] By 1595 there were seven sugar refineries in London.[37] The next period of expansion came after Barbados took to sugar production in the 1640s and London's sugar imports rose rapidly. In 1695 a petition claimed that there were 'near thirty' refining houses in the country, and an estimated 5,000 tons of brown sugar (half retained imports) were said to be refined annually.[38]

The retained tobacco also went through different hands and processing before it reached the final consumer in shops, alehouses, or coffee-houses all over the country. Similarly, furs were sold to hatters; cocoa, ginger, pimento, drugs, and spices to grocers; hides to leather-workers; and indigo and dye-woods to dry-salters, stimulating England's infant textile-finishing industries. Colonial

[32] Carole Shammas, *The Pre-Industrial Consumer in England and America* (Oxford, 1990), pp. 81–83; Noel Deerr, *History of Sugar*, 2 vols. (London, 1950), II, pp. 458–60.

[33] Shammas, *Pre-Industrial Consumer*, pp. 77–80; Jordan Goodman, *Tobacco in History: The Culture of Dependence* (London, 1995), pp. 59–89.

[34] Thomas Tryon, *The Way to Health, Long Life and Happiness* (London, 1691), p. 128.

[35] Davis, 'English Trade', p. 162.

[36] In the first twenty years of Elizabeth's reign imports of sugar remained at about £18,000 p.a., whereas three years following the defeat of the Armada at least £100,000 worth of sugar was captured at sea by English privateers: K. R. Andrews, 'The Economic Aspects of Elizabethan Privateering', unpublished Ph.D. thesis, London, 1951, p. 154; Deerr, *History of Sugar*.

[37] BL, Lansdowne MSS, 83, f. 6.

[38] Anon., *The Case of the Refiners of Sugar in England, Stated* (London, 1695).

expansion had, as predicted by early enthusiasts, enabled England to substitute her own products for imports and embark on a wide range of new industries.

Of course, not every dream was realized. The fashionability of silks and rising imports had stimulated successful attempts to establish a home industry, but this depended entirely on imported raw silk. From the days of first settlement by the Virginia Company right down to the last colonial project in Georgia, projectors hoped to establish raw silk production.[39] All attempts failed. On the other hand, the English settlers in the Caribbean did produce raw cotton, and by the 1660s they were making a major contribution to supplying the rapidly expanding cotton textile industry in Lancashire.[40] Trade with the East introduced English consumers to cotton textiles and established a taste for the lightweight, washable, and easily patterned fabrics.[41] Raw materials from the new lands in the West enabled England to make her own. In the 1680s there were proposals to set up cotton manufacturing in the islands, but the commissioners of the customs were firm in their refusal to countenance such ideas. The exchange of raw materials for manufactures remained the mercantilist ideal.[42]

The commodity imports in Table 18.7 do not include bullion as it was not recorded in the port books, but there is ample evidence of its importance. In the early seventeenth century England obtained American silver by trading with the Iberian monopoly fleets via Seville and Lisbon or, particularly in wartime, by plunder, and some contraband trade. But after the seizure of Jamaica in 1655 the English were able to develop an entrepôt trade on the same lines as the Dutch in Curaçao. Slaves and manufactured goods were sold to Spanish colonists in exchange for bullion, cocoa, indigo, and hides. Lord Inchiquin, the Governor of Jamaica, estimated that Jamaica's bullion exports were worth £100,000 in 1691, and it is noteworthy that the East India Company was able to fulfil its bullion requirements by purchase in London until 1695.[43]

While the American trade was highly praised by contemporaries for providing valuable raw materials and bullion, the East India trade was less universally

[39] Francis Bacon, 'An Essay on Plantations', in *Select Tracts Relating to Colonies* (London, 1732), p. 3; 'Account of the Design of Trustees for Establishing the Colony of Georgia in America', BL Sloane MSS, 3986, f. 38.

[40] BL Add. MSS, 36,785.

[41] A. P. Wadsworth and J. de la Mann, *The Cotton Trade and Industrial Lancashire* (Manchester, 1931); Beverley Lemire, *Fashion's Favourite: The Cotton Trade and the Consumer in Britain, 1600–1800* (Oxford, 1991).

[42] Molesworth to Lords of Trade, 17 Jan. 1686, C[olonial] O[ffice] 138/5, f. 72; Report from Commissioners of Customs, May 1686, CO 138/5, f. 142.

[43] Nuala Zahedieh, 'The Merchants of Port Royal, Jamaica, and the Spanish Contraband Trade, 1655–1692', *WMQ*, Third Series, XLIII (1986), pp. 570–93, and 'Trade, Plunder and Economic Development in Early English Jamaica, 1655–89', *EcHR*, Second Series, XXXIX (1986), pp. 205–22; Chaudhuri, *Trading World of Asia*, pp. 165–73.

TABLE 18.8. *East India Company imports, 1686*

	£ sterling	%
Chinaware and porcelain	1,477	0.5
Coffee	4,017	1.2
Indigo	—	—
Black pepper	7,458	2.3
Saltpetre	10,605	3.3
Raw silk	17,800	5.5
Tea	371	0.0
Textiles	259,498	80.4
Other	21,406	6.8
TOTAL	322,632	100.0

Source: Chaudhuri, *Trading World of Asia*, pp. 508, 519–48.

popular.[44] Imports were worth almost as much as commodity imports from the plantations (Table 18.1), but raw materials such as pepper, spices, indigo, dyestuffs, saltpetre, raw silk, and tea accounted for less than 30 per cent of total value by the end of the century (Table 18.8). The bulk of the cargoes consisted of cotton textiles, which underwent very rapid expansion from an annual average of 162,005 pieces in the 1660s to an annual average of 760,195 pieces in the 1680s, or about fourteen yards per head of the English population.[45] The peak import of 1,760,315 pieces worth £668,866 in 1684 was not approached for eighty years.

The success of Asian textiles began to cause anxiety in the 1670s, and pressure mounted for protection for the domestic woollen and silk industries, with widespread riots and disturbances in the 1690s. The government responded by requiring the East India Company to export domestic manufactures (essentially wool textiles) to the value of £100,000 per year. In 1721 it forbade the importation of printed Indian calicoes except for re-export to the colonies, although plain white calico imports were permitted.[46] But Cary noted how 'wonderfully fashion prevails', and taste did not revert to traditional fabrics to revive the ailing woollen industry.[47]

Meanwhile, as indicated earlier, the Lancashire textile industry took advantage of the firmly established market for cotton products, and both it and the English silk industry thrived behind protective barriers. Furthermore, the capacity to dye

[44] Cary, *Essay on Trade*, pp. 48–51.

[45] Carole Shammas, 'The Decline of Textile Prices in England and British America Prior to Industrialization', *EcHR*, Second Series, XLVII (1994), p. 502.

[46] Patrick K. O'Brien, Trevor Griffiths, and Philip Hunt, 'Political Components of the Industrial Revolution: Parliament and the English Cotton Textile Industry, 1660–1774', *EcHR*, Second Series, XLIV (1991), pp. 395–423.

[47] Cary, *Essay on Trade*, p. 53.

and print plain cotton cloth developed rapidly, using raw materials imported from America and India. Although Indian competition may well have prejudiced the woollen industry, it did stimulate innovation and expansion in other areas of textile production and finishing.[48]

Exports

The promise that plantations would increase demand for English manufactures and employment was a major theme of colonial projects from the first.[49] By 1686 English colonists were producing commodities which gave them purchasing power of almost £1 million in London. As noted earlier, the English market could not absorb all the goods imported from the colonies or supply all their wants. Perhaps half were re-exported and exchanged for European goods.

Another large part of the proceeds of colonial commodities was used to buy labour—the fundamental prerequisite for extensive growth. Given the availability of land and the high returns to work in the staple-producing regions, they depended on bound labour from the first, and as no region, except New England, achieved natural increase until the very end of the century, the supply had to be imported.[50] White indentured servitude dominated on the mainland throughout the century, but gave way to black slavery in the Caribbean after sugar profits raised the returns to work and enhanced the planter's ability to pay.[51] The slave population of the British West Indies rose from about 15,000 in 1650 to about 115,000 in 1700, and in 1686 the Royal African Company's slave cargoes to Jamaica, acquired in Africa in exchange for manufactured exports, approached half the value of the island's exports.[52] The customs ledgers for 1699 to 1702 suggest that this was a typical level, as they record annual average exports to Africa of £116,933 (2.4 per cent of total exports from England), almost half the value of those shipped directly to the West Indies (£262,035).[53]

[48] Wadsworth and Mann, *Cotton Trade*; Lemire, *Fashion's Favourite.*

[49] Richard Eburne, *A Plain Pathway to Plantations* (London, 1624); R. Gray, *A Good Speed to Virginia* (1609); Carl Bridenbaugh, *Vexed and Troubled Englishmen* (New York, 1908); Nuala Zahedieh, 'London and the Colonial Consumer in the Late Seventeenth Century', *EcHR*, Second Series, XLVII (1994), pp. 239–61.

[50] On the development of indentured servitude, see A. E. Smith, *Colonists in Bondage: White Servitude and Convict Labour in America, 1607–1776* (Chapel Hill, NC, 1947); David W. Galenson, *White Servitude in Colonial America: An Economic Analysis* (Cambridge, 1981).

[51] David W. Galenson, 'White Servitude and the Growth of Black Slavery in Colonial America', *JEcH*, XLI (1981), pp. 39–49; H. McD. Beckles and A. Downes, 'The Economics of Transition to the Black Labour System in Barbados, 1630–1680', *Journal of Interdisciplinary History*, XVIII (1987), pp. 227–28.

[52] John J. McCusker and Russell R. Menard, *The Economy of British America, 1607–1789* (Chapel Hill, NC, 1985), p. 34. Naval Officers' Returns, Jamaica, 1686, CO 142/13. On the Royal African Company, see above pp. 255–59.

[53] Cust[oms] 3/1–6.

The colonists also imported food and wine (much of it from Ireland and the Wine Islands), but the remainder of colonial export earnings was used to buy a wide range of miscellaneous goods required for life and work in the plantations.[54] In 1686 329 ships sailed directly from London to the colonies carrying, apart from re-exports, 598 different English commodities worth (in official values) about £212,000, and 95 per cent of them were manufactures of all sorts imaginable (Table 18.9). The total was fairly evenly divided between North America and the West Indies where, although there was a smaller white population, the use of slave labour greatly enhanced white per-capita incomes (Tables 18.9 and 18.10).[55]

TABLE 18.9. *Exports of English goods from London to plantations, 1686* (£ sterl.)

West Indies	
Barbados	69,359
Jamaica	30,974
Leewards	10,993
TOTAL	111,326
North America	
Bermuda	615
Carolina	5,495
Chesapeake	35,107
Middle Colonies	17,152
New England	40,700
Newfoundland	24
Hudson Bay	1,448
TOTAL	100,541

Source: London Port Books, E190/139/1; 141/5; 136/4. Values as in Table 18.3.

TABLE 18.10. *Per-capita consumption of imports from London*

Colony	White population in 1680	Value of imports from London, 1686 (£ sterl.)	Per-capita imports (£ sterl.)
Barbados	20,000	69,359	3.46
Jamaica	*c.*8,000	30,974	3.87
New England	68,000	40,700	0.59
Chesapeake	55,600	35,107	0.63

Sources: Col. 1: Dunn, *Sugar and Slaves*, pp. 87–88; Zahedieh, 'Trade, Plunder and Economic Development', p. 212; McCusker and Menard, *Economy of British America*, pp. 103, 136. Col. 2: Table 18.6 above. Values as in Table 18.3.

[54] On the Irish provision trade, see Nash, 'Irish Atlantic Trade in the Seventeenth and Eighteenth Century'.

[55] Child, *Discourse of Trade*, pp. 207–08.

The colonial export trade had a number of important novel features, including a new product diversity. Since the Middle Ages England had exported raw wool and woollen cloths and little else: woollens accounted for 90 per cent of London's exports in 1640 and still made up 75 per cent of exports to Europe in the 1690s.[56] But the colonial trades were different—American consumers required a wide array of miscellaneous manufactures. Clothing and textiles dominated, comprising over half the total, but the London Port Books for 1686 indicate that woollens comprised about 25 per cent of the value of English manufactures sent to North America and (not surprisingly, in view of the climate) less than 10 per cent of those sent to the West Indies. Meanwhile, silks accounted for about a quarter of exports to both regions. Cottons, linens, lace, ready-made clothing, stockings, gloves, hats, wigs, and haberdashery are also included in the clothing and textile category and, in the case of London, added about 10 per cent to the value of the city's market.

Other exports further reflected the diversity of colonial needs and heavy reliance on the mother country to supply them—cargoes included glass for windows, beds, upholstery, and furnishings of all sorts, chariots and coaches, billiards and playing-cards, spectacles and looking-glasses, parrot cages, and even tombstones.[57] The broad range of manufactured goods shipped to the colonies in the late seventeenth century suggests that extensive growth across the Atlantic had, as colonial projectors had promised, generated additional employment for those left behind.

It was not only the size of the colonial market which made it important but also its nature. The long distance of the trade encouraged moves towards bulk production and a more standardized product. Whilst fashion and novelty were important, there was less possibility of a face-to-face relationship between producer and consumer and much less scope for bespoke goods, particularly for accessories such as hats, which were shipped in boxes of a dozen or a gross. Thus, producers could make medium or long runs of a uniform product in standard sizes, which enhanced opportunities for cost-cutting and, no doubt, hastened the concentration of trade into the hands of men with large amounts of capital at their disposal. Indeed, recent research indicates that the system of production emerging in late seventeenth-century London industries was characterized by the existence of a small number of wealthy entrepreneurs who maintained centralized workshops employing large numbers of workers to perform the more complex and capital-intensive processes with a high degree of division of labour. They put out materials on credit to dependent producers to perform the simpler processes or to fulfil orders when their workshop capacity was at its limit.[58]

[56] Davis, 'English Foreign Trade', pp. 150–66.

[57] Zahedieh, 'London and the Colonial Consumer', pp. 250–51.

[58] Ibid. David Corner, 'The Tyranny of Fashion: The Case of the Felt-Hatting Trade in the Late Seventeenth and Eighteenth Centuries', *Textile History*, XXII (1991), pp. 153–78.

But innovation was not confined to organizational techniques. There was also a greatly increased use of machinery. Some had been invented long before, such as the knitting frame invented in 1589 or the Dutch loom introduced in 1616, but were not much used until the end of the century. Other examples of new ingenuity include multi-spindle mills for silk-throwers, wheel-cutting machines in watch-making, and a tobacco-shredding machine.[59] There were many reasons for the accelerated take-up of new technology, including rising real wages, the decline of the guilds, and influxes of skilled European immigrants, particularly in the 1680s, but the new expanding opportunities to market wares in the colonies added to the pressure in the same direction.

As indicated above, large numbers took a stake in colonial trade and risked some goods. But by the end of the seventeenth century a fairly small number of major players had emerged to dominate colonial export trades, and although they needed to indulge expensive whims of their colonial clients in the shape of elaborate clothing, carriages, and other luxuries, the bulk of their business lay in providing large quantities of hats, shoes, stockings, ribbons, and other items, batch-produced to a standard pattern. Levels of merchant concentration are very striking in these trades: for example, in the North American trade twelve merchants shipped 60 per cent of the hats, and although few of these men were primarily producers many did become involved in varying degrees in the finance and organization of production.

It was particularly tempting to play a facilitating role in an industry such as silk-weaving, which used an expensive, imported raw material and marketed much of its product overseas. For example, the merchant James Brailsford and his brother Thomas were heavily involved in silk hose production. On James's death in 1678 the partnership had small parcels of raw silk out with forty-two separate weavers and a large parcel worth £483 with Thomas Colborne, a thrower who organized all the stages of throwing, reeling, weaving, trimming, and finishing stockings and ribbons. Litigation shows that the Brailsfords not only provided the raw material but also advanced money to purchase equipment, including a 'great screw press for silk stockings'. The Brailsfords clearly took stockings and ribbons in return for the raw silk (the inventory lists five parcels containing 2,339 pairs of stockings in the warehouse in 1678), and exported them to American markets via Spain, Portugal, and Port Royal, Jamaica.[60]

Thus, both raw materials and finished goods passed through the hands of merchant capitalists. They took the risk of buying raw silk which, given that

[59] Wadsworth and Mann, *Cotton Trade*, pp. 97–108; Peter Earle, *The Making of the English Middle Class* (London, 1989), pp. 19–29.

[60] C[ity] [of] L[ondon] R[ecord] O[ffice], Orphans Court Inventory, CS vol. 4, f. 22; Mayors Court Original Bills, Box 196, No. 42. Detailed correspondence survives from their Jamaican trade in C[hancery] 110/152; Zahedieh, 'The Merchants of Port Royal'.

supply was limited and intermittent, was subject to violent price fluctuations, and they marketed the finished product in distant, risky markets. Their credit enabled small entrepreneurs to increase productivity by extending putting-out arrangements, increasing division of labour, and adopting new machinery. The availability of merchant capital and the incentive of a growing market help explain the rapid expansion of the silk industry, which was claimed to employ about 40,000 people in London in the 1690s, and its precocity in adopting new technology before other branches of the textile industry.

The needs, then, of the 250,000 or so Englishmen living in what were effectively detached counties west of Cornwall, with little industry of their own and a protected market, offered an important stimulus to English industry both because of the size of the demand and its quality: a more standardized, uniform product market offering opportunities for enhanced labour productivity.

Meanwhile, European traders in Asia were unable to market Western products at prices that would generate a large demand for them. It was particularly difficult to sell woollen clothes in a warm climate, although there was a small demand in Persia and some consumption for furnishings, floor-coverings, and tents elsewhere. Without public pressure the East India Company would probably have exported only bullion, being able to profit comfortably on the exchange rate in Asia, but the export of treasure was highly unpopular and the price paid for government support of the monopoly was to send a proportion of exports in commodities, although it was seldom much over 10 per cent.[61]

Commercial Developments

The rapid expansion of England's transoceanic trade in the seventeenth century was undoubtedly one of the factors contributing to the series of changes in the financial world, culminating in what has been described as a 'revolution'.[62] The links were various: at a simple level, colonial expansion provided new opportunities for investment which attracted merchants and capital from abroad, especially after the Navigation Acts made it more difficult for foreigners to trade directly with English possessions. The Jews were a particularly striking example. They already played a prominent role in importing and processing American products, together with the bullion and jewel trades centred on Amsterdam, and having been readmitted to England after the Civil War they lost no time in securing a footing in England's colonial trade, bringing with them valuable

[61] Chaudhuri, *Trading World of Asia.*

[62] P. G. M. Dickson, *The Financial Revolution in England: A Study in the Development of Public Credit, 1688–1756* (London, 1967); Henry Roseveare, *The Financial Revolution, 1660–1760* (London, 1991).

commercial and exchange skills and well-established networks of contacts from Spanish America to India. By the 1680s there were communities of about 300 Jews in both Barbados and Jamaica, and they included seven of London's twenty-one largest West India merchants.[63] They continued to be particularly interested in contraband trade with Spanish America, a major source of bullion, and in the 1680s four of the East India Company's suppliers of bullion were Jews.[64]

Transoceanic trade provided an important stimulus to commercial innovation, including the development of joint-stock organization. This was initially seen as a means to raise large amounts of capital and spread risk, but by the later seventeenth century shares were being traded and an informal stock market had emerged in the alleys between Cornhill and Lombard Street with its own language, rules, and values. The market increased commercial liquidity and the circulation of commercial capital—brokers, jobbers, and price lists all emerged to expedite the rapidly growing business.

The long turn-around times in transoceanic trade (see Map 1.1) stimulated refinements in credit practices to smooth the long chains linking a network of domestic suppliers and distributors with overseas customers. The multilateral system of payments, with England as a hub or clearing-house where balances were settled between different regions, further encouraged improvements in commercial instruments such as bills of exchange, as well as their more widespread use. Even in the late seventeenth century Child would remark that 'we have been so long accustomed to buy and sell goods by verbal contract only that rich and poor men for some time will be apt to think it a diminution of their reputation to have bills under their hands and seals demanded of them for goods bought'.[65] But in transoceanic trade merchants were of necessity less squeamish. As bills became common, they began to be transferred by endorsement in the late seventeenth century, and legal decisions of 1693 and 1696 established—with some exceptions—free negotiability.[66] Looking at Amsterdam, Barbour suggested that familiarity with the bill of exchange may have encouraged acceptance of other forms of paper: merchants' notes, receipts for bullion deposited in the bank, or merchandise stored in a warehouse, debentures of industrial companies—all these passing freely from hand to hand were a valuable addition to the money supply.[67]

[63] Zahedieh, 'The Capture of the *Blue Dove*, 1664: Policy, Profits, and Protection in Early English Jamaica', in R. A. McDonald, ed., *West Indies Accounts: Essays on the History of the British Caribbean and the Atlantic Economy in Honour of Richard Sheridan* (Kingston, Jamaica, 1996), pp. 29–47. See also her 'Credit, Risk and Reputation', pp. 21–23.

[64] Chaudhuri, *Trading World of Asia*, pp. 166–67.

[65] Child, *Discourse of Trade*, p. 91.

[66] For a detailed account of the use of bills of exchange, see James Steven Rogers, *The Early History of the Law of Bills and Notes: A Study of the Origins of Anglo-American Commercial Law* (Cambridge, 1995).

[67] Violet Barbour, *Capitalism in Amsterdam in the Seventeenth Century* (Baltimore, 1950).

Long-distance trade also stimulated the development of brokerage, commission, and wholesale services in the major ports together with increased expertise in buying, appraising and classifying, and selling exotic commodities. The dangers of the trade stimulated a range of innovations designed to improve control through better information, management, and accounting.[68] A merchant needed to write dozens of letters a week and keep basic accounts, which encouraged improvements in schools and training to produce a sufficient number 'able to write perfect good hands and to have full knowledge and use of arithmetic and merchants accounts'.[69] Commercial publications, from price lists to instruction manuals, proliferated; institutions such as Lloyd's Coffee House emerged as centres of intelligence; bookkeeping took on a more systematic appearance, although it must be said that it remained fairly elementary, and the East India Company did not produce annual balance sheets until 1704. Marine insurance began to develop in London and the major outports.[70] By the end of the seventeenth century the accumulation and refinement of commercial skills in London made it look set to overtake Amsterdam as Europe's major entrepôt, shipping centre, commodity market, and market for capital.

England's transoceanic trade was not large; even in 1700 it accounted for about 20 per cent of total overseas commerce. It was the rapidity of growth rather than its absolute scale which drew fascinated attention from contemporaries and later historians. But although still quite small, the trade does seem to have had a strategic significance in late seventeenth-century economic development. In the shipping industry the long distance of the trade meant a high ratio of shipping capacity to volume of trade, and the plantation trade in particular provided a major stimulus to the merchant fleet. The import trade from America allowed England to substitute colonial products for foreign supplies and also stimulated a range of finishing and processing industries, whilst that from the East pioneered a market for cotton textiles, encouraging imitation and import substitution by domestic industry as well as growth of textile printing. In the export trade, colonial demand for a wide range of miscellaneous manufactures, different from traditional exports and concentrated in relatively few hands, encouraged merchants and wholesalers to invest in production, bringing about a broadening and deepening of England's manufacturing base. There was diversification into new industries, such as silk-making, hat-making, and a multitude of smaller trades such as card-making.

[68] Ian K. Steele, *The English Atlantic, 1675–1740: An Exploration of Communication and Community* (Oxford, 1986).

[69] Child, *Discourse of Trade*, p. 5.

[70] Violet Barbour, 'Marine Risks and Insurance in the Seventeenth Century', *Journal of Economic and Business History*, I (1928–29), pp. 561–96.

Finally, the expansion of transoceanic trade played a major role in attracting foreign capital and stimulating the financial innovations which have been dubbed a 'commercial revolution'. Colonial expansion was not a sufficient condition for economic development, as demonstrated in Spain and Portugal, but it was certainly an important positive stimulus, as recognized by contemporaries. The fact that Englishmen seized the opportunities opened up by transoceanic commerce goes a long way towards explaining English development in this period.

Select Bibliography

KENNETH R. ANDREWS, *Trade, Plunder and Settlement: Maritime Enterprise and the Genesis of the British Empire, 1480–1630* (Cambridge, 1984).

BERNARD BAILYN and LOTTE BAILYN, *Massachusetts Shipping, 1697–1714: A Statistical Study* (Cambridge, Mass., 1959).

G. L. BEER, *The Origins of the British Colonial System, 1578–1660*, 2 vols. (New York, 1908).

ROBERT BRENNER, *Merchants and Revolutionaries: Commercial Change, Political Conflict and London's Overseas Traders, 1550–1653* (Cambridge, 1993).

K. N. CHAUDHURI, *The English East India Company: A Study of an Early Joint Stock Company, 1600–1640* (London, 1965).

—— *The Trading World of Asia and the English East India Company, 1660–1760* (Cambridge, 1978).

RALPH DAVIS, 'English Foreign Trade, 1660–1700', *Economic History Review*, Second Series, VI (1954), pp. 150–66.

—— *The Rise of the English Shipping Industry in the Seventeenth and Eighteenth Centuries* (Newton Abbot, 1962).

K. G. DAVIES, *The Royal African Company* (London, 1957).

F. J. FISHER, 'London's Export Trade in the Early Seventeenth Century', *Economic History Review*, Second Series, III (1950).

LAWRENCE A. HARPER, *The English Navigation Laws: A Seventeenth Century Experiment in Social Engineering* (New York, 1939).

S. R. H. JONES and S. VILLE, 'Efficient Transactors or Rent-Seeking Monopolists? The Rationale for Early Chartered Trading Companies', *Journal of Economic History*, LVI (1996), pp. 898–915.

PATRICK K. O'BRIEN, TREVOR GRIFFITHS, and PHILIP HUNT, 'Political Components of the Industrial Revolution: Parliament and the English Cotton Textile Industry, 1660–1774', *Economic History Review*, XLIV (1991), pp. 395–423.

JACOB M. PRICE and P. G. E. CLEMENS, 'A Revolution of Scale in Overseas Trade: British Firms in the Chesapeake Trade, 1675–1775', *Journal of Economic History*, XLVII (1987), pp. 1–43.

HENRY ROSEVEARE, '"Wiggins' Key" Revisited: Trade and Shipping in the Later Seventeenth-Century Port of London', *Journal of Transport History* (1985), pp. 1–20.

DAVID HARRIS SACKS, *The Widening Gate: Bristol and the Atlantic Economy* (Berkeley and Los Angeles, 1991).

G. V. SCAMMELL, *The First Imperial Age: European Overseas Expansion, c.1400–1715* (London, 1989).

Ian K. Steele, *The English Atlantic, 1675–1740: An Exploration of Communication and Community* (Oxford, 1986).

A. P. Wadsworth and J. de la Mann, *The Cotton Trade and Industrial Lancashire* (Manchester, 1931).

Nuala Zahedieh, 'London and the Colonial Consumer in the Late Seventeenth Century', *Economic History Review*, XLVII (1994), pp. 239–61.

19

The Emerging Empire: The Continental Perspective, 1650–1713

JONATHAN I. ISRAEL

It first became evident to other European states that England possessed outstanding advantages as a colonizing power, and that her Empire might soon outstrip all others, in the 1650s. This heightened awareness of England's exceptional capacity for maritime and colonial expansion arose, in part, from England's newly acquired naval superiority over the Dutch shown during the First Anglo-Dutch War (1652–54), a supremacy at sea that had not been foreseen on the eve of that conflict and which initially caused some surprise; and, in part, from the growing assertion, from 1651, of English dominance in the Caribbean. The English conquest of Jamaica from the Spaniards in 1655 caused as much alarm in Amsterdam, Hamburg, and Paris as in Madrid. Any lingering doubts there may have been in Europe that England now possessed a more formidable capacity to subjugate and colonize lands outside Europe than any other European power were dispelled by the astounding news of the Anglo-Portuguese marriage treaty of 1661 whereby Portugal, facing renewed pressure from Habsburg Spain, sought Charles II's help and protection. To procure this, Portugal conceded Tangier and Bombay to the English, as part of Catherine de Braganza's marriage dowry, thereby providing England with crucial new points of entry in North Africa and India.

These developments fundamentally altered European perceptions of England's overseas Empire. Where previously she had been a secondary power, and her colonies in Ireland and North America had appeared marginal, suddenly fear of English mastery of the seas and of the Indies, East and West, and therefore of the trade of the world, became a pervasive reality influencing the thinking of statesmen and diplomats throughout western Europe. Nor were these anxieties of the 1650s and early 1660s in any way eased during subsequent decades. On the contrary, they tended to intensify throughout the crucially formative period down to the Peace of Utrecht in 1713.

By the middle of the eighteenth century Britain was without any doubt the supreme maritime and colonial power and hub of global commerce. This momentous shift, furthermore, was achieved in the face not just of a growing, almost universal, anxiety over the rise of English, and after 1707 British, power on the continent, but of the full-scale armed opposition, at different times, of all of England's main colonial and maritime rivals—the French, Spanish, and Dutch. Yet this European resistance to the relentless growth of England's Empire was mostly sporadic and piecemeal, and virtually never—except briefly during the Second Anglo-Dutch War (1664–67)—involved any serious attempt at global strategic co-operation against England on the part of her main rivals. This somewhat paradoxical fact poses the question of how precisely England's rapid expansion was perceived on the continent during the period, and why it was that more effective methods of combating her burgeoning Empire were not devised.

The unexpected superiority of English seapower during the First Anglo-Dutch War greatly alarmed the ruling Dutch regent élite. Since the heavy defeats suffered by the Dutch, at Portuguese hands, in northern Brazil during the late 1640s, they had given up their ambitions to carve out a large empire in the New World. But the Dutch were still entrenched as the foremost European military and naval power in Asia and Africa and had built up a general primacy in world trade. However, it seemed clear that this general ascendancy over the seaborne trade of the world would not last long if the English navy dominated the seas and if the English could interfere at will with Dutch merchant shipping and their fisheries.

By the summer of 1653 the Dutch leaders found themselves caught in a harsh dilemma. On the one hand, there was no way that they could immediately reverse the series of major setbacks which their war fleets had suffered at English hands in the North Sea and the Channel. But, on the other hand, it was impossible for them to cut their losses and simply accept English superiority at sea. For that would mean that the English would have their way in all the numerous disputes over colonies, commerce, and rights of maritime access and passage which were generating Anglo-Dutch friction virtually throughout the world. To have accepted defeat in 1653 would have put the entire fabric of Dutch shipping, fisheries, colonies, and commerce at the disposal and mercy of the English.

Thus it was that after the heavy defeats in the summer of 1653 the Dutch States General initiated an unprecedented programme of naval reform and reorganization and the construction of new, more heavily armed, warships.[1] At a fairly late stage in the war the Dutch also commenced a major privateering war against English merchant shipping. But what chiefly enabled the Dutch to extricate themselves from their predicament without, in the end, losing any colonies or

[1] On the restructuring and professionalization of the Dutch navy after 1653, see J. R. Bruijn, 'The Dutch Navy in its Political and Social Economic Setting of the Seventeenth Century', in Charles Wilson and David Proctor, eds., *1688: The Seaborne Alliance and Diplomatic Revolution* (London, 1989), pp. 45–58, and J. R. Bruijn, *The Dutch Navy of the Seventeenth and Eighteenth Centuries* (Columbia, SC, 1993), pp. 72–82.

trade to the English, or conceding English superiority at sea, was their remarkable success in the latter stages of the war in combining seapower with strategic collaboration with other European states to paralyse England's seapower and direct maritime trade beyond English waters. Especially successful was the Dutch alliance with Denmark-Norway: throughout the latter part of the conflict, Dutch-Danish naval forces kept the Danish Sound completely closed to English shipping, bringing England's Baltic traffic to an almost total halt.[2]

At the same time the States General played on the growing tension between Spain and England, the Pensionary of Holland, Adriaen Pauw, assuring the Spanish ambassador at The Hague, as early as September 1652, that the arrogance and aggressiveness being shown by the English in all parts of the globe was as much a menace to Spain's empire and interests as to the Dutch.[3] Subsequently, while the Spanish court took care not to become entangled with England, being still at war with France until 1659, there were nevertheless clear signs that Spain was tilting more towards the Dutch than the English and adopting an accommodating stance with regard to Dutch naval operations around the Straits of Gibraltar. After their victory over the English in the battle off Livorno in March 1653, the Dutch were able to station a strong force in the Straits and effectively shut the English out of the Mediterranean (Map 3.2).

Meanwhile, the Dutch United East India Company, or VOC, made use of its naval superiority in Asian seas to paralyse English shipping from the coasts of Japan, China, and (present day) Indonesia to the Persian Gulf. Thus, even though the English won all the major naval battles in home waters, the Dutch succeeded in neutralizing the superior fire-power and weight of the English 'first-rates' by dispersing their navy to some extent and disrupting England's sea-lanes away from home waters. Eventually, Cromwell's England agreed to make peace with the Dutch in 1654 without winning any colonies or maritime concessions.[4]

Discussion about the Anglo-Dutch conflict in the capitals of western Europe reveals an acute awareness of the implications of England's newly acquired naval supremacy both for the European balance of power and all the seaborne empires outside Europe. The Council of State in Madrid judged in 1652 that England was basically now much stronger than the Dutch Republic and that English maritime expansion was likely to pose major problems for Spain. Despite their lack of sympathy for the regicide regime in London, Spanish ministers pondered the possibility of seeking close relations, or an alliance, with England, thus sacrificing

[2] Jonathan I. Israel, *Dutch Primacy in World Trade, 1585–1740* (Oxford, 1989), pp. 210–11.

[3] Consulta of the *Consejo de Estado*, Madrid, 14 Sept. 1652, f2., A[rchivo] G[eneral] [de] S[imancas] Estado 2079.

[4] Israel, *Dutch Primacy*, pp. 212–13; Jonathan I. Israel, *The Dutch Republic: Its Rise, Greatness and Fall, 1477–1806* (Oxford, 1995), p. 772.

their relations with the Dutch. They knew that any move in the opposite direction towards alignment with the United Provinces was bound to incur English hostility. Even so, Spanish statesmen came to the conclusion that Spain's interests were best served by aligning with the Dutch rather than with England. There were two main reasons for this. The first and most important, and the one which ensured a slowly strengthening strategic collaboration between Spain and the United Provinces throughout the last half-century (1650–1700) of the Habsburg era in Spain, was French expansionism in Europe and, in particular, French designs on the Spanish Netherlands. Despite its small size, the heavily fortified southern Netherlands was, from a military and strategic point of view, one of the crucial zones of Europe, and Spanish courtiers were convinced that they could only defend and retain their Low Countries base in alliance with the Dutch. They also calculated that Dutch fears of France in Europe, and the regents' desire that the southern Netherlands should remain as a buffer between France and themselves, ensured the durability and reliability of such Spanish–Dutch collaboration.[5]

The second reason for the Spanish preference for a pro-Dutch, rather than a pro-English, stance was that until the mid-1660s the Spanish crown persistently endeavoured to recover Portugal and, with Portugal, the Portuguese colonial empire which had been under Spain between 1580 and 1640. It was reasonable to suppose that the Dutch Republic would support the Spanish ambition to reconquer Portugal, Brazil, and the rest of the Portuguese empire, while the English, who were cultivating close links with Portugal, were unlikely to further any such ambition. Nor was this an idle expectation. Under the terms of the Dutch–Spanish peace, signed at Münster in 1648, Spain had recognized Dutch title to the conquests made in Brazil by the West India Company, and, despite qualms about handing over colonial territory to heretics, the Council of State in Madrid repeatedly reminded the States General in The Hague that, in return for Dutch naval assistance in blockading Portugal, Spain was willing to restore northern Brazil to the Dutch.

During the years 1652–54 Spanish ministers preferred to lean towards the Dutch rather than the English, but felt that while they remained locked in war with France they could not enter into open confrontation with England.[6] But no sooner had the English and Dutch made peace in 1654 than Parliament, under Oliver Cromwell's guidance, began to make aggressive demands on Spain which led to the Anglo-Spanish War of 1655–60. While Cromwell allied with France and proclaimed that Spain was still a menace in Europe, there was little doubt in European capitals that the chief motive for this new English maritime offensive

[5] Consulta of the *Consejo de Estado*, Madrid, 30 April 1652, AGS Estado 2078, and consulta of the *Consejo de Estado*, Madrid, 14 Sept. 1652, AGS Estado 2079.

[6] Consultas of the *Consejo de Estado*, Madrid, 16 and 20 Feb. 1653, AGS Estado 2081.

was a desire to seize Spanish colonies in the New World, plunder the treasure which Spain derived from her American viceroyalties, and acquire a grip over the vital sea-lanes converging on the Straits of Gibraltar, the strategic importance of which the Dutch had so vividly demonstrated during the previous war.[7] At that time no comparable narrow stretch of water anywhere had so many merchant fleets regularly sailing through or, as with the Spanish transatlantic convoys, based nearby.

It was now the turn of the Spaniards to try to entangle the Dutch with England. Being weak at sea and already at war with France on land, Spain had few available strategic options. The Dutch, who were only just beginning to build up their newly reorganized navy, and to recover from the damage they had suffered, showed no interest in intervening directly on the side of the Spaniards, even though Amsterdam's merchants noted every English success, and above all their conquest of Jamaica, with undisguised enmity. However, unlike the Dutch in their war with Parliamentary England, the Spanish court did decide to take up the cause of the exiled Stuart King, Charles II.[8] By helping Charles with subsidies, winning his friendship, and welcoming exiled English Royalists in the Spanish Netherlands, Spain hoped to weaken the English Republic and also ensure, should Charles ever regain his throne, that English aggression at sea, and designs on Spain's American empire, would cease. Meanwhile, English fleets dominated Spain's coasts and sea-lanes.

The news that the Stuart monarchy was indeed about to be restored in 1660 was greeted in both Spain and the United Provinces not just with relief, but with a vigorous determination not to let slip the apparent opportunity to curb what they saw as English aggression and arrogance at sea and in the colonial world. It seemed likely that Charles II, once restored to his British thrones, would be in a precarious position in respect of his troublesome subjects, and especially Parliament. By supporting the British Crown, winning Charles's friendship, and cultivating amicable relations with his court and advisers, it was hoped that the unresolved maritime and colonial disputes could be speedily settled and that the relentless English pressure on the Dutch and Spanish colonial empires of the past decade could be brought to an end.

Peace negotiations between Spain and England commenced. The Dutch lost no time in discarding their previous coolness towards Charles. He, however, did not forget the indifference of the States General to his plight over the years, nor their spurning of his offer of an alliance against Parliament in 1653. During the several

[7] Rafael Valladares Ramírez, 'Inglaterra, Tánger y el "estrecho compartido": los inicios del asentamiento inglés en el Mediterráneo occidental durante la guerra hispano-portuguesa (1641–1661)', *Hispania*, LI (1991), pp. 982–83.
[8] T. Venning, *Cromwellian Foreign Policy* (London, 1995), pp. 115–16.

months that Charles spent in Holland before returning to Britain in 1660, he found himself positively besieged with offers of friendship and goodwill from the Dutch provinces and city governments.[9] In the hope of securing amicable relations and a treaty of alliance, together with at least some offers of compromise in the maritime sphere and possibly even cancellation of the Navigation Act (1651)—a measure chiefly aimed against, and detested by, the Dutch—the States of Holland and States General resolved to present Charles with the most illustrious gift which the Republic had ever bestowed. At Amsterdam's instigation, the 'Dutch Gift' of 1660 was of unprecedented magnificence, consisting of most of the best Italian paintings to be found in the United Provinces, including Titians, Tintorettos, and Veroneses, besides Dutch pictures, Roman antiquities, and a handsome yacht for good measure.

The results of all this diplomatic fawning were profoundly disappointing to Spain and the Dutch alike. 'His Majesty heartily thanked' the Dutch ambassadors 'for so worthy a present and express'd his willingness to enter into a neerer alliance with them',[10] but he subsequently refused to modify, much less revoke, the Navigation Act and made no moves whatever to adopt a more accommodating stance on maritime issues. On the contrary, Charles's setting up of the Royal African Company (1660) led to a rapid escalation of Anglo-Dutch friction in West Africa, while the tension between the English and Dutch in the Caribbean, New Netherland, and the East Indies tended to intensify rather than lessen.[11] The Dutch, who had been at war with Portugal since 1657 in an effort to compel the Portuguese to return the territory which the West India Company had lost in Brazil, were also deeply perturbed by the alacrity with which Charles took Portugal under his protection, in an alliance which seemed likely to extend beyond Europe to what remained of the Portuguese empire in India.

But if the Dutch were dismayed by Charles II's attitude and alignment with Portugal, the Spanish King, Philip IV, was even more disgusted.[12] In Madrid the fortified city of Tangier was regarded as a crucial element in controlling the sea-lanes around the Straits of Gibraltar. Both that enclave and Bombay were regarded as the rightful property of the Spanish crown, which the Portuguese had usurped, and the English had no right whatsoever to accept as pledges from the Portuguese. Under the treaty which the Spanish crown had signed with Charles in Brussels in April 1656, the future English monarch had promised, in return for Spanish

[9] Herbert H. Rowen, *John de Witt, Grand Pensionary of Holland, 1625–1672* (Princeton, 1978), pp. 442–47.

[10] Quoted in A. M. S. Logan, *The Cabinet of the Brothers Gerard and Jan Eynst* (Amsterdam, 1979), p. 86.

[11] Charles Wilson, *Profit and Power: A Study of England and the Dutch Wars*, 2nd edn. (The Hague, 1978), pp. 111–26; Israel, *The Dutch Republic*, pp. 748–58; see above pp. 255–59.

[12] R. A. Stradling, *Europe and the Decline of Spain* (London, 1981), p. 146.

backing and subsidies, to assist Spain to reconquer Portugal and Brazil and also to arrange the return of recent English conquests from the Spaniards in the Caribbean.[13] Consequently, the Anglo-Portuguese marriage treaty of 1661 was regarded in Spain as a personal affront, a betrayal by Charles of the Spanish monarch.[14] In June 1661 secret instructions were sent from Madrid to the Spanish ambassador at The Hague that he was to do all in his power to sow discord between the Dutch and English and was, with all vigour, to renew Spain's offer to the States General of an offensive alliance against Portugal by land and sea, and again to declare to the 'United provinces that it is His Majesty's desire to fulfil what was offered in the [Dutch–Spanish] peace treaty about restitution of the regions which they formerly occupied in Brazil should [Philip IV] recover Portugal'.[15] But the Dutch provinces were divided over whether to continue the war with Portugal which, at that stage, was being chiefly fought in India and, with Amsterdam anxious to settle and resume trade, the Spanish offer was declined.[16]

Yet despite the failure of the Dutch to respond to the Spanish proposal that the two powers should combine forces to overwhelm England's ally, Portugal, Charles II's overseas policy was not without evident risks. The launching of the Royal African Company, the Anglo-Portuguese alliance, and the English occupation of Tangier and Bombay were sensational events. They confirmed England's new status as a leading power in all continents and as would-be mistress of the seas, an Empire relentlessly set on expansion and ready to antagonize several different leading European states simultaneously in pursuit of her maritime and colonial aims. By 1662 the Anglo-Dutch friction in almost all parts of the globe had again become acute, and there was a marked upsurge of hostility towards the English, and Charles II in particular, amongst both the regents and the Dutch public. Nor was the resentment of the Spanish court likely to be quickly assuaged. But the real danger from England's point of view, as at least some members of Charles's court appreciated, was less that England was likely to remain isolated diplomatically for some considerable time than that, with the Franco-Spanish conflict at an end since 1659, there was a distinct possibility that England's continued expansion overseas would soon bring all three of her main colonial rivals—France, Spain, and the United Provinces—together. Some form of co-ordinated action might bring the triumphant progress of England's Empire to a halt and cut it back. Lord Chancellor Clarendon reminded the English ambassador in The Hague, Sir George Downing, in August 1661 that 'we have yet no alliance made with France, Spain, or the United Provinces', and of the 'danger that would ensue if they three should

[13] Venning, *Cromwellian Foreign Policy*, p. 116.

[14] Valladares Ramírez, 'Inglaterra, Tánger y el "estrecho compartido"', pp. 984–87.

[15] Esteban de Gamarra to Philip IV, The Hague, 12 July 1661, AGS Libros de La Haya 44, f. 35.

[16] Israel, *The Dutch Republic*, pp. 753–54.

enter into an alliance to our prejudice'.[17] In August 1661 it seemed, in London, that there were worrying signs of a pending Dutch–Spanish naval collaboration against England as well as Portugal, and of a possible joint Dutch–Spanish attack on Tangier.

The young French King, Louis XIV, whose personal rule began in 1661, was eager to advance French overseas commerce and colonization and, especially in the first decade of his personal rule, was willing to devote substantial resources both to extending and strengthening France's colonial empire and to building up the French navy. His minister in charge of finance and economic affairs, Jean-Baptiste Colbert, was tireless in his efforts to promote French industry and overseas commerce, and placed particular stress on developing the French colonies and stimulating France's long-distance trade with all continents. Emigration to the French colonies received an unprecedented degree of encouragement, among other methods, by providing dowries at the king's expense for poor girls willing to marry in the New World. During this decade the population of New France doubled while the number of French colonists on Saint-Domingue (the western half of Hispaniola) tripled.[18] The produce shipped from the French West Indies to metropolitan France each year began to rise steeply in both quantity and value.

But while French colonial policy was now altogether more thrusting and vigorous than it had been before 1661, it was to be a consistent feature of French colonial expansion down to the 1690s that it was markedly more antagonistic towards the Dutch and Spanish than towards the English.[19] This persistent tilt in French overseas policy was not fortuitous but was a direct outgrowth of French expansionist and mercantilist aims in Europe. Louis XIV's basic strategy in Europe was to build French supremacy on the ruins of Spain's former hegemony and, in particular, to annex the Spanish Netherlands which would, in turn, have put both the United Provinces and the Rhineland at his mercy. At the same time, because the Dutch at that stage had a much larger trade with France than the English, and because it was Dutch rather than English manufactures and colonial products which had heavily penetrated the French market, the aggressive mercantilist measures and tariff increases introduced by Louis and Colbert were chiefly aimed against the Dutch rather than the English.[20] Louis's generally friendly attitude towards Charles II and James II and his desire to align with the Stuarts

[17] Clarendon to Downing, London, 30 Aug. 1661, in T. H. Lister, *Life and Administration of Edward, First Earl of Clarendon*, 3 vols. (London, 1837–38), III, p. 169.

[18] Philip Boucher, *Les Nouvelles Frances: France in America, 1500–1815: An Imperial Perspective* (Providence, RI, 1989), p. 45.

[19] Ibid., p. 54; Israel, *Dutch Primacy*, pp. 282–91.

[20] Paul Butel, 'France, the Antilles, and Europe in the Seventeenth and Eighteenth Centuries', in James D. Tracy, ed., *The Rise of Merchant Empires: Long-Distance Trade in the Early Modern World, 1350–1750* (Cambridge, 1990), p. 159.

in his European policy was to be an additional reason why, for some three decades, the French tended to avoid entanglement with the English outside of Europe also, a tendency as noticeable in the New World as in Africa and Asia. It was a strategy which was to have momentous consequences both for Europe and the colonial empires of the European powers. For clearly this persistent tilt in French policy against the Dutch and Spanish rather than the English in the period before the Glorious Revolution was the factor which, more than any other, rendered impossible any sustained concerted action to halt, and roll back, English colonial and maritime expansion.

Nevertheless, the growing friction between the English and Dutch during the opening years of Louis's reign did pose something of a dilemma for the French court. Louis wished to put the Dutch in their place; but at the same time he did not wish simply to hand over mastery of the seas and of distant continents to the English. If the English, who were seen as the stronger side in terms of fire-power, were to win a crushing victory over the Dutch in the widely expected Second Anglo-Dutch War, this would further French interests neither in the Indies nor in Europe, since Charles II would then be both more powerful abroad and more secure at home. Accordingly, Louis signed a defensive treaty with the Dutch in 1662 and made up his mind to give them just sufficient assistance in the pending war to prevent their being overwhelmed by the English.[21]

Consequently, the Dutch Republic entered the Second Anglo-Dutch War with considerably greater strategic advantages than she had entered the First, despite the fact that the Dutch leadership had still by no means succeeded in closing the gap between their navy and that of the English in terms of 'first-rates' and fire-power. In this bitter struggle the Dutch received some strategic support from both France and Spain, as well as Denmark-Norway, and it is obvious that this was a major factor in the series of defeats which the English suffered during those years. It was also a clear indication of how the expansion of England's overseas Empire could, at that stage, have been reversed had French policy been different.[22]

Yet while it is true that the Second Anglo-Dutch War was, to a greater extent than any previous European conflict, a war about empire outside Europe—in Asia, Africa, and the Americas—a struggle caused essentially by colonial and maritime rivalry, it cannot be said that the Dutch objective was to halt, or reverse, English maritime and colonial expansion as such. Rather, Dutch war aims were limited to attempting to administer a sufficient check to the English at sea to compel them to cease their interference with Dutch shipping and fisheries, and to defend those colonies which the English were trying to seize or, as in the cases of New Netherland and the Dutch Guinea forts, actually had seized.

[21] Rowen, *John de Witt*, pp. 465–72. [22] Israel, *Dutch Primacy*, pp. 269–79.

Within Europe, Louis chiefly aided the Dutch by sending troops to check the invasion of the Republic's eastern provinces by England's ally, the Prince-Bishop of Münster. Outside Europe the only region where the French intervened directly in the fighting was the Caribbean, but here they played a crucial role. For while the Dutch on their own were able to mount a successful counter-offensive against the English in West Africa in 1664, their attempt to repeat this success in the Caribbean came to nothing. De Ruyter's attack on Barbados in April 1665 was easily repulsed, and after the departure of his fleet from the Caribbean, the English launched a broad offensive. The purpose of this, in Charles II's own words, was to 'root the Dutch out of all places in the West Indies ... especially Curaçao, if God give success'.[23] The Buccaneers recruited by the Governors of Jamaica and Barbados, on the King's orders, to assist with this work overran Saint Eustatius, renaming the island New Dunkirk in July 1665. Meanwhile English regulars captured Saba, Tobago (which the Dutch had been colonizing in recent years), and all the Dutch colonies in western Guiana except Berbice. It was essentially as a result of French intervention that the English offensive was halted and then rolled back during 1666 and the early part of 1667. Louis sent out a substantial force to the Caribbean, as a result of which the French captured the islands of St Christopher (St Kitts), Tobago (August 1666), Antigua (December 1666), Montserrat, and Saint Eustatius, while the Dutch were able to reconquer Essequibo and Pomeroon (see Map 10.1). In February 1667 a relatively modest force, fitted out by the States of Zeeland, of five vessels and a thousand men under Abraham Crijnssen, captured the English colony of Surinam, changing the name of Fort Willoughby at Paramaribo to Fort Zeelandia. By early 1667 the English Empire in the Caribbean and Guianas looked likely at the very least to be drastically curtailed.

Spain's strategic support for the Dutch was also important. Dutch privateers were allowed to operate from Cadiz and other Spanish ports and openly to sell off captured English prizes. 'All the English merchants upon the coast', reported the English envoy in Madrid to London in July 1665, 'complain of the Spaniards' partiality towards the Dutch.'[24] So unwelcome were the English made to feel at Cadiz that the English consul there reported in April 1666 that 'noe English shipping has traded here above the twelve months'.[25] In the spring of 1666 there were again fears that the Spaniards and Dutch were planning a joint attack on Tangier.[26]

The Second Anglo-Dutch War was a defeat for England, but by no means the serious setback to her maritime and colonial ambitions which it seemed it might become early in 1667. For as we have seen, Louis had no real interest (or so he

[23] *C[alendar] [of] S[tate] P[apers], America and the West Indies*, 1661–68, p. 329.

[24] Fanshaw to Arlington, Madrid, 19/29 July 1665, S[tate] P[apers] 94/49, f. 43.

[25] Wescombe to Arlington, Cadiz, 28 April 1666, SP 94/50, f. 151.

[26] Southwell to Arlington, Madrid, 30 March 1666; ibid., f. 206.

judged) in confronting England and no intention of making the maritime and colonial conflict his chief priority. Once it became clear that the English were not going to overwhelm the Republic, or win undisputed mastery of the seas, Louis lost all desire to help the Dutch and fixed his attention on the Spanish Netherlands. After the inconclusive Battle of Nevis (May 1667), in which a combined Franco-Dutch fleet of eighteen ships fought a smaller English fleet, Franco-Dutch strategic collaboration all but ceased. Louis made no move to reinforce his garrisons in the Caribbean, whereas Charles sent out large-scale reinforcements.[27] Meanwhile, the entry of the French army into the Spanish Netherlands not only initiated the War of Devolution (1667–68) between France and Spain, but transformed the strategic situation throughout Europe and the wider world. The Dutch were greatly alarmed lest the French should overwhelm the Spanish Netherlands, a development which the Holland regents believed would have ruinous consequences for their Republic and its trade. They suddenly became anxious to conclude their conflict with England as soon as possible in order to concentrate on curbing French expansionism in Europe.

During the final weeks of the Anglo-Dutch War, the Dutch, following their attack on the Medway, enjoyed naval superiority in the Channel and the North Sea, but the English were able to regain the upper hand in the Caribbean. Although the French beat off an attack on St Christopher, the English recovered Antigua and Montserrat, destroyed a French force at Martinique, and finally raided Cayenne in September 1667 and recaptured Surinam in October. However, the Peace of Breda, ending the war, had been concluded on 31 July, and under its terms all captured Dutch colonies in the West Indies, including Surinam, were to be returned to the Republic. Subsequently, in April 1668, Surinam was returned to Dutch control. However, lacking French support, the Dutch were unable also to obtain restitution of New Netherland at the peace table, although had Louis's policy been otherwise there can be little doubt, given the circumstances, that they could easily have done so. For on top of the naval defeats and the almost complete paralysis of English trade on all fronts, including the East Indies (where the Dutch United East India Company had again swept the English from the seas), the Great Plague and Fire of London in 1666 had left the English temporarily in an extremely weak position. Nor would there have been any difficulty in laying down reciprocal Franco-Dutch guarantees for the defence of New France, New Netherland, and the French and Dutch Antilles and Guianas.

Although Louis captured Lille in August 1667, the Spanish forces in the southern Netherlands continued to resist and the French made only slow progress. The invasion was finally brought to a halt in 1668 by the so-called Triple Alliance, a

[27] C. Ch. Goslinga, *The Dutch in the Caribbean* (Assen, 1971), pp. 405–08.

coalition of the United Provinces, England, and Sweden, but which Louis chose to regard as essentially Dutch-inspired. From that point on, his hostility to the Dutch was to be the guiding thread of his entire foreign and colonial policy over the next decade. Consequently, during the next ten years or so, first the rising tension between France and the Dutch Republic, and then the Franco-Dutch War of 1672–77 entirely overshadowed, and for the most part nullified, the efforts of all the continental colonial powers to confront or oppose English maritime and colonial expansion. The French practically ceased all opposition to English activity in North America, the Caribbean, and all other spheres. At the same time the Dutch, hoping to win English support in the approaching struggle with France, strove hard down to 1672 to avoid maritime and colonial friction with the English. Similarly, the Spaniards, who between 1661 and 1667 had continually sought to embroil the Dutch with the English, between 1667 and 1672 were just as persistent in promoting Anglo-Dutch disengagement in order to free the Dutch to concentrate their attention on the preservation of the Spanish Netherlands.[28]

The five years in which no European power sought to oppose English maritime and colonial expansion ended with the French invasion of the United Provinces in 1672, which at the same time marked the outbreak of the Third Anglo-Dutch War (1672–74). Louis had succeeded in winning Charles II to his side and the French attacked the Dutch by land and sea jointly with England and the German ecclesiastical principalities of Cologne and Münster. France and England were not intending to dismember the Dutch Republic entirely, but it was certainly their aim to destroy the Republic's military and naval power, annex some Dutch territory, strip the Republic of its most valuable commerce, and deprive it of most of its colonies in Asia, Africa, and the Americas. But while Louis wished to work hand in hand with England in liquidating the Dutch overseas empire, it was not his intention that England should be allowed to become mistress of the seas, of the East India trade, of the Guinea trade, and of the former Dutch colonies.

Under the plans drawn up since the late 1660s by Colbert and Louis, it was expected that Dutch dominance in the East Indies, India, and Ceylon would now collapse and that the benefits from that collapse would accrue primarily to the French.[29] To ensure that this happened, Louis had sent out a powerful naval and military force in 1670 with orders to seize the Dutch forts in Ceylon and around the southern tip of India. Following the anticipated Dutch surrender in Europe, Louis and Colbert also intended to annex Curaçao, Elmina (Mina), and the other

[28] Queen Regent to Gamarra, Madrid, 28 May 1667, AGS Libros de La Haya 55, f. 312; K. H. D. Haley, *An English Diplomat in the Low Countries: Sir William Temple and John de Witt, 1665–1672* (Oxford, 1986), pp. 28–30, 225.

[29] *Lettres, instructions et mémoires de Colbert*, ed. Pierre Clément, 8 vols. (Paris, 1861–82), II, pp. 658–59; Israel, *Dutch Primacy*, p. 296.

principal Dutch colonies in the Caribbean and West Africa and absorb these into the French empire and overseas trading system.

Louis and Charles assailed the Dutch Republic and its empire with overwhelming force. During June 1672 the French and their Münsterite allies overran the eastern provinces of the Republic, captured Utrecht, and advanced to within a few miles of Amsterdam itself. But the final line of Dutch defence, the so-called 'waterline', a flooded stretch of territory extending from the Zuider Zee to the Maas, held, and final defeat was staved off. Meanwhile, the Dutch war fleet under De Ruyter had succeeded in surprising the combined Anglo-French fleet in Southwold Bay, on the east coast of England, as it was preparing to cross to the Dutch coast. De Ruyter damaged enough of the English 'first-rates' to blunt the initial Anglo-French maritime offensive and then fought a series of brilliant defensive battles, each time forcing the English back from the Dutch coasts.

In 1672 the Dutch found themselves in a desperate situation. But after surviving the initial momentum of the Anglo-French attacks, the Republic began to receive some valuable strategic support from other European powers: the Habsburg Empire, Brandenburg, and Spain, as well as Denmark-Norway; and it began to seem that the outcome of the struggle in the maritime sphere and in Asia, Africa, and the Americas might turn out to be different from what the French and English had expected.

Spain by this time was much reduced as a military and naval power. But she still possessed important resources and her colonial empire was still the largest of the European seaborne empires. Spain, like most of the small states of Italy and Germany, was horrified by the English collusion with France against the Dutch. Not only would the destruction of Dutch power mean the end of Spanish rule in the southern Netherlands, it would also mean that Louis would be the undisputed arbiter of Europe and that England would have helped him to achieve his hegemony. Besides this, it seemed certain that an Anglo-French victory would mean the end of the effective isolation of Spanish America from large-scale intervention from outside. Since the early 1660s it had been the policy of the Spanish crown to rely chiefly on the Dutch West India Company and the Curaçao slave depot for imports of black slaves into the Spanish colonies, and other commercial contacts, on the grounds that the Dutch, unlike the English or French, posed no political or strategic danger to the Spanish Indies.[30] Remove the Dutch from the equation and place transatlantic seaborne commerce, including the slave trade, entirely in English or French hands and there would be little prospect, especially in a context of Anglo-French collusion, of sealing off Spanish America from large-scale penetration, disruption, and perhaps dismemberment by rival colonial powers.

[30] Israel, *Dutch Primacy*, pp. 240–44.

Moreover, in the colonial context, it was clearly the English rather than the French who posed the principal threat. For if Charles was shamelessly helping Louis to the unchallenged mastery of Europe, from the perspective of the Spanish court (as indeed from that of Holland), it seemed that France was helping England to become the undisputed mistress of the seas and of the continents beyond Europe. Charles persisted in trying to win over the Spanish court but to no avail. Shortly before the outbreak of war, Charles's envoy in Madrid reported to London that 'there is little hope of bringing these people to what His Majesty desires for they are so pleased with their league with Holland that they will heare of nothing that crosses it; they say that the Dutch may be relyed upon but the English are so uncertaine that they are not to be trusted'.[31] Already in 1670 another English diplomat in Madrid had warned Charles that, while there had not been any clashes between the Dutch and Spaniards in the New World since 1648, the growing friction between the English and Spaniards in the Caribbean and Central America was helping to drive both the Spanish governors in the New World and the Spanish court into a 'stricter correspondence and more frequent and useful intercourse with [the Dutch]'.[32]

Given the scale of the onslaught they faced, the Dutch maritime counter-offensive against English trade, shipping, and colonies was remarkably effective. In the circumstances, there was only one way that the Republic could strike back at England and her Empire, and that was by launching a large-scale raiding and privateering campaign. With hundreds of ships and thousands of seamen laid up in Dutch and other ports—for, given the combined English and French naval might ranged against them, the States General had no alternative but to suspend Dutch commercial navigation in European waters indefinitely, and to forbid the fishing fleets to go out—vast numbers of ships and seamen were available to be signed on as privateers. These went out in packs, in all directions, to attack the English sea-lanes.[33] In all they had captured at least 700 to 800 vessels by the time the war ended, which was without doubt the heaviest maritime setback, measured in terms of losses of merchant shipping, which England's Empire suffered down to the First World War.

It was partly owing to the success of this astounding Dutch counter-offensive at sea that England withdrew from the war in 1674 without having conquered any colonies or gained any maritime advantages. But the success of the Dutch privateering campaign was in turn partly due to the Republic's strategic collaboration with Spain. For without the facilities they enjoyed in the Spanish ports it would

[31] Sunderland to Arlington, Madrid, 6 April 1672, SP 94/59, f. 206.

[32] Godolphin to Charles II, Madrid, 29 July 1670, SP 94/57, f. 37.

[33] J. R. Bruijn, 'Dutch Privateering during the Second and Third Anglo-Dutch Wars', *Acta Historiae Nederlandicae*, XI (1979), pp. 79–93; Israel, *Dutch Primacy*, pp. 298–99.

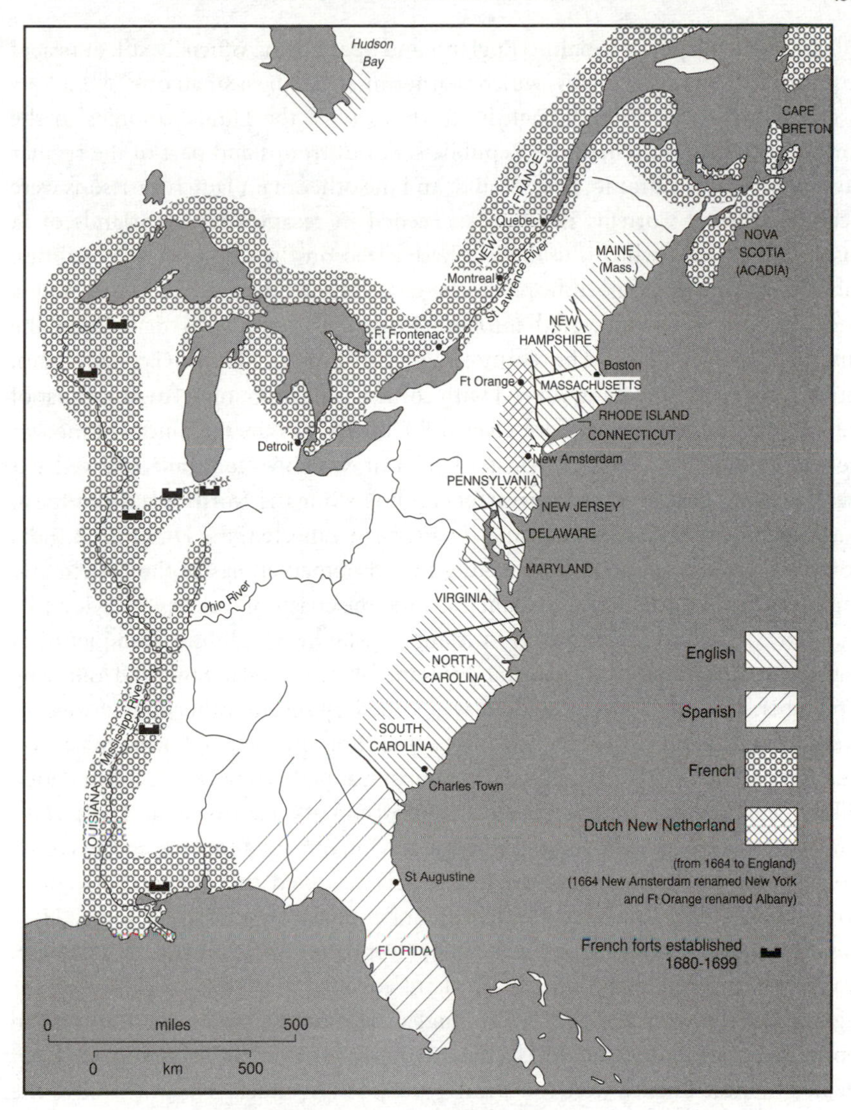

MAP 19.1. North America in the Late Seventeenth Century

not have been possible for several different Dutch privateering packs to operate continually around the coasts of Spain and Portugal and in the Straits of Gibraltar; and it was precisely this uninterrupted pressure which enabled the Dutch to paralyse English and French seaborne trade with southern Europe and the Mediterranean. 'There is no likelihood', the English envoy in Madrid commented gloomily in December 1673, 'of any ships escaping the Dutch that aventure to saile towards any port of Spaine [England and Spain being officially still at peace] or the Straits, without convoy, which neither must not be a small one.'[34]

To parry the French and English efforts to seize the Dutch colonies in the Caribbean and the Guianas, the Republic sent out troops and part of the regular navy early in 1673. Curaçao, Paramaribo, and the other main Dutch garrisons were secured. Admiral Cornelis Evertsen succeeded in recapturing the islands of St Eustatius and Saba which the English had seized on the outbreak of hostilities. Subsequently he sailed northwards to the coast of the former New Netherland, a land still not really integrated into the English colonies, and demanded the surrender of New York. The entire colony, including Albany (Fort Orange), surrendered without a fight, indeed with some enthusiasm, on 9 August, most of the white inhabitants being themselves still Dutch.[35] For the remainder of the war the port of New York, or 'New Amsterdam' as it was now again called, served as a useful forward base for Dutch privateers raiding along the North American coast.

Meanwhile, contrary to what might have been expected, the Dutch East India Company proved successful in crushing the combined efforts of the French and English to break the Dutch ascendancy around the coasts of India and Ceylon (see Map 12.1). After occupying Reunion Island in May 1671, Admiral Blanquet de la Haye, with nine warships and several thousand men, arrived at Surat the following September. Here he revictualled and was joined by several other French vessels, after which the French force sailed for Ceylon. But after seizing Trincomalee, on the east coast of Ceylon, de la Haye was almost trapped by the Dutch commander, Rijkloff van Goens, who had received reinforcements from Batavia. De la Haye could withdraw only with some difficulty, leaving behind a fort which the Dutch soon captured. The main French force then occupied the former Portuguese stronghold of São Tomé, on the Coromandel coast of south-east India. Here they were blockaded by a Dutch Company fleet by sea and the Raja of Golconda, in alliance with the Dutch Company, by land. Meanwhile there were several minor engagements between the Dutch and English around the coasts of India, and in February 1673 a Dutch United East India Company fleet appeared off Bombay but decided that the English were too strongly fortified to attack. The outcome of the war in India was decided by a battle off the Indian east coast, near Masulipatam, on 1 September 1673, between a fleet of ten English ships and a larger VOC fleet: the defeat of the English rendered inevitable a French surrender to the Dutch, which duly happened in September 1674.[36] After the surrender most of the French troops

[34] Godolphin to Williamson, Madrid, 6 Dec. 1673, SP 94/61, f. 197.

[35] On the attitude of the New Netherlanders to English rule in 1673–74, see D. Merwick, *Possessing Albany, 1630–1710: The Dutch and English Experiences* (Cambridge, 1990), pp. 188–89.

[36] C. R. Boxer, 'The Third Dutch War in the East (1672–74)', *Mariner's Mirror*, XVI (1930), pp. 344–45, 359, 361.

and seamen were evacuated from India and returned to Madagascar and France, though a small force was left in possession of Pondicherry, which later became the French headquarters in India.

After Louis XIV was forced to withdraw part of his army from the United Provinces to face the armies of the Emperor and Brandenburg on the Rhine, the conflict settled into a stalemate and ended with the Franco-Dutch Peace of Nijmegen in 1678. During the negotiations serious differences emerged between the Dutch Stadholder, William III (1672–1702), and the Holland regents over their stance towards France.[37] William thought in terms of continuing Franco-Dutch hostility, and chiefly emphasized the need to stick closely to the Republic's allies and keep up a common front, together with the Emperor, Brandenburg, and Spain, against France. The regents, by contrast, showed little interest in backing the territorial demands of the Republic's allies and chiefly stressed the need to reach a viable and lasting set of compromises with Louis on commercial, maritime, and colonial issues. Provided Louis was prepared to cancel his more aggressive mercantilist measures, such as his tariff list of 1667, and respect the security of the Republic, many of the regents seemed more than willing to settle on a long-term basis with France.

In 1677–78 Louis did cancel his tariff list and made other commercial concessions to the Dutch. This was followed by a vigorous revival of Dutch trade with France which was to continue until 1688. This situation encouraged some of the regents to think about a long-term amicable relationship with France. In other circumstances Louis himself, despite his personal antipathy to the Republic, might well have been tempted to stick to his new policy of accommodation towards the Dutch as a way of detaching them from the increasingly formidable coalition of his European enemies led by the Habsburg Emperor.

It is true that in the decade 1678–87 there were relatively few signs of increasing tension between the French and English in the Americas, or of any tendency towards Franco-Dutch collaboration in the colonial world of the sort which became a lifeline to the French colonial empire in the middle decades of the eighteenth century. The 1680s witnessed La Salle's two famous voyages down the Mississippi and a growing French presence in North America to the west of the English colonies, a presence which was military and strategic as well as economic and religious. But to the French court it still appeared that the Dutch, not the English, were the main barrier to the advancement of France's maritime interests and colonial empire. The Dutch were still the leading European power in the Indian subcontinent as well as in South-East Asia (see Map 12.1). In 1682 Dutch

[37] D. J. Roorda, 'The Peace of Nijmegen', in J. A. H. Bots, ed., *The Peace of Nijmegen, 1676–1679* (Amsterdam, 1980), pp. 24–25.

troops occupied the Sultanate of Bantam, at the western end of Java, expelling both the English and the French. Until the beginning of the eighteenth century the Dutch were also still the strongest European power along the coast of West Africa. Added to this, Franco-Spanish hostility remained intense owing to renewed French pressure on the Spanish Netherlands in the early 1680s. At that stage the French court seemed more interested in plans to attack New Spain than in considering how to curb the steady growth of the English presence in North America and the Caribbean.

Nevertheless, there was a strong tendency among the Dutch regents, especially at Amsterdam and Rotterdam, to try to placate Louis, to acquiesce in the annexation of part of the Spanish Netherlands by France (as long as most of Flanders and Brabant, including Antwerp, Bruges, and the vital Scheldt estuary, remained out of French hands), and to preserve the newly burgeoning Dutch trade with France. Had Louis been prepared to put up with the mounting influx of Dutch manufactures and colonial products into France—and the thus-far dismal failure of his East India schemes—for the sake of detaching the Dutch from his enemies, there is little doubt that William III would not have been able in 1688 to mobilize the States General against France and Stuart England or use the Dutch army and navy for his military expedition to England.[38] It is impossible to say for certain that there would have been no Glorious Revolution in Britain in 1688–89 or in the following years had there been no armed Dutch intervention in Britain. We can be reasonably certain, however, that if the Franco-Dutch accommodation had continued uninterrupted after 1687, the year in which Louis resumed his *guerre du commerce* against the Dutch and reintroduced his former measures designed to curb Dutch trade with France, there would have been no Dutch involvement in any attempt to dethrone James II and no Dutch military and naval alliance with England against France.[39]

As it was, Louis did resume his economic war against the Dutch in 1687, as well as intensifying his pressure on the Spanish Netherlands and Cologne. The regents decided that both their commerce and their security were now under dire threat and that they had little choice but to prepare for war with France. Moreover, they eventually concluded, in the summer of 1688, that if they were to guard against the possibility of another joint Anglo-French attack on themselves, on the model of 1672, and stand a fair chance of defeating France, their wisest course was to take advantage of James II's domestic difficulties to intervene in Britain with all the force at their disposal, help put William on the British thrones in place of James, and thereby turn England round against France.

[38] Jonathan I. Israel, 'The Dutch Role in the Glorious Revolution', in Israel, ed., *The Anglo-Dutch Moment: Essays on the Glorious Revolution and its World Impact* (Cambridge, 1991), pp. 105–20.

[39] Ibid., pp. 114–19.

William III's strategy succeeded brilliantly.[40] By May 1689 the kingdoms of England and Scotland had been brought into an alliance with the United Provinces against France in a war which, in its initial stages, was fought chiefly in Ireland and Flanders. The Glorious Revolution forged a global strategic alliance between the English and the Dutch, greatly weakening the strategic position of France in Europe and enhancing the security not only of the United Provinces but, in the medium term, also of the southern Netherlands and the Rhineland. It also immensely weakened the position of France outside Europe. Not only was the colonial conflict between the Dutch and English now at an end, but during the ensuing Nine Years War (1688–97) the French outside Europe found themselves embroiled with all three of their main colonial rivals. The French and English fought each other most notably on the borders of Canada and New York, in what North Americans call 'King William's War'. The French were assailed by the Dutch, most notably in India, the Dutch company capturing Pondicherry in 1693 and holding it until 1699.[41] Lastly, the French and Spaniards fought each other in the Caribbean. In 1696 the Spaniards established their fort at Pensacola, primarily as a check to French ambitions in Louisiana. Moreover, if it was the French who lost most from the situation that developed at sea and outside Europe in the 1690s, it was unquestionably the English who gained most. In theory the English and Dutch were allies against the French on equal terms. But in practice the Dutch had no choice but to devote most of their resources to the gruelling land war in the Low Countries and the Rhineland, leaving the English with the opportunity to allocate a much higher proportion of their military and naval resources to the war at sea and the struggle outside Europe. The 1690s was a decade in which the English noticeably gained ground relative to the Dutch in the Caribbean, West Africa, and in India, as well as successfully confronting the French.[42]

During the short five-year interval between the Peace of Rijswijk (1697), which ended the Nine Years War, and the outbreak of the War of the Spanish Succession (1702–13), European politics were increasingly overshadowed by the approaching demise of the Habsburg dynasty in Spain, which came with the death of Charles II in 1700, and the question of the Spanish succession. Should the Bourbon candidate, Louis XIV's grandson Philip of Anjou (d. 1746), succeed to the Spanish

[40] On the Dutch military occupation of London in 1688–90, see ibid., pp. 125–41.

[41] Paul Kaeppelin, *La Compagnie des Indes Orientales et François Martin* (Paris, 1908), pp. 314–33; K. N. Chaudhuri and Jonathan I. Israel, 'The East India Companies and the Revolution of 1688–89', in Israel, ed., *Anglo-Dutch Moment*, pp. 422–27.

[42] The Dutch Director-General on the Guinea Coast discussed this English progress at Dutch expense in his reports to the West India Company directors in the Netherlands, dated Elmina 1 March and 8 May 1699: see Algemeen Rijksarchief, The Hague, Archives of the West India Company, XCVII, ff. 5^{v}–6 and 56–57; on the shift in India, see Chaudhuri and Israel, 'The East India Companies', pp. 418–26, 427–29.

throne and, with it, possession of Spanish America and the Philippines, as well as the southern Netherlands and Spanish territories in Italy, the resulting interlocking of France and Spain, and of the French and Spanish colonial empires, would render these together the most powerful political, economic, and strategic bloc in the world—at least if the obstacle of Anglo-Dutch maritime supremacy could be overcome. In the late 1690s Louis strongly reinforced the French colony of Saint-Domingue and established the new colony of Louisiana, as well as fixing a garrison at Detroit to protect the route between New France and Louisiana. All this was done in anticipation of the pending strategic alignment of the French and Spanish colonial empires. Shortly after Charles's death, Philip was duly summoned to Madrid and acknowledged as king of Spain and the Spanish Indies. The next year the *Asiento* for the supply of slaves to Spanish America was transferred to the French Guinea Company, and various other steps were taken to tighten the interdependence between the French and Spanish empires.

In 1702 England and the United Provinces, together with Austria, declared war on France and the new Bourbon king of Spain. Neither maritime power could afford to see the Spanish Indies, the Spanish trade, and the southern Netherlands fall into the hands of the French. But the Dutch regents went to war only after some hesitation, and might well have been persuaded not to do so had they been offered some guarantees for their commerce in Spain and Spanish America, and had Louis refrained from occupying the Spanish Netherlands on behalf of his grandson.

Despite the potential strength of the Franco-Spanish alliance, in the colonial war which followed the French found themselves severely squeezed, chiefly owing to the impact of the Anglo-Dutch maritime blockade of the French ports and their weakness at sea. In India the French were tightly hemmed in by the Dutch. In the Americas their position quickly became precarious. Louisiana was cut off from France for years at a time and hung on only by a thread. New France, though resilient, proved vulnerable to mounting pressure from New England. Incursions from New England in 1709–10 led to the capture of the Port Royal region of Nova Scotia and, despite the defeat of the English invasion of 1711, at the close of the war France was obliged to cede Newfoundland, Nova Scotia, and Hudson Bay to Britain.

But the maritime and Imperial supremacy of Britain at that point was, to a considerable degree, dependent on the alliance with the Dutch. Had the latter been kept out of the war at the outset, or had Louis succeeded in his efforts in 1709–10 to buy the Dutch regents off with a separate Franco-Dutch peace, there can be little doubt that the French and not the allies would have had the upper hand in the continental war and that there could have been no maritime and commercial blockade of France. With the Dutch neutral, neither could there have been any British interruption of the trade of the French and Spanish colonies with France and Spain. We can never know to what extent the outcome of the colonial war would have been different if the French colonies had been supplied by the Dutch. In all likelihood it would have made a dramatic difference. But that is speculation. As matters stood it was clearly only Britain among the four leading colonial powers which was able to make significant gains.

During the secret Franco-Dutch peace negotiations of 1709–10 Louis offered the Dutch cancellation of the various anti-Dutch economic measures introduced in France since 1687, concessions in the southern Netherlands, an agreement for sharing the Spanish America trade and the slaving *Asiento*, and the transfer of the Spanish throne to the Austrian Habsburgs, provided King Philip was compensated with Naples and Sicily.[43] Not surprisingly the regents were tempted, fully realizing the momentousness of the decision they had to make. But it proved impossible to reach agreement as to exactly how Philip would be removed from Spain, Louis flatly refusing to employ French troops against his own grandson. At the same time the regents knew perfectly well that if they broke ranks with the allies and laid down their arms, only for Louis to break his promises to them as he had so often done in the past, then there would be no way that they could enforce their deal with France. In those circumstances the Republic would simply fall between two stools, losing all leverage with both the allies and France. In the end the States General decided they simply could not trust Louis and had no alternative but to fight on, hand in hand with Britain and Austria.

Incensed with the Dutch, Louis turned to London, giving the new Tory ministry there the opportunity to stage one of the most sensational coups in the history of the British Empire. Britain, it emerged, was ready to do a separate deal with France and was even willing to leave Philip on the throne of Spain and Spanish America provided Louis granted sweeping maritime and colonial concessions to Britain in particular. The deal was done: by the terms of the Treaty of Utrecht in 1713 Gibraltar, Minorca, and the slave *Asiento* for Spanish America, as well as Newfoundland, Nova Scotia, and Hudson Bay were handed over to Britain, while the almost pathetic Dutch plea for Puerto Rico as colonial compensation was rejected. So furious was the Dutch public with 'perfidious Albion' that there was talk on both sides of the Channel of a fourth Anglo-Dutch War. But in the end the Republic, like Austria, was powerless to do other than acquiesce. As regards the European balance of power, and her own security, Britain was satisfied with the stipulation that the French and Spanish thrones should never be united and with the transfer of the southern Netherlands to Austria, along with Naples and Milan.

As a result of the Glorious Revolution and its aftermath, the Williamite campaigns in Ireland and Scotland and the events of the War of the Spanish

[43] J. G. Stork-Penning, *Het Grote Werk* (Groningen, 1958), pp. 280–85, 416–19.

Succession, Britain was now unquestionably Europe's dominant maritime and colonial power. It was evident that all the rival colonial empires were now in a strikingly weak position in relation to Britain's Empire and that for the time being there was no longer any viable basis for strategic collaboration on the part of the other colonial powers against Britain. With Gibraltar and Port Mahon (Minorca) garrisoned by Britain, the Royal Navy was advantageously placed to control the Straits of Gibraltar, dominate the southern flank of Europe, and regulate the commerce of the Mediterranean. It was now Britain, and not France or the United Provinces, which had a special status, guaranteed by treaty, in the trade with Spanish America. With her latest territorial gains in North America, Britain's colonies had been made secure and New France, seemingly, outflanked. On all sides, it was apparent that Britain was now poised to create the greatest Empire in terms of territories, trade, and shipping that the world had ever seen.

Select Bibliography

PHILIP BOUCHER, *Les Nouvelles Frances: France in America, 1500–1815: An Imperial Perspective* (Providence, RI, 1989).

C. R. BOXER, 'The Third Dutch War in the East (1672–74)', *The Mariner's Mirror*, XVI (1930).

J. R. BRUIJN, 'The Dutch Navy in its Political and Social Economic Setting of the Seventeenth Century', in Charles Wilson and David Proctor, eds., *1688: The Seaborne Alliance and Diplomatic Revolution* (London, 1989).

—— *The Dutch Navy of the Seventeenth and Eighteenth Centuries* (Columbia, SC, 1993).

K. H. D. HALEY, *The British and the Dutch: Political and Cultural Relations through the Ages* (London, 1988).

JONATHAN I. ISRAEL, *Dutch Primacy in World Trade, 1585–1740* (Oxford, 1989).

—— *The Dutch Republic. Its Rise, Greatness and Fall, 1477–1806* (Oxford, 1995).

—— ed., *The Anglo-Dutch Moment: Essays on the Glorious Revolution and its World Impact* (Cambridge, 1991).

J. R. JONES, *The Anglo-Dutch Wars of the Seventeenth Century* (London, 1996).

RICHARD L. KAGAN and GEOFFREY PARKER, eds., *Spain, Europe and the Atlantic World: Essays in Honour of J. H. Elliott* (Cambridge, 1995).

STEVEN C. A. PINCUS, *Protestantism and Patriotism: Ideologies and the Making of English Foreign Policy, 1650–1668* (Cambridge, 1996).

D. J. ROORDA, 'The Peace of Nijmegen', in J. A. H. Bots, ed., *The Peace of Nijmegen, 1676–1679* (Amsterdam, 1980).

HERBERT H. ROWEN, *John de Witt, Grand Pensionary of Holland, 1625–1672* (Princeton, 1978).

JAMES D. TRACY, ed., *The Rise of Merchant Empires: Long-Distance Trade in the Early Modern World, 1350–1750* (Cambridge, 1990).

T. VENNING, *Cromwellian Foreign Policy* (London, 1995).

CHARLES WILSON, *Profit and Power: A Study of England and the Dutch Wars*, 2nd edn. (The Hague, 1978).

20

The Glorious Revolution and America

RICHARD S. DUNN

In 1689 a dramatic series of uprisings broke out in English America. News that William of Orange had overthrown James II triggered copycat rebellions in many of the colonies, starting with Massachusetts. On 18 April in Boston a band of rebels seized Sir Edmund Andros, the royal Governor of the Dominion of New England, and jailed him with his leading supporters. The Dominion immediately dissolved, and in Massachusetts, New Hampshire, Plymouth, Rhode Island, and Connecticut the colonists reinstituted the governments that had been in place when James II ascended the throne in 1685. Agitation quickly spread south. In New York, which had been James's proprietary colony before he became King, insurgents seized control on 31 May from Lieutenant-Governor Francis Nicholson (who then fled to England), and—not wishing to reinstitute their deposed master's proprietary government—set up a Committee of Safety under the leadership of Jacob Leisler. In Maryland there was further rebellion, in this case against the absentee Catholic proprietor, Lord Baltimore. On 1 August an armed band known as the Protestant Associators, led by John Coode, forced the proprietary Governor, William Joseph, to surrender. One week previous to this on the Caribbean island of Antigua the chief planters induced the royal Governor of the Leeward Islands, Sir Nathaniel Johnson—the most outspoken supporter of James II among the American Governors—to resign his office to Christopher Codrington and sail away.[1]

Thus the Glorious Revolution spread from England to America. Or did it? Historians disagree violently about the meaning of transatlantic events in 1688–89, and about the larger pattern of Anglo-American relations from 1675 to 1700. To begin with, some celebrate the Revolution of 1688 in England as a principled victory of Protestant parliamentary government over Catholic absolutism, while others dismiss it as a shabby Dutch *coup d'état*.[2] Students of English colonial policy

[1] For a general overview of the rebellions in Massachusetts, New York, and Maryland, see David S. Lovejoy, *The Glorious Revolution in America* (New York, 1972). Lovejoy excludes the English West Indies colonies from his discussion. For matters of detail, see the chapters in this volume on the several areas of Colonial North America.

[2] To point out a few of the historiographical benchmarks, G. M. Trevelyan presents the traditional Whig view in *The English Revolution, 1688–1689* (Oxford, 1938); John Miller argues for James II's

quarrel sharply as to whether the home government was pursuing commercial or Imperial goals, and whether the Crown acted with purposeful vigour or with drifting incompetence in the years leading up to and away from the Revolution.[3] Yet most commentators do agree on one point—that however much the colonists supposed they were participating in the Glorious Revolution, they benefited very little by joining in the attack against James II. During the 1690s William and Mary continued most of the deposed King's centralizing and Imperial policies in America, and the Crown and the English merchant community continued to forge a transatlantic business system in which the colonies became satellites of the mother country. The Massachusetts and New York rebels failed to accomplish their principal political and religious objectives, and only the Maryland rebels succeeded in obtaining most of what they wanted. All in all, it seems that the American uprisings were minor skirmishes with superficial relation to the revolution at home.[4]

This chapter argues to the contrary that the Glorious Revolution was a genuinely transatlantic phenomenon, and that the colonial protests against James II's style of government reshaped English policy and American society in enduring ways.[5] The colonial rebels in 1689 shared, with most Englishmen at home, common objections to James's absolutism and to his Catholicism. They were not aiming for independence as in 1776, and many of them welcomed a closer, more collaborative relationship with the post-revolutionary home government. The colonists' settlement with the Crown in the 1690s, while more restrictive than the bargain struck between Parliament and Crown at home, eradicated the most autocratic features of James II's colonial rule, and also bolstered the ultra-Protestant and anti-

commitment to religious and political principles in *James II: A Study in Kingship* (Hove, 1978); John Childs examines the King's use of a standing army in *The Army, James II, and the Glorious Revolution* (New York, 1980); Lucille Pinkham presents a hostile account of *William III and the Respectable Revolution* (Cambridge, Mass., 1954); whereas Robert Beddard emphasizes the positive achievement of William and his Whig supporters in 'The Unexpected Whig Revolution of 1688', in Beddard, ed., *The Revolutions of 1688* (Oxford, 1991), pp. 11–101.

[3] Charles McLean Andrews presents the classic case for an emerging commercial Empire in *The Colonial Period of American History*, 4 vols. (New Haven, 1934–38), IV, chaps. 3–6. Stephen Saunders Webb argues for a powerfully centralized militaristic Empire; see his *Lord Churchill's Coup: The Anglo-American Empire and the Glorious Revolution Reconsidered* (New York, 1995). J. M. Sosin maintains to the contrary that late Stuart policy toward America was always crippled by drift, ignorance, and incompetence; see his *English America and the Revolution of 1688: Royal Administration and the Structure of Provincial Government* (Lincoln, Nebr., 1982).

[4] This is K. G. Davies's view of 'The Revolutions in America', in Beddard, ed., *The Revolutions of 1688*, pp. 246–70.

[5] Richard R. Johnson, 'The Revolution of 1688–9 in the American Colonies', in Jonathan I. Israel, ed., *The Anglo-Dutch Moment: Essays on the Glorious Revolution and its World Impact* (Cambridge, 1991), pp. 215–40, develops much the same argument as I do except that Johnson virtually ignores developments in the English West Indies.

Catholic character of religious life in English America. Furthermore, James's overthrow initiated a twenty-five-year war with Louis XIV, in which the Crown needed the co-operation of the colonists in order to conduct military campaigns against the French in the West Indies and North America between 1689 and 1713. The Crown's efforts to enlist colonial co-operation helped to consolidate a compromise style of Imperial administration in America that the home government sustained from the 1690s into the 1760s. Thus, the Glorious Revolution was a climactic event in seventeenth-century Anglo-American history. The American participants, in pressing William and Mary to modify Crown colonial policy, articulated local political and social tensions that had been disrupting life in English America throughout the 1670s and 1680s. The revolutionary settlement resolved many of these tensions. It notably broadened the ruling class in Maryland and Massachusetts, and more generally galvanized American society in somewhat the same way as the revolution at home galvanized the English state. And the events of 1688–89 also exposed a fundamental and permanent rift in outlook between the two sections of English America—the mainland colonies in North America and the island colonies in the Caribbean.

Down to the mid-1670s most of the mainland and island colonies had shared two common characteristics: semi-independence from England and narrowly élitist government. In the West Indies as in North America the leading planters had evolved their own institutional patterns and social structure with little external supervision. To be sure, the sugar islands were all Crown colonies, directly managed by the King, whereas the mainland colonies, except Virginia, were all governed privately by proprietors or corporations. But in 1668 and 1670 the Barbados Assembly had petitioned Charles II for a royal charter that would turn this colony into a self-sustaining corporation like Massachusetts, Connecticut, and Rhode Island, and in 1675 the Virginia government similarly petitioned for a royal charter confirming the authority of their Assembly and guaranteeing no taxation without consent. The royal Governor of Virginia, Sir William Berkeley, like his counterparts, Modyford in Jamaica and Willoughby in Barbados, was a local magnate with a large estate who acted as spokesman for an inner circle of big planters in his colony. In Jamaica, Sir Thomas Modyford ruled as an independent potentate, disregarding instructions from home and conducting his own foreign policy in which he commissioned buccaneering ships to raid Spanish commerce and sack Spanish settlements. In most of the mainland colonies there was even more autonomy. The chartered proprietors of New York, New Jersey, Maryland, and Carolina had *carte blanche* to govern in any fashion that they could persuade their colonists to accept. The four New England colonies of Massachusetts, Plymouth, Connecticut, and Rhode Island were virtually independent. There was no recorded official communication between the Crown and the Massachusetts Bay Company between 1666 and 1674,[6] and during these years the Puritan colonists openly flouted the English Navigation Laws.

In the mid-1670s several of the American colonies experienced domestic crises that exposed the fault-lines within their narrowly based governments. In New York, the temporary Dutch recapture of the colony in 1673–74 stirred up resentment within the large Dutch population against the Duke of York's restrictive regime, in which the chief offices were all appointive and only the richest merchants and largest landholders were admitted into the leadership cadre. Massachusetts had a far more participatory institutional structure than New York, but the bloody Indian war of 1675–76 put tremendous strain on a system where only a minority of adult males—the Puritan church members—were eligible to vote or to hold office. In Virginia, Bacon's Rebellion of 1676 was precipitated by disaffected colonists who rose up against Berkeley's élitist style of management. Here, as in New York, office-holding was monopolized by the Governor's favourites, and the followers of Nathaniel Bacon—though apparently not Bacon himself—demanded a larger legislative voice and an active share in decision-making. In Maryland, the 'Huy and Crye' rebellion of 1676 was led by Protestant insurgents who had somewhat parallel grievances against Lord Baltimore's autocratic regime, which catered to the chief planters and to the small Catholic minority in this colony. In the Caribbean colonies, where élite government was more firmly established, there were no equivalent protests. The biggest sugar planters enjoyed exclusive control in Barbados during the 1670s, and were becoming increasingly dominant in Jamaica and the Leeward Islands.[7]

Around 1675—just at the time of troubles in Massachusetts, Virginia, and Maryland—the home government embarked on a new policy designed to shatter colonial autonomy by binding every plantation directly to the Crown. In 1673 the English Parliament had legislated the most comprehensive Navigation Act to date, and in 1675 Charles II created a new executive Council, the Lords of Trade and Plantations, to supervise the enforcement of the Navigation Acts in the colonies and to collect more American revenue. William Blathwayt, the first Whitehall bureaucrat with a clear plan for strong royal authority in America, was put in charge of the plantation office. Edward Randolph, prototype of a new professional class of colonial officials, was sent to investigate New England in 1676, and three royal commissioners with 1,000 troops arrived in Virginia in 1677 to settle Bacon's

[6] See Nathaniel B. Shurtleff, ed., *Records of the Governor and Company of the Massachusetts Bay in New England*, 5 vols. in 6 (Boston, 1853–54), IV, pt. 2, and the plantation office's New England entry book for 1661–79, C[olonial] O[ffice] 5/903.

[7] See Richard S. Dunn, *Sugar and Slaves: The Rise of the Planter Class in the English West Indies, 1624–1713* (Chapel Hill, NC, 1972), chaps. 3–5.

Rebellion.[8] In the royal colonies of Jamaica and Virginia, the King's advisers sought to limit the power of the Legislative Assemblies, which were seen as the chief source of obstruction. New Governors—the Earl of Carlisle for Jamaica, Lord Culpeper for Virginia—were directed to make their respective Assemblies ratify a new body of laws prepared by the Colonial Office, including a perpetual revenue law. All future legislation would be drafted by the Governor and his Council, and all future Assemblies would meet only after receiving permission from the King. Carlisle and Culpeper turned out to be more interested in feathering their own nests than in following the King's orders, and they never imposed the new body of laws. But the Virginia Assembly passed a perpetual revenue law in 1680, and the Jamaica Assembly passed a twenty-year revenue act in 1683.[9] In both colonies the royal Governor's salary was now secure, and autonomy from England was gone for good.

To manage the Crown Colonies, the home government selected men who were quite different from Berkeley, Modyford, and Willoughby: royal Governors without American estates or American vested interests. Many were army or navy officers with the habit of command, who felt innately superior to the bumpkin provincials they encountered in America. Obtaining their posts through court connections, they were often looking for personal profit. Lord Howard of Effingham, the Governor of Virginia, wrote a revelatory series of letters to his wife in which he explained how he expected to send home £1,500 per annum out of £2,500 in salary and perquisites.[10] Sir Richard Dutton operated on a more spectacular scale in Barbados; between 1680 and 1685 he seems to have extracted some £18,000 in salary and perquisites while paying out only £3,000 in expenses.[11] But men such as Dutton and Howard also aggressively challenged the local Assemblies and the local planter élites.

In the proprietary colonies of New York and Maryland there was a parallel trend toward authoritative administration between 1675 and 1685. James, Duke of York, gave a preview of his royal style in his ducal province of New York—the only English colony in America without a representative Assembly. Sir Edmund

[8] See Stephen Saunders Webb, 'William Blathwayt, Imperial Fixer', *William and Mary Quarterly* (hereafter *WMQ*), Third Series, XXV (1968), pp. 3–21; Michael Garibaldi Hall, *Edward Randolph and the American Colonies, 1676–1703* (Chapel Hill, NC, 1960), chap. 2; and Wilcomb E. Washburn, *The Governor and the Rebel: A History of Bacon's Rebellion in Virginia* (Chapel Hill, NC, 1957), chap. 7.

[9] The Crown's battle with the Jamaica Assembly is abundantly documented in CO 138/3, and in the following B[ritish] L[ibrary] volumes: Add. MSS, 25120; Sloane MSS, 2724; Egerton MSS, 2395. The parallel campaign against the Virginia House of Burgesses can be traced in CO 5/1355.

[10] Howard to Lady Howard, 23 Feb., 18 April 1684, Howard of Effingham Papers, II, pp. 15, 22, Library of Congress.

[11] When Dutton returned to Barbados from a visit to England, he charged his Lieutenant-Governor with misconduct so as to avoid paying him the salary he owed him, and additionally fined him £11,000. See CO 29/3, pp. 248–49, 295–97; Bodleian Library, Clarendon Papers 88, p. 41.

Andros, who governed for the Duke from 1674 to 1680, was a no-nonsense executive who tried to annex New Jersey and Connecticut, and who levied taxes and customs duties without popular consent. When James found that these tactics did not collect as much revenue as he wanted, he permitted his next Governor, Thomas Dongan, to summon an Assembly in 1683. This legislative body drafted a 'Charter of Libertyes and Priviledges' that was supposed to protect New Yorkers from future taxation without representation.[12] But no further Assemblies were convened in New York during the next five years. In Maryland, the third Lord Baltimore, a Catholic like the Duke of York, had a similar managerial approach. He quarrelled with his Assembly every time it met, and concentrated patronage in a narrow circle of councillors. The Maryland Council was mostly Catholic, and more than half the members were tied by blood or marriage to the proprietary family, which effectively blocked advancement or power-sharing for the Protestant majority in the colony.[13]

The biggest challenge for the Crown was how to deal with the remaining proprietary and corporate colonies that had received extensive royal chartered privileges between 1612 and 1664. During the final decade of Charles's reign the King's advisers sought to curb or annul these colonial charters—in tandem with their remodelling of chartered town corporations in England in the early 1680s.[14] Their chief target was the Massachusetts Bay Company, because the Puritans who governed Massachusetts insisted that the charter they received from Charles I in 1629 gave them the right to manage their own affairs without royal supervision. Randolph catalogued the misdeeds of the Massachusetts Bay Company for the Lords of Trade, and led a strenuous campaign against the Bay charter. The colony government countered with delaying tactics, twice sending agents to England—in 1676 and 1682—who had no authority to negotiate revisions in the charter. Wearied by this stalling, the Crown prosecuted the company by writ of *quo warranto* ('by what right...'). The Massachusetts leaders might have salvaged some of their liberties by compromising, as the Virginia and Jamaica Assemblies had done. But Increase Mather, the leading Puritan clergyman, urged his people not to submit, and they followed his advice. In October 1684 the Massachusetts Bay Company was liquidated and the colonists found themselves under direct royal rule.

Charles II's colonial management was often slipshod. For example, the Bermuda Company was prosecuted by writ of *quo warranto* in 1680, and the Crown took control of Bermuda when the company charter was condemned in 1684. But

[12] Lovejoy, *The Glorious Revolution in America*, pp. 114–19.

[13] Lois Green Carr and David William Jordan, *Maryland's Revolution of Government, 1689–1692* (Ithaca, NY, 1974), pp. 38–40.

[14] See Philip S. Haffenden, 'The Crown and the Colonial Charters', *WMQ*, Third Series, XV (1958), pp. 297–311, 452–66.

the King's advisers had nothing to do with the Bermuda prosecution, which was conducted as a private speculation by a minor courtier named Francis Burghill who wanted to become the first royal Governor. The King had no desire to annex this miniature island colony, which he considered to be more trouble than it was worth, and when he found himself saddled with Bermuda he reappointed the existing Company Governor instead of Burghill.[15] A more conspicuous example of royal carelessness was Charles's grant of a proprietary charter to the radical Quaker activist William Penn in 1681. Again, the King's advisers did not wish to put a Quaker pacifist in control of a potentially valuable and strategically situated colony. But Penn secured the patronage of James, Duke of York, and outmanœuvred his opponents in the Colonial Office. Penn shared none of Charles's or James's political aims, and in 1682 he publicized a benevolent Frame of Government for his 'holy experiment' in Pennsylvania—just when the Stuarts were trying to clamp down on participatory government throughout America.[16] As it turned out, Charles soon had an opportunity to reconsider his gift. Penn quarrelled with his neighbour, Lord Baltimore, concerning the boundary between Pennsylvania and Maryland, and both proprietors came to London in 1684 to ask the King for help. William Blathwayt gleefully announced to Governor Howard of Virginia that Charles II was preparing a *quo warranto* against Lord Baltimore, and that 'Prince Pen declares himself ready to resign his Principality, the Propriety of Land being reserved to him'. This, observed Blathwayt, 'will make the king great and extend his reall empire in those parts'.[17] But Blathwayt was too optimistic. All royal action against Maryland and Pennsylvania was set aside when Charles II died in February 1685 and his brother James succeeded to the throne.

The new King was a more doctrinaire absolutist than Charles, and he continued the centralizing and aggrandizing practices of 1675–85. But he had never taken close interest in his ducal province of New York, and in 1685–88 he treated the rest of his American domain in much the same offhand manner. The Lords of Trade worked less vigorously than they had under Charles II, and colonial policy decisions were made haphazardly. The King was most likely to intervene whenever he saw a chance of making money. For example, as soon as he heard in 1687 that a wrecked treasure ship had been salvaged off Bermuda, James II whipped off a letter to Governor Robinson ordering him to collect one-half rather than one-tenth of this treasure as the royal share.[18] James left the proprietary governments of

[15] See Richard S. Dunn, 'The Downfall of the Bermuda Company: A Restoration Farce', *WMQ*, Third Series, XX (1963), pp. 499–505.

[16] The founding of Pennsylvania, 1680–84, is fully documented in Mary Maples Dunn and Richard S. Dunn, eds., *The Papers of William Penn*, 4 vols. (Philadelphia, 1981–87), II.

[17] Blathwayt to Howard, 9 Dec. 1684, Blathwayt Papers, XIV, Colonial Williamsburg.

[18] James II to Robinson, 21 Oct. 1687, CO 38/2/128–31.

Pennsylvania and Maryland alone, probably because Penn was actively trying to line up support for him among English Dissenters while Baltimore was a fellow Catholic. But all of the remaining private colonies came under attack. No colonial charter was technically annulled during James's reign, but the Rhode Island Assembly accepted a royal takeover in 1686, the Connecticut General Court in 1687, and the New Jersey proprietors in 1688. The Carolina proprietors were also ready to surrender; one of them announced in 1686, 'I shall be as unwilling to dispute his Majesty's pleasure as any man'.[19] Charter government in America was apparently dissolving.

James II and his advisers evidently wished to consolidate all of the American colonies into three or four viceroyalties on the Spanish model. Only one of these was actually established: the Dominion of New England, which incorporated eight previously separate colonies into a single province that extended from the Delaware River to the Canadian border. Sir Edmund Andros was given the Governor-Generalship of this vast territory, which he ruled without a Legislative Assembly. He remodelled the lawcourts, reduced New England's local self-government to one town meeting per year, levied new taxes without consent, and jailed those few colonists who protested openly. Andros also promoted the Church of England, enforced the Navigation Acts, and challenged all existing property titles in order to impose new real-estate taxes.[20] James II did not get around to combining his southern mainland colonies into a single viceroyalty, but Governor Howard of Virginia urged him to do so, seeing a chance for better profits if he ruled over an enlarged Chesapeake domain. Howard's management technique was rather similar to Andros's. He legislated and taxed by proclamation when he could not get the House of Burgesses to accept his directives, reduced the power of the county courts, squeezed new profits from fees and real-estate taxes, and kept prisoners without trial.[21] In the Caribbean, the King in 1686 commissioned the Duke of Albemarle as Governor-General of Jamaica, with a handsome salary and honorific privileges such as the power to confer knighthood.[22] Albemarle came to Jamaica in the hope of replenishing his squandered fortune; he had already netted £50,000 by investing £800 in the recovery of a sunken Spanish silver galleon near

[19] William L. Saunders, ed., *Colonial Records of North Carolina*, 10 vols. (Raleigh, NC, 1886–90), I, p. 353.

[20] This last policy brought Andros into sharp conflict with those members of his Dominion Council who had invested in speculative land companies. See Theodore B. Lewis, 'Land Speculation and the Dudley Council of 1686', *WMQ*, Third Series, XXXI (1974), pp. 255–72.

[21] H. R. McIlwaine, ed., *Legislative Journals of the Council of Colonial Virginia*, 3 vols. (Richmond, Va., 1918–19), I, pp. 66–74; H. R. McIlwaine, ed., *Journals of the House of Burgesses of Virginia, 1659/60–1693* (Richmond, Va., 1914), pp. 267–70.

[22] Albemarle wanted the King to grant him even greater power, amounting to sovereign authority over Jamaica. The negotiations over his appointment are in CO 138/5/220–335.

Hispaniola, and was hoping to find more buried treasure.[23] The West Indian colonists saw him as an Andros-style viceroy, but once he arrived in Jamaica he reverted to Modyford's style of rule. Quite unlike Andros, who allied himself with the largest merchants and planters in New York and New England, Albemarle joined with the buccaneers and the small planters in Jamaica. He toppled the chief sugar planters from their accustomed Council and judicial seats, and employed an armed gang to secure the election of his own supporters to a new Assembly.

James II's economic policy for the colonies was as recklessly aggrandizing as his administrative policy. In 1685 Parliament granted him a new duty on sugar and tobacco, calculated to produce an additional £100,000 for the royal Treasury. This tax was supposed to be passed on to the English consumer, but in fact it was borne by the American producer; in 1686 the price of sugar in London sank to a record low. The colonists' supply of African slave labourers was monopolized by a London corporation, the Royal African Company, in which the King was chief stockholder and company president. This Company never supplied the West Indian sugar planters with as many slaves as they wanted, and ignored the North American slave market altogether, but complaints against the Company brought no results since the royal Governors in the West Indies were agents of the Company. And in 1687 and 1688 James II was asked to charter a new West India Company which promised further profits to the Crown. This projected company, to be presided over by the Duke of Albemarle, would be funded by a joint stock of £500,000 from London investors, and would take over the entire sugar trade, thus controlling all commerce between the West Indies and England. This scheme fell through, but the chorus of grateful addresses to the King from the English Caribbean Assemblies, thanking him for rescuing them from total destruction, shows how vulnerable the sugar planters now felt they were.[24]

It is easy to sentimentalize the political changes in English America, 1675–88, by dwelling upon grasping Governors, emasculated Assemblies, and the destruction of chartered liberties. The fact is that many colonists were anxious for closer union with the home government. The pre-1675 style of political and economic autonomy had isolated them from the English business community, and the leading merchants and planters, both mainland and island, were eager to jettison some of their old local independence in exchange for better connections with Whitehall

[23] Estelle Ward, *Christopher Monck, Duke of Albemarle* (London, 1915), pp. 234–70.

[24] Information about the projected West India or South American Company can be found in Dalby Thomas, *An Historical Account of the Rise and Growth of the West-India Colonies* (London, 1690); BL, Sloane MSS, 3984, pp. 210–11; *Journals of the Assembly of Jamaica*, I, pp. 108–09; CO 29/3/471–73 and T 70/57/25–26. For addresses to James II against the Company, see *Journals of the Assembly of Jamaica*, I, p. 123; CO 29/3/479–81 (Barbados); and CO 155/1/172–83 (Nevis).

officials and London merchants. In Jamaica, the big sugar planters welcomed royal intervention in the 1670s against the buccaneers who, under Governor Modyford's protection, had siphoned off their indentured servants and discouraged slave ships from coming to Jamaica. But during James's reign the big planters in all of the sugar islands became increasingly outraged as they saw their political powers stolen by the new royal Governors and their sugar profits stolen by the King's taxes. Likewise in New England, the most entrepreneurial of the non-Puritan merchants welcomed the annulment of the Massachusetts charter in 1684, and accepted office in Andros's Dominion government in 1686. But these entrepreneurs were quickly affronted by Andros's conquest style of administration, especially when he regulated their overseas trade and blocked their efforts at land speculation. By 1689 they were making common cause with the old unreconstructed Puritan leaders in New England.

There is an instructive parallel between the course of events in England and America between 1685 and 1688. On opposite shores of the Atlantic James II and his Governors ruled in a fashion calculated to alienate most people. The King bypassed Parliament, and his Governors bypassed the colonial Assemblies. The King incited religious hysteria by openly favouring the tiny Catholic minority in England and appointing as many Catholics as he could to high offices, and there was a comparable anti-papist frenzy in Maryland, New York, and several of the other colonies where Catholics were prominent office-holders. Furthermore, James's administration was hollow at the core, both in England and America. The King was a cipher in international politics, unwilling and unable to defend England's strategic interests against France. Despite his zeal for military governance, he lacked the firepower to participate in a major war. In England his standing army was far inferior to the Bourbon and Habsburg armies in Europe, and only five companies of soldiers were stationed throughout his vast holdings in America. A garrison state, perhaps, but not a very effective one.

By 1688 there was a disembodied quality to life in the colonies. In the islands, the leadership ranks were thinned because many of the leading planters were living in England as absentees. The Legislative Assemblies, so vigorous a scant dozen years before, were largely silenced. In New England, although almost everyone was alienated by Andros's policy, no one dared to organize an open protest. Increase Mather, champion of the old Puritan orthodoxy, slipped off to England in 1688 in order to appeal to James II against Andros. Throughout America Protestants became paranoid about the threat, as they saw it, of Catholic conspiracy. Settlers on the New England frontier and in the Chesapeake backcountry supposed that French papists were inciting the Indians to attack them. Jamaicans objected when Governor Albemarle's chief adviser, a Catholic priest named Dr Thomas Churchill, was sent to England as the colony agent. In Barbados Governor Stede supposed that a Jesuit missionary from Martinique was a French spy, but dared not send him away for fear of vexing the King.[25] The Leeward Island colonists were alarmed when their Governor, Sir Nathaniel Johnson, cultivated cordial relations with the French at Martinique.[26] Especially in St Kitts—where the indentured servants were mostly Irish Catholic, and the French occupied half the island—fear of popery and of French attack was downright paralysing.

Never before, and probably never since, were such toadying letters and grovelling addresses sent to Whitehall from America. Each notable English event—the King's accession, Monmouth's defeat, the Queen's pregnancy—was received with mounting spasms of rapture. And when the fateful news arrived in November 1688 that the Queen had given birth to a son, Governor Howard of Virginia glowed at 'the happy, happy news of the birth of the Prince of Wales'.[27] In Maryland Governor William Joseph instructed the Assembly to legislate a perpetual anniversary celebration of the birthday of James's Catholic heir.[28] In New York there was feasting, bonfires, and, to quote Edward Randolph, 'nothing but God bless the prince and drinking his health and loud acclamations were heard that night'.[29] And in Jamaica Governor Albemarle toasted the Prince so immoderately that he plunged into a fit of jaundice and died.[30]

News of the revolutionary events at home slowly trickled into the colonies. In December 1688 word reached Boston that William of Orange had invaded England. By January 1689 this information had filtered into the Chesapeake and Caribbean colonies. In February ships landing at Antigua and Philadelphia reported James II's flight to France. But in April the information was still unofficial; no orders had come from the new English government. James II's Governors behaved with the nervousness of men who feared that they were losing power: Andros and Howard both embargoed all shipping in order to hide news from England. In Maryland Governor Joseph ordered the planters to deliver all their guns to the colony arsenal for repairs, and prorogued the April 1689 meeting of the Maryland Assembly. The rumour spread that the papist councillors in Maryland were conspiring with the Indians to kill off all Protestants. In March and April backcountry settlers in Virginia and Maryland were gathering in armed

[25] Stede's circumspect accounts of the visiting Jesuit, written in 1688, are in CO 29/3/471–75 and CO 29/4/24–25.

[26] Johnson also permitted the Catholics in St Kitts and Montserrat to establish their own churches and clergy, CO 153/3, pp. 316–17, 418–22.

[27] Howard to Lord Sunderland, 28 Nov. 1688, Howard of Effingham Papers, I, Library of Congress.

[28] CO 5/718/71–76.

[29] Robert N. Toppan and A. T. S. Goodrick, eds., *Edward Randolph*, 7 vols. (Boston, 1898–1909), VI, pp. 263–65.

[30] Dr Hans Sloane's medical report on the Duke's fatal drinking bout is in BL, Sloane MSS, 3984, pp. 283–84.

bands.[31] And in Massachusetts Andros reported uneasily: 'There's a general buzzing among the people, great with expectation of their old charter, or they know not what.' Two days later Boston rose in revolt.

The rebellion in Massachusetts and elsewhere in America was bloodless, as in England, because James II's Governors, like their master, offered no resistance. In Boston Andros had little chance to resist, for the revolt of 18 April 1689 was carefully planned and vigorously executed. The whole town suddenly appeared in arms, and militia from neighbouring towns streamed in with alacrity. When some 2,000 militiamen marched against his garrison of fourteen redcoats, Sir Edmund decided to surrender. The rebels kept Andros and his most hated associates in prison until February 1690, and then shipped them back to England.[32] In New York, where opposition to the existing regime was much less well organized, Lieutenant-Governor Nicholson handled the crisis very feebly. Instead of taking warning from the Boston revolt, he sat passively amid a rising clamour for the proclamation of William and Mary, and watched the surrounding towns mutiny against him. When the city militia also rioted on 31 May, he surrendered the keys of Fort James to the militia captains. Ten days later he sailed for England.[33]

In Maryland Governor Joseph and the proprietary Council were more pugnacious than Nicholson. They learned of William and Mary's accession in April, but refused to proclaim them—probably because, as one of the Catholic councillors put it, they were praying for James II's 'happy restoration without bloodshed'.[34] Opposition to the proprietary government gathered force, and in July John Coode, a habitual malcontent, began to raise a rebel army. On 25 July the rebels, who called themselves Protestant Associators, issued a declaration announcing that they were rising in defence of William and Mary and of the Protestant religion. Joseph and his councillors mustered 160 men to defend Lord Baltimore's government, but when an overwhelming force of 700 armed Associators confronted them, the proprietary leaders signed articles of surrender on 1 August without firing a shot. One of the articles banned all Catholics from office in Maryland. The deposed officials were granted safe conduct to their homes, but were not permitted to leave for England nor to send letters, while the Associators

[31] William Hand Browne and others, eds., *Archives of Maryland*, 72 vols. (Baltimore, 1883–1972), VIII, pp. 56, 67, 70–71; H. R. McIlwaine and others, eds., *Executive Journals of the Council of Colonial Virginia*, 6 vols. (Richmond, Va., 1925–66), I, pp. 103–06.

[32] Seven accounts of the Boston revolt are printed in Charles M. Andrews, ed., *Narratives of the Insurrections, 1675–1690* (New York, 1915), pp. 170–267. See also Robert Earle Moody and Richard Clive Simmons, eds., *The Glorious Revolution in Massachusetts: Selected Documents, 1689–1692* (Boston, 1988).

[33] Three accounts of the New York revolt are printed in Andrews, *Narratives of the Insurrections*, pp. 320–401. See also J. R. Brodhead, *History of the State of New York*, 2 vols. (New York, 1853–71), II, pp. 557–69.

[34] *Archives of Maryland*, VIII, p. 88.

despatched a loyal address to William and Mary.[35] Events in neighbouring Virginia suggest that Baltimore's councillors might have forestalled the Associators had they proclaimed the new monarchs in April. The Virginia colonists were also restive in the spring of 1689, and their royal Governor, Lord Howard of Effingham, had departed for England in February, but when the Virginia Council proclaimed William and Mary on 26 April, agitation faded out in this colony.[36]

In contrast with the mainland colonies, there was no open revolt, though many months of tension, in the English West Indies. In Barbados Governor Stede managed by slow stages to transmute his servile loyalty to James II into an equally unctuous devotion to William III, and by October 1689 the Assembly had gained enough confidence to ask the home government to drop James II's sugar tax.[37] In Jamaica Governor Albemarle's death in October 1688 left the colony torn between two factions—the pro-Albemarle small planters and the anti-Albemarle big planters—both bereft of leadership. The Duke's supporters kept control temporarily, ruling by martial law. But in May 1689 it was learned that both James II (in November 1688) and William III (in February 1689) had cancelled all of Albemarle's proceedings, whereupon Albemarle's enemies reoccupied their former posts.[38] In the Leeward Islands there was greater alarm. Governor Johnson was a loyal Jacobite who learned 'to my great trouble' in February 1689 that his royal master had fled to France. Of all James II's American Governors, he alone announced in May 1689 that he wished to resign because he could not accept the Revolution. An intercepted letter from the French Governor of Martinique seemed to indicate that Johnson was conspiring to betray his government to the enemy. In May 1689 a band of Irish Catholic servants sacked many of the English plantations on St Kitts, and in July the French planters on the island invaded the English half of St Kitts. Obviously the Leeward Island planters had far better grounds for overthrowing their Governor than the colonists in Massachusetts, New York, or Maryland—yet they were afraid to do anything so drastic. Finally Johnson did resign. On 24 July he commissioned Christopher Codrington as Governor in his place and sailed away to Carolina. One week later the English garrison on St Kitts surrendered to the French.[39]

In North America several features of the Revolution merit emphasis. In the first place, while the Massachusetts, New York, and Maryland rebels all claimed to be following William III's splendid example, these three uprisings were each

[35] Ibid., VIII, pp. 107–10, 154–56.

[36] *Executive Journals of the Council of Colonial Virginia*, I, pp. 101–02, 106–07.

[37] CO 29/4, pp. 103–19, 159–64; CO 31/3, pp. 182–83, 195–97.

[38] CO 138/6, pp. 144–65, 210–26; CO 140/4, pp. 261–62, 268, 273–75; *Journals of the Assembly of Jamaica*, I, pp. 134–36.

[39] CO 152/37, pp. 35, 47, 68–69; CO 153/3/427–31; CO 153/4, pp. 106–10, 119–58; CO 155/2/73.

distinctly different in character. In Massachusetts, where almost everyone was opposed to the Dominion government, the colonists united decisively against Andros on 18 April—but then differed about what course to take after the Dominion was overthrown. The majority wanted to restore the charter government and the Puritan church–state nexus that they had lost in 1684, in effect to revert to the good old days, while a significant minority wanted a more broadly based government that would include non-Puritans as well. In New York, where ethnic, religious, and class cleavages were sharper than in Massachusetts, the colonists never acted in unity. Many New Yorkers, the Dutch in particular, were eager to embrace their new Dutch Protestant King. Some were fiercely anti-Catholic, some wanted more self-government, some resented the inner circle of office-holders who had dominated affairs under James. The members of this ruling élite, including the biggest merchants and landholders in the colony, had prospered during James's regime and were opposed to the revolt from the start. In Maryland the factional division was simpler than in New York. Here the rebel Associators arrayed themselves against the supporters of Lord Baltimore, and invoked anti-Catholicism to rally the Protestant majority to their cause. Significantly, the Associators wanted William and Mary to annul a royal charter and assume direct control of the Maryland government, whereas the Puritans in Massachusetts wanted the new monarchs to restore a royal charter and abandon direct control of the Bay government.

The rebels' methods also differed. The Boston revolt was led, Cotton Mather tells us, by 'some of the principal Gentleman' of the town. Actually, the fifteen men who summoned Andros to surrender were a carefully balanced coalition—five officers of the old Massachusetts chartered government, five of Andros's Dominion councillors, and five hitherto private citizens.[40] This coalition symbolized New England's united opposition to Andros, but lacked a spokesman to hold things together once the Dominion was toppled. The Principal Gentlemen quickly organized themselves into a Council of Safety, but this provisional government lasted only five weeks. When they summoned a Convention of the Massachusetts towns in May 1689—in imitation of William's Convention at Westminster in January 1689—the majority of towns voted to resurrect the charter government that had been annulled in 1684.[41] However, the Convention elected several prominent non-Puritans as magistrates, and thus preserved bipartisan support for the rebellion.

In New York there was no equivalent to the Principal Gentlemen, but there certainly was a rebel spokesman: Jacob Leisler. In May 1689, as Nicholson's

[40] Richard S. Dunn, *Puritans and Yankees: The Winthrop Dynasty of New England, 1630–1717* (Princeton, 1962), pp. 254–56.

[41] Court Records, VI, pp. 2–36, Massachusetts Archives.

government disintegrated amid seething rumours of popish conspiracy, Leisler was a militia captain in New York City. After Nicholson's departure he established himself by mid-June as the most decisive leader among the insurgents. Leisler has been variously portrayed as a demagogue, a populist, and a Calvinist zealot,[42] and perhaps he is best seen as combining all of these characteristics. Before 1689 he had been a successful merchant, and had engaged in bitter lawsuits with Nicholas Bayard, a leading member of James II's New York administration. Leisler rose to power by stages, being elected captain of the fort in June, and Commander-in-Chief in August; he finally assumed the title of Lieutenant-Governor in December 1689. He managed to keep power for a year and a half, ruling with the aid of a Council and an Assembly elected in 1690. But his command was always contested, especially in Albany and in eastern Long Island, and he had great difficulty collecting taxes. During 1690 his regime became increasingly dictatorial and desperate, as he freely arrested and imprisoned his critics on charges of sedition and treason. By the close of his stormy rule, New Yorkers had divided themselves into two fiercely partisan factions: the Leislerians and the Anti-Leislerians.[43]

In Maryland the rebel leader John Coode seems at first glance to have played much the same role as Jacob Leisler. Both men were provocateurs, rather in the style of Nathaniel Bacon in Virginia in 1676, but Coode proved to be a less dominant figure than Leisler or Bacon. He led the initial revolt in July 1689, and took the title of Commander-in-Chief, but after the first few months was no longer in charge. The Maryland Associators pursued a more cautious course than Leisler and his partisans. Having ousted the proprietary government, they kept power until 1692 without exercising much central authority. Starting in August 1689 the Associators' Convention—another imitation of William III's Convention—met twice a year. The members of this body were men of considerable social and economic status but scant political experience, because few of them had enjoyed Lord Baltimore's patronage. They refrained from taking vindictive action when their proprietary opponents defied their administration, and were rewarded in May 1690 when they received a letter from the King requesting them to continue in power temporarily. This gave them the legitimacy they needed. At the local level,

[42] David William Voorhees, who has examined Leisler's career most fully and carefully, argues that he and his followers were chiefly motivated by radical Calvinism. See his 'The "Fervent Zeale" of Jacob Leisler', *WMQ*, Third Series, LI (1994), pp. 447–72; and '"In Behalf of the true Protestants religion": The Glorious Revolution in New York', unpublished Ph.D. dissertation, New York University, 1988.

[43] Robert C. Ritchie, *The Duke's Province: A Study of New York Politics and Society, 1664–1691* (Chapel Hill, NC, 1977), chap. 9; Thomas J. Archdeacon, *New York City, 1664–1710: Conquest and Change* (Ithaca, NY, 1976), chap. 5; Joyce D. Goodfriend, *Before the Melting Pot: Society and Culture in Colonial New York, 1664–1730* (Princeton, 1992), chaps. 4–5; and Randall Herbert Balmer, *A Perfect Babel of Confusion: Dutch Religion and English Culture in the Middle Colonies* (New York, 1989), chap. 2.

the county courts now met regularly and the magistrates preserved order. Many of the small planters, landless labourers, and servants in Maryland seem to have supported the Associators' rebellion, but they did not sit in the Convention. All surviving evidence indicates that the struggle in this colony was between two propertied groups: those who were aspiring to power versus those who already held power.[44]

The rebel colonies, from Massachusetts to Maryland, made some effort to collaborate. Two Connecticut delegates visited Manhattan in June 1689 to help Leisler proclaim William and Mary, and the New York and Maryland governments began a friendly correspondence. Coode told Leisler how he welcomed 'so near and convenient a friendship, especially since our circumstances are so alike, and the common danger so equally threatening'. But when Leisler asked for 100 Maryland soldiers to guard the New York frontier against French and Indian attack, Coode replied that he could not help because the distance was too great and his own province was too unsettled.[45] None the less, delegates from Massachusetts, Plymouth, Connecticut, and New York did agree in May 1690 to attempt a three-pronged invasion of French Canada, thus demonstrating to William and Mary the loyalty and value of their revolutionary governments. One column would attack Montreal via Lake Champlain, another would make a diversionary feint into Maine, while the largest force would assault Quebec by sea. Unfortunately, this scheme completely backfired. The naval attack on Quebec was a comic failure. The overland expedition got only one-third of the way to Montreal before it turned back. Leisler was so furious that he rushed up to Albany, arrested General Fitzjohn Winthrop of Connecticut, who had commanded the expedition, and tried to court-martial him. Winthrop managed to escape, but he bore no love for Leisler. 'Never', he protested, 'did I see such a pitiful beastly fellow.'[46] Obviously any effective colonial war against French Canada was going to need home supervision.

In the English island colonies the French menace was much more tangible than in North America. Since the 1660s Anglo-French warfare in the Caribbean had been highly destructive. Between 1666 and 1713 St Kitts changed hands seven times, Montserrat and Antigua were sacked twice each, and Jamaica and Nevis once each, with many thousand settlers captured and dispersed, their slaves taken, and their plantations wiped out. The Leeward Islanders, in particular, remembered the last French war of 1666–67, when all four islands had been ransacked. The English planters, being heavily outnumbered by their black slaves, were also wary of slave insurrections; the most recent slave uprisings had occurred in Jamaica in 1685,

[44] Carr and Jordan, *Maryland's Revolution of Government*, chap. 6.

[45] Edmund B. O'Callaghan, ed., *The Documentary History of the State of New-York*, 4 vols. (Albany, NY, 1850–51), II, pp. 42–44, 181–84, 266–69.

[46] Winthrop Papers, VI, p. 177, Massachusetts Historical Society.

Barbados in 1686, and Antigua in 1687.[47] Thus the island colonists looked to William and Mary for help in 1689. With Albemarle dead in Jamaica, Johnson decamped from the Leeward Islands, and many of the leading planters absentees in England, supervision and support by the new government was desperately needed.

Between 1689 and 1692 agents from all of the American colonies lobbied furiously at Whitehall—with highly variegated results. They discovered that many of the men who had shaped or conducted Charles II's and James II's colonial affairs were still in place. William Blathwayt continued as the central figure in the Plantation Office. Edward Randolph, arriving in London in 1690 after spending eight months in a Boston jail, was soon sent back to America to inspect the collection of customs duties. Sir Edmund Andros and Francis Nicholson, both deposed in 1689, were likewise reappointed after the Revolution as royal Governors—this time in Virginia and Maryland. The colonial agents discovered too that much of Charles's and James's centralizing policy was also still in place. The new King was far too busy with other matters, particularly the war against Louis XIV in Europe, to spend much time on American colonial policy. Yet William III did have a fairly consistent colonial agenda. He and his ministers insisted that the Navigation Acts be strictly enforced, and that military governors be put in charge of the colonies in order to wage effective war against the French. But the new King, with his Calvinist background, showed some sympathy for the colonists' complaint that James II had tried to Catholicize America (or, in the case of New England, that he had tried to foist the Anglican church upon Protestant Dissenters). And William showed little interest in sustaining James's viceregal system of colonial administration, or his monopolistic economic policy. Fundamentally, the new monarchs accepted the principle that Englishmen in America should enjoy representative self-government as at home, but popular legislature was everywhere to be balanced by royal executive in English America.

In the revolutionary settlement of Maryland, the rebel Associators achieved far greater success than their counterparts in Massachusetts and New York. The King's ministers accepted the rebels' charge that Lord Baltimore had badly misruled his colony, and they suspended the proprietor's chartered powers of government. The Crown appointed a Protestant English soldier, Lionel Copley, as the first royal Governor of Maryland, and appointed a Council made up of Associators. Baltimore protested vigorously but unsuccessfully, though he was permitted to keep proprietary control over the land in the colony and to receive much of the colony revenue. When Copley arrived in Maryland in April 1692 he formed a political partnership with the men who had led the rebellion in 1689, though John Coode

[47] The Jamaican slave revolt is discussed in CO 138/6, pp. 79, 92; CO 140/4, pp. 84–100, 105–08, 169; and *Journals of the Assembly of Jamaica*, I, pp. 81–83. For Barbados, see CO 31/1/675. For Antigua, see CO 155/1/95–109; see above pp. 232–33.

and several of the other Associator leaders were shoved aside as too fractious. The Anglican church was established, and Catholics and Quakers found themselves barred from public office. But despite religious restrictions the governing cadre was now notably larger than in the proprietary era and much more open to new talent. From the 1690s onward the Maryland Assembly became far more assertive and better organized than it had been, and the tensions and dislocations that had stirred rebellion in this colony in 1676, 1681, and 1689 were largely resolved.[48]

In the revolutionary settlement of Massachusetts, the rebel agents put up a strong effort but were forced to capitulate to the home government's wishes. In 1689 Increase Mather was unable to persuade either King or Parliament to restore the old Bay charter, and in 1690 the Lords of Trade summarily dismissed all charges against Governor Andros. A new royal charter for Massachusetts was hammered out, clause by clause, in strenuous negotiation between Mather and Blathwayt—in which Blathwayt won the most-contested points, but Mather secured significant concessions. In the Massachusetts charter of 1691 the franchise qualification was property-holding rather than church membership; the Governor was appointed by the Crown; the House of Representatives nominated the Council; and the Governor's executive appointments required the consent of Council. While the old Bible commonwealth was gone for good, the new Massachusetts legislature was more powerful than in other royal colonies, and the royal Governor was somewhat weaker. This compromise solution well suited the non-Puritan merchants who had joined the 1689 coalition against the Dominion of New England, and it had the effect, as in Maryland, of expanding the governing class significantly. Elsewhere in New England, Connecticut and Rhode Island were permitted to retain their self-governing charters, though Plymouth Colony was now permanently absorbed into Massachusetts.[49]

In the revolutionary settlement of New York, the rebels fared very poorly. The Lords of Trade quickly agreed that a new royal Governor should be despatched to this colony to replace Leisler's regime, and the King assigned Colonel Henry Sloughter to the task, giving him a Council staffed by Leisler's chief enemies—the exact opposite of the decision for Maryland. When Sloughter reached New York in 1691 Leisler delayed relinquishing his command, and Sloughter retaliated by arresting him and bringing him to trial and execution for treason. The old élite, who had controlled the colony under James II, returned to power in a vengeful mood. But though Leisler was dead, his faction lived on. For twenty years, from 1691 to 1710, the Leislerians kept the memory of their martyred leader alive by

[48] Carr and Jordan, *Maryland's Revolution of Government*, chaps. 5–6.

[49] Richard R. Johnson, *Adjustment to Empire: The New England Colonies, 1675–1715* (New Brunswick, NJ, 1981), chap. 3; Michael G. Hall, *The Last American Puritan: The Life of Increase Mather, 1639–1723* (Middletown, Conn., 1988), chap. 7.

feuding continually with their anti-Leislerian enemies. During these two decades the royal Governors fomented this factional rivalry by allying themselves with one or the other side. Thus, in New York there was no agreed-upon settlement, and the legacy of 1689 was a bitterly partisan political environment that hampered economic development and did nothing to resolve the ethnic and social divisions within the colony.

Ironically, the Caribbean colonists, who had not risen up on behalf of William and Mary in 1689, achieved greater success in the revolutionary settlement than any of the mainland colonists. The absentee sugar planters who lived in England joined forces with the London sugar merchants to lobby at Whitehall and Westminster for their interest. As many as sixty Jamaica merchants and planters, resident in England, could be mustered to sign petitions denouncing Governor Albemarle. Edward Littleton, a Barbados absentee planter, published a London tract in 1689 entitled *The Groans of the Plantations* in which he told the new government that the sugar colonies had been ruinously over-taxed and mismanaged by Charles II and James II. Littleton's argument had great weight. Throughout the 1690s William III's government gave special favour to the West Indian sugar interest. The King supplied much greater military aid to the island colonies than to North America. The Royal African Company, patronized by Charles II and James II, lost its monopoly on the African slave trade, and the volume of slave traffic to the English islands immediately doubled as new traders entered the business. In 1693 the government dropped James II's sugar tax of 1685, while the companion tax on Chesapeake tobacco was made permanent. And the style of government in the islands was significantly altered. Throughout the 1690s Christopher Codrington served as Governor of the Leeward Islands and Sir William Beeston was Governor of Jamaica—both opponents of Stuart centralization in their youth, and both very big sugar planters. In 1690 Codrington gathered a force of 2,500 men, invaded St Kitts, and retook the island from the French in a three-week campaign. Throughout the 1690s the English generally outfought the French in the Caribbean, thanks to naval support and fresh troops from home, a regiment from Barbados, and spirited local leadership. Backed by their absentee colleagues in London, Codrington and Beeston symbolized the return of home rule in the English West Indies.

While the mainland colonists won fewer concessions from William and Mary than the island colonists, 1689 marked a major turning point for them as well. Americans such as Increase Mather who came to England to fight for 'liberties' that they could not secure nevertheless gained self-confidence from their stubborn battles with bureaucrats such as Blathwayt, and they also gained a more cosmopolitan understanding of the realities of Anglo-American life. The Revolution made it obvious that the North American colonists, for better or worse, must operate within a transatlantic system, with London as the metropolitan core. Ambitious planters and merchants quickly learned their role as junior partners in this system. And American intellectuals quickly found ways to assert in positive fashion their provincial identity. The effort by Mather's son Cotton to proclaim the special Ultra-Protestant meaning of New England Puritan society in his monumental *Magnalia Christi Americana* (1702), and Robert Beverley's more modest effort to describe his secular Chesapeake society in *The History and Present State of Virginia* (1705), show how a new generation of Americans was proudly articulating its provincial culture for English readers 3,000 miles away.

It has already been noted how the revolutions in Massachusetts and Maryland enlarged and energized the leadership cadres within these colonies. The same process was also taking place in Virginia, where no upheaval occurred in 1689. With the expansion of the African slave trade during the 1690s, the most entrepreneurial of the Chesapeake tobacco planters were for the first time buying large numbers of slaves in emulation of the Caribbean sugar planters. Here was the nucleus of a powerful ruling class, far wealthier in land and labour than the Chesapeake gentry had been back in the 1670s, that would dominate politics and society in Virginia and Maryland throughout the eighteenth century. The leading Virginia gentry sat on the Council, which was a seasoned and powerful body in the 1690s, and they more than held their own in dealing with Governors Andros and Nicholson between 1690 and 1705. These two gentlemen had learned their own set of lessons from the débâcle of 1689, and both of them acted less arbitrarily and more constructively in William's service than they had in James's. Yet Andros and Nicholson found that their executive authority was continually challenged by the expansive ambitions of the Virginia planter class.

William Blathwayt and his Plantation Office associates at Whitehall were not satisfied with the compromise character of the settlement made between Crown and colonists in 1689–92, and they kept trying to complete the administrative centralization of the English colonial system. These efforts were largely unsuccessful. In 1696 both King and Parliament did act to tighten colonial policy. Parliament passed a new Navigation Act that established Vice-Admiralty courts in America to enforce commercial regulation, while the King created a new supervisory body, the Board of Trade and Plantations, in substitution for the Lords of Trade. Blathwayt was the most vigorous member of this new Board. For several years he and his colleagues assembled evidence to show that the proprietary and corporate colonies in North America were violating the Navigation Acts and hampering the war against France. But when the Board of Trade tried to get Parliament in 1701–02 to pass a Reunification Bill that would bring all remaining chartered colonies under direct Crown control, the Bill failed. William Penn, who in 1688–89 had almost lost his colony because he sided with James against William, joined with agents from the other private colonies to defeat this manœuvre. In effect, the compromise settlement of 1689–92 remained in place until the 1760s.[50]

Perhaps the most fundamental result of the Glorious Revolution in America was the emergence of two varieties of colonial relationship, a West Indian kind and a North American kind. The West Indian relationship was tailored to the requirements of the big sugar planters. These people, whose control over island politics and society had been severely challenged between 1675 and 1688, were once again in full charge of their local governments after 1689 even though many of them now lived in England. And they knew that they needed a lot of help from the Crown in order to sustain their prosperity. The sugar planters asked William III for reduced Crown taxes, expanded slave imports, better military support, and full protection against foreign sugar competition. The revolutionary settlement gave them these things, crystallizing their dependent colonial status. As for the North American colonists, they wanted a looser relationship with the Crown, with less political and economic dependency. Though they failed to gain as much leeway as they wanted in 1689–92, they did escape from the stifling restrictions imposed by Charles II and James II, and the revolutionary settlement effectually broadened their local self-government and strengthened their local self-determination. In the early eighteenth century the mainland colonists demonstrated that their sector of the Empire was considerably more dynamic than the West Indian sector. They doubled their population every twenty years; they started expanding into the interior of the continent; they attracted new migrants who made their society more heterogeneous in ethnicity and more pluralistic in religion; their politics became more participatory and their economy more diversified—with widening opportunities for both élite and middling entrepreneurs. None of these creative developments could have happened had James II and his heirs remained in control. Which is why the colonial protests of 1689 matter, and why the Glorious Revolution reshaped English policy and American society in enduring ways.

[50] Ian K. Steele, *Politics of Colonial Policy: The Board of Trade in Colonial Administration, 1696–1720* (New York, 1968).

Select Bibliography

CHARLES M. ANDREWS, ed., *Narratives of the Insurrections, 1675–1690* (New York, 1915).

ROBERT BEDDARD, 'The Unexpected Whig Revolution of 1688', in Beddard, ed., *The Revolutions of 1688* (Oxford, 1991).

LOIS GREEN CARR and DAVID WILLIAM JORDAN, *Maryland's Revolution of Government, 1689–1692* (Ithaca, NY, 1974).

RICHARD S. DUNN, *Puritans and Yankees: The Winthrop Dynasty of New England, 1630–1717* (Princeton, 1962).

Richard S. Dunn, *Sugar and Slaves: The Rise of the Planter Class in the English West Indies, 1624–1713* (Chapel Hill, NC, 1972).

Joyce D. Goodfriend, *Before the Melting Pot: Society and Culture in Colonial New York, 1664–1730* (Princeton, 1992).

Philip S. Haffenden, 'The Crown and the Colonial Charters', *William and Mary Quarterly*, Third Series, XV (1958), pp. 297–311, 452–66.

Michael Garibaldi Hall, *Edward Randolph and the American Colonies, 1676–1703* (Chapel Hill, NC, 1960).

Richard R. Johnson, *Adjustment to Empire: The New England Colonies, 1675–1715* (New Brunswick, NJ, 1981).

David S. Lovejoy, *The Glorious Revolution in America* (New York, 1972).

Robert C. Ritchie, *The Duke's Province: A Study of New York Politics and Society, 1664–1691* (Chapel Hill, NC, 1977).

J. M. Sosin, *English America and the Restoration Monarchy of Charles II: Transatlantic Politics, Commerce, and Kinship* (Lincoln, Nebr., 1981).

—— *English America and the Revolution of 1688: Royal Administration and the Structure of Provincial Government* (Lincoln, Nebr., 1982).

Ian K. Steele, *Politics of Colonial Policy: The Board of Trade in Colonial Administration, 1696–1720* (New York, 1968).

David William Vorhees, 'The "Fervent Zeale" of Jacob Leisler', *William and Mary Quarterly*, Third Series, LI (1994), pp. 447–72.

Stephen Saunders Webb, 'William Blathwayt, Imperial Fixer', *William and Mary Quarterly*, Third Series, XXV (1968), pp. 3–21.

—— *1676: The End of American Independence* (New York, 1984).

—— *Lord Churchill's Coup: The Anglo-American Empire and the Glorious Revolution Reconsidered* (New York, 1995).

21

Navy, State, Trade, and Empire

G. E. AYLMER

The growing importance of the colonial trade was recognized by the government in 1660 when a royal commission for a Council of Trade was required to strike a balance of exports and imports 'as to the public account or good of the state and nation'.[1] If, however, we take up a historical vantage point anywhere before the 1700s, Britain's future Imperial domination would seem far from assured or predetermined. Indeed, it is incorrect even to use the term 'Britain' before the Act of Union in 1707; until then Scotland could, and up to a point did, still pursue its own colonial and commercial policy. Ireland and the plantations—as the English overseas territories were usually known—were within what was already a considerable transoceanic customs union, a mercantilist commercial system. As the chapters by Michael Braddick and others in this volume have shown, England was appreciably more of a maritime and Imperial power by the end of the seventeenth century than had been the case sixty, fifty, or even forty years earlier.

The restored monarchy of 1660 built on the foundations of the Republic, only discarding its sole continental bridgehead. Although there was an outcry a few years later, when Edward Hyde, Earl of Clarendon—Charles II's chief minister—was accused of having profited personally from the sale of Dunkirk to the French, this should be seen in context. Jamaica, which had been captured from Spain under the Protectorate, was retained, while Tangier and Bombay were both acquired as part of Charles II's marriage settlement with the crown of Portugal. In addition, the Commonwealth's Navigation Act of 1651 was extended by a further series of statutes from 1660 to 1673 and then codified more or less definitively in 1696. In that year too the successive Councils and Committees of Trade and Plantations were superseded by the Board of Trade, although this body did not have the powers or the status of a department of state, and there was never to be a single governmental bureau with sole responsibility for the central administration of the overseas Empire. Meanwhile further territorial acquisitions had been made, in a piecemeal and sometimes haphazard fashion, as has also been explained elsewhere in this volume: New York in 1664 and then more permanently in 1674,

[1] Charles II, an undated draft, State Papers Domestic, SP 29/19/20.

the Carolinas and New Jersey in the 1660s and 1670s; Pennsylvania in the early 1680s; other small islands and even parts of islands in the Caribbean, more forts and 'factories' or trading stations on the coasts of West Africa and of the Indian subcontinent. Yet we should remember that Tangier was abandoned in 1684 and not replaced by another naval base at the western entrance to the Mediterranean until the capture of Gibraltar from Spain in 1704. As early as 1670–72 English warships were using Port Mahon in the Balearic Islands as a base for revictualling, repairs, and minor refitting. This, however, was on sufferance from the Spanish government, and was only a partial anticipation of the actual British possession of Minorca during the next century (1708–56 and 1763–82).

Over this same span of time the Royal Navy came to play a more prominent part in the life of the country. With some continuity from Charles I's ship-money fleets in the 1630s and much more from the time of the Republic (1649–60), a standing, peacetime navy became more firmly established and more generally accepted, never being regarded with the same political—indeed ideological—suspicion as a standing army. The state became progressively less dependent on the hiring or commandeering of merchant vessels on the outbreak of war; its ships were increasingly its own in time of war as well as peace. On the other hand, the navy was still crucially dependent on seamen from the commercial and fishing fleets being recruited in time of war or sudden crisis, either by enticement or by seizure through the instrument of the press-gang. From the 1660s Parliament grew accustomed to voting large sums in direct taxation specifically for the navy. Not surprisingly, MPs and, we may begin to say, 'public opinion' in a wider sense also came to expect value for money, and were liable to turn nasty if the Crown and the Admiralty failed to deliver the goods. This can be seen as early as 1667–68 when—in an echo of 1626 and 1628—defeats in war led to Parliamentary outbursts. This was to be a continuing theme right through to the twentieth century. The willingness of Parliament to supply money, and the concern of the public over how it was spent, are themselves proof that priorities had changed and that trade and empire were seen as matters of national importance.

It would be a serious mistake to think of English (shortly to be British) naval history at this or any other time as an unbroken succession of glorious victories. By the latter stages of the First Anglo-Dutch War (1652–54) the English Commonwealth had undoubtedly gained the upper hand in the narrow seas, although by no means globally even then, suffering a severe minor defeat in the western Mediterranean. If Oliver Cromwell and the new Protectorate government had been prepared to provide the necessary logistical back-up for a continuing blockade of the Dutch coast, the United Provinces would have had to accept much more severe peace terms as the price of restoring their all-important seaborne trade with safe freedom of movement in and out of their ports. Whether in the longer run this would have made a great deal of difference is another matter, and may well be doubted. The Second Dutch War of 1664–67 was less commercial and maritime in motivation, that is, from the point of view of England under Charles II, the undoubted aggressor. After gaining some initial victories, there was a failure to follow these up. The Dutch too—as is shown in the chapter by Jonathan Israel—were modernizing and professionalizing their navy, in spite of the extraordinary handicap of its being managed by no less than five separate admiralties, under the orders of at least three of the seven autonomous constituent states. By the latter stages of the war their fleet was led by one of the greatest sea commanders of all time: M. A. de Ruyter. In 1667 they exacted a humiliating price for the English decision to lay up most of the great ships of the line while peace negotiations were pending. Not only did the Dutch sail up the River Medway, burning several of England's largest ships and towing away the finest of all, but they cruised almost at will along the southern and eastern coasts of England, disrupting convoys and threatening further assaults.

By the time of the Third Dutch War (1672–74) there had been a double diplomatic revolution. Reacting to French entry into the second war in 1666 and (in the case of some at least among Charles II's ministers) provoked by genuine alarm at the prospect of Louis XIV's France conquering the whole of the southern, or Spanish Netherlands, the three leading northern powers—England, the United Provinces, and Sweden—had entered into what came to be called the Triple Alliance, which looked like a defensive bloc against further French aggression. But the King's heart was never in this policy; indeed, for him it was perhaps no more than a concession to the Crown's parliamentary critics and to the growing anti-French element within his own Council. The policy was abruptly reversed by the Treaty of Dover in 1670; even more dramatically so by the secret clauses of that agreement, which Charles gambled, successfully, on not becoming public knowledge until long after. Thus, in the Third Dutch War England joined in the French onslaught against the Netherlands. By land Louis's armies won tremendous victories and came very near to conquering the seven provinces; at sea the allied fleets were greatly superior in numbers to the Dutch, but the campaigns were a classic case of divided command leading to indecision and missed opportunities. The Dutch were forced on to the defensive by the larger allied fleets, and having suffered traumatic defeats on land were fighting for their very survival. What the outcome would have been if this war had continued must remain unknown. Partly under renewed parliamentary pressure, and partly to keep his freedom of manœuvre in other respects, Charles abandoned his allies, making a separate compromise peace with the Dutch, now under the semi-regal rule of William III of Orange (Charles's nephew, who also became his brother James's son-in-law a few years later). In the treaty of 1674 the Dutch agreed to cede New York permanently, but their other concessions were not extensive, especially considering that they were still at war with France.

In 1662 a small expedition was sent out to assert England's title to Bombay, but these claims were not made good until 1665, while only three years later the new colony was handed over to the East India Company. English activity in the eastern seas and around the Indian subcontinent remained almost wholly in the hands of the Company and its freelance rivals, known as 'interlopers'.[2] The Royal Navy only began to play a significant role in these waters during the wars against France in the eighteenth century. The larger of the Company's ships were unusually heavily armed and protected, and indeed constituted the only exception to the generalization that merchant- and warship-design diverged almost totally from the mid-seventeenth century, as is fully explained in N.A.M. Rodger's chapter. Moreover, since investment in the Company proved attractive to monarchs, ministers, lesser officials, and MPs, its activities both by sea and on land should not be seen as private enterprise in the conventional sense, but rather as a kind of state imperialism by proxy.

Likewise, immediately after the Restoration investment in the Royal African Company, which enjoyed a monopoly of the English share in the slave trade across the Atlantic, reads like a roll-call of royalty, ministers of state, and courtiers. Admittedly as reconstructed in the 1670s, the Company had a much stronger merchant element, which put it on a sounder financial basis. Even so, it should be seen as a branch of Empire and not simply as a trading venture like, for example, the Levant Company in the eastern Mediterranean and the territories of the Turkish empire. In spite of having to maintain forts, related to the export of gold from West Africa to England rather than the shipment of slaves to the Americas, the Royal African Company managed to hold its own against 'interlopers' until its monopoly was called in question after 1688. In consequence of that, its decline was steep; more and more of the slaves arriving in the Caribbean from West Africa were carried by interlopers' ships, and in 1698 the Company formally abandoned its claim to a monopoly and began to license private traders, whose share of the market continued to grow.

The often inconsistent, if not contradictory, nature of English policy is illustrated by the grant to the Hudson's Bay Company in 1670. In the very same year that Charles II was to reverse his foreign policy and make an alliance with France, he granted wide-ranging monopoly rights of trade and settlement in what is now the Canadian Arctic to his cousin, Prince Rupert, and a syndicate of courtiers and financiers. This posed an inevitable challenge to the potential northward expan-

[2] See above, pp. 276–84.

sion of New France, although military conflict in that remote region did not begin until after the further reversal of English foreign policy in 1689.

The Netherlands was to remain a major European colonial power, especially in the Far East, but it would never again challenge England (or Britain) as a maritime and imperial competitor. The case with France was very different. It may well be that Louis XIV's priorities were always dynastic and continental, but the work of his great minister, J.-B. Colbert, led to the development of a French navy which was formidable in both size and quality. Much to Louis's subsequent regret, he remained a neutral observer in 1688 during William's preparations against England, and then throughout the successful invasion which led to the overthrow of his uncle and father-in-law, King James II. To say that William's unopposed landing on the south Devon coast represented a total defeat for the English navy may be true in a formal sense, but is highly misleading in reality. The conventional view is that an unusual, positively freakish spell of easterly winds carried William's invading fleet safely down the Channel while Lord Dartmouth, James's Commander-in-Chief, remained mewed up in the Thames Estuary. Apart from the fact that William initially sailed in a north-westerly direction towards the Yorkshire coast before turning south, a truly determined and talented admiral would have got his big ships 'warped out' (i.e. hauled out by cable); in fact, several of Dartmouth's captains and other officers were secret Orangist sympathizers who had no intention of trying to intercept and give battle to the Dutch fleet. When eventually it did get out, after having to turn back once off Kent, the English fleet sailed round to the south coast, made no attempt to molest William's forces or to interrupt his supply lines, and after James's flight to France placed itself under the Prince's orders, months before his formal installation as King William III together with his wife, Queen Mary II, as joint monarchs in the spring of 1689.

Soon the English and Dutch navies were acting together as allies in William's continental coalition against France (1689–97). Not that the maritime powers, as they can now without exaggeration be described, by any means had things all their own way. They failed to prevent James landing in Ireland with a medium-sized French army or to isolate and totally blockade him once he had got there, while the year after this the English were defeated in a major fleet action by the French in the Channel. In spite of recovering from these setbacks, winning a double victory off the French coast two years later, and safeguarding William's reconquest of Ireland, when the allies in turn attempted amphibious attacks on the French coast these were an expensive failure. Treachery contributed to this, as English Jacobite sympathizers gave advanced warning to the enemy. Nor were the French swept from the seas by the allied navies. In fact, whether measured by the number of battleships (defined as those large and powerful enough to fight 'in the line', exchanging broadsides with the enemy's line), or by estimated total tonnage, the

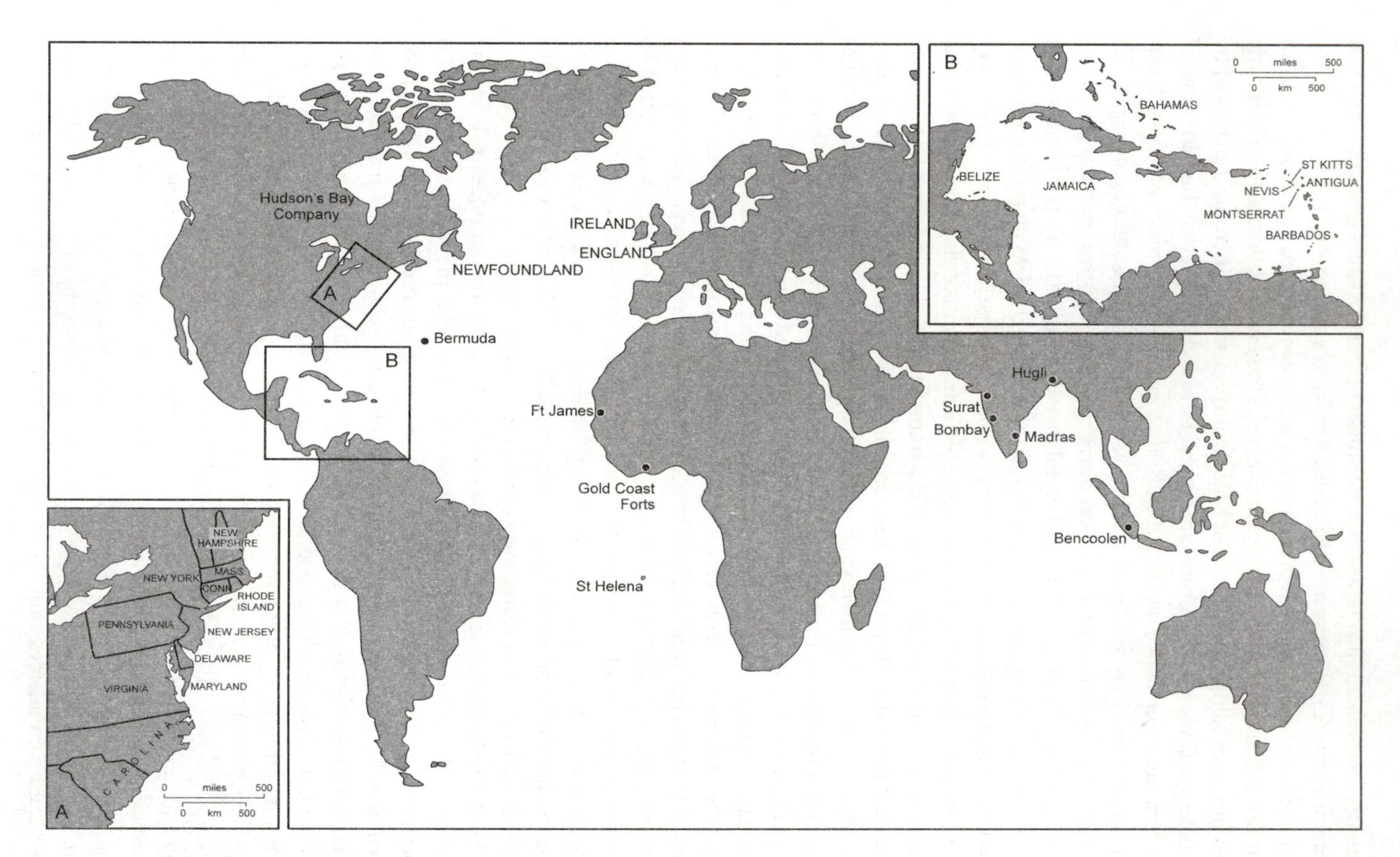

MAP 21.1. England Overseas in 1689

French navy was actually larger than the English from 1670 until around 1697–1705.[3] This was in spite of a major English building programme, initiated in 1677 and substantially completed by 1682, and another in the 1690s. Over and above this, the French still maintained a considerable force of oared galleys in the Mediterranean, besides a sailing battle-fleet based on Toulon. A further massive building programme, organized by Colbert's successors from 1689 to 1693, was halted on Louis's orders due to financial crisis and a decision to give absolute priority to French land forces; many of these new ships, even those effectively completed, were never used in a fleet action. But the so-called *guerre de course*, conducted by French privateers and fast-sailing commerce raiders, if not as grave a threat as the German U-boat campaigns in the two world wars of the twentieth century, was still remarkably successful and damaging to English trade and shipping.

Generally speaking, the larger a country's merchant marine and the more far-flung its overseas trading interests, the more potentially vulnerable it is to commerce raiding and action by the enemy against its overseas trade. Thus, in the war of 1652–54, while English merchant shipping suffered severely, Dutch losses in ships and cargoes were even greater. The same was true, but by a much narrower margin, in the second and third wars (of 1664–67 and 1672–74). By the time of the wars with France (1689–97 and 1702–13) British shipping was at least as vulnerable as Dutch shipping to French attacks. Although the Dutch merchant marine remained the largest in the world until well into the eighteenth century, Britain had more to lose and less to gain from sea warfare against commerce than did France. French merchant shipping was far from negligible, but by the 1690s–1700s the situation of the two countries was not so different in this regard from that of Spain and England a hundred and more years before.[4]

Even by the time of the second Anglo-French conflict, the so-called War of the Spanish Succession (1702–13), British naval primacy was largely due to all possible rivals having, at least for the time being, opted out of the naval building race. The battle-fleets alike of Britain's allies—the Netherlands and Portugal—and of her enemies—France and Spain—simply dwindled away. In the early eighteenth century, as again after 1815, Britain was to maintain an unnecessarily large number of big ships; for the protection of trade and Empire, the need was for more smaller vessels of the right type and quality.[5]

[3] Different authorities disagree about the exact dates and the proper units of measurement. See Robert Gardiner, ed., and Brian Lavery (consultant), *The Line of Battle: The Sailing Warship, 1650–1840* (London, 1992); Jan Glete, *Navies and Nations: Warships, Navies and State Building in Europe and America, 1500–1860*, 2 vols. (Stockholm, 1993); George Modelski and William R. Thompson, *Seapower in Global Politics, 1494–1993* (Basingstoke, 1988).

[4] See chap. by John C. Appleby.

[5] I. R. Mather, 'The Role of the Royal Navy in the English Atlantic Empire, 1660–1720', unpublished D.Phil. thesis, Oxford, 1995.

Naturally numbers and size are not everything. The seaworthiness of ships and seamanship of their crews, the quality of their armaments, the successful strategic use of seapower by monarchs, Cabinets, and Boards of Admiralty, and finally the tactical skills, courage, and endurance shown in the implementation of naval strategy were all vital components. Between the 1680s and the 1720s it is not fanciful to see the emergence of a naval tradition. At its best this spelt innovation, heroism, and victories, but it could all too easily degenerate into a complacent and dangerously obscurantist mystique; even at its most successful, the connection of seapower with trade and Empire was only partial, and intermittent, if none the less sometimes decisive. Therefore only with the advantage of hindsight can we identify this period as a turning point.

Besides the ships, their armaments, and crews, the provision of adequate food and drink was one of the biggest challenges to naval administration. The larger the fleet and the longer that it was to be at sea, operating away from its home ports, the greater the problem of victualling. From 1660 until the winter of 1683–84 the English navy relied on contractors, who undertook to provide victuals at so much money per man per day; and for much of this period there was only a single, in effect monopolistic, contractor, whose honesty, efficiency, and creditworthiness were thus an absolutely crucial factor in the deployment of the country's power at sea. The change from contracting, either with a single victualler or with a syndicate, to direct management by salaried commissioners followed hard on the final abandonment of tax-farming, notably in the Excise, and its replacement by fiscal management through state servants. Indeed, the one may be seen as a change on the supply side of government finance, the other comparably on the demand side, and their respective introductions in such rapid succession was no coincidence. Direct management did not solve everything, of course. Individual ships' pursers and victualling agents ashore could still be incompetent, dishonest, or both. There does, however, seem to have been some genuine improvement in naval victualling by the opening decades of the eighteenth century compared with the 1690s and earlier.

England was slowly becoming a more urbanized and commercialized society, a process in which the colonial trades played a growing part. Yet the political system at home was still dominated, not to say controlled, by the landed classes: the peers in the House of Lords and the representatives of the gentry in the Commons. There were, of course, MPs who were not landowners, such as army and navy officers, civil administrators, courtiers, lawyers, merchants, and financiers. But the proportion of non-landowners in the House did not increase in any spectacular way. Even if the active men of business were drawn chiefly from these minority groups, taxes could not be voted without the agreement of the back-bench gentry MPs, many (perhaps even the majority) of whom had no direct maritime or commercial connections, and did not live on the seacoasts of the country. Yet, even if most of them were normally inarticulate, there does seem to have been a growing awareness of the importance to the 'state and nation' of the navy, trade, and Empire. The best-known late-twentieth-century historian of British seapower has given first place to economic determinants, in the sense of these having underpinned, if not always having directly caused, colonial and naval developments.[6] Others would prefer to think in terms of the proposition that, the more overseas trade came to involve commitments (whether or not involving the extension of territorial possessions) in the non-European world, the greater the need for the kind of naval forces which could keep sea communications open and protect trade routes. This required ever-increasing fiscal and administrative support. The actual quest for additional overseas territories of the kind which came to be known as colonies of settlement was not, until at least some decades later, the principal cause or consequence of these changes. In theory England, then Great Britain, could have come to possess the largest merchant and fishing fleets and the strongest navy of any European power without having held such extensive territorial possessions. In practice there was interaction here too. Some colonies of settlement—notably the tobacco coast of Virginia and Maryland and the sugar-producing islands of the Caribbean—played a decisive part in the growth and above all the diversification of English foreign trade, most particularly the re-export of such imports to continental Europe. On the other hand, even by around 1700 the economic contribution to the Empire of New England, New York, and Pennsylvania is less obvious to historians and was certainly unclear to most contemporaries. Massachusetts indeed, as other chapters have abundantly demonstrated, was regarded as an awkward customer, needing to be firmly handled in order to become a useful part of the Empire rather than a chronic source of infringement and evasion of its mercantile regulations. The relative importance of North America and the Baltic region in supplying timber and naval stores for the Royal Navy is difficult to establish. The latest view is that the Baltic was always the larger source for these supplies. None the less, masts were arriving from Massachusetts as early as the 1660s, while two acts of Parliament passed during Anne's reign reserved certain kinds of timber and naval stores, found mainly in New England, exclusively for use by the navy.

Besides their economic significance for the nascent Empire, the colonies varied widely in other respects. This can be seen in the reasons for their original founding and for their later development. Thus, on the mainland of North America the drive for material betterment had been combined with the quest for freedom from ecclesiastical interference and religious persecution. This religious motivation had

[6] Paul M. Kennedy, *The Rise and Fall of British Naval Mastery* (1976; London, 1983).

been at its very strongest in the tiny settlement of New Plymouth, but powerful in Massachusetts, New Haven, Connecticut, and Rhode Island, also in Maryland, and likewise later in Pennsylvania; it was weaker in Virginia and scarcely discernible in New York or Carolina. In the Caribbean and the Atlantic islands material motives almost totally eclipsed religion except for the ill-fated, short-lived settlement on Providence Island and the Cromwellian vision which led almost incidentally to the capture of Jamaica. In Africa and Asia trade rather than settlement provided the basic economic motive; here too religion is hard to find, though a genuine Christian missionary motive was to emerge in the future.

Another way of looking at England's colonies by the end of the seventeenth century is according to how they were governed. Naturally this includes their relations with the home government as well as their internal political systems, and—except for the 1640s and 1650s—that meant their connection with the English Crown. At the beginning (from the 1600s to the 1620s) what may be called the 'company' model had been dominant, by which the monarch granted a charter to a corporate body, formed much like existing trading companies. But even before the settlement of New England had begun on any scale (apart from the Plymouth Pilgrims) this had received a serious check with the downfall of the Virginia Company in 1623–24 and the assumption of direct rule by King James and his Council. Contemporaries did not use the term until much later, but in retrospect Virginia can reasonably be called the first 'Crown colony'. It was to be crucial for later developments that the infant elements of representative government were not abolished when the link with the Crown was made more direct with a royally appointed Governor and other office-holders. Paradoxically, the next substantial addition to what would later become Crown colonies was acquired when there was no King or Queen but a Lord Protector ruling over a republic. The Restoration did not bring about any substantial change in Jamaica's status, though its strategic significance was altered by the making of peace with Spain after 1660 and by the renewed enmity with the Dutch and later with France. There too the growth of a settler population led to the establishment of an elected or representative element in the island's government. Far and away the most important chartered company colony from its beginnings in 1629–30 until the loss of its charter in 1684 was Massachusetts Bay. As has been shown in the chapters by Virginia Anderson and Richard Dunn, Massachusetts then came under various forms of direct rule, punctuated by the revolutionary upheaval of 1689; the new charter of the 1690s made it in effect a Crown colony, though one in which royal control was always to be weaker and more contested than anywhere else in the eighteenth-century Empire. The settlements of Connecticut and Rhode Island, which had originally been secessions from Massachusetts, were initially governed under a similar model. Rather ironically, the revised charter of Connecticut (which had by then absorbed New Haven), secured by the younger John Winthrop in the early 1660s, was to survive the *quo warranto* campaign of the 1680s, and remained the basis of the colony's relationship to the Imperial authority until American Independence. Rhode Island's charter was probably left alone because of the colony's unimportance, a view which was broadly justified except for the as yet unforeseen rise of Newport as a trading and shipping centre. Those colonies where the company actually constituted the government must be distinguished from the forts and trading posts, originally known as 'factories', which were established and governed by trading companies with their headquarters in London—the East India, Royal African, and Hudson's Bay Companies. The Bermuda Company, which was also snuffed out in 1684, had been a kind of hybrid; out of it came another small Crown colony.

Meanwhile a third type of colonial government had come into existence, starting with the acquisition of small individual West Indian islands in the 1620s but extending to the North American mainland by the 1630s. These were proprietary grants by royal charter to favoured individuals, or sometimes to groups of people (but not organized as companies), who were given extensive rights of jurisdiction as well as trade, settlement, and political control over the territories in question. The various proprietary grants which had been made by James and Charles I of islands in the Caribbean had all been effectively extinguished by 1663, in some cases compensation being paid to the strongest claimants, and the islands were all brought under direct royal rule. Surprisingly, in spite of some ups and downs during the rule of the Puritans in England, the Roman Catholic family of Calvert (Lords Baltimore) kept their highly privileged proprietorship over Maryland until 1689; they even recovered control of the governorship, though without their earlier rights of jurisdiction and landownership, in the early eighteenth century. In the 1660s a massive grant entrusted the Carolinas to a group of highly influential ministers and courtiers. In spite of political differences among themselves and changes of personnel, the Carolina Proprietors kept their privileges and control over the government of the colony, although the settlements were divided into what were to become North and South Carolina from the 1690s. Not until the 1720s did the heirs of the original Proprietors bow out and the two colonies come under direct royal control. As its name suggests, New York began its history in England's Empire as a proprietary grant to the King's brother, James, Duke of York. It became a Crown colony more or less automatically on his accession to the throne in 1685, and in spite of internal conflicts continued in this relationship to the Crown under William and Mary and their successors from 1689 until Independence. Again, as elsewhere, representative institutions survived from the 1680s, perhaps only because James's grandiose Dominion of New England lasted such a short time.

The early history of New Jersey is confused and difficult to summarize. James and his functionaries tried intermittently and unsuccessfully to extend his proprietary claims across the Hudson River; in fact his only expansionist success as proprietor of New York was in the opposite direction, in prising the whole of Long Island away from its earlier links to New Haven–Connecticut. By the 1670s–1680s there were two groups of proprietors for East and West Jersey respectively, neither fully accepting the existence, let alone the claims, of the other. Latterly there were strong Quaker elements in both. The Jersey proprietors seem to have lacked both the incentive and the power to maintain themselves, and the two settlements came together as the single royal colony of New Jersey in the early 1700s.

Undoubtedly the most remarkable of all proprietary grants was that made to William Penn in the early 1680s: another reminder that later Stuart policy was never monolithic, or—to take a more favourable view—that Charles and James II never discarded some commitment to religious toleration. In fact the status of Pennsylvania, the government of which also claimed what later became the separate colony of Delaware, came under most grave threat after the Revolution of 1688–89. Penn was discredited as a personal friend, indeed a political ally of James II, and his greatest achievement, not as the founder of a major colony but as a political operator, was to prevent the loss of his charter in the 1690s. As will be seen in the next volume of this *History*, there were occasions in the eighteenth century when it looked as if all the colonies, at least in America, would be reduced to a uniform status under the Crown. But this did not happen, and the various forms described here were to survive until the American Revolution (and, in the case of Britain's Empire in India, until much later than that).

These constitutional distinctions must not be made to explain too much. Differences of climate, economic potential, native and settler populations, and the cultural patterns of values and beliefs which developed both in the settlements themselves and among those involved with them in the home country were always at least as important, and arguably for the most part a good deal more so.

Colonies were seen to exist for the glory of the monarch and the benefit of the mother country. At the same time, those who had studied the history of classical Greece and Rome as part of their education would know that, on reaching a certain stage of maturity, such communities had a tendency to break away and to set up for themselves. Nothing was permanent in human affairs, but while an empire existed it was there to be exploited; foreign trade likewise should not only benefit the individuals and companies directly engaged in it, but should enrich and strengthen the country as a whole. In order to safeguard trade and Empire, a navy was essential, moreover, a navy which was both larger and different in character from one designed merely to meet the needs of defending the shores of Britain and Ireland against foreign attack. Human rationality and foresight were seldom able to assess these needs exactly and then to translate them into consistent policies. Perhaps ironically, even the construction and maintenance of a battle-fleet in excess of the country's and the Empire's strategic requirements may have had a positive effect on the growth of the domestic economy. So we should not exaggerate either the scale or the inevitability of the future growth of England's commercial, maritime, and imperial strength at the turn of the seventeenth-eighteenth centuries. The extent of this power and its increase in the years which followed were due in part to input and commitment, but also to the country's position in relation to the other European powers, notably France, the Netherlands, and Spain. The next volume of this *History* shows how and why the story unfolded as it did, when Britain became the foremost European Imperial power. In that process, navy, state, trade, and Empire would become increasingly identified in people's minds, if not always in all the realities of everyday life. It is difficult, if not impossible, to imagine how these developments could have come about without the efforts and experiences of the seventeenth and even of the sixteenth century.

Select Bibliography

JEREMY BLACK and PHILIP WOODFINE, eds., *The British Navy and the Use of Naval Power in the Eighteenth Century* (Leicester, 1988).

C. R. BOXER, *The Anglo-Dutch Wars of the 17th Century* (for the National Maritime Museum, London, 1974).

J. S. BROMLEY and A. N. RYAN, 'Navies', in J. S. Bromley, ed., *The New Cambridge Modern History*, Vol. VI, *The Rise of Great Britain and Russia, 1688–1715/25* (Cambridge, 1970), chap. XXII, s. 3.

J. R. BRUIJN, *The Dutch Navy of the 17th and 18th Centuries* (Columbia, SC, 1993).

BERNARD CAPP, *Cromwell's Navy: The Fleet and the English Revolution, 1648–1660* (Oxford, 1989).

J. D. DAVIES, *Gentlemen and Tarpaulins: The Officers and Men of the Restoration Navy* (Oxford, 1991).

K. G. DAVIES, *The Royal African Company* (London, 1957).

RALPH DAVIS, *The Rise of the English Shipping Industry in the Seventeenth and Eighteenth Centuries* (London, 1962).

MICHAEL DUFFY, ed., *Parameters of British Naval Power, 1650–1850* (Exeter, 1992).

J. P. W. EHRMAN, *The Navy in the War of William III, 1689–97: Its State and Direction* (Cambridge, 1953).

FRANK FOX, *Great Ships: The Battlefleet of King Charles II* (Greenwich, 1980).

ROBERT GARDINER, ed., and BRIAN LAVERY (consultant), *The Line of Battle: The Sailing Warship, 1650–1840* (London, 1992).

JAN GLETE, *Navies and Nations: Warships, Navies and State Building in Europe and America, 1500–1860*, 2 vols. (Stockholm, 1993).

RICHARD HARDING, *The Evolution of the Sailing Navy, 1509–1815* (London, 1994).

J. R. HILL, ed., with B. RANFT, *The Oxford Illustrated History of the Royal Navy* (Oxford, 1995).

SARI R. HORNSTEIN, *The Restoration Navy and English Foreign Trade, 1674–1688: A Study in the Peacetime Use of Sea Power* (Aldershot, 1991).
D. W. JONES, *War and Economy in the Age of William III and Marlborough* (Oxford, 1988).
PAUL M. KENNEDY, *The Rise and Fall of British Naval Mastery* (1976; London, 1983).
BRIAN LAVERY, *The Arming and Fitting of British Ships of War, 1600–1815* (London, 1987).
GEORGE MODELSKI and WILLIAM R. THOMPSON, *Seapower in Global Politics, 1494–1993* (Basingstoke, 1988).

CHRONOLOGY

Year	Britain and Ireland	Europe
1481		
1487		
1492		Jews expelled from Spain
1496	Henry VII authorizes John Cabot and his sons to make voyage (in 1497) to North America	
1497		
1498		
1504		
1509	Accession of Henry VIII	
1511		
1513		
1516		
1517		31 October: Martin Luther's 95 Theses
1518		
1521		
1523		
1526		
1529		Imperial Diet at Speyer; word 'Protestant' coined
1531		
1533		

The Wider World	Arts and Sciences	Year
Earliest possible date of first English voyage to reach coast of North America		1481
Portuguese expedition under Bartholomeu Dias passes Cape of Good Hope		1487
Christopher Columbus's first transatlantic voyage		1492
		1496
John Cabot's voyage to North America		1497
John Cabot lost on second voyage		1498
1504–8 First known Norman and Breton voyages to Newfoundland	Michelangelo Buonarroti begins to sculpt *David*	1504
Conjectural North American voyage of Sebastian Cabot	Sebastian Brant, *The Ship of Fools* translated by Alexander Barclay	1509
	Erasmus, *Moriae Encomium (In Praise of Folly)*	1511
	Niccolò Machiavelli, *Il Principe (The Prince)*	1513
	Thomas More, *Utopia*	1516
	*c.*1518–20 John Rastell, *The Four Elements*	1518
Spanish forces under Hernán Cortés overthrow Aztec Empire in Mexico		1521
	St Ignatius Loyola, *Spiritual Exercises*	1523
	P. A. Paracelsus proposes his *Theory of Disease* in Basle	1526
		1529
Francisco Pizarro leads his first attack on Cuzco, Inka capital		1531
Willoughby and Chancellor reach Archangel		1533

Year	Britain and Ireland	Europe
1534	Henry VIII issues the Act of Supremacy	
1536		
1543		
1545		Council of Trent meets
1546		War of Schmalkalden begins
1547	Accession of Edward VI	End of Schmalkaldic war
1553	Accession of Mary I	
1555		Peace of Augsburg
1556		Ferdinand I Holy Roman Emperor
1558	Accession of Elizabeth I	
1559		
1562		Wars of Religion begin in France
1564		Maximilian II Holy Roman Emperor
1565		Dutch revolt against Spain begins
1568		Revolt of Morisco population of Granada
1570		
1571	Attempts to plant the Ards and Clandeboyne, Co. Down begins	
1572		23/24 Aug. Massacre of St Bartholomew's Day, Paris
1573		Henry de Valois elected King of Poland
1574		
1576	First of Martin Frobisher's three expeditions in search of North-west Passage	Rudolf II Holy Roman Emperor

The Wider World	Arts and Sciences	Year
First voyage of Jacques Cartier to the gulf of St Lawrence		1534
	Jean Calvin publishes his *Institution de la religion chrétienne* in Basle	1536
	M. Kopernik writes on *Heliocentrism*	1543
		1545
		1546
		1547
Earliest regular English voyages to Guinea begin		1553
Establishment of the Muscovy Company	Accounts of English Guinea voyages published	1555
		1556
		1558
	Philip Melanchthon, *De lege naturae* Works by Abelard, Boccaccio, Calvin, Dante, and Erasmus placed on the Papal Index of Prohibited Books	1559
Establishment of Anglo-French/ Huguenot settlement on coast of Florida		1562
John Hawkins begins slaving voyages		1564
Spanish destroy Anglo-French settlement in Florida		1565
	George Buchanan, 'In Colonias Brasilienses, vel Sodomitas', *Brasilia*	1568
	Andrea Palladio, *Quattro Libri della Architectura*	1570
		1571
		1572
		1573
Sir Richard Grenville proposes colonizing South America		1574
Frobisher's first expedition to Newfoundland		1576

Year	Britain and Ireland	Europe
1577		
1578	Minority of James VI	
1579–85	War followed by plantation in the Province of Munster in Ireland	
1580		Annexation of Portugal by Philip II of Spain
1581		
1582		
1583		

CONFLICT BETWEEN ENGLAND AND SPAIN

Year	Britain and Ireland	Europe
1584	Attacks on Spanish property	
1585	Plantation of Munster begins	Earl of Leicester Governor-General of the Netherlands
1586		
1587		
1588	Defeat of Spanish Armada	
1589–95	James VI launches five 'fire and sword' campaigns along the Western Seaboard	
1590		
1591		Siege of Paris begins

The Wider World	Arts and Sciences	Year
1577–80 Francis Drake circumnavigates globe	John Dee, *General and Rare Memorials... of Navigation* Jean Bodin, *De la République*	1577
Sir Humphrey Gilbert sets out on his first abortive transatlantic colonizing expedition		1578
		1579
		1580
Establishment of the Levant Company		1581
	Stephen Parmenius, *De Navigatione... Carmen επιβατικον*	1582
Sir Humphrey Gilbert's second expedition to the North American mainland (fails)		1583
Sir Walter Ralegh's expedition to Guiana Francis Amadas and Arthur Barlowe reconnoitre eastern coast of North America First Roanoke Voyage	Richard Hakluyt, *A Particuler Discourse (Discourse on Western Planting)*	1584
Barbary Company incorporated First settlement of Roanoke Drake's expedition to the West Indies Exploration of the Chesapeake Bay John Davis begins search for North-west Passage		1585
Sir Francis Drake sacks St Augustine, Florida Roanoke settlement fails		1586
Chartered English trade voyage to Senegambia region Second Roanoke settlement begun		1587
	Thomas Hariot, *A Briefe and True Report of the Newfound Land of Virginia*	1588
	Richard Hakluyt, *The Principale Navigations*	1589
Roanoke settlers lost		1590
	Edmund Spenser, engaged on *The Færie Queene*	1591

Year	Britain and Ireland	Europe
1591		Habsburg–Ottoman Fifteen Years War begins
1592	Foundation of the University of Dublin, Trinity College	
1594	Nine Years War in Ireland begins	
1595	First attempt to plant islands of Lewis and Harris	
1596		
1598		Edict of Nantes: end of French Religious Wars
1600		
1603	Accession of James I and Union of the Crowns Pacification of the Borders begins Increasing numbers of Scottish settlers colonize Counties Antrim and Down	
1604	Anglo-Spanish Peace Treaty (Peace of London)	
1605		
1606		
1607–8	Flight of the Earls; revolt of Sir Cahir O'Dogherty paves way for plantation of Ulster	
1608		
1609	Plantation of Ulster launched Statutes of Iona	Moriscos expelled from Spain

The Wider World	Arts and Sciences	Year
		1591
Licence issued for Sierra Leone trade		1592
		1594
Last voyage of Drake and Hawkins to the Caribbean		1595
	Edmund Spenser, *A View of the Present State of Ireland* completed Walter Ralegh, *The Discoverie of the Large, Rich and Bewtiful Empire of Guiana* George Chapman, *De Guiana, Carmen Epicum*	1596
	c.1599–1603 Alonso de Ercilla, *La Araucana*, trans. George Carew as *The Historie of Araucana*	1598
31 Dec. English East India Company Charter		1600
		1603
Settlement on the River Wiapoco in Guiana		1604
Attempted settlement in the Lesser Antilles		1605
Virginia Company of London Charter, and of Plymouth	Michael Drayton, *To the Virginia Voyage*	1606
c.1607 Sierra Leone redwood trade initiated by John Davis Jamestown, Virginia, established First permanent English settlement in the Chesapeake English colony at Sagadahoc, Maine	First performance of C. Monteverdi's *Orfeo*	1607
First English ship at Surat	J. Lippershey constructs a telescope in Middleburg	1608
First Royal Charter for the Virginia Company Henry Hudson establishes Dutch claim to New Netherland First permanent settlement at Quebec	Z. Janssen constructs a microscope in Amsterdam	1609

Year	Britain and Ireland	Europe
1609		
1610		
1612		Matthias Holy Roman Emperor
1613		Beginning of the Romanov dynasty with Mikhail Romanov
1614		General Diet of Central European estates at Linz
1615		

THIRTY YEARS WAR

Year	Britain and Ireland	Europe
1618	War with Spain	thirty years war begins
1619		Ferdinand II Holy Roman Emperor
1620		
1621		Foundation of Dutch West India Company
1622		
1623		
1624		
1625	Accession of Charles I Act of Revocation in Scotland	
1627	Île de Rhé expedition	
1628		
1629		Edict of Restitution in Holy Roman Empire
1630		

The Wider World	Arts and Sciences	Year
'Starving Time' begins in the Chesapeake		1609
First English settlement in Newfoundland		1610
Settlement of Bermuda begun	William Shakespeare, *The Tempest*	1612
Opening of factory at Hirado, Japan Grant of trading rights, Surat		1613
Marriage of John Rolfe to Pocahontas		1614
Sir Thomas Roe's embassy to Mughal Emperor		1615
First Guinea Company chartered Death of Powhatan		1618
First General Assembly held in Jamestown		1619
Plymouth Plantation established Mayflower Compact signed Voyage of the *Mayflower* made	Francis Bacon, *Instauratio Magna*	1620
Treaty signed between Ampanoags and Plymouth Colony		1621
Opechancanough launches large-scale uprising in Virginia Attempted Amerindian 'massacre' of settlers in the Chesapeake Capture of Hormuz by English; Portuguese expelled		1622
Amboina Massacre; closing of Far East factories		1623
Collapse of Virginia Company St Christopher colony established by Thomas Warner	Martin Luther's German Bible placed on the *Index Liberarum Prohibitarum*	1624
Virginia made a Royal Colony Sir Francis Wyatt first Royal Governor, Barbados	Samuel Purchas, *Hakluytus Posthumous or Purchas His Pilgrims*	1625
Barbados colony established		1627
Guinea Company taken over by Nicholas Crispe	William Harvey proposes his theory of the Circulation of Blood in London	1628
Charles I grants Carolina to Sir Robert Heath Massachusetts Bay Charter		1629
Massachusetts Bay Colony founded		1630

Year	Britain and Ireland	Europe
1630		
1631		
1632	Wentworth Lord Deputy of Ireland	
1633		
1634		
1636		
1637		Ferdinand III Holy Roman Emperor
1638		
1639	Bishop's Wars in Scotland (Covenanter Risings) begin	
1639	Wars of the Three Kingdoms begin	
1640	Short and Long Parliaments called in England	Revolts in Catalonia and Portugal against Spanish rule
1641	Outbreak of the Irish rebellion (Ulster)	
1642	English Civil War begins	
1643		

The Wider World	Arts and Sciences	Year
Great migration of English settlers to New England begins		1630
Launching of first New England-built ship, *The Blessing of the Bay*		1631
Maryland Charter	George Sandys, *Ovid's Metamorphoses English'd*	1632
Kormantin and other factories established on the Gold Coast		
	George Herbert, *The Church Militant*	1633
First Connecticut towns established Virginia divided into eight counties, each with own court and officials; spread of population beyond James River basin Lord Baltimore founds St Mary's city, Maryland		1634
Roger Williams founds Providence, Rhode Island Founding of Harvard College		1636
Antinomian Controversy in Massachusetts Pequot War (Puritan 'massacre' of the Pequot Indians in New England) New Haven Colony begins	Descartes, *Discours sur la méthode*	1637
New Sweden established on the Delaware Fundamental Orders of Connecticut signed	William Davenant, *Madagascar*	1638
Barbadians elect Assembly Grant of Madras to English		1639
White population of Virginia and Maryland 8,000 Sharp decline in farm price of tobacco		1640
Beginning of English slave trade to Barbados		1641
		1642
	E. Torricelli constructs a mercury barometer in Rome	1643

Year	Britain and Ireland	Europe
1644		
1645		
1646	End of Civil War	
1648		Dutch-Spanish peace signed at Munster: end of Thirty Years War
1649	Oliver Cromwell's expedition to Ireland	
1650	Cromwell's campaign against the Scots begins	
1651	First Navigation Act	
1651–52		

FIRST ANGLO-DUTCH WAR

Year	Britain and Ireland	Europe
1652	War with Dutch	
1653		
1654	Oliver Cromwell's 'Western Design' End of Dutch War	
1655		

ANGLO-SPANISH WAR

Year	Britain and Ireland	Europe
1655	War with Spain beings	
1657		Leopold I Holy Roman Emperor
1658		
1659		Treaty of the Pyrenees ends war between France and Spain

The Wider World	Arts and Sciences	Year
Large-scale Indian attack by Opechancanough: 500 colonists killed, Powhatans defeated by 1646	R. Descartes writes on Analytical Geometry in Amsterdam	1644
Richard Ingle's rebellion in Maryland: estates of leading Catholics plundered		1645
	John Eliot translates Bible into Massachusetts dialect of Algonquian	1646
		1648
Emigration of Puritan settlers from Virginia to Maryland		1649
Francis Willoughby Governor of Barbados		1650
First Indian 'Praying Town' established in Natick, Massachusetts	Thomas Hobbes, *Leviathan*	1651
Extension of Guinea Company's monopoly		
Maryland and Virginia acknowledge parliamentary rule		1651–52
Barbados yields to Asycues's siege		1652
Squatters settle Albemarle Sound, Virginia		1653
'Western Design' for Jamaica	Luis de Camoens, *Lusiads*, trans. Richard Fanshawe	1654
Conquest of New Sweden by New Netherland in North America		1655
English capture Jamaica from Spain		
		1655
Admiral Blake captures Spanish treasure fleet off Tenerife		1657
East India Company permanent joint-stock with new charter		1658
	William Davenant, *The Cruelty of the Spaniards in Peru*	
	Jan Amos Komensky (Comenius), *Opera didacticaomnia*	
	William Davenant, *The History of Sir Francis Drake*	1659

Year	Britain and Ireland	Europe
1660	Restoration of Charles II Second Navigation Act New Charter for East India Company	
1660s		
1661	Anglo-Portuguese marriage treaty: England gains Tangier and Bombay	
1662		Louis XIV's personal rule begins
1663	Navigation Act: Staple Act	
1664		Habsburg–Ottoman War

SECOND ANGLO-DUTCH WAR

Year	Britain and Ireland	Europe
1664	War with Dutch begins	
1665	Great Plague in London	
1666	Great Fire of London	

The Wider World	Arts and Sciences	Year
Company of Royal Adventurers into Africa chartered by Charles II (Royal African Company) Royal authority restored in colonies White population of the Chesapeake reaches 24,000 as immigration into region continues		1660
Increased production in Virginia and Maryland leads to continuing decline in price of tobacco		1660s
James Fort (Gambia) founded Barbados' slave and servant codes		1661
Halfway Covenant drafted Royal Adventurers enter slave trade	Royal Society for the Improvement of Natural Knowledge founded	1662
Royal Adventurers Trading into Africa granted new Charter Charles II grants Carolina to 8 Lords Proprietors	Governor William Berkeley's *Discourse and View of Virginia* advocates a mixed economy and less reliance on tobacco	1663
English conquest of New Netherland Barbadian settlement on the Cape Fear River Thomas Modyford Governor of Jamaica Jamaica slave code William Berkeley, Governor of Virginia and Carolina proprietor commissions William Drummond as Governor of Albemarle County, North Carolina Proprietary Charter in New York		1664
		1664
The Duke's Laws issued in New York Second Charter of Carolina Connecticut annexes New Haven Colony Dutch attack Barbados	John Dryden, *The Indian Queen*	1665
	Isaac Newton formulates the Laws of Gravity G. Leibnitz publishes on Differential Calculus	1666

Year	Britain and Ireland	Europe
1667	Treaty of Breda ends the Second Anglo-Dutch War	
1668		
1669		
1670		

THIRD ANGLO-DUTCH WAR

Year	Britain and Ireland	Europe
1672	War with Dutch begins	French invade the United Provinces Franco-Dutch War begins
1673	Navigation Act	
1674	End of Third Anglo-Dutch War	
1675	Lords of Trade and Plantations appointed by Charles II to supervise colonies	
1676		
1677		
1679	Treaties of Nijmegen and Fontainebleau	
1680s		

The Wider World	Arts and Sciences	Year
	John Milton, *Paradise Lost* John Dryden, *The Indian Emperour* and *Annus Mirabilis*	1667
East India Company take over Bombay		1668
Fundamental Constitutions of Carolina Antigua slave code		1669
English expedition reaches Carolina coast; colony established on the Ashley River Hudson's Bay Company Charter Montserrat slave and servant legislation		1670
Royal Africa Company chartered		1672
Dutch United East India Company fleet fails to take Bombay	John Dryden, *Amboyna*	
Dutch recapture New Netherland Battle of Masulipatam, India		1673
New Netherland restored to England		1674
First Quaker settlement in West Jersey		
King Philip's (Metacom) War in New England begins		1675
'Huy and Crye' rebellion in Maryland		1676
Bacon's Rebellion in Virginia: Bacon's followers sack Jamestown		
Culpeper's Rebellion, North Carolina begins		1677
Proprietors order settlers to move to the site of Charleston, South Carolina		1679
Tobacco depression begins, Carolina Slaves imported in larger numbers after 1680 to Carolina La Salle's two voyages down the Mississippi		1680s

Year	Britain and Ireland	Europe
1681		
1682		
1683		Ottoman siege of Vienna
1684		French claim Louisiana
1685	Duke of York becomes James II and VII	Louis XIV revokes the Edict of Nantes
1686		
1687		
1688	Triple Alliance: England, United Provinces, and Sweden	

WAR OF THE LEAGUE OF AUGSBURG

Year	Britain and Ireland	Europe
1689	War with France Convention Parliament offers English throne to William of Orange and Mary: Glorious Revolution	Peter I (the Great) Tsar
1690	James II defeated by William III at Battle of the Boyne	

The Wider World	Arts and Sciences	Year
Quaker settlement in Pennsylvania; Charles II grants colony of Pennsylvania to William Penn		1681
The Frame of Government of Pennsylvania Dutch troops occupy Bantam, Java, expelling English and French		1682
Beginning of Scottish settlement in East New Jersey 'Charter of Libertyes and Priviledges', New York		1683
Scots make short-lived settlement at Stuart's Town, South Carolina Massachusetts Bay Company charter annulled Bermuda Company charter annulled		1684
1,500 Huguenots arrive in the colonies		1685–95
Duke of Albemarle Governor of Jamaica War between English and Mughals in Bengal		1686
Dominion of New England established, and Andros appointed Governor 1686		
	Sir Isaac Newton, *Principia*	1687
	Aphra Behn, *Oroonoko*	1688

(KING WILLIAM'S WAR)

The Wider World	Arts and Sciences	Year
The Glorious Revolution in America: overthrow of proprietory rule Rebellion in Boston against Governor Andros Rebellion in New York against Lt-Gov. Nicholson Protest in Leeward Islands against Governor Johnson Rebellion in Maryland against Lord Baltimore Capture of St Kitts by the French War disrupts Atlantic commerce	John Locke, *Second Treatise of Government*	1689
		1690

Year	Britain and Ireland	Europe
1690		
1691	Treaty of Limerick ends war in Ireland	
1692		
1694		
1696	Legitimacy of Scottish office-holding in the Colonies called into question by the Navigation Acts Board of Trade replaces Lords of Trade as manager of colonies	
1697	Peace of Rijswijk	
1698		
1700		Charles II of Spain succeeded by Philip of Anjou Third or 'Great Northern War' begins
1701	Nevis restricts Irish immigration Parliament rejects Reunification Bill for direct royal rule over all American colonies	
1702	Accession of Queen Anne	

The Wider World	Arts and Sciences	Year
New England and New York colonists invade Canada Governor Codrington recaptures St Kitts Calcutta settlement	John Locke, *Essay Concerning Human Understanding*	1690
Execution of Jakob Leisler by Governor Sloughter New Massachusetts charter		1691
Keithian Schism in Pennsylvania Royal government established in Maryland Witch trials in Salem, Massachusetts Anglican church established in North America Abortive slave revolt in Barbados Anglo-French fighting in Africa Unofficial clashes with the Dutch West India Company		1692
	First performance of A. Scarlatti's *Pirro e Demetrio*	1694
Navigation Act establishes Vice-Admiralty Courts in America	First performance of Henry Purcell's *Dido and Aeneas*	1696
		1697
'Ten per Cent' Act ends Royal African Company's monopoly of the African trade New East India Company chartered	T. Savery invents the steam pump in England	1698
Population of Virginia and Maryland reaches nearly 100,000 (85,000 whites, 13,000 blacks)	John Locke's *Essay Concerning Human Understanding* placed on the Papal Index of Prohibited Books	1700
Darien colony abandoned		1701
Surrender of East and West Jersey Proprietaries		1702

Year	Britain and Ireland	Europe
	WAR OF THE SPANISH SUCCESSION ('QUEEN ANNE'S WAR')	
1702	War with France	
1704	Battle of Blenheim Gibraltar captured	
1705		Joseph I Holy Roman Emperor
1706		
1707	Act of Union between England and Scotland	
1708		
1709		
1711		Charles VI Holy Roman Emperor
1712		
1713	Peace of Utrecht: Britain gains Gibraltar, Minorca	
1714	Accession of George I	Peace of Rastatt between the Habsburg Empire and France
1715		
1718	Act for Transportation of Convicts to North America	Peace of Passarowitz between the Habsburg and Ottoman Empires
1719		
1729		

The Wider World	Arts and Sciences	Year
		1702
Destruction of Spanish missions, northern Florida, by South Carolina Expedition England gains Gibraltar		1704
Virginia's slave laws codified	Robert Beverley, *The History and Present State of Virginia*	1705
Incorporation of Bath, first town in North Carolina Church of England established in South Carolina		1706
		1707
Black majority in South Carolina's population		1708
	First performance of G. F. Handel's *Agrippina and Rinaldo*	1709
Tuscorora War begins		1711
Separate Governor appointed for North Carolina		1712
Peace of Utrecht: Britain gains Newfoundland, Nova Scotia, Hudson Bay, and the *Asiento* for Spanish America		1713
		1714
Yamasee War, South Carolina		1715
	G. Fahrenheit makes a mercury thermometer in Amsterdam	1718
Governor replaces proprietors' official in South Carolina; Crown asked to assume control in South Carolina		1719
Seven of eight proprietors in North Carolina sell their rights to the Crown		1729

INDEX